Lecture Notes in Computer Science 5154

Commenced Publication in 1973
Founding and Former Series Editors:
Gerhard Goos, Juris Hartmanis, and Jan van Leeuwen

Elisabeth Oswald   Pankaj Rohatgi (Eds.)

Cryptographic Hardware and Embedded Systems – CHES 2008

10th International Workshop
Washington, D.C., USA, August 10-13, 2008
Proceedings

 Springer

Volume Editors

Elisabeth Oswald
University of Bristol
Department of Computer Science
Merchant Venturers Building, Woodland Road, BS8 1UB, Bristol, UK
E-mail: elisabeth.oswald@bristol.ac.uk

Pankaj Rohatgi
IBM T.J. Watson Research Center
19 Skyline Drive, Hawthorne, NY 10532, USA
E-mail: rohatgi@us.ibm.com

Library of Congress Control Number: 2008931306

CR Subject Classification (1998): E.3, E.4, D.4.6, C.2.0, I.3.1

LNCS Sublibrary: SL 4 – Security and Cryptology

ISSN	0302-9743
ISBN-10	3-540-85052-X Springer Berlin Heidelberg New York
ISBN-13	978-3-540-85052-6 Springer Berlin Heidelberg New York

Springer is a part of Springer Science+Business Media

springer.com

© International Association for Cryptologic Research 2008
Printed in Germany

Typesetting: Camera-ready by author, data conversion by Scientific Publishing Services, Chennai, India
Printed on acid-free paper   SPIN: 12441693   06/3180   5 4 3 2 1 0

Preface

These are the proceedings of the 10th Workshop on Cryptographic Hardware and Embedded Systems (CHES), held in Washington D.C., USA, August 10–13, 2008. This workshop was sponsored by the International Association for Cryptologic Research (IACR).

The CHES 2008 workshop attracted 107 submissions from 23 countries, of which the program committee selected 27 papers for publication. The review process followed strict standards: each paper received at least four reviews; members of the program committee were restricted to submitting at most two papers. The 42 Program Committee members from 13 countries were selected carefully to ensure that different fields, such as hardware and software implementations, active and passive implementation attacks, cryptanalysis and cryptography including random number generation, embedded systems, and trusted computing, were well represented and a balance between academia and industry was achieved. Counting all Program Committee members, external reviewers, and the Program Co-chairs, we had 158 people contributing to the review process. We would like to thank all Program Committee members and external reviewers for their contribution to the review process.

In just 10 years, the CHES workshop has grown to become the flagship event in its area, attracting high-profile papers and attendees from academia and industry. This excellence is reflected in the quality of the contributed papers and invited talks. In cooperation with the CHES Steering Committee, the Program Committee awarded the CHES 2008 Best Paper Award to two contributions: "Attack and Improvement of a Secure S-box Calculation Based on the Fourier Transform" by Jean-Sébastien Coron, Christophe Giraud, Emmanuel Prouff and Matthieu Rivain, and "Time-Area Optimized Public-Key Engines: MQ-Cryptosystems as Replacement for Elliptic Curves?" by Andrey Bogdanov, Thomas Eisenbarth, Andy Rupp and Christopher Wolf. The purpose of the award is to formally acknowledge excellence in research. We would like to congratulate the authors of these two papers. In addition to presentations of peer-reviewed papers there were excellent invited presentations. At the time of compiling the proceedings, an invited talk by Adi Shamir on "RSA: Past, Present and Future", and an invited talk by Ernie Brickell from Intel on "A Vision for Platform Security" had been confirmed.

In order to celebrate the 10th anniversary of CHES, the workshop program included a tour of the National Cryptologic Museum in Fort Mead and a talk by Christof Paar and Çetin Kaya Koç on the history of CHES. In addition there was a rump session and a panel discussion. Special thanks for making these possible and taking care of the local organization go to the General Co-chairs Kris Gaj and Jens-Peter Kaps (both from George Mason University). We are also greatly indebted to the CHES Steering Committee for their guidance and support throughout the process of putting this program together. The peer review process and the production of these proceedings were greatly facilitated by the IACR Webreview System. Shai Halevi (IBM) receives our sincere gratitude for providing and maintaining this software, and for always being prepared to help.

We would also like to acknowledge and thank our sponsors, many of whom have generously supported the workshop over the years. At the time of writing this preface a number of companies had been confirmed as sponsors: Cryptography Research, Inc., CygnaCom Solutions, escrypt GmbH, IBM Research, Oberthur Technologies, Philips Intrinsic-ID, Research Center of Information Security (RCIS) Japan, and Thomson R&D France.

Finally, we would like to thank all the researchers and authors from all over the world who submitted their work to the CHES 2008 conference and whose efforts create the vibrant field of research that CHES is proud to represent.

August 2008   Elisabeth Oswald
                                                                Pankaj Rohatgi

CHES 2008

Workshop on Cryptographic Hardware and Embedded Systems
Washington DC, USA, August 10–13, 2008

Sponsored by the *International Association for Cryptologic Research*

General Co-chairs

Kris Gay, George Mason University
Jens-Peter Kaps, George Mason University

Program Co-chairs

Elisabeth Oswald, University of Bristol
Pankaj Rohatgi, IBM Research

Program Committee

Daniel V. Bailey	RSA Laboratories, USA
Lejla Batina	Katholieke Universiteit Leuven, Belgium
Feng Bao	Institute for Infocomm Research, Singapore
Daniel J. Bernstein	Univ. of Illinois, Chicago, USA
Suresh Chari	IBM Research, USA
Christophe Clavier	Gemalto, France
Jean-Sebastien Coron	University of Luxembourg, Luxembourg
Markus Dichtl	Siemens AG, Germany
Louis Goubin	Université de Versailles, France
Anwar Hasan	Univ. of Waterloo, Canada
Joshua Jaffe	Cryptography Research, USA
Marc Joye	Thomson R&D, France
Çetin Kaya Koç	Oregon State University, USA
Markus Kuhn	University of Cambridge, UK
Klaus Kursawe	Philips Research, Netherlands
Ruby Lee	Princeton University, USA
Kerstin Lemke-Rust	T-Systems, Germany
Arjen Lenstra	EPFL, Switzerland, and Alcatel-Lucent Bell Laboratories, USA
Stefan Mangard	Infineon Technologies, Germany
Mitsuru Matsui	Mitsubishi Electric, Japan
Máaire McLoone	Queens University Belfast, UK

David Naccache	ENS, France
Katsuyuki Okeya	Hitachi, Japan
Christof Paar	Ruhr-Universität Bochum, Germany
Dan Page	Univ. of Bristol, UK
Pascal Paillier	Gemalto, France
Emmanuel Prouff	Oberthur Card Systems, France
Jean-Jacques Quisquater	Université Catholique de Louvain, Belgium
Anand Raghunathan	NEC labs, USA
Josyula R. Rao	IBM Research, USA
Ahmad-Reza Sadeghi	Ruhr-Universität Bochum, Germany
Akashi Satoh	AIST, Japan
Erkay Savas	Sabanci University, Turkey
Patrick Schaumont	Virginia Tech, USA
Jean-Pierre Seifert	Samsung R&D, USA
Berk Sunar	Worcester Polytechnic Institute, USA
Masahiko Takenaka	Fujitsu Laboratories Ltd, Japan
Kris Tiri	Intel, USA
Elena Trichina	Spansion, France
Ingrid Verbauwhede	Katholieke Universiteit Leuven, Belgium
Colin Walter	Comodo CA, UK
Johannes Wolkerstorfer	TU Graz, Austria

External Reviewers

Onur Acıiçmez	Thomas Eisenbarth	Kouichi Itoh
Manfred Aigner	Takashi Endo	Tetsuya Izu
Kahraman Akdemir	Benoit Feix	Charanjit Jutla
Toru Akishita	Martin Feldhofer	Marcelo Kaihara
Frédéric Amiel	Berndt M. Gammel	Jens-Peter Kaps
Frederik Armknecht	Sergiu Ghetie	Anton Kargl
Muhammad Asim	Benedikt Gierlichs	Markus Kasper
Guido Bertoni	Kevin Gotze	Timo Kasper
Sumeer Bhola	Aline Gouget	Chong Hee Kim
Alex Biryukov	Rob Granger	Ovunc Kocabas
Andrey Bogdanov	Vanessa Gratzer	Masanobu Koike
Joseph Bonneau	Johann Großschädl	Konrad Kulikowski
Joppe Bos	Jorge Guajardo	Hans Lähr
Arnaud Boscher	Shay Gueron	T. Lan
Marco Bucci	Sylvain Guilley	Tanja Lange
Philippe Bulens	Tim Güneysu	Albert Levi
David Champagne	Xu Guo	Yingxi Lu
Zhimin Chen	Ghaith Hammouri	Raimondo Luzzi
Benoit Chevallier-Mames	Matt Henricksen	François Macé
Emmanuelle Dottax	Christoph Herbst	Sandra Marcello
Saar Drimer	Naofumi Homma	Mark Marson

Table of Contents

Random Number Generation

Side-Channel Analysis 2

Cryptography and Cryptanalysis

Implementations 2

Attack and Improvement of a Secure S-Box Calculation Based on the Fourier Transform

Jean-Sébastien Coron[1], Christophe Giraud[2], Emmanuel Prouff[2],
and Matthieu Rivain[1,2]

[1] University of Luxembourg
jean-sebastien.coron@uni.lu
[2] Oberthur Technologies
{c.giraud,e.prouff,m.rivain}@oberthurcs.com

Abstract. At CHES 2006, a DPA countermeasure based on the Fourier Transform was published. This generic countermeasure aims at protecting from DPA any S-box calculation used in symmetric cryptosystems implementations. In this paper, we show that this countermeasure has a flaw and that it can be broken by first order DPA. Moreover, we have successfully put into practice our attack on two different S-box implementations. Finally, we propose an improvement of the original countermeasure and we prove its security against first order DPA.

1 Introduction

The processing of a cryptographic algorithm on a physical device may leak information about the manipulated data. To exploit this information, Side Channel Attacks (SCA) were introduced in 1996, *cf.* [8]. It is today composed of a large variety of attacks that differ in the attack model, the nature of the side channels they target or the leakage treatments they perform. The *Differential Power Analysis* (DPA) introduced in [9] is probably the one which has received the most attention in the literature. This attack has indeed been demonstrated to be very powerful against unprotected cryptographic implementations, where it allows the attacker to recover the value of a secret key with only a few leakage measurements. Roughly speaking, a DPA is a statistical attack that correlates a physical leakage with the values of particular intermediate variables (called *sensitive variables* in this paper) that depend on both a public value and the secret key. To avoid information leakage and its exploitation by DPA, the manipulation of sensitive variables must be protected by adding countermeasures to the algorithm.

A very common countermeasure to protect block cipher implementations from DPA is to mask every sensitive variable with a randomly generated variable (called *mask*) and then to perform the calculations by only manipulating the masked variable and/or the mask. When such a technique is applied, a problem occurs which is usually referred in the literature as the *mask correction Problem*. It relies on the difficulty of masking the calculation of non-linear sub-functions (*e.g.* the so-called *S-boxes*), without ever manipulating an intermediate variable that depends on sensitive data. Many papers have been published that aim at providing a solution to this problem (see for instance [1,7,10,11,12]). At CHES

E. Oswald and P. Rohatgi (Eds.): CHES 2008, LNCS 5154, pp. 1–14, 2008.

2006, Prouff, Giraud and Aumônier proposed in [11] a solution that may be of particular interest when the input/output dimensions of the function to protect are small and when the masks values are regenerated many times during the algorithm processing. Moreover, the solution is provided together with a proof of security that allows the reader to formally validate its security. In this paper, we show that contrary to what is claimed in [11], a DPA attack can be successfully mounted against this countermeasure. We exhibit the flaw upon which our attack is based and we present how to successfully exploit it to recover the value of a secret parameter. Finally, we propose an improvement of the countermeasure proposed in [11] and we prove its security *versus* DPA in a realistic model.

2   Preliminaries

In the rest of the paper, we say that a variable is *sensitive with respect to DPA* (shortened to *sensitive variable* in the context of the present paper) if it is a non-constant function of a plaintext and a secret key. A DPA (also called first order DPA in the literature when it is compared to higher order DPA) exploits the leakage about a single intermediate sensitive variable. Hereafter, we recall the formal definition of the security against DPA (see for instance [2,4,11]).

Definition 1. *A cryptographic algorithm is said to be secure against DPA if all its intermediate variables are independent of any sensitive variable.*

Conversely, an algorithm is said to admit a *first order flaw* if one of its intermediate variables depends on a sensitive variable.

A common countermeasure against DPA is to add (by bitwise or modular addition) a random value called the *mask* to each sensitive variable. Masks and masked variables propagate throughout the cipher in such a way that every intermediate variable is independent of any sensitive variable. This strategy, called *first order masking*, ensures that the instantaneous leakage is independent of any sensitive variable, thus rendering DPA ineffective.

As pointed out for instance in [6,1], the tricky part when masking the implementation of an algorithm is to deal with the following problem, called *mask correction Problem*:

Problem 1. Let F be a (n, m)-function (that is a function from $\mathbb{F}_2^n$ into $\mathbb{F}_2^m$). From a masked input $Z \oplus R_1 \in \mathbb{F}_2^n$, the mask $R_1 \in \mathbb{F}_2^n$ and an output mask $R_2 \in \mathbb{F}_2^m$, compute $F(Z) \oplus R_2$ without introducing any first order flaw.

3   Secure S-Box Calculation Based on the Fourier Transform

In [11], an algorithm claimed to solve Problem 1 is proposed. The method is based on the involutivity property of the *Fourier Transform*. Before describing it, let us first recall some basics about the transformation itself.

Algorithm 1. Computation of an arithmetically masked S-box output from a boolean masked input

INPUTS: A masked input $\tilde{Z} = Z \oplus R_1$, the input mask R_1 and a lookup table $\widehat{F}$

OUTPUT: The 3-tuple $((-1)^{(\tilde{Z} \oplus R_2) \cdot R_1} F(Z) + R_3 \mod 2^n, R_3, R_2)$ where R_2 and R_3 are random values.

---

1. Pick up three n-bit randoms R_2, R_3 and R_4
2. $result \leftarrow 2^n R_3 + R_4$
3. **for** a **from** 0 **to** $2^n - 1$ **do**
4. $T_1 \leftarrow \mathrm{SSP}(a, \tilde{Z})$ $[T_1 = (-1)^{a \cdot \tilde{Z}}]$
5. $T_2 \leftarrow \tilde{Z} \oplus a$ $[T_2 = \tilde{Z} \oplus a]$
6. $T_2 \leftarrow T_2 \oplus R_2$ $[T_2 = \tilde{Z} \oplus a \oplus R_2]$
7. $T_2 \leftarrow \mathrm{SSP}(R_1, T_2)$ $[T_2 = (-1)^{R_1 \cdot (\tilde{Z} \oplus a \oplus R_2)}]$
8. $T_2 \leftarrow T_1 \times T_2$ $[T_2 = (-1)^{a \cdot \tilde{Z} \oplus R_1 \cdot (\tilde{Z} \oplus a \oplus R_2)}]$
9. $T_2 \leftarrow T_2 \times \widehat{F}(a)$ $[T_2 = \widehat{F}(a)(-1)^{a \cdot \tilde{Z} \oplus R_1 \cdot (\tilde{Z} \oplus a \oplus R_2)}]$
10. $result \leftarrow result \boxplus T_2$ $[result = (2^n R_3 + R_4) \boxplus \sum_{i \in \{0,a\}} \widehat{F}(i)(-1)^{i \cdot \tilde{Z} \oplus R_1 \cdot (\tilde{Z} \oplus i \oplus R_2)}]$
11. **end**
12. $result \leftarrow result \gg n$ $[result = (-1)^{(\tilde{Z} \oplus R_2) \cdot R_1} F(Z) + R_3 \mod 2^n]$
13. **return** $(result, R_3, R_2)$

For every (n, m)-function F, the Fourier transform $\widehat{F}$ of F is defined for every $Z = (Z_0, \cdots, Z_{n-1}) \in \mathbb{F}_2^n$ by:

$$\widehat{F}(Z) = \sum_{a \in \mathbb{F}_2^n} F(a)(-1)^{a \cdot Z} \ , \tag{1}$$

where $\cdot$ denotes the scalar product defined by $a \cdot Z = \bigoplus_{i=0}^{n-1} a_i Z_i$.

It is well known that this transformation is involutive, which means that $\widehat{\widehat{F}} = 2^n F$ or equivalently that:

$$F(Z) = \frac{1}{2^n} \sum_{a \in \mathbb{F}_2^n} \widehat{F}(a)(-1)^{a \cdot Z}, \ Z \in \mathbb{F}_2^n \ . \tag{2}$$

Let R_1, R_2, R_3 and R_4 be 4 random masks belonging to $\mathbb{F}_2^n$, and let Z denotes a sensitive variable. The algorithm proposed in [11] to process $F(Z) + R_3 \mod 2^n$ securely from $\tilde{Z} = Z \oplus R_1$ and R_1, implements the right-hand side calculus of the following relation (which is a slightly modified version of Relation (2)):

$$(-1)^{(\tilde{Z} \oplus R_2) \cdot R_1} F(Z) + R_3 \mod 2^n$$

$$= \left\lfloor \frac{1}{2^n} \left(R' + \sum_{a \in \mathbb{F}_2^n} \widehat{F}(a)(-1)^{a \cdot \tilde{Z} \oplus R_1 \cdot (\tilde{Z} \oplus a \oplus R_2)} \mod 2^{2n} \right) \right\rfloor \ , \tag{3}$$

where $R' = 2^n R_3 + R_4$.

Let SSP denote the signed scalar product $X, Y \mapsto (-1)^{X \cdot Y}$, let $\boxplus$ denote the addition modulo 2^{2n} and let $\times$ denote the multiplication of two values belonging to $\{-1, 1\}$. We recall hereafter the algorithm proposed in [11] to process the right-hand side of (3) securely.

Finally, it is proposed in [11] to use the method described in [5] in order to transform the arithmetic masking of the output of Algorithm 1 into a boolean masking.

The authors of [11] had proposed a proof of security *versus* DPA for the countermeasure defined by Algorithm 1, but as we will see in the next section, the proof is flawed and the countermeasure is not secure against DPA.

4   DPA against the Fourier Transform Based S-Box Calculation

4.1   First Order Flaw

Unlike what is claimed in [11], the implementation of Algorithm 1 is not immune against DPA. Indeed, the variable $V = a \cdot \widetilde{Z} \oplus R_1 \cdot (\widetilde{Z} \oplus a \oplus R_2)$ processed at Step 8 brings information about the sensitive variable Z (recalling $\widetilde{Z} = Z \oplus R_1$). To exhibit the dependency between V and Z, let us first rewrite V as follows:

$$
\begin{aligned}
V &= a \cdot \widetilde{Z} \oplus R_1 \cdot (\widetilde{Z} \oplus a \oplus R_2) \\
&= a \cdot (Z \oplus R_1) \oplus R_1 \cdot (\widetilde{Z} \oplus a \oplus R_2) \\
&= a \cdot Z \oplus R_1 \cdot (\widetilde{Z} \oplus R_2) \ .
\end{aligned}
$$

The relation above shows that the intermediate variable V equals the sensitive variable $a \cdot Z$ (a being a loop index) masked with the scalar product $R_1 \cdot (\widetilde{Z} \oplus R_2)$. Since R_2 is uniformly distributed and is independent of both Z and R_1, then so does the variable $\widetilde{Z} \oplus R_2$. The flaw of the method proposed in [11] comes from the fact that the scalar product of two uniformly distributed random variables does not output an uniformly distributed random variable. For example, the product $b_1 \cdot b_2$ of two random bits b_1 and b_2 equals 0 with probability $3/4$, and equals 1 with probability $1/4$. More generally, for n-bit random variables we have the following lemma.

Lemma 1. *Let X and Y be two random variables uniformly distributed over $\mathbb{F}_2^n$ and mutually independent. Then the scalar product $X \cdot Y$ satisfies*

$$
\Pr[X \cdot Y = 0] = \frac{1}{2} + \frac{1}{2^{n+1}} \ . \tag{4}
$$

Proof. We have:

$$
P[X \cdot Y = 0] = P[X \neq 0] \cdot P[X \cdot Y = 0 | X \neq 0] + P[X = 0] \cdot P[X \cdot Y = 0 | X = 0] \ .
$$

Since the Boolean function $y \in \mathbb{F}_2^n \mapsto x \cdot y$ is linear and not null for every $x \neq 0$, we have $\#\{x \cdot y = 1\} = \#\{x \cdot y = 0\} = 2^{n-1}$. This, together with the fact that X and Y are independent, implies $P[X \cdot Y = 0 | X \neq 0] = \frac{1}{2}$. Since $P[X \cdot Y = 0 | X = 0] = 1$ and $P[X \neq 0] = \frac{2^n - 1}{2^n}$, we deduce (4). $\diamond$

Remark 1. In the security proof conducted in [11], it is stated that the uniform distribution of X and Y implies the one of $X \cdot Y$. We show in Lemma 1 that this assertion is actually wrong.

Lemma 1 implies that the distribution of $R_1 \cdot (\widetilde{Z} \oplus R_2)$ has a bias $\frac{1}{2^{n+1}}$ with respect to the uniform distribution. Since the sensitive variable $a \cdot Z$ is masked with a biased mask, the variable V defined in (4) leaks information on $a \cdot Z$. This information can be used to recover Z by DPA.

4.2   DPA Attack

A DPA attack [9] targets the leakage $L(b)$ generated by the processing of a sensitive bit b in order to recover information about a secret which we denote here by $k^\star$. It can be performed with only a few information about the leakage and it actually only assumes that the expectation of $L(b)$ depends on the value of b. Let us first recall the outlines of the attack in the general case where b can be expressed as:

$$b = f(X, k^\star) , \tag{5}$$

where f is a Boolean function and X is a public variable.

Description. To perform a DPA, the target algorithm is executed several times, say N, for a sequence of values $(x_i)_{i \leq N}$ taken by X. For each execution, the attacker measures the leakage l_i generated by the processing of b. Then, the resulting *leakage measurement sequence* $(l_i)_{i \leq N}$ is involved to (in)validate a key hypothesis k on $k^\star$. For such a purpose, the attacker first computes the *sequence of guesses* $(b_i)_{i \leq N}$ which are the predicted values of the bit b processed in the successive executions: namely, for every $i \leq N$ we have $b_i = f(x_i, k)$. Then, the leakage measurements are separated in two categories: the ones for which the predicted bit b_i is equal to 1, and the ones for which it is equal to 0. Finally, the so-called differential Δ_k corresponding to the difference between the mean values of the two sets is computed:

$$\Delta_k = \frac{\sum_{i=1}^{N} b_i \times l_i}{\sum_{i=1}^{N} b_i} - \frac{\sum_{i=1}^{N} (1 - b_i) \times l_i}{\sum_{i=1}^{N} (1 - b_i)} . \tag{6}$$

If the key hypothesis is correct then the expectation satisfies:

$$E[\Delta_{k^\star}] = E[L(1)] - E[L(0)] . \tag{7}$$

If the key hypothesis is incorrect then a *ratio* $\alpha \in [0, 1]$ of the b_i's is wrongly predicted and the expectation of the differential satisfies:

$$E[\Delta_k] = (1 - 2\alpha)\big(E[L(1)] - E[L(0)]\big) . \tag{8}$$

Since α is usually around $\frac{1}{2}$, we have $E[\Delta_{k \neq k^\star}] \simeq 0$. This implies that, for a sufficiently large N, the correct key hypothesis is such that Δ_k is of maximum amplitude.

Remark 2. Depending on the function f, it may happen that the correct key hypothesis is not the single one for which Δ_k is of maximum amplitude. Indeed, a key hypothesis such that $\alpha = 1$ also results in a differential of maximal amplitude. According to (6), this differential and the one corresponding to the correct key hypothesis have exactly the same amplitude but have opposite signs. To differentiate them the attacker needs to determine the polarity of $E[L(1)]-E[L(0)]$.

DPA Attack Exploiting a Biased Mask. Let us now consider the case where the target bit b is masked, namely:

$$b = f(X, k^\star) \oplus R \ , \tag{9}$$

where R is a random bit.

If R is uniformly distributed over $\mathbb{F}_2$, then no successful DPA attack is possible. Indeed, in that case b equals 0 (*resp.* 1) with probability $\frac{1}{2}$ independently of $k^\star$. Conversely, when the distribution of R is biased compared to the uniform distribution, then the distribution of b depends on $f(X, k^\star)$, which renders DPA possible. In the following, we denote by $\varepsilon \neq 0$ the bias such that $P[R = 0] = \frac{1}{2}+\varepsilon$.

The DPA works in the same way as in the unmasked case. The sequence of guesses is still defined as $b_i = f(x_i, k)$ (since R is not predictable) and the differential Δ_k is computed according to (6). The randomization provided by R implies that the bit effectively processed equals $f(x_i, k^\star)$ with probability $\frac{1}{2} + \varepsilon$. One deduces that, for the correct key hypothesis, a portion $\frac{1}{2} + \varepsilon$ of the b_i's is correctly predicted while a portion $\frac{1}{2} - \varepsilon$ is wrongly predicted in average. This implies that the expectation of the differential for the correct key hypothesis satisfies:

$$E[\Delta_{k^\star}] = \left(\frac{1}{2} + \varepsilon\right)\left(E[L(1)] - E[L(0)]\right) + \left(\frac{1}{2} - \varepsilon\right)\left(E[L(0)] - E[L(1)]\right) \ ,$$

that is:

$$E[\Delta_{k^\star}] = 2\varepsilon \times \left(E[L(1)] - E[L(0)]\right) \ .$$

Hence the expectation of $\Delta_{k^\star}$ is divided by a factor $\frac{1}{2\varepsilon}$ compared to an unprotected implementation (this also holds for the differentials Δ_k obtained for wrong key hypotheses – see Appendix A –). This implies, according to the analysis in [3], that the number of required leakage measurements is roughly multiplied by $(\frac{1}{2\varepsilon})^2$. A more detailed analysis is conducted in Appendix A where we give the exact distribution of Δ_k, assuming that the leakage noise has a Gaussian distribution.

As a result, Lemma 1 implies that a DPA on Algorithm 1 exploiting the flaw exhibited in Section 4.1 is expected to require about 2^{2n} times more leakage measurements than a DPA when no masking is used. Since Algorithm 1 is only interesting for a small value of n (*e.g.* $n = 4$), this factor is not prohibitive.

4.3   DPA Attack on the Flaw

In this section, we apply the DPA attack described in Section 4.2 in order to exploit the flaw exhibited in Section 4.1. More precisely, our attack targets a bit

b which is a scalar product $a \cdot Z$ masked with a biased mask $R = R_1 \cdot (\tilde{Z} \oplus R_2)$, that is

$$b = a \cdot Z \oplus R . \tag{10}$$

We recall that a refers to a loop index in Algorithm 1 and that its value can be chosen by the attacker among $\{0, \cdots, 2^n - 1\}$. The sensitive variable Z is the sensitive S-box input and it can be written as a function of a public variable X and a piece of secret data $k^\star$. The way our attack is performed depends on this function which can take several forms. In the sequel we consider two usual cases.

The first one is referred as the *linear case* and assumes:

$$Z = X \oplus k^\star .$$

This occurs for instance in AES and in FOX algorithms for the first round S-box calculation.

The second case, referred as the *non-linear case*, assumes the existence of a non-linear transformation ϕ such that:

$$Z = \phi(X \oplus k^\star) .$$

This occurs for instance in the AES algorithm implemented using the *composite field method* [10,11] (see [11, §4.1] for details). In that case, ϕ is the non-linear $(8, 4)$-function which from $a \in \mathbb{F}_{256}$ processes $d \in \mathbb{F}_{16}$ according to the notations of [10,11].

The Linear Case. We consider here the case where the targeted bit can be expressed as $b = a \cdot (X \oplus k^\star) \oplus R$ that is:

$$b = a \cdot X \oplus a \cdot k^\star \oplus R . \tag{11}$$

The bit b in (11) only depends on one secret binary value $a \cdot k^\star$. Therefore, a DPA on b will provide at most one bit of information on $k^\star$. Hence, recovering the whole secret $k^\star$ requires to perform a DPA attack on b for t different loop indices a_0, ..., a_{t-1}.

When mounting a DPA attack on b for a particular loop index a, the sequence of guesses can only take one of the two following forms: $(a \cdot x_i)_i$ or $(a \cdot x_i \oplus 1)_i$. According to (6), these two sequences result in two differentials that are opposite one to each other. The attacker does not know *a priori* which of these differentials correspond to the correct key hypothesis. Indeed, depending on the device, the polarity $(-1)^s$ of the good differential $\Delta_{a \cdot k^\star}$ may be positive or negative. In other terms, the DPA allows the attacker to recover the value of $a \cdot k^\star \oplus s$, where $k^\star$ and s are unknown.

Since the polarity s is the same for all the loop indices a, then performing t DPA attacks for t different loop indices a_0, ..., a_{t-1} provides the attacker with a system of t equations and $n + 1$ variables (the polarity bit s and the n bits of $k^\star$). Solving this system requires to have at least $t = n + 1$ equations. After choosing n indices a_i having linearly independent vectorial representations in $\mathbb{F}_2^n$ and after defining $a_n = a_0 \oplus a_1$, it can be checked that solving the system allows the attacker to unambiguously determine the value of $k^\star$.

The Non-linear Case. We now consider the case where b satisfies:

$$b = a \cdot \phi(X \oplus k^\star) \oplus R . \tag{12}$$

For a non-linear ϕ, the attack is analogous to a classical DPA on some output bit of *e.g.* a DES or AES S-box [9]. The non-linearity of ϕ ensures that for the correct key hypotheses a peak of maximal amplitude will appear while for most other key hypothesis no peak will appear. This enables to fully recover $k^\star$.

In this section, we have described how to exploit the leakage on a sensitive bit which is masked with a biased random bit. In the linear case, the attack requires to perform $n + 1$ DPAs while only one DPA is needed in the non-linear case. In the following section, we present experimental results for these two attacks.

5   Experimental Results

We put into practice the attacks described in Section 4.2 for two S-box implementations on an 8-bit smart card. Both attacks exploited the power consumption resulting from several S-box calculations.

Regarding the linear case, we performed the attack on the S-box calculation of FOX algorithm during the first round protected by the method described in [11]. In this case, the sensitive bits we targeted are of the form $a \cdot (X \oplus k^\star) \oplus R$, where $a, X, k^\star \in \mathbb{F}_2^4$. Following the outlines of the attack described in Section 4.3 for the linear case, we have applied $4 + 1$ DPAs on five different loop iterations of Algorithm 1, namely one DPA for every $a \in \{1, 2, 4, 8, 3\}$.

Figure 1.a represents the value of $\sum_{i=0}^3 \Delta_{a_i \cdot k}$, where $a_i = 2^i$, obtained after 20 000 executions of the algorithm. The full black curve corresponds to the correct subkey value $k^\star$ and the dotted black curve corresponds to the complementary of this value. As expected, these two candidates are such that the highest peaks of the differential vectors $\Delta_{a_i \cdot k}$ are either all positive or all negative, hence leading to the highest amplitudes for $\sum_{i=0}^3 \Delta_{a_i \cdot k}$. As explained in Section 4.3, we then computed the differential $\Delta_{a \cdot k^\star}$ for $a = a_0 \oplus a_1 = 3$. Figure 1.c illustrates this computation. The polarity of the highest peak of $\Delta_{3 \cdot k^\star}$ being negative, one deduces that the correct subkey value $k^\star$ corresponds to the full black curve in Figure 1.a.

Figures 1.b and 1.d represent respectively the convergence of the peak of maximal amplitude for $\sum_{i=0}^3 \Delta_{a_i \cdot k}$ and for $\Delta_{3 \cdot k^\star}$ according to the number of power consumption measurements. By analyzing these curves, we deduce that the value of the 4-bit subkey $k^\star$ is recovered by using about 8 000 executions of the algorithm.

Regarding the non-linear case, we attacked the AES S-box calculation using the composite field method in order to perform the inversion in $\mathbb{F}_2^4$ instead of $\mathbb{F}_2^8$ and the method of [11] to protect this inversion (see [11, § 4.1] for more details). In that case, the targeted bit is of the form $a \cdot \phi(X \oplus k^\star) \oplus R$ where $X, k^\star \in \mathbb{F}_2^8$, $a \in \mathbb{F}_2^4$ and $\phi : \mathbb{F}_2^8 \to \mathbb{F}_2^4$. Figure 2.a represents the value of the differentials Δ_k's for $k \in \mathbb{F}_2^8$ and $a = 1$, when 200 000 executions of the algorithm are used. It can be seen that the correct subkey $k^\star$ (plotted in black) is easily distinguishable.

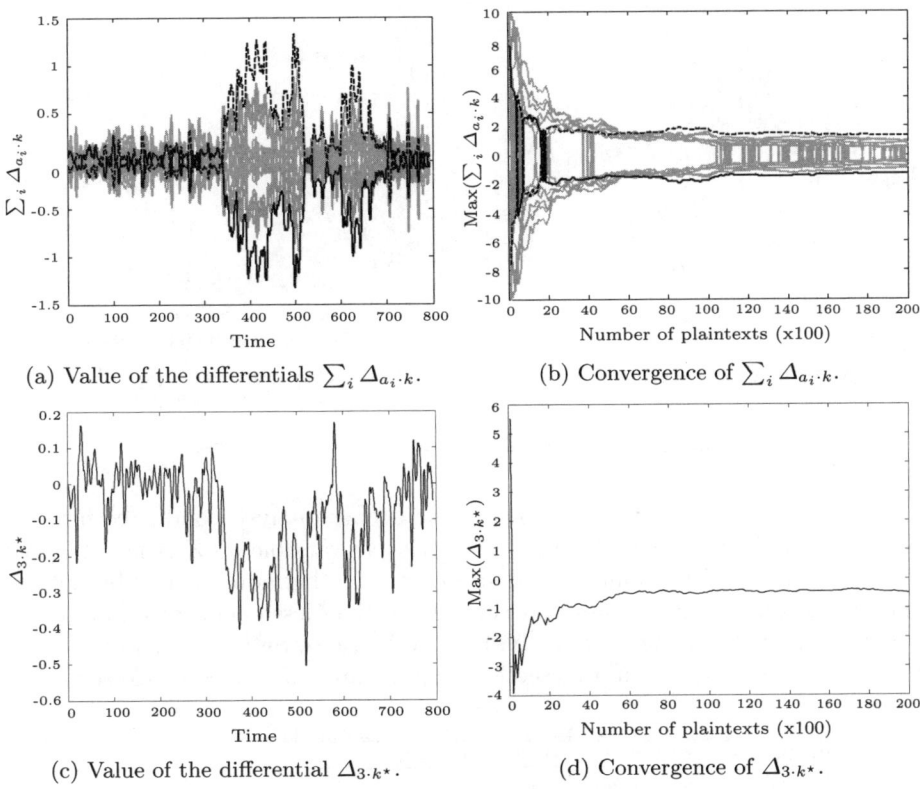

(a) Value of the differentials $\sum_i \Delta_{a_i \cdot k}$.

(b) Convergence of $\sum_i \Delta_{a_i \cdot k}$.

(c) Value of the differential $\Delta_{3 \cdot k^\star}$.

(d) Convergence of $\Delta_{3 \cdot k^\star}$.

Fig. 1. Practical DPA attack – the linear case

Figure 2.b represents the convergence of the maximum peak amplitude for the differentials according to the number of power consumption measurements. The analysis of these curves shows us that the value of the 8-bit subkey $k^\star$ is recovered after about $100\,000$ executions of the algorithm.

6   An Improved Version of a Secure S-Box Calculation

In the following we propose an improvement of Algorithm 1 that allows to circumvent the flaw depicted in Section 4.1 and also leads to a more efficient implementation.

The new algorithm is still a secure calculation of a Fourier Transform but it is based on a slightly modified version of (3) which we rewrite in the following form:

$$(-1)^{R_2} F(Z) + R_3 \bmod 2^n$$

$$= \left\lfloor \frac{1}{2^n} \left(R' + \sum_{a \in \mathbb{F}_2^n} \widehat{F}(a)(-1)^{R_2 \oplus a \cdot \widetilde{Z} \oplus a \cdot R_1} \bmod 2^{2n} \right) \right\rfloor , \quad (13)$$

where $\widetilde{Z} = Z \oplus R_1$, $R_2 \in \mathbb{F}_2$, $(R_1, R_3, R_4) \in (\mathbb{F}_2^n)^3$ and $R' = 2^n R_3 + R_4$.

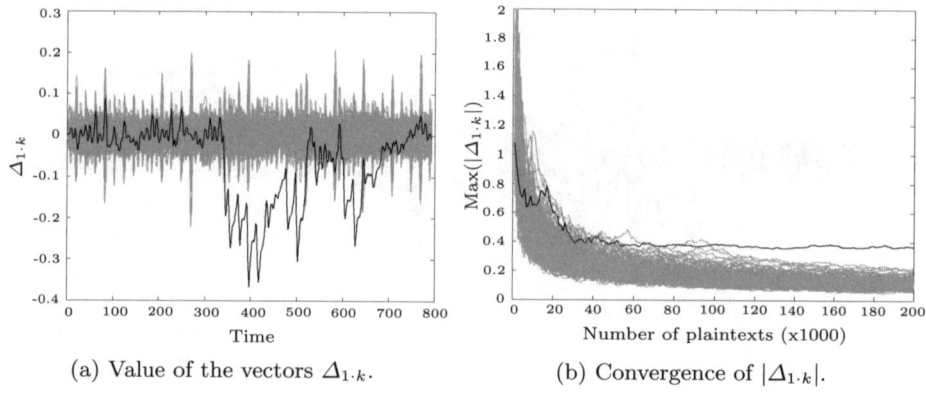

(a) Value of the vectors $\Delta_{1 \cdot k}$.

(b) Convergence of $|\Delta_{1 \cdot k}|$.

Fig. 2. Practical DPA attack – the non-linear case

After a brief look at (13) (and before the deeper analysis conducted later on in this section), we can notice that the sensitive variable $a \cdot Z$ is now masked with the uniformly distributed random bit R_2. Furthermore, it may be noticed that the exponent in the summation in (13) involves less operations than in (3).

Let us denote by SP the function $X, Y \mapsto X \cdot Y$ and by SFT the function $X, T \mapsto \widehat{F}(X)(-1)^T$. As we prove in this section, Algorithm 2 implements (13) securely.

Algorithm 2. First order Secure S-box calculation

INPUTS: A masked value $\widetilde{Z} = Z \oplus R_1$ and the mask R_1

OUTPUT: The 3-tuple $((-1)^{R_2} F(Z) + R_3 \mod 2^n, R_3, R_2)$, where R_2 and R_3 are random values.

---

1. Generate a random bit R_2
2. Generate two n-bit random R_3 and R_4
3. $result \leftarrow 2^n R_3 + R_4$
4. **for** a **from** 0 **to** $2^n - 1$ **do**
5. $T_1 \leftarrow \text{SP}(a, \widetilde{Z})$ $[T_1 = a \cdot \widetilde{Z}]$
6. $T_1 \leftarrow T_1 \oplus R_2$ $[T_1 = R_2 \oplus a \cdot \widetilde{Z}]$
7. $T_2 \leftarrow \text{SP}(a, R_1)$ $[T_2 = a \cdot R_1]$
8. $T \leftarrow T \oplus T$ $[T = R \oplus a \cdot Z]$
9. $T_1 \leftarrow \text{SFT}(a, T_1)$ $[T_1 = \widehat{F}(a)(-1)^{R_2 \oplus a \cdot Z}]$
10. $result \leftarrow result \boxplus T_1$ $[result = (2^n R_3 + R_4) \boxplus \sum_{i \in \{0, a\}} \widehat{F}(i)(-1)^{R_2 \oplus i \cdot Z}]$
11. **end**
12. $result \leftarrow result \gg n$ $[result = (-1)^{R_2} F(Z) + R_3 \mod 2^n]$
13. **return** $(result, R_3, R_2)$

Efficiency Analysis. Although Algorithm 2 is more secure than Algorithm 1, it is also faster. For each loop, Algorithm 2 requires two XORs, two calls to the function SP and one call to the lookup table SFT. Therefore, for each loop Algorithm 1 performs 2 extra multiplications compared to Algorithm 2. Combining this result with the fact that function SP is slightly faster than function SSP, we deduce that our method is faster than the one proposed in [11].

Security Analysis. In Table 1, we list the intermediate variables of Algorithm 1 that involve a sensitive variable. The values which only depend on the loop counter or on a random value are obviously omitted.

Table 1. The different sensitive values manipulated during Algorithm 2

Step	Instruction	Masked Value	$Mask(s)$
5.1	register $\leftarrow$ $\quad$ $\widetilde{Z}$	$\widetilde{Z}$	R_1
5.2	$T_1 \quad \leftarrow \quad \mathrm{SP}(a, \widetilde{Z})$	$a \cdot \widetilde{Z}$	$a \cdot R_1$
6	$T_1 \quad \leftarrow \quad T_1 \oplus R_2$	$R_2 \oplus a \cdot \widetilde{Z}$	$R_2 \oplus a \cdot R_1$
8	$T_1 \quad \leftarrow \quad T_1 \oplus T_2$	$R_2 \oplus a \cdot Z$	R_2
9	$T_1 \quad \leftarrow \mathrm{SFT}(a, T_1)$	$\widehat{F}(a)(-1)^{R_2 \oplus a \cdot Z}$	R_2
10	$result \leftarrow result \boxplus T_1$	$(2^n R_3 + R_4) \boxplus \sum_i \widehat{F}(i)(-1)^{R_2 \oplus i \cdot Z}$	(R_2, R_3, R_4)
11	$result \leftarrow result \gg n$	$(-1)^{R_2} F(Z) + R_3 \bmod 2^n$	R_3

As it can be checked in Table 1, the intermediate variables manipulated at Steps 5.1, 6, 8, 9, 10 and 11 are additively masked with a uniformly distributed random variable (resp. R_1, $R_2 \oplus a \cdot R_1$, R_2, R_2, $R_3 \| R_4$ and R_3) which is independent of the sensitive variable. Those intermediate variables are therefore independent of the sensitive variable Z.

The intermediate variable at Step 5.2 can be rewritten $a \cdot Z \oplus a \cdot R_1$. When a equals 0, this variable equals 0 whatever Z and R_1. Otherwise, for every $a \neq 0$ the variable $a \cdot R_1$ is uniformly distributed and independent of Z. We deduce that $a \cdot Z \oplus a \cdot R_1$ (and hence $a \cdot \widetilde{Z}$) is independent of Z whatever a.

Therefore, we have proved that all the intermediate variables manipulated during the execution of Algorithm 1 are independent of Z, which implies that our method is secure against first order DPA.

7 Conclusion

In this paper, we have shown that a provably secure DPA countermeasure published at CHES 2006 has a flaw. We have explained how this flaw can be exploited to mount an efficient attack on S-box implementations protected by this countermeasure. Our attack is not only theoretical since we have successfully put it into practice on two different S-box implementations: the AES S-box using the composite field method and the FOX S-box.

Finally, we have proposed an improvement of the CHES 2006 countermeasure for which we prove the resistance against first order DPA. Moreover we showed that our improvement is not only more secure but can also be implemented more efficiently than the original countermeasure.

References

1. Akkar, M.-L., Giraud, C.: An Implementation of DES and AES, Secure against Some Attacks. In: Koç, Ç.K., Naccache, D., Paar, C. (eds.) CHES 2001. LNCS, vol. 2162, pp. 309–318. Springer, Heidelberg (2001)
2. Blömer, J., Guajardo, J., Krummel, V.: Provably Secure Masking of AES. In: Handschuh, H., Hasan, M.A. (eds.) SAC 2004. LNCS, vol. 3357, pp. 69–83. Springer, Heidelberg (2004)
3. Clavier, C., Coron, J.-S., Dabbous, N.: Differential power analysis in the presence of hardware countermeasures. In: Paar, C., Koç, Ç.K. (eds.) CHES 2000. LNCS, vol. 1965, pp. 252–263. Springer, Heidelberg (2000)
4. Coron, J.-S., Prouff, E., Rivain, M.: Side Channel Cryptanalysis of a Higher Order Masking Scheme. In: Paillier, P., Verbauwhede, I. (eds.) CHES 2007. LNCS, vol. 4727, pp. 28–44. Springer, Heidelberg (2007)
5. Goubin, L.: A Sound Method for Switching between Boolean and Arithmetic Masking. In: Koç, Ç.K., Naccache, D., Paar, C. (eds.) CHES 2001. LNCS, vol. 2162, pp. 3–15. Springer, Heidelberg (2001)
6. Goubin, L., Patarin, J.: DES and Differential Power Analysis – The Duplication Method. In: Koç, Ç.K., Paar, C. (eds.) CHES 1999. LNCS, vol. 1717, pp. 158–172. Springer, Heidelberg (1999)
7. Gueron, S., Parzanchevsky, O., Zuk, O.: Masked Inversion in $GF(2^n)$ Using Mixed Field Representations and its Efficient Implementation for AES. In: Nedjah, N., Mourelle, L.M. (eds.) Embedded Cryptographic Hardware: Methodologies and Architectures, pp. 213–228. Nova Science Publishers (2004)
8. Kocher, P.: Timing Attacks on Implementations of Diffie-Hellman, RSA, DSS, and Other Systems. In: Koblitz, N. (ed.) CRYPTO 1996. LNCS, vol. 1109, pp. 104–113. Springer, Heidelberg (1996)
9. Kocher, P., Jaffe, J., Jun, B.: Differential Power Analysis. In: Wiener, M.J. (ed.) CRYPTO 1999. LNCS, vol. 1666, pp. 388–397. Springer, Heidelberg (1999)
10. Oswald, E., Mangard, S., Pramstaller, N., Rijmen, V.: A Side-Channel Analysis Resistant Description of the AES S-box. In: Gilbert, H., Handschuh, H. (eds.) FSE 2005. LNCS, vol. 3557, pp. 413–423. Springer, Heidelberg (2005)
11. Prouff, E., Giraud, C., Aumonier, S.: Provably Secure S-Box Implementation Based on Fourier Transform. In: Goubin, L., Matsui, M. (eds.) CHES 2006. LNCS, vol. 4249. Springer, Heidelberg (2006)
12. Rivain, M., Dottax, E., Prouff, E.: Block Ciphers Implementations Provably Secure Against Second Order Side Channel Analysis. Cryptology ePrint Archive, Report 2008/021 (2008), http://eprint.iacr.org/

A   Distribution of the Differentials

In this section, we investigate the distribution of the differential Δ_k when the attack targets a masked bit $b = f(X, k^\star) \oplus R$ where R is a random bit satisfying $P[R = 0] = \frac{1}{2} + \varepsilon$. Our analysis includes the unmasked case by setting ε to $\frac{1}{2}$.

We make the usual assumption that the leakage has a Gaussian distribution:

$$L(b) \sim \mathcal{N}\left(\mu - \frac{\delta}{2}(-1)^b, \sigma^2\right) , \tag{14}$$

where μ, δ and σ are constants and δ equals $E[L(1)] - E[L(0)]$.

The leakage measurement l_i obtained for the ith encryption can thus be expressed as:

$$l_i = \mu - \frac{\delta}{2}(-1)^{b_i^\star + r_i} + \eta_i \, , \tag{15}$$

where, for the ith encryption, $b_i^\star$ is the unmasked value of b (i.e. $b_i^\star = f(x_i, k^\star)$), r_i is the mask value and η_i is the noise in the leakage measurement.

We make the additional assumption that for every key hypothesis k, the sequence of guesses satisfies: $\#\{i; b_i = 0\} = \#\{i; b_i = 1\} = N/2$. This assumption is realistic since the functions $f(\cdot, k)$ are usually *balanced* (i.e. $\#\{x; f(x, k) = 1\} = \#\{x; f(x, k) = 0\}$) and since the x_i's are usually uniformly distributed. It allows us to rewrite (6) as:

$$\Delta_k = -\frac{2}{N}\left(\sum_{i=1}^{N}(-1)^{b_i} l_i\right) \, . \tag{16}$$

This relation together with (15) leads to:

$$\Delta_k = \frac{\delta}{N}\sum_{i=1}^{N}(-1)^{b_i + b_i^\star + r_i} - \frac{2}{N}\sum_{i=1}^{N}(-1)^{b_i}\eta_i$$

$$= \frac{\delta}{N}\left(\sum_{\substack{i=1 \\ b_i = b_i^\star}}^{N}(-1)^{r_i} - \sum_{\substack{i=1 \\ b_i \neq b_i^\star}}^{N}(-1)^{r_i}\right) - \frac{2}{N}\sum_{i=1}^{N}(-1)^{b_i}\eta_i$$

Recalling that α is the *ratio* of the b_i's that are wrongly predicted (i.e. $\alpha = \#\{i; b_i \neq b_i^\star\}/N$) and after rewriting $(-1)^{r_i}$ as $1 - 2r_i$, we get:

$$\Delta_k = \delta(1 - 2\alpha) + \frac{2\delta}{N}\left(\sum_{\substack{i=1 \\ b_i \neq b_i^\star}}^{N} r_i - \sum_{\substack{i=1 \\ b_i = b_i^\star}}^{N} r_i\right) - \frac{2}{N}\sum_{i=1}^{N}(-1)^{b_i}\eta_i \, .$$

Since r_i is distributed over $\mathbb{F}_2$ with $P[r_i = 1] = 1/2 - \varepsilon$ then for every $I \subseteq \{1, \cdots, N\}$, the sum $\sum_{i \in I} r_i$ has a binomial distribution with parameter $(\#I, 1/2 - \varepsilon)$. Moreover, since η_i has a Gaussian distribution $\mathcal{N}(0, \sigma^2)$, then the sum $\sum_{i=1}^{N}(-1)^{b_i}\eta_i$ has a Gaussian distribution $\mathcal{N}(0, N\sigma^2)$. This way, we obtain:

$$\Delta_k \sim \mathcal{N}\left(\delta(1 - 2\alpha), \frac{4\sigma^2}{N}\right) + \frac{2\delta}{N}\mathcal{B}\left(\alpha N, \frac{1}{2} - \varepsilon\right) - \frac{2\delta}{N}\mathcal{B}\left((1 - \alpha)N, \frac{1}{2} - \varepsilon\right) \, .$$

After approximating $\mathcal{B}(n, p)$ by $\mathcal{N}(np, np(1 - p))$ (which is almost exact when $n \geq 30$, $np > 5$ and $n(1 - p) > 5$), we finally get:

$$\Delta_k \sim \mathcal{N}\left(2\varepsilon \times \delta(1 - 2\alpha), \frac{4\sigma^2 + \delta^2(1 - 4\varepsilon^2)}{N}\right) \, .$$

This relation shows that the biased masking results in a reduction of the expectation of Δ_k and in an increase of its variance. The expectation is divided by a factor $1/2\varepsilon$ while its variance is multiplied by a factor $1 + \delta^2(1 - 4\varepsilon^2)/\sigma^2$. When the leakage signal-to-noise ratio is low, $i.e.$ $\sigma \gg \delta$, then the biais has a weak influence on the variance and its main effect is the reduction of the expectation. According to [3] this results in an increase of the number of required leakage measurements by a factor $(1/2\varepsilon)^2$. If the leakage signal-to-noise ratio is not that low, the increase of the variance is significant and the number of required leakage measurements is multiplied by $(1/2\varepsilon)^2\big(1 + \delta^2(1 - 4\varepsilon^2)/\sigma^2\big)$.

Collision-Based Power Analysis of Modular Exponentiation Using Chosen-Message Pairs

Naofumi Homma[1], Atsushi Miyamoto[1], Takafumi Aoki[1],
Akashi Satoh[2], and Adi Shamir[3]

[1] Graduate School of Information Sciences, Tohoku University
{homma,miyamoto}@aoki.ecei.tohoku.ac.jp, aoki@ecei.tohoku.ac.jp
[2] National Institute of Advanced Industrial Science and Technology
akashi.satoh@aist.go.jp
[3] Weizmann Institute of Science
adi.shamir@weizmann.ac.il

Abstract. This paper proposes new chosen-message power-analysis attacks against public-key cryptosystems based on modular exponentiation, which use specific input pairs to generate collisions between squaring operations at different locations in the two power traces. Unlike previous attacks of this kind, the new attacks can be applied to all the standard implementations of the exponentiation process: binary (left-to-right and right-to-left), m-ary, and sliding window methods. The SPA countermeasure of inserting dummy multiplications can also be defeated (in some cases) by using the proposed attacks. The effectiveness of the attacks is demonstrated by actual experiments with hardware and software implementations of RSA on an FPGA and the PowerPC processor, respectively. In addition to the new collision generation methods, a high-accuracy waveform matching technique is introduced to detect the collisions even when the recorded signals are noisy and the clock has some jitter.

Keywords: side-channel attacks, power-analysis attacks, RSA, modular exponentiation, waveform matching.

1 Introduction

Physical attacks on cryptographic modules using side-channel information are attracting extensive attention. In order to reveal the secret parameters, the power dissipation, the electromagnetic radiation, or the operating times related to internal operations are analyzed. Two of the best known attacks are Simple Power Analysis (SPA) and Differential Power Analysis (DPA) proposed by Kocher et al. [1,2].

The original concept of side-channel attacks against modular exponentiation [3] is to look for some physical phenomena which differentiates between multiplication and squaring operations. Messerges presented a variety of power-analysis attacks against RSA with some experimental results [4]. However, most of the

E. Oswald and P. Rohatgi (Eds.): CHES 2008, LNCS 5154, pp. 15–29, 2008.

implementations of modular exponentiation nowadays use the same sequence of instructions to implement multiplications and squarings, and for random inputs, it is very difficult to distinguish between these two operations. In order to cause secret information to leak via the power waveforms, chosen-message attacks that use specific data specialized for a particular cryptographic module were proposed [5,6,7,8,9,10].

The timing attacks against RSA with Montgomery multiplication [11] and/or CRT algorithm in [5,6] measures the operating times caused by extra calculations depending on input data. The SPA with adaptively chosen messages [7] can be applied to an RSA implementation using CRT based on Garner's algorithm, in which an extra modular reduction is performed at the end of the operation according to the input data. The DPA using the Hamming weight of an intermediate value [8] was also applied to RSA with CRT. These attacks focused on specific RSA implementations, and thus information about the implementation is indispensable to reveal the secret keys. The first three attacks can be defeated by inserting dummy operations, and the DPA of [8] cannot be applied to implementations using the Montgomery algorithm.

Over the last few years, several researchers have proposed to use a power analysis technique which is a mixture of the simple and the differential approaches. This technique compares two segments of power consumption data (within a single execution or in two different executions) and uses the result to determine whether the values operated on were the same or different. For example, when we perform two multiplications $a \times b$ and $c \times d$, we expect the power consumption curves to be similar when $a = c$ and $b = d$, and different in all other cases. This can give us a simple equality oracle, even though it may be extremely difficult to determine the actual values of a, b, c, and d from the complex waveforms. This is not a standard SPA technique since we do not try to understand the details of each waveform, and it is not a standard DPA since it is not based on the statistical analysis of large collections of power traces. We propose to call such attacks on pairs of waveforms CPA (Comparative Power Analysis).

One of the simplest attacks of this type was proposed by Yen et al [10]. It uses the particular input data of $N - 1$ where N is the modulus, which has the special property that all its powers are either 1 or -1. However, a simple countermeasure is to block the special message $N - 1$, and the attack can only be applied to implementations using a left-to-right binary method.

Another attack of this type is the "doubling attack" of Fouque and Valette [9]. They used the two related input messages X and X^2 to cause collisions between adjacent time frames in the two power waveforms, where squaring operations are performed. Since every message X can be part of such a message pair, it is harder to block potentially harmful messages. As in the case of Yen's method, these attacks can only be applied to the left-to-right binary method, and the authors make this point explicit in the title of their paper: "The Doubling Attack - Why Upwards is Better than Downwards".

In this paper we propose new power-analysis attacks using input pairs which can be successfully applied to all the standard implementations of the exponentiation function, including both left-to-right and right-to-left binary methods, m-ary (window), and sliding window methods. The major new element of these attacks is the observation that an attacker can easily choose pairs of messages that generate collisions between their power traces at arbitrary time frames (which need not be the same or adjacent) even though he does not know the factorization of the modulus and thus cannot extract modular roots. Information about the locations of such non-adjacent collisions in the power traces is then used to identify the bit pattern of the secret exponent. In the proposed attack, the relationship between the two input messages can cope flexibly with the many variants of exponentiation algorithms, including those which were immune to previous attacks.

We demonstrate the practical effectiveness of the proposed attacks against hardware and software implementations of RSA using a Xilinx FPGA with a PowerPC processor core. In this experiment, a high-accuracy waveform matching technique is introduced to find collisions between squaring patterns that appear at different time frames even when the signal is noisy and the clock has some jitter.

The remainder of this paper is organized as follows: Section 2 presents an overview of modular exponentiation algorithms and describes power-analysis attacks using a chosen-message pair. In Section 3, the new power-analysis attacks using chosen-message pairs against binary and m-ary methods are proposed. Section 4 describes the experimental results using actual RSA hardware and software implementations. Finally, Section 5 contains some concluding remarks.

2   Preliminary and Related Attacks

2.1   Modular Exponentiation Algorithms

Modular exponentiation is one of the most important arithmetic operations for public-key cryptography, such as the RSA scheme and the ElGamal encryption scheme, and for the Diffie-Hellman key agreement. Basically, there are two types of efficient exponentiation algorithms: binary methods and m-ary (or window) methods [12,13].

The binary method performs multiplications and squarings sequentially according to the bit pattern of the exponent. There are two variations of the algorithm. The left-to-right binary method starts at the exponent's MSB and works downward. The right-to-left binary method, on the other hand, starts at the exponent's LSB and works upward. **ALGORITHM 1** shows the left-to-right binary method, where k indicates the bit length of the secret keys. Each multiplication (or squaring) operation requires a large number of clock cycles due to the long operand length depending on the implementation. The binary method is frequently used in smartcards and embedded devices, due to its simplicity and low resource consumption.

The m-ary method processes more than one bit of the exponent in each iteration cycle, in which the exponent uses a representation with base m. **ALGORITHM 2** shows the m-ary method in which the exponent is processed from

ALGORITHM 1
LEFT-TO-RIGHT BINARY METHOD

Input:	$X, N,$
	$E = (e_{k-1}, ..., e_1, e_0)_2$
Output:	$Z = X^E \bmod N$
1 :	$Z := 1;$
2 :	**for** $i = k - 1$ **downto** 0
3 :	$Z := Z * Z \bmod N;$
4 :	**if** $(e_i = 1)$ **then**
5 :	$Z := Z * X \bmod N;$
6 :	**end if**
7 :	**end for**

ALGORITHM 2
m-ARY METHOD

Input:	$X, N,$
	$E = (e_{k-1}, ..., e_1, e_0)_{2^m},$
	for $m \geq 1.$
Output:	$Z = X^E \bmod N$
1 :	$g_0 := 1;$
2 :	**for** $i = 1$ **to** $2^m - 1$
3 :	$g_i := g_{i-1} * X;$ — $g_i = X^i$
4 :	**end for**
5 :	$Z := 1;$
6 :	**for** $i = k - 1$ **downto** 0
7 :	**for** $l = 1$ **to** m
8 :	$Z := Z * Z \bmod N;$
9 :	**end for**
10:	$Z := Z * g_{e_i} \bmod N;$
11:	**end for**

the MSB down to the LSB. The powers $g_i \bmod N$ $(i = 0, 1, 2, ..., 2^m - 1)$ are pre-computed and used in multiplication. The intermediate value Z is raised to the power of 2^m by repeating the squaring operation m times. The m-ary method requires fewer clock cycles but more memory resources compared with the binary methods, and thus is often used for software implementation on processors with large memory resources. The sliding window method is an extension of the m-ary method to reduce the amount of pre-computation by using the presence of zero bits in the exponent.

2.2 SPA Using a Chosen-Message Pair against Modular Exponentiation

The doubling attack [9] uses the two related inputs X and X^2. The secret exponent is revealed by detecting collisions of squaring operations in two power traces. Fig. 1 illustrates an image of the doubling attack against the left-to-right binary method in **ALGORITHM 1** with the secret key exponent of "101001..." The doubling attack can generate a collision between a squaring operation at the $i + 1$-th cycle in the power trace of X and a squaring operation at the i-th cycle in that of X^2 only if the corresponding key bit e_i is 0. The collision for squaring is detected by comparing the power traces, and thus we do not have to know the intermediate data being processed. The doubling attack works on modular exponentiation based on left-to-right binary methods including those using the blinding countermeasures shown in [14].

A different attack which uses the message pair X and $-X$ $(= N - X \bmod N)$ was proposed by Yen et al [10]. Fig. 2 illustrates an image of this attack against the left-to-right binary method. When the key bit e_i is 0, a collision between power traces can be observed for the two squaring operations during the same iteration cycle.

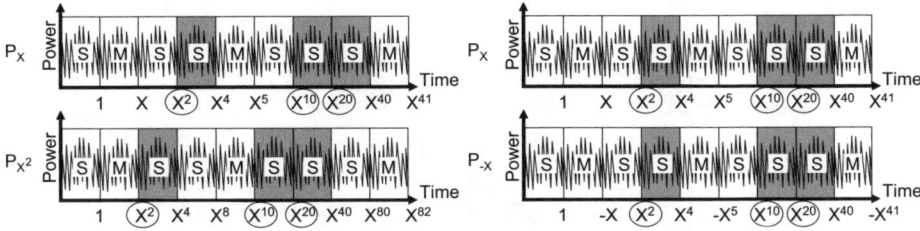

Fig. 1. Doubling attack. [9]   **Fig. 2.** Yen's attack. [10]

Both attacks exploit the fact that the values which are squared depend on the bits of the secret exponent. As mentioned in [9], it is hard to apply the attack to exponentiation algorithms such as right-to-left algorithms and window methods that perform squaring operations independently of the secret exponent.

3   The New Attacks

The above two attacks generate collisions of squaring operations at the adjacent or the same time frames in two power traces. In contrast, the proposed attacks generate a collision between two power traces at two arbitrary time frames by using two input messages with a more flexible relationship. One input gives a power trace including an unknown (multiplication or square) operation depending on a target key bit to be estimated, which is called a target operation. The other input gives a power trace including a square operation, the input of which can be determined by the known sub-key bits, referred to as the reference operation. The partial traces for the target and reference operations are called target and reference waveforms, respectively. The collision between the target and reference waveforms is used to estimate the target key bit.

Our attacks provide direct and backward estimations of the key exponent using the collision. The direct estimation simply compares the target (squaring or multiplication) operation with the reference (squaring) operation to identify the target operation corresponding to the key bit. The backward estimation identifies the target operation by comparing a squaring operation following the target operation with the reference operation. Unlike all the previous techniques, these new estimation techniques can be applied to all the standard exponentiation techniques (including both left-to-right and right-to-left binary methods, m-ary methods and the sliding window methods).

The simple trick we use in order to generate a collision at any pair of locations in two power traces is to find a solution for any equation of the form $Y^\alpha = Z^\beta \bmod N$, where α and β are given constants. Note that the attacker does not know the factorization of N and thus cannot solve this equation by extracting modular roots. However, he can choose an arbitrary value R and compute $Y = R^\beta \bmod N$ and $Z = R^\alpha \bmod N$, which is clearly a solution for the equation. This method is also applicable for CRT implementation that uses the prime

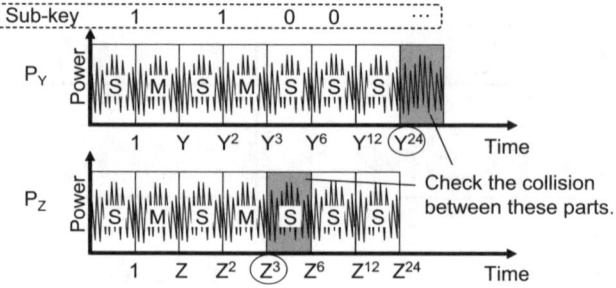

Fig. 3. Attack on the binary method (direct estimation)

factors p and q of N as the moduli since the message pair Y and Z satisfies $Y^\alpha = Z^\beta \bmod p$ and $Y^\alpha = Z^\beta \bmod q$.

3.1   Attack on Binary Methods

First, the direct estimation of the binary method shown in **ALGORITHM 1** is described. Suppose that the sub-key bits $E^{(j)}$ ($= e_{k-1}, ..., e_{k-j}$) of the secret exponent E have already been obtained. In order to estimate the next key bit $e_{k-(j+1)}$, a message pair is used, which causes a collision between the target and reference operations performed at different time frames. If a collision is observed, the target operation is a squaring (i.e., $e_{k-(j+1)} = 0$). If no collision is observed, then the operation is a multiplication (i.e., $e_{k-(j+1)} = 1$). Once $e_{k-(j+1)}$ is obtained, the remaining bits $e_{k-(j+2)}, ..., e_0$ are sequentially computed in the same manner.

The message pair Y and Z is given as $Y^\alpha = Z^\beta (Y \neq Z)$, where the α and β satisfy

$$\alpha = 2E^{(j)}, \tag{1}$$

$$\beta = \left\lfloor \frac{\alpha}{2^t} \right\rfloor \quad (0 \leq t \leq j), \tag{2}$$

respectively. Here, Y^α is the input for the target operation performed by $e_{k-(j+1)}$, and Z^β is the input for the reference operation. If $e_{k-(j+1)} = 0$, the operation of Y^α is the same as that of Z^β. In contrast, if $e_{k-(j+1)} = 1$, the operation of Y^α is a multiplication, and is different from that of Z^β. As a result, the bit $e_{k-(j+1)}$ is obtained by comparing the target waveforms of Y^α and the reference waveform of Z^β.

Fig. 3 shows an example of the direct (bit/digit) estimation of **ALGO-RITHM 1**. Suppose that the attacker already knows the first four bits ($E^{(4)} = 1100_2$). In this condition, α and β are given as $\alpha = 24$ and $\beta = 1, 3, 6, 12$, or 24. In order to estimate the next key bit, a message pair Y and Z, which meets the condition $Y^{24} = Z^3$ (i.e., $\alpha = 24$ and $\beta = 3$) is used. Here, Y^{24} is the input for the target operation, and Z^3 is the input for the reference operation. If $\beta = 24$ ($Y^{24} = Z^{24}$), then $Y = r$ and $Z = -r$. Therefore, this attack is identical to

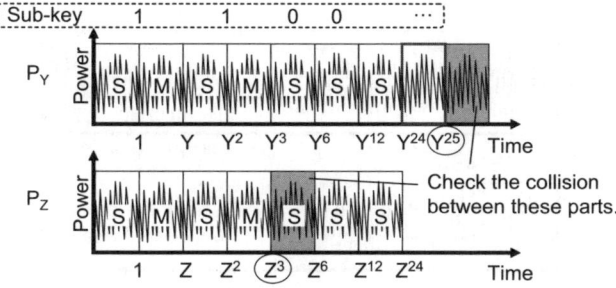

Fig. 4. Attack on the binary method (backward estimation)

Yen's attack [10]. If $\beta = 12$ ($Y^{24} = Z^{12}$), then $Y = r$ and $Z = r^2$, which is identical to the doubling attack [9]. Thus, these attacks are special cases of the present direct estimation.

Now, the backward estimation of **ALGORITHM 1** is explained. To estimate the key bit $e_{k-(j+1)}$, a squaring operation following the target operation for $e_{k-(j+1)}$ is investigated. Unlike the direct estimation, the bit value of $e_{k-(j+1)}$ (0 or 1) is estimated first, and the input message pair is then selected so that the power waveform for the squaring *following* the target operation would match the waveform for the reference operation. Assuming that $e_{k-(j+1)} = 1$, the message pair Y and Z is selected so as to meet the condition $Y^{\alpha+1} = Z^{\beta}$. If the estimation of $e_{k-(j+1)}$ is correct, the operating sequence and data for the squaring of $Y^{\alpha+1}$ are the same as those of Z^{β}, and the two waveforms of the squaring would be identical. In contrast, if the estimation is incorrect, the two square waveforms would be different.

Fig. 4 shows an example of the backward (bit/digit) estimation against the binary method. Assuming that the target key bit is 1, and the message pair is selected to meet the condition $Y^{25} = Z^3$. If the estimation is correct, a multiplication $Y^{24} \times Y$ is performed as the target operation and the result of Y^{25} is fed to the following squaring. Therefore, the same input values Y^{25} and Z^3 ($= Y^{25}$) are used for the squaring operations that generate two power waveforms to be compared. If the target key bit is 0, the target operation is squaring, and the input of the following squaring is Y^{48} ($= Y^{24 \times 2}$), which is not equal to Z^3, and thus the two waveforms for the squaring do not match.

As described above, the direct estimation compares the two waveforms generated by the reference (square) and the target (unknown) operations with the same input data to determine the target operation. In contrast, the backward estimation compares the two waveforms generated by square operations to determine the input data to the squaring following the target (unknown) operation. In order to determine the operation or the data using waveform matching, the proposed method controls the relation between the messages Y and Z as Equations (1) and (2).

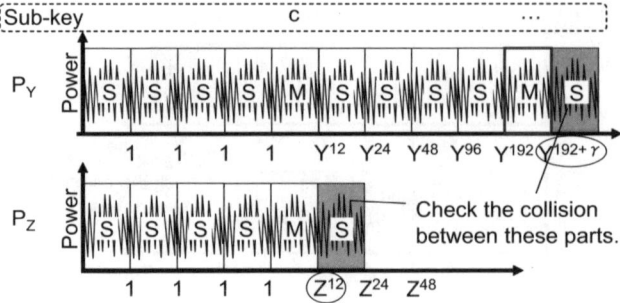

Fig. 5. Attack on the m-ary methods (backward estimation)

3.2   Attack on m-Ary Methods

The backward estimation has no additional advantage over the direct estimation for attacking the conventional binary method. However, the backward estimation is essential when attacking the m-ary method shown in **ALGORITHM 2**. This algorithm always performs a multiplication after raising the intermediate result to the power of 2^m (i.e., m squaring operations). Therefore, the direct estimation, which detects the multiplication performed only if the corresponding key bit is 1, cannot be applied. Suppose that the m-bit sub-keys $E^{(j)} = (e_{k-1}, ..., e_{k-j})_{2^m}$ of the secret exponent E have already been obtained. To estimate the next sub-key $e_{k-(j+1)}$, the waveform of the squaring following the target multiplication is investigated. At the beginning of the attack, the target sub-key $e_{k-(j+1)}$ is assumed as γ $(0 \leq \gamma \leq 2^m - 1)$, and the message pair Y and Z is selected to meet the condition $Y^{\alpha+\gamma} = Z^\beta$, where the α and β are given as

$$\alpha = 2^m E^{(j)}, \tag{3}$$

$$\beta = \left\lfloor \frac{\alpha}{2^{mt}} \right\rfloor \ (0 \leq t \leq j), \tag{4}$$

respectively. If the estimation is correct $(e_{k-(j+1)} = \gamma)$, the input data $Y^{\alpha+\gamma}$ to the squaring following the target multiplication is the same as the Z^β input in the reference squaring, and thus the waveforms for the two squaring operations would match. Even if the estimation is wrong, the correct sub-key can be obtained after 2^m trials at most.

Fig. 5 shows an example of the attack against the m-ary algorithm of **AL-GORITHM 2**, where $m = 4$. When the sub-key $e_{k-1} = 12$ is already known, α and β can be given by $\alpha = 192$ and $\beta = 12$. Assuming that e_{k-2} is γ, a message pair Y and Z is selected to meet the condition $Y^{192+\gamma} = Z^{12}$. If the estimation is correct, the input of the squaring $(Y^{192+\gamma})$ following the target operation is equal to that of the reference squaring (Z^{12}), and these inputs would make identical waveforms. In this case, the correct sub-key e_{k-2} can be estimated with at most $2^4 = 16$ trials.

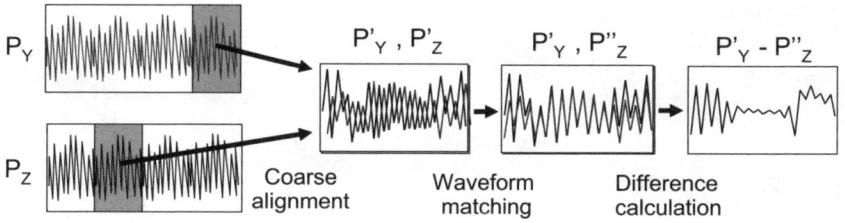

Fig. 6. Identification of operations using waveform matching

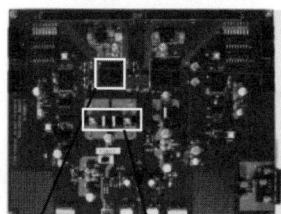

FPGA   Measuring points
(Xilinx Virtex-II Pro xc2vp7)

EXPERIMENTAL FPGA BOARD (SASEBO)	
FPGA	Virtex-II Pro xc2vp7
Crystal oscillator	24-MHz
Resistance value	1 Ohm
Power supply voltage	3.3 V
EXPERIMENTAL EQUIPMENT	
Digital oscilloscope	Agilent MSO6104A
Probe	Coaxial cable (50 Ohm)

Fig. 7. Evaluation board   **Fig. 8.** Experimental conditions

4   Experiments

4.1   Identification of Operations by Waveform Matching

The proposed attacks create collisions between target and reference power waveforms at time frames which can be far apart, whereas previous attacks compare the waveforms at adjacent time frames or at the same time frame, as shown in Figs. 1 and 2. Therefore, a flexible and precise matching technique which can overcome the cumulative effect of clock jitter and noise is crucial for collision detection. In the following, the phase-based waveform matching technique [15], which can match waveform positions with a resolution higher than the sampling resolution, is used. Fig. 6 shows an overview of the identification method. Given two power traces P_Y and P_Z, we first cut out the waveform segments that include the target and reference operations, P_Y' and P_Z', respectively. The segments can easily be recognized because each multiplication or square operation consumes less power around the boundaries of the operation. The waveform segments are then aligned precisely using the phase-based waveform matching technique. Finally, the difference between the waveforms is calculated to evaluate the equality of the operations or data being processed.

4.2   Experimental Results

RSA hardware and software using the Montgomery multiplication algorithm were implemented on the Xilinx FPGA platform Side-channel Attack Standard

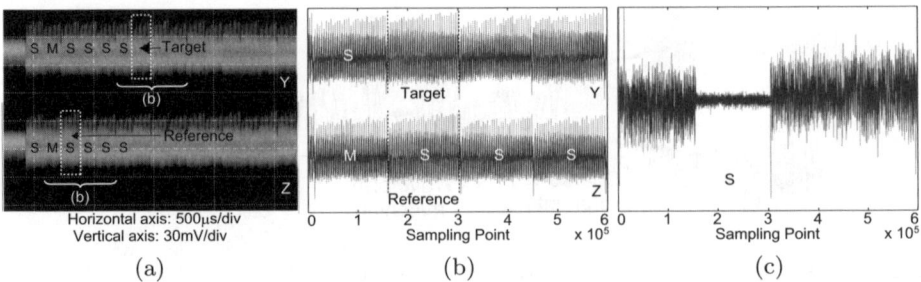

Fig. 9. Results of hardware implementation (target: squaring):(a) power traces of Y and Z, (b) waveform segments, and (c) differential waveform

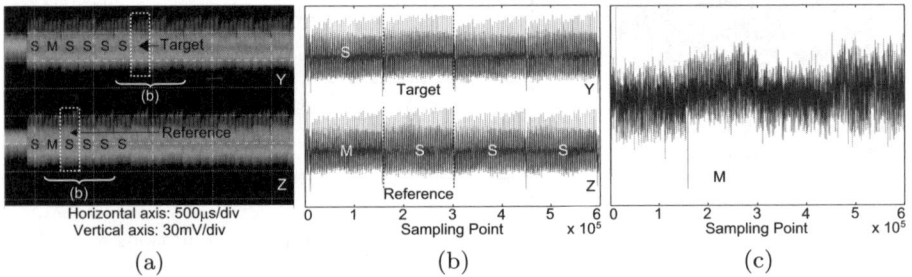

Fig. 10. Results of hardware implementation (target: multiplication):(a) power traces of Y and Z, (b) waveform segments, and (c) differential waveform

Evaluation BOard (SASEBO) [16] shown in Fig. 7. The RSA hardware with the FPGA's embedded multipliers performs 1,024-bit modular exponentiation using the binary method. On the other hand, the RSA software is executed as a PowerPC processor macro in the FPGA, where both binary and 4-ary methods are applied to a 256-bit exponent due to memory limitations.

The power traces were monitored using an oscilloscope (Agilent MSO 6104A) at 400 Msamples/sec for software and 800 Msamples/sec for hardware as voltage drops caused by the resistor inserted between the FPGA ground pin and the ground plane. Fig. 8 summarizes the experimental conditions.

Figs. 9 and 10 show the experimental results of the direct estimation using power traces generated by the RSA hardware with two different keys. The measured power waveforms in Figs. 9 (a) and 10 (a) are aligned on the reference and target time frames as (b), and then the differential waveforms in (c) are calculated. In order to reduce the noise distortion of the differential waveform, low-pass filtering techniques, as well as phase-based waveform matching, are applied. The result is extremely clean, producing a greatly reduced difference signal when the two squared values are the same. In Figs. 9 and 10, the first four bits of the exponents are the same and are known as "1101", and each 5-th key bit will be identified. As described in the example operation of Fig. 3, a message pair Y and Z that satisfies $Y^{24} = Z^3$ is used for the identification. The amplitude

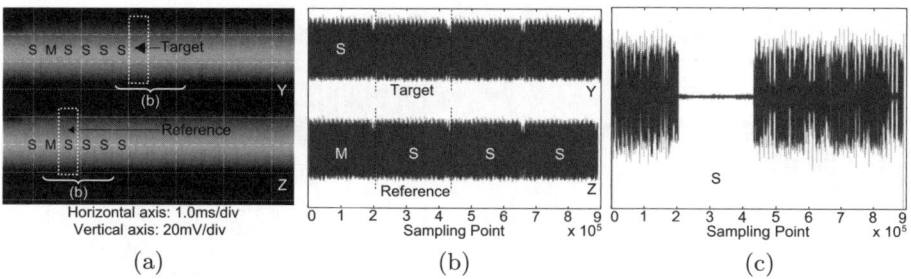

Fig. 11. Results of software implementation (target: squaring):(a) power traces of Y and Z, (b) waveform segments, and (c) differential waveform

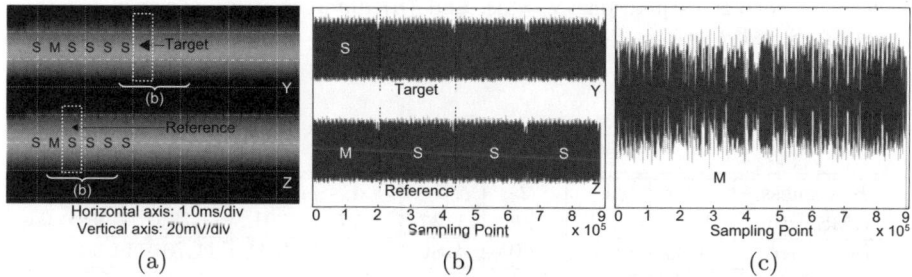

Fig. 12. Results of software implementation (target: multiplication):(a) power traces of Y and Z, (b) waveform segments, and (c) differential waveform

of the differential waveform in Fig. 9 (c) remains around zero, and thus the target (unknown) and reference (square) operations are the same. As a result, the target operation is squaring, and the 5-th key bit is identified as 0. In contrast, the differential waveform in Fig. 10 (c) indicates that the target and reference operations do not match. Therefore, the target operation is multiplication, and the 5-th key bit is revealed to be 1. Figs. 11 and 12 show the experimental results of the software implementation of RSA with the same algorithm and parameters used in Figs. 9 and 10, respectively. By applying the same matching techniques used for the hardware implementation, the secret key bits (target operations) can be easily identified.

Fig. 13 shows the differential waveforms derived from the backward estimation applied to the RSA software using the 4-ary method, where the known sub-key is 12. As described in Section 3.2 using the example operation of Fig. 5, a message pair Y and Z that meets the condition $Y^{192+\gamma} = Z^{12}$ was executed by the RSA software. The parameter γ denotes the next unknown 4-bit sub-key, and thus all sixteen possible sub-keys $0000 \sim 1111$ were tested. Figs. 13 (a) and 13 (b) show the differential waveforms for the correct sub-key ($\gamma = 3$) and for one of the fifteen incorrect sub-keys ($\gamma = 4$), respectively. The correct waveform is easily distinguished from the incorrect waveforms. For additional details, Root Mean Square (RMS) and maximum errors in the differential waveforms are shown in

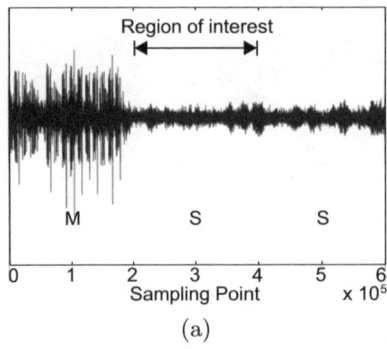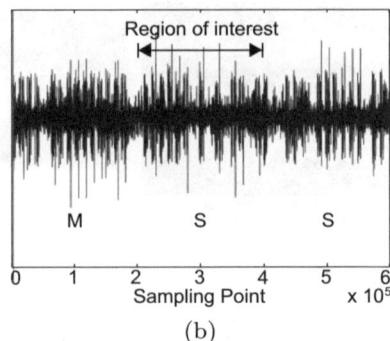

Fig. 13. Results of software implementation based on the 4-ary method:(a) differential waveform of correct estimation ($\gamma = 3$), and (b) differential waveform of incorrect estimation ($\gamma = 4$)

Table 1. RMS and maximum errors of differential waveforms

Key guess	0	1	2	**3**	4	5	6	7
RMS error	1.92	2.11	1.98	**1.27**	1.77	2.91	1.75	1.95
Max. error	11.39	11.55	12.05	**4.86**	11.76	12.41	11.70	11.50
Key guess	8	9	a	b	c	d	e	f
RMS error	1.96	1.89	1.74	2.11	1.90	1.82	2.21	2.07
Max. error	11.78	11.52	11.43	12.53	12.29	11.07	12.83	12.55

Table 1. In addition to visual observation, Table 1 can be used to automate the computation of the correct key bits.

The above results demonstrate that the proposed attacks can defeat both binary and m-ary methods. The m-ary method was not implemented in hardware due to memory limitations. But the proposed attack would defeat RSA hardware with the m-ary method as well as RSA software implementations, judging from the results of RSA hardware with the binary method. In addition to the logical approach, signal processing techniques such as phase-based matching and filtering greatly reduced the noise disturbing the correlation check between the target and reference waveforms. The same squaring operations can then be identified by numerical (RMS and maximum error) evaluation as well as visual observation. Although waveforms are not shown in the present study, the right-to-left binary method under the same condition described above was also defeated by the proposed attacks. Furthermore, the proposed attacks can be adapted to sliding window methods by combining the attacks against the binary and m-ary methods. These results clearly indicate that the proposed attacks are better than the previous attacks, which can only be applied to some of the implementations.

5   Conclusions

In this paper, we proposed new power-analysis attacks using chosen-message pairs against a variety of modular exponentiation algorithms. The message pairs are selected to have an exponential relationship in order to identify the same squaring operations which are performed at different time frames as determined by the bit pattern of the secret exponent. The proposed attacks can be adapted to all the standard exponentiation algorithms such as left-to-right/right-to-left binary methods, m-ary methods, and sliding window methods. Notice that standard message padding techniques such as OAEP provide no protection against our attacks: even though the chosen Y and Z ciphertexts are unlikely to produce validly padded plaintexts, this fact will be discovered only after the modular exponentiations will take place, and thus the attacker can recover the secret exponent even when no plaintexts are provided by the decryption process.

The effectiveness of the proposed attacks was demonstrated by experiments on RSA hardware/software implementations with the Montgomery multiplication algorithm. We also introduced signal processing techniques to reduce the expected noise distortion in the waveform comparison process. The proposed attacks derived the secret exponents from both binary methods and m-ary methods independently of the implementation platform. The values of the message pair can be selected arbitrarily. Therefore, the proposed attacks can also be applied to CRT implementations with/without the Montgomery multiplication algorithm, in which the relationship is controllable. In addition, dummy multiplication inserted as an SPA countermeasure for the left-to-right binary method can easily be detected by the new backward estimation technique which compares a squaring waveform following the true or dummy multiplication waveform with the reference waveform.

The right-to-left binary method with the squaring-and-multiply-always technique [17] and the blinding techniques [3] can still be used as effective countermeasures against the proposed attacks. Note however that the blinding techniques for the exponent and the message should be used simultaneously because each one of them separately can be defeated by the proposed attacks. For example, the mask updating technique in [3,14] is vulnerable to the proposed attacks as suggested in [9]. With regard to m-ary methods, the randomized m-ary methods [18,19] would also work as countermeasures.

The proposed chosen-message attacks provide a flexible relationship between two input messages and can generate waveform collisions in different time frames. The phase-based waveform matching with filtering technique enables high-accuracy alignment and collision detection between reference and target waveforms in any time frames independently of the algorithms, implementations, and platform. As a whole, the proposed methods and techniques make it possible to apply comparative power-analysis attacks to additional RSA implementations, using a very small number of chosen messages. Further research is being conducted to expand the applicable scope of the attacks even further (e.g., to exponentiation algorithms based on addition chains), and to overcome a variety of possible countermeasures.

References

1. Kocher, P., Jaffe, J., Jun, B.: Differential power analysis. In: Wiener, M.J. (ed.) CRYPTO 1999. LNCS, vol. 1666, pp. 388–397. Springer, Heidelberg (1999)
2. Kocher, P., Lee, R., McGraw, G., Raghunathan, A.: Security as a new dimension in embedded system design. In: Proc. the 41st annual conference on Design automation, pp. 753–760. ACM Press, New York (2004)
3. Kocher, P.: Timing attacks on implementations of Diffie-Hellman, RSA, DSS, and other systems. In: Koblitz, N. (ed.) CRYPTO 1996. LNCS, vol. 1109, pp. 104–113. Springer, Heidelberg (1996)
4. Messerges, T.S., Dabbish, E.A., Sloan, R.H.: Power analysis attacks of modular exponentiation in smartcards. In: Koç, Ç.K., Paar, C. (eds.) CHES 1999. LNCS, vol. 1717, pp. 144–157. Springer, Heidelberg (1999)
5. Schindler, W.: A timing attack against RSA with the Chinese remainder theorem. In: Paar, C., Koç, Ç.K. (eds.) CHES 2000. LNCS, vol. 1965, pp. 109–124. Springer, Heidelberg (2000)
6. Walter, C.D., Thompson, S.: Distinguishing exponent digits by observing modular subtractions. In: Naccache, D. (ed.) CT-RSA 2001. LNCS, vol. 2020, pp. 192–207. Springer, Heidelberg (2001)
7. Novak, R.: SPA-based adaptive chosen-ciphertext attack on RSA implementation. In: Naccache, D., Paillier, P. (eds.) PKC 2002. LNCS, vol. 2274, pp. 252–262. Springer, Heidelberg (2002)
8. Boer, B.D., Lemke, K., Wicke, G.: A DPA attack against the modular reduction within a CRT implementation of RSA. In: Kaliski Jr., B.S., Koç, Ç.K., Paar, C. (eds.) CHES 2002. LNCS, vol. 2523, pp. 228–243. Springer, Heidelberg (2003)
9. Fouque, A.P., Valette, F.: The doubling attack -why upwards is better than downawards. In: D.Walter, C., Koç, Ç.K., Paar, C. (eds.) CHES 2003. LNCS, vol. 2779, pp. 269–280. Springer, Heidelberg (2003)
10. Yen, S.M., Lien, W.C., Moon, S.J., Ha, J.C.: Power analysis by exploiting chosen message and internal collisions - vulnerability of checking mechanism for RSA-decryption. In: Dawson, E., Vaudenay, S. (eds.) Mycrypt 2005. LNCS, vol. 3715, pp. 183–195. Springer, Heidelberg (2005)
11. Montgomery, P.L.: Modular multiplication without trial division. Math. Comp. 44(170), 519–521 (1985)
12. Menezes, J.A., Oorschot, C.P., Vanstone, A.S.: Handbook of Applied Cryptography. CRC Press, Boca Raton (1997)
13. Koc, C.K.: High-speed RSA implementation, Technical Report TR201, RSA Laboratories (November 1994)
14. Coron, J.S.: Resistance against differential power analysis for elliptic curve cryptosystems. In: Koç, Ç.K., Paar, C. (eds.) CHES 1999. LNCS, vol. 1717, pp. 192–302. Springer, Heidelberg (1999)
15. Homma, N., Nagashima, S., Imai, Y., Aoki, T., Satoh, A.: High-resolution side-channel attack using phase-based waveform matching. In: Goubin, L., Matsui, M. (eds.) CHES 2006. LNCS, vol. 4249, pp. 187–200. Springer, Heidelberg (2006)
16. Side-channel Attack Standard Evaluation Board (SASEBO),
    http://www.rcis.aist.go.jp/special/SASEBO/
17. Joye, M.: Highly regular right-to-left algorithms for scalar multiplication. In: Paillier, P., Verbauwhede, I. (eds.) CHES 2007. LNCS, vol. 4727, pp. 135–147. Springer, Heidelberg (2007)

18. Walter, C.D.: MIST: An efficient, randomized exponentiation algorithm for resisting power analysis. In: Preneel, B. (ed.) CT-RSA 2002. LNCS, vol. 2271, pp. 53–66. Springer, Heidelberg (2002)
19. Itoh, K., Yajima, J., Takenaka, M.: DPA countermeasures by improving the window method. In: Kaliski Jr., B.S., Koç, Ç.K., Paar, C. (eds.) CHES 2002. LNCS, vol. 2523, pp. 303–317. Springer, Heidelberg (2003)

Multiple-Differential Side-Channel Collision Attacks on AES

Andrey Bogdanov

Horst Görtz Institute for IT Security
Ruhr University Bochum, Germany
abogdanov@crypto.rub.de,
www.crypto.rub.de

Abstract. In this paper, two efficient multiple-differential methods to detect collisions in the presence of strong noise are proposed - binary and ternary voting. After collisions have been detected, the cryptographic key can be recovered from these collisions using such recent cryptanalytic techniques as linear [1] and algebraic [2] collision attacks. We refer to this combination of the collision detection methods and cryptanalytic techniques as *multiple-differential collision attacks* (MDCA).

When applied to AES, MDCA using binary voting without profiling requires about 2.7 to 13.2 times less traces than the Hamming-weight based CPA for the same implementation. MDCA on AES using ternary voting with profiling and linear key recovery clearly outperforms CPA by requiring only about 6 online measurements for the range of noise amplitudes where CPA requires from 163 to 6912 measurements. These attacks do not need the S-box to be known. Moreover, neither key nor plaintexts have to be known to the attacker in the profiling stage.

Keywords: side-channel attacks, collision detection, multiple-differential collision attacks, AES, DPA.

1 Introduction

Side-channel attacks have become mainstream since their first publication in [3]. Differential power analysis (DPA) [4] and correlation power analysis (CPA) [5], a generalization of DPA, are probably the most wide-spread practical attacks on numerous cryptographic embedded systems such as smart-card microcontrollers [6] and dedicated lightweight ASICs [7].

Collision attacks represent another class of side-channel attack techniques being essentially based on the cryptanalytic properties of attacked cryptographic algorithms. Collision attacks on block ciphers were proposed in [8] for DES. The idea is due to Hans Dobbertin and was also discussed in the early work [9]. Since then there has been quite a bit of research in this area: [10] improves the collision attack on DES, [11] applies the technique to AES, [12] suggests a collision attack

E. Oswald and P. Rohatgi (Eds.): CHES 2008, LNCS 5154, pp. 30–44, 2008.

on an AES-based MAC construction, [13] combines collision attacks on AES with differential cryptanalysis to overcome several masked rounds.

Recently such improvements as linear collision attacks [1] and algebraic collision attacks [2] for AES have been proposed which require a very low number of measurements for the key recovery procedure to succeed with a high probability and within a feasible time span. However, these attacks as well as those in [11] and [12] are rather theoretical being substantially based on the assumption that the implementation allows the attacker to reliably detect if two given S-box instances process the same value.

The contribution of this paper is two-fold. On the theoretical side, two collision detection techniques are proposed called *binary* and *ternary voting*. We refer to the combination of the statistical collision detection methods and cryptanalytic collision attacks as *multiple-differential collision attacks (MDCA)*. On the practical side, we apply MDCA to a hardware implementation of AES for a wide range of noise amplitudes using advanced power consumption simulation.

MDCA works in the two scenarios: where profiling is either allowed (ternary voting) or not allowed (ternary voting without profiling and binary voting). Note that the notion of profiling for our collision detection techniques is different from that for template attacks [14], [15]. While template attacks require detailed knowledge of the implementation in the profiling stage, the only information needed in the profiling stage of the collision detection methods is the time interval when the S-boxes are executed.

MDCA based on the binary voting method for the given AES implementation needs about 2.7 to 13.2 times less traces than Hamming-weight based CPA in the range of noise levels we studied. While MDCA based on ternary voting without profiling does not exhibit any advantages over CPA, the required number of online measurements for ternary voting with profiling is considerably lower than that for CPA for all noise amplitudes we investigated. For instance, if $\leq 10^6$ profiling measurements are allowed, MDCA based on ternary voting with profiling and linear key recovery requires only 6 online measurements in the noise amplitude range where the standard CPA would require from 163 to 6912 measurements. A further advantage of the proposed collision detection techniques combined with the linear collision attacks is that they work with *secret S-boxes*. Moreover, ternary voting with profiling also requires *neither keys nor inputs/outputs to be known* in the profiling stage. However, as already mentioned, the attacker has to know when the S-boxes are executed within the implementation.

The remainder of the paper is organized as follows. Section 2 discusses the attack scenarios, introduces some notation and briefly mentions the linear collision attacks. Section 3 presents the multiple-differential collision detection techniques and theoretically investigates some of their properties. Section 4 characterizes the underlying least-square based binary comparison test for an AES implementation, applies MDCA to this implementation and compares the results to CPA. We conclude in Section 5.

2   Preliminaries

2.1   Attack Flows

There are two basic attack scenarios we consider: collision attacks *without profiling* and collision attacks *with profiling*. A collision attack without profiling consists of an online stage and an offline stage, while a collision attack with profiling additionally contains a profiling stage.

In the *online stage*, some random known 16-byte plaintexts $P_i = \{p_j^i\}_{j=1}^{16}$, $p_j^i \in GF(2^8)$, are sent to the attacked device implementing AES, where they are added with the first 16-byte subkey $K = \{k_j\}_{j=1}^{16}$, $k_j \in GF(2^8)$. Then each of the 16 values $a_j^i = p_j^i \oplus k_j$, $a_j^i \in GF(2^8)$, is processed by the AES S-box. The *online traces* $T_i = \{\tau_j^i\}_{j=1}^{16}$, $\tau_j^i = (\tau_{j,1}^i, \ldots, \tau_{j,l}^i) \in \mathbb{R}^l$, corresponding to these S-box calculations are acquired by the measurement equipment (e.g. they can contain such side-channel parameters as power consumption or electromagnetic radiation).

In the optional *profiling stage*, the device is triggered to perform a number of cryptographic operations with some unknown profiling inputs for some unknown keys. The *profiling traces* are acquired by the measurement equipment. The profiling stage takes place before the online stage and can be reused by several attacks on the same implementation.

The *offline stage* recovers the key. This occurs in two steps. First, collisions are detected in the online traces T_i by means of signal processing. The collision detection with profiling additionally uses the profiling traces. Second, an AES key candidate is obtained using the detected collisions and the corresponding inputs P_i. Note that one or several plaintext-ciphertext pairs produced with the attacked key may be needed to identify the correct key candidate in the offline stage.

If averaging is applied, the attacker has to be able to send several unknown equal inputs to the device and to fix some unknown key for these measurements in the profiling stage. Additionally, he has to be able to send several copies of the known random plaintexts to the implementation in the online stage.

The attack complexity is defined by three parameters. $C_{\text{profiling}}$ is the number of inputs to AES for which measurements have to be performed in the profiling stage (number of profiling measurements). Obviously, $C_{\text{profiling}} = 0$ for collision attacks without profiling. C_{online} is the number of inputs to AES for which measurements have to be performed in the online stage (number of online measurements). C_{offline} is the computational complexity of the key recovery, that is, the number of operations needed to solve the resulting systems of linear or nonlinear equations and to identify the most probable solution.

2.2   Key Recovery from S-Box Collisions

AES-128 performs 160 S-box operations in the data path for each run, which are different for different inputs, and 40 additional S-box computations in the key schedule, which remain the same for a given key. If two of these S-box instances in one or two distinct runs process the same value, there is *a generalized internal collision*. The power of the improved collision attacks [1] on AES origins from the fact that the number of generalized collisions grows quadratically with the linear increase of the number of unique inputs considered. So, even if the key schedule is ignored, there are about 40.9 colliding S-boxes for just one input and already about 555.2 collisions for 5 inputs.

When collisions have been detected, the AES key has to be recovered. In this paper we use the linear collision attacks [1] for this purpose. A *linear collision* in AES is a generalized collision within the first AES round. Given such a linear collision, the attacker obtains a binomial linear equation over $GF(2^8)$ of the form $k_{j_1} \oplus k_{j_2} = p_{j_1}^{i_1} \oplus p_{j_2}^{i_2}$ for $j_1 \neq j_2$.

Let γ be the number of different random inputs P_i to the algorithm for which collisions have to be detected in order for the key to be recovered with probability π within C_{offline} operations. In this paper, we apply the variant of linear collision attacks with $\gamma = 6$, $\pi = 0.854$ and C_{offline} equal to $2^{37.15}$ encryptions, see [1] for details and [2] for some more advanced techniques.

3   Multiple-Differential Collision Detection

The goal of the collision detection is to decide if two S-box instances in AES have had equal inputs based on side-channel traces.

For the direct binary comparison of S-box instances, the least-square based test was used in the original collision attack on AES in [11], which is essentially a computation of the Euclidean distance between two real-valued traces. Its resolution can be increased by suppressing noise through averaging.

However, there are other collision detection methods substantially using the simple binary comparison, two of which - binary voting and ternary voting - we propose in this section. Both methods can be combined with averaging. Additionally, the ternary voting test enables performance gains through profiling.

3.1   Binary Comparison

Definition. Given two traces $\tau_{j_1}^{i_1} = (\tau_{j_1,1}^{i_1}, \ldots, \tau_{j_1,l}^{i_1}) \in \mathbb{R}^l$ and $\tau_{j_2}^{i_2} = (\tau_{j_2,1}^{i_2}, \ldots, \tau_{j_2,l}^{i_2}) \in \mathbb{R}^l$, respectively corresponding to S-box j_1 for plaintext P_{i_1} and to S-box j_2 for plaintext P_{i_2}, the binary comparison test $\mathfrak{T}^{BC}$ can be defined as:

$$\mathfrak{T}^{BC}(\tau_{j_1}^{i_1}, \tau_{j_2}^{i_2}) = \begin{cases} 0 \ (\text{no collision}), \text{if } \mathfrak{S}^{BC}(\tau_{j_1}^{i_1}, \tau_{j_2}^{i_2}) > Y^{BC} \\ 1 \ (\text{collision}), \quad \text{if } \mathfrak{S}^{BC}(\tau_{j_1}^{i_1}, \tau_{j_2}^{i_2}) \leq Y^{BC}, \end{cases}$$

where Y^{BC} is a decision threshold and

$$\mathfrak{S}^{BC}(\tau_{j_1}^{i_1}, \tau_{j_2}^{i_2}) = \sum_{r=1}^{l} (\tau_{j_1,r}^{i_1} - \tau_{j_2,r}^{i_2})^2,$$

which can be seen as a correlation characteristic of two reduced templates. Let $\mathfrak{T}^{BC}$ be characterized by the following type I and II error probabilities:

$$\alpha_1 = \Pr\{\mathfrak{T}^{BC}(\tau_{j_1}^{i_1}, \tau_{j_2}^{i_2}) = 0 | a_{j_1}^{i_1} = a_{j_2}^{i_2}\},$$
$$\alpha_2 = \Pr\{\mathfrak{T}^{BC}(\tau_{j_1}^{i_1}, \tau_{j_2}^{i_2}) = 1 | a_{j_1}^{i_1} \neq a_{j_2}^{i_2}\}.$$

Note that α_1 and α_2 depend on the implementation and the value of Y^{BC}. Of course, there is a strong dependency on the noise as well. See Section 4 for estimations of α_2 with a given α_1 for one implementation example and a wide range of noise amplitudes.

Combination with Averaging. To increase the resolution of the collision detection one can use averaging. That is, each plaintext is sent t times to the device. Respectively, t measurements are performed for each plaintext. Then the obtained traces for each distinct plaintext are averaged. If the noise is due to normal distribution with the zero mean value and a standard deviation σ, then the noise amplitude of the trace averaged t times will be $\sigma/\sqrt{t}$.

3.2 Binary Voting Test

In this subsection we propose a more efficient method to suppress noise which is called *binary voting*. Like in averaging, traces for multiple copies of the same plaintexts are first obtained. However, instead of averaging, the attacker tries to detect collisions using binary comparison for each pair of the traces and applies voting to filter for correct ones.

Definition. We have to reliably detect collisions for γ different plaintexts. Then each of these plaintexts is sent M^{BV} times to the device. So we have a group $\tilde{\tau}_j^i = \{\tau_j^{i,m}\}_{m=1}^{M^{BV}}$, $\tau_j^{i,m} \in \mathbb{R}^l$, of traces for each S-box instance and each plaintext. That is, the direct application of binary voting requires $C_{\text{online}} = \gamma \cdot M^{BV}$ measurements.

The binary voting test is based on the following statistic which uses a binary comparison test (for instance, the least-square based one as defined above):

$$\mathfrak{S}^{BV}(\tilde{\tau}_{j_1}^{i_1}, \tilde{\tau}_{j_2}^{i_2}) = \sum_{m=1}^{M^{BV}} \mathfrak{T}^{BC}(\tau_{j_1}^{i_1,m}, \tau_{j_2}^{i_2,m}),$$

where the multiple traces for two S-box instances are pairwisely compared to each other. The test $\mathfrak{T}^{BV}$ to decide if there has been a collision is then defined as

$$\mathfrak{T}^{BV}(\tilde{\tau}_{j_1}^{i_1}, \tilde{\tau}_{j_2}^{i_2}) = \begin{cases} 0 \ (\text{no collision}), \text{if } \mathfrak{S}^{BV}(\tilde{\tau}_{j_1}^{i_1}, \tilde{\tau}_{j_2}^{i_2}) < Y^{BV} \\ 1 \ (\text{collision}), \quad \text{if } \mathfrak{S}^{BV}(\tilde{\tau}_{j_1}^{i_1}, \tilde{\tau}_{j_2}^{i_2}) \geq Y^{BV}, \end{cases}$$

where Y^{BV} is a decision threshold. The idea is that the distribution of statistic $\mathfrak{S}^{BV}$ will be different for $a_{j_1}^{i_1} = a_{j_2}^{i_2}$ and for $a_{j_1}^{i_1} \neq a_{j_2}^{i_2}$.

Properties. As the individual binary comparisons are independent, the distribution of $\mathfrak{S}^{BV}$ is due to the binomial law with M^{BV} experiments and success probability p. If $a_{j_1}^{i_1} = a_{j_2}^{i_2}$, the success probability is $p = p_e = 1 - \alpha_1$. If $a_{j_1}^{i_1} \neq a_{j_2}^{i_2}$, it is $p = p_{ne} = \alpha_2$. For sufficiently large group sizes M^{BV}, the distribution of $\mathfrak{S}^{BV}$ can be approximated by a normal distribution $\mathcal{N}(M^{BV}p, M^{BV}p(1-p))$. That is, the problem of collision detection is reduced to the problem of distinguishing between two normal distributions in this case. Thus, the required value of M^{BV} can be obtained using

Proposition 1. *Let α_1 and α_2 be type I and II error probabilities, respectively, for $\mathfrak{T}^{BC}$. Then the number of S-box traces in each group needed to distinguish between $a_{j_1}^{i_1} = a_{j_2}^{i_2}$ and $a_{j_1}^{i_1} \neq a_{j_2}^{i_2}$ using binary voting test $\mathfrak{T}^{BV}$ can be estimated as*

$$M^{BV} \approx \frac{(u_{1-\beta_1}\sqrt{\alpha_1(1-\alpha_1)} + u_{1-\beta_2}\sqrt{\alpha_2(1-\alpha_2)})^2}{(1 - \alpha_1 - \alpha_2)^2},$$

where:

- *β_1 and β_2 are the required type I and II error probabilities for $\mathfrak{T}^{BV}$,*
- *$u_{1-\beta_1}$ and $u_{1-\beta_2}$ are quantiles of the standard normal distribution $\mathcal{N}(0,1)$.*

Combination with Averaging. The required value of M^{BV} depends on α_1 and α_2 which in turn can be seen as functions of the noise amplitude σ. For this reason we will write $M^{BV}(\sigma)$ where this dependency is important.

The binary voting technique can be combined with averaging. The traces are first averaged t times. Then the statistic $\mathfrak{S}^{BV}$ is computed. That is, one deals with $M^{BV}(\sigma/\sqrt{t})$ instead of $M^{BV}(\sigma)$.

Since each plaintext P_i is sent $t \cdot M^{BV}(\sigma/\sqrt{t})$ times to the device, binary voting with averaging requires $C_{online} = \gamma \cdot t \cdot M^{BV}(\sigma/\sqrt{t})$ measurements. Depending on the concrete implementation and on the range of σ, the measurement complexity can be reduced, if $\gamma \cdot t \cdot M^{BV}(\sigma/\sqrt{t}) < \gamma \cdot M^{BV}(\sigma)$ for some t. In the sequel, we will refer to binary voting with averaging simply as binary voting, since binary voting with averaging for $t = 1$ corresponds to the basic binary voting.

3.3 Ternary Voting Test

Ternary voting is another statistical technique we propose to reliably detect collisions. It is based on indirect comparisons of traces, where two given S-box traces (*target traces*, a subset of online traces) are compared through a pool of other ones (*reference traces*, profiling traces if any and possibly a subset of online traces).

While the ternary voting test is less efficient than the binary voting one in terms of the overall number of traces needed, it allows for profiling. That is, the reference traces can be acquired in the profiling stage and shared by several attacks, which can significantly amplify the performance of the online stage.

Definition. Let N^{TV} be the number of S-box instances whose (reference) traces $\{\tau_m\}_{m=1}^{N^{TV}}$, $\tau_m \in \mathbb{R}^l$, are available to the attacker for some random unknown inputs $\{a_m\}_{m=1}^{N^{TV}}$, $a_m \in GF(2^8)$. Let $\tau_{j_1}^{i_1}$ and $\tau_{j_2}^{i_2}$ be the traces for two further S-box instances for which we have to decide if $a_{j_1}^{i_1} = a_{j_2}^{i_2}$. Then the ternary voting test can be defined as follows:

$$\mathfrak{T}^{TV}(\tau_{j_1}^{i_1}, \tau_{j_2}^{i_2}) = \begin{cases} 0 \text{ (no collision), if } \mathfrak{S}^{TV}(\tau_{j_1}^{i_1}, \tau_{j_2}^{i_2}) < Y^{TV} \\ 1 \text{ (collision),} \quad \text{if } \mathfrak{S}^{TV}(\tau_{j_1}^{i_1}, \tau_{j_2}^{i_2}) \geq Y^{TV}, \end{cases}$$

where

$$\mathfrak{S}^{TV}(\tau_{j_1}^{i_1}, \tau_{j_2}^{i_2}) = \sum_{m=1}^{N^{TV}} F(\tau_{j_1}^{i_1}, \tau_{j_2}^{i_2}, \tau_m)$$

with

$$F(\tau_{j_1}^{i_1}, \tau_{j_2}^{i_2}, \tau_m) = \mathfrak{T}^{BC}(\tau_{j_1}^{i_1}, \tau_m) \cdot \mathfrak{T}^{BC}(\tau_{j_2}^{i_2}, \tau_m)$$

and Y^{TV} is some decision threshold. The key idea of ternary voting is similar to that of binary voting: The distributions of $\mathfrak{S}^{TV}(\tau_{j_1}^{i_1}, \tau_{j_2}^{i_2})$ for $a_{j_1}^{i_1} = a_{j_2}^{i_2}$ and for $a_{j_1}^{i_1} \neq a_{j_2}^{i_2}$ will be different. Typically, $\mathfrak{S}^{TV}(\tau_{j_1}^{i_1}, \tau_{j_2}^{i_2})$ will be higher for $a_{j_1}^{i_1} = a_{j_2}^{i_2}$ than for $a_{j_1}^{i_1} \neq a_{j_2}^{i_2}$. To decide if there has been a collision, the attacker needs to statistically distinguish between these two cases.

Properties. To explore the behaviour of F, it is not sufficient to know the type I and II error probabilities for the binary comparison test. Let $\mathfrak{T}^{BC}$ be characterized by the simultaneous distribution of the test results depending on the relations between $a_{j_1}^{i_1}$, $a_{j_2}^{i_2}$ and a_m:

$$\chi_1 = \Pr\{\mathfrak{T}^{BC}(\tau_{j_1}^{i_1}, \tau_m) = 1, \mathfrak{T}^{BC}(\tau_{j_2}^{i_2}, \tau_m) = 1 | a_{j_1}^{i_1} = a_{j_2}^{i_2} = a_m\},$$
$$\chi_2 = \Pr\{\mathfrak{T}^{BC}(\tau_{j_1}^{i_1}, \tau_m) = 1, \mathfrak{T}^{BC}(\tau_{j_2}^{i_2}, \tau_m) = 1 | a_{j_1}^{i_1} = a_{j_2}^{i_2} \neq a_m\},$$
$$\chi_3 = \Pr\{\mathfrak{T}^{BC}(\tau_{j_1}^{i_1}, \tau_m) = 1, \mathfrak{T}^{BC}(\tau_{j_2}^{i_2}, \tau_m) = 1 | a_{j_1}^{i_1} \neq a_{j_2}^{i_2}, a_{j_1}^{i_1} = a_m, a_{j_2}^{i_2} \neq a_m\},$$
$$\chi_4 = \Pr\{\mathfrak{T}^{BC}(\tau_{j_1}^{i_1}, \tau_m) = 1, \mathfrak{T}^{BC}(\tau_{j_2}^{i_2}, \tau_m) = 1 | a_{j_1}^{i_1} \neq a_{j_2}^{i_2}, a_m \neq a_{j_1}^{i_1}, a_m \neq a_{j_2}^{i_2}\}.$$

Then the probabilities

$$p_e = \Pr\{F(\tau_{j_1}^{i_1}, \tau_{j_2}^{i_2}, \tau_m) = 1 | a_{j_1}^{i_1} = a_{j_2}^{i_2}\}$$

and

$$p_{ne} = \Pr\{F(\tau_{j_1}^{i_1}, \tau_{j_2}^{i_2}, \tau_m) = 1 | a_{j_1}^{i_1} \neq a_{j_2}^{i_2}\}$$

can be computed using

Proposition 2. If $a_{j_1}^{i_1}, a_{j_2}^{i_2}, a_m \in GF(2)^8$ are uniformly distributed and mutually independent, then

$$p_e = \frac{1}{2^8}\chi_1 + \frac{2^8-1}{2^8}\chi_2$$

and

$$p_{ne} = \frac{2}{2^8}\chi_3 + \frac{2^8-2}{2^8}\chi_4.$$

Proof. If $a_{j_1}^{i_1} = a_{j_2}^{i_2}$, two cases are possible for $F(\tau_{j_1}^{i_1}, \tau_{j_2}^{i_2}, \tau_m) = 1$:

- $a_{j_1}^{i_1} = a_{j_2}^{i_2} = a_m$ which happens with probability of $1/2^8$, and
- $a_{j_1}^{i_1} = a_{j_2}^{i_2} \neq a_m$ which happens with probability $\frac{2^8-1}{2^8}$.

If $a_{j_1}^{i_1} \neq a_{j_2}^{i_2}$, there are three cases leading to $F(\tau_{j_1}^{i_1}, \tau_{j_2}^{i_2}, \tau_m) = 1$:

- $a_{j_1}^{i_1} = a_m$, $a_{j_2}^{i_2} \neq a_m$ with probability $1/2^8$,
- $a_{j_2}^{i_2} = a_m$, $a_{j_1}^{i_1} \neq a_m$ with probability $1/2^8$, and
- $a_{j_1}^{i_1} \neq a_m$, $a_{j_2}^{i_2} \neq a_m$ with probability $(2^8 - 2)/2^8$.

The claims of the proposition follow. □

For the sake of simplicity, we first study the properties of $\mathfrak{T}^{TV}$ under the assumption that all applications of F to compute $\mathfrak{S}^{TV}$ are mutually independent. Under this assumption, $\mathfrak{S}^{TV}(\tau_{j_1}^{i_1}, \tau_{j_2}^{i_2})$ would have a binomial distribution with N^{TV} being the number of experiments and success probability $p = p_e$, if $a_{j_1}^{i_1} = a_{j_2}^{i_2}$, or $p = p_{ne}$, if $a_{j_1}^{i_1} \neq a_{j_2}^{i_2}$. Thus, for sufficiently large values of N^{TV}, $\mathfrak{S}^{TV}(\tau_{j_1}^{i_1}, \tau_{j_2}^{i_2})$ could be approximated by normal distribution $\mathcal{N}(N^{TV}p, N^{TV}p(1-p))$. Thus, similarly to binary voting, the number N^{TV} of S-box reference instances needed to distinguish between $a_{j_1}^{i_1} = a_{j_2}^{i_2}$ and $a_{j_1}^{i_1} \neq a_{j_2}^{i_2}$ could be estimated as

$$N^{TV} \approx \frac{(u_{1-\beta_1}\sqrt{p_e(1-p_e)} + u_{1-\beta_2}\sqrt{p_{ne}(1-p_{ne})})^2}{(p_e - p_{ne})^2},$$

where β_1 and β_2 are the required type I and II error probabilities for $\mathfrak{T}^{TV}$, $u_{1-\beta_1}$ and $u_{1-\beta_2}$ are quantiles of the standard normal distribution $\mathcal{N}(0,1)$.

However, the applications of F are dependent and this result can be only used to obtain a rough estimation of N^{TV}.

Procedure, Complexity, Averaging. Now we can describe the basic procedure of ternary voting in the case that the target key is fixed in the device and the plaintexts are random and known. This is what we call *ternary voting without profiling.*

The number N^{TV} of S-box reference instances as well as the number M^{TV} of different inputs for which reference traces have to be acquired depend on the noise level σ. We will write $N^{TV}(\sigma)$ and $M^{TV}(\sigma)$, when this dependency is crucial for understanding.

First, the attacker obtains traces for $M^{TV}(\sigma)$ random plaintexts. This yields τ_m for $N^{TV}(\sigma) = 160 \cdot M^{TV}(\sigma)$ different S-box instances for AES-128, if the key schedule is not considered and all the $16 \cdot 10$ S-box traces within each AES run are acquired at a time. Then, if $M^{TV}(\sigma) \geq \gamma$, no further measurements are needed. Otherwise, the attacker acquires traces for further $\gamma - M^{TV}(\sigma)$ plaintexts. Note that some of the reference traces can be interpreted as target traces (16 S-box traces corresponding to the first round in each of some γ executions of AES).

This yields the complexity of $C_{\text{online}} = \max(\gamma, M^{TV}(\sigma))$ measurements, where

$$M^{TV}(\sigma) = \left\lceil \frac{N^{TV}(\sigma)}{160} \right\rceil.$$

Like binary voting, ternary voting can be combined with averaging to achieve better resolution. In this case each trace has to be averaged t times. Thus, the complexity of ternary voting with averaging is $C_{\text{online}} = t \cdot \max(\gamma, M^{TV}(\sigma/\sqrt{t}))$. In the sequel we refer to ternary voting both with and without averaging simply as ternary voting.

Profiling. Now we are ready to describe what we refer to as *ternary voting with profiling*. Unlike binary voting, the method of ternary voting allows for profiling. In the profiling stage, reference traces are acquired only, for which the attacker has to know *neither* the key used *nor* the plaintexts. Moreover, this also works if keys are changed between blocks of t executions. The target traces are obtained in the online phase and compared based on the pre-measured reference traces.

Thus, $C_{\text{profiling}} = t \cdot M^{TV}(\sigma/\sqrt{(t)})$ measurements have to be performed in the profiling stage, each measurement comprising all 10 rounds of AES-128. Then only $C_{\text{online}} = t \cdot \gamma$ measurements are needed in the online stage, each measurement comprising only the first round for the linear key recovery. For the latter measurements we do have to know inputs. Moreover, they all have to be performed with the key to be recovered.

3.4   Required Error Probabilities of Collision Detection

The measurement complexity of the binary and ternary voting methods depends on the success probability to be achieved. Let us take q as a desirable success probability of the whole attack and estimate the required type II error probabilities β_2 for binary and ternary voting. Recall that π is the success probability of the cryptanalytic collision attack used to recover the key after the collisions have been detected.

In the linear key recovery, there are 16γ S-box instances between which a collision can occur. That is, the voting has to be performed $w = \binom{16\gamma}{2}$ times. Then β_2 can computed as

$$\beta_2 = 1 - (q/\pi)^{1/w}.$$

For instance, if $\gamma = 6$ and $q = 0.5$, one obtains $\beta_2 \approx 1.174 \cdot 10^{-4}$. Additionally, β_1 has to be low enough to enable the detection of a sufficient number of collisions.

4   MDCA and AES: A Case Study

The purpose of this section is to estimate the real-world efficiency of different MDCA variants based on an AES implementation example and to compare the methods to the standard Hamming-weight based CPA for the same AES implementation. In order to be able to perform this comparison for different noise levels σ, we carefully simulated the deterministic power consumption in Nanosim using dedicated power simulation libraries and added Gaussian noise of different amplitudes to it. The main results of the section are summarized in Table 1.

4.1 Implementation and Simulated Traces

The characteristics of $\mathfrak{T}^{BC}$ strongly depend on the signal-to-noise ratio of the implementation. To perform the estimations for a variety of noise levels, a serial VHDL implementation of the AES S-box has been performed (that is, only one S-box is calculated at a time). The deterministic power consumption for all 2^8 inputs was simulated using Synopsys Nanosim with the Dolphin Integration power consumption library SESAME-LP2 based on a 250nm technology by IHP [16]. The design was clocked at 10 MHz. The sampling rate was set to 10 Gsamples/s.

The S-box was implemented as combinatorial logic on the basis of an 8-bit register. Each S-box calculation $y = S(x)$ occurs in two clocks. In the first clock, the input x is read from the register and the output y is computed. In the second clock, the register is set to zero and the calculated output y is written to the register.

The simulated deterministic power traces obtained are noise-free. That is, there is neither electronic noise (power supply noise, clock generator noise, conducted emissions, radiated emissions, etc.) nor algorithmic noise (since only the relevant part of the circuit is considered) in these traces. To model noise we added random values due to univariate normal distribution[1] with the zero mean value and a standard deviation σ whose value characterizes the noise amplitude.

Note also that the simulated signal was not subject to a low-pass filter as it would have been the case for the real-world measurements of power consumption due to the presence of capacitances within the chip as well as on the circuit board where the power consumption measurements are performed. This would have cut off the high-frequency contribution to the signal reducing the advantage of high-resolution measurements. However, the effect of this circumstance is rather limited for the measurements of the electromagnetic radiation. A major limitation in this case is the bandwidth of the oscilloscope. Thus, we believe that the simulated traces with added Gaussian noise can be used for an initial analysis of the efficiency of our collision detection techniques. The main advantage of using the simulated power consumption is that one can add noise of different amplitudes to model the behaviour of attack methods for different devices and physical conditions.

To evaluate α_2 for this implementation, we chose Y^{BC} in $\mathfrak{T}^{BC}$ so that α_1 becomes sufficiently low by shifting Y^{BC} to the right. For this value of α_1, the

---

[1] Normal distribution is a sound noise model [17]. As a matter of fact, the noise is often distributed due to the multivariate normal distribution [17], [18]. However, only a few co-variances in the co-variance matrix of this multivariate normal distribution significantly differ from zero [18] for many implementations.

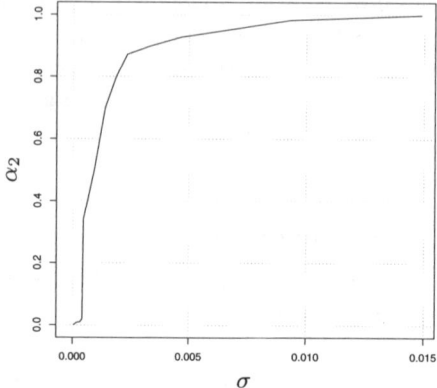

Fig. 1. Type II error probability α_2 for $\mathfrak{T}^{BC}$ as a function σ

type II error probability α_2 was estimated experimentally by executing $\mathfrak{T}^{BC}$ for random equal and unequal inputs to the S-box. We performed that for several noise amplitudes σ. The results can be found in Figure 1. Though this cannot be seen as a complete characterization of $\mathfrak{T}^{BC}$, the figure is meant to illustrate the intuition behind the multiple-differential collision detection methods.

4.2   Reference Figures for CPA

We compared the efficiency of MDCA with binary and ternary voting to the Hamming-weight based CPA [5]. The Hamming-weight power consumption model is sound for the implementation in question, since the register is first set to zero and then re-written with the target byte value. CPA was applied to the same simulated traces with the same noise amplitudes as MDCA. The number of measurements needed by CPA is denoted by C_{CPA}.

For our comparison, it was assumed that traces for all 16 S-boxes in the first round are acquired within one measurement. This is very similar to MDCA based on linear key recovery considered in this paper: The traces corresponding to the 16 S-box calculations in the first round are acquired at a time in the online stage for binary voting and ternary voting with profiling.

The number of measurements needed for CPA can be potentially reduced if guessing entropy is allowed in the offline stage of CPA. To treat this point, we assumed that CPA is successful, if it returns a correct 8-bit key chunk with probability 0.5. At the same time, it was assumed for all collision attacks that the needed success probability of the complete attack is $q = 0.5$. That is, a collision attack on AES is successful, iff it returns the correct 16-byte key with probability 0.5.

Note that power consumption models are also important for collision attacks. The right choice of a power consumption model allows the attacker to perform binary comparison more efficiently. In this paper, the consideration was restricted to the Euclidean distance of two vectors. However, other binary comparison tests can turn out to be more consistent with the power consumption of other implementations.

4.3   Online and Profiling Complexity of MDCA

In this subsection, C_{online} and $C_{\text{profiling}}$ for MDCA based on binary voting and ternary voting both with and without profiling are experimentally derived for the given implementation. The estimations are performed for the linear key recovery method with $\gamma = 6$.

Table 1. C_{online} against different values of σ for $\mathfrak{T}^{BV}$, $\mathfrak{T}^{TV}$ without profiling, $\mathfrak{T}^{TV}$ with profiling and C_{CPA}

$10^3\sigma$	0.46	0.93	2.32	3.25	4.65	6.97	9.30	11.62	13.95
C_{online}, $\mathfrak{T}^{BV}$	60	192	276	468	960	1290	1872	2976	4242
C_{online}, $\mathfrak{T}^{TV}$ w/o profiling	80	390	2605	5200	10640	23840	42320	66080	95200
C_{online}, $\mathfrak{T}^{TV}$ with profiling	6	6	6	6	6	18	30	60	120
C_{CPA}, HW based CPA	163	349	1645	4192	6912	15676	26341	39348	56025

Binary Voting. Figure 2 and Table 1 give experimental values of C_{online} for the binary voting test in a range of noise amplitudes. The values of t have been chosen that minimize the resulting number of traces needed. If σ' is the noise amplitude to be attained by averaging and σ is the given noise level, then one has to average about $t = (\sigma/\sigma')^2$ times. Thus, $C_{\text{online}} \approx \gamma\frac{\sigma^2}{\sigma'^2}M^{BV}(\sigma')$. The results demonstrate that binary voting is well-suited for our implementation providing an advantage of factor 2.7 to 13.2 for a wide range of σ.

Ternary Voting without Profiling. Figure 3 and Table 1 give concrete values of C_{online} in this case for a range of noise amplitudes. Values of t were chosen that minimize C_{online}. The performance of the ternary voting test without profiling is comparable to CPA. However, ternary voting without profiling does not exhibit any advantages over CPA in terms of measurement complexity.

Ternary Voting with Profiling. For a given σ, the attacker can reduce t which leads to a linear decrease of C_{online} and to a considerable growth of $C_{\text{profiling}}$ due to the slope of M^{TV} as a function of the noise amplitude (see Figure 3 for this dependency). We assumed that $\leq 10^6$ measurements in the profiling stage are feasible. To obtain the lowest possible online complexity within this bound on the profiling complexity, we chose t that minimizes C_{online} with $C_{\text{profiling}} \leq 10^6$ for each interesting value of σ. The resulting values of C_{online} and $C_{\text{profiling}}$ are depicted in Figure 4.3. The values of C_{online} can be also found in Table 1. Note that there is a wide spectrum of parameter choices: If there are more severe limits on $C_{\text{profiling}}$, then t and C_{online} increase. And the other way round: If the attack scenario admits for higher values of $C_{\text{profiling}}$, C_{online} can be further reduced.

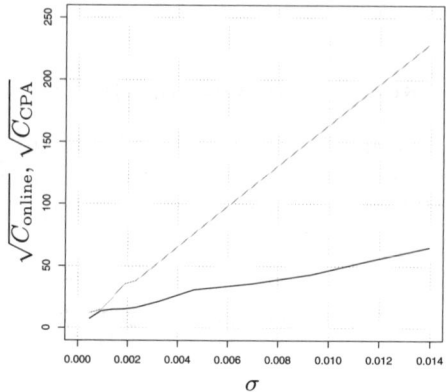

Fig. 2. Binary voting test against CPA: C_{online} (black line) and C_{CPA} (grey line) as functions of σ

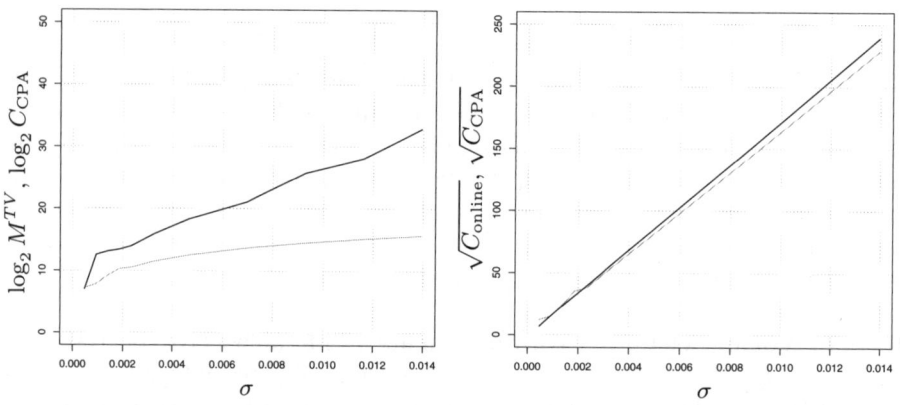

Fig. 3. Ternary voting test without profiling against CPA: $M^{TV}(\sigma)$ (on the left, black line) and C_{online} (on the right, black line) as well as C_{CPA} (both graphics, grey lines) as functions of σ

The complexity estimations for ternary voting were performed under the assumption that the attacker is able to acquire the reference traces for all S-boxes in each of the 10 AES rounds at a time. If one deals with a short-memory oscilloscope, $C_{\text{profiling}}$ increases in a linear way with respect to the decrease of the available memory volume. However, only measurements for the first round are needed for the target traces, if the linear key recovery is used.

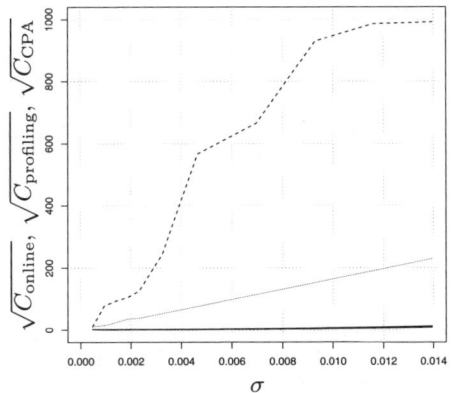

Fig. 4. Ternary voting test with profiling: C_{online} (solid black line), $C_{\mathrm{profiling}} \leq 10^6$ (dashed black line) and C_{CPA} (solid grey line) as functions of σ

5   Conclusions and Outlooks

In this paper two statistical techniques - binary and ternary voting - allowing to safely detect collisions even in the presence of considerable noise have been proposed. An AES hardware implementation with its accurately simulated power consumption has been taken as an example to demonstrate the power of the methods. This also enables us to obtain a clear dependency of the attack efficiency from the noise amplitude in a wide range of values and to soundly compare the multiple-differential techniques with CPA for the same implementation.

The binary voting method combined with linear key recovery is well applicable to AES being 2.7 to 13.2 times more efficient than CPA in terms of measurement complexity for our implementation in the explored range of noise amplitudes. Ternary voting combined with linear key recovery and profiling needs only about 6 online measurements for the range of noise amplitudes where CPA requires from 163 to 6912 measurements for the same implementation.

Techniques similar to the ones described in this work might turn out applicable to other symmetric constructions such as stream ciphers or message authentication codes and asymmetric constructions such as digital signature schemes. There can be also some potential in using MDCA-like methods to overcome certain random masking schemes for block ciphers.

Acknowledgements. The author would like to thank Christof Paar, Emmanuel Prouff and Francesco Regazzoni for fruitful discussions as well as the anonymous referees for their constructive comments.

References

1. Bogdanov, A.: Improved side-channel collision attacks on AES. In: Adams, C., Miri, A., Wiener, M. (eds.) SAC 2007. LNCS, vol. 4876, pp. 84–95. Springer, Heidelberg (2007)
2. Bogdanov, A., Pyshkin, A.: Algebraic side-channel collision attacks on AES, http://eprint.iacr.org/2007/477
3. Kocher, P.C.: Timing attacks on implementations of Diffie-Hellman, RSA, DSS and other systems. In: Koblitz, N. (ed.) CRYPTO 1996. LNCS, vol. 1109, pp. 104–113. Springer, Heidelberg (1996)
4. Kocher, P.C., Jaffe, J., Jun, B.: Differential power analysis. In: Wiener, M.J. (ed.) CRYPTO 1999. LNCS, vol. 1666, pp. 388–397. Springer, Heidelberg (1999)
5. Brier, E., Clavier, C., Olivier, F.: Correlation power analysis with a leakage model. In: Joye, M., Quisquater, J.-J. (eds.) CHES 2004. LNCS, vol. 3156, pp. 16–29. Springer, Heidelberg (2004)
6. Messerges, T.S., Dabbish, E.A., Sloan, R.H.: Investigations of power analysis attacks on smartcards. In: Smartcard 1999, USENIX Association, pp. 151–161 (1999)
7. Örs, S.B., Gürkaynak, F., Oswald, E., Preneel, B.: Power-analysis attack on an ASIC AES implementation. In: ITCC 2004, pp. 546–552. IEEE Computer Society, Los Alamitos (2004)
8. Schramm, K., Wollinger, T.J., Paar, C.: A new class of collision attacks and its application to DES. In: Johansson, T. (ed.) FSE 2003. LNCS, vol. 2887, pp. 206–222. Springer, Heidelberg (2003)
9. Wiemers, A.: Collision Attacks for Comp128 on Smartcards. In: ECC-Brainpool Workshop on Side-Channel Attacks on Cryptographic Algorithms, Bonn, Germany (2001)
10. Ledig, H., Muller, F., Valette, F.: Enhancing collision attacks. In: Joye, M., Quisquater, J.-J. (eds.) CHES 2004. LNCS, vol. 3156, pp. 176–190. Springer, Heidelberg (2004)
11. Schramm, K., Leander, G., Felke, P., Paar, C.: A collision-attack on AES: combining side channel- and differential-attack. In: Joye, M., Quisquater, J.-J. (eds.) CHES 2004. LNCS, vol. 3156, pp. 163–175. Springer, Heidelberg (2004)
12. Biryukov, A., Bogdanov, A., Khovratovich, D., Kasper, T.: Collision attacks on Alpha-MAC and other AES-based MACs. In: Paillier, P., Verbauwhede, I. (eds.) CHES 2007. LNCS, vol. 4727, pp. 166–180. Springer, Heidelberg (2007)
13. Biryukov, A., Khovratovich, D.: Two new techniques of side-channel cryptanalysis. In: Paillier, P., Verbauwhede, I. (eds.) CHES 2007. LNCS, vol. 4727, pp. 195–208. Springer, Heidelberg (2007)
14. Chari, S., Rao, J.R., Rohatgi, P.: Template attacks. In: Kaliski Jr., B.S., Koç, Ç.K., Paar, C. (eds.) CHES 2002. LNCS, vol. 2523, pp. 51–62. Springer, Heidelberg (2003)
15. Archambeau, C., Peeters, E., Standaert, F.X., Quisquater, J.J.: Template attacks in principal subspaces. In: Goubin, L., Matsui, M. (eds.) CHES 2006. LNCS, vol. 4249, pp. 1–14. Springer, Heidelberg (2006)
16. Dolphin: Description of the standard cells for the process IHP 0.25 μm. ViC specifications. SESAME-LP2. version 1.1 (2005)
17. Mangard, S., Oswald, E., Popp, T.: Power Analysis Attacks and Countermeasures for Cryptographic Smart Cards: Revealing the Secrets of Smart Cards. Springer, Heidelberg (2007)
18. Lemke-Rust, K.: Models and Algorithms for Physical Cryptanalysis. PhD thesis, Ruhr University Bochum (2007)

Time-Area Optimized
Public-Key Engines: $\mathcal{MQ}$-Cryptosystems as
Replacement for Elliptic Curves?

Andrey Bogdanov, Thomas Eisenbarth, Andy Rupp, and Christopher Wolf

Horst Görtz Institute for IT-Security
Ruhr-University Bochum, Germany
{abogdanov,eisenbarth,arupp}@crypto.rub.de,
chris@Christopher-Wolf.de, cbw@hgi.rub.de

Abstract. In this paper ways to efficiently implement public-key schemes based on $\mathcal{M}$ultivariate $\mathcal{Q}$uadratic polynomials ($\mathcal{MQ}$-schemes for short) are investigated. In particular, they are claimed to resist quantum computer attacks. It is shown that such schemes can have a much better time-area product than elliptic curve cryptosystems. For instance, an optimised FPGA implementation of amended TTS is estimated to be over 50 times more efficient with respect to this parameter. Moreover, a general framework for implementing small field $\mathcal{MQ}$-schemes in hardware is proposed which includes a systolic architecture performing Gaussian elimination over composite binary fields.

Keywords: $\mathcal{MQ}$-cryptosystems, ECC, hardware implementation, TA-product, UOV, Rainbow, amended TTS.

1 Introduction

Efficient implementations of public key schemes play a crucial role in numerous real-world security applications: Some of them require messages to be signed in real time (like in such safety-enhancing automotive applications as car-to-car communication), others deal with thousands of signatures per second to be generated (e.g. high-performance security servers using so-called HSMs - Hardware Security Modules). In this context, software implementations even on high-end processors can often not provide the performance level needed, hardware implementations being thus the only option. In this paper we explore the approaches to implement $\mathcal{M}$ultivariate $\mathcal{Q}$uadratic-based public-key systems in hardware meeting the requirements of efficient high-performance applications. The security of public key cryptosystems widely spread at the moment is based on the difficulty of solving a small class of problems: the RSA scheme relies on the difficulty of factoring large integers, while the hardness of computing discrete logarithms provides the basis for ElGamal, Diffie-Hellmann scheme and elliptic curves cryptography (ECC). Given that the security of all public key schemes used in practice relies on such a limited set of problems that are *currently* considered to be

E. Oswald and P. Rohatgi (Eds.): CHES 2008, LNCS 5154, pp. 45–61, 2008.

hard, research on new schemes based on other classes of problems is necessary as such work will provide greater diversity and hence forces cryptanalysts to spend additional effort concentrating on completely new types of problems. Moreover, we make sure that not all "crypto-eggs" are in one basket. In this context, we want to point out that important results on the potential weaknesses of existing public key schemes are emerging. In particular techniques for factorisation and solving discrete logarithms improve continually. For example, polynomial time quantum algorithms can be used to solve both problems. Therefore, the existence of quantum computers in the range of a few thousands of qbits would be a real-world threat to systems based on factoring or the discrete logarithm problem. This emphasises the importance of research into new algorithms for asymmetric cryptography.

One proposal for secure public key schemes is based on the problem of solving $\mathcal{M}$ultivariate $\mathcal{Q}$uadratic equations ($\mathcal{M}\mathcal{Q}$-problem) over finite fields $\mathbb{F}$, *i.e.* finding a solution vector $x \in \mathbb{F}^n$ for a given system of m polynomial equations in n variables each

$$\begin{cases} y_1 = p_1(x_1, \ldots, x_n) \\ y_2 = p_2(x_1, \ldots, x_n) \\ \quad \vdots \\ y_m = p_m(x_1, \ldots, x_n) \, , \end{cases}$$

for given $y_1, \ldots, y_m \in \mathbb{F}$ and unknown $x_1, \ldots, x_n \in \mathbb{F}$ is difficult, namely $\mathcal{N}\mathcal{P}$-complete. An overview over this field can be found in [14].

Roughly speaking, most work on public-key hardware architectures tries to optimise either the speed of a single instance of an algorithm (e.g., high-speed ECC or RSA implementations) or to build the smallest possible realization of a scheme (e.g., lightweight ECC engine). A major goal in high-performance applications is, however, in addition to pure time efficiency, an optimised cost-performance ratio. In the case of hardware implementations, which are often the only solution in such scenarios, costs (measured in chip area and power consumption) is roughly proportional to the number of logic elements (gates, FPGA slices) needed. A major finding of this paper is that $\mathcal{M}\mathcal{Q}$-schemes have the better time-area product than established public key schemes. This holds, interestingly, also if compared to elliptic curve schemes, which have the reputation of being particularly efficient.

The first public hardware implementation of a cryptosystem based on multivariate polynomials we are aware of is [17], where enTTS is realized. A more recent result on the evaluation of hardware performance for Rainbow can be found in [2].

1.1   Our Contribution

Our contribution is many-fold. First, a clear taxonomy of secure multivariate systems and existing attacks is given. Second, we present a systolic architecture implementing Gauss-Jordan elimination over GF(2^k) which is based on the work in [13]. The performance of this central operation is important for the overall efficiency of multivariate based signature systems. Then, a number of concrete hardware architectures are presented having a low time-area product. Here we address both rather conservative schemes such as UOV as well as more aggressively designed proposals such as Rainbow or amended TTS (amTTS). For instance, an optimised implementation of amTTS is estimated to have a TA-product over 50 times lower than some of the most efficient ECC implementations. Moreover, we suggest a generic hardware architecture capable of computing signatures for the wide class of multivariate polynomial systems based on small finite fields. This generic hardware design allows us to achieve a time-area product for UOV which is somewhat smaller than that for ECC, being considerably smaller for the short-message variant of UOV.

2 Foundations of $\mathcal{MQ}$-Systems

In this section, we introduce some properties and notations useful for the remainder of this article. After briefly introducing $\mathcal{MQ}$-systems, we explain our choice of signature schemes and give a brief description of them.

2.1 Mathematical Background

Let $\mathbb{F}$ be a finite field with $q := |\mathbb{F}|$ elements and define Multivariate Quadratic ($\mathcal{MQ}$) polynomials p_i of the form

$$p_i(x_1, \ldots, x_n) := \sum_{1 \le j \le k \le n} \gamma_{i,j,k} x_j x_k + \sum_{j=1}^{n} \beta_{i,j} x_j + \alpha_i \,,$$

for $1 \le i \le m; 1 \le j \le k \le n$ and $\alpha_i, \beta_{i,j}, \gamma_{i,j,k} \in \mathbb{F}$ (constant, linear, and quadratic terms). We now define the polynomial-vector $\mathcal{P} := (p_1, \ldots, p_m)$ which

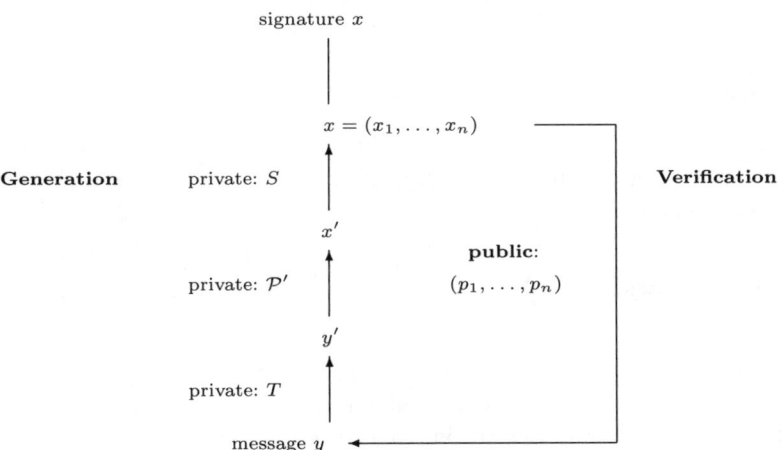

Fig. 1. Graphical Representation of the $\mathcal{MQ}$-trapdoor $(S, \mathcal{P}', T)$

yields the public key of these $\mathcal{M}ultivariate$ $\mathcal{Q}uadratic$ systems. This public vector is used for signature verification. Moreover, the private key (cf Fig.1) consists of the triple $(S, \mathcal{P}', T)$ where $S \in \mathrm{Aff}(\mathbb{F}^n), T \in \mathrm{Aff}(\mathbb{F}^m)$ are affine transformations and $\mathcal{P}' \in \mathcal{MQ}(\mathbb{F}^n, \mathbb{F}^m)$ is a polynomial-vector $\mathcal{P}' := (p'_1, \ldots, p'_m)$ with m components; each component is in $x'_1, \ldots, x'_n$. Throughout this paper, we will denote components of this private vector $\mathcal{P}'$ by a prime $'$. The linear transformations S and T can be represented in the form of invertible matrices $M_S \in \mathbb{F}^{n \times n}, M_T \in \mathbb{F}^{m \times m}$, and vectors $v_S \in \mathbb{F}^n, v_T \in \mathbb{F}^m$ i.e. we have $S(x) := M_S x + v_S$ and $T(x) := M_T x + v_T$, respectively. In contrast to the public polynomial vector $\mathcal{P} \in \mathcal{MQ}(\mathbb{F}^n, \mathbb{F}^m)$, our design goal is that the private polynomial vector $\mathcal{P}'$ does allow an efficient computation of $x'_1, \ldots, x'_n$ for given $y'_1, \ldots, y'_m$. At least for secure $\mathcal{MQ}$-schemes, this is not the case if the public key $\mathcal{P}$ alone is given. The main difference between $\mathcal{MQ}$-schemes lies in their special construction of the central equations $\mathcal{P}'$ and consequently the trapdoor they embed into a specific class of $\mathcal{MQ}$-problems.

In this kind of schemes, the public key $\mathcal{P}$ is computed as function composition of the affine transformations $S : \mathbb{F}^n \to \mathbb{F}^n$, $T : \mathbb{F}^m \to \mathbb{F}^m$ and the central equations $\mathcal{P}' : \mathbb{F}^n \to \mathbb{F}^m$, i.e. we have $\mathcal{P} = T \circ \mathcal{P}' \circ S$. To fix notation further, we note that we have $\mathcal{P}, \mathcal{P}' \in \mathcal{MQ}(\mathbb{F}^n, \mathbb{F}^m)$, i.e. both are functions from the vector space $\mathbb{F}^n$ to the vector space $\mathbb{F}^m$. By construction, we have $\forall x \in \mathbb{F}^n : \mathcal{P}(x) = T(\mathcal{P}'(S(x)))$.

2.2 Signing

To sign for a given $y \in \mathbb{F}^m$, we observe that we have to invert the computation of $y = \mathcal{P}(x)$. Using the trapdoor-information $(S, \mathcal{P}', T)$, cf Fig. 1, this is easy. First, we observe that transformation T is a bijection. In particular, we can compute $y' = M_T^{-1} y$. The same is true for given $x' \in \mathbb{F}^n$ and $S \in \mathrm{Aff}(\mathbb{F}^n)$. Using the LU-decomposition of the matrices M_S, M_T, this computation takes time $O(n^2)$ and $O(m^2)$, respectively. Hence, the difficulty lies in evaluating $x' = \mathcal{P}'^{-1}(y')$. We will discuss strategies for different central systems $\mathcal{P}'$ in Sect. 2.4.

2.3 Verification

In contrast to signing, the verification step is the same for all $\mathcal{MQ}$-schemes and also rather cheap, computationally speaking: given a pair $x \in \mathbb{F}^n, y \in \mathbb{F}^m$, we evaluate the polynomials

$$p_i(x_1, \ldots, x_n) := \sum_{1 \le j \le k \le n} \gamma_{i,j,k} x_j x_k + \sum_{j=1}^n \beta_{i,j} x_j + \alpha_i ,$$

for $1 \le i \le m; 1 \le j \le k \le n$ and given $\alpha_i, \beta_{i,j}, \gamma_{i,j,k} \in \mathbb{F}$. Then, we verify that $p_i = y_i$ holds for all $i \in \{1, \ldots, m\}$. Obviously, all operations can be efficiently computed. The total number of operations takes time $O(mn^2)$.

2.4   Description of the Selected Systems

Based on [14] and some newer results, we have selected the following suitable candidates for efficient implementation of signature schemes: enhanced TTS, amended TTS, Unbalanced Oil and Vinegar and Rainbow. Systems of the big-field classes HFE (Hidden Field Equations), MIA (Matsumoto Imai Scheme A) and the mixed-field class ℓIC — ℓ-Invertible Cycle [8] were excluded as results from their software implementation show that they cannot be implemented as efficiently as schemes from the small-field classes, *i.e.* enTTS, amTTS, UOV and Rainbow. The proposed schemes and parameters are summarised in Table 1.

Table 1. Proposed Schemes and Parameters

	q	n	m	τ	K	Solver
Unbalanced Oil	256	30	10	0.003922	10	$1 \times K = 10$
and Vinegar (UOV)		60	20		20	$1 \times K = 20$
Rainbow	256	42	24	0.007828	12	$2 \times K = 12$
enhanced TTS (v1)	256	28	20	0.000153	9	$2 \times K = 9$
(v2)				0.007828	10	$2 \times K = 10$
amended TTS	256	34	24	0.011718	4,10	$1 \times K = 4, 2 \times K = 10$

Unbalanced Oil and Vinegar (UOV)

$$p'_i(x'_1, \ldots, x'_n) := \sum_{j=1}^{n-m} \sum_{k=j}^{n} \gamma'_{i,j,k} x'_j x'_k \text{ for } i = 1 \ldots v_1$$

Unbalanced Oil and Vinegar Schemes were introduced in [10,11]. Here we have $\gamma \in \mathbb{F}$, *i.e.* the polynomials p are over the finite field $\mathbb{F}$. In this context, the variables x'_i for $1 \leq i \leq n - m$ are called the "vinegar" variables and x'_i for $n - m < i \leq n$ the "oil" variables. We also write $o := m$ for the number of oil variables and $v := n - m = n - o$ for the number of vinegar variables. To invert UOV, we need to assign random values to the vinegar variables $x'_1, \ldots, x'_v$ and obtain a linear system in the oil variables $x'_{v+1}, \ldots, x'_n$. All in all, we need to solve a $m \times m$ system and have hence $K = m$. The probability that we do *not* obtain a solution for this system is $\tau^{UOV} = 1 - \frac{\prod_{i=0}^{m-1} q^m - q^i}{q^{m^2}}$ as there are q^{m^2} matrices over the finite field $\mathbb{F}$ with $q := |\mathbb{F}|$ elements and $\prod_{i=0}^{m-1} q^m - q^i$ invertible ones [14].

Taking the currently known attacks into account, we derive the following secure choice of parameters for a security level of 2^{80}:

- Small datagrams: $m = 10, n = 30, \tau \approx 0.003922$ and one $K = 10$ solver
- Hash values: $m = 20, n = 60, \tau \approx 0.003922$ and one $K = 20$ solver

The security has been evaluated using the formula $O(q^{v-m-1}m^4) = O(q^{n-2m-1}m^4)$. Note that the first version (*i.e.* $m = 10$) can only be used with messages of less than 80 bits. However, such datagrams occur frequently in applications with power or bandwidth restrictions, hence we have noted this special possibility here.

Rainbow. Rainbow is the name for a generalisation of UOV [7]. In particular, we do not have one layer, but several layers. This way, we can reduce the number of variables and hence obtain a faster scheme when dealing with hash values. The general form of the Rainbow central map is given below.

$$p_i'(x_1', \dots, x_n') := \sum_{j=1}^{v_l} \sum_{k=j}^{v_{l+1}} \gamma_{i,j,k} x_j' x_k' \text{ for } i = v_l \dots v_{l+1}, 1 \le l \le L$$

We have the coefficients $\gamma \in \mathbb{F}$, the layers $L \in \mathbb{N}$ and the vinegar splits $v_1 < \dots < v_{L+1} \in \mathbb{N}$ with $n = v_{L+1}$. To invert Rainbow, we follow the strategy for UOV — but now layer for layer, i.e. we pick random values for $x_1, \dots, x_{v_1}$, solve the first layer with an $(v_2 - v_1) \times (v_2 - v_1)$-solver for $x_{v_1+1}, \dots, x_{v_2}$, insert the values $x_1, \dots, x_{v_2}$ into the second layer, solve second layer with an $(v_3 - v_2) \times (v_3 - v_2)$-solver for $x_{v_2+1}, \dots, x_{v_3}$ until the last layer L. All in all, we need to solve sequentially L times $(v_l - v_{l-1}) \times (v_l - v_{l-1})$ systems for $l = 2 \dots L + 1$. The probability that we do not obtain a solution for this system is $\tau^{rainbow} = 1 - \prod_{l=1}^{L} \frac{\prod_{i=0}^{v_{l+1}-v_l} q^{v_{l+1}-v_l} - q^i}{q^{v_{l+1}-v_l^2}}$ using a similar argument as in Sec. 2.4.

Taking the latest attack from [3] into account, we obtain the parameters $L = 2, v_1 = 18, v_2 = 30, v_3 = 42$ for a security level of 2^{80}, i.e. a two layer scheme 18 initial vinegar variables and 12 equations in the first layer and 12 new vinegar variables and 12 equations in the second layer. Hence, we need two $K = 12$ solvers and obtain $\tau \approx 0.007828$.

Amended TTS (amTTS). The central polynomials $\mathcal{P}' \in \mathcal{MQ}(\mathbb{F}^n, \mathbb{F}^m)$ for $m = 24, n = 34$ in amTTS [6] are defined as given below:

$$p_i' := x_i' + \alpha_i' x_{\sigma(i)}' + \sum_{j=1}^{8} \gamma_{i,j}' x_{j+1}' x_{11+(i+j \bmod 10)}' \text{ , for } i = 10 \dots 19;$$

$$p_i' := x_i' + \alpha_i' x_{\sigma(i)}' + \gamma_{0,i}' x_1' x_i' + \sum_{j=1}^{8} \gamma_{i,j}' x_{15+(i+j+4 \bmod 8)j+1}' x_{\pi(i,j)}', \text{ for } i = 20 \dots 23;$$

$$p_i' := x_i' + \gamma_{0,i}' x_0' x_i' + \sum_{j=1}^{9} \gamma_{i,j}' x_{24+(i+j+6 \bmod 10)j+1}' x_{\pi(i,j)}' \text{ , for } i = 24 \dots 33.$$

We have $\alpha, \gamma \in \mathbb{F}$ and σ, π permutations, i.e. all polynomials are over the finite field $\mathbb{F}$. We see that they are similar to the equations of Rainbow (Sec. 2.4) — but this time with sparse polynomials. Unfortunately, there are no more conditions given on σ, π in [6] — we have hence picked one suitable permutation for our implementation.

To invert amTTS, we follow the sames ideas as for Rainbow — except with the difference that we have to invert twice a 10×10 system ($i = 10 \dots 19$ and $24 \dots 33$) and once a 4×4 system, i.e. we have $K = 10$ and $K = 4$. Due to the

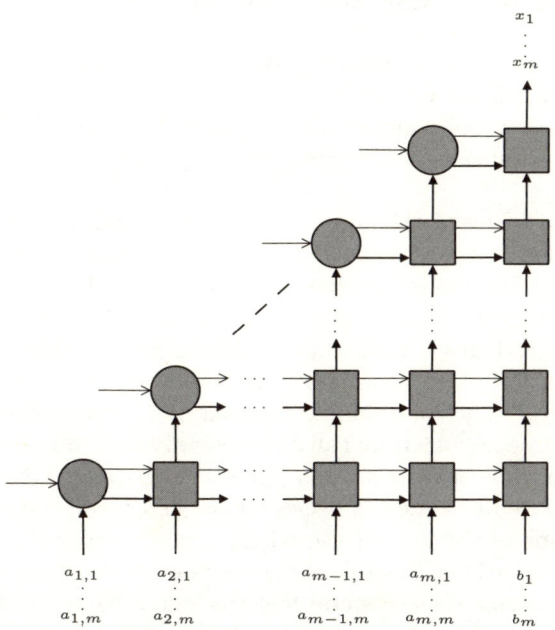

Fig. 2. Signature Core Building Block: Systolic Array LSE Solver (Structure)

structure of the equations, the probability for *not* getting a solution here is the same as for a 3-Layer Rainbow scheme with $v_1 = 10, v_2 = 20, v_3 = 24, v_4 = 34$ variables, *i.e.* $\tau^{amTTS} = \tau^{Rainbow}(10, 20, 24, 34) \approx 0.011718$.

Enhanced TTS (enTTS). The overall idea of enTTS is similar to amTTS, $m = 20, n = 28$. For a detailed description of enTTS see [16,15]. According to [6], enhanced TTS is broken, hence we do not advocate its use nor did we give a detailed description in the main part of this article, However, it was implemented in [17], so we have included it here to allow the reader a comparison between the previous implementation and ours.

3   Building Blocks for $\mathcal{MQ}$-Signature Cores

Considering Section 2 we see that in order to generate a signature using an $\mathcal{MQ}$-signature scheme we need the following common operations:

- computing affine transformations (*i.e.* vector addition and matrix-vector multiplication),
- (partially) evaluating multivariate polynomials over $\mathrm{GF}(2^k)$,
- solving linear systems of equations (LSEs) over $\mathrm{GF}(2^k)$.

In this section we describe the main computational building blocks for realizing these operations. Using these generic building blocks we can compose a signature core for any of the presented $\mathcal{MQ}$-schemes (cf Section 4).

3.1   A Systolic Array LSE Solver for GF(2^k)

In 1989, Hochet *et al.* [9] proposed a systolic architecture for Gaussian elimination over GF(p). They considered an architecture of simple processors, used as systolic cells that are connected in a triangular network. They distinguish two different types of cells, main array cells and the boundary cells of the main diagonal.

Wang and Lin followed this approach and proposed an architecture in 1993 [13] for computing inverses over GF(2^k). They provided two methods to efficiently implement the Gauss-Jordan algorithm over GF(2) in hardware. Their first approach was the classical *systolic array* approach similar to the one of Hochet *et al.*. It features a critical path that is independent of the size of the array. A full solution of an $m \times m$ LSE is generated after $4m$ cycles and every m cycles thereafter. The solution is computed in a serial fashion.

The other approach, which we call a *systolic network*, allows signals to propagate through the whole architecture in a single clock cycle. This allows the initial latency to be reduced to $2m$ clock cycles for the first result. Of course the critical path now depends of the size of the whole array, slowing the design down for huge systems of equations. Systolic arrays can be derived from systolic networks by putting delay elements (registers) into the signal paths between the cells.

We followed the approach presented in [13] to build an LSE solver architecture over GF(2^k). The biggest advantage of systolic architectures with regard to our application is the low amount of cells compared to other architectures like SMITH [4]. For solving a $m \times m$ LSE, a systolic array consisting of only m boundary cells and $m(m + 1)/2$ main cells is required.

An overview of the architecture is given in Figure 2. The boundary cells shown in Figure 3 mainly comprise one inverter that is needed for pivoting the corresponding line. Furthermore, a single 1-bit register is needed to store whether a pivot was found. The main cells shown in Figure 4 comprise of one GF(2^k) register, a multiplier and an adder over GF(2^k). Furthermore, a few multiplexers are needed. If the row is not initialised yet ($T_{in} = 0$), the entering data is multiplied with the inverse of the pivot (E_{in}) and stored in the cell. If the pivot was zero, the element is simply stored and passed to the next row in the next clock cycle. If the row is initialised ($T_{in} = 1$) the data element $a_{i,j+1}$ of the entering line is reduced with the stored data element and passed to the following row. Hence, one can say that the k-th row of the array performs the k-th iteration of the Gauss-Jordan algorithm.

The inverters of the boundary cells contribute most of the delay time t_{delay} of the systolic network. Instead of introducing a full systolic array, it is already almost as helpful to simply add delay elements only between the rows. This seems to be a good trade-off between delay time and the number of registers used. This approach we call *systolic lines*.

As described earlier, the LSEs we generate are not always solvable. We can easily detect an unsolvable LSE by checking the state of the boundary cells after $3m$ clock cycles (m clock cycles for a systolic network, respectively). If one of them is not set, the system is not solvable and a new LSE needs to be generated.

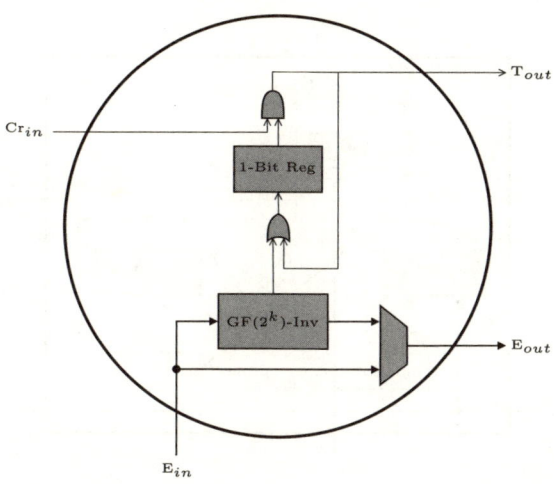

Fig. 3. Pivot Cell of the Systolic Array LSE Solver

Table 2. Implementation results for different types of systolic arrays and different sizes of LSEs over $GF(2^8)$ (t_{delay} in ns, F_{Max} in MHz)

Engine	Size on FPGA			Speed		Size on ASIC
	Slices	LUTs	FFs	t_{delay}	F_{Max}	GE (estimated)
Systolic arrays on a Spartan-3 device (XC3S1500, 300 MHz)						
Systolic Array (10x10)	2,533	4,477	1,305	12.5	80	38,407
Systolic Array (12x12)	3,502	6,160	1,868	12.65	79	53,254
Systolic Array (20x20)	8,811	15,127	5,101	11.983	83	133,957
Alternative systolic arrays on a Spartan-3						
Systolic Network (10x10)	2,251	4,379	461	118.473	8.4	30,272
Systolic Lines (12x12)	3,205	6,171	1,279	13.153	75	42,013
Systolic arrays on a Virtex-V device (XC5VLX50-3, 550 MHz)						
Systolic Array (10x10)	1314	3498	1305	4.808	207	36,136
Systolic Lines (12x12)	1,534	5,175	1,272	9.512	105	47,853
Systolic Array (20x20)	4552	12292	5110	4.783	209	129,344

However, as shown in Table 1, this happens very rarely. Hence, the impact on the performance of the implementation is negligible. Table 2 shows implementation results of the different types of systolic arrays for different sizes of LSEs (over $GF(2^8)$) on different FPGAs.

3.2   Matrix-Vector Multiplier and Polynomial Evaluator

For performing matrix-vector multiplication, we use the building block depicted in Figure 5. In the following we call this block a t-MVM. As you can see a t-MVM consists of t multipliers, a tree of adders of depth about $log_2(t)$ to compute the sum of all products $a_i \cdot b_i$, and an extra adder to recursively add up previously

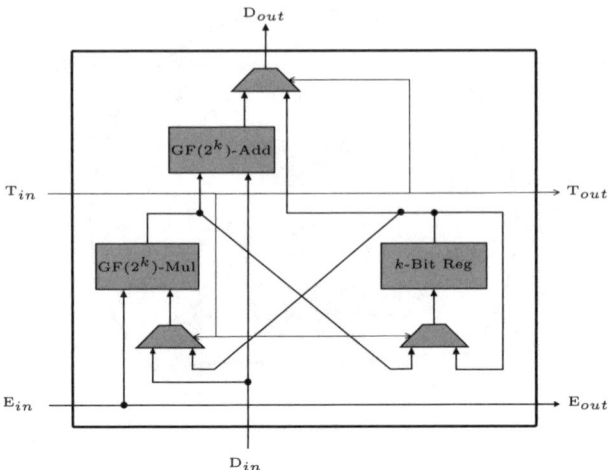

Fig. 4. Main Cell of the Systolic Array LSE Solver

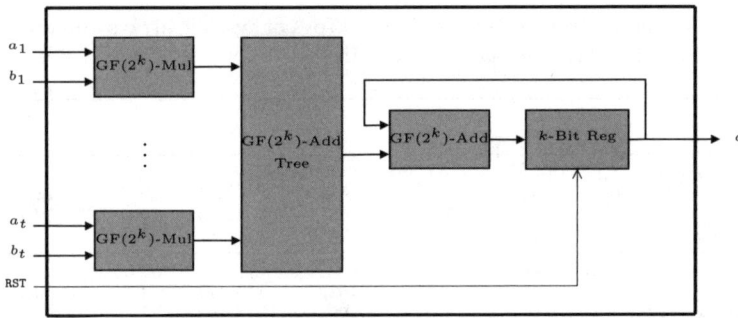

Fig. 5. Signature Core Building Block: Combined Matrix-Vector-Multiplier and Polynomial-Evaluator

computed intermediate values that are stored in a register. Using the RST-signal we can initially set the register content to zero.

To compute the matrix-vector product

$$A \cdot b = \begin{bmatrix} a_{1,1} \dots a_{1,u} \\ \vdots \qquad \vdots \\ a_{v,1} \dots a_{v,u} \end{bmatrix} \cdot \begin{bmatrix} b_1 \\ \vdots \\ b_u \end{bmatrix}$$

using a t-MVM, where t is chosen in a way that it divides[1] u, we proceed row by row as follows: We set the register content to zero by using RST. Then we

---

[1] Note that in the case that t does not divide u we can nevertheless use a t-MVM to compute the matrix-vector product by setting superfluous input signals to zero.

feed the first t elements of the first row of A into the t-MVM, *i.e.* we set $a_1 = a_{1,1}, \ldots, a_t = a_{1,t}$, as well as the first t elements of the vector b. After the register content is set to $\sum_{i=1}^{t} a_{1,i} b_i$, we feed the next t elements of the row and the next t elements of the vector into the t-MVM. This leads to a register content corresponding to $\sum_{i=1}^{2t} a_{1,i} b_i$. We go on in this way until the last t elements of the row and the vector are processed and the register content equals $\sum_{i=1}^{u} a_{1,i} b_i$. Thus, at this point the data signal c corresponds to the first component of the matrix-vector product. Proceeding in a analogous manner yields the remaining components of the desired vector. Note that the $\frac{u}{t}$ parts of the vector b are *re-used* in a periodic manner as input to the t-MVM. In Section 3.4 we describe a building block, called word rotator, providing these parts in the required order to the t-MVM without re-loading them each time and hence avoid a waste of resources.

Therefore, using a t-MVM (and an additional vector adder) it is clear how to implement the affine transformations $S : \mathbb{F}^n \to \mathbb{F}^n$ and $T : \mathbb{F}^m \to \mathbb{F}^m$ which are important ingredients of an $\mathcal{MQ}$-scheme. Note that the parameter t has a significant influence on the performance of an implementation of such a scheme and is chosen differently for our implementations (as can be seen in Section 4).

Besides realizing the required affine transformations, a t-MVM can be re-used to implement (partial) polynomial evaluation. It is quite obvious that evaluating the polynomials p_i' (belonging to the central map $\mathcal{P}'$ of a $\mathcal{MQ}$-scheme, cf Section 2) with the vinegar variables involves matrix-vector multiplications as the main operations. For instance, consider a fixed polynomial $p_i'(x_1', \ldots, x_n') = \sum_{j=1}^{n-m} \sum_{k=j}^{n} \gamma_{i,j,k}' x_j' x_k'$ from the central map of UOV that we evaluate with random values $b_1, \ldots, b_{n-m} \in \mathbb{F}$ for the vinegar variables $x_1', \ldots, x_{n-m}'$. Here we like to compute the coefficients $\beta_{i,0}, \beta_{i,n-m+1}, \ldots, \beta_{i,n}$ of the linear polynomial

$$p_i'(b_1, \ldots, b_{n-m}, x_{n-m+1}', \ldots, x_n') = \beta_{i,0} + \sum_{j=n-m+1}^{n} \beta_{i,j} x_j'.$$

We immediately obtain the coefficients of the non-constant part of this linear polynomial, *i.e.* $\beta_{i,n-m+1}, \ldots, \beta_{i,n}$, by computing the following matrix-vector product:

$$\begin{bmatrix} \gamma_{i,1,n-m+1}' & \cdots & \gamma_{i,n-m,n-m+1}' \\ \vdots & & \vdots \\ \gamma_{i,1,n}' & \cdots & \gamma_{i,n-m,n}' \end{bmatrix} \cdot \begin{bmatrix} b_1 \\ \vdots \\ b_{n-m} \end{bmatrix} = \begin{bmatrix} \beta_{i,n-m+1} \\ \vdots \\ \beta_{i,n} \end{bmatrix} \quad (1)$$

Also the main step for computing $\beta_{i,0}$ can be written as a matrix-vector product:

$$\begin{bmatrix} \gamma_{i,1,1}' & 0 & 0 & \cdots & 0 \\ \gamma_{i,1,2}' & \gamma_{i,2,2}' & 0 & \cdots & 0 \\ \vdots & \vdots & \ddots & & \vdots \\ \gamma_{i,1,n-m-1}' & \gamma_{i,2,n-m-1}' & \cdots & \gamma_{i,n-m-1,n-m-1}' & 0 \\ \gamma_{i,1,n-m}' & \gamma_{i,2,n-m}' & \cdots & & \gamma_{i,n-m,n-m}' \end{bmatrix} \cdot \begin{bmatrix} b_1 \\ \vdots \\ b_{n-m} \end{bmatrix} = \begin{bmatrix} \alpha_{i,1} \\ \vdots \\ \alpha_{i,n-m} \end{bmatrix} \quad (2)$$

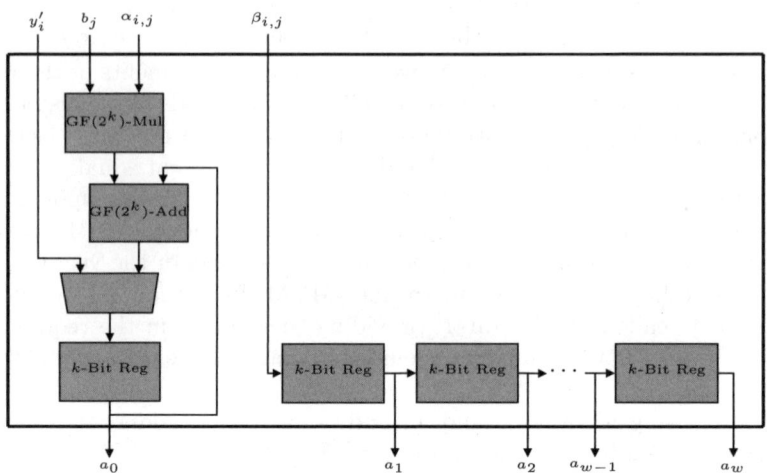

Fig. 6. Signature Core Building Block: Equation Register

Of course, we can exploit the fact that the above matrix is a lower triangular matrix and we actually do not have to perform a full matrix-vector multiplication. This must simply be taken into account when implementing the control logic of the signature core. In order to obtain $\beta_{i,0}$ from $(\alpha_{i,1} \ldots \alpha_{i,n-m})^T$ we have to perform the following additional computation:

$$\beta_{i,0} = \alpha_{i,1}b_1 + \ldots + \alpha_{i,n-m}b_{n-m}\,.$$

This final step is performed by another unit called equation register which is presented in the next section.

3.3   Equation Register

The Equation Register building block is shown in Figure 6. A w-ER essentially consists of $w + 1$ register blocks each storing k bits as well as one adder and one multiplier. It is used to temporarily store parts of an linear equation until this equation has been completely generated and can be transferred to the systolic array solver.

For instance, in the case of UOV we consider linear equations of the form

$$p_i'(b_1,\ldots,b_{n-m},x_{n-m+1}',\ldots,x_n') = y_i' \Leftrightarrow \sum_{j=1}^{n-m} \alpha_{i,j}b_j - y_i' + \sum_{j=n-m+1}^{n} \beta_{i,j}x_j' = 0$$

where we used the notation from Section 3.2. To compute and store the constant part $\sum_{j=1}^{n-m} \alpha_{i,j}b_j - y_i'$ of this equation the left-hand part of an m-ER is used

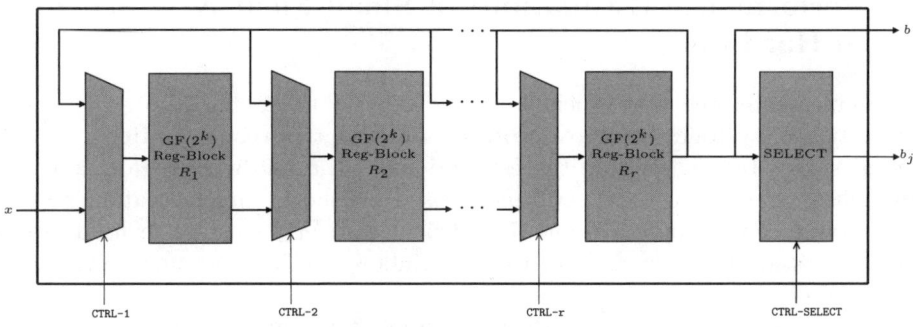

Fig. 7. Signature Core Building Block: Word Rotator

(see Figure 6): The respective register is initially set to y_i'. Then the values $\alpha_{i,j}$ are computed one after another using a t-MVM building block and fed into the multiplier of the ER. The corresponding values b_j are provided by a t-WR building block which is presented in the next section. Using the adder, y_i' and the products can be added up iteratively. The coefficients $\beta_{i,j}$ of the linear equation are also computed consecutively by the t-MVM and fed into the shift-register that is shown on the right-hand side of Figure 6.

3.4 Word Rotator

A word cyclic shift register will in the following be referred to as word rotator (WR). A (t, r)-WR, depicted in Figure 7, consists of r register blocks storing the $\frac{u}{t}$ parts of the vector b involved in the matrix vector products considered in Section 3.2. Each of these r register blocks stores t elements from $GF(2^k)$, hence each register block consists of t k-bit registers. The main task of a (t, r)-WR is to provide the correct parts of the vector b to the t-MVM at all times. The r register blocks can be serially loaded using the input bus x. After loading, the r register blocks are rotated at each clock cycle. The cycle length of the rotation can be modified using the multiplexers by providing appropriate control signals. This is especially helpful for the partial polynomial evaluation where due to the triangularity of the matrix in Equation (2), numerous operations can be saved. Here, the cycle length is $\lceil \frac{j}{t} \rceil$, where j is the index of the processed row. The possibility to adjust the cycle length is also necessary in the case $r > \frac{u}{t}$ frequently appearing if we use the *same* (t, r)-WR, i.e., fixed parameters t and r, to implement the affine transformation T, the polynomial evaluations, and the affine transformation S. Additionally, the WR provides b_j to the ER building block which is needed by the ER at the end of each rotation cycle. Since this b_j value always occurs in the last register block of a cycle, the selector component (right-hand side of Figure 7) can simply load it and provide it to the ER.

4   Performance Estimations of Small-Field $\mathcal{MQ}$-Schemes in Hardware

We implemented the most crucial building blocks of the architecture as described in Section 3 (systolic structures, word rotators, matrix-vector multipliers of different sizes). In this section, the estimations of the hardware performance for the whole architecture are performed based on those implementation results. The power of the approach and the efficiency of $\mathcal{MQ}$-schemes in hardware is demonstrated at the example of UOV, Rainbow, enTTS and amTTS as specified in Section 2.

Side-Note: The volume of data that needs to be imported to the hardware engine for $\mathcal{MQ}$-schemes may seem too high to be realistic in some applications. However, the contents of the matrices and the polynomial coefficients (*i.e.* the private key) does not necessarily have to be imported from the outside world or from a large on-board memory. Instead, they can be generated online in the engine using a cryptographically strong pseudo-random number generator, requiring only a small, cryptographically strong secret, *i.e.* some random bits.

4.1   UOV

We treat two parameter sets for UOV as shown in Table 3: $n = 60$, $n = 20$ (long-message UOV) as well as $n = 30$, $m = 10$ (short-message UOV). In UOV signature generation, there are three basic operations: linearising polynomials, solving the resulting equation system, and an affine transform to obtain the signature. The most time-consuming operation of UOV is the partial evaluation of the polynomials p'_i, since their coefficients are nearly random. However, as already mentioned in the previous section, for some polynomials approximately one half of the coefficients for the polynomials are zero. This somewhat simplifies the task of linearization.

For the linearization of polynomials in the long-message UOV, 40 random bytes are generated to invert the central mapping first. To do this, we use a 20-MVM, a (20,3)-WR, and a 20-ER. For each polynomial one needs about 100 clock cycles (40 clocks to calculate the linear terms and another 60 ones to compute the constants, see (1) and (2)) and obtains a linear equation with 20 variables. As there are 20 polynomials, this yields about 2000 clock cycles to perform this step.

After this, the 20×20 linear system over $GF(2^8)$ is solved using a 20×20 systolic array. The signature is then the result of this operation which is returned after about $4 \times 20 = 80$ clock cycles. Then, the 20-byte solution is concatenated with the randomly generated 40 bytes and the result is passed through the affine transformation, whose major part is a matrix-vector multiplication with a 60×60-byte matrix. To perform this operations, we re-use the 20-MVM and a (20,3)-WR. This requires about 180 cycles of 20-MVM and 20 bytes of the matrix entries to be input in each cycle.

For the short-message UOV, one has a very similar structure. More precisely, one needs a 10-MVM, a (10,3)-WR, a 10-ER and a 10×10 systolic array. The design requires approximately 500 cycles for the partial evaluation of the polynomials, about 40 cycles to solve the resulting 10×10 LSE over $GF(2^8)$ as well as another 90 cycles for the final affine map.

Note that the critical path of the Gaussian elimination engine is much longer than that for the remaining building blocks. So this block represents the performance bottleneck in terms of frequency and hardware complexity. Thus, the maximal frequency for both UOV variants will be bounded by about 200 MHz for XC5VLX50-3 and about 80 MHz for XC3S1500. See Table 3 for our estimations.

4.2 Rainbow

In the version of Rainbow we consider, the message length is 24 byte. That is, a 24-byte matrix-vector multiplication has to be performed first. One can take a 6-MVM and a (6,7)-WR which require about 96 clock cycles to perform the computation. Then the first 18 variables of x_i' are randomly fixed and 12 first polynomials are partially evaluated. This requires about 864 clock cycles. The results are stored in a 12-ER. After this, the 12×12 system of linear equations is solved. This requires a 12×12 systolic array over $GF(2^8)$ which outputs the solution after 48 clock cycles. Then the last 12 polynomials are linearised using the same matrix-vector multiplier and word rotator based on the 18 random values previously chosen and the 12-byte solution. This needs about 1800 clock cycles. This is followed by another run of the 12×12 systolic array with the same execution time of about 48 clock cycles. At the end, roughly 294 more cycles are spent performing the final affine transform on the 42-byte vector. See Table 3 for some concrete performance figures in this case.

4.3 enTTS and amTTS

Like in Rainbow, for enTTS two vector-matrix multiplications are needed at the beginning and at the end of the operation with 20- and 28-byte vectors each. We take a 10-MVM and a (10,3)-WR for this. The operations require 40 and 84 clock cycles, respectively. One 9-ER is required. Two 10×10 linear systems over $GF(2^8)$ need to be solved, requiring about 40 clock cycles each. The operation of calculating the linearization of the polynomials can be significantly optimised compared to the generic UOV or Rainbow (in terms of time) which can drastically reduce the time-area product. This behaviour is due to the special selection of polynomials, where only a small proportion of coefficients is non-zero.

After choosing 7 variables randomly, 10 linear equations have to be generated. For each of these equations, one has to perform only a few multiplications in $GF(2^8)$ which can be done in parallel. This requires about 10 clock cycles. After this, another variable is fixed and a further set of 10 polynomials is partially evaluated. This requires about 10 further cycles.

In amTTS, which is quite similar to enTTS, two affine maps with 24- and 34-byte vectors are performed with a 12-MVM and a (12,3)-WR yielding 48 and 102 clock cycles, respectively. Two 10×10 and one 4×4 linear systems have to be solved requiring for a 10×10 systolic array (twice 40 and once 16 clock

Table 3. Comparison of hardware implementations for ECC and our performance estimations for $\mathcal{MQ}$-schemes based on the implementations of the major building blocks (F=frequency, T=Time, L=luts, S=slices, FF=flip-flops, A=area)

Implementation	F, MHz	T, μs	L/S/FF	A,kGE	L×T
ECC over GF(2^{163}), [1], NIST, XC2V200	100	41	8,300/-/-	-	71.3
ECC over GF(2^{163}), [12], NIST, XCV200E-7	48	68.9	25,763/-/-	-	372.3
UOV $n = 60$, $m = 20$, XC5VLX50-3	209	11	15,497/4,188/4,999	166.6	35.7
UOV $n = 60$, $m = 20$, XC3S1500	83	27.7	21,167/9,203/6,828	227.5	122.8
UOV $n = 30$, $m = 10$, XC5VLX50-3	207	3.1	5,276/1,265/1,487	56.7	3.4
UOV $n = 30$, $m = 10$, XC3S1500	80	8	8,601/4,072/2,916	92.4	14.4
Rainbow $n = 42$, $m = 24$, XC5VLX50-3	105	30.3	5,929/1,681/1,869	63.7	37.6
Rainbow $n = 42$, $m = 24$, XC3S1500	79	39.1	7,114/1,968/2,377	76.4	58.2
enTTS $n = 24$, $m = 20$, [17], CMOS 0.25 μm	80#	291	-	22	-
enTTS $n = 24$, $m = 20$, XC5VLX50-3	207	1.1	4,341/1,284/1,537	44.2	1.0
enTTS $n = 24$, $m = 20$, XC3S1500	80	2.8	5,423/1,248/1,986	55.9	3.2
amTTS $n = 34$, $m = 24$, XC5VLX50-3	207	1.5	4,471/1,412/1,678	45.7	1.4
amTTS $n = 34$, $m = 24$, XC3S1500	80	3.9	6,034/2,920/2,395	61.6	4.9

For comparison purposes we assume that the clock frequency for the design is 80 MHz.

cycles). Moreover, a 10-ER is needed. The three steps of the partial evaluation of polynomials requires roughly 25 clock cycles in this case. See Table 3 for our estimations on enTTS and amTTS.

5   Comparison and Conclusions

Our implementation results (as well as the estimations for the optimisations in case of enTTS and amTTS) are compared to the scalar multiplication in the group of points of elliptic curves with field bitlengths in the rage of 160 bit (corresponding to the security level of 2^{80}) over GF(2^k), see Table 3. A good survey on hardware implementations for ECC can be found in [5].

Even the most conservative design, *i.e.* long-message UOV, can outperform some of the most efficient ECC implementations in terms of TA-product on some hardware platforms. More hardware-friendly designs such as the short-message UOV or Rainbow provide a considerable advantage over ECC. The more aggressively designed enTTS and amTTS allow for extremely efficient implementations having a more than 70 or 50 times lower TA-product, respectively. Though the metric we use is not optimal, the results indicate that $\mathcal{MQ}$-schemes perform better than elliptic curves in hardware with respect to the TA-product and are hence an interesting option in cost- or size-sensitive areas.

Acknowledgements. The authors would like to thank our college Christof Paar for fruitful discussions and helpful remarks as well as Sundar Balasubramanian, Harold Carter (University of Cincinnati, USA) and Jintai Ding (University of Cincinnati, USA and Technical University of Darmstadt, Germany) for exchanging some ideas while working on another paper about $\mathcal{MQ}$-schemes.

References

1. Ansari, B., Anwar Hasan, M.: High performance architecture of elliptic curve scalar multiplication. Technical report, CACR (January 2006)
2. Balasubramanian, S., Bogdanov, A., Rupp, A., Ding, J., Carter, H.W.: Fast multivariate signature generation in hardware: The case of Rainbow. In: ASAP 2008 (to appear, 2008)
3. Billet, O., Gilbert, H.: Cryptanalysis of rainbow. In: De Prisco, R., Yung, M. (eds.) SCN 2006. LNCS, vol. 4116, pp. 336–347. Springer, Heidelberg (2006)
4. Bogdanov, A., Mertens, M., Paar, C., Pelzl, J., Rupp, A.: A parallel hardware architecture for fast gaussian elimination over GF(2). In: FCCM 2006 (2006)
5. de Dormale, G.M., Quisquater, J.-J.: High-speed hardware implementations of elliptic curve cryptography: A survey. Journal of Systems Architecture 53, 72–84 (2007)
6. Ding, J., Hu, L., Yang, B.-Y., Chen, J.-M.: Note on design criteria for rainbow-type multivariates. Cryptology ePrint Archive, Report 2006/307 (2006)
7. Ding, J., Schmidt, D.: Rainbow, a new multivariable polynomial signature scheme. In: Ioannidis, J., Keromytis, A.D., Yung, M. (eds.) ACNS 2005. LNCS, vol. 3531, pp. 164–175. Springer, Heidelberg (2005)
8. Ding, J., Wolf, C., Yang, B.-Y.: ℓ-invertible cycles for multivariate quadratic public key cryptography. In: Okamoto, T., Wang, X. (eds.) PKC 2007. LNCS, vol. 4450, pp. 266–281. Springer, Heidelberg (2007)
9. Hochet, B., Quinton, P., Robert, Y.: Systolic Gaussian Elimination over GF (p) with Partial Pivoting. IEEE Transactions on Computers 38(9), 1321–1324 (1989)
10. Kipnis, A., Patarin, J., Goubin, L.: Unbalanced Oil and Vinegar signature schemes. In: Stern, J. (ed.) EUROCRYPT 1999. LNCS, vol. 1592. Springer, Heidelberg (1999)
11. Kipnis, A., Patarin, J., Goubin, L.: Unbalanced Oil and Vinegar signature schemes — extended version, 17 pages , 2003-06-11 (2003),
http://www.citeseer/231623.html
12. Shu, C., Gaj, K., El-Ghazawi, T.: Low latency elliptic curve cryptography accelerators for nist curves on binary fields. In: IEEE FPT 2005 (2005)
13. Wang, C.L., Lin, J.L.: A Systolic Architecture for Computing Inverses and Divisions in Finite Fields $GF(2^m)$. IEEE Trans. Comp. 42(9), 1141–1146 (1993)
14. Wolf, C., Preneel, B.: Taxonomy of public key schemes based on the problem of multivariate quadratic equations. Cryptology ePrint Archive, Report 2005/077 (May 12, 2005)
15. Yang, B.-Y., Chen, J.-M.: Rank attacks and defence in Tame-like multivariate PKC's. Cryptology ePrint Archive Report 2004/061 (September 29, 2004),
http://eprint.iacr.org
16. Yang, B.-Y., Chen, J.-M.: Building secure tame-like multivariate public-key cryptosystems: The new TTS. In: Boyd, C., González Nieto, J.M. (eds.) ACISP 2005. LNCS, vol. 3574, pp. 518–531. Springer, Heidelberg (2005)
17. Yang, B.-Y., Cheng, D.C.-M., Chen, B.-R., Chen, J.-M.: Implementing minimized multivariate public-key cryptosystems on low-resource embedded systems. In: Clark, J.A., Paige, R.F., Polack, F.A.C., Brooke, P.J. (eds.) SPC 2006. LNCS, vol. 3934, pp. 73–88. Springer, Heidelberg (2006)

Ultra High Performance ECC over NIST Primes on Commercial FPGAs

Tim Güneysu and Christof Paar

Horst Görtz Institute for IT Security, Ruhr University Bochum, Germany
{gueneysu, cpaar}@crypto.rub.de

Abstract. Elliptic Curve Cryptosystems (ECC) have gained increasing acceptance in practice due to their significantly smaller bit size of the operands compared to other public-key cryptosystems. Since their computational complexity is often lower than in the case of RSA or discrete logarithm schemes, ECC are often chosen for high performance public-key applications. However, despite a wealth of research regarding high-speed software and high-speed FPGA implementation of ECC since the mid 1990s, providing truly high-performance ECC on readily available (i.e., non-ASIC) platforms remains an open challenge. This holds especially for ECC over prime fields, which are often preferred over binary fields due to standards in Europe and the US.

This work presents a new architecture for an FPGA-based ultra high performance ECC implementation over prime fields. Our architecture makes intensive use of the DSP blocks in modern FPGAs, which are embedded arithmetic units actually intended to accelerate digital signal processing algorithms. We describe a novel architecture and algorithms for performing ECC arithmetic and describe the actual implementation of standard compliant ECC based on the NIST primes P-224 and P-256. We show that ECC on Xilinx's Virtex-4 SX55 FPGA can be performed at a rate of more than 37,000 point multiplications per second. Our architecture outperforms all single-chip hardware implementations over prime fields in the open literature by a wide margin.

Keywords: Elliptic Curve Cryptosystems, FPGA, High-Performance.

1 Introduction

With the explosive growth of Internet-based applications like ecommerce, peer-to-peer networks and distributed gaming as well as embedded ones — ranging from mobile over set-top boxes to automotive — the demand for security in such systems has also grown dramatically. In these applications, asymmetric cryptography is used to achieve a large variety of security goals. However, asymmetric cryptographic algorithms are extremely arithmetic intensive since their security assumptions rely on computational problems which are considered to be hard in combination with parameters of significant bit sizes.

Neal Koblitz and Victor Miller proposed independently in 1985 [20,17] the use of Elliptic Curve Cryptography providing similar security compared to classical cryptosystems but using smaller keys. This benefit allows for greater efficiency

E. Oswald and P. Rohatgi (Eds.): CHES 2008, LNCS 5154, pp. 62–78, 2008.

when using ECC (160–256 bit) compared to RSA or discrete logarithm schemes over finite fields (1024–4096 bit) while providing an equivalent level of security [18]. Due to this, ECC has become the most promising candidate for many new applications, especially in the embedded domain, which is also reflected by several standards by IEEE, ANSI and SECG [15,1,5,6].

In addition to many new "lightweight" applications (e.g., digital signature on RFID-like devices), there are also many new applications which call for high-performance asymmetric primitives. Even though very fast public-key algorithms can be provided for PC and server applications by accelerator cards equipped with ASICs, providing very high speed solutions in embedded devices is still a major challenge. Somewhat surprisingly, there appears to be extremely few, if any, commercially available ASICs or chip sets that provide high speed ECC and which are readily available for integration in general embedded systems. A potential alternative is provided by Field Programmable Gate Arrays (FPGA). FPGAs have evolved over the last decade to a powerful alternative for classical ASIC circuits. In addition, FPGAs provide the advantage of dynamic and flexible circuit reconfigurability allowing for rapid prototyping at little development costs. However, despite a wealth of research regarding high-speed FPGA (and high-speed software) implementation of ECC since the mid 1990s, providing truly high-performance ECC (i.e., to reach less than $100\mu s$ per point multiplication) on readily available platforms remains an open challenge. This holds especially for ECC over prime fields, which are often preferred over binary fields due to standards in Europe and the US, and a somewhat clearer patent situation.

In this work, we propose a novel hardware architecture based on reconfigurable FPGAs supporting ECC cryptography over prime fields $GF(p)$ offering the highest single-chip performance reported in literature up to now. Usually, known ECC implementations for reconfigurable logic implement the computationally expensive low-level arithmetic in configurable logic elements, allowing for greatest flexibility but offering only moderate performance. Some implementations have attempted to address this problem by using dedicated arithmetic hardware in the reconfigurable device for specific parts of the computations, like built-in 18x18 multipliers. But other components of the circuitry for field addition, subtraction and inversion have been still implemented in the FPGA's fabric which usually leads to a significant decrease in performance.

The central idea of this contribution is to relocate the arithmetic intensive operations of ECC over prime fields *entirely* in dedicated hardcore units on the FPGA actually reserved for use in Digital Signal Processing (DSP) filter applications. These DSP accelerating functions are built-in components in the static logic of modern FPGA devices capable to perform integer multiplication, addition and subtraction as well as a multiply-accumulate operation.

2   Previous Work

We briefly summarize previously published results of relevance to this contribution. There is a wealth of publication addressing ECC hardware architectures, and a good overview can be found in [8]. In the case of high speed architectures for ECC, most implementation primarily address elliptic curves over binary fields $GF(2^m)$ since the arithmetic is more hardware-friendly [22,10]. Our work, however, focuses on the prime field $GF(p)$. First implementations for ECC over prime fields $GF(p)$ have been proposed by [23,24] demonstrating ECC processors built completely in reconfigurable logic. The contribution by [19] proposes a high-speed ECC crypto core for arbitrary moduli with up to 256 bit length designed on a large number of built-in multiplier blocks of FPGA devices providing a significant speedup for modular multiplications. However, other field operations have been implemented in the FPGA fabric, resulting in a very large design (15,755 slices and 256 multiplier blocks) on a large Xilinx XC2VP125 device. The architecture presented in [7] was designed to achieve a better trade-off between performance and resource consumption. According to the contribution, an area consumption of only 1,854 slices and a maximum clock speed of 40 MHz can be achieved on a Xilinx Virtex-2 XC2V2000 FPGA for a parameter bit length of 160 bit.

Our approach to implementing an FPGA-based ECC engines was to shift *all* field operations into the integrated DSP building blocks available on modern FPGAs. We show that this approach leads to an extremely high throughput. Furthermore, our strategy frees most configurable logic elements on the FPGA for other applications and requires less power compared to a conventional design. To the best of our knowledge, this architecture offers the fastest performance for ECC computations over prime fields with up to 256 bit security in reconfigurable logic.

3   Mathematical Background

In the following, we will briefly introduce to the mathematical background relevant for this work. We will start with a short review of the Elliptic Curve Cryptosystems (ECC). Please note that only ECC over prime fields $GF(p)$ will be subject of this work since binary extensions fields $GF(2^m)$ require binary arithmetic which is not (yet) natively supported by DSP blocks.

3.1   Elliptic Curve Cryptography

Let p be a prime with $p > 3$ and $\mathbb{F}_p = GF(p)$ the Galois Field over p. Given the Weierstrass equation of an elliptic curve

$$\mathcal{E} : y^2 = x^3 + ax + b,$$

with $a, b \in GF(p)$ and $4a^3 + 27b^2 \neq 0$, points $\mathcal{P}_i \in \mathcal{E}$, we can compute tuples (x, y) also considered as points on this elliptic curve $\mathcal{E}$. Based on a group of points defined over this curve, ECC arithmetic defines the addition $\mathcal{R} = \mathcal{P} + \mathcal{Q}$ of two points $\mathcal{P}, \mathcal{Q}$ using the *tangent-and-chord* rule as the primary group operation. This group operation distinguishes the case for $\mathcal{P} = \mathcal{Q}$ (*point doubling*) and $\mathcal{P} \neq \mathcal{Q}$ (*point addition*). Furthermore, formulas for these operations vary for affine and projective coordinate representations. Since affine coordinates require the availability of fast modular inversion, we will focus on projective point representation to avoid the implementation of a costly inversion circuit. Given two points $\mathcal{P}_1, \mathcal{P}_2$ with $\mathcal{P}_i = (X_i, Y_i, Z_i)$ and $\mathcal{P}_1 \neq \mathcal{P}_2$, the sum $\mathcal{P}_3 = \mathcal{P}_1 + \mathcal{P}_2$ is defined by

$$A = Y_2 Z_1 - Y_1 Z_2 \quad B = A^2 Z_1 Z_2 - C^3 - 2C^2 X_1 Z_2 \quad C = X_2 Z_1 - X_1 Z_2$$
$$X_3 = BC \qquad Y_3 = A(C^2 X_1 Z_2 - B) - C^3 Y_1 Z_2 \quad Z_3 = C^3 Z_1 Z_2, \qquad (1)$$

where A, B, C are auxiliary variables and $\mathcal{P}_3 = (X_3, Y_3, Z_3)$ is the resulting point in projective coordinates. Similarly, for $\mathcal{P}_1 = \mathcal{P}_2$ the point doubling $\mathcal{P}_3 = 2\mathcal{P}_1$ is defined by

$$A = aZ^2 + 3X^2 \qquad B = YZ \quad C = XYB \qquad D = A^2 - 8C$$
$$X_3 = 2BD \qquad Y_3 = A(4C - D) - 8B^2 Y^2 \qquad Z_3 = 8B^3. \qquad (2)$$

Most ECC-based cryptosystems rely on the Elliptic Curve Discrete Logarithm Problem (ECDLP) and thus employ the technique of point multiplication $k \cdot \mathcal{P}$ as cryptographic primitive, i.e., a k times repeated point addition of a base point $\mathcal{P}$. Precisely, the ECDLP is the fundamental cryptographic problem used in protocols and crypto schemes like the Elliptic Curve Diffie-Hellman key exchange [9], the ElGamal encryption scheme [12] and the Elliptic Curve Digital Signature Algorithm (ECDSA) [1].

3.2   Standardized General Mersenne Primes

The arithmetic for ECC point multiplication is based on modular computations over a prime field $GF(p)$. These computations always include a subsequent step to reduce the result to the domain of the underlying field. Since the reduction is very costly for general primes due to the demand for a multi-precision division, special primes have been proposed by Solinas [26] which have been finally standardized in [21]. These primes provide efficient reduction algorithms based on a sequence of multi-precision addition and subtractions only and eliminate the need for the costly division. Special primes P-l with bitlengths $l = \{192, 224, 256, 384, 521\}$ are part of the standard. But we believe that the primes P-224 and P-256 are the most relevant bit sizes for future implementations of the next decades.

According to Algorithm 1 the modular reduction for P-224 can be performed with two 224-bit subtractions and additions. However, these four consecutive operations can lead to a potential over- and underflow in step 1. With $Z = z_1 + z_2 + z_3 - z_4 - z_5$, we can determine the bounds $-2p < Z < 3p$ reducing the number of final correction steps to two additions or subtractions to compute the correctly bounded $c \bmod p_{224}$.

Algorithm 2 presents the modular reduction for P-256 requiring two doublings, four 256-bit subtractions and four 256-bit additions. Based on the computation $Z = z_1 + 2z_2 + 2z_3 + z_4 + z_5 - z_6 - z_7 - z_8 - z_9$, the range of the result to be corrected is $-4p < Z < 5p$.

Algorithm 1. NIST Reduction with P-224 $= 2^{224} - 2^{96} + 1$

Input: Double-sized integer $c = (c_{13}, \ldots, c_2, c_1, c_0)$ in base 2^{32} and $0 \geq c \geq$ P-224^2
Output: Single-sized integer c mod P-224.
1: Concatenate c_i to following 224-bit integers z_j:

$$z_1 = (c_6, c_5, c_4, c_3, c_2, c_1, c_0), \; z_2 = (c_{10}, c_9, c_8, c_7, 0, 0, 0),$$
$$z_3 = (0, c_{13}, c_{12}, c_{11}, 0, 0, 0), \; z_4 = (0, 0, 0, 0, c_{13}, c_{12}, c_{11}),$$
$$z_5 = (c_{13}, c_{12}, c_{11}, c_{10}, c_9, c_8, c_7)$$

2: Compute $c = (z_1 + z_2 + z_3 - z_4 - z_5 \bmod \text{P-224})$

Algorithm 2. NIST Reduction with P-256 $= 2^{256} - 2^{224} + 2^{192} + 2^{96} - 1$

Input: Double-sized integer $c = (c_{15}, \ldots, c_2, c_1, c_0)$ in base 2^{32} and $0 \geq c \geq$ P-256^2
Output: Single-sized integer c mod P-256.
1: Concatenate c_i to following 256-bit integers z_j:

$$z_1 = (c_7, c_6, c_5, c_4, c_3, c_2, c_1, c_0), \; z_2 = (c_{15}, c_{14}, c_{13}, c_{12}, c_{11}, 0, 0, 0),$$
$$z_3 = (0, c_{15}, c_{14}, c_{13}, c_{12}, 0, 0, 0), \; z_4 = (c_{15}, c_{14}, 0, 0, 0, c_{10}, c_9, c_8),$$
$$z_5 = (c_8, c_{13}, c_{15}, c_{14}, c_{13}, c_{11}, c_{10}, c_9), \; z_6 = (c_{10}, c_8, 0, 0, 0, c_{13}, c_{12}, c_{11}),$$
$$z_7 = (c_{11}, c_9, 0, 0, c_{15}, c_{14}, c_{13}, c_{12}), \; z_8 = (c_{12}, 0, c_{10}, c_9, c_8, c_{15}, c_{14}, c_{13}),$$
$$z_9 = (c_{13}, 0, c_{11}, c_{10}, c_9, 0, c_{15}, c_{14})$$

2: Compute $c = (z_1 + 2z_2 + 2z_3 + z_4 + z_5 - z_6 - z_7 - z_8 - z_9 \bmod \text{P-256})$

---

4   An Efficient ECC Architecture Using DSP Cores

In this section we demonstrate how to implement ECC over NIST primes P-224 and P-256 using available DSP blocks of Xilinx Virtex-4 FPGAs.

4.1   DSP-Accelerator Blocks in FPGAs

Modern FPGA devices like Xilinx Virtex-4 and Virtex-5 as well as Altera Stratix FPGAs have been equipped with dedicated arithmetic hardcore extensions to accelerate, in particular, digital signal processing applications. These function blocks (*DSP blocks*) can be used to build a more efficient implementation in terms of performance *and* reduce at the same time the demand for logical elements. In general, DSP blocks of FPGAs can be programmed to perform basic arithmetic functions, especially multiplication, addition and subtraction of (un)signed integers. A common DSP component comprises an l_M-bit signed integer multiplier coupled with an l_A-bit signed adder, where $l_A > l_M$ holds. For enabling maximum performance, the multiplier and adder block can be augmented with pipeline registers to reduce signal propagation delays between components. Using different data paths, DSP blocks can operate on external inputs A, B, C as well as on feedback values from accumulation or even results $P_{j \pm 1}$ from a

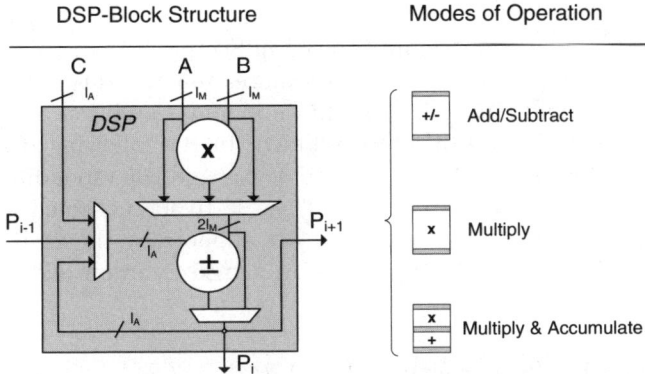

Fig. 1. Generic and simplified structure of DSP-blocks of advanced FPGA devices

neighboring DSP block. Figure 1 shows the generic DSP-block used in recent Xilinx FPGA devices [29].

4.2 ECC Engine Design Criteria

When using DSP blocks to develop a high-speed ECC design, there are several criteria which should be met to exploit their full performance. Note that the following aspects have been designed to target the requirements of Xilinx Virtex-4 FPGAs:

1. *Build DSP cascades:* Neighboring DSP blocks can be cascaded to widen or extent their atomic operand width (e.g., from 18 bit to 256 bit).
2. *Use DSP routing paths:* DSPs have been provided with inner routing paths connecting two adjacent blocks. It is advantageous in terms of performance to use these paths as frequently as possible instead of using FPGA's general switching matrix for connecting logic blocks.
3. *Consider DSP columns:* Within a Xilinx FPGA, DSPs are aligned in columns, i.e., routing paths between DSPs within the same column are efficient while a switch in columns can lead to degraded performance. Hence, DSP cascades should not exceed the column width (typically 32/48/64 DSPs per column).
4. *Use DSP pipeline registers:* DSP blocks feature pipeline stages which should be used to achieve the maximum clock frequency supported by the device (up to 500 MHz).
5. *Use different clock domains:* Optimally, DSP blocks can be operated at maximum device frequency. This is not necessarily true for the remainder of the design so that separate clock domains should be introduced (e.g. by halving the clock frequency for control signals) to address the critical paths in each domain individually.

4.3   Arithmetic Units

According to the EC arithmetic introduced in Section 3.1, an ECC engine over $GF(p)$ based on projective coordinates requires functionality for modular addition, subtraction and multiplication. Since modular addition and subtraction is very similar, both operation are combined. In the following description we will assume a Virtex-4 FPGA as reference device and corresponding DSP block arithmetic with word sizes $l_A = 32$ and $l_M = 16$ for unsigned addition and multiplication, respectively. Note that native support by the DSP blocks on a Virtex-4 device is available for up to 48-bit signed addition and 18-bit signed multiplication.

Modular Addition/Subtraction. Let $A, B \in GF(P)$ be two multi-precision operands with lengths $|A|, |B| \leq l$ and $l = \lfloor \log_2 P \rfloor + 1$. Modular addition $C = A + B \mod P$ and subtraction $C = A - B \mod P$ can be efficiently computed according to Algorithm 3:

Algorithm 3. Modular addition and subtraction

Input: A, B, P with $0 \leq A, B < P$;
     Operation flag $f \in \{0, 1\}$ denotes a subtraction when $f = 1$ and addition otherwise
Output: $C = A \pm B \mod P$
1: $(C_{\text{IN0}}, S_0) = A + (-1)^f B$;
2: $(C_{\text{IN1}}, S_1) = S_0 + (-1)^{1-f} P$;
3: Return $S_{|f - C_f|}$;

For using DSP blocks, we need to divide the l-bits operands into multiple words each having a maximum size of l_A bit due to the limited width of the DSP input port. Thus, all inputs A, B and P to the DSP blocks can be represented in the form $X = \sum_{i=0}^{n_A - 1} x_i \cdot 2^{i \cdot l_A}$, where $n_A = \lceil l / l_A \rceil$ denotes the number of words of an operand. According to Algorithm 3, we employ two cascaded DSP blocks, one for computing $s_{(0,i)} = a_i \pm (b_i + C_{\text{IN0}})$ and a second for $s_{(1,i)} = s_{(0,i)} \mp (p_i + C_{\text{IN1}})$. The resulting values $s_{(0,i)}$ and $s_{(1,i)}$ each of size $|s_{(j,i)}| \leq l_A + 1$ are temporarily stored and recombined to S_0 and S_1 using shift registers (SR). Finally, a 2-to-1 l-bit output multiplexer selects the appropriate value $C = S_i$. Figure 2 presents a schematic overview of a combined modular addition and subtraction based on two DSP blocks. Note that DSP blocks on Virtex-4 FPGAs provide a dedicated carry input c_{IN} but *no* carry output c_{OUT}. Particularly, this fact requires extra logic to compensate for duplicate carry propagation to the second DSP which is due to the fixed cascaded routing path between the DSP blocks. In this architecture, each carry is considered twice, namely in $s_{0,i+1}$ and $s_{1,i}$ what needs to be corrected. This special carry treatment requires a wait cycle to be introduced so that one l_A-bit word can be processed each two clock cycles. However, this is no restriction for our architecture since we design for *parallel* addition and multiplication so that the (shorter) runtime of an addition is completely hidden in the duration of a concurrent multiplication operation.

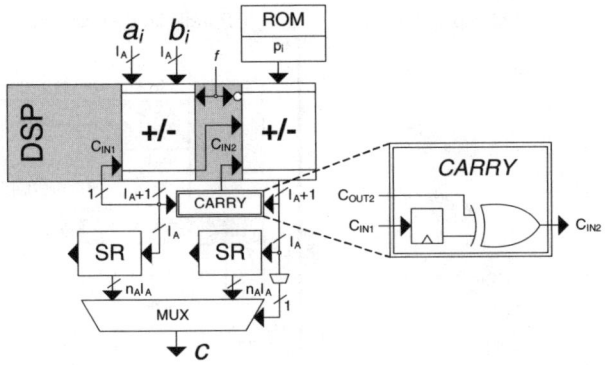

Fig. 2. Modular addition/subtraction based on DSP-blocks

Modular Multiplication. The most straightforward multiplication algorithm to implement the multiplication with subsequent NIST prime reduction (cf. Section 3.2) is the schoolbook multiplication method with a time complexity of $\mathcal{O}(n^2)$ for n-bit inputs. Other methods, like the Karatsuba algorithm [16], trade multiplications for additions using a divide-and-conquer approach. Due to the higher number of additions, this latter strategy is only preferable in case that the complexity costs of an an addition is significantly below that of a multiplication [28]. But even when neglecting any further control overhead introduced by the Karatsuba method, this does not hold for Virtex-4 devices since multiplication is comparably cheap within the DSP blocks. Let $A, B \in GF(P)$ be two multi-precision integers with bit length $l \leq \lfloor \log_2 P \rfloor + 1$. According to the limited input size l_M of DSP blocks, we split now the values A, B in $n_M = \lceil l/l_M \rceil$ words represented as $X = \sum_{i=0}^{n_M - 1} x_i \cdot 2^{il_M}$. Schoolbook multiplication computes $C = A \cdot B$ based on accumulation of $(n_M)^2$ products $C = \sum_{i=0}^{2n_M} 2^{i \cdot n_M} \sum_{j=0}^{i} a_j b_{i-j}$ providing a result C of size $|C| \leq 2n_M$. For parallel execution on n_M DSP units, we compacted the order of inner product computations as shown in Figure 3. All n_M DSP blocks operate in a loadable *Multiply-and-Accumulate* mode (MACC) so that intermediate results remain in the corresponding DSP block until an inner product $s_i = \sum_{j=0}^{i} a_j b_{i-j}$ is fully computed. Note that s_i returned from the n_M DSP blocks are not aligned and can vary in size up to $|s_i| \leq 2l_M + \log_2(n_M) = l_{ACC} = 36$ bits. Thus, all s_i need to be converted to non-redundant representation to finally form the final product of words c_i with maximum size $2l_M$ each. Hence, we feed all values into a subsequent accumulator to combine each s_i with the corresponding bits of s_{i-1} and s_{i+1}. Considering the special input constraints, timing conventions and carry transitions of DSP blocks, we developed Algorithm 4 to address the accumulation of inner products based on two DSP blocks performing l_{ACC}-bit additions.

Figure 4 gives a schematic overview of the multiplication circuit returning the full-size product C. This result has to be reduced using the fast NIST prime reduction scheme discussed in the next section.

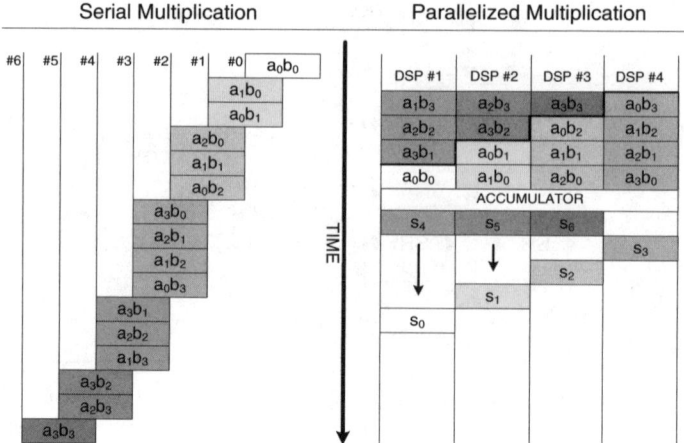

Fig. 3. Parallelizing multiplication for efficient DSP-based computation

---

Algorithm 4. Accumulation of partial product c_i

Input: Partial products s_i with bitsize $|s_i| \leq l_{ACC}$ for $i = 0 \ldots 2n_M - 1$ and $l_{ACC} = 2l_M + \log_2(n_M)$

Output: Product $C = (c_{2n_M}, \ldots, c_0)$ with bitsize $|C| \leq 2l$

1: $s_{(-1)} \to 0$; $c_{(-1)} \to 0$
2: **for** $i = 0$ to $2n_M - 2$ **by** 2 **do**
3:   $d_i \to \text{ADD}(s_{i-1}[l_{ACC} - 1 \ldots l_M], s_i[l_{ACC} \ldots 0])$
4:   $c_i \to \text{ADD}(d_i[l_{ACC} \ldots l_M], (s_{i+1}[l_M \ldots 0]|c_{i-1}[3l_M \ldots 2l_M]))$
5: **end for**
6: **return** $c = (c_{2n_M-1}, \ldots, c_0)$

Modular Reduction. At this point we will discuss the subsequent modular reduction of the $2n_M$-bit multiplication result C using the NIST reduction scheme. All fast NIST reduction algorithms rely on a reduction step (1) defined as a series multi-precision additions and subtractions followed by a correction step (2) to achieve a final value in the interval $[0, \ldots, P - 1]$ (cf. Algorithms 1 and 2). To implement (1), we decided to use one DSP-block for each individual addition or subtraction, e.g., for the P-256 reduction we reserved a cascade of 8 DSP blocks. Each DSP performs one addition or subtraction and stores the result in a register whose output is taken as input to the neighboring block (data pipeline).

For the correction step (2), we need to determine *in advance* the possible overflow or underflow of the result returned by (1) to avoid wait or idle cycles in the pipeline. Hence, we introduced a Look-Ahead Logic (LAL) consisting of a separate DSP block which exclusively computes the expected overflow or underflow. Then, the output of the LAL is used to select a corresponding reduction value which are stored as multiple $\{0, \ldots, 5P\}$ in a ROM table. The ROM values are added or subtracted to the result of (1) by a sequence of two DSP blocks

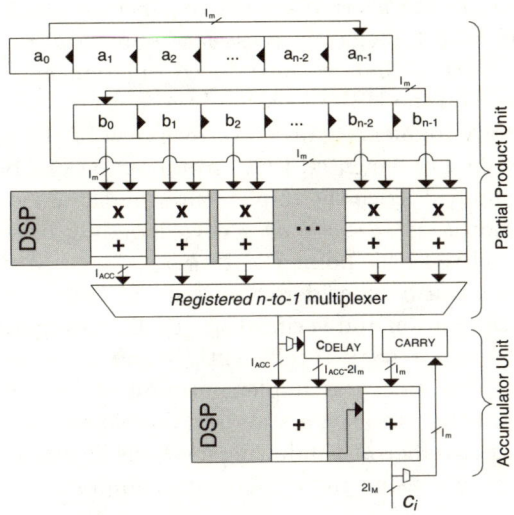

Fig. 4. An l-bit multiplication circuit employing a cascade of parallelly operating DSP blocks

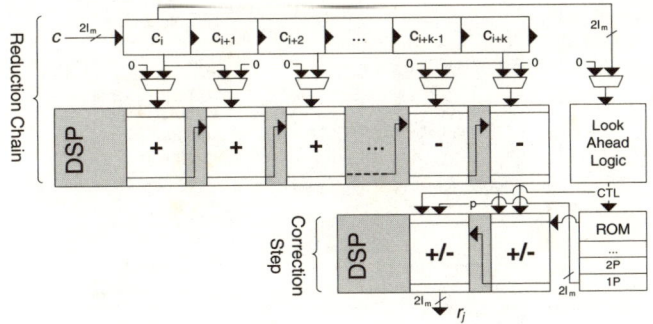

Fig. 5. Modular reduction for NIST-P-224 and P-256 using DSP blocks

ensuring that the final result is always in $\{0, \ldots, P-1\}$. Figure 5 depicts the general structure of the reduction circuit which is applicable for both primes P-224 and P-256.

4.4   ECC Core Architecture

With the basic field operations for $l-bit$ computations at hand supporting NIST primes P-224 and P-256, we have combined a modular multiplier and a modular subtraction/addition component with dual-port RAM modules (BRAM) and a state machine to build an ECC core. We have implemented an asymmetric datapath supporting two different operand lengths: the first operand provides full l-bit of data whereas the second operand is limited to 32-bit words so that several words need to be transferred serially to generate the full l-bit input. This approach allows for direct memory accesses of our *serial-to-parallel* multiplier architecture. Note further that we introduced different clock domains for the core arithmetic based on the DSP blocks and the state machines for upper layers (running at half clock frequency only). An overview of the entire ECC core is shown in Figure 6. We implemented ECC group operations based on projective Chudnowsky coordinates[1] since the implementation should support to compute a point multiplication $k \cdot \mathcal{P}$ *as well as* a corresponding linear combination $k \cdot \mathcal{P} + r \cdot \mathcal{Q}$ based on a fixed base point $\mathcal{P} \in \mathcal{E}$, $k, r \in \{1, \ldots, ord(\mathcal{P}) - 1\}$ and $\mathcal{Q} \in \langle \mathcal{P} \rangle$. Both operations can be considered as basic ECC primitives, e.g., used for ECDSA signature generation and verification [1]. The computation of $k \cdot \mathcal{P} + r \cdot \mathcal{Q}$ can make use of *Shamir's trick* to efficiently compute several point products simultaneously [12]. For this first implementation of the point multiplication and the sake of simplicity, we used a standard double-and-add (binary method) algorithm [14], but more efficient windowing methods [2] can also be implemented without significantly increasing the resource consumption.

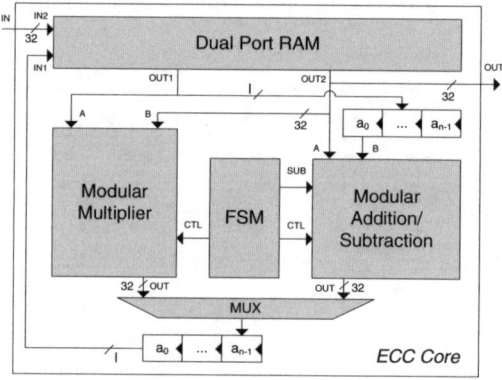

Fig. 6. Schematic overview of a single ECC core

4.5   ECC Core Parallism

Due the intensive use of DSP blocks to implement the core functionality of ECC, the resulting implementation requires only few reconfigurable logic elements on the FPGA. This allows for efficient multiple-core implementations on a single FPGA improving the overall system throughput by a linear factor n dependent on the number of cores. Note that most other high-performance implementations occupy the full FPGA due to their immense resource consumption so that these cannot easily be instantiated several times.

---

[1] ECC operations based on mixed affine-Jacobian coordinates are more efficient but more complex in hardware when considering precomputed points in Jacobian coordinates required for computing $k \cdot \mathcal{P} + r \cdot \mathcal{Q}$ as required for ECDSA signature verification.

Based on our synthesis results, the limiting factor of our architecture is the number of available DSP blocks of a specific FPGA device (cf. Section 5).

5   Implementation

The proposed architecture has been synthesized and implemented for the smallest available Xilinx Virtex-4 device (XC4VFX12-12SF363) and the corresponding results are presented in Subsection 5.1. This FPGA type offers 5,472 slices (12,288 4-input LUTs and flip flops) of reconfigurable logic, 32 DSP blocks and can be operated at a maximum clock frequency of 500 MHz. Furthermore, to demonstrate how many ECC computations can be performed using ECC core parallelism, we take a second device, the large Xilinx Virtex-4 XC4VSX55-12FF1148 providing the maximum number of 512 DSP blocks and 24,576 slices (49,152 4-input LUTs and flip flops) as a reference for a multi-core architecture.

5.1   Implementation Results

Based on the Post-Place and Route (PAR) results using Xilinx ISE 9.1 we can present the following performance and area details for ECC cores for primes P-224 and P-256 on the small XC4VFX12 device as shown in Table 1. Note that up to now the implementation for P-224 is not yet fully verified in functionality or optimized. The core for P-256, however, is already available for use in real-world products.

Table 1. Requirements and clock frequency of a single ECC core on a Virtex-4 FX 12 after PAR

Aspect	ECC Core P-224	ECC Core P-256
Slices occupied	1,580 (29%)	1,715 (31%)
4-input LUTs	1,825	2,589
Flip flops	1,892	2,028
DSP blocks	26	32
BRAMs	11	11
Frequency/Max. delay	487 MHz/2.050 ns	490 MHz/2.040 ns

5.2   Throughput of a Single ECC Core

Given an ECC core with a separate adder/subtracter and multiplier unit, we can perform a field multiplication and field addition simultaneously. By optimizing the execution order of the basic field operations, it is possible to perform all additions/subtraction required for the ECC group operation in parallel to a multiplication. Based on the runtimes of a single field multiplication, we can determine the number of required clock cycles for the operations $k \cdot \mathcal{P}$ and $k \cdot \mathcal{P} + r \cdot \mathcal{Q}$ using the implemented Double-and-Add algorithm. Moreover, we also give

Table 2. Performance of ECC operations based on a single ECC core using projective Chudnowsky coordinates on a Virtex-4 XC4VFX12 (Figures denoted with an asterisk are estimates)

Aspect	ECC Core P-224	ECC Core P-256
Cycles per MUL in $GF(p)$	58	70
Cycles per ADD/SUB in $GF(p)$	16	18
Cycles per ECC Addition (Chudnovsky)	812	980
Cycles per ECC Doubling (Chudnovsky)	580	700
Cycles $k \cdot \mathcal{P}$ (Double&Add)	219,878	303,450
Cycles $k \cdot \mathcal{P}$ (Window)	178,000*	243,000*
Cycles $k \cdot \mathcal{P} + r \cdot \mathcal{Q}$ (Double&Add)	265,959	366,905
Cycles $k \cdot \mathcal{P} + r \cdot \mathcal{Q}$ (Window)	194,000*	264,000*
Time and OP/s for $k \cdot \mathcal{P}$ (Double&Add)	452 μs/2214	620 μs/1614
Time and OP/s for $k \cdot \mathcal{P}$ (Window)	365 μs*/2740*	495 μs*/2020*
Time and OP/s for $k \cdot \mathcal{P} + r \cdot \mathcal{Q}$ (Double&Add)	546 μs/1831	749 μs/1335
Time and OP/s for $k \cdot \mathcal{P} + r \cdot \mathcal{Q}$ (Window)	398 μs*/2510*	540 μs*/1850*

estimates concerning their performance when using a window-based method [2] based on a window size $w = 4$.

Note that the specified timing considers signal propagation after complete PAR excluding the timing constraints from I/O pins since no underlying data communication layer was implemented. Hence, when being combined with an I/O protocol of a real-world application, the clock frequency will be slightly lower than specified in Table 1 and 3.

5.3   Multi-core Architecture

Since a single ECC core has obviously moderate resource requirements, it is possible to place multiple instances of the core on a larger FPGA. On a *single* XC4VSX55 device, we can implement, depending on the underlying prime field, between 16–18 ECC cores running in parallel (cf. Table 3). Due the small amount of LUTs and flip flops required for a single core, the number of available DSP blocks (and routing resources) on the FPGA is here the limiting factor.

5.4   Comparison

Based on our architecture, we can estimate a throughput of more than 37,000 point multiplications on the standardized elliptic curve P-224 per second which exceeds the throughput of all *single-chip* hardware implementation known to the authors by far. A detailed comparison with other implementations is presented in Table 4.

Table 3. PAR-Results for a multi-core architecture on a Virtex-4 XC4VSX55 device for ECC over prime fields P-224 and P-256 (Figures denoted with an asterisk are estimates)

Aspect	ECC P-224	ECC P-256
Number of Cores	18	16
Slices occupied	24,452 (99%)	24,574 (99%)
4-input LUTs	32,688	34,896
Flip flops	34,166	32,430
DSP blocks	468	512
BRAMs	198	176
Frequency/Max. delay	372 MHz/2.685 ns	375 MHz/2.665 ns
OP/s $k \cdot P$ (Double&Add)	30,438	19,760
OP/s $k \cdot P$ (Window)	37,700*	24,700*
OP/s $k \cdot P + r \cdot Q$ (Double&Add)	25,164	16,352
OP/s $k \cdot P + r \cdot Q$ (Window)	34,500*	22,700*

At this point we like to point out that the field of highly efficient *prime field* arithmetic is believed to be predominated by implementations on general purpose microprocessors rather than on FPGAs. Hence, we will also compare our hardware implementation against the performance of software solutions on recent microprocessors. Since most performance figures for software implementations are given in cycles rather than absolute times, we assumed for comparing throughputs that, on a modern microprocessor, repeated computations can be performed *without* interruption simultaneously on *all* available cores with no further cycles spent, e.g., on scheduling or other administrative tasks. Note that this is indeed a very optimistic assumption possibly overrating the performance of software implementations with respect to actual applications.

For example, a point multiplication using the highly efficient software implementation by Dan Bernstein based on floating point arithmetic for ECC over P-224 requires 839.000 cycles on an (outdated) Intel Pentium 4 [3] at 1.4GHz. According to our assumption for cycle count interpretation, this correlates to 1670 point multiplication per second.

Despite the good performance figures on this platform, we prefer to take more recent results, e.g., obtained from ECRYPT's eBATS project. According to the report from March 2007 [11], an Intel Core2 Duo running at 2.13 GHz is able to generate 1868 and 1494 ECDSA signatures based on the OpenSSL implementation for P-224 and P-256, respectively. Taking latest Intel Core2 Quad microprocessors into account, these performance figures might even double. We also compare our work to the very fast software implementation by [13] using an Intel Core2 system at 2.66 GHz. However, in this contribution the special Montgomery and non-standard curve over $\mathbb{F}_{2^{255}-19}$ is used instead of a standardized NIST prime. Despite of that, for the design based on this curve the authors report the impressive throughput of 6700 point multiplications per second.

Table 4. Selected high-performance implementations of public-key cryptosystems

Scheme	Device	Implementation	Logic	Clock	Time
This work	XC4VFX12-12	GF(p), NIST-224	1580 LS/26 DSP	487 MHz	365 μs
	XC4VFX12-12	GF(p), NIST-256	1715 LS/32 DSP	490 MHz	495 μs
	XC4VSX55-12	GF(p), NIST-224	24452 LS/468 DSP	372 MHz	26.5 μs
	XC4VSX55-12	GF(p), NIST-256	24574 LS/512 DSP	375 MHz	40.5 μs
ECC [23]	XCV1000E	GF(p), NIST-192	5708 LS	40 MHz	3 ms
ECC [19]	XC2VP125-7	GF(p), 256-bit	15755 LS/256 MUL	39.5 MHz	3.84 ms
ECC [24]	0.13 μm CMOS	GF(p), 160-bit	117500 GE	137.7 MHz	1.21 ms
ECC [3]	Intel Pentium4	GF(p), NIST-224	32 bit μP	1.4 GHz	599 μs
ECC [11]	Intel Core2 Duo	GF(p), NIST-256	64 bit μP	2.13 GHz	669[a] μs
ECC [13]	Intel Core2 Duo	GF($2^{255} - 19$)	64 bit μP	2.66 GHz	145 μs
RSA[4]	XC40250XV	1024-bit	6826 CLB	45.2 MHz	3.1 ms
RSA[27]	XC4VFX12-10	1024-bit (DSP)	3937 LS/17 DSP	400 MHz	1.71 ms
RSA[25]	0.5 μm CMOS	1024-bit	28,000 GE	64 MHz	46 ms

[a] Note that this figure reflects a full ECDSA signature generation rather than a point multiplication.

For a fair comparison with software solutions it should be considered that a single Virtex-4 SX 55 costs about US$ 1,170[2]. Recent microprocessors like the Intel Core2 Duo, however, are available at only about a quarter of that price. With this in mind, we might not be able to beat all software implementation in terms of the cost-performance ratio, but we still like to point out that our FPGA-based design - as the fastest reported hardware implementation so far - definitely closes the performance gap between software and hardware implementations for ECC over prime fields. Furthermore, we like to emphasize again that all software related performance figures are based on very optimistic assumptions.

6   Conclusion

We presented a novel ECC implementation for fields over NIST primes P-224 and P-256. Due to the exhaustive utilization of DSP blocks, which are contained as hardcores in modern FPGA devices, we are able to perform the critical components computing low-level integer arithmetic operations nearly at maximum device frequency. Furthermore, considering a multi-core architecture on a Virtex-4 XC4VSX55 FPGA, we can achieve a throughput of more than 24,000 and 37,000 point multiplications per second for P-256 and P-224, respectively, what significantly exceeds the performance of all other hardware implementation known to the authors and comes close to the cost-performance ratio provided by the fastest available software implementations in the open literature.

---

[2] Market price for a single device in May 2008.

References

1. ANSI X9.62-2005. American National Standard X9.62: The Elliptic Curve Digital Signature Algorithm (ECDSA). Technical report, Accredited Standards Committee X9 (2005), http://www.x9.org
2. Avanzi, R.M., Cohen, H., Doche, C., Frey, G., Lange, T., Nguyen, K., Vercauteren, F.: Handbook of Elliptic and Hyperelliptic Curve Cryptography. Chapman & Hall/CRC (2005)
3. Bernstein, D.J.: A software implementation of NIST P-224. In: Presentation at the 5th Workshop on Elliptic Curve Cryptography (ECC 2001), October 29-31, 2001, University of Waterloo (2001), http://cr.yp.to/nistp224/timings.html
4. Blum, T., Paar, C.: High radix Montgomery modular exponentiation on reconfigurable hardware. IEEE Transactions on Computers 50(7), 759–764 (2001)
5. Certicom research. Standards for Efficient Cryptography — SEC 1: Elliptic Curve Cryptography. Version 1.0 (September 2000), http://www.secg.org/secg_docs.htm
6. Certicom research. Standards for Efficient Cryptography — SEC 1: Recommended Elliptic Curve Domain Parameters. Version 1.0 (September 2000), http://www.secg.org/secg_docs.htm
7. Daly, A., Marnane, W., Kerins, T., Popovici, E.: An FPGA implementation of a GF(p) ALU for encryption processors. Elsevier - Microprocessors and Microsystems 28(5–6), 253–260 (2004)
8. de Dormale, G.M., Quisquater, J.-J.: High-speed hardware implementations of elliptic curve cryptography: A survey. J. Syst. Archit. 53(2-3), 72–84 (2007)
9. Diffie, W., Hellman, M.: New directions in cryptography. IEEE Trans. Inf. Theory 22, 644–654 (1976)
10. Eberle, H., Gura, N., Chang-Shantz, S.: A cryptographic processor for arbitrary elliptic curves over $GF(2^m)$. In: Application-Specific Systems, Architectures, and Processors (ASAP), pp. 444–454 (2003)
11. ECRYPT. eBATS: ECRYPT Benchmarking of Asymmetric Systems. Technical report (March 2007), http://www.ecrypt.eu.org/ebats/
12. ElGamal, T.: A public key cryptosystem and a signature scheme based on discrete logarithms. IEEE Trans. Inf. Theory 31, 469–472 (1985)
13. Gaudry, P., Thomé, E.: The mp𝔽q library and implementing curve-based key exchanges. SPEED: Software Performance Enhancement for Encryption and Decryption, 49–64 (2007)
14. Hankerson, D., Menezes, A., Vanstone, S.: Guide to Elliptic Curve Cryptography. Springer, New York (2004)
15. Institute of Electrical and Electronics Engineers. IEEE P1363 Standard Specifications for Public Key Cryptography (2000)
16. Karatsuba, A., Ofman, Y.: Multiplication of multidigit numbers on automata. Soviet Physics—Doklady 7(7), 595–596 (1963)
17. Koblitz, N.: Elliptic curve cryptosystems. Mathematics of Computation 48, 203–209 (1987)
18. Lenstra, A.K., Verheul, E.R.: Selecting Cryptographic Key Sizes. Journal of Cryptology 14(4), 255–293 (2001)
19. McIvor, C., McLoone, M., McCanny, J.: An FPGA elliptic curve cryptographic accelerator over GF(p). In: Irish Signals and Systems Conference (ISSC), pp. 589–594 (2004)

20. Miller, V.: Uses of elliptic curves in cryptography. In: Williams, H.C. (ed.) CRYPTO 1985. LNCS, vol. 218, pp. 417–426. Springer, Heidelberg (1986)
21. National Institute of Standards and Technology (NIST). Recommended Elliptic Curves for Federal Government Use (July 1999),
    http://csrc.nist.gov/csrc/fedstandards.html
22. Orlando, G., Paar, C.: A High-Performance Reconfigurable Elliptic Curve Processor for GF(2^m). In: Paar, C., Koç, Ç.K. (eds.) CHES 2000. LNCS, vol. 1965, pp. 41–56. Springer, Heidelberg (2000)
23. Orlando, G., Paar, C.: A scalable GF(p) elliptic curve processor architecture for programmable hardware. In: Koç, Ç.K., Naccache, D., Paar, C. (eds.) CHES 2001. LNCS, vol. 2162, pp. 356–371. Springer, Heidelberg (2001)
24. Satoh, A., Takano, K.: A scalable dual-field elliptic curve cryptographic processor. IEEE Transactions Computers 52, 449–460 (2003)
25. Savas, E., Tenca, A.F., Ciftcibasi, M.E., Koc, C.K.: Multiplier architectures for GF(p) and GF(2^n). IEE Proc. Comput. Digit. Tech. 151(2), 147–160 (2004)
26. Solinas, J.A.: Generalized Mersenne Numbers. Technical report (September 09, 1999)
27. Suzuki, D.: How to maximize the potential of FPGA Resources for Modular Exponentiation. In: Paillier, P., Verbauwhede, I. (eds.) CHES 2007. LNCS, vol. 4727, pp. 272–288. Springer, Heidelberg (2007)
28. Weimerskirch, A., Paar, C.: Generalizations of the Karatsuba Algorithm for Efficient Implementations. Technical report, Ruhr-Universität-Bochum, Germany (2003)
29. Xilinx. Xilinx Virtex 4, 5 and Spartan 3A FPGAs (2008),
    http://www.xilinx.com/products/silicon_solutions/

Exploiting the Power of GPUs for Asymmetric Cryptography

Robert Szerwinski and Tim Güneysu

Horst Görtz Institute for IT Security, Ruhr University Bochum, Germany
{szerwinski,gueneysu}@crypto.rub.de

Abstract. Modern Graphics Processing Units (GPU) have reached a dimension with respect to performance and gate count exceeding conventional Central Processing Units (CPU) by far. Many modern computer systems include – beside a CPU – such a powerful GPU which runs idle most of the time and might be used as cheap and instantly available co-processor for general purpose applications.

In this contribution, we focus on the efficient realisation of the computationally expensive operations in asymmetric cryptosystems on such off-the-shelf GPUs. More precisely, we present improved and novel implementations employing GPUs as accelerator for RSA and DSA cryptosystems as well as for Elliptic Curve Cryptography (ECC). Using a recent Nvidia 8800GTS graphics card, we are able to compute 813 modular exponentiations per second for RSA or DSA-based systems with 1024 bit integers. Moreover, our design for ECC over the prime field P-224 even achieves the throughput of 1412 point multiplications per second.

Keywords: Asymmetric Cryptosystems, Graphics Processing Unit, RSA, DSA, ECC.

1 Introduction

For the last twenty years graphics hardware manufacturers have focused on producing fast Graphics Processing Units (GPUs), specifically for the gaming community. This has more recently led to devices which outperform general purpose Central Processing Units (CPUs) for specific applications, particularly when comparing the MIPS (million instructions per second) benchmarks. Hence, a research community has been established to use the immense power of GPUs for general purpose computations (GPGPU). In the last two years, prior limitations of the graphics application programming interfaces (API) have been removed by GPU manufacturers by introducing unified processing units in graphics cards. They support a general purpose instruction set by a native driver interface and framework.

In the field of asymmetric cryptography, the security of all practical cryptosystems rely on hard computational problems strongly dependant on the choice of parameters. But with rising parameter sizes (often in the range of 1024–4096

E. Oswald and P. Rohatgi (Eds.): CHES 2008, LNCS 5154, pp. 79–99, 2008.

bits), however, computations become more and more challenging for the underlying processor. For modern hardware, the computation of a *single* cryptographic operation is not critical, however in a many-to-one communication scenario, like a central server in a company's data processing centre, it may be confronted with hundreds or thousands of simultaneous connections and corresponding cryptographic operations. As a result, the most common current solution are cryptographic accelerator cards. Due to the limited market, their price tags are often in the range of several thousands euros or US dollars. The question at hand is whether commodity GPUs can be used as high-performance public-key accelerators.

In this work, we will present novel implementations of cryptosystems based on modular exponentiations and elliptic curve operations on recent graphics hardware. To the best of our knowledge, this is the first publication making use of the CUDA framework for GPGPU processing of asymmetric cryptosystems. We will start with implementing the extremely wide-spread *Rivest Shamir Adleman* (RSA) cryptosystem [30]. The same implementation based on modular exponentiation for large integers can be used to implement the *Digital Signature Algorithm* (DSA), which has been published by the US National Institute of Standards and Technology (NIST) [25]. Recently, DSA has been adopted to elliptic curve groups in the ANSI X9.62 standard [2]. The implementation of this variant, called ECDSA, is the second major goal of this work.

2   Previous Work

Lately, the research community has started to explore techniques to accelerate cryptographic algorithms using the GPU. For example, various authors looked at the feasibility of the current industry standard for *symmetric* cryptography, the Advanced Encryption Standard (AES) [21,31,18,9]. Only two groups, namely Moss *et al.* and Fleissner, have aimed for the efficient implementation of modular exponentiation on the GPU [24,14]. Their results were not promising, as they were limited by the legacy GPU architecture and interface (cf. the next section). To the best of our knowledge there are neither publications about the implementation of these systems on modern, GPGPU-capable hardware nor on the implementation of elliptic curve based systems.

We aim to fill this gap by implementing the core operations for both systems efficiently on modern graphics hardware, creating the foundation for the use of GPUs as accelerators for public key cryptography. We will use Nvidia's current flagship GPU series, the G80 generation, together with its new GPGPU interface CUDA.

3   Using GPUs for General-Purpose Applications

The following section will give an overview over traditional GPU computing, followed by a more in-depth introduction to Nvidia's general purpose interface CUDA.

3.1   Traditional GPU Computing

Roughly, the graphics pipeline consist of the stages *transform & light, assemble primitives, rasterise* and *shade*. First GPUs had all functions needed to implement the graphics pipeline hardwired, but over time more and more stages became *programmable* by introducing specialised processors, e.g. vertex and fragment processors that made the transform & light and shading stages, respectively, more flexible.

When processing power increased massively while prices kept falling, the research community thought of ways to use these resources for computationally intense tasks. However, as the processors' capabilities were very limited and the API of the graphics driver was specifically built to implement the graphics pipeline, a lot of overhead needed to be taken into account. For example, all data had to be encoded in textures which are two dimensional arrays of pixels storing colour values for red, green, blue and an additional alpha channel used for transparency. Additionally, textures are *read-only* objects, which forced the programmers to compute one step of an algorithm, store the result in the frame buffer, and start the next step using a texture reference to the newly produced pixels. This technique is known as *ping-ponging*. Most GPUs did only provide instructions to manipulate floating point numbers, forcing GPGPU programmers to map integers onto the available mantissa and find ways to emulate bit-logical functions, e.g., by using look-up tables.

These limitations have been the main motivation for the key GPU manufacturers ATI/AMD and Nvidia to create APIs specifically for the GPGPU community and modify their hardware for better support: ATI's solution is called Close To the Metal (CTM) [1], while Nvidia presented the Compute Unified Device Architecture (CUDA), a radically new design that makes GPU programming and GPGPU switch places: The underlying hardware of the G80 series is an accumulation of *scalar* common purpose processing units ("unified" design) and quite a bit of "glue" hardware to efficiently map the graphics pipeline to this new design. GPGPU applications however directly map to the target hardware and thus graphics hardware can be programmed without any graphics API whatsoever.

3.2   Programming GPUs Using Nvidia's CUDA Framework

In general, the GPU's immense computation power mainly relies on its inherent parallel architecture. For this, the CUDA framework introduces the **thread** as smallest unit of parallelism, i.e., a small piece of concurrent code with associated state. However, when compared to threads on microprocessors, GPU threads have much lower resource usage and lower creation and switching cost. Note that GPUs are only effective when running a *high number* of such threads. A group of threads that is executed *physically* in parallel is called **warp**. All threads in one warp are executed in a *single instruction multiple data* (SIMD) fashion. If one or more thread(s) in the *same* warp need to execute different instructions, e.g., in case of a data-dependent jump, their execution will be serialised and the threads are called *divergent*. As the next level of parallelism, a (thread) **block** is a group of threads that can communicate with each other and synchronise their execution. The maximum number of threads per block is limited by the hardware. Finally, a group of blocks that have same dimensionality and execute the same CUDA program *logically* in parallel is called **grid**.

To allow optimal performance for different access patterns, CUDA implements a hierarchical memory model, contrasting the flat model normally assumed on computers. Host (PC) and device (GPU) have their own memory areas, called *host memory* and *device memory*, respectively. CUDA supplies optimised functions to transfer data between these separate spaces.

Each thread possesses its own **register file**, which can be read and written. Additionally, it can access its own copy of so-called **local memory**. All threads in the same *grid* can access the same on-chip read- and writable **shared memory** region. To prevent hazards resulting from concurrent execution of threads synchronisation mechanisms must be used. Shared memory is organised in groups called banks that can be accessed in parallel. All threads can access a read- and writable memory space called **global memory** and read-only regions called **constant memory** and **texture memory**. The second last is optimised for one-dimensional locality of accesses, while the last is most effective when being used with two-dimensional arrays (matrices). Note that the texture and constant memories are the only regions that are cached. Thus, all accesses to the off-chip regions global and local memory have a high access latency, resulting in penalties when being used too frequently.

The hardware consists of a number of so-called *multiprocessors* that are build from SIMD processors, on-chip memory and caches. Clearly, one processor executes a particular thread, the same warp being run on the multiprocessor at the same time. One or more blocks are mapped to each multiprocessor, sharing its resources (registers and shared memory) and get executed on a time-sliced basis. When a particular block has finished its execution, the scheduler starts the next block of the grid until all blocks have been run.

Design Criteria for GPU Implementations. To achieve optimal performance using CUDA, algorithms must be designed to run in a multitude of parallel threads and take advantage of the presented hierarchical memory model. In the following, we enumerate the key criteria necessary for gaining the most out of the GPU by loosely following the CUDA programming guide [27] and a talk given by Mark Harris of Nvidia [17].

A. *Maximise use of available processing power*
   A1. **Maximise independent parallelism** in the algorithm to enable easy partitioning in threads and blocks.
   A2. **Keep resource usage low** to allow concurrent execution of as many threads as possible, i.e., use only a small number of registers per thread and shared memory per block.
   A3. **Maximise arithmetic intensity**, i.e., match the arithmetic to bandwidth ratio to the GPU design philosophy: GPUs spend their transistors

on ALUs, not caches. Bearing this in mind allows to hide memory access latency by the use of independent computations (*latency hiding*). Examples include using arithmetic instructions with high throughput as well as re-computing values instead of saving them for later use.

A4. **Avoid divergent threads** in the *same* warp.

B. *Maximise use of available memory bandwidth*

B1. **Avoid memory transfers between host and device** by shifting more computations from the host to the GPU.

B2. **Use shared memory** instead of global memory **for variables**.

B3. **Use constant or texture memory** instead of global memory **for constants**.

B4. **Coalesce global memory accesses**, i.e., choose access patterns that allow to combine several accesses in the same warp to one, wider access.

B5. **Avoid bank conflicts** when utilising shared memory, i.e., choose patterns that result in the access of *different* banks per warp.

B6. **Match access patterns** for constant and texture memory **to the cache design**.

CUDA Limitations. Although CUDA programs are written in the C language together with extensions to support the memory model, allow synchronisation and special intrinsics to access faster assembler instructions, it also contains a number of limitations that negatively affect efficient implementation of public key cryptography primitives. Examples are the lack for additions/subtractions with carry as well as the missing support for inline assembler instructions[1].

4   Modular Arithmetic on GPUs

In the following section we will give different ways do realise *modular arithmetic* on a GPU efficiently, keeping the aforementioned criteria in mind. For the RSA cryptosystem we need to implement arithmetic modulo N, where N is the product of two large primes p and q: $N = p \cdot q$. The arithmetic of both DSA systems, however, is based on the prime field $GF(p)$ as the lowest-level building block. Note that the DSA systems both use a *fixed* – in terms of sessions or key generations – prime p, thus allowing to choose special primes at build time that have advantageous properties when reducing modulo p. For example, the US National Institute of Standards and Technology (NIST) proposes a set of *generalised Mersenne primes* in the *Digital Signature Standard* (DSS) [25, Appendix 6]. As the RSA modulus N is the product of the two secret primes p and q that will be chosen secretly *for each* new key pair, we cannot optimise for the modulus in this case.

---

[1] Nvidia published their own (abstract) assembler language PTX [28], however as of CUDA version 1.0 one kernel *cannot* contain code both generated from the C language and PTX.

Modular Addition and Subtraction. In general, addition $s \equiv a + b \bmod m$ of two operands a and b, where $0 \leq a, b < m$, is straightforward, as the result of the plain addition operation $a + b$ always satisfies $0 \leq a + b < 2m$ and therefore needs at maximum one subtraction of m to fulfil $0 \leq s < m$. Due to the SIMD design, we require algorithms that have a uniform control flow in all cases and compute both $a + b$ and $a + b - m$ and decide afterwards which is the correctly reduced result, cf. Criterion A4. Subtraction $d \equiv a - b \bmod m$ can be treated similarly: we compute both $a - b$ and $a - b + m$ and use a sign test at the end to derive the correctly reduced result.

Modular Multiplication. Multi-precision modular multiplication $r \equiv a \cdot b \bmod m$ is usually the most critical operation in common asymmetric cryptosystems. In a straightforward approach to compute r, we derive a double-sized product $r' = ab$ first and reduce afterwards by multi-precision division. Besides the quadratic complexity of standard multiplication, division is known to be very costly and should be avoided whenever possible. Thus, we will discuss several multiplication strategies to identify an optimal method for implementation on GPUs.

4.1   Modular Multiplication Using Montgomery's Technique

In 1985 Peter L. Montgomery proposed an algorithm [23] to remove the costly division operation from the modular reduction. Koç et al. [6] give a survey of different implementation options. As all multi-precision Montgomery multiplication algorithms feature no inherent parallelism except the possibility to pipeline, we do *not* consider them optimal for our platform and implement the method with the lowest temporary space requirement of $n + 2$ words, coarsely integrated operand scanning (CIOS), as a reference solution only (cf. to Algorithm 1).

4.2   Modular Multiplication in Residue Number Systems (RNS)

As an alternative approach to conventional base-2^w arithmetic, we can represent integers based on the idea of the Chinese Remainder Theorem, by encoding an integer x as a tuple formed from its residues x_i modulo n relatively prime w-bit moduli m_i, where $|x|_{m_i}$ denotes $x \bmod m_i$:

$$\langle x \rangle_{\mathcal{A}} = \langle x_0, x_1, \ldots, x_{n-1} \rangle_{\mathcal{A}} = \langle |x|_{m_0}, |x|_{m_1}, \ldots, |x|_{m_{n-1}} \rangle_{\mathcal{A}} \tag{1}$$

Here, the ordered set of relatively prime moduli $(m_0, m_1, \ldots, m_{n-1})$, gcd $(m_i, m_j) = 1$ for all $i \neq j$, is called *base* and denoted by $\mathcal{A}$. The product of all moduli, $A = \prod_{i=0}^{n-1} m_i$ is called *dynamic range* of $\mathcal{A}$, i.e., the number of values that can be *uniquely* represented in $\mathcal{A}$. In other words, all numbers in $\mathcal{A}$ get implicitly reduced modulo A. Such a representation in RNS has the advantage that addition, subtraction and multiplication can be computed *independently* for all residues:

$$\langle x \rangle_{\mathcal{A}} \circ \langle y \rangle_{\mathcal{A}} = \langle |x_0 \circ y_0|_{m_0}, |x_1 \circ y_1|_{m_1}, \ldots, |x_{n-1} \circ y_{n-1}|_{m_{n-1}} \rangle_{\mathcal{A}}, \circ \in \{+, -, \cdot\} \tag{2}$$

Algorithm 1. Montgomery Multiplication for Multi-Precision Integers (CIOS Method) [6]

Require: Modulus M and radix $R = 2^{wn}$ s.t. $R > M$ and $\gcd(R, M) = 1$; $M_0' = (-M^{-1} \bmod R) \bmod 2^w$, two unsigned integers $0 \le A, B < M$ in Montgomery form, i.e. $X = (X_{n-1}X_{n-2}\ldots X_0)_{2^w}$ for $X \in \{A, B, M\}$.

Ensure: The product $C = ABR^{-1} \pmod{M}$, $0 \le C < M$, in Montgomery form.

1:   $T \leftarrow 0$
2:   **for** i **from** 0 **to** $n - 1$ **do**
3:      $c \leftarrow 0$
4:      **for** j **from** 0 **to** $n - 1$ **do** {Multiplication}
5:         $(c, T_j) \leftarrow A_j \cdot B_i + T_j + c$
6:      **end for**
7:      $(T_{n+1}, T_n) \leftarrow T_n + c$

8:      $m \leftarrow T_0 \cdot M_0' \bmod 2^w$ {Reduction}
9:      $(c, T_0) \leftarrow m \cdot M_0 + T_0$
10:     **for** j **from** 1 **to** $n - 1$ **do**
11:        $(c, T_{j-1}) \leftarrow m \cdot M_j + T_j + c$
12:     **end for**
13:     $T_{n-1} \leftarrow T_n + c$
14:     $T_n \leftarrow T_{n+1} + c$
15: **end for**
16: **return** $(T_{n-1}T_{n-2}\ldots T_0)_{2^w}$

---

which allows carry-free computations[2] and multiplication without partial products. However, some information involving the whole number x cannot be easily computed. For instance, sign and overflow detection and comparison of magnitude are hard, resulting from the fact that residue number systems are no weighted representation. Furthermore, division and as a result reduction modulo an arbitrary modulus $M \ne A$ is *not* as easy as in other representations.

But similar to the basic idea of Montgomery multiplication, one can create a modular multiplication method for input values in RNS representation as shown in Algorithm 2, which involves a second base $\mathcal{B} = (\tilde{m}_0, \tilde{m}_1, \ldots, \tilde{m}_{n-1})$ with corresponding dynamic range B. It computes a value $v = XY + fM$ that is equivalent to $0 \bmod A$ and $XY \bmod M$. Thus, we can safely divide by A, i.e., multiply by its inverse modulo B, to compute the output $XYA^{-1} \pmod{M}$. Note that the needed reduction modulo A to compute f is *free* in $\mathcal{A}$.

All steps of the algorithm can be efficiently computed in parallel. However, a method to convert between both bases, a *base extension* mechanism, is needed. We take three different options into account: the method based on a Mixed Radix System (MRS) according to Szabó and Tanaka [37], as well as CRT-based methods due to Shenoy and Kumaresan [33], Kawamura et al. [20] and Bajard et al. [3]. We present a brief introduction of these methods, but for more detailed information about base extensions, please see the recent survey at [5].

---

[2] Inner-RNS operations still contain carries.

Algorithm 2. Modular Multiplication Algorithm for Residue Number Systems [20]

Require: Modulus M, two RNS bases $\mathcal{A}$ and $\mathcal{B}$ composed of n distinct moduli m_i
  each, $\gcd(A, B) = \gcd(A, M) = 1$ and $B > A > 4M$.
  Two factors X and Y, $0 \le X, Y < 2M$, encoded in both bases and in Montgomery
  form, i.e. $\langle X \rangle_{\mathcal{A} \cup \mathcal{B}}$ and $\langle Y \rangle_{\mathcal{A} \cup \mathcal{B}}$, $X = xA \pmod{M}$ and $Y = yA \pmod{M}$.
Ensure: The product $C = XYA^{-1} \pmod{M}$, $0 \le C < 2M$, in both bases and
  Montgomery form.

1: $\langle u \rangle_{\mathcal{A} \cup \mathcal{B}} \leftarrow \langle X \rangle_{\mathcal{A} \cup \mathcal{B}} \cdot \langle Y \rangle_{\mathcal{A} \cup \mathcal{B}}$
2: $\langle f \rangle_{\mathcal{A}} \leftarrow \langle u \rangle_{\mathcal{A}} \cdot \langle -M^{-1} \rangle_{\mathcal{A}}$
3: $\langle f \rangle_{\mathcal{A} \cup \mathcal{B}} \leftarrow \text{BaseExtend}(\langle f \rangle_{\mathcal{A}})$
4: $\langle v \rangle_{\mathcal{B}} \leftarrow \langle u \rangle_{\mathcal{B}} + \langle f \rangle_{\mathcal{B}} \cdot \langle M \rangle_{\mathcal{B}}$ $\{\langle v \rangle_{\mathcal{A}} = 0$ by construction$\}$
5: $\langle w \rangle_{\mathcal{B}} \leftarrow \langle v \rangle_{\mathcal{B}} \cdot \langle A^{-1} \rangle_{\mathcal{B}}$
6: $\langle w \rangle_{\mathcal{A} \cup \mathcal{B}} \leftarrow \text{BaseExtend}(\langle w \rangle_{\mathcal{B}})$
7: **return** $\langle w \rangle_{\mathcal{A} \cup \mathcal{B}}$

4.3 Base Extension Using a Mixed Radix System (MRS)

The classical way to compute base extensions is due to Szabó and Tanaka [37].
Let $(m_0, \ldots, m_{n-1})$ be the MRS base *associated* to $\mathcal{A}$. Then, each integer x can
be represented in a *mixed radix system* as

$$x = x_0' + x_1' m_0 + x_2' m_0 m_1 + \cdots + x_{n-1}' m_0 \ldots m_{n-2}. \tag{3}$$

The MRS digits x_i' can be derived from the residues x_i by a recursive strategy:
where $m_{(i,j)}^{-1}$ are the pre-computed inverses of m_j modulo m_i. To convert x from

$$x_0' = x_0 \pmod{m_0} \tag{4}$$
$$x_1' = (x_1 - x_0') m_{(1,0)}^{-1} \pmod{m_1}$$

$$\vdots$$

$$x_{n-1}' = (\cdots ((x_n - x_0') m_{(n-1,0)}^{-1} - x_1') m_{(n-1,1)}^{-1} - \cdots - x_{n-2}') m_{(n-1,n-2)}^{-1} \pmod{m_{n-1}}$$

this representation to a target RNS base, we could reduce Equation (3) by each
target modulus $\widetilde{m}_k$, involving pre-computed constants $\widetilde{c}_{(k,i)} = \left| \prod_{l=0}^{i-1} m_l \right|_{\widetilde{m}_k}$. But
instead of creating a table for all $\widetilde{c}_k$, a recursive approach is more efficient in our
situation, eliminating the need for table-lookups [4], and allowing to compute all
residues in the target base in parallel:

$$|x|_{\widetilde{m}_k} = \left| (\cdots ((x_{n-1}' m_{n-2} + x_{n-2}') m_{n-3} + x_{n-3}') m_{n-4} + \cdots + x_1') m_0 + x_0 \right|_{\widetilde{m}_k} \tag{5}$$

4.4 Base Extension Using the Chinese Remainder Theorem (CRT)

Recall the definition of the CRT and adopt it to the source base $\mathcal{A}$ with dynamic
range A:

$$x = \sum_{k=0}^{n-1} \hat{A}_k \left| \frac{x_k}{\hat{A}_k} \right|_{m_k} - \alpha A, \qquad \alpha < n \tag{6}$$

where $\hat{A}_k = A/m_k$ and α is an integer s.t. $0 \le x < A$. Note that α is strictly upper-bounded by n. When reducing this equation with an arbitrary target modulus, say $\tilde{m}_i$, we yield

$$|x|_{\tilde{m}_i} = \left| \sum_{k=0}^{n-1} \left| \hat{A}_k \right|_{\tilde{m}_i} \delta_k - |\alpha A|_{\tilde{m}_i} \right|_{\tilde{m}_i}, \qquad \delta_k = \left| x_k \cdot \hat{A}_k^{-1} \right|_{m_k} \tag{7}$$

where $\left| \hat{A}_k \right|_{\tilde{m}_i}$, $\left| \hat{A}_k^{-1} \right|_{m_k}$ and $|A|_{\tilde{m}_i}$ are pre-computed constants. Note that the δ_k do *not* depend on the target modulus and can thus be reused in the computation of a different target residue.

This is an efficient way to compute all residues modulo the target base, provided we know the value of α. While involving a couple of look-ups for the constants as well, the instruction flow is highly uniform (cf. Criterion A4) and fits to our SIMD architecture, i.e., we can use n threads to compute the n residues of x in the target base in parallel (cf. Criterion A1).

The first technique to compute such an α is due to Shenoy and Kumaresan [33] and requires a *redundant modulus* $m_r \ge n$ that is relatively prime to all other moduli m_j and $\tilde{m}_i$, i.e., $\gcd(A, m_r) = \gcd(B, m_r) = 1$. Consider Equation 7, set $\tilde{m}_i = m_r$ and rearrange it to the following:

$$|\alpha|_{m_r} = \left| |A^{-1}|_{m_r} \cdot \left(\sum_{k=0}^{n-1} \left| \hat{A}_k \right|_{m_r} \delta_k - |x|_{m_r} \right) \right|_{m_r}. \tag{8}$$

Since $\alpha < n \le m_r$ it holds that $\alpha = |\alpha|_{m_r}$ and thus Equation 8 computes the exact value of α, involving the additional constant $|A^{-1}|_{m_r}$.

Kawamura *et al.* propose a different technique that approximates α using fixed-point computations [20]. Consider Equation 7, rearrange it and divide by A:

$$\alpha = \sum_{k=0}^{n-1} \frac{\delta_k}{m_k} - \frac{|x|_{\tilde{m}_i}}{A} = \left\lfloor \sum_{k=0}^{n-1} \frac{\delta_k}{m_k} \right\rfloor. \tag{9}$$

Next, they approximate α by using $\text{trunc}_r(\delta_k)$ as numerator and 2^w as denominator and adding a properly chosen offset σ, where $\text{trunc}_r(\delta_k)$ sets the last $w - r$ bits of δ_k to zero:

$$\alpha' = \left\lfloor \sum_{k=0}^{n-1} \frac{\text{trunc}_r(\delta_k)}{2^w} + \sigma \right\rfloor = \left\lfloor \frac{1}{2^r} \sum_{k=0}^{n-1} \lfloor \delta_k/2^{w-r} \rfloor + \sigma \right\rfloor, \tag{10}$$

Thus, the approximate value α' can be computed in fixed-point arithmetic as integer part of the sum of the r most-significant bits of all δ_k. Provided σ is chosen correctly, Equation 10 will compute $\alpha' = \alpha$, and the resulting base extension will be exact.

Finally, Bajard *et al.* follow the most radical approach possible [3]: they allow an offset of $\alpha A \le (n - 1)A$ to occur in Equation 7 and thus do not need to compute α at all. After the first base extension we have $f' = f + \alpha A$ and thus

$w' = w + \alpha M$, i.e., the result w' will contain a maximum offset of $(n-1)M$, and thus be equivalent to $w \mod M$. However, this technique needs additional measures of precaution in the multiplication algorithm, which predominantly condense in the higher dynamic ranges needed.

4.5 Multiplication Modulo Generalised Mersenne Primes

For some cryptosystems like DSA, arithmetic in an underlying prime field is required. Taking advantage of the special structure of Mersenne primes, the reduction modulo p after a multiplication can be carried out very efficiently. Using such a method, we can compute r' using a standard multi-precision multiplication method first, followed by a reduction algorithm that is specific for the given prime. In this work, we will use an algorithm to efficiently compute multiplications modulo P-224, where P-224 is the 224 bit prime proposed by NIST [25]. Algorithm 3 performs the complete reduction for this prime with only two additions and two subtractions of 224 bit integers and a subsequent correction step to determine the correct value of $r \equiv r' \mod p$, since $-2p \leq r' < 3p$ must be considered. Note that this final correction step additionally needs the same amount of computations, as we have to avoid data-dependant branches (cf. Criterion A4).

Algorithm 3. NIST Reduction for P-224 $= 2^{224} - 2^{96} + 1$

Require: Double-sized integer $r' = (r'_{13}, \ldots, r'_2, r'_1, r'_0)$ in base 2^{32} and $0 \leq r' < $ P-224^2
Ensure: Single-sized integer $r \equiv r' \mod$ P-224, $0 \leq r < $ P-224.
 1: Concatenate r'_i to following 224-bit integers t_j:

$t_1 = (r'_6, r'_5, r'_4, r'_3, r'_2, r'_1, r'_0)$, $t_2 = (r'_{10}, r'_9, r'_8, r'_7, 0, 0, 0)$, $t_3 = (0, r'_{13}, r'_{12}, r'_{11}, 0, 0, 0)$
$t_4 = (0, 0, 0, 0, r'_{13}, r'_{12}, r'_{11})$, $t_5 = (r'_{13}, r'_{12}, r'_{11}, r'_{10}, r'_9, r'_8, t_7)$

 2: Compute $r'' = t_1 + t_2 + t_3 - t_4 - t_5$
 3: **return** $r = r'' \mod$ P-224

---

5 Implementation

In this section we will describe the implementation of two primitive operations for a variety of cryptosystems: first, we realise modular exponentiation on the GPU for use with RSA, DSA and similar systems. Second, for ECC-based cryptosystems we present an efficient point multiplication method which is the fundamental operation, e.g., for ECDSA or ECDH [16].

5.1 Modular Exponentiation Using the CIOS Method

We implemented the CIOS Method as introduced in Algorithm 1 for sequential execution since it does *not* include any inherent parallelism. Fan *et al.* describe efficient ways to pipeline such an algorithm for the use on multi-core systems [13].

This would however need fairly complex coordination and memory techniques and thus will not be considered further for our implementation, cf. Criteria A4 and B4-B6.

As all modular exponentiations are independent, we let each thread compute exactly one modular exponentiation in parallel with all others. Resulting from that, this solution only profits from coarse-grained parallelism. We assume the computation of distinct exponentiations, each having the *same* exponent t – for example RSA signatures using the same key – and thus need to transfer only the messages P_i for each exponentiation to the device and the result P_i^t (mod N) back to the host. As a result, every thread executes the same control flow, fulfilling Criterion A4. To accelerate memory transfers between host and device, we use page-locked host memory and pad each message to a fixed length that forces the starting address of each message to values that are eligible for global memory coalescing (cf. Criteria B1 and B4).

For modular exponentiation based on Algorithm 1, we applied the straightforward binary right-to-left method [35]. During exponentiation, each *thread* needs three temporary values of $(n+2)$ words each that get used as input and output of Algorithm 1 in a round-robin fashion by pointer arithmetic. Thus, $3(n+2)$ words are required. This leads to 408 bytes and 792 bytes for 1024 bits and 2048 bit parameters, respectively. Each multiprocessor features 16384 bytes of shared memory, resulting in a maximum number of $\lfloor 16386/408 \rfloor = 40$ and $\lfloor 16386/792 \rfloor = 20$ threads per multiprocessor for 1024 and 2048 bits, respectively, if we use shared memory for temporary values. Clearly, both solutions are inefficient when considering that each multiprocessor is able to execute 768 threads per block in principle (i.e., we favour Criterion A2 over B2).

Thus, we chose to store the temporary values in *global memory*. We have to store the values *interleaved* so that memory accesses of one word by all threads in a warp can be combined to *one* global memory access. Hence, for a given set of values $(A, B, C, \ldots)$ consisting each of $n + 2$ words $X = (x_0, x_1, \ldots, x_{n+1})$, we store all first words $(a_0, b_0, c_0, \ldots)$ for all threads in the same block, then all second words $(a_1, b_1, c_1, \ldots)$, and so on (cf. Criterion B4).

Moreover, we have to use *nailing* techniques, as CUDA does not yet include add-with-carry instructions. Roughly speaking, nailing reserves one or more of the high-order bits of each word for the carry that can occur when adding two numbers. To save register and memory space, however, we store the full word of w bits per register and use bit shifts and **and**-masking to extract two nibbles, each providing sufficient bits for the carry (cf. Criterion A3). This can be thought of decomposing a 32 bit addition in two 16 bit additions plus the overhead for carry handling.

5.2   Modular Exponentiation Using Residue Number Systems

Computations in residue number systems yield the advantage of being inherently parallel. According to Algorithm 2 all steps are computed in *one* base only, except for the first multiplication. Thus, the optimal mapping of computations to threads is as follows: each thread determines values for one modulus in the two bases. As a result, we have coarse-grained (different exponentiations) and fine-grained parallelism (base size), fulfilling Criterion A1. We call n' the number of residues that can be computed in parallel, i.e., the number of threads per encryption. The base extension by Shenoy et al. needs a *redundant* residue starting from the first base extension to be able to compute the second base extension. To reflect this fact, we use two RNS bases $\mathcal{A}$ and $\mathcal{B}$, having n moduli each, and an additional residue m_r resulting in $n' = n + 1$. For all other cases, it holds that $n' = n$.

Considering the optimal number of bits per modulus, we are faced with $w = 32$ bit integer registers on the target hardware. Thus, to avoid multi-precision techniques, we can use moduli that are smaller than 2^w. The hardware can compute 24 bit multiplications faster than full 32 bit multiplications. However, CUDA does *not* expose an intrinsic to compute the most-significant 16 bits of the result. Using 16 bit moduli would waste registers and memory and increase the *number of memory accesses* as well. Thus, we prefer *full* 32 bit moduli to save storage resources at the expense of higher computational cost (cf. Criteria A2 and A3).

For Algorithm 1 to work, the dynamic ranges A and B and the modulus M have to be related according to $B > A > 2^2 M$, or $B > A > (2+n)^2 M$ when using Bajard's method. For performance reasons, we consider *full warps* of 32 threads only, resulting in a slightly reduced size of M. The figures for all possible combinations can be found in Table 6 in the Appendix. For input and output values, we assume that all initial values will have been already converted to both bases (and possibly the redundant modulus m_r) and that output values will be returned in the same encoding. Note that it would be sufficient to transfer values in *one* base only and do a base extension for all input values (cf. Criterion B1, transferring values in both bases results in a more compact kernel together with a slightly higher latency). Different from the CIOS method, temporary values can be kept local for each thread, i.e., every thread stores its assigned residues in registers. Principally all operations can be performed *in parallel* on different residues and – as a result – the plain multiplication algorithm does *not* need any synchronisations. However, both properties do *not* hold for the base extension algorithms.

Mixed Radix Conversion. Recall that the mixed radix conversion computes the mixed radix representation from all residues in the source base first and uses this value to compute the target residues. The second step involves the computation of n' residues and can be executed in parallel, i.e., each thread computes the residue for 'its' modulus. As a result, we have to store the n MRS digits in shared memory to make them accessible to all threads (cf. Criteria A1 and B2). The first step however is the main caveat of this algorithm due to its highly divergent nature as each MRS digit is derived from the residue of a temporary variable in a *different* modulus (and thus thread) and depends on all previously computed digits, clearly breaking Criterion A4 and resulting in serialisation of executions. Additionally, note that threads having already computed an MRS digit do not generate any useful output anymore.

CRT-Based Conversion. The first step for all CRT-based techniques is to compute the δ_k for each source modulus and can be carried out by one thread for each value. Second, all n' threads compute a weighted sum involving δ_k and a modulus-dependent constant. Note that all threads need to access *all* δ_k and thus δ_k have to be stored in shared memory (cf. Criterion B2). Third, α has to be derived, whose computation is the main difference in the distinguished techniques. α is needed by *all* threads later and thus needs to be stored in shared memory as well. After computing α all threads can proceed with their independent computations.

Bajard's method does not compute α and consequently needs no further operations. For Shenoy's method, the second step above is needed for the redundant modulus m_r as well, which can be done in parallel with all other moduli. Then, a *single* thread computes α and writes it to shared memory. The redundant residue m_r comes at the price of an additional thread, however the divergent part needed to compute α does only contain one addition and one multiplication modulo m_r. Kawamura's method needs to compute the sum of the r most significant bits of all δ_k. While the right-shift of each δ_k can be done using *all* threads, the sum over all shifted values and the offset has to be computed using a *single* thread. A final right-shift results in the integer part of the sum, namely α.

Comparison and Selection. Clearly, Bajard's method is the fastest since it involves no computation of α. Shenoy's method only involves a small divergent part. However, we pay the price of an additional thread for the redundant modulus, or equivalently decrease the size of M. Kawamura's technique consists of a slightly larger divergent part, however it does neither include look-ups nor further reduces the size of M.

Not all base extension mechanisms can be used for both directions required for Algorithm 2. For Bajard's method, consider the consequence of an offset in the second base extension: we would compute some w'' in base $\mathcal{A}$ that is *not equal* to the w' in $\mathcal{B}$. As a result, neither $\langle w' \rangle_{\mathcal{A}}$ nor $\langle w'' \rangle_{\mathcal{B}}$ could be computed leading to an invalid input for a subsequent execution of Algorithm 2. Thus, their method is only available for $\mathcal{A} \to \mathcal{B}$ conversions. Shenoy's method can only be used for the *second* base extension as there is no efficient way to carry the redundant residue through the computation of f modulo A. The technique by Kawamura *et al.* would in principle be available for both conversions. However, the sizes of both bases would be different to allow proper reduction in the $\mathcal{A} \to \mathcal{B}$ case, thus we exclude this option from our consideration. Table 1 shows the available and the practical combinations.

Table 1. Base Extension Algorithm Combinations

		$\mathcal{A} \to \mathcal{B}$			
		MRC (M)	Shenoy (S)	Kawamura (K)	Bajard (B)
$\mathcal{B} \to \mathcal{A}$	MRC (M)	•	○	○	•
	Shenoy (S)	•	○	○	•
	Kawamura (K)	•	○	○	•
	Bajard (B)	○	○	○	○

5.3   Point Multiplication Using Generalised Mersenne Primes

For realising the elliptic curve group operation, we chose mixed affine-Jacobian coordinates [8] to avoid costly inversions in the underlying field and thus concentrated on efficient implementation of modular multiplication, the remaining time critical operation. For this, we used a straightforward schoolbook-type multiplication combined with the efficient reduction technique for the generalised Mersenne prime presented in Algorithm 3.

As for the CIOS method, there is no intrinsic parallelism except pipelining in this approach (cf. Criterion A1). Thus, we use one thread per point multiplication. We assume the use of the same base point P per point multiplication kP and *varying* scalars k. Thus, the only input that has to be transferred are the scalars. Secondly, we transfer the result in projective Jacobian coordinates back to the host. For efficiency reasons, we encode all coordinates interleaved for each threads in a block again.

We used shared memory to store all temporary values, nailed to 28 bits to allow schoolbook multiplication without carry propagation. Thus, we need 8 words per coordinate. Point addition and doubling algorithms were inspired by libseccure [29]. With this approach shared memory turns out to be the limiting factor. Precisely, we require 111 words per point multiplication to store 7 temporary coordinates for point addition and modulo arithmetic, *two* points and each scalar. This results in 444 bytes of shared memory and a maximum of $\lfloor 16384/444 \rfloor = 36$ threads per multiprocessor. This leaves still room for improvements as Criterion A1 is *not* fulfilled. However, due to internal errors in the toolchain, we were not (yet) able to compile a solution that uses global memory for temporary values instead. Note that the left-to-right binary method for point multiplication demands only one temporary point. However, for the sake of a homogeneous flow of instructions we compute both possible solutions per scalar bit and use a small divergent section to decide which of them is the desired result (cf. Criterion A4).

6   Conclusion

With the previously discussed implementations on GPUs at hand, we finally need to identify the candidate providing the best performance for modular exponentiation.

6.1   Results and Applications

Before presenting the benchmarking results of the best algorithm combinations we show our results regarding the different base extension options for the RNS method. The benchmarking scheme was the following: first, we did an exhaustive search for the number of registers per thread that can principally be generated by the toolchain. Then, we benchmarked all available execution configurations for these numbers of registers. To make the base extension algorithms comparable, we would have to repeat this for all possible combinations, as shown in

Table 2. Results for different Base Extension Techniques (RNS Method)

Base Ext.		Throughput (1024 bits)	Throughput (2048 bits)
$\mathcal{A} \rightarrow \mathcal{B}$	$\mathcal{B} \rightarrow \mathcal{A}$	[Enc/s] (rel.)	[Enc/s] (rel.)
M	M	194 (46%)	28 (50%)
B	M	267 (63%)	38 (67%)
B	K	408 (97%)	55 (98%)
B	S	419 (100%)	56 (100%)

Table 1. However to reduce the complexity of benchmarking, it suffices to measure all possible combinations in the first row and all possible combinations in the second column to gain figures for all available combinations. The results for the particular best configuration can be found in Table 2.

Clearly, the mixed radix based approach also used in [24] cannot compete with CRT-based solutions. Kawamura *et al.* is slower than the method of Shenoy *et al.* , but performs only slightly worse for the 2048 bit range. Figure 1 shows the time over the number of encryptions for the four cases and the 1024 bit and 2048 bit ranges, respectively.

Both graphs show the characteristic behaviour: Depending on the number of blocks that are started on the GPU and the respective execution configuration we get stair-like graphs. Only multiples of the number of warps per multiprocessor and the number of multiprocessors result in optimal configurations that fully utilise the GPU. However, depending on the number of registers per thread and the amount of shared memory used other configurations are possible and lead to smaller steps in between.

Optimised Implementations. Beside the reference implementation based on the CIOS algorithm, we selected as best choice the CRT-RNS method based on a combination of Bajard's and Shenoy's methods to compute the first and second base extension of Algorithm 2, respectively.

The selection of the implementation was primarily motivated to achieve high throughput rather than a small latency. Hence, due to the latency, not all implementations might be suitable for all practical applications. To reflect this, we present figures for data throughput as well as the initial latency t_{min} required at the beginning of a computation. Note that our results consider optimal configurations of warps per block and blocks per grid only. Table 3 shows the figures for modular exponentiation with 1024 and 2048 bit moduli and elliptic curve point multiplication using NIST's P-224 curve.

The throughput is determined from the number of encryptions divided by the elapsed time. Note that this *includes* the initial latency t_{min} at the beginning of the computations. The corresponding graphs are depicted in Figure 2. Note the relatively long plateau when using the CIOS technique. It is a direct result from having coarse-grained parallelism only: the smallest number of encryptions that can be processed is 128 times higher than for the RNS method. Its high offset is due to storing temporary values in global memory: memory access latency is

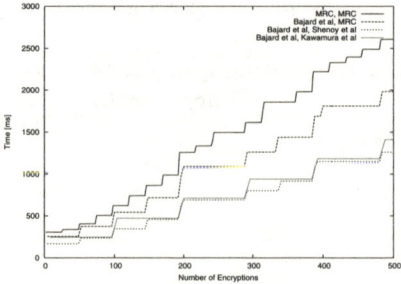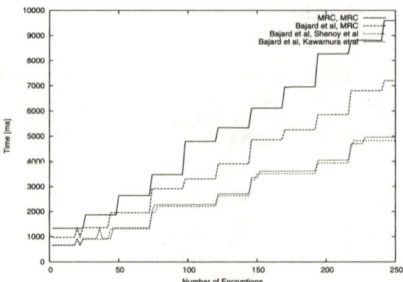

Fig. 1. Results For Modular Exponentiation with about 1024 (left) and 2048 bit (right) Moduli For Different Base Extension Methods, based on a Nvidia 8800 GTS Graphics Card

Table 3. Results for Throughput and Minimum Latency t_{min} on a Nvidia 8800 GTS Graphics Card

Technique	Throughput		Latency t_{min}	OPs at t_{min}
	[OPs/s]	[ms/OP]	[ms]	
ModExp-1024 CIOS	813.0	1.2	6930	1024
ModExp-1024 RNS	439.8	2.3	144	4
ModExp-2048 CIOS	104.3	9.6	55184	1536
ModExp-2048 RNS	57.9	17.3	849	4
ECC PointMul-224	1412.6	0.7	305	36

hidden by scheduling independent computations, however the time needed to fetch/store the first value in each group cannot be hidden.

Clearly, the CIOS method delivers the highest throughput at the price of a high initial latency. For interactive applications such as online banking using TLS this will be a major obstacle. However, non-interactive applications like a *certificate authority* (CA) might benefit from the raw throughput[3]. Note that both applications will share the *same* secret key for all digital signatures when using RSA. In case of ECC (ECDSA) however, *different* exponents were taken into account.

The residue number system based approach does only feature roughly half of the throughput but provides a more immediate data response. Thus, this method seems to be suitable even in interactive applications. Last but not least elliptic curve cryptography clearly outperforms modular exponentiation based techniques not only due to the much smaller parameters. With respect to other hardware and software implementations compared against our results in the next section, we present an ECC solution which outperforms most hardware devices and comes close the the performance of recent dual-core microprocessors.

---

[3] Also consider the top model of Nvidia's next series of GPUs, the GeForce 9800GX2, that can be used in a four-card setup.

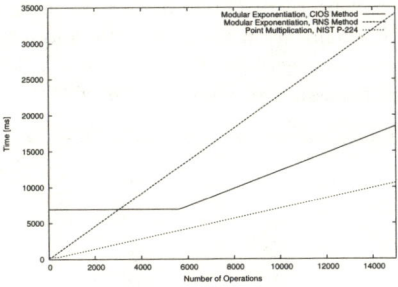 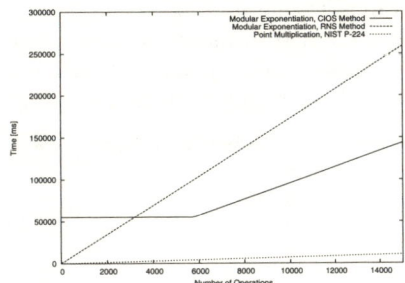

Fig. 2. Results For Modular Exponentiation with about 1024 (left) and 2048 bit (right) Moduli and Elliptic Curve Point Multiplication on NIST's P-224 Curve, based on a Nvidia 8800 GTS Graphics Card

6.2   Comparison with Previous Implementations

Due to the novelty of general purpose computations on GPUs and since directly comparable results are rare, we will take reference to recent hardware and software implementations in literature as well. To give a feeling for the different GPU generations we include Table 4.

Table 4. Comparison of Nvidia GPU platforms

GPU	Shader clock [MHz]	Shaders	Fill Rate [GPixels/s]	Mem Bandwidth [GB/s]	CUDA
7800GTX			13.2	54.4	no
8800GTS	1200	92	24.0	64.0	yes
8800GTX	1350	128	36.8	86.4	yes
9800GX2	1500	2 · 128	76.8	128.0	future

Moss *et al.* implemented modular exponentiation for 1024 bit moduli on Nvidia's 7800GTX GPU [24], using the same RNS approach but picking different base extension mechanisms. The authors present the *maximum* throughput only that has been achieved at the cost of an unspecified but high latency. Fleissner's recent analysis on modular exponentiation for GPUs is based on 192 bit moduli but relates the GPU performance solely to the CPU of his host system.

Costigan and Scott implemented modular exponentiation on IBM's Cell platform, i.e., a Sony Playstation 3 and an IBM MPM blade server, both running at 3.2 GHz [10]. We only quote the best figures for the Playstation 3 as they call the results for the MPM blade preliminary. The Playstation features one PowerPC core (PPU) and 6 *Synergistic Processing Elements* (SPUs). Software results have been attained from ECRYPT's eBATS project [11]. Here, we picked a recent Intel Core2 Duo with 2.13 GHz clock frequency. Since mostly all figures for software relate to cycles, we assumed that repeated computations can be

Table 5. Comparison of our designs to results from literature. The higher throughput values the better. ModExp-i denotes modular exponentiation using an i-bit modulus. PointMul-i denotes point multiplication on elliptic curves over $\mathbb{F}_p$, where p is a i-bit prime. Results that used the Chinese remainder theorem are marked with "CRT".

Reference	Platform & Technique	ModExp-1024	ModExp-1024, CRT	ModExp-2048	ModExp-2048, CRT	ECC PointMul-160	ECC PointMul-224	ECC PointMul-256
Our Design	Nvidia 8800GTS GPU, CIOS algorithm	**813.0**		**104.3**				
	Nvidia 8800GTS GPU, RNS arithmetic	439.8		57.9				
	Nvidia 8800GTS GPU, ECC NIST-224						1412.6	
[24] Moss	Nvidia 7800GTX GPU, RNS arithmetic	175.4						
[10] Costigan	Sony Playstation 3, 1 PPU, 6 SPUs		909.2		**401.4**			
[22] Mentens	Xilinx xc2vp30 FPGA	471.7	1724.1		235.8	1000.0		440.5
[32] Schinianakis	Xilinx xc2vp125 FPGA, RNS arithmetic						413.9	
[36] Suzuki	Xilinx xc4fx12 FPGA, using DSPs	584.8		79.4				
[26] Nozaki	0.25μm CMOS, 80 MHz, 221k GE	238.1		34.2				
[11] eBATS	Intel Core2 2.13 GHz		1447.5		300.4	**2623.4** [a]	**1868.5**[a]	1494.8[a]
[15] Gaudry	Intel Core2 2.66 GHz							**6900**[b]

[a] Performance for ECDSA operation including additional modular inversion and multiplication operation.
[b] Special elliptic curve in Montgomery form, non-compliant to ECC standardised by NIST.

performed *without* interruption on *all* available cores so that no further cycles are spent, e.g., on scheduling or other administrative tasks. Note that this is a very optimistic assumption possibly overrating the performance of microprocessors with respect to actual applications. We also compare our work to the very fast software implementation by [15] on an Intel Core2 system at 2.66 GHz but which uses the special Montgomery and non-standard curve over $\mathbb{F}_{2^{255}-19}$.

To the best of our knowledge, Mentens published the best results for public key cryptography on reconfigurable hardware so far [22]. She used a Field Programmable Gate Array (FPGA) of Xilinx' Virtex-II Pro family, namely the xc2vp30-7FF1152. Schinianakis *et al.* implemented elliptic curve cryptography on the same family of FPGAs but using RNS arithmetic for the underlying field [32]. Suzuki implemented the modular exponentiation on FPGAs taking advantage of the included digital signal processors (DSPs) on a board from Xilinx' Virtex 4 FX family [36].

Nozaki *et al.* designed an RSA circuit in 0.25 μm CMOS technology, that needs 221k gate equivalents (GE) [26] and uses RNS arithmetic with Kawamura's base extension mechanism.

6.3   Further Work

Elliptic curves in Hessian form feature highly homogeneous formulae to compute all three projective coordinates in point additions [19,34]. However, the curves standardised by ANSI and NIST *cannot* be transformed to Hessian form. Furthermore, point doublings can be converted to point additions by simple coordinate rotations. Thus, it is possible to compute point doublings and additions for all three coordinates in parallel. A future study will show the applicability to graphics hardware.

References

1. Advanced Micro Devices, Inc. (AMD), Sunnyvale, CA, USA. ATI CTM Guide, Release 1.01 (2006)
2. American National Standards Institute (ANSI). Public key cryptography for the financial services industry: The elliptic curve digital signature algorithm (ECDSA) (ANSI X9.62:2005) (2005)
3. Bajard, J.-C., Didier, L.-S., Kornerup, P.: Modular multiplication and base extension in residue number systems. In: Burgess, N. (ed.) Proceedings ARITH15, the 15th IEEE Symposium on Computer Arithmetic, Vail, Colorado, USA, pp. 59–65 (June 2001)
4. Bajard, J.-C., Meloni, N., Plantard, T.: Efficient RNS bases for cryptography. In: Proceedings of IMACS 2005 World Congress, Paris, France (July 2005)
5. Bajard, J.-C., Plantard, T.: RNS bases and conversions. Advanced Signal Processing Algorithms, Architectures, and Implementations XIV 5559(1), 60–69 (2004)
6. Koç, Ç.K., Acar, T., Kaliski Jr., B.S.: Analyzing and comparing Montgomery multiplication algorithms. IEEE Micro 16(3), 26–33 (1996)
7. Koç, Ç.K., Naccache, D., Paar, C. (eds.): CHES 2001. LNCS, vol. 2162. Springer, Heidelberg (2001)
8. Cohen, H., Frey, G. (eds.): Handbook of elliptic and hyperelliptic curve cryptography. Chapman & Hall/CRC Press, Boca Raton (2005)
9. Cook, D.L., Ioannidis, J., Keromytis, A.D., Luck, J.: CryptoGraphics: Secret key cryptography using graphics cards. In: Menezes, A. (ed.) CT-RSA 2005. LNCS, vol. 3376. Springer, Heidelberg (2005)
10. Costigan, N., Scott, M.: Accelerating SSL using the vector processors in IBM's Cell broadband engine for Sony's Playstation 3. In: SPEED 2007 Workshop Record [12] (2007), http://www.hyperelliptic.org/SPEED/
11. ECRYPT. eBATS: ECRYPT benchmarking of asymmetric systems. Technical report (2007), http://www.ecrypt.eu.org/ebats/
12. ECRYPT European Network of Excellence in Cryptography. Software Performance Enhancement for Encryption and Decryption (SPEED), 2007 Workshop Record, Amsterdam, The Netherlands (June 2007),
http://www.hyperelliptic.org/SPEED/
13. Fan, J., Skiyama, K., Verbauwhede, I.: Montgomery modular multiplication algorithm for multi-core systems. In: SPEED 2007 Workshop Record [12] (2007),
http://www.hyperelliptic.org/SPEED/
14. Fleissner, S.: GPU-accelerated Montgomery exponentiation. In: Shi, Y., van Albada, G.D., Dongarra, J., Sloot, P.M.A. (eds.) ICCS 2007. LNCS, vol. 4487, pp. 213–220. Springer, Heidelberg (2007)
15. Gaudry, P., Thomé, E.: The mpF$_q$ library and implementing curve-based key exchanges. In: SPEED 2007 Workshop Record [12], pp. 49–64 (2007),
http://www.hyperelliptic.org/SPEED/
16. Hankerson, D., Menezes, A.J., Vanstone, S.: Guide to Elliptic Curve Cryptography. Springer, New York (2003)
17. Harris, M.: Optimizing CUDA. In: Supercomputing 2007 Tutorial, Reno, NV, USA (November 2007)

18. Harrison, O., Waldron, J.: AES encryption implementation and analysis on commodity graphics processing unit. In: Paillier, P., Verbauwhede, I. (eds.) CHES 2007. LNCS, vol. 4727, pp. 209–226. Springer, Heidelberg (2007)
19. Hisil, H., Carter, G., Dawson, E.: Faster group operations on special elliptic curves. Cryptology ePrint Archive, Report 2007/441 (2007), http://eprint.iacr.org/
20. Kawamura, S., Koike, M., Sano, F., Shimbo, A.: Cox-rower architecture for fast parallel Montgomery multiplication. In: Preneel, B. (ed.) EUROCRYPT 2000. LNCS, vol. 1807, pp. 523–538. Springer, Heidelberg (2000)
21. Manavski, S.A.: CUDA compatible GPU as an efficient hardware accelerator for AES cryptography. In: Proceedings of IEEE's International Conference on Signal Processing and Communication ICSPC 2007, pp. 65–68 (November 2007)
22. Mentens, N.: Secure and Efficient Coprocessor Design for Cryptographic Applications on FPGAs. PhD thesis, Katholieke Universiteit Leuven, Leuven-Heverlee, Belgium (June 2007)
23. Montgomery, P.L.: Modular multiplication without trial division. Mathematics of Computation 44(170), 519–521 (1985)
24. Moss, A., Page, D., Smart, N.: Toward acceleration of RSA using 3d graphics hardware. In: Galbraith, S.D. (ed.) Cryptography and Coding 2007. LNCS, vol. 4887, pp. 369–388. Springer, Heidelberg (2007)
25. National Institute of Standards and Technology (NIST). Digital signature standard (DSS) (FIPS 186-2) (January 2000)
26. Nozaki, H., Motoyama, M., Shimbo, A., Kawamura, S.: Implementation of RSA algorithm based on RNS Montgomery multiplication. In: Koç, Ç.K., Naccache, D., Paar, C. (eds.) CHES 2001. LNCS, vol. 2162, pp. 364–376. Springer, Heidelberg (2001)
27. Nvidia Corporation, Santa Clara, CA, USA. Compute Unified Device Architecture (CUDA) Programming Guide, Version 1.0 (June 2007)
28. Nvidia Corporation, Santa Clara, CA, USA. Parallel Thread Execution (PTX) ISA Version 1.0, Release 1.0 (June 2007)
29. Poettering, B.: seccure – SECCURE elliptic curve crypto utility for reliable encryption, version 0.3 (August 2006), http://point-at-infinity.org/seccure/
30. Rivest, R., Shamir, A., Adleman, L.: A method for obtaining digital signatures and public key cryptosystems. In: Communications of the ACM, vol. 21, pp. 120–126 (February 1978)
31. Rosenberg, U.: Using graphic processing unit in block cipher calculations. Master's thesis, University of Tartu, Tartu, Estonia (2007)
32. Schinianakis, D.M., Kakarountas, A.P., Stouraitis, T.: A new approach to elliptic curve cryptography: an RNS architecture. In: Proceedings of IEEE's 14th Mediterranian Electrotechnical Conference (MELECON 2006), pp. 1241–1245 (May 2006)
33. Shenoy, A.P., Kumaresan, R.: Fast base extension using a redundant modulus in RNS. In: IEEE Transactions on Computers, vol. 38, pp. 292–297 (February 1989)
34. Smart, N.P.: The Hessian form of an elliptic curve. In: Koç, Ç.K., et al. (eds.) [7], pp. 118–125
35. Stinson, D.R.: Cryptography. Theory and Practice, 3rd edn. Taylor & Francis, Abington (2005)
36. Suzuki, D.: How to maximize the potential of FPGA resources for modular exponentiation. In: Paillier, P., Verbauwhede, I. (eds.) CHES 2007. LNCS, vol. 4727, pp. 272–288. Springer, Heidelberg (2007)
37. Szabó, N.S., Tanaka, R.I.: Residue Arithmetic and its Applications to Computer Technology. McGraw-Hill Inc., USA (1967)

A   Appendix

Table 6. Modulus Sizes for Modular Multiplication Using RNS

1st Base Ext.	2nd Base Ext.	1024 bit range	2048 bit range
Bajard *et al.*	Shenoy *et al.*	981	2003
	Others	1013	2035
Others	Shenoy *et al.*	990	2014
	Others	1022	2046

High-Performance Concurrent Error Detection Scheme for AES Hardware

Akashi Satoh[1], Takeshi Sugawara[2], Naofumi Homma[2], and Takafumi Aoki[2]

[1] Research Center for Information Security,
National Institute of Advanced Industrial Science and Technology (AIST)
Sotokanda, Tokyo, Japan
akashi.satoh@aist.go.jp
[2] Graduate School of Information Sciences, Tohoku University
Sendai, Miyagi, Japan
{sugawara,homma}@aoki.ecei.tohoku.ac.jp,
aoki@ecei.tohoku.ac.jp

Abstract. This paper proposes an efficient concurrent error detection scheme for hardware implementation of the block cipher AES. The proposed scheme does not require an additional arithmetic unit, but simply divides the round function block into two sub-blocks and uses the sub-blocks alternately for encryption (or decryption) and error detection. The number of clock cycles is doubled, but the maximum operating frequency is increased owing to the shortened critical path of the sub-block. Therefore, the proposed scheme has a limited impact on hardware performance with respect to size and speed. AES hardware with the proposed scheme was designed and synthesized using a 90-nm CMOS standard cell library with size and speed optimization options. The compact and high-speed implementations achieved performances of 2.21 Gbps @ 16.1 Kgates and 3.21 Gbps @ 24.1 Kgates, respectively. In contrast, the performances of AES hardware without error detection were 1.66 Gbps @ 12.9 Kgates for the compact version and 4.22 Gbps @ 30.7 Kgates for the high-speed version. There is only a slight difference between the performances with and without error detection. The performance overhead caused by the error detection is evaluated at the optimal balance between size and speed and was estimated to be 14.5% at maximum. Conversely, the AES hardware with the proposed scheme had better performance in some cases. If pipeline operation is allowed, as in the CTR mode, throughputs can easily be boosted by further dividing the sub-blocks. Although the proposed error detection scheme was applied to AES in the present study, it can also be applied to other algorithms efficiently.

1 Introduction

The fault injection attack is a physical attack to obtain internal secret information from cryptographic modules by causing a malfunction in operating units or the sequencer logic using electrical noise injection on the power source or clock signal or by illuminating the module by an electronic beam. In 1996, Boneh,

E. Oswald and P. Rohatgi (Eds.): CHES 2008, LNCS 5154, pp. 100–112, 2008.

Demillo, and Lipton [1] proposed a fault injection attack against public key cryptosystems, and Biham and Shamir [2] extended this attack to symmetric key cryptosystems. Since then, research on the fault injection attack has been rapidly evolved [3-5], and several papers have proposed attacks on the standard block cipher AES [7-13].

On the other hand, several countermeasures that detect errors in processing have also been proposed [14-29]. Fig. 1 summarizes the conventional error detection schemes for block cipher hardware with a loop architecture that iteratively uses one round function block. The figures illustrate error detection schemes for encryption process, but the same schemes can be applied to decryption circuits and to implementations merging encryption and decryption datapaths.

In Fig. 1(a), the data in register RegX is processed by the round function block for encryption (Enc), and then an error detection code, such as a parity bit, is generated. The code is compared with an expected value output from another data path (Predict) [14, 17-20]. It is very easy to calculate the expected value for linear functions by using a small amount of hardware resources, and thus several studies have proposed error detection codes for the non-linear substitution function S-box [15, 16, 21-23]. The operation "Predict" is much simpler than "Enc" and usually outputs a smaller number of bits, and thus it is impossible to detect all of the error patterns. Therefore, the trade-off between overhead of the additional circuit, "Predict", and the error detection ratio should be considered carefully.

In Fig. 1(b), two encryption operations for the same data in the register RegX are performed by duplicated round function blocks, and the results are compared [24]. The architecture of Fig. 1(c) has encryption and decryption datapaths, and the data in RegX is encrypted and soon decrypted. The result is then compared with the original data in RegY [24, 25]. These two schemes have a disadvantage in that the hardware size is almost double compared to that of the circuit without error detection.

The scheme of Fig. 1(d) encrypts the same data twice using one round function block and two results are compared [26, 27]. In Fig. 1(e), the round function block supports both encryption and decryption, and confirms that encrypted data can be decrypted correctly. This scheme can also be applied efficiently to the round function $F(x)$ with the characteristic of $x = F(F(x))$ [28]. The drawback of these schemes is that twice as many clock cycles are required.

Fig. 1(f) is similar to Fig. 1(d), where two encryptions are performed to confirm that the same encrypted data are generated, but the round function block is divided into two sub-blocks and encryption and error detection (another encryption) are performed simultaneously in each sub-block [29]. Hardware size and the number of clock cycles are almost the same between these schemes, but the maximum operating frequency of Fig. 1(f) is much higher than any other scheme in Fig. 1 because the critical path (the round function block) is halved.

Fig. 1(f) is the best scheme in terms of circuit size and speed, but the use of the same datapath for two encryptions (one of which is for error detection) causes a major problem. When an attacker injects an electron beam to cryptographic

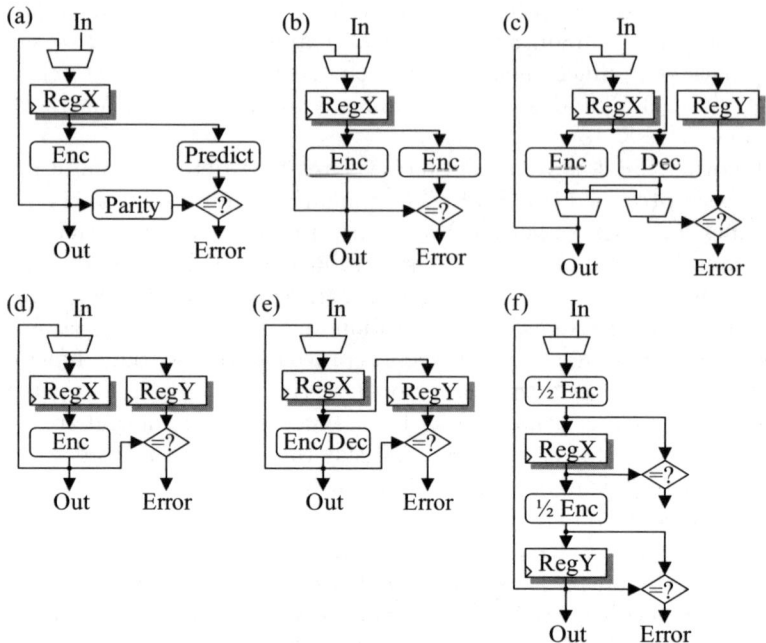

Fig. 1. Conventional error detection schemes (Encryption)

circuit, it is very difficult to control the beam precisely in order to make an error in only one clock period. In contrast, it is incomparably easy to keep the beam on during certain periods and to keep the circuit in failure. In this case, the same error occurs repeatedly and thus the scheme of Fig. 1(f) that repeats the same encryption twice for data checking cannot detect the error. The beam might cause different types of errors in each cycle, but defects on transistor devices and metal interconnections in LSI chips always make the same error, and thus the scheme of Fig. 1(f) is unworkable for these static errors.

In order to solve these problems, this paper proposes a new error detection scheme that performs encryption (or decryption) and error detection simultaneously in different operating blocks with limited impact on hardware size and speed. AES hardware using the proposed scheme is designed and synthesized using an ASIC library, and the effectiveness of the scheme is evaluated.

2   Proposed Error Detection Scheme

2.1   Normal AES Circuit

Fig. 2 shows a block diagram of an AES circuit using a loop-architecture based on the compact implementation proposed in references [30] and [31], which does not support error detection feature. A 128-bit input is encrypted (or decrypted)

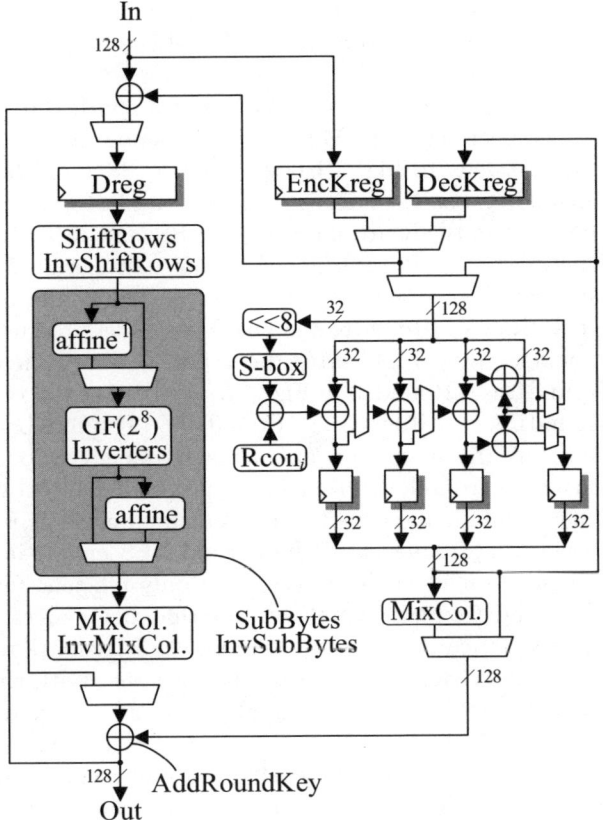

Fig. 2. Normal AES circuit

with a 128-bit secret key in 10 clock cycles. The encryption and decryption paths are merged by sharing $GF(2^8)$ inverters in S-boxes and common terms between the permutation functions MixColumns and InvMixColumns. The circuit size is almost halved in comparison to an implementation with two different datapaths for encryption and decryption. In order to merge the datapaths, the location of AddRoundKey and InvMixColumns (shown as InvMixCol. in Fig. 2) is switched from the original order. Then, the MixColumns function block is placed at the output of the key scheduler on the right in Fig. 2 to compensate the side effect. In the next section, the proposed error detection scheme is explained in contrast with this normal architecture.

2.2   AES Circuit with the Proposed Scheme

The proposed scheme uses a datapath that supports both encryption and decryption, which is similar to that shown in Fig. 2, and divides the merged round function block into pre- and post-blocks. Then, one of the blocks is used for encryption (or decryption), and another block is used for decryption (or encryption) for error detection. Fig. 3 shows the outline of the proposed scheme in the encryption mode. Decryption can be carried out in a similar way. SR and ISR denote ShiftRows and InvShiftRows, respectively, SB and ISB denote SubBytes and InvSubBytes, respectively, and MX and IMX denote MixColumns and InvMixColumns, respectively. In Fig. 3(b), the order of ISB and ISR is switched to share components between the encryption (Enc.) and decryption (Dec.) flows of Fig. 3(a). Then SR and ISR are merged, and SB and ISR are merged, and a half round function block, BlockS, is composed. The permutation functions MX and IMX are also merged and compose another half round block, BlockM, with two 128-bit XORs (AddRoundKey). These two blocks are used alternately for encryption (or decryption) and error detection, as shown in Fig. 3(c), and each round of Round1, $\cdots$, Round10 in Fig. 3(a) is processed in two clock cycles as Round1X, Round1Y, $\cdots$, Round10X, Round10Y. The number of operating cycles is doubled, but the maximum operating frequency is boosted because the critical path of the round function block is divided into two sub-blocks. Therefore, this has a minor impact on the operating speed. It is also possible to increase the operating frequency of the normal AES circuit in Fig. 1 by dividing the round function block. However, it is only efficient for the Electric Code Book (ECB) and Counter (CTR) modes that can process 128-bit data blocks independently but cannot increase the speed for feedback modes, such as Cipher Block Chaining (CBC). When speed performance with the CTR is the first priority, the proposed architecture can also respond to this requirement by increasing the number of pipeline stages from 2 to $2n$. For example, it is easy to perform two encryptions (or decryptions) and two decryption (or encryption) as error detections by dividing sub-block BlockS and BlockM into two smaller sub-blocks each.

In Fig. 3(c), the XOR output from Round0 is processed by the SR and SB functions of BlockS in the clock cycle Round 1X, and the result is fed to BlockS and BlockM. In the following cycle Round 1Y, the inverse operation of Round1X is performed by BlockS, and the result is compared with the input to BlockS in the previous cycle Round1X for error detection. At the same time, the MX and XOR (AddRoundKey) operations are executed by BlockM to continue the encryption process. In the next cycle Round2X, BlockS performs the following encryption process, and BlockM checks the previous result. In a similar manner, the remainder of the encryption and error detection operations are executed by BlockS and BlockM interchangeably. The same round function blocks are used for encryption and error detection, but these operations are different, and thus static errors caused by defects in LSIs can be detected, while the scheme of Fig. 1(f) cannot find the errors, where the same operation is executed twice by the same function block for encryption and error detection.

Fig. 4 shows the datapath architecture of the AES circuit using the proposed error detection scheme. This architecture does not switch the order of AddRoundKey and InvMixColumns to share the XOR gates for AddRoundKey, as in Fig. 2. The critical path of the round function block in Fig. 2 is shortened by

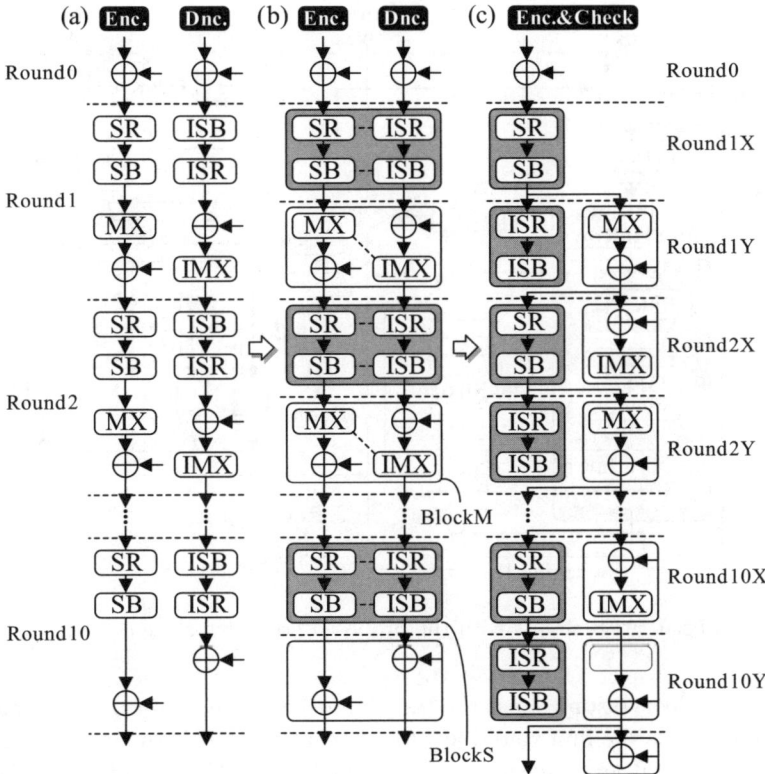

Fig. 3. Proposed error detection scheme for AES (Encryption)

sharing the XOR gate, but the additional MixColumns block is required at the output port of the key scheduler. In contrast, when the proposed scheme that divides the round function block into two sub-blocks was applied, implementations without sharing the XOR gates showed better performance in balance between size and speed. When the signal delay time for the round function block is shortened by the division, the key scheduler becomes the critical path. Therefore, the scheduler is also divided in two by inserting a register and uses two clocks to generate one round key. In Fig. 4, the datapaths of the round function block and the key scheduler are divided at the end of S-boxes for simplicity, but pipeline registers are actually placed inside the S-boxes in order to balance the signal delay times before and after the registers.

Even if the round function block works correctly, the key scheduler can also be attacked [11, 12, 13], or malfunction in a control counter may output intermediate data soon after the first round key is XORed without waiting for the completion of 10-round operations [3]. In order to prevent this, the key scheduler in Fig. 4 compares the round-key generated in the round key register with the pre-calculated keys in the key registers DecKreg or EncKreg in the final round of encryption or decryption, respectively. The register DecKreg holds the first

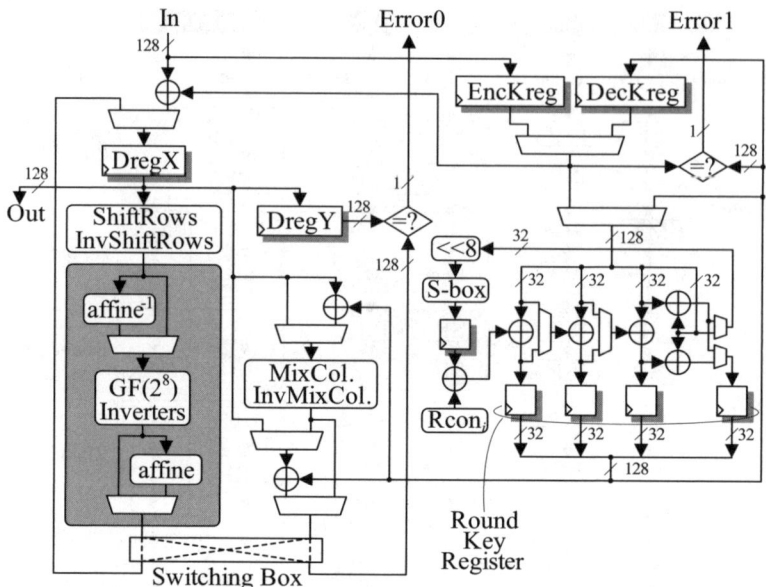

Fig. 4. AES circuit with the proposed error detection scheme

round-key for decryption that is the last round-key for encryption, and the register EncKreg holds the first round-key for encryption that is the last round-key of decryption. Even if an attacker can flip a few bits in the control counter to skip the round operations, it is impossible to control the unknown 128-bit round-key to match the final value.

2.3 Example Operation

Fig. 5 shows the example encryption process of the AES circuit with the proposed error detection scheme. It is assumed that the initial key for decryption K10 has been calculated from the initial key K0 for encryption, and the keys K0 and K10 are stored in registers EncReg and DecReg, respectively. In Fig. 5(a), a plaintext input XORed with the initial key K0 has been stored in the data register DregX as D0, and the first half of the round function (Shiftrows and SubBytes) is applied to the data D0, and then the result D1X is fed back to the register DregX. At the same time, the data D0 is transferred to the register DregY for error detection, and the key register generates the first round-key K1 from K0.

In Fig. 5(b), the datapath for encryption in Fig. 5(a) is used for decryption as error detection. The data D1X in DregX is processed by InvShiftRows and InvSubBytes, and the result is compared with the data D0 in RegY. In the other data path, the last half of the round function, MixColumns and AddroundKey (XOR with the round-key K1), is applied to the data D1X, and the result of the first round function is obtained in DregX as D1.

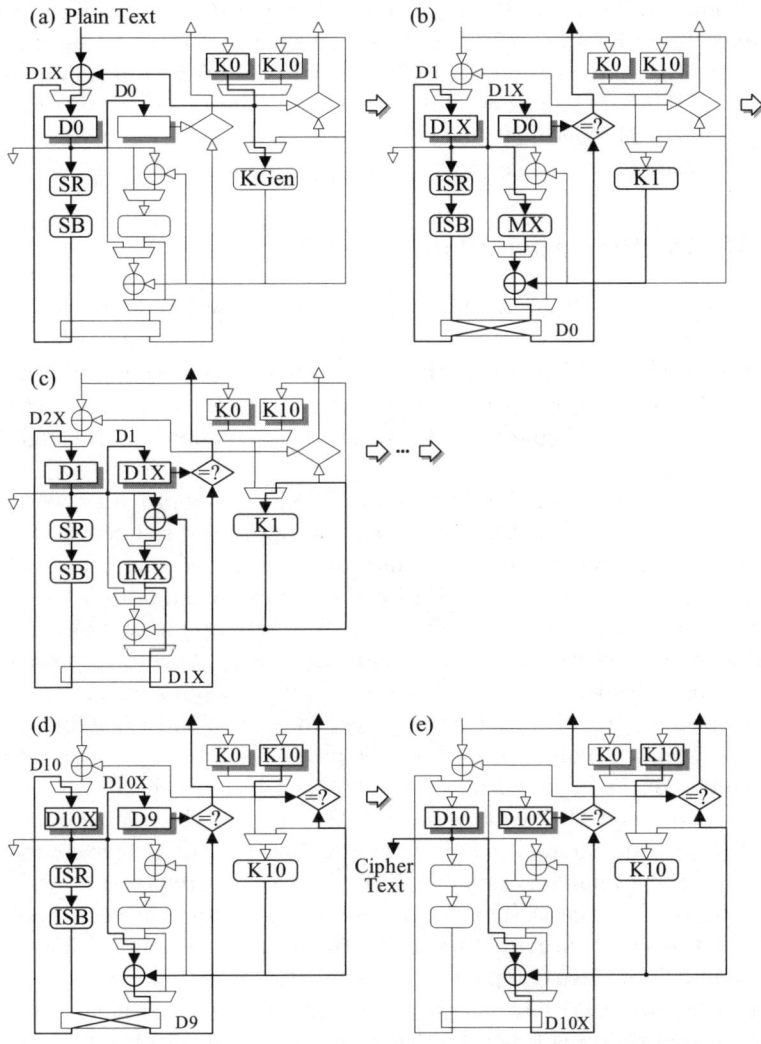

Fig. 5. Example operation of the proposed AES circuit

In Fig. 5(c), the same encryption datapath of Fig. 5(a) encrypts the data D1 in DregX to D2X, and the datapath on the right (InvMixColumns and XOR) decrypts the same data D1 to D1X for error detection. The output from the right datapath is then compared with the data in RegY. In a similar manner, the encryption and error detection process are continuously performed.

Fig. 5(d) shows the operation in the final round, where AddRoundKey with the 10-th round key K10 for encryption, and InvShiftRows and InvSubBytes are performed for error detection. As shown in Fig. 3(c), the MixColumns block is bypassed for this final round. In order to check whether the sequencer logic and key scheduler worked correctly and all 10 rounds are processed without skip, the final round key generated in the round key register is compared with the pre-calculated key K10 in EncKreg. The ciphertext D10 can be output in this cycle, but it is output in the next cycle of Fig. 5(e) after confirming that D10 can return to D10X. The next plaintext cannot be input before this final check and thus requires 21 clocks, 20 clocks (= 10 rounds × 2 clocks) + one additional clock for the final check, to encrypt (or decrypt) one data block.

3   ASIC Performance Comparison

Table 1 shows a comparison of the performance between the AES circuits with and without the proposed error detection scheme, as shown in Figs. 2 and 4. The designs were synthesized by a Synopsis Design Compiler using a 90-nm CMOS standard cell library. In addition to size and speed optimizations, implementations that achieve the highest hardware efficiency, defined as throughput per gate, are shown.

The signal delay time for the round function block is approximately halved by using the proposed scheme, but the maximum operating frequency is not doubled because of the setup and hold times of the inserted register. In addition, the proposed scheme requires an additional clock cycle and additional hardware resources for error detection. Therefore, simple prediction may indicate that the proposed scheme is slower and larger than the simple AES circuit without the error detection scheme. However, the throughputs of compact implementations are 2.21 Gbps with 16.1 Kgates for the proposed scheme and 1.66 Gbps with 12.9 Kbps for the simple architecture. Thus, the proposed scheme is faster. Moreover, the gate counts of the high-speed versions are 24.1 Kgates with 3.21 Gbps for the proposed scheme and 30.7 Kgates with 4.22 Gbps for the simple architecture. Thus, the proposed scheme is smaller. This is because the longer combinatorial logic path in the round function block of the simple architecture causes wide variations in logic synthesis. The range of gate counts and throughputs in Table 1 are ×2 for the simple architecture, while this range is within ×1.5 for the proposed scheme. To achieve compact implementation, it is important to reuse gate logic, even though the critical path becomes longer, and to use smaller cells, even though their drivability is lower. On the other hand, parallel processing without

Table 1. Hardware performance comparison

Archi-tecture	Clock Cycles	Size (gates)	Maximum Frequency (MHz)	Through-put (Mbps)	Hardware Efficiency (Kbps/gate)	Optimi-zation
Proposed (Fig. 4)	21	16,099	362.32	2,208.40	137.18	Size
		17,087	406.50	2,477.70	145.01	Efficiency
		24,114	526.32	3,208.00	133.04	Speed
Normal (Fig. 2)	10	12,949	129.37	1,655.90	127.88	Size
		20,003	265.25	3,395.20	169.48	Efficiency
		30,708	330.03	4,224.40	137.57	Speed

(90-nm CMOS, 1 gate = 2-input NAND, worst condition).

sharing gate logic and use of large cells with higher drivability are efficient for high-speed implementation. This means that smaller circuits become slower and faster circuits become larger. Therefore, the simple implementation with a wide range of synthesis optimization had smaller but "slower" performance for the compact implementation, and the high-speed version is faster but "larger" than the proposed architecture.

The results indicate that total hardware performance cannot be determined by simply measuring gate counts and throughput, and thus the performance overhead caused by the error detection circuit cannot be evaluated either. Therefore, as the criterion, we use the balance between hardware size and operating speed, that is, the hardware efficiency is defined as the throughput per gate. However, the hardware efficiency still varies somewhat depending on the synthesis constraints. Consequently, the optimal balance between size and speed, i.e., the highest hardware efficiency, was chosen as the score of the hardware performance. To investigate the highest hardware efficiency, logic synthesis was repeated several times by changing the constraints. Then, the proposed AES architecture and the simple AES architecture achieved efficiencies of 145.0 Kbps/gate (= 2.48 Gbps/17.1 Kgates) and 169.5 Kbps/gate (= 3.40 Gbps/20.0 Kgates), respectively. The efficiency of the proposed scheme is 85.5% compared to the simple architecture, and thus we can say that the performance overhead of the error detection scheme is at most 14.5%. Meanwhile, in many cases, the AES circuit with the error detection showed better performances. These results clearly demonstrate the advantage of the proposed scheme.

4   Conclusion

This paper proposed an error detection scheme for the AES circuit, and evaluated its performance using a 90-nm standard cell library. The scheme divides a round function block into two sub-blocks and uses them alternatively for encryption (or decryption) and error detection. Therefore, no extra calculation block is needed, even though only a pipeline register, a selector and a comparator are added. The number of operating cycles is doubled, but the operating frequency is boosted because the round function block in the critical path is halved. Therefore, the scheme has only a minor impact on hardware performance.

Logic synthesis was repeated by changing the optimization conditions, and the AES circuit with the proposed scheme achieved a range of 16.1 ~ 24.1 Kgates for hardware size and 2.21 ~ 3.21 Gbps for throughput. Those of the simple architecture without error detection are 12.9 ~ 30.7 Kgates and 1.66 ~ 4.22 Gbps. The simple implementation has a longer combinatorial logic path, which leads to a wider range of performance optimization. These different ranges make it difficult to compare the performance between the proposed and simple architectures. Therefore, the highest hardware efficiency (throughput/gate), which gives the optimal balance between hardware speed and size was chosen for the performance comparison. The hardware efficiencies are 145.0 kbps/gate for the proposed scheme and 169.4 Kbps/gate for the simple implementation, and thus the performance overhead due to the error detection is only 14.5%. In addition, the AES circuit with the proposed scheme had better performance than the simple implementation depending on the constraints of logic synthesis.

Although the round function block was divided by 2 in the above implementations, it should be possible to increase the number of pipeline stages to 4, 6, and 8, in which half of the stages are used for encryption and the other half are used for error detection. This is a very efficient way to achieve a much higher throughput when pipeline operation, such as that for the CTR mode, is possible. The proposed scheme does not depend greatly on the algorithm, and thus it can also be applied to hardware implementations of several coding algorithms, as well as cryptographic hardware. As a result, the proposed error detection scheme has significant advantages in both efficiency and versatility.

We have developed experimental ASIC and FPGA boards called SASEBO (Side-channel Attack Standard Evaluation BOard) and have distributed these boards to research institutes in an attempt to contribute to establish standard evaluation criteria and test requirements for cryptographic modules against physical analysis attacks including fault injection attacks. A cryptographic ASIC chip with countermeasures is currently under development, and the AES circuit proposed in this paper will be implemented on the chip. Detailed technical information and specifications about the experimental chip and the boards will be disclosed on the Website of the SASEBO project [32].

References

1. Boneh, D., Demillio, R., Liotin, R.: On the Importance of Checking Crypto-graphic Protocols for Fault. In: Fumy, W. (ed.) EUROCRYPT 1997. LNCS, vol. 1233, pp. 37–51. Springer, Heidelberg (1997)
2. Biham, E., Shamir, A.: Differential Fault Analysis of Secret Key Cryptosys-tems. In: Kaliski Jr., B.S. (ed.) CRYPTO 1997. LNCS, vol. 1294, pp. 513–525. Springer, Heidelberg (1997)
3. Anderson, R., Kuhn, M.: Low Cost Attacks on Tamper Resistant Devices. In: Christianson, B., Lomas, M. (eds.) Security Protocols 1997. LNCS, vol. 1361, pp. 125–136. Springer, Heidelberg (1998)
4. Bar-El, H., Choukri, H., Naccache, D., Tunstall, M., Whelan, C.: The Sorcerer's Apprentice Guide to Fault Attack. IACR ePrint archive, Report 2004/100 (2004)
5. Giraud, G., Thiebeauld, H.: A Survey on Fault Attacks. In: Proc. Sixth Smart Card Research and Advanced Application IFIP Conf. (CARDIS 2004), pp. 159–176 (August 2004)
6. National Institute of Standards and Technology (NIST), Advanced Encryption Standard (AES) FIPS Publication 197 (November 2001),
   http://csrc.nist.gov/publications/fips/fips197/fips-197.pdf
7. Blömer, J., Seifert, J.-P.: Fault Based Cryptanalysis of the Advanced Encryption Standard (AES). In: Wright, R.N. (ed.) FC 2003. LNCS, vol. 2742, pp. 162–181. Springer, Heidelberg (2003)
8. Blömer, J., Krummel, V.: Fault Based Collision Attacks on AES. In: Breveglieri, L., Koren, I., Naccache, D., Seifert, J.-P. (eds.) FDTC 2006. LNCS, vol. 4236, pp. 106–120. Springer, Heidelberg (2006)

9. Piret, G., Quisquater, J.-J.: A Differential Fault Attack Technique against SPN Structures, With Application to the AES avd Khazad. In: Walter, C.D., Koç, Ç.K., Paar, C. (eds.) CHES 2003. LNCS, vol. 2779, pp. 77–88. Springer, Heidelberg (2003)

10. Dusart, P., Letourneux, G., Vivolo, O.: Differential Fault Analysis on AES. Cryptology ePrint Archive, Report2003/010 (2003), http://eprint.iacr.org/2003/010.pdf

11. Chen, C.-N., Yen, S.-M.: Differential Fault Analysis on AES Key Schedule and Some Countermeasures. In: Safavi-Naini, R., Seberry, J. (eds.) ACISP 2003. LNCS, vol. 2727, pp. 118–129. Springer, Heidelberg (2003)

12. Giraud, C.: DFA on AES. In: Dobbertin, H., Rijmen, V., Sowa, A. (eds.) AES 2005. LNCS, vol. 3373, pp. 27–41. Springer, Heidelberg (2005)

13. Takahashi, J., Fukunaga, T., Yamakoshi, K.: DFA Mechanism on the AES Key Schedule. In: Proc. Fault Diagnosis and Tolerance in Cryptography (FDTC 2007), pp. 62–72 (September 2007)

14. Bertoni, G., Breveglieri, L., Koren, I., Maistri, P., Piuri, V.: Error Analysis and Detection Procedures for a Hardware Implementation of the Advanced Encryption Standard. IEEE Trans. Comp. Special Issue on Cryptographic Hardware and Embedded Software 52(4), 492–505 (2003)

15. Bertoni, G., Breveglieri, L., Koren, I., Maistri, P.: An Efficient Hardware-Based Fault Diagnosis Scheme for AES Performances and Cost. In: Proc. the 19th IEEE Int. Sym. Defect and Fault Tolerance in VLSI Systems (DFT 2004), pp. 130–138 (October 2004)

16. Breveglieri, L., Koren, I., Maistri, P.: Incorporating Error Detection and Online Reconfiguration into a Regular Architecture for the Advanced Encryption Standard. In: Proc. the 20th IEEE Int. Sym. Defect and Fault Tolerance in VLSI Systems (DFT 2005), pp. 72–80 (October 2005)

17. Karri, R., Kuznetsov, G., Gossel, M.: Parity-Based Concurrent Error Detection of Substitution-Permutation Network Block Ciphers. In: Walter, C.D., Koç, Ç.K., Paar, C. (eds.) CHES 2003. LNCS, vol. 2779, pp. 113–124. Springer, Heidelberg (2003)

18. Karpovsky, M., Kulikowski, K.J., Taubin, A.: Robust Protection against Fault-Injection Attacks on Smart Cards Implementing the Advanced Encryption Standard. In: Proc. 2004 International Conference on Dependable Systems and Networks (DSN 2004), pp. 93–101 (July 2004)

19. Karpovsky, M., Kulikowski, K.J., Taubin, A.: Differential Fault Analysis Attack Resistant Architectures for the Advanced Encryption Standard. In: Proc. Sixth Smart Card Research and Advanced Application IFIP Conference (CARDIS 2004), pp. 177–192 (August 2004)

20. Yen, C.-H., Wu, B.-F.: Simple Error Detection Methods for Hardware Implementation of Advanced Encryption Standard. IEEE Trans. Comp. 55(6), 720–731 (2006)

21. Wu, K., Karri, R., Kuznetsov, G., Goessel, M.: Low Cost Concurrent Error Detection for the Advanced Encryption Standard. In: Proc. The 2004 Int. Test Conf., pp. 1242–1248 (October 2004)

22. Kermani, M.M., Masoleh, A.R.: Parity-Based Fault Detection Architecture of S-box for Advanced Encryption Standard. In: Proc. the 21st IEEE Int. Symp. De-fect and Fault-Tolerance in VLSI Systems (DFT 2006), pp. 572–580 (December 2006)

23. Kermani, M.M., Masoleh, A.R.: A Structure-independent Approach for Fault Detection Hardware Implementations of the Advanced Encryption Standard. In: Proc. Fault Diagnosis and Tolerance in Cryptography (FDTC 2007), pp. 47–53 (September 2007)

24. Wu, K., Mishra, P., Karri, R.: Concurrent Error Detection of Fault-Based Side-Channel Cryptanalysis of 128-Bit RC6 Block Cipher. Special Issue on Defect and Fault Tolerance in VLSI Systems. Microelectronics Journal 34(1), 31–39 (2003)
25. Karri, R., Wu, K., Mishra, P., Kim, Y.: Concurrent Error Detection Schemes for Fault-Based Side-Channel Cryptanalysis of Symmetric Block Ciphers. IEEE Trans. CAD of Integrated Circuits and Systems 21(12), 1509–1517 (2002)
26. Anghel, L., Nicolaidis, M.: Cost Reduction and Evaluation of a Temporary Faults Detecting Technique. In: Proc. Design Automation and Test in Europe (DATE 2000), pp. 591–597 (March 2000)
27. Maistri, P., Vanhauwaert, P., Leveugle, R.: A Novel Double-Data-Rate AES Architecture Resistant against Fault Injection. In: Proc. Fault Diagnosis and Tolerance in Cryptography (FDTC 2007), pp. 54–61 (September 2007)
28. Joshi, N., Wu, K., Karri, R.: Concurrent Error Detection Schemes for Involution Ciphers. In: Joye, M., Quisquater, J.-J. (eds.) CHES 2004. LNCS, vol. 3156, pp. 400–412. Springer, Heidelberg (2004)
29. Malkin, T.G., Standaert, F.-X., Yung, M.: A Comparative Cost/Security Analysis of Fault Attack Countermeasures. In: Breveglieri, L., Koren, I., Naccache, D., Seifert, J.-P. (eds.) FDTC 2006. LNCS, vol. 4236, pp. 159–172. Springer, Heidelberg (2006)
30. Satoh, A., Morioka, S., Takano, K., Munetoh, S.: A Compact Rijndael Hardware Architecture with S-box Optimization. In: Boyd, C. (ed.) ASIACRYPT 2001. LNCS, vol. 2248, pp. 239–254. Springer, Heidelberg (2001)
31. Chodowiec, P., Gaj, K.: Very Compact FPGA Implementation of the AES Algorithm. In: D.Walter, C., Koç, Ç.K., Paar, C. (eds.) CHES 2003. LNCS, vol. 2779, pp. 319–333. Springer, Heidelberg (2003)
32. Side-channel Attack Standard Evaluation Board (SASEBO), http://www.rcis.aist.go.jp/special/SASEBO/

A Lightweight Concurrent Fault Detection Scheme for the AES S-Boxes Using Normal Basis

Mehran Mozaffari-Kermani and Arash Reyhani-Masoleh

Department of Electrical and Computer Engineering,
The University of Western Ontario
London, Ontario, Canada
{mmozaff,areyhani}@uwo.ca

Abstract. The use of an appropriate fault detection scheme for hardware implementation of the Advanced Encryption Standard (AES) makes the standard robust to the internal defects and fault attacks. To minimize the overhead cost of the fault detection AES structure, we present a lightweight concurrent fault detection scheme for the composite field realization of the S-box using normal basis. The structure of the S-box is divided into blocks and the predicted parities of these blocks are obtained. Through an exhaustive search among all available composite fields and transformation matrices that map the polynomial basis representation in binary field to the normal basis representation in composite field, we have found the optimum solution for the least overhead S-box and its parity predictions. Finally, using FPGA implementations, the complexities of the proposed schemes are compared to those of the previously reported ones. It is shown that the FPGA implementations of the S-box using normal basis representation in composite fields outperform the traditional ones using polynomial basis for both with and without fault detection capability.

Keywords: Advanced encryption standard, fault detection, normal basis, S-box.

1 Introduction

The AES was approved by NIST in 2001 [1] and is currently replaced the previous Data Encryption Standard in many applications. In encryption, the AES accepts a 128-bit plaintext and a key as the inputs, where the key size can be selected as 128, 192 or 256 bits. In the AES-128, which is hereafter referred to as AES, the ciphertext is generated after 10 rounds, where each encryption round (except for the final round) consists of four transformations [1].

Among the four transformations in the encryption of the AES, only the S-box operation is non-linear. There exist several fault detection schemes devised for detecting the faults in the hardware implementation of this operation, see for example [2], [3], [4], [5], [6], [7], and [8]. In this regard, the schemes in [2], [4], [5], [6], and [7] are independent of the way this transformation is implemented

E. Oswald and P. Rohatgi (Eds.): CHES 2008, LNCS 5154, pp. 113–129, 2008.
© International Association for Cryptologic Research 2008

in hardware. In [2], redundant unit is proposed for the fault detection of the S-box, where an inverse S-box is placed after the S-box. Although such an scheme detects any faults in the S-box or the inverse S-box, its overhead is at least 100%. The approach in [4] and [5] is based on storing the one-bit predicted parity of the S-box in a table and comparing it with the actual parity. Theoretically, this causes the error coverage of 50% for a single S-box. In [6], a multiplication approach for the fault detection of the multiplicative inversion of the S-box is presented. In this approach, the result of the multiplication of the input and the output of the multiplicative inversion is compared to the actual result.

There exist some other fault detection schemes that are suitable for a specific implementation of the S-box, see for example [3] and [8]. The fault detection approach presented in [3] is based on the table look-up S-boxes which may not be preferable for high performance implementations. Therefore, for applications requiring high performance AES implementations, the S-box is implemented using logic gates in the composite field [9]. This reduces the area complexity of the implementations. In addition, through pipelining, the working frequencies of the hardware implementations can be increased [10].

Since direct calculation of the multiplicative inversion is costly [9], [11], composite field arithmetic is used to perform a low cost inversion. It is noted that the inversion in $GF(2^8)$ can be implemented by mapping the binary field to the composite field using polynomial or normal bases. It is shown in [9] that the S-box structure using normal basis in composite field requires lower gate count as compared to its counterparts using polynomial basis. In this paper, we have implemented both types of the S-boxes on FPGAs and have shown that the ones using normal basis has lower complexities than the one using polynomial basis. Furthermore, we show that the parity predictions for the proposed fault detection scheme using normal basis has lower gate count and time complexity in comparison with those presented in [8] which uses polynomial basis.

In this paper, we propose a lightweight concurrent parity-based fault detection scheme for the S-box using normal basis. This scheme can also be applied to the inverse S-box. Through an exhaustive search, we obtain the least area and delay overhead S-box and its fault detection scheme for the optimum composite field. In this regard, our comparisons through FPGA implementations show that the presented scheme is more efficient than the previously reported ones. Furthermore, considering random fault injection, high error coverage is achieved for the presented scheme.

The organization of this paper is as follows: In Section 2, preliminaries regarding the AES S-box and its implementation using composite fields and normal basis are explained. The proposed fault detection scheme for the S-box is presented in Section 3. Moreover, in this section, the time and space complexities of the proposed scheme are analyzed. In Section 4, the presented fault detection scheme for the S-box and the previously reported ones are implemented on FP-GAs and they are compared in terms of time and space complexities. Finally, conclusions are made in Section 5.

2   Preliminaries

In this section, we first describe the S-box operation. Then, the composite field realization of the S-box using normal basis is explained.

2.1   The S-Box

The S-box is a nonlinear operation which takes an 8-bit input and generates an 8-bit output. In the S-box, the irreducible polynomial of $P(x) = x^8 + x^4 + x^3 + x + 1$ is used to construct the binary field $GF(2^8)$. Let $X \in GF(2^8)$ and $Y \in GF(2^8)$ be the input and the output of the S-box, respectively. Then, the S-box consists of the multiplicative inversion, i.e., $X^{-1} \in GF(2^8)$, followed by an affine transformation. The affine transformation consists of the matrix $\boldsymbol{A}$ and the vector $\boldsymbol{b}$ to generate the output as

$$
\boldsymbol{y} = \boldsymbol{A}\boldsymbol{x}^{-1} + \boldsymbol{b} = \begin{pmatrix} 1\,0\,0\,0\,1\,1\,1\,1 \\ 1\,1\,0\,0\,0\,1\,1\,1 \\ 1\,1\,1\,0\,0\,0\,1\,1 \\ 1\,1\,1\,1\,0\,0\,0\,1 \\ 1\,1\,1\,1\,1\,0\,0\,0 \\ 0\,1\,1\,1\,1\,1\,0\,0 \\ 0\,0\,1\,1\,1\,1\,1\,0 \\ 0\,0\,0\,1\,1\,1\,1\,1 \end{pmatrix} \boldsymbol{x}^{-1} + \begin{pmatrix} 1 \\ 1 \\ 0 \\ 0 \\ 0 \\ 1 \\ 1 \\ 0 \end{pmatrix} , \tag{1}
$$

where, $\boldsymbol{y}$ and $\boldsymbol{x}^{-1}$ are vectors corresponding to the field elements Y and X^{-1}, respectively.

In the following, we explain the composite field realization of the multiplicative inversion using normal basis. Then, in the next section, we propose the parity-based fault detection scheme of the S-box using this realization.

2.2   Multiplicative Inversion Using Composite Fields and Normal Basis

Let us briefly explain the composite field arithmetic to calculate the multiplicative inversion over $GF(2^8)$. In what follows, we use capital Roman letters such as X and Y for the elements in the binary field $GF(2^8)$. Furthermore, small Greek letters such as η_h, η_l, ν represent the elements in $GF(2^4)$. Finally, capital Greek letters such as Φ and Ω are utilized for the elements in $GF(2^2)$.

The transformation matrix $\boldsymbol{\Psi}$ transforms a field element $X = \sum_{i=0}^{7} x_i \alpha^i$ in the binary field $GF(2^8)$ to the corresponding representation in the composite field $GF(2^8)/GF(2^4)$. The result of this transformation is the polynomial $X = \eta_h u^{16} + \eta_l u$ (see Fig. 1), with the multiplications modulo the irreducible polynomial $u^2 + \tau u + \nu$. It is noted that the coefficients η_h and η_l are field elements in the sub-field $GF(2^4)$ representing X in terms of the normal basis $[U^{16}, U]$ [12]. The decomposition can be further applied to represent $GF(2^4)$ as a linear polynomial over $GF(2^2)$ with multiplications modulo the irreducible polynomial of $v^2 + \Omega v + \Phi$ which uses the normal basis $[V^4, V]$. Moreover, one can

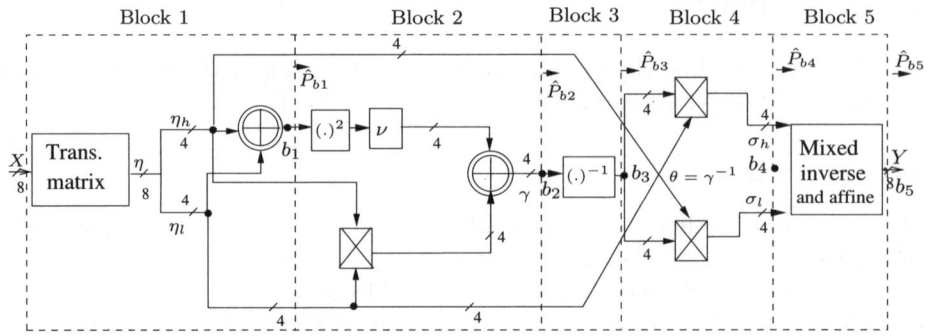

Fig. 1. The S-box using composite field and normal basis [12] and its fault detection blocks

represent $GF(2^2)$ as a linear polynomial over $GF(2)$ with multiplications modulo the irreducible polynomial of $w^2 + w + 1$ using the normal basis $[W^2, W]$. After calculating the inversion in the composite field, the inverse transformation matrix $\boldsymbol{\Psi}^{-1}$ is used to transform the composite field representation to the field element $Y = \sum_{i=0}^{7} y_i \alpha^i$ in $GF(2^8)$.

For calculating the multiplicative inversion, the most efficient choice is to let $\Omega = \tau = 1$ in the above irreducible polynomials [9], [12]. Then, we have the following for the multiplicative inversion using normal basis [12]

$$(\eta_h u^{16} + \eta_l u)^{-1} = [\theta \eta_h] u^{16} + [\theta \eta_l] u, \qquad (2)$$

where, $\theta = (\eta_h \eta_l + (\eta_h^2 + \eta_l^2)\nu)^{-1}$ (see the output of block 3 in Fig. 1). As seen in (2), the multiplicative inversion consists of a number of multiplications, an inversion, a squaring and modulo-2 additions in $GF(2^4)$. In the next section, while we derive the parity predictions for the S-boxes, we will explain these in more details. Then, we derive the most efficient coefficients ν and Φ for the presented fault detection scheme.

3   Fault Detection Scheme

In this paper, we use multiple stuck-at fault model at the logic level. This type of fault, which forces multiple nodes to be stuck at logic one (for stuck-at one) or zero (for stuck-at zero) independent of the fault-free logic values, has been frequently used in the literature, see for example [16]. It is noted that the presented scheme is independent of the life time of the faults. Thus, both permanent and transient stuck-at faults lead to the same fault coverage.

In the parity-based fault detection scheme of a block of logic gates, the parity of the block is predicted and it is compared to the actual parity. The result of this comparison is the error indication flag of the corresponding block. This method has been utilized in the literature to develop a fault detection scheme for different applications, see for example [3], [13], [14], [15].

We have divided the S-box into 5 blocks similar to what is done in [8]. This results in low overhead parity predictions while maintaining the fault detection required for the security-constrained environments. This is shown in Fig. 1. Let b_i be the output of block i in Fig. 1, where $b_1 = \eta_h + \eta_l, b_2 = \gamma, b_3 = \theta, b_4 = \sigma$, and $b_5 = Y$. As seen in this figure, the first block consists of the transformation matrix that changes an element in polynomial basis to the composite field. Moreover, the last block (block 5) is obtained by mixing the inverse and affine transformation matrices. The remaining three blocks are for the multiplicative inversion, where, the hardware realization of equation (2) has been depicted. In this figure, the modulo-2 additions, consisting of 4 XOR gates, are shown by two concentric circles with a plus inside. Furthermore, the multiplications in $GF(2^4)$ are shown by rectangles with crosses inside. In the remaining of this section, the five predicted parities of the outputs of five blocks of the S-box (b_1-b_5 in Fig. 1) are obtained. The predicted parity of the output of block i is a Boolean function of the inputs of block i. These parity predictions are denoted by $\hat{P}_{b1}$, $\hat{P}_{b2}$, $\hat{P}_{b3}$, $\hat{P}_{b4}$, and $\hat{P}_{b5}$ in Fig. 1. It is noted that we have exhaustively searched for the best possible choice of ν and Φ to find the least overhead parity predictions using composite field and normal basis, the details of which are to follow.

3.1   Least Overhead Parity Predictions

The implementation complexities of different blocks of the S-box are dependent on the choice of the coefficients $\nu \in GF(2^4)$ and $\Phi \in GF(2^2)$ in the irreducible polynomials $u^2 + u + \nu$ and $v^2 + v + \Phi$ used for the composite field. Therefore, the area/delay complexities of the predicted parities of these blocks are also affected for different choices of ν and Φ. It is noted that only the values of these coefficients that make the polynomials irreducible are acceptable. Therefore, it can be derived that the only two acceptable values for Φ are $\Phi = w^2 = \{10\}_2$ and $\Phi = w = \{01\}_2$. Furthermore, among the 16 values for ν, the following 8 make the polynomial of $u^2 + u + \nu$ irreducible and thus are possible: $\nu \in \{\{\Phi 00\}_2, \{00\Phi\}_2, \{\Phi^2 00\}_2, \{00\Phi^2\}_2, \{\Phi 11\}_2, \{11\Phi\}_2, \{\Phi^2 11\}_2, \{11\Phi^2\}_2\} = \{$
$\{0100\}_2, \{0001\}_2, \{1000\}_2, \{0010\}_2, \{0111\}_2, \{1101\}_2, \{1011\}_2, \{1110\}_2\}$.

In what follows, we are going to compare different implementations of the predicted parities of the blocks in the S-box considering different combinations of ν and Φ to reach a low complexity fault detection scheme.

Blocks 1 and 5 of the S-box. Based on the possible values of ν and Φ, the transformation matrices in blocks 1 and 5 of the S-box, denoted as $\mathbf{\Psi}$ and $\mathbf{\Psi}^{-1}$/affine, can be constructed using the algorithm presented in [17] with a slight modification for normal basis. One possible way to find the least complex transformation matrices is to calculate the Hamming weights, i.e., the number of non-zero elements, of the matrices $\mathbf{\Psi}$ and $\mathbf{\Psi}^{-1}$/affine. It is noted in [9] that instead of considering the Hamming weights, subexpression sharing is used for obtaining the low complexity implementations. We have exhaustively searched for the least overhead transformation matrices and their parity predictions combined, the results of which are presented in Table 1. In this table, for every

Table 1. Area/delay complexities of blocks 1 and 5 of the S-box and their predicted parities for possible values of νs and Φs

Φ	ν	$H(\Psi)+H$ (Ψ^{-1}/affine)	Total area of blocks 1 and 5	Total delay of blocks 1 and 5	Total area of $\hat{P}_{b1}$ and $\hat{P}_{b5}$	Total delay of $\hat{P}_{b1}$ and $\hat{P}_{b5}$
10	0001	57	28X		5X	
	0010	57	32X		5X	
	0100	57	34X		5X	
	1000	57	30X		5X	
	0111	67	34X		3X	
	1011	65	30X		5X	
	1101	67	34X		3X	
	1110	65	31X	$7T_X$	5X	$4T_X$
01	0001	57	32X		5X	
	0010	57	32X		5X	
	0100	57	29X		5X	
	1000	57	34X		5X	
	0111	65	34X		5X	
	1011	67	37X		3X	
	1101	65	34X		5X	
	1110	67	32X		3X	

$X = XOR$, T_X = Delay of an XOR.

possible combination of ν and Φ, the Hamming weights of Ψ and Ψ^{-1}/affine for the least complex cases are tabulated in column 3. Also, the number of gates needed for the low complexity implementation of blocks 1 and 5 are presented in column 4 of the table. Furthermore, the total number of XOR gates needed for the predicted parities of blocks 1 and 5 of the S-box, i.e., $\hat{P}_{b1}$ and $\hat{P}_{b5}$, and the delays associated with them are also shown in the table.

Block 2: As shown in Fig. 1, block 2 of the S-box consists of a multiplication, an addition, a squaring and a multiplication by constant ν in $GF(2^4)$. The multiplication in $GF(2^4)$ presented in [12], is depicted in Fig. 2a. As seen in this figure, it consists of three multiplications, additions and a multiplication by constant Φ in $GF(2^2)$. Moreover, the multiplication in $GF(2^2)$ is shown in this figure. The following lemmas are used for deriving the predicted parity of the multiplication in $GF(2^4)$ and block 2, respectively. It is noted that all proofs are presented in Appendix A.

Lemma 1. *Let* $\lambda = (\lambda_3, \lambda_2, \lambda_1, \lambda_0)$ *and* $\delta = (\delta_3, \delta_2, \delta_1, \delta_0)$ *be the inputs of a multiplier in* $GF(2^4)$. *The predicted parity of the result of the multiplication of* λ *and* δ *in* $GF(2^4)$ *is independent of* Φ *and can be derived as*

$$\hat{P}_\pi = \lambda_3\delta_3 + \lambda_2\delta_2 + \lambda_1\delta_1 + \lambda_0\delta_0. \tag{3}$$

Lemma 2. *The predicted parity of block 2, i.e.,* $\hat{P}_{b2}$ *in Fig. 1, depends on the choice of the coefficients* $\nu \in GF(2^4)$ *and* $\Phi \in GF(2^2)$ *in the irreducible polynomials* $u^2 + u + \nu$ *and* $v^2 + v + \Phi$ *used for the composite field.*

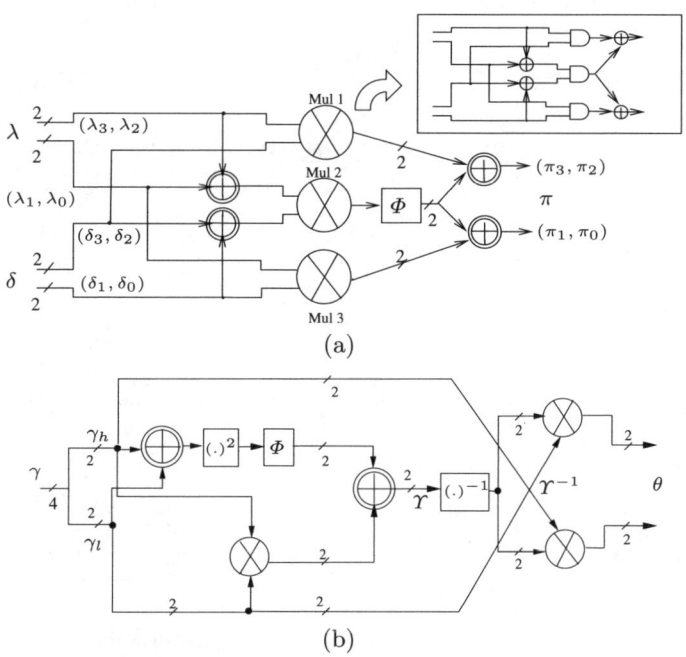

Fig. 2. (a) Multiplication and (b) Inversion in $GF(2^4)$ [12]

The proof is presented in Appendix A.

Using Lemma 1 and Lemma 2 and Fig. 1, we can state the following to predict the parity of block 2. The proof is presented in Appendix A.

Lemma 3. *The predicted parity of block 2, i.e., $\hat{P}_{b2}$, can be derived as shown in Table 2.*

Table 2 shows the predicted parities for different combinations of ν and Φ and their area/delay complexities. Moreover, the complexities for block 2 are shown in this table. As seen in Table 2, the delay overhead for both the original block and its parity prediction is the same for all the cases. Whereas, the area in terms of the number of gates are different for different values of ν and Φ.

Block 3: Block 3 in Fig. 1 consists of an inversion in $GF(2^4)$. The hardware implementation for this block has also been shown in Fig. 2b [12]. As seen in this figure, the inversion in $GF(2^4)$ is dependent on the two possible choices of Φ and is the same for different values of ν. Therefore, depending on the choice of Φ, there are two possible choices for this block and its parity prediction. It is noted that for both of these implementations, the area and the critical path delay are the same. The following theorem is used for obtaining the predicted parity of block 3, i.e., $\hat{P}_{b3}$, the proof of which is presented in Appendix A.

Table 2. Parity predictions and complexities of block 2 of the S-box in Fig. 1 for possible values of ν and Φ

Φ	ν	Area of block 2	Delay of block 2	Predicted parity ($\hat{P}_{b2}$)	Area of $\hat{P}_{b2}$	Delay of $\hat{P}_{b2}$
	0001	28X+9A		$(\eta_7 \vee \eta_3) + (\eta_6 \vee \eta_2) + (\eta_4 \vee \eta_0) + \eta_5\eta_1$	3X+3O+1A	
	0010	29X+9A		$(\eta_7 \vee \eta_3) + (\eta_5 \vee \eta_1) + (\eta_4 \vee \eta_0) + \eta_6\eta_2$	3X+3O+1A	
	0100	28X+9A		$(\eta_6 \vee \eta_2) + (\eta_5 \vee \eta_1) + (\eta_4 \vee \eta_0) + \eta_7\eta_3$	3X+3O+1A	
10	1000	29X+9A		$(\eta_7 \vee \eta_3) + (\eta_6 \vee \eta_2) + (\eta_5 \vee \eta_1) + \eta_4\eta_0$	3X+3O+1A	
	0111	28X+9A		$(\eta_4 \vee \eta_0) + \eta_7\eta_3 + \eta_6\eta_2 + \eta_5\eta_1$	3X+3A+1O	
	1011	29X+9A		$(\eta_7 \vee \eta_3) + \eta_6\eta_2 + \eta_5\eta_1 + \eta_4\eta_0$	3X+3A+1O	
	1101	28X+9A		$(\eta_6 \vee \eta_2) + \eta_7\eta_3 + \eta_5\eta_1 + \eta_4\eta_0$	3X+3A+1O	
	1110	29X+9A	$6T_X$ $+1T_A$	$(\eta_5 \vee \eta_1) + \eta_7\eta_3 + \eta_6\eta_2 + \eta_4\eta_0$	3X+3A+1O	$2T_X$ $+1T_A$
	0001	29X+9A		$(\eta_6 \vee \eta_2) + (\eta_5 \vee \eta_1) + (\eta_4 \vee \eta_0) + \eta_7\eta_3$	3X+3O+1A	
	0010	28X+9A		$(\eta_7 \vee \eta_3) + (\eta_6 \vee \eta_2) + (\eta_5 \vee \eta_1) + \eta_4\eta_0$	3X+3O+1A	
	0100	29X+9A		$(\eta_7 \vee \eta_3) + (\eta_6 \vee \eta_2) + (\eta_4 \vee \eta_0) + \eta_5\eta_1$	3X+3O+1A	
01	1000	28X+9A		$(\eta_7 \vee \eta_3) + (\eta_5 \vee \eta_1) + (\eta_4 \vee \eta_0) + \eta_6\eta_2$	3X+3O+1A	
	0111	29X+9A		$(\eta_6 \vee \eta_2) + \eta_7\eta_3 + \eta_5\eta_1 + \eta_4\eta_0$	3X+3A+1O	
	1011	28X+9A		$(\eta_5 \vee \eta_1) + \eta_7\eta_3 + \eta_6\eta_2 + \eta_4\eta_0$	3X+3A+1O	
	1101	29X+9A		$(\eta_4 \vee \eta_0) + \eta_7\eta_3 + \eta_6\eta_2 + \eta_5\eta_1$	3X+3A+1O	
	1110	28X+9A		$(\eta_7 \vee \eta_3) + \eta_6\eta_2 + \eta_5\eta_1 + \eta_4\eta_0$	3X+3A+1O	

$A = AND, \{+, X\} = XOR, \{\vee, O\} = OR.$
$T_X =$ Delay of an XOR, $T_A =$ Delay of an AND= Delay of an OR.

Theorem 1. *Let* $\gamma = (\gamma_3, \gamma_2, \gamma_1, \gamma_0)$ *be the input and* $\theta = (\theta_3, \theta_2, \theta_1, \theta_0)$ *be the output of an inverter in* $GF(2^4)$. *Then, for* $\Phi = w^2 = \{10\}_2$, *the predicted parity of block 3, i.e.,* $\hat{P}_{b3}$, *can be found as*

$$\hat{P}_{b3} = \hat{P}_\theta = \overline{\gamma_2\gamma_0}(\gamma_3 + \gamma_1) + \gamma_3\gamma_1(\gamma_2 + \gamma_0). \tag{4}$$

Also, for $\Phi = w = \{01\}_2$ *we have*

$$\hat{P}_{b3} = \hat{P}_\theta = \overline{\gamma_3\gamma_1}(\gamma_2 + \gamma_0) + \gamma_2\gamma_0(\gamma_3 + \gamma_1). \tag{5}$$

Block 4: Block 4 of the S-box consists of two multiplications in $GF(2^4)$. According to Lemma 1, the area/delay overhead of the multiplications in $GF(2^4)$ and that of their predicted parity are the same for both $\Phi = w = \{01\}_2$ and $\Phi = w^2 = \{10\}_2$. Moreover, as seen in Fig. 1, we have $\hat{P}_{b4} = \hat{P}_{\eta_h\theta} + \hat{P}_{\eta_l\theta} = \hat{P}_{(\eta_h+\eta_l)\theta}$. Then, according to (3) in Lemma 1 with the inputs of $\eta_h + \eta_l$ and θ, one can find $\hat{P}_{b4}$ as

$$\hat{P}_{b4} = (\eta_7 + \eta_3)\theta_3 + (\eta_6 + \eta_2)\theta_2 + (\eta_5 + \eta_1)\theta_1 + (\eta_4 + \eta_0)\theta_0. \tag{6}$$

It is noted that as seen in Fig. 1, for the implementation of $\hat{P}_{b4}$, the modulo-2 additions of $\eta_7 + \eta_3$, $\eta_6 + \eta_2$, $\eta_5 + \eta_1$, and $\eta_4 + \eta_0$ are already available at the input of block 2. Therefore, implementing (6) only needs 3 XORs and 4ANDs.

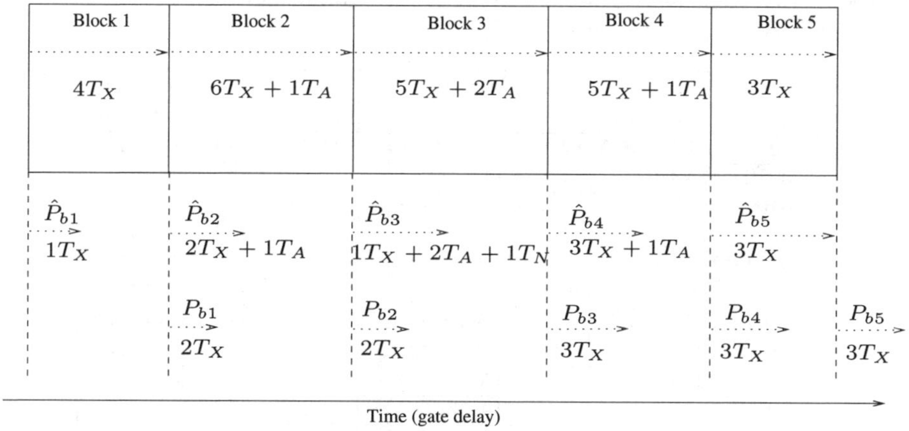

Block 1	Block 2	Block 3	Block 4	Block 5
$4T_X$	$6T_X + 1T_A$	$5T_X + 2T_A$	$5T_X + 1T_A$	$3T_X$
$\hat{P}_{b1}$	$\hat{P}_{b2}$	$\hat{P}_{b3}$	$\hat{P}_{b4}$	$\hat{P}_{b5}$
$1T_X$	$2T_X + 1T_A$	$1T_X + 2T_A + 1T_N$	$3T_X + 1T_A$	$3T_X$
	P_{b1}	P_{b2}	P_{b3}	P_{b4}	P_{b5}
	$2T_X$	$2T_X$	$3T_X$	$3T_X$	$3T_X$

Time (gate delay)

Fig. 3. Time complexity of the presented concurrent fault detection scheme for the 5 blocks of the S-box

3.2   Complexity Analysis

Based on the above discussions, the delay overhead of the predicted parities of the 5 blocks in the S-box is the same for different combinations of ν and Φ, i.e., the total delay of the predicted parities is $14T_X + 4T_A$. This delay overhead can overlap the delays for the implementations of the 5 blocks in Fig. 1. We use Fig. 3 for explaining this delay overhead in more details. As seen in this figure, the time complexity of the presented concurrent fault detection scheme for the 5 blocks of the S-box is shown. For this reason, the delays for the parity predictions, i.e., the delays for $\hat{P}_{b1}$-$\hat{P}_{b5}$, as well as the delays for the actual parity calculations[1], i.e., the delays for P_{b1}-P_{b5}, are depicted in this figure. As seen in Fig. 3, the delays for 5 parity predictions can overlap the time needed for computations in the corresponding blocks. After finding the predicted parity for a block, say block i, the actual parity of this block is obtained during the time needed for the computation of block $i + 1$. As seen in Fig. 3, the only delay overhead for this concurrent scheme is the delay of the actual parity of block 5 which is $3T_X$.

Using the discussions presented in this section and the results of Tables 1 and 2, the total gate count of all blocks of the S-box and their parity predictions for different combinations of ν and Φ are shown in Table 3. As seen in this table, if we only consider the area complexities of the parity predictions, the following four composite fields have the least area: $\Phi = \{10\}_2$ and $\nu \in \{\{0111\}_2, \{1101\}_2\}$ and also $\Phi = \{01\}_2$ and $\nu \in \{\{1011\}_2, \{1110\}_2\}$. As seen from Table 3, the gates needed for implementing these low-area parity predictions are 12 XORs, 11 ANDs, 1 OR and 1 NOT. However, the results of the table show that none of these has the least area for the S-box and its fault detection circuit together. As seen in Table 3, among all the 16 possible combinations of ν and Φ, the composite

---

[1] Binary trees of XOR gates are used.

Table 3. Area complexities of blocks 1 to 5 of the S-box and their predicted parities for possible values of νs and Φs

Φ	ν	Area of blocks 1 to 5	Area of $\hat{P}_{b1}$ to $\hat{P}_{b5}$	Total area of the S-box and its parity predictions
	0001	**119X+36A**	**14X+9A+3O+1N**	**133X+45A+3O+1N**
	0010	124X+36A	14X+9A+3O+1N	138X+45A+3O+1N
	0100	125X+36A	14X+9A+3O+1N	139X+45A+3O+1N
10	1000	122X+36A	14X+9A+3O+1N	136X+45A+3O+1N
	0111	125X+36A	12X+11A+1O+1N	137X+47A+1O+1N
	1011	122X+36A	14X+11A+1O+1N	136X+47A+1O+1N
	1101	125X+36A	12X+11A+1O+1N	137X+47A+1O+1N
	1110	123X+36A	14X+11A+1O+1N	137X+47A+1O+1N
	0001	124X+36A	14X+9A+3O+1N	138X+45A+3O+1N
	0010	123X+36A	14X+9A+3O+1N	137X+45A+3O+1N
	0100	121X+36A	14X+9A+3O+1N	135X+45A+3O+1N
01	1000	125X+36A	14X+9A+3O+1N	139X+45A+3O+1N
	0111	126X+36A	14X+11A+1O+1N	140X+47A+1O+1N
	1011	128X+36A	12X+11A+1O+1N	140X+47A+1O+1N
	1101	126X+36A	14X+11A+1O+1N	140X+47A+1O+1N
	1110	123X+36A	12X+11A+1O+1N	135X+47A+1O+1N

$X = XOR$, $A = AND$, $O = OR$, $N = NOT$.

field shown in bold face, i.e., $\Phi = w^2 = \{10\}_2$ and $\nu = \{00\Phi^2\}_2 = \{0001\}_2$, has the least area for the S-box and its fault detection circuit combined. It is interesting to note that after area optimization, this field has also been suggested in [9] for reaching the least area S-box using composite field.

From the previous section, we reach the following parity predictions for the 5 blocks in order to obtain the least overhead S-box and its fault detection circuit in Fig. 1

$$\hat{P}_{b1} = x_7 + x_5, \tag{7}$$

$$\hat{P}_{b2} = (\eta_7 \vee \eta_3) + (\eta_6 \vee \eta_2) + (\eta_4 \vee \eta_0) + \eta_5\eta_1, \tag{8}$$

$$\hat{P}_{b3} = \overline{\gamma_2\gamma_0}(\gamma_3 + \gamma_1) + \gamma_3\gamma_1(\gamma_2 + \gamma_0), \tag{9}$$

$$\hat{P}_{b4} = (\eta_7 + \eta_3)\theta_3 + (\eta_6 + \eta_2)\theta_2 + (\eta_5 + \eta_1)\theta_1 + (\eta_4 + \eta_0)\theta_0, \tag{10}$$

$$\hat{P}_{b5} = \sigma_7 + \sigma_5 + \sigma_4 + \sigma_3 + \sigma_2, \tag{11}$$

where, $\vee$ represents an OR operation.

We conclude this section with the calculation of the error coverage of the presented scheme. As seen in Fig. 1, since the 5 blocks of the S-box do not overlap, the fault detection of each block is independent of those of the others. It is noted that using parities, the probability of detecting (or not detecting) the faults by the error indication flag of each block is $\frac{1}{2}$. Therefore, using the mentioned fault model, for the error coverage of each S-box we have $100 \times (1 - (\frac{1}{2})^5)\% = 97\%$.

4   Comparisons

In this section, we compare the area and the delay of the presented scheme with those of the previously reported ones. For this reason, first the gate count and the gate delays of the schemes are obtained and compared. Then, the implementations on the Xilinx [18] FPGAs are presented.

4.1   Area and Time Complexities

For deriving the area overhead of the presented fault detection scheme, we assume that 2-input AND and OR gates require 6 transistors each using the full CMOS technology. Also, 2-input XOR and XNOR gates can be implemented using 10 transistors each [19] and a NOT gate can be realized using 2 transistors assuming that PMOS and NMOS need the same chip area. Therefore, the space complexities of a 2-input AND (OR) and a NOT gate are equivalent to 0.6 and 0.2 XOR gates, respectively.

In the previous section, the total gate count for the predicted parities of 5 blocks of the S-box was derived as 14 XORs, 9 ANDs, 3 ORs and 1 NOT which is equivalent to 21.4 XORs. In addition, 23 XORs and 5 XORs are needed for obtaining the actual parities and the comparisons of the predicted and the actual parities, respectively. Therefore, the equivalent gates for the total area overhead is obtained as $21.4 + 28 = 49.4$ XOR gates. Moreover, as seen in Table 3, the corresponding S-box implementation needs 119 XORs and 36 ANDs which is equivalent to 140.6 XOR gates. Therefore, the percentage of area overhead is approximately $\frac{49.4}{140.6} \simeq 35\%$.

The complexity of the presented fault detection scheme can be compared to the other fault detection schemes of the S-box using composite fields. The original area of the S-boxes and the overheads of these fault detection schemes in terms of equivalent XOR gates are presented in Table 4. The S-box presented in [11] has been hardware optimized in [20] and is extensively used in the literature, see for example [21], [22]. The gate count for the predicted parities of this S-box in [20] is derived as 23 XORs, 10 ANDs and 1 XNOR [8]. In addition, similar to the scheme in this paper, 28 XORs are required for obtaining the actual parities and their comparisons with the predicted parities. Therefore, the equivalent gates for the total area overhead is obtained as 58 XORs. Moreover, this S-box needs 123 XORs and 36 ANDs, equivalent to 144.6 XOR gates, resulting in the area overhead of approximately 40%. In addition, for comparison, we have derived the parity predictions of the S-box using polynomial basis, presented in [23] which is used in the literature, see for example [24], [25], [26]. Table 4 shows the total equivalent gate count for the fault detection scheme of this S-box, comprising the actual and the predicted parities and comparisons. As seen in this table, the gate overhead for the fault detection scheme of this S-box is around 38%.

Table 4. Area overhead comparison of the parity-based fault detection schemes

S-box	[11], [20], [21], [22]	[23], [24], [25], [26]	[27]	**Presented**
FDS[a]	[8]	Applied[b]	Applied[b]	This work
S-box XORs	144.6	144.6	141.6	**140.6**
FDS XORs[c]	58	56	56.4	**49.4**
Area overhead	40%	38%	39%	**35%**

[a] Fault detection scheme.
[b] We have applied the technique proposed in [8] to derive the predicted parities for the 5 blocks of the S-boxes presented in [23]-[27].
[c] The area complexity overhead of the fault detection scheme is dependent on the way the S-box is implemented. Therefore, the numbers of XOR gates are different for different S-box realizations.

Finally, using subexpression sharing for the implementation of the S-box in [27], the area overhead of the fault detection scheme is approximately 39% (see Table 4). As seen in this table, all the above S-boxes and their fault detection S-boxes are less compact than the scheme presented in this paper. It is noted that similar to the presented fault detection scheme, the delay overhead of these schemes is $4T_X$ comprising $3T_X$ for calculating the actual parity of block 5 plus one T_X for its comparison with the predicted parity of this block.

4.2 FPGA Implementations

In the following, we have implemented the S-boxes using look-up table (LUT) and the ones presented in [20], [23], and [27] which use polynomial basis (PB) representation in composite field. We have also implemented the fault detection schemes proposed in [2] and [3] which are based on the LUT implementation of the S-box and the one presented in [8] which is based on the S-box of [20]. Moreover, we have applied similar technique presented in [8] and derived formulations for the S-boxes of [23] and [27] to implement their fault detection schemes. All the schemes are implemented on the Xilinx Virtex[TM]-E and Virtex[TM]-II Pro FPGAs [18] and are compared with the one presented in this paper. For the implementations, VHDL has been used as the design-entry language for the Xilinx ISE[TM] version 9.1i. Furthermore, the synthesis is performed using XST[TM].

For the presented scheme in this paper, we have implemented the S-box presented in the previous section and the fault detection circuits, i.e., the equations (7)-(11). The results of the implementations have been tabulated in Table 5. In this table, the synthesis optimization goal is set as area with medium effort. The number of slices used for the implementations on the target devices and the minimum clock periods (delays) are presented in this table. It is noted that we have not used sub-pipelining in the implementations of the S-boxes using composite fields since the results are intended for finding the space complexity of the S-boxes and the overhead of their fault detection schemes.

Table 5. Comparisons of the implementation of the fault detection scheme of the S-box using normal basis (NB) with those of other schemes on Xilinx FPGAs

FPGA family	S-box		Slice			Delay (ns)		
(Device)	Structure	FDS	Original	FDS	Overhead[a]	Original	FDS	Overhead[a]
	LUT	[2]	88	188	113.6%	6.280	8.621	37.3%
	LUT	[3]	88	206	134.1%[b]	6.280	8.242	31.2%
Virtex-E	PB [20]	[8]	33	42	27.3%	17.976	19.079	6.1%
(xcv50e-8)	PB [23]	Applied[c]	38	50	31.6%	15.875	17.077	7.8%
	PB [27]	Applied[c]	37	47	27.0%	19.133	19.912	4.1%
	NB	**This work**	**31**	**39**	**25.8%**	**16.517**	**17.360**	**5.1%**
	LUT	[2]	69	150	117.4%	3.826	5.398	41.0%
	LUT	[3]	69	159	130.4%[b]	3.826	4.287	12.0%
Virtex-2 Pro	PB [20]	[8]	33	42	27.3%	9.375	10.317	10.0%
(xc2vp2-7)	PB [23]	Applied[c]	38	50	31.6%	8.285	9.582	15.7%
	PB [27]	Applied[c]	37	47	27.0%	9.986	10.832	8.4%
	NB	**This work**	**31**	**39**	**25.8%**	**9.339**	**10.026**	**9.8%**

[a] Overhead=$\frac{FDS-original}{original} \times 100$.

[b] The high area overhead is because of using two blocks of 256×9 memory cells to generate the predicted parity bit and the 8-bit output of the S-box [3].

[c] We have applied the technique proposed in [8] to derive the predicted parities for the 5 blocks of the S-boxes presented in [23] and [27].

The results of the comparison of the presented fault detection scheme for the S-box using normal basis with those of the other schemes have also been presented in Table 5. Using pipelined distributed memories, we have implemented the fault detection scheme presented in [2], which is based on using redundant units for the S-box of table look-ups. Furthermore, the fault detection scheme proposed in [3] is implemented. This scheme uses 512×9 memory cells to generate the predicted parity bit and the 8-bit output of the S-box [3]. The results in Table 5 show that for both of these schemes the area overhead is more than 100%. We have also implemented the fault detection scheme presented in [8] which uses the original S-box proposed in [20]. This S-box uses the polynomial basis representation in composite field. Our implementations show that the implementation of [20] is more area-efficient on FPGAs than the ones presented in [23] and [27]. However, the one presented in [23] is the fastest one compared to [20] and [27]. Moreover, we have applied the fault detection schemes presented in [8] to the S-boxes in [23] and [27]. Those fault detection schemes have also been implemented and the implementation results are also shown in this table.

As seen in bold faces in the table, the presented S-box is the most compact one among the other S-boxes with and without the fault detection scheme. It is interesting to note that the least area required for the S-box implementation using normal basis on FPGAs complies with the least gate count reported in [12] for such a composite field. Moreover, except for the scheme in [27], the post place and route timing overhead of the presented scheme is less than the other schemes. It is interesting to note that the presented scheme has less delay for the fault detection S-box compared to the scheme for [27]. This delay can overlap the computation time of the next transformation in the AES encryption.

5   Conclusions

In this paper, we have presented a high performance parity-based concurrent fault detection scheme of the S-box using normal basis for the advanced encryption standard. We have exhaustively searched for the least complex S-box as well as its fault detection circuit and have presented closed formulations for the parity predictions of each block of the S-box. We have implemented a number of proposed S-boxes and their fault detection schemes from the literature on FPGAs and compared them with the one presented here. Our FPGA implementations using area optimized syntheses show that the S-box using normal basis is more compact than the one using polynomial basis. Moreover, the cost of the FPGA implementation of the presented fault detection scheme is 25.8% slice overhead with negligible timing delay. It is noted that similar parity-based fault detection scheme can be obtained for the inverse S-box in the AES decryption.

Acknowledgments

The authors would like to thank the reviewers of CHES 2008 for their comments. This work has been supported by an NSERC Discovery grant awarded to A. Reyhani-Masoleh.

References

1. Federal Information Processing Standards Publication 197, Advanced Encryption Standard (AES), NIST (2001),
   http://csrc.nist.gov/publications/fips/fips197/fips-197.pdf
2. Karri, R., Wu, K., Mishra, P., Yongkook, K.: Fault-based Side-Channel Cryptanalysis Tolerant Rijndael Symmetric Block Cipher Architecture. In: DFT 2001, pp. 418–426. IEEE Computer Society Press, San Francisco (2001)
3. Bertoni, G., Breveglieri, L., Koren, I., Maistri, P., Piuri, V.: Error Analysis and Detection Procedures for a Hardware Implementation of the Advanced Encryption Standard. IEEE Trans. on Computers, special issue on Cryptographic Hardware and Embedded Systems 52(4), 492–505 (2003)
4. Bertoni, G., Breveglieri, L., Koren, I.: An Efficient Hardware-based Fault Diagnosis Scheme for AES: Performances and Cost. In: DFT 2004, pp. 130–138. IEEE Computer Society Press, Cannes (2004)
5. Breveglieri, L., Koren, I.: Maistri: Incorporating Error Detection and Online Reconfiguration into a Regular Architecture for the Advanced Encryption Standard. In: DFT 2005, pp. 72–80. IEEE Computer Society Press, Monterey (2005)
6. Karpovsky, M., Kulikowski, K.J., Taubin, A.: Differential Fault Analysis Attack Resistant Architectures for the Advanced Encryption Standard. In: Quisquater, J.J., Paradinas, P., Deswarte, Y., Abou El Kalam, A. (eds.) CARDIS 2004, vol. 153, pp. 177–192. Kluwer, Toulouse (2004)

7. Yen, C.H., Wu, B.F.: Simple Error Detection Methods for Hardware Implementation of Advanced Encryption Standard. IEEE Trans. on Computers 55(6), 720–731 (2006)
8. Mozaffari-Kermani, M., Reyhani-Masoleh, A.: Parity-based Fault Detection Architecture of S-box for Advanced Encryption Standard. In: DFT 2006, pp. 572–580. IEEE Computer Society Press, Arlington (2006)
9. Canright, D.: A Very Compact Rijndael S-box. Technical Report: NPS-MA-05-001, Naval Postgraduate School (2005)
10. Hodjat, A., Verbauwhede, I.: Area-Throughput Trade-Offs for Fully Pipelined 30 to 70 Gbits/s AES Processors. IEEE Trans. on Computers 55(4), 366–372 (2006)
11. Satoh, A., Morioka, S., Takano, K., Munetoh, S.: A Compact Rijndael Hardware Architecture with S-Box Optimization. In: Boyd, C. (ed.) ASIACRYPT 2001. LNCS, vol. 2248, pp. 239–254. Springer, Heidelberg (2001)
12. Canright, D.: A Very Compact S-Box for AES. In: Rao, J.R., Sunar, B. (eds.) CHES 2005. LNCS, vol. 3659, pp. 441–455. Springer, Heidelberg (2005)
13. Cardarilli, G.C., Ottavi, M., Pontarelli, S., Re, M., Salsano, A.: Fault Localization, Error Correction, and Graceful Degradation in Radix 2 Signed Digit-based Adders. IEEE Trans. on Computers 55(5), 534–540 (2006)
14. Cardarilli, G.C., Pontarelli, S., Re, M., Salsano, A.: A Self Checking Reed Solomon Encoder: Design and Analysis. In: DFT 2005, pp. 111–119. IEEE Computer Society Press, Monterey (2005)
15. Nicolaidis, M.: Carry Checking/Parity Prediction Adders and ALUs. IEEE Trans. on VLSI Systems. 11(1), 121–128 (2003)
16. Monnet, Y., Renaudin, M., Leveugle, R.: Designing Resistant Circuits against Malicious Faults Injection Using Asynchronous Logic. IEEE Trans. on Computers 55(9), 1104–1115 (2006)
17. Zhang, X., Parhi, K.K.: On the Optimum Constructions of Composite Field for the AES Algorithm. IEEE Trans. on Circuits and Systems II: Express Briefs 53(10), 1153–1157 (2006)
18. Xilinx, http://www.xilinx.com/
19. Zimmermann, R., Fichtner, W.: Low-power Logic Styles: CMOS versus Pass-transistor Logic. IEEE Journal of Solid-State Circuits 32(7), 1079–1090 (1997)
20. Zhang, X., Parhi, K.K.: High-Speed VLSI Architectures for the AES Algorithm. IEEE Trans. on VLSI Systems. 12(9), 957–967 (2004)
21. Morioka, S., Satoh, A.: An Optimized S-Box Circuit Architecture for Low Power AES Design. In: Kaliski Jr., B.S., Koç, Ç.K., Paar, C. (eds.) CHES 2002. LNCS, vol. 2523, pp. 172–186. Springer, Heidelberg (2003)
22. Standaert, F.X., Rouvroy, G., Quisquater, J.J., Legat, J.D.: Efficient Implementation of Rijndael Encryption in Reconfigurable Hardware: Improvements and Design Tradeoffs. In: D.Walter, C., Koç, Ç.K., Paar, C. (eds.) CHES 2003. LNCS, vol. 2779, pp. 334–350. Springer, Heidelberg (2003)
23. Wolkerstorfer, J., Oswald, E., Lamberger, M.: An ASIC Implementation of the AES SBoxes. In: Preneel, B. (ed.) CT-RSA 2002. LNCS, vol. 2271, pp. 67–78. Springer, Heidelberg (2002)
24. Trichina, E.: Combinational Logic Design for AES Subbyte Transformation on Masked Data. In: Cryptology eprint archive: Report 2003/236, IACR, Report 2003/236 (2003), http://eprint.iacr.org/
25. Mangard, S., Aigner, M., Dominikus, S.: A Highly Regular and Scalable AES Hardware Architecture. IEEE Trans. on Computers. 52(4), 483–491 (2003)

26. Mangard, S., Pramstaller, N., Oswald, E.: Successfully Attacking Masked AES Hardware Implementations. In: Rao, J.R., Sunar, B. (eds.) CHES 2005. LNCS, vol. 3659, pp. 157–171. Springer, Heidelberg (2005)
27. Mentens, N., Batina, L., Preneel, B., Verbauwhede, I.: A Systematic Evaluation of Compact Hardware Implementations for the Rijndael S-Box. In: Menezes, A. (ed.) CT-RSA 2005. LNCS, vol. 3376, pp. 323–333. Springer, Heidelberg (2005)

Appendix A: Proofs

Proof of Lemma 1. According to Fig. 2a, for the inputs $\Lambda = (\Lambda_1, \Lambda_0)$ and $\Delta = (\Delta_1, \Delta_0)$, the two-bit result of the multiplication in $GF(2^2)$, $\Pi = (\Pi_1, \Pi_0)$, can be derived as $\Pi_1 = \Delta_1\Lambda_0 + \Delta_0\Lambda_1 + \Delta_0\Lambda_0$ and $\Pi_0 = \Delta_1\Lambda_0 + \Delta_0\Lambda_1 + \Delta_1\Lambda_1$. Furthermore, multiplication by two possible values of Φ, i.e., $\Phi = w^2 = \{10\}_2$ and $\Phi = w = \{01\}_2$, can be obtained by putting $\Delta = \Phi$. Then, we have $\Pi_1 = \Lambda_0$ and $\Pi_0 = \Lambda_1 + \Lambda_0$ for $\Phi = w^2 = \{10\}_2$ and $\Pi_1 = \Lambda_1 + \Lambda_0$ and $\Pi_0 = \Lambda_1$ for $\Phi = w = \{01\}_2$. Consequently, one can derive the coordinates of π according to Fig. 2a and these discussions for the operations in the multiplication $GF(2^4)$. Therefore, for $\Phi = w^2 = \{10\}_2$ we have

$$\pi_3 = \lambda_3(\delta_3 + \delta_1 + \delta_0) + \lambda_2(\delta_1 + \delta_2) + \lambda_1(\delta_3 + \delta_2 + \delta_1 + \delta_0) + \lambda_0(\delta_3 + \delta_1),$$
$$\pi_2 = \lambda_3(\delta_2 + \delta_1) + \lambda_2(\delta_3 + \delta_2 + \delta_0) + \lambda_1(\delta_3 + \delta_1) + \lambda_0(\delta_2 + \delta_0),$$
$$\pi_1 = \lambda_3(\delta_3 + \delta_2 + \delta_1 + \delta_0) + \lambda_2(\delta_3 + \delta_1) + \lambda_1(\delta_3 + \delta_2 + \delta_1) + \lambda_0(\delta_3 + \delta_0), \quad (12)$$
$$\pi_0 = \lambda_3(\delta_3 + \delta_1) + \lambda_2(\delta_2 + \delta_0) + \lambda_1(\delta_3 + \delta_0) + \lambda_0(\delta_2 + \delta_1 + \delta_0).$$

Also, for $\Phi = w = \{01\}_2$ we have the result as

$$\pi_3 = \lambda_3(\delta_3 + \delta_2 + \delta_1) + \lambda_2(\delta_3 + \delta_0) + \lambda_1(\delta_3 + \delta_1) + \lambda_0(\delta_2 + \delta_0),$$
$$\pi_2 = \lambda_3(\delta_3 + \delta_0) + \lambda_2(\delta_2 + \delta_1 + \delta_0) + \lambda_1(\delta_2 + \delta_0) + \lambda_0(\delta_3 + \delta_2 + \delta_1 + \delta_0),$$
$$\pi_1 = \lambda_3(\delta_3 + \delta_1) + \lambda_2(\delta_2 + \delta_0) + \lambda_1(\delta_3 + \delta_1 + \delta_0) + \lambda_0(\delta_2 + \delta_1), \quad (13)$$
$$\pi_0 = \lambda_3(\delta_2 + \delta_0) + \lambda_2(\delta_3 + \delta_2 + \delta_1 + \delta_0) + \lambda_1(\delta_2 + \delta_1) + \lambda_0(\delta_3 + \delta_2 + \delta_0).$$

Modulo-2 adding the coordinates of (12) or (13) gives (3) and the proof is complete. In addition, another proof can be obtained by observing Fig. 2a and noting that the output of the multiplication by Φ is added to both of the results, i.e., it is added to both (π_3, π_2) and (π_1, π_0). Therefore, it is canceled in finding the predicted parity.   □

Proof of Lemma 2. Considering the fact that $\hat{P}_{b2} = \hat{P}_{(\eta_h + \eta_l)^2\nu} + \hat{P}_{\eta_h\eta_l}$, one can use Lemma 1 to obtain $\hat{P}_{\eta_h\eta_l}$ independent of the values of ν and Φ. However, $\hat{P}_{(\eta_h + \eta_l)^2\nu}$ depends on the elements ν and Φ. This is because of having squaring in $GF(2^4)$, i.e., $(\eta_h + \eta_l)^2$, and also a multiplication by ν to obtain $\hat{P}_{(\eta_h + \eta_l)^2\nu}$. Therefore, the predicted parity of block 2 is also dependent on these values and the proof is complete.   □

Proof of Lemma 3. One can use Lemma 1 to obtain $\hat{P}_{(\eta_h + \eta_l)^2\nu}$ and $\hat{P}_{\eta_h\eta_l}$ in $\hat{P}_{b2} = \hat{P}_{(\eta_h + \eta_l)^2\nu} + \hat{P}_{\eta_h\eta_l}$. $\hat{P}_{\eta_h\eta_l}$ can be easily found using Lemma 1. Furthermore, using Lemma 1 with the inputs being $\lambda = (\eta_h + \eta_l)^2$ and $\delta = \nu$ one can obtain $\hat{P}_{(\eta_h+\eta_l)^2\nu}$. Noting that the possible values for Φ are $\Phi = w^2 = \{10\}_2$ and $\Phi = w = \{01\}_2$, one can find the corresponding possible $(\eta_h + \eta_l)^2$ using (12) and (13). This is achieved by putting both inputs in (12) or (13) as $\eta_h + \eta_l$. Then, for $\Phi = w^2 = \{10\}_2$ we have

$$
\begin{aligned}
(\eta_h + \eta_l)^2 =& (\eta_7 + \eta_6 + \eta_5 + \eta_3 + \eta_2 + \eta_1, \eta_6 + \eta_5 + \eta_4 + \eta_2 + \eta_1 + \eta_0, \\
& \eta_7 + \eta_5 + \eta_4 + \eta_3 + \eta_1 + \eta_0, \eta_7 + \eta_6 + \eta_4 + \eta_3 + \eta_2 + \eta_0), \quad (14)
\end{aligned}
$$

and for $\Phi = w = \{01\}_2$ we have

$$
\begin{aligned}
(\eta_h + \eta_l)^2 =& (\eta_7 + \eta_5 + \eta_4 + \eta_3 + \eta_1 + \eta_0, \eta_7 + \eta_6 + \eta_4 + \eta_3 + \eta_2 + \eta_0, \\
& \eta_7 + \eta_6 + \eta_5 + \eta_3 + \eta_2 + \eta_1, \eta_6 + \eta_5 + \eta_4 + \eta_2 + \eta_1 + \eta_0). \quad (15)
\end{aligned}
$$

One can obtain the predicted parities of block 2, i.e., $\hat{P}_{b2} = \hat{P}_{(\eta_h+\eta_l)^2\nu} + \hat{P}_{\eta_h\eta_l}$, for all the possible combinations of ν and Φ. The results are presented in Table 2. $\quad\square$

Proof of Theorem 1. According to Fig. 2b, $\hat{P}_\theta = \hat{P}_{\Upsilon^{-1}\gamma_h} + \hat{P}_{\Upsilon^{-1}\gamma_l} = \hat{P}_{\Upsilon^{-1}(\gamma_h+\gamma_l)}$. Then, according to the predicted parity of the multiplication in $GF(2^2)$ in the proof of Lemma 1, we have $\hat{P}_{\Upsilon^{-1}(\gamma_h+\gamma_l)} = \Upsilon_1^{-1}(\gamma_3+\gamma_1)+\Upsilon_0^{-1}(\gamma_2+\gamma_0)$. Moreover, considering the fact that the inversion in $GF(2^2)$ is free, i.e., $\Upsilon^{-1} = (\Upsilon_0, \Upsilon_1)$, we reach $\hat{P}_\theta = \Upsilon_0(\gamma_3 + \gamma_1) + \Upsilon_1(\gamma_2 + \gamma_0)$. Then, according to the formulations for the multiplication in $GF(2^2)$ and knowing that the squaring in $GF(2^2)$ is free, finding the coordinates of Υ for two values of Φ is straightforward and the proof is complete. $\quad\square$

RSA with CRT: A New Cost-Effective Solution to Thwart Fault Attacks

David Vigilant

Cryptography Engineering, Gemalto Security Labs
david.vigilant@gemalto.com

Abstract. Fault attacks as introduced by Bellcore in 1996 are still a major threat toward cryptographic products supporting RSA signatures. Most often on embedded devices, the public exponent is unknown, turning resistance to fault attacks into an intricate problem. Over the past few years, several techniques for secure implementations have been published, all of which suffering from inadequacy with the constraints faced by embedded platforms. In this paper, we introduce a novel countermeasure mechanism against fault attacks in RSA signature generation. In the restricted context of security devices where execution time, memory consumption, personalization management and code size are strong constraints, our countermeasure is simply applicable with a low computational complexity. Our method extends to all cryptosystems based on modular exponentiation.

Keywords: Bellcore attack, Chinese Remainder Theorem, Fault attacks, RSA, Software countermeasure, Modular exponentiation.

1 Introduction

1.1 Restricted Context

Throughout the paper, we will be considering constrained embedded architectures on which one seeks to simultaneously optimize the following:

Execution Time. The secure RSA-CRT signature computation has to be performed in reasonable time. Without giving concrete bounds, the time overhead added by the countermeasure must remain negligible compared to the whole RSA signature calculation. This is of prime importance for micro-controllers running under a clock frequency of only a few megahertz.

Memory Consumption. Countermeasures require extra RAM memory buffers to store security parameters. 2K RSA is now supported as a standard functionality and we impose that the whole memory consumption remains comprised between 1 and 2K bytes.

Personalization Management. The availability of input key parameters is very strict. Only the input message m, as well as the key elements p, q, d_p, d_q, i_q

E. Oswald and P. Rohatgi (Eds.): CHES 2008, LNCS 5154, pp. 130–145, 2008.

are known while performing the signature and no extra variable parameter can be stored in non-volatile memory. This constraint stems from mass-production requirements where the personalization of unusually formatted keys in the device is costly and no customizable key container is available in EEPROM nor Flash to store anything different from the classical RSA-CRT key sets [1].

Code Size. On micro-controllers that have little ROM, the code size will be of a great concern. The extra code size added by the countermeasure must remain negligible compared to the whole code size of the signature. To minimize the code, it is preferable to design a simple countermeasure based on already existing arithmetic bricks.

1.2   The Bellcore Attack and Related Countermeasures

Invasive attacks on a hardware device consist in disturbing its expected behavior and making it work abnormally in order to infer sensitive data. They were introduced in the late nineties. As the technological response of hardware manufacturers evolves, new hardware countermeasures are being added regularly. However it is widely believed that those can only be effective if combined with efficient software countermeasures. Embedded devices are especially exposed to this category of attacks since the attacker has the hardware fully available in hands. A typical example is the original Bellcore attack [2] which allows an attacker to retrieve the RSA private key given one faulty signature.

Since the discovery of the Bellcore attack, countermeasures have been proposed by the research community. In 1997, Shamir proposed an elegant countermeasure [3] assuming that the private exponent d is known when running an RSA signature generation in CRT mode. In practice, however, this parameter is hardly available. Aumüller et al. [4] in 2002, Blömer et al. [5] in 2003, Joye and Ciet [6] and Giraud [7] in 2005, and Kim and Quisquater [8] in 2007 also proposed CRT secure implementations of RSA. All these countermeasures have a dramatic impact either on execution time, memory consumption or personalization management constraints. As an example, Aumüller et al. set out an efficient countermeasure [4] in 2002 using a small prime on which evaluating Euler's totient function is trivial. We will see in the sequel that, on the one hand, this countermeasure gives good performances. On the other hand, the selection of a random prime constitutes a real disadvantage.

This paper presents a simple alternative countermeasure thwarting fault attacks on RSA with CRT. Compared to prior techniques, our countermeasure is cost-effective regarding all considered constraints.

In Section 2, we make a brief review of the Bellcore attack and we show the disadvantages of previous propositions in the defined context. Our secure exponentiation algorithm and its application to RSA in the CRT mode is shown in Section 3. We then analyze its security under a fault model described in Section 4, where brief estimates in terms of time execution, memory consumption, personalization management and code size are undertaken. Finally Section 5 concludes this paper.

2   Related Work

2.1   RSA-CRT System

RSA was introduced in 1977 by Rivest, Shamir and Adleman [9]. In the so-called straightforward mode, (N, e) is the RSA public key and (N, d) the RSA private key such that $N = pq$, where p and q are large prime integers, $\gcd((p-1), e) = \gcd((q-1), e) = 1$ and $d = e^{-1} \bmod (p-1)(q-1)$. The RSA signature of a message $m < N$ is given by $S = m^d \bmod N$.

As the computing power of crypto-enabled architectures increases, RSA key sizes inflate overtime. 2K RSA is now a standard functionality. It is a strong constraint on embedded devices as processors have little RAM memory and run under a clock frequency of a few megahertz. RSA is more efficient in Chinese Remainder Theorem mode than in straightforward mode. The RSA-CRT domain is composed of an RSA public key (N, e) and an RSA private key (p, q, d_p, d_q, i_q) where $N = pq$, p and q are large prime integers, $\gcd((p-1), e) = \gcd((q-1), e) = 1$, $d_p = e^{-1} \bmod (p-1)$, $d_q = e^{-1} \bmod (q-1)$ and $i_q = q^{-1} \bmod p$. As it handles data with half the RSA modulus size, RSA with CRT is theoretically about four times faster and is therefore better suited to embedded devices. The RSA signature in CRT mode is described in Figure 1.

Input: message m, key (p, q, d_p, d_q, i_q)
Output: signature $m^d \in \mathbb{Z}_N$

$S_p = m^{d_p} \bmod p$
$S_q = m^{d_q} \bmod q$
$S = S_q + q \cdot (i_q \cdot (S_p - S_q) \bmod p)$
return (S)

Fig. 1. Naive CRT implementation of RSA

2.2   The Bellcore Attack against RSA with CRT

In 1996, the Bellcore Institute introduced a differential fault attack [2] which is still weakening the RSA-CRT signature security today. On embedded platforms, this attack is usually considered as "easy" since the attacker has full access to the device. Disturbing the calculation of either $S_p = m^{d_p} \bmod p$ or $S_q = m^{d_q} \bmod q$ can be achieved in ways such as voltage glitches, laser or temperature variation. Once the precise disturbance is obtained the attack succeeds, and allows an attacker to retrieve the RSA prime factors with a single gcd calculation. By construction, $S = S_q + q \cdot (i_q \cdot (S_p - S_q) \bmod p) = S_p + p \cdot (i_p \cdot (S_q - S_p) \bmod q)$. Noting S the correct signature and $\tilde{S}$ the faulty signature where either S_p or S_q (but not both) is incorrect for the same input message, $\gcd(S - \tilde{S}, N)$ is either q or p. A standard improvement of the Bellcore attack [10] leads to retrieving the factorization of N without the genuine signature by calculating $\gcd((\tilde{S}^e - m)$ mod $N, N) \in \{p, q\}$. Thus, the RSA private elements p and q are recovered and, as a consequence, the whole RSA-CRT private key is recovered.

2.3   Previous Countermeasures

Shamir's Method and Generalizations. One year after the discovery of the Bellcore attack, Shamir proposed an elegant countermeasure [3] where the method consists in computing $S_p^* = m^d$ mod pr and $S_q^* = m^d$ mod qr separately and in checking the consistency of S_p^* and S_q^* by testing whether $S_p^* = S_q^*$ mod r. A more efficient variant suggests to choose r prime and reduce d modulo $(p-1)(r-1)$ and $(q-1)(r-1)$. However, requiring the RSA straightforward-mode private exponent d, while performing an RSA signature generation in CRT mode, is unpractical since the key material is given in CRT format [1]. This parameter is most often not known and it would be unacceptable in our context to personalize d for each device. d could be computed from p, q, d_p and d_q, but as no key container would be available to store it, the computation of d would be mandatory at each RSA signature. As described in [11], this would lead to an unreasonable execution time overhead since we need to invert $(p-1)$ modulo $(q-1)$. Moreover, the CRT recombination is not protected at all since injecting a fault in i_q during the recombination allows the gcd attack.

Other improvements of Shamir's method which include the protection of the recombination were proposed later. As an example, Aumüller et al. [4] in 2002 proposed a careful implementation that also protects the CRT recombination. As opposed to Shamir's method, only d_p and d_q (and not d) are required. The algorithm is fully described in Figure 2. The proposal uses the efficient variant of the method where the parameter t is prime. Therefore the solution gives good performances. Compared to the naive CRT implementation of RSA, only two extra exponentiations modulo t and a few modular reductions are required. This solution presents a big disadvantage: the way the random prime is selected. Is it fixed or picked at random in a fixed table? (If this prime is recovered, does it make new flaws appear?). Is it different on each device? (This would impact personalization management). Is it generated at random for each signature? (This would lead to an unacceptable slowdown).

Interestingly, other solutions combining generalizations of Shamir's method and infective computation were proposed. The main idea of this combination consists in infecting the signature S whenever a fault is induced, such that the gcd attack is no more feasible on the faulty signature S', i.e. $S' \neq S$ mod p and $S' \neq S$ mod q. This concept was introduced in 2001 by Yen, Kim, Lim and Moon [12]. Later, Blömer, Otto and Seifert suggested a countermeasure [5] based on infective computation in 2003. Unfortunately, as for Shamir's original method, it requires the availability of d. Moreover, some parameters t_1 and t_2 required by the countermeasure have to satisfy quite strong properties: amongst the required properties, it is needed that: $\gcd(t_1, t_2) = \gcd(d, \varphi(t_1)) = \gcd(d, \varphi(t_2)) = 1$, where φ represents the Euler's totient function. t_1 and t_2 should normally be generated one time with the RSA key and the same values used throughout the

---

Input: message m, key (p, q, d_p, d_q, i_q)
32-bit prime integer t
Output: signature $m^d \in \mathbb{Z}_N$

$p' = pt$
$d_p' = d_p + random_1 \cdot (p - 1)$
$S_p' = m^{d_p'} \bmod p'$
if $(p' \bmod p \neq 0)$ **or** $(d_p' \bmod (p-1) \neq d_p)$ **then**
    return (error)
end if

$q' = qt$
$d_q' = d_q + random_2 \cdot (q - 1)$
$S_q' = m^{d_q'} \bmod q'$
if $(q' \bmod q \neq 0)$ **or** $(d_q' \bmod (q-1) \neq d_q)$ **then**
    return (error)
end if

$S_p = S_p' \bmod p$
$S_q = S_q' \bmod q$
$S = S_q + q \cdot (iq \cdot (S_p - S_q) \bmod p)$
if $(S - S_p' \neq 0 \bmod p)$ **or** $(S - S_q' \neq 0 \bmod q)$ **then**
    return (error)
end if

$S_{pt} = S_p' \bmod t$
$S_{qt} = S_q' \bmod t$
$d_{pt} = d_p' \bmod (t - 1)$
$d_{qt} = d_q' \bmod (t - 1)$
if $S_{pt}^{d_{qt}} \equiv S_{qt}^{d_{pt}} \bmod t$ **then**
    return (S)
else
    return (error)
end if

Fig. 2. Aumüller et al.'s secure CRT implementation of RSA

lifetime of the key, but t_1 and t_2 cannot be stored in this strong personalization context. Therefore the generation of t_1 and t_2 at each signature is not negligible. Compared to Aumüller et al.'s countermeasure, the BOS algorithm requires the generation of t_1 and t_2, two evaluations of the totient function φ on t_1 and t_2

and two inversions. This constitutes a real disadvantage in terms of simplicity and execution time.

Joye and Ciet also set out an elegant countermeasure based on infective computation [6]. Their generalization of Shamir's method is more efficient than BOS since, compared to Aumüller et al.'s countermeasure, one only needs to compute $\varphi(t_1)$ and $\varphi(t_2)$ for two random numbers t_1 and t_2. However, evaluations are not negligible as they imply a full factorization of t_1 and t_2. As a consequence, Joye and Ciet's countermeasure is not satisfactory in terms of execution time.

Last year, Kim and Quisquater proposed a CRT implementation of RSA defeating fault attacks and all known side-channel attacks [8], based on combination of Shamir's method and infective computation too. However, their proposed scheme requires either one inversion modulo N, or to update and store three unusually formatted parameters of size $|N|$, at each signature. As defined in Section 1.1, no key container is available in non-volatile memory and therefore, this solution becomes hardly acceptable in terms of execution time.

Giraud's Method. In 2005, Giraud proposed an efficient way [7] to protect RSA with CRT against fault attacks. His countermeasure is based on the properties of the Montgomery-ladder exponentiation algorithm [13]. Using this exponentiation algorithm, we compute successively (m^{d_p}, m^{d_p-1}) and (m^{d_q}, m^{d_q-1}). The Montgomery-Ladder algorithm infects both results whenever a fault is induced. The two recombined values S and $S' = m^{d_q-1} + q \cdot (i_q \cdot (m^{d_p-1} - m^{d_q-1}) \bmod p)$ are computed and the final verification $S = mS'$ is made. This solution is also SPA-safe. Unfortunately, the memory consumption is clearly prohibitive since it requires the storage of m, S_p, S_q, S'_p and S'_q in RAM during the calculation of S. For large RSA key sizes, this countermeasure seems hardly feasible in portable devices.

This shows that devising a CRT implementation of RSA that thwarts the Bellcore attack and meets the strong requirements of embedded systems remains a hard problem.

3   Our Secure RSA with CRT

3.1   Mathematical View

We consider a generic exponentiation of a message m to the exponent d modulo N. We perform the exponentiation modulo NR where R is for example a 64-bit random integer. We impose that N and R are coprime, i.e. $\gcd(N, R) = 1$.

Let α be such that $\begin{cases} \alpha \equiv 0 \bmod R \\ \alpha \equiv 1 \bmod N \end{cases}$ and β be such that $\begin{cases} \beta \equiv 1 \bmod R \\ \beta \equiv 0 \bmod N \end{cases}$

Applying the Chinese Remainder Theorem, we get the existence and the uniqueness of α and β in $\mathbb{Z}_{NR}$. We build these integers using Garner's algorithm:

$$\alpha = R \cdot (R^{-1} \bmod N) = 1 - [N \cdot (N^{-1} \bmod R)] \bmod NR$$

$$\beta = N \cdot (N^{-1} \bmod R) = 1 - [R \cdot (R^{-1} \bmod N)] \bmod NR$$

Considering R now such that $R = r^2$, where r is for example a 32-bit random number, we get the following result:

Theorem 1 (Exponentiation Identity in $\mathbb{Z}_{Nr^2}$). *Let N and r be integers such that $\gcd(N, r) = 1$, let $\beta = N \cdot (N^{-1} \bmod r^2)$ and $\alpha = 1 - \beta \bmod Nr^2$. For any $m \in \mathbb{Z}_{Nr^2}$ and for any $d \in \mathbb{N}^*$,*

$$(\alpha m + \beta \cdot (1 + r))^d = \alpha m^d + \beta \cdot (1 + dr) \bmod Nr^2$$

We refer to Appendix A for a proof and related mathematical details. Theorem 1 provides a way to perform a secure exponentiation in any ring $(\mathbb{Z}_N, +, \cdot)$, $N \in \mathbb{N}^*$.

3.2 A Secure Exponentiation Algorithm

We want to perform an exponentiation m^d of an integer $m < N$ over $\mathbb{Z}_N$. Pick a random integer r coprime with N and compute $\beta = N \cdot (N^{-1} \bmod r^2)$ and $\alpha = 1 - \beta \bmod Nr^2$. Applying Theorem 1, in order to exponentiate the element m and verify that no disturbance occurred, proceed as follows:

1. Compute $\hat{m} = \alpha m + \beta \cdot (1 + r) \bmod Nr^2$
2. Verify that $\hat{m} = m \bmod N$ and in case of inequality return "error detected"
3. Compute $S_r = \hat{m}^d \bmod Nr^2$ and $S = S_r \bmod N \ (= m^d \bmod N)$
4. Verify that $S_r = \alpha S + \beta \cdot (1 + dr) \bmod Nr^2$ and in case of inequality return "error detected"

By virtue of equalities $\beta = \beta^2$ and $\alpha\beta = 0$ in $\mathbb{Z}_{Nr^2}$ (by construction of α and β), the consistency of S_r can also be verified by any one of the following checks:

1. $\beta S_r = \beta \cdot (1 + dr) \bmod Nr^2$
2. $N \cdot (S_r - \beta \cdot (1 + dr)) = 0 \bmod Nr^2$
3. $S_r = 1 + dr \bmod r^2$

The optimal choice will depend on the hardware architecture and the algorithmic context. This countermeasure may be applied to any cryptographic scheme based on exponentiation in $(\mathbb{Z}_N, +, \cdot)$, $N \in \mathbb{N}^*$ (RSA [9], Diffie-Hellman key exchange [14], ElGamal [15], ...). Here we underline its application to the CRT implementation of RSA, where it appears to be particularly relevant.

3.3 Application to RSA with CRT

As p and q are prime, r is automatically coprime with p and q ,we define: $\beta_p = p \cdot (p^{-1} \bmod r^2)$, $\alpha_p = 1 - \beta_p \bmod pr^2$, $\beta_q = q \cdot (q^{-1} \bmod r^2)$ and $\alpha_q = 1 - \beta_q \bmod qr^2$. Figure 3 shows a possible application of our countermeasure to RSA with CRT. Exponentiations S_{pr} and S_{qr} are performed over $\mathbb{Z}_{pr^2}$ and $\mathbb{Z}_{qr^2}$. We verify that each exponentiation has not been disturbed by checking:

$$\beta_p S_{pr} = \beta_p \cdot (1 + d'_p r) \bmod pr^2 \quad \text{and} \quad \beta_q S_{qr} = \beta_q \cdot (1 + d'_q r) \bmod qr^2.$$

We pick up two 64-bit random integers R_3 and R_4. We then transform:

$$S_{pr} \text{ into } S'_p \text{ s.t. } \begin{cases} S'_p \equiv S_p \bmod p \\ S'_p \equiv R_3 \bmod r^2 \end{cases} \quad \text{and } S_{qr} \text{ into } S'_q \text{ s.t. } \begin{cases} S'_q \equiv S_q \bmod q \\ S'_q \equiv R_4 \bmod r^2 \end{cases}$$

Next, the resulting signature is recombined over $\mathbb{Z}_{Nr^2}$:

$$S = S'_q + q \cdot \left[i_q \cdot (S'_p - S'_q) \bmod pr^2 \right] \ ,$$

and, we perform the final consistency check:

$$S = R_4 + qi_q \cdot (R_3 - R_4) \bmod r^2 \ .$$

If all verifications are positive, we return the result $S \bmod N$.

3.4   Recommendations

The quality of the random number generator must be verified. We recommend to choose r such that $i_q \neq 0 \bmod r$. Indeed if $r \mid i_q$, the fault detection probability is reduced since the verification $N \cdot [S - R_4 - qi_q \cdot (R_3 - R_4)] \equiv 0 \bmod Nr^2$ is true even though the result of $S_p - S_q \bmod pr^2$ or q has been modified. So we recommend to renew the generation of the random r while r divides i_q. r must be as large as possible within the limits of the hardware architecture. Since we can see r as a security parameter, the larger it is, the higher the fault detection probability. Indeed, the highest success probability of an attack is $2^{-(|r|-1)} \ln 2$ (see Section 4.1 and Appendix B for more details). So we suggest that r should be at least a 32-bit random integer. Finally, we choose r with most significant bit equal to one, in order to optimize the security level. We also choose r odd in order to optimize the efficiency of the inversion.

4   Analysis

4.1   Resistance against Fault Attacks

The following fault model defines what an attacker is able to do by assumption. By disturbing the device, we mean that an attacker can:

- modify a value in memory obtaining a totally random result uncorrelated to the original value (as known as permanent fault);
- modify a value when it is handled in local registers, without modifying the global value in memory. The value handled obtained is fully random looking to the attacker and uncorrelated to the original value (as known as transient fault);

The design does not address attackers who can:

- modify the code execution. Processor instructions cannot be replaced or removed while executing code. Such an attacker might have the power to dump EEPROM and obtain the secret key;

Input: message m, key (p, q, d_p, d_q, i_q)
32-bit random integer r
64-bit random integers R_1, R_2, R_3 and R_4
Output: signature $m^d \in \mathbb{Z}_N$

$p' = pr^2$, $m_p = m \bmod p'$
$i_{pr} = p^{-1} \bmod r^2$, $\beta_p = p i_{pr}$ and $\alpha_p = 1 - \beta_p \bmod p'$
$\hat{m}_p = \alpha_p m_p + \beta_p \cdot (1 + r) \bmod p'$
if $(\hat{m}_p \neq m \bmod p)$ **then**
    return (error)
end if
$d'_p = d_p + [R_1 \cdot (p - 1)]$
$S_{pr} = \hat{m}_p^{d'_p} \bmod p'$
if $(\beta_p S_{pr} \neq \beta_p \cdot (1 + d'_p r) \bmod p')$ **or** $(d'_p \neq d_p \bmod (p - 1))$ **then**
    return (error)
end if
$S'_p = S_{pr} - \beta_p \cdot (1 + d'_p r - R_3)$

$q' = qr^2$, $m_q = m \bmod q'$
$i_{qr} = q^{-1} \bmod r^2$, $\beta_q = q i_{qr}$ and $\alpha_q = 1 - \beta_q \bmod q'$
$\hat{m}_q = \alpha_q m_q + \beta_q \cdot (1 + r) \bmod q'$
if $(\hat{m}_q \neq m \bmod q)$ **or** $(m_p \bmod r^2 \neq m_q \bmod r^2)$ **then**
    return (error)
end if
$d'_q = d_q + [R_2 \cdot (q - 1)]$
$S_{qr} = \hat{m}_q^{d'_q} \bmod q'$
if $(\beta_q S_{qr} \neq \beta_q \cdot (1 + d'_q r) \bmod q')$ **or** $(d'_q \neq d_q \bmod (q - 1))$ **then**
    return (error)
end if
$S'_q = S_{qr} - \beta_q \cdot (1 + d'_q r - R_4)$

$S = S'_q + q \cdot (i_q \cdot (S'_p - S'_q) \bmod p')$
$N = pq$
if $(N \cdot [S - R_4 - q i_q \cdot (R_3 - R_4)] \neq 0 \bmod Nr^2)$ **or** $(q i_q \neq 1 \bmod p)$
then
    return (error)
end if
return $(S \bmod N)$

Fig. 3. Our secure CRT implementation of RSA

- inject a permanent fault in the input elements, the message m as well as the key (p, q, d_p, d_q, i_q). We suppose that input elements are given along with an integrity value that can be verified whenever during the signature;
- Change the Boolean result of a conditional check. An expression "if $a = b$" has a result *true* or *false* that cannot be modified. We made here a compromise on the level of security. Indeed, contrary to some other methods based on infective computations, our design uses conditional checks. However it would be possible to replace these checks by unconditional infections of the computation.

We consider the CRT implementation of RSA described in Figure 3 and we assume the recommendations discussed in Section 3.4 have been followed. Noting $|a|$ the bit size of a and $\underline{a}$ the faulty value of a, let us review some fault scenarios and identify the associated success probabilities (probabilities are more detailed in Appendix B):

- Modifying p or r in a transient way during the calculation of p' or modifying p' in a permanent way before the check of $\hat{m}_p$ (The same holds for q'):
$\Pr[\hat{m}_{\underline{p}} = m \bmod p] \approx 2^{-(|p|-1)} \ln 2$
After the check of $\hat{m}_p$, if the permanent fault occurs only during the exponentiation:
$\Pr[\beta_p S_{\underline{pr}} = \beta_p \cdot (1 + d'_p r) \bmod p'] \approx 2^{-(|p'|-1)} \ln 2$
- Modifying m in a transient way during the calculation of $\hat{m}_p$ or modifying $\hat{m}_p$ in a permanent way before the check (The same holds for $\hat{m}_q$):
$\Pr[\hat{m}_{\underline{p}} = m \bmod p] \approx 2^{-(|p|-1)} \ln 2$
- Modifying m in a permanent way after the first exponentiation (we may also consider that m is associated with an integrity value that is verified):
$\Pr[m_{\underline{q}} \bmod r^2 = m_p \bmod r^2] \approx 2^{-(2|r|+1)}$
If the permanent fault occurs after the check of $\hat{m}_p$:
$\Pr[\beta_p S_{\underline{pr}} = \beta_p \cdot (1 + d'_p r) \bmod p'] = \Pr[\hat{m}_{\underline{p}} = 1 + r \bmod r^2] \approx 2^{-2|r|+1}$
- Modifying p or r^2 in a transient way during the calculation of i_{pr}, or modifying i_{pr} in a permanent way (The same holds for i_{qr}):
$\Pr[(\alpha_p m + \beta_p \cdot (1+r) = m \bmod p) \cap (\alpha_{\underline{p}} m + \beta_p \cdot (1+r) = (1+r) \bmod r^2)] = 0$
- Modifying p or i_{pr} in a transient way during the calculation of β_p or modifying β_p in a permanent way (The same holds for β_q):
$\Pr[(\alpha_p m + \beta_{\underline{p}} \cdot (1+r) = m \bmod p) \cap (\alpha_p m + \beta_{\underline{p}} \cdot (1+r) = (1+r) \bmod r^2)] = 0$
- Modifying β_p or p' in a transient way during the calculation of α_p or modifying α_p in a permanent way (The same holds for α_q):
$\Pr[\beta_p S_{\underline{pr}} = \beta_p \cdot (1 + d'_p r) \bmod p'] = \Pr[\alpha_{\underline{p}} = 0 \bmod r^2] \approx 2^{-2|r|+1}$
- Modifying $(p - 1)$ or d_p in a transient way during the calculation of d'_p or modifying d'_p in a permanent way (The same holds for d'_q):
$\Pr[d'_{\underline{p}} = d_p \bmod (p - 1)] \approx 2^{-(|p|-1)} \ln 2$
- Modifying d'_p in a transient way during the computation of S_{pr} (The same holds for S_{qr}):
$\Pr[\beta_p S_{\underline{pr}} = \beta_p \cdot (1 + d'_p r) \bmod p'] = \Pr[d'_{\underline{p}} = d'_p \bmod r] \approx 2^{-(|r|-1)} \ln 2$

- Modifying $\hat{m}_p$ or p' in a transient way during the computation of S_{pr} (The same holds for S_{qr}):
  $$\Pr[\beta_p \underline{S_{pr}} = \beta_p \cdot (1 + d'_p r) \bmod p'] = \Pr[\hat{m}_p = 1 + r \bmod r^2] \approx 2^{-2|r|+1}$$
- Modifying S_{pr}, $\beta_p \cdot (1 + d'_p r)$, R_3 or p' in a transient way during the computation of S'_p, or modifying S'_p in a permanent way (The same holds for S'_q):
  $$\Pr[S - R_4 - qi_q \cdot (R_3 - R_4) = 0 \bmod r^2] \approx 2^{-2|r|+1}$$
- Modifying S'_p, S'_q, p', q, i_q or S'_q in a transient way during the recombination:
  $$\Pr[N \cdot (S - R_4 - qi_q \cdot (R_3 - R_4)) = 0 \bmod Nr^2] \approx 2^{-2|r|+1}$$

4.2   Side-Channel Analysis

Although side-channel analysis is not studied in this paper, the design should be combined with adapted extra countermeasures against side-channel attacks.

4.3   Performance Analysis

Execution Time. The most expensive steps are the two inversions. They are performed on parameters with length twice the length of r. Noting $i_{pr0} = p^{-1} \bmod r$ and $i_{qr0} = q^{-1} \bmod r$, we make use of tricks to compute i_{pr} and i_{qr} from i_{pr0} and i_{qr0}. Indeed let $p = p_0 + p_1 r \bmod r^2$ and $i_{pr1} = [-i_0 p_1 - (i_0 p_0 - 1)] \cdot i_0 \bmod r$. Then $i_{pr} = r i_{pr1} + i_{pr0}$ (The same holds for i_{qr}). Thus, only two inversions modulo r are needed to compute i_{pr} and i_{qr}. If r is for example a 32-bit value and implementation is carried out on a 32-bit chip architecture, an SPA-safe extended binary gcd algorithm can be implemented very efficiently since loops of the algorithm would be composed of comparisons, shifts, subtractions and additions on 32-bit single precision data. In this context, the execution time added by our countermeasure would be clearly less costly than Aumüller et al.'s countermeasure [4]. On smaller micro-controllers, execution time will depend on the hardware architecture, but a good approximate being that the two inversions can be considered at most as costly as two exponentiations modulo t (if $|t| = |r|$). Our proposal is therefore more efficient than Joye and Ciet's solution [6] where two extra totient calculations are needed. We can also consider that our algorithm is about as efficient as Giraud's countermeasure [7], if our exponentiation algorithm only has the property that an attacker cannot distinguish squarings from multiplications. In the case of RSA with CRT where the exponents are masked, the exponentiation algorithm could be unbalanced contrary to Montgomery-Ladder algorithm [13]. If we suppose that the modulus and the exponent are randomized by a 64-bit random integer, we perform about $\lfloor \frac{|p|}{2} \rfloor - 96$ and $\lfloor \frac{|q|}{2} \rfloor - 96$ fewer modular multiplications for each exponentiation, but with larger operands. As an example, if the implementation is carried out on a 32-bit architecture, one Montgomery modular multiplication with two operands of length k 32-bit words, theoretically requires $2k(k + 1)$ single-precision multiplications. Thus, one Montgomery-Ladder exponentiation requires about $128k^2(k+1)$ single-precision multiplications with clear data, versus $96(k + 2)^2(k + 3)$ for a classical exponentiation with randomized data. As a consequence, for p and q greater than about 640 bits, our algorithm would be slightly more efficient than Giraud's one. Under this size, it would be the opposite.

Memory Consumption. Our countermeasure requires about as much memory as Aumüller et al.'s [4] and Joye and Ciet's implementation [6]. Obviously, it requires far less memory than Giraud's proposal [7] where memory consumption is a real disadvantage. We can consider in Figure 3 that β_p, β_q are not kept in RAM during the calculations of S'_p and S'_q since i_{pr} and i_{qr} can be stored on the stack. β_p and β_q can be calculated "on-the-fly" when needed. In the same way for the value m_p, only $m_p \bmod r^2$ can be stored on the stack. The instant when memory consumption is the highest occurs during the recombination (as in a classical RSA-CRT signature), except that S'_p, respectively S'_q, have length $|p| + 2|r|$, and $|q| + 2|r|$. The final result has length $|N| + 2|r|$. Some crypto-processors are not able to perform the final verification $(S - R_4 - qi_q \cdot (R_3 - R_4)) \cdot N \equiv 0 \bmod Nr^2$ if N is a 2K integer, since the co-processor register size may be limited to 2K. In this case, the final verification can be replaced with $S - R_4 - qi_q \cdot (R_3 - R_4) \equiv 0 \bmod r^2$.

Personalization Management. The proposed implementation only requires the usual parameters needed for the computation, the input message m and the classical RSA-CRT key set (p, q, d_p, d_q, i_q).

Code Size. The countermeasure is mainly based on arithmetic operations already developed for the RSA-CRT signature. Only the modular inversion, which is also based on classical arithmetic operations, should be implemented. The code of the modular inversion is often contained in products that supply the RSA signature as they supply the RSA key generation too. Even if the code of modular inversion must be added, this leads to an acceptable code size overhead.

5   Conclusion

This paper presents an original algorithm which computes secure exponentiations in an arbitrary integer ring $(\mathbb{Z}_N, +, \cdot)$ where $N \in \mathbb{N}^*$. Our countermeasure mechanism can be applied to secure any cryptosystem requiring exponentiations in rings or finite fields of integers, such as Diffie-Hellman key exchange [14], El Gamal decryption [15], RSA in straightforward mode [9], Schnorr [16], DSA [17], KCDSA [18] and so forth. However, it is especially relevant in the case of RSA with CRT where it constitutes an efficient defense line against Bellcore attack.

Reviewing related work on CRT implementation of RSA and considering simultaneously all practical constraints faced by cryptographic devices, our solution matches all desirable requirements.

Although here side-channel attacks have not been studied, our CRT implementation of RSA can be simply associated with appropriate countermeasures against simple and differential side-channel attacks.

Acknowledgments. The author wishes to thank Pascal Paillier, Mathieu Chartier and the CHES2008 reviewers for helpful remarks on the preliminary version of this paper.

References

1. Sun Microsystems Inc.: Javacard 2.2.2 - application programming interface. Technical report (2006)
2. Boneh, D., DeMillo, R.A., Lipton, R.J.: On the importance of checking cryptographic protocols for faults. In: Fumy, W. (ed.) EUROCRYPT 1997. LNCS, vol. 1233, pp. 37–51. Springer, Heidelberg (1997)
3. Shamir, A.: Method and apparatus for protecting public key schemes from timing and fault attacks, U.S. Patent Number 5,991,415 (also presented at the rump session of EUROCRYPT 1997) (November 1999)
4. Aumüller, C., Bier, P., Fischer, W., Hofreiter, P., Seifert, J.P.: Fault attacks on rsa with crt: Concrete results and practical countermeasures. In: Kaliski Jr., B.S., Koç, Ç.K., Paar, C. (eds.) CHES 2002. LNCS, vol. 2523, pp. 260–275. Springer, Heidelberg (2003)
5. Blömer, J., Otto, M., Seifert, J.P.: A new crt-rsa algorithm secure against bellcore attacks. In: CCS 2003: Proceedings of the 10th ACM conference on Computer and communications security, pp. 311–320. ACM, New York (2003)
6. Joye, M., Ciet, M.: Practical fault countermeasures for chinese remaindering based rsa. In: Breveglieri, L., Koren, I. (eds.) 2nd Workshop on Fault Diagnosis and Tolerance in Cryptography - FDTC 2005 (2005)
7. Giraud, C.: Fault resistant rsa implementation. In: Breveglieri, L., Koren, I. (eds.) 2nd Workshop on Fault Diagnosis and Tolerance in Cryptography — FDTC 2005, pp. 142–151 (2005)
8. Kim, C.H., Quisquater, J.J.: How can we overcome both side channel analysis and fault attacks on rsa-crt? In: Breveglieri, L., Gueron, S., Koren, I., Naccache, D., Seifert, J.P. (eds.) FDTC, pp. 21–29 (2007)
9. Rivest, R.L., Shamir, A., Adelman, L.M.: A method for obtaining digital signatures and public-key cryptosystems. Technical Report MIT/LCS/TM-82 (1977)
10. Joye, M., Lenstra, A.K., Quisquater, J.J.: Chinese remaindering based cryptosystems in the presence of faults. Journal of Cryptology: the journal of the International Association for Cryptologic Research 12(4), 241–245 (1999)
11. Joye, M., Paillier, P.: Gcd-free algorithms for computing modular inverses. In: D.Walter, C., Koç, Ç.K., Paar, C. (eds.) CHES 2003. LNCS, vol. 2779, pp. 243–253. Springer, Heidelberg (2003)
12. Yen, S.M., Kim, S., Lim, S., Moon, S.: Rsa speedup with residue number system immune against hardware fault cryptanalysis. In: Kim, K.-c. (ed.) ICISC 2001. LNCS, vol. 2288, pp. 397–413. Springer, Heidelberg (2002)
13. Joye, M., Yen, S.: The montgomery powering ladder. In: Kaliski Jr., B.S., Koç, Ç.K., Paar, C. (eds.) CHES 2002. LNCS, vol. 2523, pp. 291–302. Springer, Heidelberg (2003)
14. Diffie, W., Hellman, M.E.: New directions in cryptography. IEEE Transactions on Information Theory IT-22(6), 644–654 (1976)
15. ElGamal, T.: A public-key cryptosystem and a signature scheme based on discrete logarithms. In: Blakely, G.R., Chaum, D. (eds.) CRYPTO 1984. LNCS, vol. 196, pp. 10–18. Springer, Heidelberg (1985)

16. Schnorr, C.P.: Efficient signature generation by smart cards. Journal of Cryptology 4(3), 161–174 (1991)
17. National Institute of Standards and Technology: Digital Standard Signature. Federal Information Processing Standards Publications 186 (1994)
18. Lim, C.H., Lee, P.J.: A study on the proposed korean digital signature algorithm. In: Ohta, K., Pei, D. (eds.) ASIACRYPT 1998. LNCS, vol. 1514, pp. 175–186. Springer, Heidelberg (1998)

A   Proof of Theorem 1

Claim. Let N and R be integers such that $\gcd(N, R) = 1$, let $\beta = (N \cdot (N^{-1} \bmod R))$ and $\alpha = 1 - \beta \bmod NR$. Then α and β are non zero elements verifying the following properties:

1. $\alpha^2 = \alpha \bmod NR$
2. $\beta^2 = \beta \bmod NR$
3. $\alpha\beta = 0 \bmod NR$ (α and β are zero divisors in $(\mathbb{Z}_{NR}, +, \cdot)$)

Proof. This trivially comes from the definition of α and β.

Lemma 1. *Let N and r be integers such that $\gcd(N, r) = 1$, let $\beta = N \cdot (N^{-1} \bmod r^2)$ and $\alpha = 1 - \beta \bmod Nr^2$. Then, for any $d \in \mathbb{N}^*$ and any pair $(A, B) \in (\mathbb{Z}_{Nr^2} \times \mathbb{Z}_{Nr^2})$:*

$$(\alpha A + \beta B)^d = \alpha A^d + \beta B^d \bmod Nr^2 \qquad (1)$$

Proof. Let us take $R = r^2$. Since $\alpha\beta = 0 \bmod Nr^2$, for any $d \in \mathbb{N}^*$ and for any $(A, B) \in (\mathbb{Z}_{Nr^2})^2$, we get:

$$(\alpha A + \beta B)^d = (\alpha A)^d + (\beta B)^d \bmod Nr^2 = \alpha A^d + \beta B^d \bmod Nr^2 \ ,$$

as $\alpha^d = \alpha$ and $\beta^d = \beta$ modulo Nr^2.

Lemma 2. *Let N and r be coprime integers and $\beta = N \cdot (N^{-1} \bmod r^2)$. For any $d \in \mathbb{N}^*$, we have:*

$$\beta \cdot (1 + r)^d = \beta \cdot (1 + dr) \bmod Nr^2 \qquad (2)$$

Proof. Since $\beta = 0 \bmod N$, the equation holds modulo N. It also holds modulo r^2 since $\beta = 1 \bmod r^2$ and for any $d \in \mathbb{N}^*$, $(1 + r)^d = 1 + dr \bmod r^2$. By Chinese remaindering, the equation therefore holds modulo Nr^2. □

Finally, combining Equations (1) and (2), we get the exponentiation identity of Theorem 1, for any $m \in \mathbb{Z}_{Nr^2}$ and for any $d \in \mathbb{N}^*$:

$$(\alpha m + \beta \cdot (1 + r))^d = \alpha m^d + \beta \cdot (1 + dr) \bmod Nr^2$$

B Details Concerning Success Probabilities of Fault Attacks

Let us consider the fault model defined in 4.1. Assume that the attacker modifies a value A $(A = B \bmod C)$ and obtains a random value $\underline{A}$ uncorrelated to A. We give here a generic expression of a success probability for passing the test $\underline{A} = B \bmod C$ where C is a t-bit integer. We force $2^{t-1} < C < 2^t$, $C = 1 \bmod 2$. According to our recommendations in Section 3.4, r is odd, its most significant bit is one and we can deduce the same property for p. We suppose that C is uniform. We note E the event that the fault is undetected, $\Pr[E]$ the total probability of E, $\Pr[E \mid C]$ the probability of E assuming C, $\Pr[c = C]$ the probability of taking an element c in the considered set S such that $c = C$. Since the random result obtained is uniformly distributed, we know that:

$$\Pr[E \mid C] = \frac{1}{C} \tag{3}$$

We want to compute $\Pr[E]$. Let $S = \{C \text{ s.t. } 2^{t-1} < C < 2^t \text{ and } C = 1 \bmod 2\}$. From the total probability Theorem, we have:

$$\Pr[E] = \sum_{C \in S} (\Pr[E \mid C] \cdot \Pr[c = C]) \tag{4}$$

Since C is uniform:

$$\Pr[c = C] = \frac{1}{|S|} \tag{5}$$

Replacing Identities (3) and (5) in Equation (4), we get:

$$\Pr[E] = \frac{1}{|S|} \cdot \sum_{C \in S} \frac{1}{C}$$

Let $\bar{S} = \{C \text{ s.t. } 2^{t-1} < C < 2^t \text{ and } C = 0 \bmod 2\}$, then:

$$\sum_{C \in S \cup \bar{S}} \frac{1}{C} = [\ln C]_{2^{t-1}}^{2^t} = \ln(2^t) - \ln(2^{t-1}) = t \ln 2 - (t-1) \ln 2 = \ln 2$$

Since, $|S| = |\bar{S}|$, we may approximate:

$$\Pr[E] = \frac{1}{|S|} \cdot \sum_{C \in S} \frac{1}{C} \approx \frac{1}{|S|} \cdot \frac{1}{2} \sum_{C \in S \cup \bar{S}} \frac{1}{C} = \frac{1}{|S|} \cdot \frac{\ln 2}{2}$$

Hence:

$$\Pr[E] \approx \frac{1}{|S|} \cdot \frac{ln2}{2} = \frac{1}{2^{t-2}} \cdot \frac{ln2}{2} = 2^{-(t-1)} \ln 2$$

This explains the probability values $2^{-(|p|-1)} \ln 2$, $2^{-(|p'|-1)} \ln 2$ and $2^{-(|r|-1)} \ln 2$.

Given the same C, we now assume that the attacker modifies a value A ($A = B \bmod C^2$) and obtains a random value $\underline{A}$ uncorrelated to A. We apply the same argument, we compute the success probability for passing the test $\underline{A} = B \bmod C^2$. In this case:

$$\Pr[E \mid C] = \frac{1}{C^2} \tag{6}$$

The Identity (5) still applies here. Hence, replacing Identities (5) and (6) in Equation (4):

$$\Pr[E] = \frac{1}{|S|} \cdot \sum_{C \in S} \frac{1}{C^2}$$

$$\sum_{C \in S \cup \bar{S}} \frac{1}{C^2} = \left[-\frac{1}{C} \right]_{2^{t-1}}^{2^t} = -\frac{1}{2^t} + \frac{1}{2^{t-1}} = -\frac{1}{2^t} + \frac{2}{2^t} = 2^{-t}$$

In the same way, we may approximate:

$$\Pr[E] = \frac{1}{|S|} \cdot \sum_{C \in S} \frac{1}{C^2} \approx \frac{1}{|S|} \cdot \frac{1}{2} \sum_{C \in S \cup \bar{S}} \frac{1}{C^2} = \frac{1}{|S|} \cdot \frac{1}{2^{t+1}}$$

And therefore:

$$\Pr[E] \approx \frac{1}{|S|} \cdot 2^{-(t+1)} = 2^{-(t-2)} \cdot 2^{-(t+1)} = 2^{-2t+1}$$

This leads to the probability value $2^{-(2|r|+1)}$.

A Design for a Physical RNG
with Robust Entropy Estimators

Wolfgang Killmann[1] and Werner Schindler[2]

[1] T-Systems ISS GmbH
Rabinstr. 8
53111 Bonn, Germany
Wolfgang.Killmann@t-systems.com
[2] Bundesamt für Sicherheit in der Informationstechnik (BSI)
Godesberger Allee 185–189
53175 Bonn, Germany
Werner.Schindler@bsi.bund.de

Abstract. We briefly address general aspects that reliable security evaluations of physical RNGs should consider. Then we discuss an efficient RNG design that is based on a pair of noisy diodes. The main contribution of this paper is the formulation and the analysis of the corresponding stochastic model which interestingly also fits to other RNG designs. We prove a theorem that provides tight lower bounds for the entropy per random bit, and we apply our results to a prototype of a particular physical RNG.

Keywords: Physical RNG, stochastic model, entropy.

1 Introduction

Many cryptographic mechanisms require random numbers, e.g. as session keys, signature parameters, ephemeral keys (DSA, ECDSA), zero-knowledge protocols, challenge response-protocols, nonces. Inappropriate RNGs may allow to break principally strong cryptosystems, e.g. if an adversary is able to determine session keys. *Ideal RNGs* generate random numbers that are uniformly distributed on their range and independent. An ideal RNG, however, is a mathematical construction (lastly a fiction). Following [11] (cf. [21] for further explanations) 'real-world' RNGs can be divided into two classes, which contain the *true RNGs* (TRNGs) and the *deterministic RNGs* (DRNGs; aka pseudo-random number generators), respectively. The TRNGs fall into two subclasses: *Physical TRNGs* use non-deterministic effects of electronic circuits (e.g. shot noise from Zener diodes, inherent semiconductor thermal noise, free running oscillators) or physical experiments (e.g., time between emissions of radioactive decay, quantum photon effects). *Non-physical non-deterministic RNGs* exploit non-deterministic events (e.g., system time, hard disk seek time, RAM content, user interaction). So-called *hybrid RNGs* combine design elements from both, TRNGs and DRNGs.

E. Oswald and P. Rohatgi (Eds.): CHES 2008, LNCS 5154, pp. 146–163, 2008.

Unlike for deterministic RNGs it seems hardly possible to specify approved designs for physical RNGs (in a strict sense) since security-relevant properties do not only depend on the generic design but also on its implementation. A designer of a physical RNG is faced with two challenges. At first he has to develop an appropriate design, and then he has to implement it carefully. The second task may be even more difficult, namely providing evidence that the generic RNG design and its implementation are indeed appropriate.

In the last years several designs of physical RNGs have been proposed [4, 5, 6, 7, 9] etc., and several evaluation guidances and standards were developed and became effective [1, 2, 11, 13, 17]. These documents define properties that strong RNGs should fulfil, and the evaluation guidances explain how these criteria shall be verfied. A comprehensive treatment of evaluation aspects for physical RNGs are given in [22].

In Section 2 we briefly address central aspects and goals that reliable security evaluations of physical RNGs should consider. In Section 3 we discuss an RNG design that exploits a pair of noisy diodes. Section 4 contains the main contribution of our paper. We formulate and analyze a stochastic model that describes this design and, interestingly, also fits to further RNG designs. In particular, we prove a theorem that allows to quantify a tight lower bound for the average entropy per random bit. We apply our results to a particular physical RNG where we derive lower entropy bounds per random bit that are very close to 1. Finally we explain a generic online test scheme that is tailored to RNG designs which belong to the analyzed stochastic model.

2 Security Evaluation of Physical RNGs: Fundamental Aspects

In this section we address central aspects that are relevant for security evaluations of physical RNGs. For a comprehensive treatment of this matter we refer the interested reader to [21, 22, 19].

2.1 Entropy

With regard to Section 4 we extend the definition of Shannon entropy to random variables with infinite range. More precisely, to a random variable X that assumes values in a countable (finite or infinite) set Ω (e.g. $\Omega = \mathbb{N}_0$) we assign the term

$$H(X) := - \sum_{\omega \in \Omega} \text{Prob}(X = \omega) \log_2(\text{Prob}(X = \omega)). \tag{1}$$

As usual, we set $0 \cdot \log_2(0) := 0$. Following the common convention we denote the Shannon entropy briefly as 'entropy' in the remainder.

Remark 1. (i) We point out that $H(X) \in [0, \infty]$ where $H(X) = \infty$ is possible for infinite Ω. The 'auxiliary' random variables $V_{(s')}$, which will be relevant in Section 4, yet have finite entropy for any $s' \in (0, \infty)$ (cf. [20], Lemma 2(ii)).

(ii) Random numbers that are generated by physical RNGs can usually be modelled by stationary stochastic processes (cf. Sect. 4). At least the internal random numbers (cf. Subsect. 2.2) typically assume values in $\Omega = \{0, 1\}$, and for all cases of practical relevance the Shannon entropy per internal random bit should be close to 1. Hence the Shannon entropy provides a sound estimate for the average guessing workload, justifying the use of the Shannon entropy for physical RNGs in place of the more conservative min-entropy. For physical RNGs it is usually much easier to compute the Shannon entropy than the min-entropy (cf. [21], Subsect. 5.2, for a more comprehensive treatment of this matter). We mention that it may be necessary to apply the min-entropy in place of the Shannon entropy in specific guessing problems with very imbalanced probability distributions (cf. [15]).

2.2   Central Definitions and Goals of a Security Evaluation

The core of a physical RNG is its *noise source*, which usually generates a time-continuous analog signal that is digitized after uniform time intervals. The digitized values are called *das random numbers* where 'das' abbreviates *digital analog signal*. The das-random numbers may be algorithmically postprocessed, giving the so-called *internal random numbers*. Algorithmic postprocessing may increase the entropy per bit, but only at cost of performance (data compression). If the entropy of the das-random numbers is sufficiently large the algorithmic postprocessing may be saved in favour of higher throughput. Online and tot tests shall detect non-tolerable weaknesses while the RNG is in operation. Upon external request the RNG outputs *external random numbers*.

The main part of a security evaluation considers the generic design and its implementation. The central goal is to quantify (at least a lower bound for) the entropy per random bit. Unfortunately, entropy cannot be measured as voltage or temperature. Instead, entropy is a property of random variables and not of observed realizations (here: random numbers). In particular, entropy cannot be guaranteed by passing a collection of statistical blackbox tests [14, 16] since typically even weak pseudorandom sequences pass these tests [19, 21, 22]. To quantify entropy one has to study the distribution of the random numbers, or more precisely, the distribution of the underlying random variables.

Definition 1. *Random variables are denoted with capital letters. Realizations of these random variables, i.e. values that are assumed by these random variables, are denoted by the respective small letters. For instance, the das random numbers $r_1, r_2, \ldots$ are interpreted as realizations of random variables $R_1, R_2, \ldots$. We denote the internal random numbers and the underlying random variables by $y_1, y_2, \ldots$ and $Y_1, Y_2, \ldots$, respectively.*

External random numbers are not under control of the RNG designer. Since the external random numbers are usually concatenations of the internal random numbers it is natural to focus on the *conditional entropy*

$$H(Y_{n+1} \mid Y_1 = y_1, \ldots, Y_n = y_n) \tag{2}$$

which corresponds to the real-life situation that an adversary knows a subsequence $y_1, y_2, \ldots, y_n$ of internal random numbers, e.g. due to openly transmitted challenges or session keys which the adversary received legitimately.

The random variables $R_1, R_2, \ldots$ describe the stochastic behaviour of the das random numbers. Their distribution clearly depends on the noise source and the digitization mechanism. Usually, it is not feasible to determine these distributions exactly. At least in a strict sense the exact distribution depends on the characteristics of the components of the particular noise source, and these characteristics may differ to some extent even for RNGs from the same production series. A sound security evaluation of a physical RNG should be based on a *stochastic model*.

Stochastic Model. Ideally, the stochastic model comprises a *family of distributions* that contains the true distribution of the internal random numbers. At least, the stochastic model should specify a family of probability distributions that contains the distribution of the das-random numbers or even merely of 'auxiliary' random variables *provided that these random variables enable the verification of a lower entropy bound for the internal random numbers*. We follow this approach in Sect. 4, for instance.

Example 1. (Repeated tossing of a single coin) Since coins have no memory it is reasonable to assume that the random variables R_j are independent and binomially $B(1, p)$-distributed with unknown parameter $p \in [0, 1]$, defining a one-parameter family of probability distributions. Given a particular coin the parameter p can be estimated by tossing the coin a large number of times. Substituting the gained estimate $\tilde{p}$ into the entropy formula yields an estimate for the entropy. The entropy of the internal random numbers depends on p and the algorithmic postprocessing (if there is any).

For 'real life' RNGs the stochastic model is usually more complicated than in Example 1, often depending on several parameters. For most RNG designs it is reasonable to assume that the sequence $R_1, R_2, \ldots$ is stationary (i.e. time-invariant; Definition 2), at least within time periods that are large compared to the output rate. Drifts of process parameters within the life cycle of the RNG (e.g. due to ageing effects) are not problematic if the distribution remains in the acceptable part of the specified class of distributions. In a first step we are interested in

$$H(R_{n+1} \mid R_1 = r_1, \ldots, R_n = r_n) \tag{3}$$

for any history $r_1, \ldots, r_n$, or at least in the average conditional entropy

$$H(R_{n+1} \mid R_1, \ldots, R_n). \tag{4}$$

For dependent random variables the calculation of (4) is in general easier than (3). At least if (4) is too small a suitable (data-compressing) postprocessing algorithm should be applied to the das random numbers that increases the average entropy per bit ([22], Sect. 5). (Of course, even if not necessarily needed, a strong cryptographic postprocessing algorithm with memeory may serve as an additional security anchor.)

Due to tolerances of components, ageing effects, a total breakdown of the noise source or (depending on the conditions of use) maybe active attacks the RNG may output considerably weaker random numbers than the RNG proto-types which were investigated in the lab. Online tests and tot tests ('total failure test') shall detect non-tolerable weaknesses while the RNG is in operation. Un-fortunately, there do not exist statistical tests that are universally strong for any RNG design. Instead, these tests should be tailored to the stochastic model of the das random numbers. The statistical tests may be supported by physical sensors. The second task of a security evaluation is thus to verify the effective-ness of the online and tot tests and the consequence of noise alarms [18, 19, 22]. We will briefly address relevant aspects in Section 6.

Remark 2. A reasonable stochastic model is the core of any CC (Common Cri-teria) evaluation with regard to the evaluation guidance AIS 31 [2, 13], which has been effective in Germany since 2001. We point out that besides physical RNGs with cryptographic postprocessing the international ISO norm [11] also permits physical RNGs without cryptographic postprocessing provided that a sound stochastic model confirms that the random numbers have enough entropy and that effective online tests are applied.

3   An RNG Design Based on Two Noisy Diodes

Figure 1 illustrates an RNG design that exploits two identical noisy diodes. (E.g.) Zener diodes have a reverse avalanched effect (depending on the diode type 3 - 4 Volt or about 10 V) and generate more than 1 mV noisy voltage with a frequency of about 10 MHz. The outlets of both diodes provide symmetrical input to an operational amplifier that amplifies the difference of the voltages. We point out that, depending on the implementation, the device and the conditions of use, a design with only one noisy diode may be more vulnerable to manipulations by active adversaries, e.g. by external electromagnetic fields. The circuit of the AC coupling, the negative feedback for the operational amplifier, the stabilizing mechanism for the power supply or compensating effects of temperature are omitted in the graphic. The output of the operational amplifier (with very high amplification rate) is fed into a Schmitt trigger. The mean voltage of the amplifier output signal is about the middle of the two threshold values of the Schmitt trigger. Due to the steep edges of the input and usage of the 0-1-upcrossings only the hysteresis effect should be negligible. Moreover, the proposed design only exploits 0-1-crossings. The output signal of the Schmitt trigger consists of zeros ('low') and ones ('high'). The time lengths of these signals is random.

Each 0-1 crossing (up-crossing) within the Schmitt trigger clocks an inter-mediate flip-flop. This flip-flop inverts the D-input of a second (final) flip-flop, which is latched by a clock after constant time intervals. The number of 0-1-crossings within the nth clock cycle gives the das random number r_n. Hence

$y_{n+1} = y_n \oplus r_{n+1} \pmod 2$ where y_n and y_{n+1} denote the internal random numbers in Step n and $n + 1$, respectively. (We mention that more efficient algorithmic postprocessing algorithms than the addition $\pmod 2$ may exist but this is outside the scope of this paper.)

Unlike for related designs that exploit both 0-1- and 1-0-crossings it is irrelevant whether the intervals between 0-1- and 1-0-crossings and the intervals between 1-0- and 0-1-crossings are identically distributed. This feature increases robustness at cost of halving the output rate.

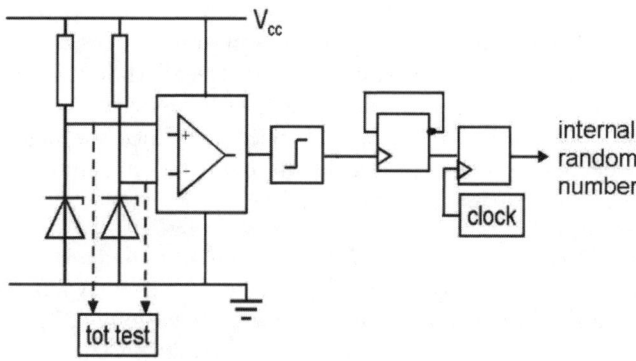

Fig. 1. RNG with two noisy diodes: generic design

The uncertainty on the number of switchings of the Schmitt trigger per time interval is crucial for the entropy of the random numbers. Hence the ratio beteen the cycle length of the clock and the average length between two consecutive 0-1-crossings should not be selected too small. If the distribution of the interval lengths changes considerably, causing a smaller or larger number of switchings within the particular clock cycles, this may have significant influence on the entropy per output bit. Online and tot test should detect such behaviour (cf. Subsect. 6). The tot test may separately check the generation of the noisy voltage for each diode in order to detect a total breakdown or abnormality of the noise.

4   Formulation and Analysis of the Stochastic Model

In this section we formulate and analyze a stochastic model for the RNG design discussed in the previous section. Interestingly, the same stochastic model fits to to other RNG designs as well (cf. Remark 3(ii), (iii)). Theorem 1 collects the main results.

In the following we assume that the analogue part of the noise source is in equilibrium state (since a sufficient amount of time has passed since the start of the RNG; a fraction of a second should suffice). We begin with the analysis of the das random numbers $r_0, r_1, \ldots$ at time $t = 0$. The internal random numbers $y_1, y_2, \ldots$ are latched at equidistant times $s_1 := s, \ldots, s_j := js, \ldots$ where $s > 0$

denotes the cycle length of the clock that latches the final flip-flop (cf. Fig. 1). Recall that the das random number r_n denotes the number of 0-1-switchings of the Schmitt trigger within the time interval $I_n := (s_{n-1}, s_n] = ((n-1)s, ns]$. Clearly

$$y_n \equiv y_{n-1} + r_n \equiv y_0 + r_1 + \cdots + r_n \pmod{2} \quad \text{for } n \geq 1 \tag{5}$$

where y_0 denotes the internal random number at time $t = 0$. Our goal is to determine a lower bound for

$$H(R_{n+1} \mid R_1, \ldots, R_n) \quad \text{and finally for} \quad H(Y_{n+1} \mid Y_0, Y_1, \ldots, Y_n), \tag{6}$$

the average conditional entropy per das-random number, resp. the average conditional entropy per internal random number. Recall that the second formula corresponds to the real-world situation where an adversary knows several internal random numbers $y_0, y_1, y_2, \ldots, y_n$ (cf. Sect. 2). Since the algorithmic post-processing is very elementary results on the das random numbers can directly be transferred to the internal random numbers.

Definition 2. *As usually, iid stands for 'independent and identically distributed'. A sequence of random variables $X_1, X_2, \ldots$ or $\ldots, X_{-1}, X_0, X_1, \ldots$ is called (strictly) stationary if for each integer $r \geq 1$ the distribution of $(X_{m+1}, \ldots, X_{m+r})$ does not depend on the shift parameter m. The generalized variance of the sequence $X_1, X_2, \ldots$ is defined as*

$$\sigma^2 = \mathrm{Var}(X_1) + 2 \sum_{i=2}^{\infty} E\left((X_1 - \mu)(X_i - \mu)\right). \tag{7}$$

The sequence $X_1, X_2, \ldots$ is called q-dependent if the vectors $(X_a, \ldots, X_b)$ and $(X_c, \ldots, X_d)$ are independent whenever $c - b > q$.

As usually, $N(\mu, \sigma^2)$ denotes a normal distribution with mean μ and variance σ^2. The cumulative distribution function of the standard normal distribution $N(0,1)$ is denoted with Φ, i.e. $\Phi(x) = \int_{-\infty}^{x} e^{-t^2/2} \, dt / \sqrt{2\pi}$ for $x \in \mathbb{R}$.

Stochastic Model. We interpret the lengths $t_1, t_2, \ldots$ of the time intervals between consecutive 0-1-switchings as realizations of a q-dependent stationary stochastic process $T_1, T_2, \ldots$. We set $\mu := E(T_1)$ and $\sigma_T^2 := \mathrm{Var}(T_1)$ while the generalized variance of $T_1, T_2, \ldots$ simplifies to

$$\sigma^2 = \sigma_T^2 + 2 \sum_{i=2}^{q+1} E\left((T_1 - \mu)(T_i - \mu)\right) \tag{8}$$

We assume $\sigma_T^2 > 0$ (otherwise the das-random numbers were deterministic), $E(|T_j|^3) < \infty$ (needed for the proof of Lemma 2(iii); cf. also Remark 3(iii)) and $\mathrm{Prob}(T_1 = 0) = 0$.

The term z_n denotes the index of the first 0-1-switching that follows after time $s_n = ns$ (i.e., when the clock latches the nth time) while $w_n := t_{z_n} - s_n$. That is, w_n equals the time span from s_n to the next 0-1-switching. In particular,

$w_0 + t_1 + \cdots + t_{z_n - 1} \leq s_n < w_0 + t_1 + \cdots + t_{z_n}$. Recall that the stochastic model of an RNG shall enable to determine (at least a lower bound for) the conditional entropy $H(Y_{n+1} \mid Y_0, \ldots, Y_n)$. This defines our central goal.

More abstract, the corresponding random variables can be described as follows:

$$T_1, T_2, \ldots \quad \text{are stationary} \tag{9}$$

$$R_n := Z_n - Z_{n-1} \quad \text{with} \tag{10}$$

$$Z_n := min_{m \in \mathbb{N}} \{W_0 + T_1 + T_2 + \ldots + T_m > s_n\} \tag{11}$$

Remark 3. (i) Relations (9) to (11) remain valid if we substitute the two noisy diodes by a single noisy diode.

(ii) We note that (9) to (11) also fits to a RNG design, which was introduced in [23] and later analyzed in [8,20]. This noise source consists of two independent ring oscillators. To simplify analysis we assumed $W_0 = 0$ in [20]. Since the ratios $(s_n - s_{n-1})/\mu$ and thus the das random numbers $r_1, r_2, \ldots$ were extremely large this simplification had little impact.

(iii) The assumption that the T_j are q-dependent may be relaxed as long as a version of the central limit theorem for dependent random variables remains valid (cf. Lemma 2(iii)).

(iv) Due to the nature of shot noise one may assume that q is very small, presumably $q \leq 1$ (cf. Sect. 5).

(v) In our context s should be selected considerably larger than μ so that at least one 0-1-switching should occur in each time interval $(sn, s(n + 1)]$ with overwhelming probability. Then z_n equals the index of the first 0-1-switching within this interval.

With regard to Remark 3(i), (ii) it should be profitable to study the system (9) to (11) under general (weak) assumptions as well as for specific conditions on the distribution of the T_j (e.g., for iid or Markovian T_j). Note, however, that although (9) to (11) fit to several RNG designs the distributions of the random variables $T_1, T_2, \ldots$ and, consequently, the distribution of $R_1, R_2, \ldots$ and $Y_1, Y_2, \ldots$ may be very different. Lemma 1 below considers the 'transfer' of the stationarity property.

Lemma 1. *(Stationarity Lemma) Let $\ldots, T'_{-1}, T'_0, T'_1, \ldots$ denote a doubly infinite sequence of stationary random variables with $\mathrm{Prob}(T'_j \in [0, s)) = 1$ and $\mathrm{Prob}(T'_j = 0) < 1$. Assume that the sequence $\ldots, S'_{-1}, S'_0, S'_1, \ldots$ fulfils $S'_{j+1} - S'_j \equiv T'_{j+1}(\mathrm{mod}\ s)$ for each integer j. Assume further that S'_J is uniformly distributed on $[0, s)$ and independent from the random variables $\ldots, T'_{-1}, T'_0, T'_1, \ldots$ for a particular integer J.*

(i) S'_j is uniformly distributed on $[0, s)$ for each integer j, and the random variables $\ldots, S'_{-1}, S'_0, S'_1, \ldots$ are stationary.

(ii) For $j \geq 1$ let z'_j denote the jth index $m > 0$ for which $S'_m < S'_{m-1}$, and $W'_j := S'_{z_j}$. For $R'_j = Z'_j - Z'_{j-1}$ the random vectors (W'_j, R'_j) and the random variables W'_j, R'_j and $Y' := f(R'_j)$ (with $f: \mathbb{R} \to \mathbb{R}$) are stationary.

Proof. For $k \geq 0$ trivially $S'_{J+k} \equiv S'_J + T'_{J+1} + \cdots + T'_{J+k} (\mathrm{mod}\, s)$, and the independence of S'_J and $T'_{J+1} + \cdots + T'_{J+k}$ proves the first assertion of (i). The case $k < 0$ can be handled analogously. We point out that the sequence $(S'_j - S'_{j-1})(\mathrm{mod}\, s) \equiv T'_j (\mathrm{mod}\, s)$ is stationary. We claim that S'_{J+j} and $(T'_i, \ldots, T'_k)$ are independent for any triple of integers (j, i, k) with $i \leq k$. Let $M := \{J + 1, \ldots, J+j, i, \ldots, k\}$ and assume $j \geq 0$ for the moment. Then $\mathrm{Prob}(S'_{J+j} \in A \mid T'_\tau = t'_\tau$ for all $\tau \in M\} = \mathrm{Prob}(S'_J + T'_{J+1} + \cdots + T'_{J+j} (\mathrm{mod}\, s) \in A \mid T'_\tau = t'_\tau$ for all $\tau \in M\} = \mathrm{Prob}(S_J \in (A - t'_{J+1} - \cdots - t'_{J+j})(\mathrm{mod}\, s)) = \mathrm{Prob}(S'_J \in A)$ for each Borel subset $A \subseteq [0, s)$ and any realizations $t'_{J+1}, \ldots, t'_{J+j}, t'_i, \ldots, t'_k$ since the random variables S'_J and $(T'_{J+1}, \ldots, T'_{J+j}, T'_i, \ldots, T'_k)$ are independent, and S_J is uniformly distributed on $[0, s)$. This proves the claim for $j \geq 0$. For $j \leq 0$ we have $S'_J \equiv S'_{J+j} + T_{J+j+1} + \cdots + T'_J (\mathrm{mod}\, s)$, and the claim can be shown analogously. Let k and j be fixed for the moment. By the preceding $\mathrm{Prob}(S'_{j+1}, (T'_{j+2}, \ldots, T'_{j+k}) \in A \times B) = \mathrm{Prob}(S'_{j+1} \in A)\mathrm{Prob}(T'_{j+2}, \ldots, T'_{j+k} \in B) = \mathrm{Prob}(S'_1 \in A)\mathrm{Prob}(T'_2, \ldots, T'_k \in B) = \mathrm{Prob}(S'_1, (T'_2, \ldots, T'_k) \in A \times B)$ for any Borel subsets $A \subseteq [0, s)$ and $B \subseteq [0, s)^{k-1}$. Hence $(S'_1, T'_2, \ldots, T'_k)$ and $(S'_{j+1}, T'_{j+2}, \ldots, T'_{j+k})$ are identically distributed. Let the diffeomorphism $\chi_k : [0, s)^k \to [0, s)^k$ be given by $\chi(x_1, \ldots, x_k) := (x_1, x_1 + x_2 (\mathrm{mod}\, s), \ldots, x_1 + \cdots + x_k (\mathrm{mod}\, s))$. Since $(S'_{j+1}, S'_{j+2}, \ldots, S'_{j+k}) = \chi_k(S'_{j+1}, T'_{j+2}, \ldots, T'_{j+k})$, the random vectors $(S'_1, S'_2, \ldots, S'_k)$ and $(S'_{j+1}, S'_{j+2}, \ldots, S'_{j+k})$ are identically distributed. Since j and k were arbitrary, this completes the proof of (i).

Let $j_1 > 0$ denote the smallest index for which $S'_{j_1} < S'_{j_1 - 1}$. Divide the random variables $\ldots, S'_{-1}, S'_0, S'_1, \ldots$ into increasing subsequences $\ldots, (\ldots, S'_{j_1 - 1})$, $(S'_{j_1}, \ldots, S'_{j_2 - 1}), (S'_{j_2}, \ldots), \ldots$ such that $S'_{j_m - 1} > S'_{j_m}$. (As $\mathrm{Prob}(T'_j = 0) < 1$ these subsequences are finite with probability 1.) Alternatively, these subsequences can be described by the sequence $(W'_j, R'_j)_{j \in Z}$ (and index j_0). For any $k \geq 1$, integers $r_1, \ldots, r_k \geq 1$ and subsets $A_1, \ldots, A_k \subseteq [0, s)$ the probability $\mathrm{Prob}((W'_{1+\tau}, R'_{1+\tau}) \in A_1 \times \{r_1\}, \ldots, (W'_{k+\tau}, R'_{k+\tau}) \in A_k \times \{r_k\})$ depends on the distribution of the $r := (r_1 + \cdots + r_k + 2)$-tuple $(S'_{j_1 - 1}, \ldots, S'_{j_1 + r - 2})$. Since the sequence $\ldots, (S'_1, \ldots, S'_r), (S'_2, \ldots, S'_{r+1}), \ldots$ is stationary the above probability is independent of τ. This proves the stationarity of $(W'_j, R'_j)_{j \in Z}$. The random variables W'_j, R'_j and Y'_j are functions of (W'_j, R'_j), which completes the proof of (ii).

Assumption 1. Unlike $\mathrm{Prob}(T'_j \geq s)$ in Lemma 1 the probability $\mathrm{Prob}(T_j \geq s)$ may be not 0 but negligible if $\mu \ll s$. It is reasonable to assume that for 'large' indices j the term $T_1 + \cdots + T_j (\mathrm{mod}\, s)$ is uniformly distributed on $[0, s)$ ($\to$ uniformity assumption on S'_j), and that $T_1, T_2, \ldots$ may be assumed to be stationary. Note that the intervals between the 0-1 switchings from the start of the RNG to time $t = 0$ can be described by random variables T_j with negative indices. The assumptions on the T_j seem to be natural and very mild, and with regard to Lemma 1 (and its proof) we assume in the following that besides the T_j also $(R_j)_{j \in \mathbb{N}}$, $(W_j)_{j \in \mathbb{N}_0}$, $(R_j (\mathrm{mod}\, 2))_{j \in \mathbb{N}}$ and finally $(Y_j)_{j \in \mathbb{N}}$ are stationary.

Definition 3. *The cumulative distribution functions of the random variables T_j and W_n are denoted by $G_T(\cdot)$ and $G_W(\cdot)$. For $u \in (0, \infty)$ the random variable*

$V_{(u)} := \inf \left\{ \tau \in \mathbb{N} \mid \sum_{j=1}^{\tau+1} T_j > u \right\} = \sup \left\{ \tau \in \mathbb{N} \mid \sum_{j=1}^{\tau} T_j \leq u \right\}$ *quantifies the number of 0-1-switchings in the interval* $[0, u]$ *if* $W_0 \equiv 0$.

Lemma 2 collects some useful properties that will be needed later. Note that (12) formally confirms the intuition that the knowledge of more random numbers should not weaken the adversary's position. We point out that (12) might become false without the stationarity property, namely when R_n (for what reasons ever!) is easier to guess than R_{n+1}.

Lemma 2

(i) $H(R_n \mid R_0, R_1, \ldots, R_{n-1}) \geq H(R_{n+1} \mid R_0, R_1, \ldots, R_n)$ *and*   (12)
$\qquad H(Y_n \mid Y_0, Y_1, \ldots, Y_{n-1}) \geq H(Y_{n+1} \mid Y_0, Y_1, \ldots, Y_n)$ *for all* $n \in \mathbb{N}$.

In particular, $\lim_{n \to \infty} H(R_{n+1} \mid R_1, \ldots, R_n)$ *and* $\lim_{n \to \infty} H(Y_{n+1} \mid Y_1, \ldots, Y_n)$
exist.
(ii) For $k \geq 1$ *we have*

$$\text{Prob}(V_{(u)} = k) = \text{Prob}\,(T_1 + \cdots + T_k \leq u) - \text{Prob}\,(T_1 + \cdots + T_{k+1} \leq u). \quad (13)$$

Further,

$$\text{Prob}(V_{(u)} = 0) = 1 - \text{Prob}\,(T_1 \leq u)\,, \quad \text{Prob}(V_{(u)} = \infty) = 0 \quad \text{and} \quad (14)$$
$$H(V_{(u)}) < \infty. \quad (15)$$

(iii) The distributions of the random variables $(\sum_{j=1}^{k} T_j - k\mu)/(\sqrt{k}\sigma)$ *tend to the standard normal distribution as* k *tends to infinity. In particular,*

$$\text{Prob}\left(\frac{T_1 + \cdots + T_k - k\mu}{\sqrt{k}\sigma} \leq x\right) \longrightarrow_{k \to \infty} \Phi(x). \quad (16)$$

for each $x \in \mathbb{R}$.
If the random variables $T_1, T_2, \ldots$ *are iid the condition* $E(|T_j|^3) < \infty$ *may be dropped, and in particular* $\sigma^2 = \sigma_T^2$
(iv) Let $u = v\mu$ *with* $v \gg 1$. *Then*

$$\text{Prob}\,(V_{(v\mu)} = k) \approx \Phi\left(\frac{v-k}{\sqrt{k}} \cdot \frac{\mu}{\sigma}\right) - \Phi\left(\frac{v-(k+1)}{\sqrt{k+1}} \cdot \frac{\mu}{\sigma}\right) \quad \text{for } k \geq 1 \quad (17)$$
$$\text{Prob}\,(V_{(v\mu)} = 0) \approx 1 - \Phi\left((v-1)\frac{\mu}{\sigma}\right). \quad (18)$$

The distribution of the random variable $V_{(v\mu)}$ *(or more precisely, its approximation given by (17) and (18)) depends only on the ratios* μ/σ *and* $u/\mu = v$ *but not on the absolute values of the parameters* $\mu, \sigma^2, u = v\mu$. *The mass of* $V_{(v\mu)}$ *is essentially concentrated on those* k's *with* $k \approx v$. *Unless* k *is very small the interval*

$$J_k := \left[\frac{v-(k+1)}{\sqrt{k+1}} \cdot \frac{\mu}{\sigma}, \frac{v-k}{\sqrt{k}} \cdot \frac{\mu}{\sigma}\right) \quad \text{has length} \approx \frac{\mu}{\sigma} \cdot \frac{v+k}{2k^{3/2}} \quad (19)$$

(v) (iid case) If the random variables $T_1, T_2, \ldots$ are iid then

$$\text{Prob}(W_n \leq x) = \frac{1}{\mu} \int_0^x (1 - G_T(u)) \, du =: G_W(x). \qquad (20)$$

(Note that if $\text{Prob}(W_n \leq x)$' is substituted by $\lim_{n \to \infty} \text{Prob}(W_n \leq x)$ assertion (20) remains valid even if the sequence $(W_n)_{n \in \mathbb{N}_0}$ is not stationary.) If $G_T(\cdot)$ is continuous (or equivalently, if $\text{Prob}(T_1 = y) = 0$ for all $y \in [0, \infty)$) then $G_W(\cdot)$ has density $g(x) := (1 - G_T(x))/\mu$.

Proof. By Assumption 1 the random variables R_j and Y_j are stationary. Hence, (e.g.)

$$H(Y_n \mid Y_1, \ldots, Y_{n-1}) = H(Y_{n+1} \mid Y_2, \ldots, Y_n) \geq H(Y_{n+1} \mid Y_1, \ldots, Y_n),$$

and since entropy is non-negative this verifies (i). Assertions (ii), (iii) and the first assertions of (iv) follow from Lemma 1 and Lemma 2(ii) in [20]. We merely mention that (iii) applies a version of the Central Limit Theorem for dependent random variables that was proved in [12]. The remaining assertions in (iv) demand elementary but careful computations. (Note that $(\sqrt{k+1} - \sqrt{k})(\sqrt{k+1} + \sqrt{k}) = 1$ and $\sqrt{k} \approx \sqrt{k+1}$.) The remark in brackets and (20) were shown in [10] (4.10), and the last assertion of (v) follows by differentiation.

Under mild regularity assumptions on the $T_1, T_2, \ldots$ plausible heuristic arguments indicate that

$$H(Y_{n+1} \mid Y_1, \ldots, Y_n) \geq \min\{H(V_{(s-u)}(\text{mod} 2)) \mid u \in [0, \mu + a\sigma)\} G_W(\mu + a\sigma). \qquad (21)$$

even for moderate parameter $a > 0$. We point out that for $n = 0$ or if the T_j are iid (21) is valid for any $a \geq 0$. Due to the lack of space we omit details. Theorem 1 collects the main results of this paper. Theorem 1 focuses on the entropy of the internal random numbers. Cancelling the term '(mod 2)' in (21), (24), (25) and (26) yields entropy estimates for the das random numbers. Equation (29) can be used to compute the autocovariance function and the autocorrelation function of the random variables $R_1, R_2, \ldots$.

Theorem 1. *(i)*

$$\text{Prob}(R_{n+1} = k) \approx \int_0^s \text{Prob}(V_{(s-u)} = k - 1) \, G_W(du) \text{ for } k \in \mathbb{N}_0 \qquad (22)$$

$$\text{Prob}(R_{n+1}(\text{mod } 2)) \approx \int_0^s \text{Prob}(V_{(s-u)} \equiv k - 1(\text{mod } 2)) \, G_W(du) \text{ for } k \in \{0, 1\} (23)$$

$$H(R_{n+1}(\text{mod } 2)) \geq H(R_{n+1}(\text{mod } 2) \mid W_n) \approx \int_0^s H(V_{(s-u)}(\text{mod } 2)) \, G_W(du) (24)$$

with equality for iid random variables T_j.
(ii) Substituting the integrands in (22) to (24) by $\text{Prob}(V_{(s-u)} = k-1 \mid W_0 = u)$, $\text{Prob}(V_{(s-u)} \equiv k - 1(\text{mod } 2) \mid W_0 = u)$, and $H(V_{(s-u)}(\text{mod } 2) \mid W_0 = u)$, resp.,

provides equality also for the general case. For dependent T_j these conditional terms implicitly define conditions on the random variables $T_1, T_2, \ldots$ and thus on $V_{(s-u)}$.

(iii) (iid case) If the sequence $T_1, T_2, \ldots$ is iid

$$H(Y_{n+1} \mid Y_0, \ldots, Y_n) \geq \int_0^s H(V_{(s-u)}(\mathrm{mod}\,2))\, G_W(du) \quad \text{for all } n \in \mathbb{N}. \quad (25)$$

If $G_T(\cdot)$ is continuous the right-hand side of (25) reads

$$\int_0^s H(V_{(s-u)}(\mathrm{mod}\,2))\, \frac{1}{\mu}(1 - G_T(u))\, du. \quad (26)$$

(iv) $E((R_1 + \cdots + R_j)^k) = \int_0^{js} E((V_{(js-u)} + 1)^k \mid W_0 = u)\, G_W(du) \quad (27)$

$$\approx \int_0^{js} E((V_{(js-u)} + 1)^k)\, G_W(du) \quad \text{for each } k \in \mathbb{N}\,(28)$$

with equality for iid random variables T_j. The stationarity of the R_j implies

$$E((R_1 + \ldots + R_j)^2) = j E(R_1^2) + 2 \sum_{i=2}^{j} (j + 1 - i) E(R_1 R_i) \quad (29)$$

Proof. By stationarity $(R_{n+1} \mid W_n = u)$ is distributed as $(V_{(s-w_n)} + 1 \mid W_0 = u)$, and thus $(R_{n+1}(\mathrm{mod}\,2) \mid W_n = u)$ as $(V_{(s-w_n)} + 1(\mathrm{mod}\,2) \mid W_0 = u)$. Formulae (22) to (24) and (ii) follow immediately from the stationarity of the random variables $R_1, R_2, \ldots$ and $W_1, W_2, \ldots$. Within this proof ν_n and $\nu_{n|y_0,\ldots,y_n}$ denote the distribution of W_n, resp. of the conditional random variable $(W_n \mid Y_0 = y_0, \ldots, Y_n = y_n)$. In this notation

$$H(Y_{n+1} \mid Y_0 = y_0, \ldots, Y_n = y_n) \geq H(Y_{n+1} \mid Y_0 = y_0, \ldots, Y_n = y_n, W_n) \quad (30)$$

$$= \int_0^{\infty} H(Y_{n+1} \mid Y_j = y_j, j \leq n; W_n = u)\, \nu_{n|y_0,\ldots,y_n}(du)$$

If the T_j are iid for all $n \in \mathbb{N}$ the vector $(T_{z_n+1}, T_{z_n+1+2}, \ldots)$ is distributed as $(T_1, T_2, \ldots)$, regardless of u and the history $y_0, \ldots, y_n$. In particular, since $H(Y_{n+1} \mid \cdot) = H(Y_{n+1} - Y_n(\mathrm{mod}\,2) \mid \cdot) = H(R_{n+1}(\mathrm{mod}\,2) \mid \cdot)$ the integrand of the right-hand side of (30) only depends on u. More precisely, for any $y_0, \ldots, y_n$ the integrand equals $H(V_{(s-u)} + 1(\mathrm{mod}\,2)) = H(V_{(s-u)}(\mathrm{mod}\,2))$. Altogether

$$H(Y_{n+1} \mid Y_0, \ldots, Y_n, W_n)$$

$$= \sum_{y_0,\ldots,y_n \in \{0,1\}} \mathrm{Prob}(Y_0 = y_0, \ldots, Y_n = y_n) \int_0^{\infty} H(V_{(s-u)}(\mathrm{mod}\,2))\, \nu_{n|y_1,\ldots,y_n}(du)$$

$$= \int_0^{\infty} H(V_{(s-u)}(\mathrm{mod}\,2))\, \nu_n(du) = \int_0^s H(V_{(s-u)}(\mathrm{mod}\,2))\, G_W(du)$$

in the iid case. The last equation follows from the fact that $\mathrm{Prob}(W_{n+1} > s) = 1 - G_W(s) \approx 0$ since $s >> \mu$. This proves (25), and (26) follows immediately from Lemma 2(v). The sum $R_1 + \cdots + R_n = Z_n - Z_0$ is distributed as $V_{(ns-W_0)} + 1$, which proves (27). For iid T_j the history (expressed by W_0) is irrelevant, yielding (28). The stationarity of the T_j finally yields (29).

Remark 4. (i) (robustness) Formulae (24), (25) and (26) (with and without '(mod 2)') provide entropy estimators for the das random numbers and the internal random numbers that seem to be robust against at least moderate deviations of the distribution of the random variables $T_1, T_2, \ldots$. In fact, by (17) and (18) the entropy $H(V_{(s-u)})$ essentially depends on the ratios $(s - u)/\mu$ and μ/σ. The density $(1 - G_T(\cdot))/\mu$ in (26) is monotonically decreasing, which additionally supports robustness.

(ii) (approximation errors) Theorem 1 tacitly applies the normal approximations (17) and (18). For large ratios s/μ this should not cause serious problems unless very small 'entropy defects' $\epsilon := 1 - H(Y_{n+1} \mid Y_1, \ldots, Y_n)$ shall be verified (cf. Sect. 5); for small ratios s/μ one should be careful anyway. The convergence rate of the central limit theorem and thus the meaning of 'small' depends on the distribution of the random variables $T_1, T_2, \ldots$. Fortunately, for the conditional entropy $H(Y_{n+1} \mid Y_1, \ldots, Y_n)$ the sum $\sum_{k \equiv 0(\bmod 2)} \mathrm{Prob}(V_{(s-u)} = k)$ is relevant so that one may expect that approximation errors in Lemma 2(iv) cancel out each other to a large extent.

To be on the safe side (especially for very small ϵ) one may study the approximation errors in (17) and / or in $H(V_{(s-u)}(\bmod 2))$ for the relevant distribution. For this purpose stochastic simulations may be applied where pseudorandom numbers t_j are generated according to the distribution of the random variables $T_1, T_2, \ldots$. A similar approach can be followed with experimental data from measurements (cf. (iii)). If the T_j are independent one may operate with Fourier transforms. Concerning (17) it seems to be reasonable to concentrate on integers k in a vicinity of s/μ, resp. for $(s - u)/\mu$ with small u.

(iii) Theorem 1 considers the stationary distribution of the random variables W_j but it can also be adjusted to experimental data in a straight-forward way. To apply (22), (23), (24), (25) and (28) one uses a sequence of measured time spans $t_1, t_2, \ldots$ between consecutive 0-1-crossings to obtain an empirical distribution for the stationary distribution of $W_1, W_2, \ldots$ (tacitly assuming ergodicity). The formulae are then applied with this empirical distribution in place of G_W. For Theorem 1(ii) and (27) (relevant for dependent T_j's) the procedure is similar but more costly since only subsequences of $t_1, t_2, \ldots$ can be used to obtain the conditional distributions $(\cdot \mid u)$. Of course, in this empirical approach statistical deviations add to the approximation errors mentioned in (ii).

Remark 5. In [4] a design of a physical RNG is investigated that also exploits the switchings of a comparator. The amplified noise is also modelled as a stationary stochastic process, and the autocorrelation function of the random numbers are computed. We mention that unlike the present paper reference [4] yet considers idealized assumptions (Gaussian white noise etc.), which clearly simplify analysis. [4] exploits the number of comparator switchings within fixed time periods for an online test (cf. Sect. 6). For an introduction into the field of stationary stochastic processes we refer the interested reader e.g. to [24].

5   Practical Experiments

As pointed out in Remark 3 relations (9) to (11) fit to various RNG designs. The distribution of the random variables T_j and thus of R_j and Y_j depend on the particular design but also on the concrete implementation. To get 'real' das random numbers we performed measurements on a prototype of a particular physical RNG (cf. Fig. 2 and Acknowledgement) for which the design left from the first flip-flop coincides with the generic design discussed in Section 3.

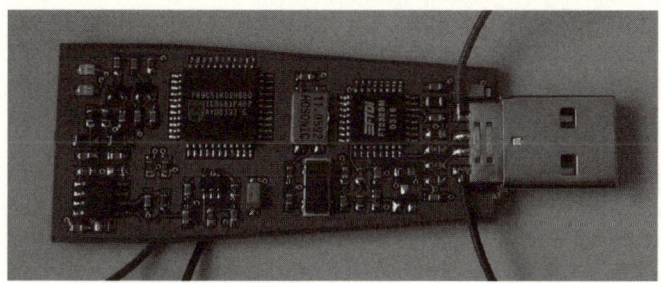

Fig. 2. RNG prototype used for measurements

Maximum-Likelihood tests indicate that the one-dimensional empirical distribution of the times between consecutive 0-1-crossings can be well approximated by a Gamma distribution with shape parameter 3.0949 and rate 0.0240. In Fig. 3 the circles show the percentiles of the empirical distribution, and the curve shows the percentile of Gamma distribution with the indicated parameters.

We applied Theorem 1 (more precisely, (25) and (28) and (29)) to a set of $\approx 620\,000$ measured time spans $t_1, t_2, \ldots$ between consecutive 0-1-crossings to obtain Table 1 (cf. Remark 4(iii)). We estimated $\mu = E(T_1)$ by $\widetilde{\mu} = 128.85 ns$ and $\mathrm{Var}(T_1)$ by $\widetilde{\sigma}_T^2 = 5314.0$. The estimates for the autocovariances $\mathrm{cov}(T_j, T_{j+\tau}) = E(T_j T_{j+\tau}) - E(T_j)E(T_{j+\tau})$ were $-2.08, -10.08, 5.56, 3.80$ and -1.18 for the shift parameters $\tau = 1, \ldots, 5$. Compared to $\widetilde{\sigma}_T^2$ these values are very small, and experiments with various measurement sets support the conjecture that the true autocovariances are essentially 0. We point out that also contingency tests did not contradict the hypothesis that the random variables T_j and T_{j+1} are independent (97 from 99 tests on significance level 0.01 were passed).

The correlation coefficient of random variables X and Y is given by $\mathrm{corr}(X, Y) = \mathrm{cov}(X, Y)/\sqrt{\mathrm{Var}(X)\mathrm{Var}(Y)}$. We applied Theorem 1 directly to the experimental data and to their Gamma approximation (Table 1). Especially for the small clock lengths $s = 7.497\widetilde{\mu}$ and $s = 9.996\widetilde{\mu}$ the exact conditional entropy $H(Y_{n+1} \mid Y_1, \ldots, Y_n)$ might differ somewhat from the estimates in Table 1

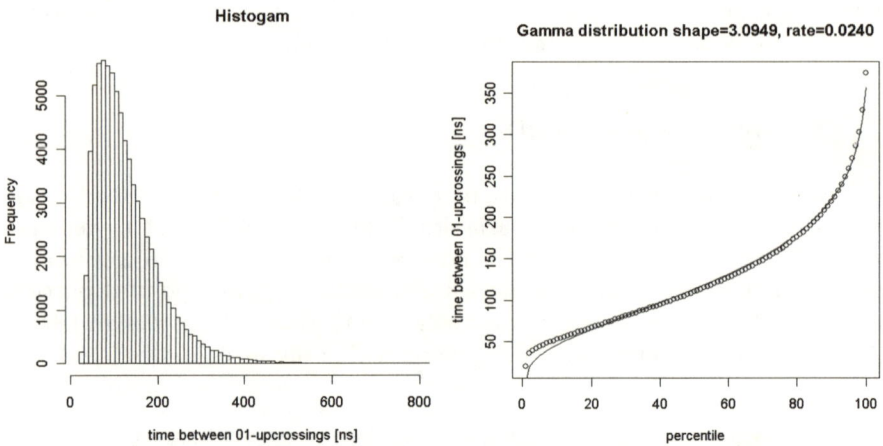

Fig. 3. Empirical distribution of the time between 0-1 crossings: histogram and percentiles

(cf. Remark 4(ii)). Table 1 suggest that the true conditional entropies should be indeed very close to 1, especially for $s = 15.017\widetilde{\mu}$, which gives an output of slightly more than 500 kBit internal random numbers per second. For a k-fold convolution (let's say for $k \in \{10, \ldots, 20\}$) of a gamma distribution with the above-mentioned parameters the normal approximation and thus approximation (17) should be pretty good. Numerical experiments indicate that for $s = 15.017\widetilde{\mu}$ the entropy defect $\epsilon = 1 - H(Y_{n+1} \mid Y_1, \ldots, Y_n)$ (cf. Remark 4) should be smaller than (at least) $< 10^{-4}$. Smaller bounds seem to be realistic but (in our opinion) deserve more elaborate analysis.

It is easy to see that the random variables R_n and R_{n+1} are negatively correlated: A 'large' value r_n (resp., a small value r_n) is an indicator that w_n is also large (resp., that w_n is small), and thus r_{n+1} is likely to be small (resp., r_{n+1} to be large). Apart from the autocorrelation coefficients corr(R_1, R_2) and corr(R_1, R_3) the results obtained by the direct application of Theorem 1 to the experimental data and to their Gamma approximation are essentially equal. To obtain the autocorrelation coefficients we had to apply (28) and (29) iteratively. In particular since the terms $E(R_j^2)$ dominate estimation errors clearly propagate to the autocorrelation coefficients. The results for the Gamma approximation are more reasonable since $|\text{corr}(R_1, R_3)|$ is considerably smaller than $|\text{corr}(R_1, R_2)|$ and both values decrease for larger s, what was expected. Increasing the sample size should also yield better results for the direct use of the experimental data.

6   Online Tests

The conditional entropies $H(R_{n+1} \mid R_0, \ldots, R_n)$ and $H(Y_{n+1} \mid Y_0, \ldots, Y_n)$ are closely related to the entropy of the random variables $V_{(s-u)}$ and $V_{(s-u)}(\bmod 2)$, respectively. If the ratio $(s-u)/\mu$ is not too small $H(V_{(s-u)})$ essentially depends

Table 1. Experimental Results

	$s=7.497\widetilde{\mu}$	$s=9.996\widetilde{\mu}$	$s=9.996\widetilde{\mu}$ (Gamma approx.)	$s=15.017\widetilde{\mu}$	$s=15.017\widetilde{\mu}$ (Gamma approx.)
$E(R_1)$	7.493	9.994	9.996	15.014	15.017
$\mathrm{Var}(R_1)$	2.701	3.502	3.519	5.107	5.141
$\mathrm{corr}(R_1,R_2)$	-0.034	-0.034	-0.041	-0.011	-0.028
$\mathrm{corr}(R_1,R_3)$	0.022	0.010	0.0001	0.019	0.00009
$H(R_{n+1}\,|\,R_1,\ldots,R_n)$	2.631	2.850	2.858	3.155	3.163
$H(Y_{n+1}\,|\,Y_1,\ldots,Y_n)$	0.99990	1.00000	0.99999	1.00000	1.00000

only on the ratios μ/σ and $(s-u)/\mu$ (17). Moreover, 'small' arguments u provide the essential contribution to the integrals from Theorem 1. Hence it is natural (and effective) to estimate the process parameters $\mu = E(T_j)$ and the generalized variance σ^2 of $T_1, T_2, \ldots$ while the RNG is in operation. Unfortunately, this required an internal clock with high resolution, which may be too costly for many applications.

Alternatively, one may check the process parameters μ and σ^2 indirectly, namely by estimating the mean value $\mu_R := E(R_j)$ and the generalized variance σ_R^2 of the stationary sequence $R_1, R_2, \ldots$. In a first step intervals I_μ and I_{σ^2} should be specified which contain 'suitable' values of the process parameters μ and σ^2. By Theorem 1(iv) one computes sets I_{μ_R} and $I_{\sigma_R^2}$ that contain μ_R and σ_R^2 if μ and σ^2 are contained in I_μ and I_{σ^2}. It seems to be reasonable if the online tests consider the mean and maybe also the generalized variance of $R_1, R_2, \ldots$. Generically,

- Estimate μ_R: Compute the arithmetic mean $\mathrm{av}(r_1, \ldots, r_m) := (r_1 + \cdots + r_m)/m$.
- Estimate σ_R^2 or a related parameter from das random numbers $r_{m+1}, \ldots, r_{m+M}$.

The respective test fails if the estimator lies outside a particular regions. Such basis tests may directly serve as online tests, or they can be integrated into a more sophisticated procedure that covers the tasks of the tot test, self test and online test. Due to lack of space we cannot deepen this aspect here but refer the interested reader to [18], [22], Sect. 6, or [13], Example 7. In any case the probability for a failure of a single test must be determined to specify appropriate test rules.

The distribution of $\mathrm{av}(R_1, \ldots, R_m)$ can be computed with (22) with upper integration boundary ms in place of s. The second basis test should be tailored to the distribution of the random variables R_j, which is determined by the RNG. The generalized variance σ_R^2 can be estimated directly, or a relevant set of covariances $\mathrm{cov}(R_n, R_{n+k})$ may be estimated. A precise computation of the failure probability, i.e. that the test value lies outside a specified set, is more complicated than for the arithmetic mean. This may be done on basis of theoretical considerations, or by stochastic simulations (with pseudorandom numbers $\widetilde{t}_1, \widetilde{t}_2, \ldots$ that are generated according to the specified distribution of the random variables T_j), or on basis of measurement series. We point out that under suitable circumstances the second type of online test may be dropped, e.g. when within the class of distributions that contains the true distribution of $R_1, R_2, \ldots$ ($\rightarrow$ stochastic model) the generalized variance σ^2 is a function of μ.

7 Final Remarks

We addressed general requirements that should be considered in security evaluations of physical RNGs. We formulated and analyzed a stochastic model that describes the stochastic behaviour of a particular RNG design that exploits two noisy diodes. Interestingly, this stochastic model also fits to other designs, which makes its understanding important. Theorem 1 collects the main results of this paper, which allow to establish tight lower bounds for the entropy per internal random random number. We applied our results to a particular physical RNG, and we briefly touched the field of online tests.

Acknowledgement. The authors would like to thank Frank Bergmann, who courteously provided the RNG prototype, and Joachim Schüth for performing measurements.

References

1. AIS 20: Functionality Classes and Evaluation Methodology for Deterministic Random Number Generators. Version 1 (02.12.1999) (mandatory if a German IT security certificate is applied for; English translation) (1999),
www.bsi.bund.de/zertifiz/zert/interpr/ais20e.pdf
2. AIS 31: Functionality Classes and Evaluation Methodology for Physical Random Number Generators. Version 1 (25.09.2001) (mandatory if a German IT security certificate is applied for; English translation) (2001),
www.bsi.bund.de/zertifiz/zert/interpr/ais31e.pdf
3. ANSI X9.82, Random Number Generation (Draft Version)
4. Bagini, V., Bucci, M.: A Design of Reliable True Number Generators for Cryptographic Applications. In: Koç, Ç.K., Paar, C. (eds.) CHES 1999. LNCS, vol. 1717, pp. 204–218. Springer, Berlin (1999)
5. Bucci, M., Germani, L., Luzzi, R., Trifiletti, A., Varanonuovo, M.: A High-Speed Oscillator-Based Truly Random Number Source for Cryptographic Applications. IEEE Trans. Computers 52, 403–409 (2003)
6. Bucci, M., Lucci, R.: Design of Testable Random Bit Generators. In: Rao, J.R., Sunar, B. (eds.) CHES 2005. LNCS, vol. 3659, pp. 147–156. Springer, Berlin (2005)
7. Bock, H., Bucci, M., Luzzi, R.: An Offset-Compensated Oscillator-Based Random Bit Source for Security Applications. In: Joye, M., Quisquater, J.-J. (eds.) CHES 2004. LNCS, vol. 3156, pp. 268–281. Springer, Berlin (2004)
8. Dichtl, M.: How to Predict the Output of a Hardware Random Number Generator. In: Walter, C.D., Koç, Ç.K., Paar, C. (eds.) CHES 2003. LNCS, vol. 2779, pp. 181–188. Springer, Berlin (2003)
9. Dichtl, M., Golic, J.: High-Speed True Random Number Generation with Logic Gates Only. In: Paillier, P., Verbauwhede, I. (eds.) CHES 2007. LNCS, vol. 4727, pp. 45–62. Springer, Berlin (2007)

10. Feller, W.: An Introduction to Probability Theory and Its Application, vol. 2. Wiley, New York (1965)
11. ISO / IEC 18031 Random Bit Generation (November 2005)
12. Hoeffding, W., Robbins, H.: The Central Limit Theorem for Dependent Random Variables. Duke Math. J. 15, 773–780 (1948)
13. Killmann, W., Schindler, W.: A Proposal for: Functionality Classes and Evaluation Methodology for True (Physical) Random Number Generators. Version 3.1, 25.09.2001, mathematical-technical reference of [2] (English translation) (2001), www.bsi.bund.de/zertifiz/zert/interpr/trngk31e.pdf
14. Marsaglia, G.: Diehard (Test Suite for Random Number Generators), www.stat.fsu.edu/~geo/diehard.html
15. Pliam, J.O.: The Disparity Between the Work and the Entropy in Cryptology (01.02.1999), eprint.iacr.org/complete/
16. Rukhin, A., et al.: A Statistical Test Suite for Random and Pseudorandom Number Generators for Cryptographic Applications. NIST Special Publication 800–22 with revisions dated (15.05.2001), csrc.nist.gov/rng/SP800-22b.pdf
17. Schindler, W.: Functionality Classes and Evaluation Methodology for Deterministic Random Number Generators. Version 2.0, 02.12.1999, mathematical-technical reference of [1] (English translation) (1999), www.bsi.bund.de/zertifiz/zert/interpr/ais20e.pdf
18. Schindler, W.: Efficient Online Tests for True Random Number Generators. In: Koç, Ç.K., Naccache, D., Paar, C. (eds.) CHES 2001. LNCS, vol. 2162, pp. 103–117. Springer, Heidelberg (2001)
19. Schindler, W., Killmann, W.: Evaluation Criteria for True (Physical) Random Number Generators Used in Cryptographic Applications. In: Kaliski Jr., B.S., Koç, Ç.K., Paar, C. (eds.) CHES 2002. LNCS, vol. 2523, pp. 431–449. Springer, Heidelberg (2003)
20. Schindler, W.: A Stochastical Model and Its Analysis for a Physical Random Number Generator Presented at CHES 2002. In: Paterson, K.G. (ed.) Cryptography and Coding 2003. LNCS, vol. 2898, pp. 276–289. Springer, Heidelberg (2003)
21. Schindler, W.: Random Number Generators for Cryptographic Applications. In: Koç, Ç.K. (ed.) Cryptographic Engineering. Signals and Communication Theory. Springer, Berlin (to appear)
22. Schindler, W.: Evaluation Criteria for Physical Random Number Generators. In: Koç, Ç.K. (ed.) Cryptographic Engineering. Signals and Communication Theory. Springer, Berlin (to appear)
23. Tkacik, T.: A Hardware Random Number Generator. In: Kaliski Jr., B.S., Koç, Ç.K., Paar, C. (eds.) CHES 2002. LNCS, vol. 2523, pp. 450–453. Springer, Heidelberg (2003)
24. Yaglom, A.M.: Correlation Theory of Stationary and Related Random Functions. Springer Series in Statistics, vol. 1. Springer, New York (1987)

Fast Digital TRNG
Based on Metastable Ring Oscillator

Ihor Vasyltsov, Eduard Hambardzumyan,
Young-Sik Kim, and Bohdan Karpinskyy

Samsung Electronics, SoC R&D Center, System LSI, Korea
ihor.vasiltsov@samsung.com

Abstract. In this paper, a new true random number generator (TRNG), based entirely on digital components is proposed. The design has been implemented using a fast random number generation method, which is dependent on a new type of ring oscillator with the ability to be set in metastable mode. Earlier methods of random number generation involved employment of jitter, whereas the proposed method leverages the metastability phenomenon in digital circuits and applies it to a ring oscillator. The new entropy employment method allows an increase in the TRNG throughput by significantly reducing the required entropy accumulating time. Samples obtained from simulation of TRNG design have been evaluated using AIS.31 and FIPS 140-1/2 statistical tests. The results of these tests have proven the high quality of generated data. Corners analysis of the TRNG design was also performed to estimate the robustness to technology process and environment variations. Investigated in FPGA technology, phase distribution highlighted the advantages of the proposed method over traditional architectures.

Keyword: Digital TRNG, Metastable Ring Oscillator, AIS.31, FPGA.

1 Introduction

The security of most cryptographic systems relies on unpredictability and irreproducibility of digital key-streams that are used for encryption and/or signing of confidential information. These key-streams are generated by random number generators (RNG), which are further split into two classes: true random number generators (TRNG) and deterministic random number generators (DRNG) [1], [2]. The key difference between TRNG and DRNG lies in the entropy source component. For TRNG, an analog physical process (electronic thermal noise, radioactive decay, etc.) is used, while for DRNG, a random number called seed is used [1], [2]. Since the seed value is constant, it must be refreshed regularly to maintain the required security level. This seed value is generated by a TRNG, so any security system should be comprised of a TRNG as the key part. Compromising on the TRNG means compromising on the whole security system. That's why a great degree of attention is paid to TRNG as the fundamental security component that guarantees the quality of the whole security system.

E. Oswald and P. Rohatgi (Eds.): CHES 2008, LNCS 5154, pp. 164–180, 2008.

In this paper, we introduced a TRNG based entirely on digital designs. For this purpose, a new type of ring oscillator was created. To validate the theoretical background of the proposed method, we implemented and simulated it in the Cadence Design Environment (CDE). Additionally, we performed the FPGA implementation for phase distribution investigation. The samples obtained were statistically evaluated according to AIS.31 and FIPS 140-1/2 standards [3], [4].

This paper contains the following sections: Section 2 describes the basic concept of digital TRNG and technology state of the art. Section 3 describes metastable ring oscillator theory, implementation and simulation, statistical evaluation, and robustness investigation. Section 4 describes the investigations in FPGA implementation and finally, Section 5 gives the conclusion of this paper.

2   Digital TRNG

Traditional TRNGs are based on a precise analog design requiring special custom layout. The migration of such TRNG products to a new platform or technology is complicated since it involves a heavy custom re-design, an increased budget, and more time-to-market. TRNG design, which is based entirely on digital components, is free from such drawbacks. By significantly reducing the need to custom re-design, it facilitates product migration. Hereafter, we will use the term *Digital TRNG* in this paper to explain this totally digital synthesizable design.

The first scheme considered as totally Digital TRNG was based on coupled oscillators. This method produces randomness from the phase noise in free-running oscillators. The output of the fast oscillator is sampled on the rising edge of a slower clock using a D flip-flop [5]. The main physical phenomenon used as an entropy source in such architectures is jitter, which is defined as the short-term variation of signal's significant instants from their ideal positions in time, due to the existence of thermal and shot noise in a semiconductor device. Oscillator jitter causes uncertainty in the exact sample values, ideally producing a random bit for each sample. By carefully selecting the ratio between the two oscillator frequencies, an artificially enhanced randomness can be achieved. But such synchronization of oscillators requires special custom design that increases the complexity of development. So, straightforward implementation of such a scheme cannot be achieved easily.

Another problem with such a scheme is that it necessitates wait for jitter accumulation and only after that accumulated entropy can be sampled as random data. The length of waiting time depends on the technology specification and component parameters, and usually takes from a few hundreds to several thousands of oscillator periods, limiting the throughput up to 1 Mbits/sec, which is considered critical for high-performance security applications.

There were many efforts to decrease the jitter accumulation time. For example, Jun and Kocher employed the hybrid TRNG [6], wherein the thermal noise source modulated the frequency of the slower clock. The variable, noise-modulated slower clock triggers the measurements of the fast clock. Drift between the two clocks thus provide the source of random binary digits. But such architecture cannot be considered as purely digital because direct noise amplification circuit requires analog design. Another example of the mixed usage of digital and analog TRNGs is presented by Trichina, Bucci, Seta and Luzzi [7].

To overcome the de-synchronization of the sampling oscillator, another approach was used in [8], where Sunar, Martin and Stinson proposed to use a plurality of free running ring oscillators (RO), outputs of which are XORed. According to the authors, properly selected numbers of oscillators and their periods guarantee that the entire spectrum will be populated with transition zones. Also, sampling the waveform only in such zones would provide enough entropy. The area cost for this solution is huge. For example, in [9] even a minimal TRNG design based on 110 free running 3-cascades ring oscillators occupies 565 slices in Xilinx Virtex FPGA, what is more than the lightest known AES implementations [10]. Additionally, in [11] there were serious concerns about the unrealistic assumptions of the theoretical model used in [8] which raised questions about the practical implementation of such a Digital TRNG architecture. Bock, Bucci and Luzzi proposed a scheme where the oscillators are re-synchronized before each bit generation [12]. As a result, the periodical behavior typical for the oscillator-based source is suppressed and each bit generation restarts from the same state as with a direct-amplification source. Fischer and Drutarovsky proposed to sample the jittered signal by several shifted in-time flip-flops, aiming to guarantee that at least one of them will correspond to the random jitter [13]. However, obtained throughput was low. For the implementation in Altera APEX EP20K200 FPGA with a 88.245 MHz internal clock, it generated only 69 kbps.

Another type of Digital TRNG exploits the metastability of RS latches and edge-triggered flip-flops (for example, see [14]). The output of such a flip-flop may become unpredictable if the input and clock signals are such that the setup and/or hold times are violated. For example, when the data input signal is forced to change at nearly the same time as the clock signal the output signal then stabilizes on a random, typically biased value after a random amount of time. The metastability of D-type flip-flops can be exploited together with the jitter of underlying ring oscillator signals by using D-type flip-flops for sampling the ring oscillator signals. In any case, naturally occurred metastability events are relatively rare and when they occur are sensitive to temperature and voltage changes [14]. So, TRNGs, which are based solely on naturally occurred metastability events are relatively slow and do not appear to be very reliable.

Tkacik proposed the use of two oscillators of different sizes that were clocking linear feedback shift register and cellular automata shift register [15]. The investigation of individual statistical characteristics of LFSR and CASR outputs showed the presence of some weakness. To improve the design their outputs were XORed. Such architecture includes a pseudo randomness properties and does not comply with the AIS.31 P2.d)(vii) requirements for getting desirable statistical raw data characteristics [1], [2]. A theoretical attack for this TRNG is described by Dichtl in [16].

Golić introduced Fibonacci and Galois ring oscillators, which are both defined as generalizations of a typical ring oscillators [17]. He claimed that the high-speed output oscillating signal has both pseudo and true randomness properties. True randomness accumulates from unpredictable variations in the delay of internal logic gates that get propagated and enhanced through feedback, possibly in a chaotic manner, and also from internal metastability events. It is suggested that further randomness due to metastability may be induced within a sampling unit (e.g., a D-type flip-flop) as well as that the mutual coupling effect between the oscillating and sampling signals may be significantly reduced by the pseudo random noise-like form of the oscillating signal. Recently, the inherited pseudo randomness property of Fibonacci and Galois ring oscillators was fixed by using restarting mode, which makes the generator stateless and excludes pseudo randomness as described in [11].

In spite of the many proposals for hardware-based TRNGs, finding an efficient and robust method for high-speed generation of true random numbers that can be implemented by using only logic gates in digital semiconductor technology remains a challenge. The ideal method should be efficient in terms of gate count, achievable speed, and power consumption. Further in this paper, the authors propose an original method which can be used for Digital TRNG implementation.

3   Metastable Ring Oscillator

3.1   Metastability Employment

To increase the throughput of the Digital TRNG based on jitter phenomena in ring oscillators, the available solutions require either a custom layout design or huge area costs. In this paper, we suggest the use of another physical phenomenon as entropy source in oscillators – metastability.

It is known that for any digital component with threshold level near the metastable state, the circuit behavior becomes totally stochastic and depends on the characteristics of the circuit noise [18]. Thus, a metastable state is the perfect entropy source. But, due to the mismatch of transistors, temperature imbalance within a chip, ionizing radiation, or any other parasitic fluctuation of the output voltages, the probability that the physical flip-flop circuit will stay in the metastable region is very small [19]. Therefore, straightforward employment of metastability phenomena in flip-flop circuits is inefficient due to the rare occurrence of natural metastability event [14] .

Thus, it is required to build a circuit with the ability to be put into a metastable state. Our investigation in CMOS technology showed that such a circuit could be implemented on an inverter. In Fig.1, the generic scheme of metastability employment based on a CMOS inverter is shown. If the inverter is connected into the loop by a switch, the output voltage converges to metastability level and stays there as long as required (see Fig.1b))[1]. Due to inherited thermal noise, the output voltage stochastically fluctuates around the metastable level.

---

[1] This state is stable as long as input and output are connected, and becomes metastable when the control signal allows the oscillator to run.

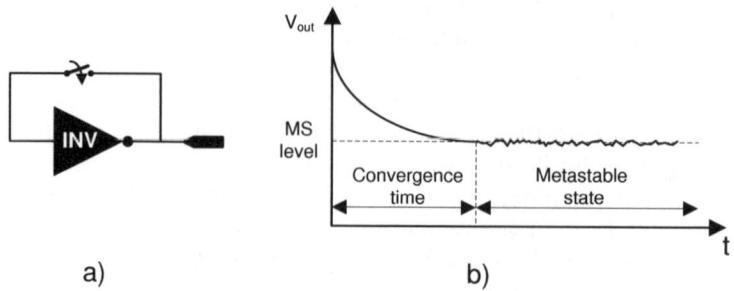

Fig. 1. Metastability employment scheme based on CMOS inverter a), and its convergence process b)

When a ring oscillator is composed of such schemes, after disconnecting the feedback loop, the initial state of the ring oscillator is completely defined by the entropy from stochastic fluctuations of each inverter (here we neglected the deterministic disturbances propagated through the power supply; such a special case was considered separately and showed that our design is robust for realistic $\pm 10\%$ voltage variation). In Fig.2, the explanation of metastability employment in an inverter-based ring oscillator circuit is shown.

1. *Initialization.* The initialization is done by putting the RO system into the metastable point (threshold voltage level). The momentary voltage value of

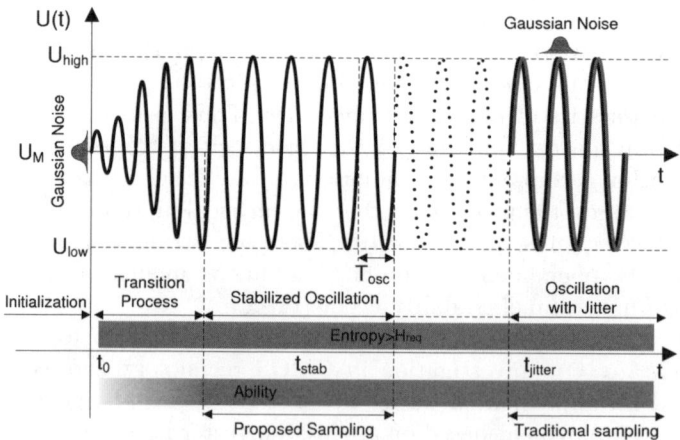

Fig. 2. Metastability employment in the inverter-based ring oscillator. Entropy exists at the beginning of the oscillation and transition periods, because initial voltage is defined by thermal noise. Because of low amplitude value and not stabilized period, the sampling is postponed until amplitude value is high enough and setup/hold time condition is satisfied. Usually it takes only few periods, so appeared latency is negligible comparatively to jitter accumulation process.

the initial noise influences the RO system and causes the oscillations, which at the beginning are very low by amplitude (and can be recovered by following momentary voltage values with bigger amplitude). Thus, the initial voltage value of an RO system is defined by the noise and already inherits enough entropy.

2. *Transition Process.* This process is semi-deterministic (almost does not increase entropy). Deterministic part consists of amplifying the noise signal obtained at the initialization mode. But due to the continuous influence of noise, this deterministic signal can be recovered and the initial entropy level can even be increased. Sampling in this period is not applied because the signal voltage value could be significantly lower than required[2].

3. *Stabilized Oscillations.* Full-range amplitude oscillations at stabilized periods allow for effective sampling, because of the inherited entropy from the initialization mode.

As can be seen from Fig.2, the main advantage of the proposed method is the significant decrease in the latency of TRNG due to earlier sampling times. Compare: with jitter accumulating it is required to wait a few hundreds/thousands of RO oscillation periods and for the method proposed in this paper it is enough to wait only few periods.

3.2   Generic Meta-RO Architecture

Based on the theoretical assumptions from the previous section, we propose an original architecture of a metastable ring oscillator (Meta-RO) as shown in the Fig.3. This architecture consists of:

- an odd plurality of inverters that can form either independent entropy source components while in metastable mode, or a traditional RO while in generation mode;
- a corresponding number of Switching Components (referred as MUXes) for re/dis-connecting inverters between two modes;
- a Control Clock Generator to control the random number generation process by switching between metastability (MS) and generation (Gener.) mode to guarantee the proper entropy collecting and entropy acquiring;
- a Sampling Component (referred as D flip-flop) for sampling the collected entropy from Meta-RO;
- a Delay Component to synchronize the sampling process with generating random data process by pre-defined delay.

The proposed method operates as follows (see Fig.3). First, the Control Clock Generator switches the system into MS mode by sending the corresponding signals to the Switching Components to disconnect each inverter from the others and connect it into a loop (this helps to apply the metastability point to the input of every inverter after a while). Since each inverter is disconnected from the other and the threshold point voltage is applied to its input, they form a set of *independent noise sources.*

---

[2] The gain of inverters of the modern technology is big enough, so usually transition process is very short.

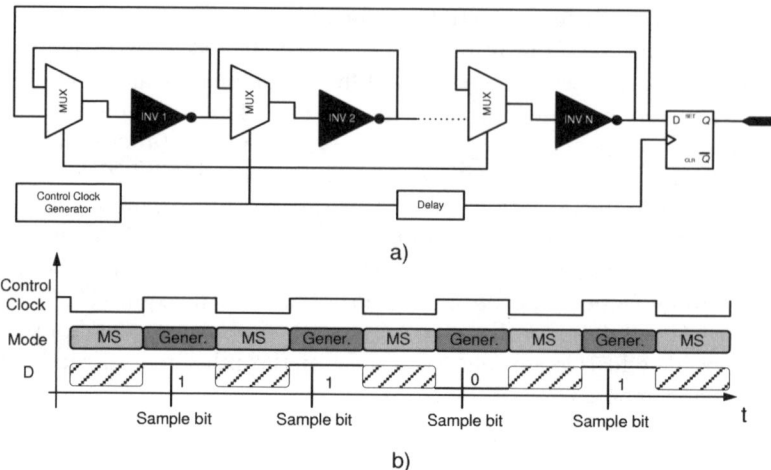

Fig. 3. Generic Meta-RO architecture a) and operational diagram b). The set of inverters could be used to form independent entropy sources (in metastable mode) or a regular ring oscillator to amplify and resolve the obtained random state.

After a while, the system is switched into the Generation mode, where inverters are re-connected to each other to form a traditional RO. Since in the previous MS mode the value of each inverter output was defined by random noise, the momentary voltages inside the RO are also random, causing high entropy. After sampling a random bit, the TRNG system again is switched to MS mode to collect a new random value. Since for whole process it is required to wait just several periods of RO oscillation, the total TRNG throughput can be increased significantly compared to traditional jitter employment architectures.

3.3   Implementation in Cadence Design Environment

For appropriate and accurate investigation of the proposed architecture, Meta-RO5st (a 5-stage metastable ring oscillator) has been implemented in Cadence Virtuoso Environment version 5.10.41 within a 65nm technology process library.

The specifics of our investigation are such that even if we are investigating a Digital TRNG case to consistently prove the proposed Meta-RO architecture, we still have to provide analog simulation with transient analysis of random data generation. In this case, the realistic implementation of the proposed method into existent ASIC technology will verified[3].

The whole design of the core of the Meta-RO5st architecture (FIFO, external control and interfaces not included) covered up to 70 transistors. Taking into

---

[3] The relevancy of the simulation to the real chip processes still is an open question. In this paper the authors could not solve it completely, but at least consider the technology process and temperature variations. Another advantage of the simulation consists in the absence of complex patterns in the power supply lines, which complicates the distinguishing between true and pseudo randomness.

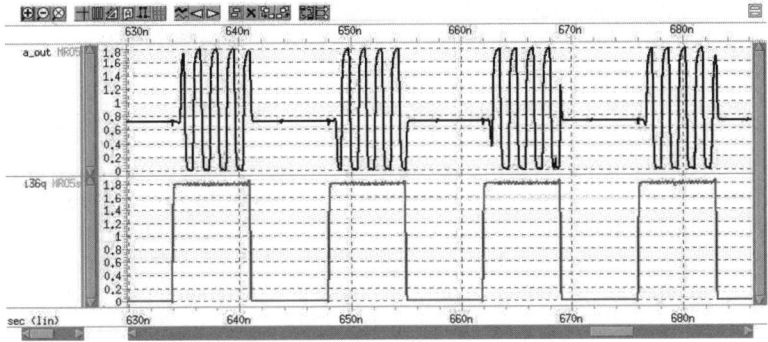

Fig. 4. Results of Meta-RO5st simulation. From the figure it is clear the difference between MS and Generation mode following the control clock signal.

account the nominal parameters of CMOS transistor in 65nm technology, the raw estimation for the covered area is about $1\mu m^2$, which is the smallest area estimation for the known Digital TRNGs.

Simulation was performed by Virtuoso Spectre Circuit Simulator. This simulator allows the use of an embedded transient noise feature during simulation which gives a realistic estimation for the internal noise value and behavior inside the device.

In Fig.4, an example of Meta-RO5st simulation is shown. The figure clearly shows that in MS mode the Meta-RO comes to the metastability point.

3.4   Statistical Evaluation

There are several standards and criteria for evaluating random number generators including PRNG and TRNG. FIPS 140-1/2 [3], [4] is one of the most accepted standard series. In FIPS 140-1, four statistical tests are presented for evaluating RNG used in crypto systems. Note that the statistical tests in FIPS 140-2 are almost the same as in FIPS 140-1, except for the thresholds and ranges of each test. (The statistical tests in FIPS 140-2 are stricter than those in FIPS 140-1.) However, in the later version of FIPS 140-2, the statistical requirements for the RNG are omitted as a result of amendment. AIS.31 [1] is a German standard for the necessary properties of secure TRNGs and their evaluations. This standard includes 9 statistical tests for the evaluation of random output from TRNG. Detailed description of the test and methodology on how to use it can be found in [1] and [2]. Note that statistical tests T0–T5 required a relatively strict statistical quality of the sample since they are applied to the output of a post-processing. Furthermore, T1–T4 are exactly the same as the statistical tests in FIPS 140-1. T6 is a uniform distribution test consisting of two sub-tests. T7 is a comparative test for multinomial distributions that consists of two sub-tests. Finally T8 is an entropy test that corresponds to Coron's entropy estimation. Note that the last 3 statistical tests T6–T8 required relatively loose conditions since these tests are applied for the direct output of TRNG.

In this evaluation, we performed statistical tests for the random samples from Spectre simulation. Because of the complexity of analog simulation (large number of parameters, high precision, large number of simulated and stored points, etc.) the obtaining of a big sample was limited. To perform appropriate simulation instead of one long simulation 20 experiments (every for 7 μs) with different noise seed have been run. Sampling period equals 7ns, giving throughput above 140 Mbits/sec. In total a sample of 20,000 bits was obtained. Raw sample inherits Bias = 0.484075796 and Shannon Entropy = 0.999268198. The size of this random sample was too short to apply the original AIS.31 statistical tests. Instead, we used the modified version of AIS.31 with re-estimated boundaries for every test. In Table 1 a summary on the results of the AIS.31 test is shown. Tests T0, T6-2, T7-1, T7-2, and T8 are not available because of the sample size. As it is shown in the table, the generated sample passed the tests, except T1 for FIPS 140-2. Detailed investigation showed that reason of fail was the stronger boundaries for the bias in the FIPS 140-2 test[4].

Table 1. Statistical test on Meta-RO5st (20 kbits simulated by Spectre CDE)

Test	AIS.31	FIPS 140-1	FIPS 140-2
T1: Monobit Test	P	P	F
T2: Poker Test	P	P	P
T3: Run Test	P	P	P
T4: Long Run Test	P	P	P
T5: Autocorrelation Test	P	NA	NA
T6-1: Uniform Test Results	P	NA	NA

3.5 Corners Analysis

One of the major challenges facing semiconductor companies today is how to increase yield. The ability to predict and improve yield becomes even more vital as processes move to geometries under 100 nm. To account for process variations, an IC designer not only has to design for good electrical performance, but also for high manufacturing yield. There are many factors that effect yield. Manufacturing issues such as defect density on the silicon, maturity of the process, and effectiveness of design rules all affect yield. Another factor is how the design reacts to technological process variation and environment conditions (for example, high/low temperatures and voltage fluctuations) simultaneously. So, to be convinced of the robustness of our design to technological process and environment variations, special investigation must be performed.

Corners simulation is perhaps the most widely used method to test for process, temperature, and voltage variations. With this method, a designer determines the worst case corners, or conditions, under which the design will be expected to function. The process variations mean the variation on used pmos and nmos transistors. They can be "slow" or "fast", so there are possible 4 corners (SS,

---

[4] The obtained value equaled 9681, while acceptance boundaries were [9725, 10275].

SF, FS and FF). This kind of simulation is very important because parameters of used transistors in real scheme can be very different, causing design malfunctioning.

To estimate the robustness of the proposed design to process and temperature variations (PTVA), the Corners analysis for 65 nm technology library was run in CDE. Process variations ran all 4 possible technology variation sets (FF, SS, FS, and SF) while temperature changed from −25 to 100 with step = 25 degrees of Celsius. Similar to the nominal case, the sampling period equaled 7 ns, giving throughput above 140 Mbits/sec. For every specific PTVA point a 2,600 bits sample was generated. For every PVTA point the bias was estimated, the data is collected in Table 2.

Table 2. Bias estimation for Corners analysis on Meta-RO5st

PVA	Temperature					
	−25	0	25	50	75	100
FF	0.4665	0.4896	0.5135	0.5281	0.5442	0.5565
SS	0.3892	0.3689	0.3792	0.4073	0.4323	0.4515
FS	0.4119	0.4258	0.4377	0.4496	0.4558	0.4577
SF	0.4808	0.5039	0.5046	0.4865	0.4711	0.4554

The analysis of Table 2 showed that the technology process and temperature variation significantly influenced the quality of the generated data. We can propose three approaches to solve this problem.

The *most common method* consists of decreasing the operation rate. In this case, the period of the metastability mode is proportionally increasing, causing longer time for convergence and assuring a metastable state is reached (see Fig. 1b)).

The *second most common approach* consists of applying a post-processing to the raw data to increase the original entropy. There are many post-processing schemes: XOR, von Neumann, resilient, etc [1], [2], [8], [17], [21]–[23]. Von Neumann corrector stands as the most powerful method of significantly reducing the existing bias (in spite of degradation in performance by factor 4 in average). The general method is described in [21], and modern advanced methods are represented in [22] and [23]. Fig. 5 is the result of statistical evaluation of previously generated samples (Meta-RO5st Corners analysis) after post-processing by von Neumann corrector. Since the sample size was too short, only an online test could be applied [1]. This test is intended to detect some kinds of statistical defects from the sampled random sequences. As can be seen in the figure, the post-processed data passed the online test for every PTVA point. The potential throughput was decreased approximately 4 times and was estimated as 35 Mbits/sec.

The *third approach* consists of balancing the design. The parasitic RC characteristic of a digitizer circuit influences the loads of the last inverter in Meta-RO, causing change of the output voltage value from the original metastable level.

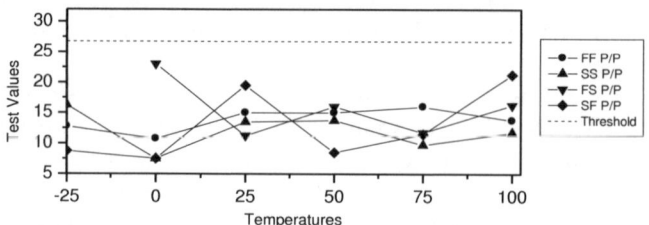

Fig. 5. Online test values via temperature for different process variations after post-processing by von Neumann

Therefore the metastable levels between the last and other inverters in RO are mismatched, causing some bias to the generated data. If the output of every inverter is similarly loaded, then the difference in the metastability level between inverters will be minimized, reducing the bias. So, another approach consists of balancing the digitizer circuits.

Table 3 shows the bias estimation for data generated by a simulation of balanced Meta-RO5st design with decreased operation rate period (T= 20ns allows to get throughput of 50 Mbits/sec). Again, for every specific PTVA point 2,600 bits sample was generated. The analysis showed that only 2 PVTA points (marked as * in the table) are slightly out of the AIS.31 acceptable boundaries [0.475, 0.525]. First, it must be noted that boundaries [0.475, 0.525] were defined for a 20 kbits sample, and for a 2,600 bits sample they could be wider. Also, we believe that further decreasing of the operation rate will refine the bias in those points as well.

Table 3. Bias estimation for Corner analysis on Meta-RO5st (balanced design)

	Temperature					
PVA	−25	0	25	50	75	100
FF	0.5169	0.4940	0.4967	0.4785	0.4924	0.5006
SS	0.5111	0.5075	0.5120	0.5117	0.5111	0.5155
FS	0.4618*	0.4672*	0.4880	0.5016	0.5170	0.5100
SF	0.4757	0.5137	0.5019	0.5110	0.5100	0.5019

Also, similar stable results (with usage of balanced Meta-RO5st design) were obtained for 150 nm semiconductor technology. The properties of Digital TRNG for the following variations were investigated: PVA (FF, FS, SF and SS), temperature (−40, −25, 25 and 125 of Celsius) and supply voltage variation (1.45 V and 1.9 V with 50 mv noise harmonic at 20 MHz and 100 kHz).

Thus, any of the methods listed above (as well a combination) could be used for building a Meta-RO–based TRNG robust to process and environment variations.

4   Investigation in FPGA Technology

In order to provide a proof of the proposed Meta-RO concept we conducted the experiments in FPGA technology (Xilinx XC2V3000–5). We noted that straightforward implementation of the Verilog code of Meta-RO5st design is not possible, because the logic synthesizer performs unnecessary design optimization, causing malfunctioning of Meta-RO. To avoid this, special constraints had to be used. Additionally, every logic function in FPGA is implemented by a look-up table, the dynamic properties of which are different from the properties of inverters or other gates. That is why the designer has to be very careful while implementing a Meta-RO in FPGA.

Direct measurement of the Meta-RO5st analog signal by oscilloscope (see Fig. 6) confirms that Meta-RO5st digital TRNG functioned properly and followed the theoretical assumption discussed above. We can see during metastability mode how the voltage is converged, arriving at metastable level. When the control signal takes a high value, the generation mode is started.

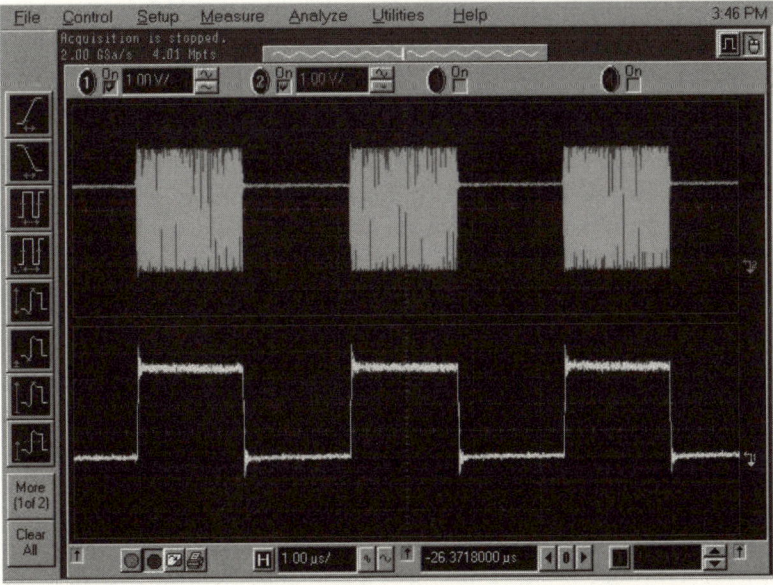

Fig. 6. Random number generation process in FPGA technology. Digital TRNG output is switched between metastable and generation state following the control signal.

To check pseudo randomness properties we used the Dichtl and Golić idea [11] for measuring the data from the same initial conditions. In Fig. 7 the results of the measurement of several consequent D-TRNG runs are shown. In the figure, the horizontal axis is the time, the period of time shown for each run is $100\,\mu s$. The vertical axis is the output voltage of the sampled signal. To guarantee the

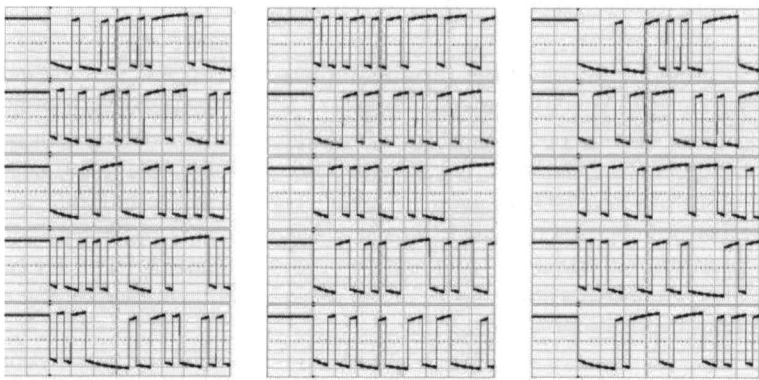

Fig. 7. Consequent runs of Meta-RO5st after restarting. Since after restarting, every generated sample is different, this is evidence that output of the proposed D-TRNG is not defined by a deterministic source.

same initial conditions we must wait a few minutes between consequent runs, powering off the FPGA board. Every run in the figure corresponds to a different sample, i.e., the output of D-TRNG is not defined by a deterministic source.

To confirm the advantages of the proposed method, it is necessary to compare the phase distribution characteristics of Meta-RO and traditional ring oscillator. In [20], Bucci and Luzzi introduced the concept of stateless generator. The stateless hypothesis can be fulfilled by resetting TRNG to a constant value for every state variable in both the entropy source and the post-processor, before the generation of a new bit. For a random number generator built on a traditional RO, this means resetting the RO to some constant value before generating every new bit. Thus, in the following experiments we examined the phase distribution for traditional RO with Reset and Meta-RO5st (unbalanced).

In Fig. 8 the measurement of Meta-RO5st is shown[5]. We measured the time of the first transition of the signal starting from 30 ns to 40 ns after switching to generation mode. Since the period of Meta-RO5st oscillation is about 10 ns, we can interpret this measurement as a phase distribution in generation mode. Compared to the phase distribution of a traditional 5-stage ring oscillator (see Fig. 9), we noted that the phase distribution of Meta-RO5st was spread over the complete period of oscillation. This effect allows faster entropy accumulation for random number generation compared to traditional jitter-based TRNG. Thus, digital TRNG based on Meta-RO provides higher entropy for significantly increased throughput. Additionally, period-wide phase distribution of Meta-RO guarantees some minimal entropy accumulating (far different from zero) in any instance of time during sampling, significantly decreasing the risk of random number quality degradation due to parasitic synchronization of Meta-RO with other processes in the system.

---

[5] Agilent oscilloscope "Measuring Jitter Using Histogram" feature and methodology has been used for this experiment.

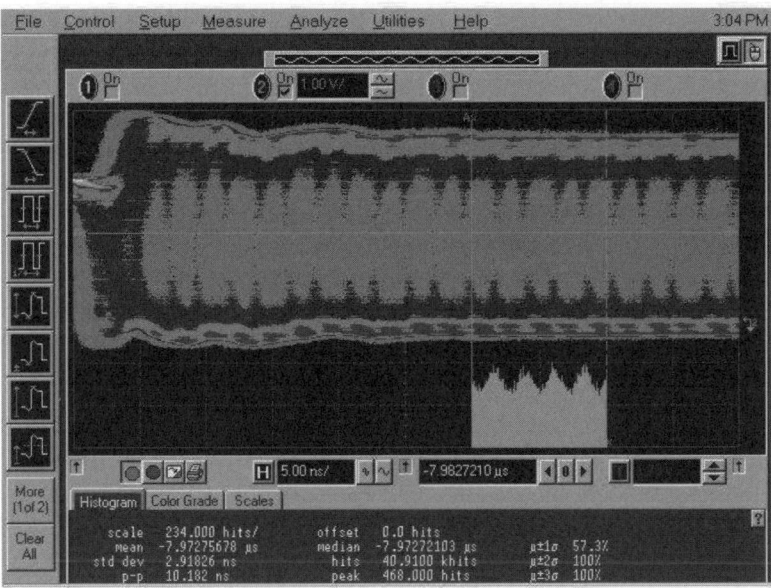

Fig. 8. Histogram of phase distribution in Meta-RO5st digital TRNG. The phase distribution occupies the whole period of the Meta-RO oscillations, significantly increasing the entropy.

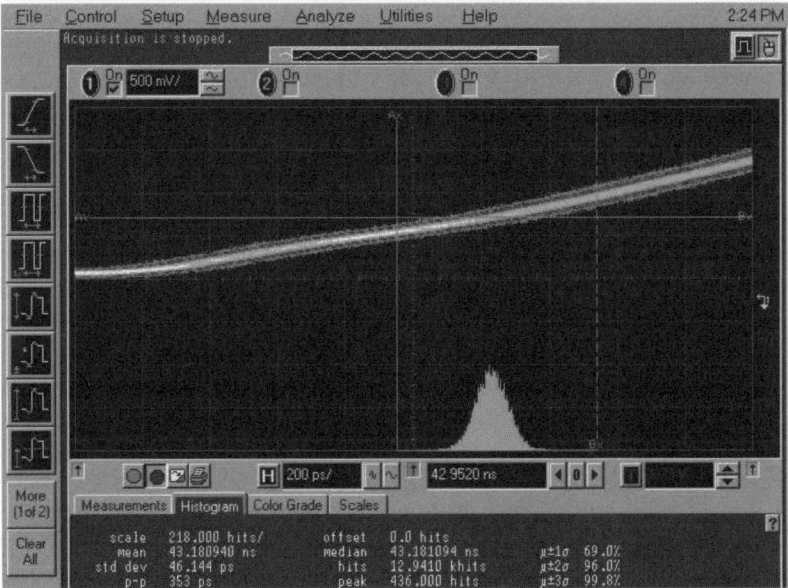

Fig. 9. Histogram of phase distribution in traditional 5-stage RO with reset (measured for rise transition from 30 ns after restart)

Table 4. Summary of the statistical tests on Meta-RO5st (FPGA implementation)

Test Suite	Tests	Without post-processing, %	With post-processing, %
FIPS 140-1/2	T1-T4	68	100
AIS.31 Class P1	T0-T4	68	100
	T5 (Autocorrelation)	100	Not needed
AIS.31 Class P2	T0-T4	68	100
	T5 (Autocorrelation)	100	Not needed
	T6-T8	88	Not allowed
NIST STS	Spectrum test	100	Not needed

For FIPS 140-1/2 and AIS.31 tests, evaluation was made completely over 1 Gbits of data samples. The preliminary investigation showed that the statistical properties of the samples vary during the generation. The reason for such instability can be explained by the fact that the FPGA design is sensitive to temperature fluctuations and voltage supply noise. Improving FPGA operation and environment conditions (using a stable power supply source and installing a cooler over the FPGA) allowed us to obtain more satisfactory results, summarized in Table 4.

As it can be seen from the table, our FPGA design has no correlation problem, i.e., in 1 Gbit of total data there was no single failure in either the AIS.31 T5 Autocorrelation test or the NIST STS Spectrum test[6]. There are still some bias weaknesses, however, which could be fixed by post-processing (where applicable). Thus, our FPGA design successfully passes FIPS 140-1/2 and AIS.31 Class P1, but problems may arise with AIS.31 Class 2. Taking into account the fact that FPGA implementation is not very stable compared to ASIC, we can expect that real ASIC implementation will have no such weaknesses.

5   Conclusion

In this paper, a method for true random number generation was proposed. The highlight of this method lies in the usage of metastability phenomena in the ring oscillator for entropy accumulating, compared to traditional methods based on jitter. For practical realization of this method, a special ring oscillator architecture with the ability to be set in metastable mode was discovered. This ring oscillator is based on digital components only and does not require special custom design.

For validation of the proposed method, a Meta-RO5st (5-stage metastable ring oscillator) component was implemented and simulated in Cadence. Collected samples were tested according to AIS.31 and FIPS 140-1/2 standard

---

[6] National Institute of Standards and Technology. A Statistical Test Suite for the Validation of Random Number Generators and Pseudo Random Number Generators for Cryptographic Applications. http://csrc.nist.gov/groups/ST/toolkit/rng/documents/SP800-22b.pdf

requirements and inherit Bias $= 0.48407$ and Shannon Entropy $= 0.99926$ for raw samples. The throughput reached 140 Mbits/sec in nominal conditions. To compensate for process and temperature variations, the sampling rate was decreased, and as a result the throughput reached 35–50 Mbits/sec. The estimated area for 65 nm semiconductor technology is approximately $1 \mu m^2$ (for Digital TRNG core only).

Physical experiments in FPGA technology showed that phase distribution of the proposed metastable RO occupies the complete oscillating period with stronger entropy value, allowing faster entropy accumulating for random number generation. Thus, Digital TRNG based on Meta-RO provides high entropy for significantly increased throughput. Statistical evaluation showed that our FPGA design could successfully pass FIPS 140-1/2 and AIS.31 Class P1. Further improvements in FPGA operation environment conditions could increase the quality of the proposed TRNG to pass AIS.31 Class P2.

The patent for this method of true random number generation and Meta-RO architecture is pending.

Acknowledgement

We deeply appreciate the support of Markus Dichtl, whose useful comments and notes significantly increase the quality and value of the paper.

References

1. Killmann, W., Schindler, W.: AIS 31: Functionality Classes and Evaluation Methodology for True (Physical) Random Number Generators, version 3.1, Bundesamt für Sicherheit in der Informationstechnik (BSI), Bonn (2001)
2. Schindler, W., Killmann, W.: Evaluation Criteria for True (Physical) Random Number Generators Used in Cryptographic Applications. In: Kaliski Jr., B.S., Koç, Ç.K., Paar, C. (eds.) CHES 2002. LNCS, vol. 2523, pp. 431–449. Springer, Heidelberg (2003)
3. FIPS PUB 140-1: Security requirements for cryptographic modules (1994)
4. FIPS PUB 140-2: Security requirements for cryptographic modules (2001)
5. Fairfield, R., Mortenson, R., Coulthart, K.: An LSI random number generator (RNG). In: Blakely, G.R., Chaum, D. (eds.) CRYPTO 1984. LNCS, vol. 196, pp. 203–230. Springer, Heidelberg (1985)
6. Jun, B., Kocher, P.: The Intel random number generator, White paper for Intel Corporation, Cryptography Research Inc. (April 1999), http://www.cryptography.com/resources/whitepapers/IntelRNG.pdf
7. Trichina, E., Bucci, M., De Seta, D., Luzzi, R.: Supplemental Cryptographic Hardware for Smart Cards. IEEE Micro. 21(6), 26–35 (2001)
8. Sunar, B., Martin, W., Stinson, D.: A provably secure true random number generator with built-in tolerance to active attacks. IEEE Trans. Computers 56(1), 109–119 (2007)
9. Schellekens, D., Preneel, B., Verbauwhede, I.: FPGA vendor agnostic true random number generator. In: 16th Int. Conf. Field Programmable Logic and Applications - FPL 2006, pp. 1–6 (2006)

10. Chodowiec, P., Gaj, K.: Very Compact FPGA Implementation of the AES Algorithm. In: Walter, C.D., Koç, Ç.K., Paar, C. (eds.) CHES 2003. LNCS, vol. 2779, pp. 319–333. Springer, Heidelberg (2003)
11. Dichtl, M., Golić, J.: High-Speed True Random Number Generation with Logic Gates Only. In: Paillier, P., Verbauwhede, I. (eds.) CHES 2007. LNCS, vol. 4727, pp. 45–62. Springer, Heidelberg (2007)
12. Bock, H., Bucci, M., Luzzi, R.: Offset-compensated oscillator-based random bit source for security applications. In: Joye, M., Quisquater, J.-J. (eds.) CHES 2004. LNCS, vol. 3156, pp. 268–281. Springer, Heidelberg (2004)
13. Fischer., V., Drutarovsky, M.: True Random Number Generator Embedded in Reconfigurable Hardware. In: Kaliski Jr., B.S., Koç, Ç.K., Paar, C. (eds.) CHES 2002. LNCS, vol. 2523, pp. 415–430. Springer, Heidelberg (2003)
14. Epstein, M., Hars, L., Krasinski, R., Rosner, M., Zheng, H.: Design and implementation of a true random number generator based on digital circuits artifacts. In: Walter, C.D., Koç, Ç.K., Paar, C. (eds.) CHES 2003. LNCS, vol. 2779, pp. 152–165. Springer, Heidelberg (2003)
15. Tkacik, T.: A hardware random number generator. In: Kaliski Jr., B.S., Koç, Ç.K., Paar, C. (eds.) CHES 2002. LNCS, vol. 2523, pp. 450–453. Springer, Heidelberg (2003)
16. Dichtl, M.: How to predict the output of a hardware random number generator. In: Walter, C.D., Koç, Ç.K., Paar, C. (eds.) CHES 2003. LNCS, vol. 2779, pp. 181–188. Springer, Heidelberg (2003)
17. Golić, J.D.: New methods for digital generation and postprocessing of random data. IEEE Trans. Computers 55(10), 1217–1229 (2006)
18. Horstmann, J., Eichel, H., Coates, R.: Metastability behavior of CMOS ASIC flip-flops in theory and test. IEEE J. Solid-State Circuits 24(1), 146–157 (1989)
19. Kacprzak, T., Albicki, A.: Analysis of metastable operation in RS CMOS flip-flops. IEEE J. Solid-State Circuits 22(1), 57–64 (1987)
20. Bucci, M., Luzzi, R.: Design of testable random bit generators. In: Rao, J.R., Sunar, B. (eds.) CHES 2005. LNCS, vol. 3659, pp. 147–156. Springer, Heidelberg (2005)
21. Neumann, J.: Various techniques for use in connection with random digits. In: Von Neumann's Collected Works, vol. 5, pp. 768–770. Pergamon (1963)
22. Peres, Y.: Iterating von Neumann's Procedure For Extracting Random Bits. The Annals of Statistics 20(3), 590–597 (1992)
23. Juels, A., Jakobsson, M., Shriver, E., Hillyer, B.: How to turn loaded dice into fair coins. IEEE Trans. Inf. Theory 46(3), 911–921 (2000)

Efficient Helper Data Key Extractor on FPGAs

Christoph Bösch[1,*], Jorge Guajardo[2], Ahmad-Reza Sadeghi[1],
Jamshid Shokrollahi[1,**], and Pim Tuyls[2]

[1] Horst-Görtz-Institute for IT-Security, Ruhr-University Bochum, Germany
{christoph.boesch,jamshid.shokrollahi,ahmad.sadeghi}@trust.rub.de
[2] Philips Research Europe, Eindhoven, The Netherlands
{jorge.guajardo,pim.tuyls}@philips.com

Abstract. Physical Unclonable Functions (PUFs) have properties that make them very attractive for a variety of security-related applications. Due to their inherent dependency on the physical properties of the device that contains them, they can be used to uniquely bind an application to a particular device for the purpose of IP protection. This is crucial for the protection of FPGA applications against illegal copying and distribution. In order to exploit the physical nature of PUFs for reliable cryptography a so-called helper data algorithm or fuzzy extractor is used to generate cryptographic keys with appropriate entropy from noisy and non-uniform random PUF responses. In this paper we present for the first time efficient implementations of fuzzy extractors on FPGAs where the efficiency is measured in terms of required hardware resources. This fills the gap of the missing building block for a full FPGA IP protection solution. Moreover, in this context we propose new architectures for the decoders of Reed-Muller and Golay codes, and show that our solutions are very attractive from both the area and error correction capability points of view.

Keywords: Physical Unclonable Functions, Intrinsic PUF, Fuzzy Extractor, Helper Data Algorithm, FPGAs, Implementation.

1   Introduction

Virtually all keyed cryptographic primitives, regardless of whether they are based on public-key or private-key cryptography, assume the secrecy of the key used to encrypt/sign a given message. Since the late 90's, there has been a lot of interest in developing methods to guard against key compromise at the protocol level but also at the physical level [1,2,3]. By physical level, we mean mechanisms which can make the platform where cryptographic primitives run (more) secure to key compromise. One of the most interesting of these methodologies is the idea of Physical Unclonable Functions (PUFs) as introduced in [1]. A PUF is a primitive that maps challenges T_i to responses R_i, which are highly dependent on the physical properties of the device in which the PUF is contained or embedded.

---

* Part of this work was done while the author was at Philips Research Europe.
** Current contact address: jamshid.shokrollahi@de.bosch.com

E. Oswald and P. Rohatgi (Eds.): CHES 2008, LNCS 5154, pp. 181–197, 2008.
© International Association for Cryptologic Research 2008

We will write $R_i \leftarrow \mathsf{PUF}(T_i)$ to denote the response R_i of a PUF to a challenge T_i. Physical Unclonable Functions have essentially two parts: i) a physical part and ii) an operational part. The physical part is a physical system that is very difficult to clone. It inherits its unclonability from uncontrollable process variations during manufacturing. In the case of PUFs on an IC such process variations are typically deep-submicron variations such as doping variations in transistors. The operational part corresponds to the function. In order to turn the physical system into a *function* a set of challenges T_i (stimuli) has to be available to which the system responds with a set of sufficiently different responses R_i. Examples of PUFs include optical PUFs [1], silicon PUFs [4], coating PUFs [2], Intrinsic-PUFs [5], and LC-PUFs [6]. Regardless of their particular instantiation, their unclonability, and tamper evidence properties have made PUFs very useful tools in IP protection and secure key storage applications.

IP Protection For FPGAs. Field Programmable Gate Arrays (FPGAs) are gaining widespread acceptance as substitutes for ASICs in many applications. In fact their re-programmability has made them very attractive in the embedded market, where software and functionality updates can be common and desirable by customers. As a result of this shift, it is increasingly the case that the functionality of an embedded system is presented in the form of a bit configuration file or, in the case of microprocessors, in the form of a program. Thus, the very property that makes FPGAs so attractive (their programmability) also makes it very easy for counterfeiters to copy an IP developer's configuration file and create a similar product without the up-front cost of Intellectual Property (IP) development. This problem was introduced most recently[1] by Simpson and Schaumont [8]. In particular, the authors in [8] showed that by using a PUF on an FPGA they could develop protocols that allow binding of a particular IP to a particular FPGA. Their protocols also allow proving authenticity of the IP to the hardware platform. In [5], the authors further reduce the computation and communication complexity of the protocols in [8] and introduce the idea of Intrinsic-PUFs based on the start-up values of SRAM memory values. Both based their protocols on symmetric-key primitives. In [9], the authors observe that by introducing public-key cryptography, the corresponding private-key does not need to ever leave the FPGA, even during the enrollment stage, thus increasing the security of the overall system. A common characteristic of all PUF-based protocols in [5,8,9] is the derivation of a key(s) from the PUF, which is used to encrypt a piece of IP and authenticate its origin. In the remainder of the paper, we will refer to the encrypting operation for ease of presentation but it is clear that our discussion extends to the computation of Message Authentication Codes (MACs) and/or signatures on a particular IP block.

The Need for a Helper Data Algorithm. Notice that PUF responses are noisy by nature. In other words, two calls to the PUF with the same challenge T_i will produce two different but closely related responses R_i, R_i', where the measure of closeness can be defined via a distance function. We will make the distance

---

[1] See [7] for earlier references to the problem.

function more explicit in Sect. 2. Intuitively, the distance function should be small among responses originating from the same device and very large for PUF responses originating from different devices. Nevertheless, it is clear that the plain PUF response can not be used as the key, since this would mean that the data encrypted under response R_i could not be decrypted with response R'_i, even if both responses originate from the same PUF embedded in the same device[2]. In order to derive reliable and uniform strings from (imperfect) sources of randomness, such as a PUF, the concept of a fuzzy extractor or helper data algorithm were introduced in [10,11].

Related Work. To our knowledge, there is no previous description of the complexities and design choices made to implement a helper data algorithm on hardware and, more specifically, on FPGAs. In both [12,13] the noisy nature of a PUF is acknowledged. Their solution to the problem is to add an error correcting stage based on BCH codes. Other codes are not considered and no detailed explanation of how to choose the code is given. Gassend [14] also considers the problem of noisy measurements in PUFs by considering Hamming codes and product codes. The solutions based on product codes in [14] is only able to correct up to two errors. Gassend gets around this problem by trying different challenges until the response has a sufficiently small number of errors that they can be solved. It is worth noticing that a similar problem to the one we are considering is present in biometrics. In fact, the first fuzzy extractor construction [15] was aimed at biometric applications. Dodis et al. [11] also describe a software implementation of a fuzzy extractor based on BCH codes. Somewhat related to our construction is the construction of Hao et al. [16] where they implement a two stage error correcting scheme for biometric applications (iris recognition). The scheme in [16] uses first a Hadamard code and then a Reed-Solomon code in a concatenated manner. Notice that the authors in [16] do not consider the hardware implementation of their schemes. In addition, Reed-Solomon codes are optimized for burst errors and thus, are not applicable to our solution since errors present in PUF responses tend to be random.

Our Contributions. In this paper, we focus on the study and implementation of fuzzy extractors on FPGAs, as [5,8,9] assume the existence of such a block but do not provide explicit constructions nor investigate the hardware costs of fuzzy extractors on FPGAs. Our work can be seen as the final block necessary to generate cryptographic keys and, thus, allows for the construction of full IP-protection solutions on FPGAs. We focus on making an efficient choice of code. By efficient, we mean two things. First, we aim to be able to reconstruct the same key with high probability. In other words, given a code we want to achieve an error probability (the probability that an error pattern happens that can not be corrected by the chosen error correcting code) of at least $10^{-6} \approx 2^{-20}$. We argue in Sect. 3.2 that this is a conservative estimate, which can be applied for most applications. In this respect, we show empirically that from the codes considered,

---

[2] This would only work if $R_i = R'_i$, which in general is highly unlikely.

the best codes (meaning those that can achieve a low error probability) are BCH codes [17,18].

Our second efficiency measure refers to hardware resources. In particular, once we have achieved a certain error probability, we desire that the error correcting decoding algorithm implementation be as area efficient as possible. This, in fact, is a key requirement and makes our work fundamentally different from other helper data algorithm implementations. In particular, the aim of our solution is not the implementation of a helper data algorithm on an FPGA by itself. Rather, our aim is to implement a helper data algorithm in as little hardware as possible and, in the process, allow for the secure deployment of IP. The IP block, in fact, is the one that should determine the FPGA resources, not the helper data algorithm. In our search for an area efficient solution, we turned to different code constructions. We find that concatenation of codes as introduced by Forney [19], allows for the use of codes that are much simpler to implement and possibly more area efficient than BCH codes. In particular, an odd repetition code followed by a Reed-Muller code or a Golay code can satisfy our error probability requirements. We expect that such construction will incur in considerable area savings with respect to a construction based on BCH codes only. We also propose new architectures for the decoders of Reed-Muller and Golay codes, which are of independent interest. In addition, we identify which universal hash function constructions from those already known in the literature are most suitable for small area implementations. These results are described with focus on an implementation results targeting a Spartan-3E Xilinx FPGA, which is a typical FPGA used in low cost applications.

Notation. Algebraically a binary linear code $\mathcal{C}$ with message length k and codeword length n is a k-dimensional subspace of $\mathbb{F}_2^n$. The messages specify each element of the subspace and the codewords are their representations in $\mathbb{F}_2^n$. Given two codewords $\mathbf{v} = (v_1, v_2, \ldots, v_n)$, and $\mathbf{w} = (w_1, w_2, \ldots, w_n)$, with $v_i, w_i \in \mathbb{F}_2$, the Hamming distance between the two words, denoted by d_H, is the number of coordinates in which $\mathbf{v}$ and $\mathbf{w}$ differ. The minimum distance $d_{\min}$ of a linear code $\mathcal{C}$ is the smallest Hamming distance between any two different codewords in $\mathcal{C}$. For linear codes the minimum distance is equal to the minimum non-zero weight in $\mathcal{C}$. We write an $[n, k, d]$-code to mean a binary code $\mathcal{C}$ of length n, cardinality 2^k (encoding messages of length k), and minimum distance d. A linear code with minimum distance d has error correcting capability or error correcting distance $t = \lfloor \frac{d_{\min}-1}{2} \rfloor$. An important data structure related to the linear code is the generator matrix G whose rows are elements of a basis for the linear code. For a binary linear $[n, k, d]$-code, we can write the generator matrix in the standard form as $G = (I_k|P)$, where I_k is the $k \times k$ identity matrix and P is a $k \times (n - k)$ matrix. The parity check matrix is then found as $H = (P^T|I_{n-k})$. This is an $n - k$ by n matrix such that the inner product of any codeword with any column of H equals zero. Encoding a message $\mathbf{m}$ is accomplished by computing $\mathbf{v} = \mathbf{m}G$. The syndrome of a received word $\mathbf{r} = \mathbf{v} + \mathbf{e}$, where $\mathbf{v}$ and $\mathbf{e}$ are a codeword and error, respectively, is defined as $S_r = H\mathbf{r} = H\mathbf{e}$. We refer the reader to [20,21] as standard references for error correcting codes.

2 Helper Data Algorithms

PUF responses can not be used as a key (as in e.g. [2]) in a cryptographic primitive for two reasons. First, PUF responses are obtained through measurements on physical systems, which are typically noisy. This leads to a problem since cryptographic functions are very sensitive to noise on their inputs. Second, PUF responses are not uniformly distributed. Hence, even if there was no noise, the response would not form a cryptographically secure key. In order to deal with both issues a Helper Data Algorithm (HDA) or Fuzzy Extractor or has to be used. In the remainder of this paper, we will use the two terms interchangeably. For the precise definition of a Fuzzy Extractor and Helper Data algorithm we refer to [10,11].

In general a helper data algorithm deals with both issues (noise and non-uniformity of keys) by implementing first an *information reconciliation phase* and second, by applying a *privacy amplification* or randomness extraction primitive. In order to implement those two primitives, helper data W are generated during the *enrollment phase*. During this phase, carried out in a trusted environment, a probabilistic procedure called Gen is run. Later, during the *key reconstruction* or authentication phase, the key is reconstructed based on a noisy measurement R_i' and the helper data W. During this phase, a procedure called Rep is performed. We present one of the constructions for such procedures previously described in [11]. Other constructions as well as constructions for other metrics can be found in [11]. Notice that all constructions have an error correcting stage. Optimizing such stage will be our focus in the next sections.

Construction Based on Code Offset. In order to implement the procedures Gen and Rep an error correction code $\mathcal{C}$ and a set $\mathcal{H}$ of universal hash functions [22] is required. The parameters $[n, k, d]$ of the code $\mathcal{C}$ are determined by the length of the responses R and the number of errors t that have to be corrected. The distance d of the code is chosen such that t errors can be corrected. The Gen-procedure takes as input a PUF response(s) R and produces as output a key K and helper data $W = (W_1, W_2)$, i.e., $(K; W) = (K; (W_1, W_2)) \leftarrow$ Gen(R). This is achieved as follows. First, a code word $C_S \leftarrow \mathcal{C}$ is chosen at random from $\mathcal{C}$. Then, a first helper data vector equal to $W_1 = C_S \oplus R$ is generated. Furthermore, a hash function h_i is chosen at random from $\mathcal{H}$ and the key K is defined as $K \leftarrow h_i(R)$. The helper data W_2 is set to i. During the key reconstruction phase the procedure Rep is run. It takes as input a noisy response R' from the same PUF and helper data W and reconstructs the key K *i.e.* $K \leftarrow$ Rep(R', W). This is accomplished according to the following steps: (1) *Information Reconciliation*: Using the helper data W_1, $W_1 \oplus R'$ is computed. Then, the decoding algorithm of $\mathcal{C}$ is used to obtain C_S. From C_S, R is reconstructed as $R = W_1 \oplus C_S$; and (2) *Privacy amplification*: The helper data W_2 is used to choose the correct hash function $h_i \in \mathcal{H}$ and to reconstruct the key as $K = h_i(R)$. Notice that we have implicitly assumed the use of a binary code. The security of the above constructions has been established in [10,11].

3   Searching for Good Linear Codes and Efficient HDAs

We will model the noise present in PUF responses as a binary symmetric channel (BSC). In particular, in a BSC, the bit error probability p_b specifies the probability that a transmitted information bit is received in error. Then, with probability $1 - p_b$ the sent information bit equals the received one. We assume that all bits are independent, which turns out to be a good assumption as shown in [9,5]. In [9], the authors also show that the probability that a string of n bits has more than t errors is given by:

$$P_{total} = \sum_{i=t+1}^{n} \binom{n}{i} p_b^i (1 - p_b)^{n-i} = 1 - \sum_{i=0}^{t} \binom{n}{i} p_b^i (1 - p_b)^{n-i} \tag{1}$$

Notice that the value of P_{total} will determine the minimum distance of the code and thus, the size of the code. We argue that a conservative value is $P_{total} \leq 10^{-6}$. To see this, we relate the failure error probability of our system to the error probability of the hardware platform (in this case FPGAs), which is given in terms of the Failure-In-Time (FIT) unit. Given a FIT rate λ, the probability that a failure will occur until time t is given by $P_{\text{Failure until time } t}(t) = 1 - \exp(-\lambda t)$. For both Xilinx and Altera devices, the lowest FIT rate that we found in [23,24] was five for older devices. All device families manufactured in newer process technology have a FIT rate higher than twelve. Assuming conservatively a FIT rate equal to five, for a 15-year period the resulting failure probability is 6.610^{-4}. Thus, it is clear that assuming $P_{total} \leq 10^{-6}$ is quite conservative for any realistic application (i.e. applications that should last more than a month).

3.1   The Naive Approach: Simple Codes

We consider codes which can be used to correct random errors (as opposed to burst errors) in a received word $\mathbf{r}$. Thus, we do not consider Reed-Solomon codes, which have very good burst error correcting capabilities, as well as convolutional codes for similar reasons. We also discarded LDPC codes [25], which are very efficient but require very large and sparse binary matrices, thus making them resource intensive in hardware applications (see e.g. [26,27] for designs targeting FPGAs, which occupy more than 50% of a high-end FPGA). We do not consider Hadamard codes explicitly but notice that they are equivalent to first-order Reed-Muller codes. Similarly, the Hamming code is a $[2^m - 1, 2^m - m - 1, 3]$-code and can therefore correct only one error. Thus, it is not very useful to decode received vectors with high error rates as in the applications we are considering. In order to attain the desired error probability of 10^{-6}, we simply start by looking at what can be achieved via straight forward use of the following codes: repetition code, Reed-Muller codes of the first order[3], binary Golay code, and binary BCH codes. We refer to [28] for extensive tables for different error probabilities. For our particular case, we summarize the relevant code parameters in Table 1. In Table 1,

---

[3] Reed-Muller codes of higher order offer better error correction performance at a considerable higher cost in decoder complexity. Thus, we do not consider them.

Table 1. Results for different codes with $p_b = 0.15$. A code denoted with a star $(^*)$ means it has been shortened.

Code	$[n, k, d]$	$t = \lfloor d/2 \rfloor$	P_{total}	source bits for 171 bits
Repetition	$[33, 1, 33]$	16	1.0010^{-6}	5643
Reed-Muller	$[256, 9, 128]$	63	2.0410^{-5}	4864
Reed-Muller	$[512, 10, 256]$	127	2.5410^{-9}	9216
Golay	$[23, 12, 7]$	3	0.4604	345
BCH	$[511, 19, 239]$	119	2.9710^{-7}	4599
BCH	$[1023, 46, 439]$	219	1.8510^{-8}	4092
BCH	$[1020, 43, 439]^*$	219	1.4410^{-8}	**4080**

the last column refers to the number of SRAM source bits required to obtain 171 "error-free" bits which can then be hashed to obtain 128 random and uniformly distributed bits. This is based on the amount of entropy in SRAM PUFs reported in [5]. Then, the last column in Table 1 can be computed as $n\lceil 171/k \rceil$, where n and k, refer to the code parameters. We observe that in this table, we have only considered the code as stated in the first column or a shortened version of it in the case of the $[1020, 43, 439]$-BCH code. Shortening a code[4] is one of many different code modifications and one which we found useful empirically. We also notice that the number of errors that a shortened code can correct is at least t. However, correcting the additional error patterns enabled by the code shortening results in additional decoder complexity. Notice that neither the Golay code nor the $[256, 9, 128]$-Reed-Muller code provide our desired error probability and that the BCH codes provide a very low error rate. Thus, the question that we ask is if we can extract a 128-bit cryptographically secure key with less than 4080 bits of SRAM.

3.2 A New Construction Based on Concatenated Codes

Notice that the previous scheme has several disadvantages. First, a scheme based on the repetition code alone, although low complexity, requires more than 5000 bits of SRAM. Second, although we have not discussed the complexity of the decoders yet, BCH decoder algorithms are very complex and, thus, we expect it to be expensive in terms of area. Thus, in this section we propose a new scheme based on concatenation of two error correcting codes $\mathcal{C}_1$ and $\mathcal{C}_2$ [19] to get less complexity while achieving the same or comparable error probabilities. Given two codes $\mathcal{C}_1$ and $\mathcal{C}_2$ with parameters $[n_1, k_1, d_1]$ and $[n_2, k_2, d_2]$ respectively, the concatenated code $\mathcal{C}_c$ is a $[n_c, k_c, d_c]$-code with $n_c = n_1 n_2$, $k_c = k_1 k_2$ and $d_c = d_1 d_2$. Notice that very long codes can be constructed from considerably shorter ones. Furthermore, a concatenated code can correct (depending on construction) random and burst errors simultaneously and the decoding complexity of two short codes is lower than the complexity of the entire code. Based

---

[4] One way to shorten an $[n, k, d]$-code, is to set i information symbols to zero to obtain an $[n - i, k - i, d]$-code.

Algorithm 1. Gen_c Algorithm for Concatenated Codes

Require: An $[n_1, k_1, d_1]$-code $\mathcal{C}_1$, an $[n_2, k_2, d_2]$-code $\mathcal{C}_2$, a family $\mathcal{H}$ of universal hash functions, and a PUF response R of size $s_R = l_2 \cdot n_2$ bits, where $l_2 = \lceil \frac{l_1 \cdot n_1}{k_2} \rceil$ and $l_1 = \lceil \frac{s_K}{k_1} \rceil$ or $l_1 = \lceil \frac{s_K}{k_1} \rceil + 1$.

Ensure: Helper data (W_1, W_2) and a key K of size s_K

1: Set $l_1 \leftarrow \lceil \frac{s_K}{k_1} \rceil$ if k_2 divides $l_1 \cdot n_1$, otherwise $l_1 \leftarrow \lceil \frac{s_K}{k_1} \rceil + 1$

2: Generate uniformly at random code words $\mathbf{v_{1i}}$ from $\mathcal{C}_1$, for $i = 1, 2, \ldots, l_1$.

3: Form the string u by concatenating the binary representation of $\mathbf{v_{1i}}$ for $i = l_1, \ldots, 2, 1$. At the end $u = (u_1, u_2, \cdots, u_{l_u})$, where $u_i \in \{0, 1\}$ and $l_u = l_1 \cdot n_1$.

4: Set $l_2 \leftarrow \lceil \frac{l_u}{k_2} \rceil$. If k_2 does not divide l_u, extend u by adding $l_2 k_2 - l_u$ zero bits to it. The resulting string u' is of size $l_2 \cdot k_2$ bits.

5: Write $u' = (U_1', U_2', \ldots, U_{l_2}')$, where U_i' are words of size k_2 bits.

6: For $i = 1, 2, \ldots, l_2$, compute $\mathbf{v_{2i}} \leftarrow \mathsf{Encode}_{\mathcal{C}_2}(U_i')$, where $\mathsf{Encode}_{\mathcal{C}_2}$ is the encoding algorithm for the code $\mathcal{C}_2$.

7: Form the string w by concatenating the binary representation of $\mathbf{v_{2i}}$ for $i = 1, 2, \ldots, l_2$. At the end $w = (w_1, w_2, \cdots, w_{l_w})$, where $w_i \in \{0, 1\}$ and $l_w = l_2 \cdot n_2$.

8: Set $W_1 \leftarrow w \oplus R$, where $\oplus$ is the bitwise logical XOR operation.

9: Choose a random hash function $h_i \in \mathcal{H}$

10: Set $W_2 \leftarrow i$

11: Set R_K to the first $(l_2 - 1) \cdot n_2$ bits of R. This essentially ignores n_2 bits of the response R.

12: Set $K \leftarrow h_i(R_K)$

---

on our discussion on fuzzy extractors in Sect. 2, our new constructions for the procedures Gen and Rep are described in Algorithms 1 and 2, respectively.

Before considering specific examples, we discuss what the error probability will be for our concatenated codes. Intuitively, the main idea of our construction is to first use a rather simple code, let's say $\mathcal{C}_2$ to bring the number of errors down. Then, with the second code, $\mathcal{C}_1$, the remaining errors are corrected. By a clever choice of the first code also the second code, has to correct only a few errors making the scheme more efficient. A similar idea is presented in [29] as a way to cope with extremely noisy channels. In particular, [29] reduced the error probability by using a repetition code and then combine the first stage with a more powerful code. For example, a simple calculation with (1) will demonstrate that just using the $[3, 1, 3]$ repetition code, it is possible to bring the error probability from 15% to 6%. In general, the resulting error probability can be estimated as follows. Given two codes $\mathcal{C}_1, \mathcal{C}_2$ with parameters $[n_1, k_1, d_1; t_1 = \lfloor (d_1 - 1)/2 \rfloor]$ and $[n_2, k_2, d_2; t_2 = \lfloor (d_2 - 1)/2 \rfloor]$, respectively, the Rep_c-procedure will first decode with $\mathsf{Decode}_{\mathcal{C}_2}$ and the result will be decoded with $\mathsf{Decode}_{\mathcal{C}_1}$. Thus, the error probabilities P_2 and P_1 after decoding with the decoding algorithms of $\mathcal{C}_2$ and $\mathcal{C}_1$, respectively, correspond to:

$$P_2 = \sum_{i=t_2+1}^{n_2} \binom{n_2}{i} p_b^i (1 - p_b)^{n_2-i} = 1 - \sum_{i=0}^{t_2} \binom{n_2}{i} p_b^i (1 - p_b)^{n_2-i} \qquad (2)$$

Algorithm 2. Rep_c Algorithm for Concatenated Codes

Require: Helper data (W_1, W_2), the decoding algorithms $Decode_{C_1}$ and $Decode_{C_2}$ corresponding to the $[n_1, k_1, d_1]$-code C_1 and $[n_2, k_2, d_2]$-code C_2, respectively, and a noisy PUF response R' of size $s_R = l_2 \cdot n_2$ bits, where l_2 and l_1 are as determined in Algorithm 1.

Ensure: A key K of size s_K

1: Set $\widetilde{w} \leftarrow W_1 \oplus R'$, where $\oplus$ is the bitwise logical XOR operation. This results in a bit string $\widetilde{w} = (\widetilde{w}_1, \widetilde{w}_2, \cdots, \widetilde{w}_{l_w})$, where $\widetilde{w}_i \in \{0, 1\}$ and $l_w = l_2 \cdot n_2$.

2: Set $\widetilde{\mathbf{v}}_{2i} = (\widetilde{w}_{(i-1)n_2+1}, \widetilde{w}_{(i-1)n_2+2}, \ldots, \widetilde{w}_{in_2})$ for $i = 1, 2, \ldots, l_2$.

3: Compute $\mathbf{v}'_{2i} \leftarrow Decode_{C_2}(\widetilde{\mathbf{v}}_{2i})$ and recover the perturbed string $\widetilde{u}' = (\widetilde{U}'_1, \widetilde{U}'_2, \ldots, \widetilde{U}'_{l_2})$, where $\widetilde{U}'_i$ are words of size k_2 bits.

4: If zero bits were added during the Gen_c procedure, delete them and obtain a string $\widetilde{u} = (\widetilde{u}_1, \widetilde{u}_2, \cdots, \widetilde{u}_{l_u})$, where $\widetilde{u}_i \in \{0, 1\}$ and $l_u = l_1 \cdot n_1$. Otherwise (if no zero bits were added) set $\widetilde{u} \leftarrow \widetilde{u}'$.

5: Set $\mathbf{v}'_{1i} = (\widetilde{u}_{(i-1)n_1+1}, \widetilde{u}_{(i-1)n_1+2}, \ldots, \widetilde{u}_{in_1})$ for $i = 1, 2, \ldots, l_1$.

6: Compute $\mathbf{v}_{1i} \leftarrow Decode_{C_1}(\mathbf{v}'_{1i})$ and recover the original string $u = (u_1, u_2, \cdots, u_{l_u})$, where $u_i \in \{0, 1\}$ and $l_u = l_1 \cdot n_1$.

7: Perform Steps 4 through 12 of Algorithm 1 to recover K.

$$P_1 = \sum_{i=t_1+1}^{n_1} \binom{n_1}{i} P_2^i (1 - P_2)^{n_1-i} = 1 - \sum_{i=0}^{t_1} \binom{n_1}{i} P_2^i (1 - P_2)^{n_1-i}$$

where p_b is the bit error probability of the source, in our case the noise in the PUF response. Notice that P_i is the *word* error probability. In other words, the probability that a word will be in error after decoding. This is equal to the bit error probability in the case of the repetition code but not in the case of Golay, Reed-Muller or BCH codes. However, it is well known [30] that the resulting *bit* error probability is always less or equal to the word error probability as estimated in (2). Thus, we are being conservative in our estimates and the results in Table 2 correspond to worst case error probabilities. We report in Table 2 the best constructions that we found. Extensive tables for different PUF bit-error probabilities can be found in [28]. Our first observation about Table 2 is that we can achieve probabilities $\leq 10^{-6}$ not using BCH codes. This is a nice outcome of the construction, since this allows us to consider other codes which accept a more efficient implementation. Nevertheless, BCH codes error correction capabilities are indisputable. A second and perhaps more important observation is that when we combine a repetition code with a BCH code in a concatenated construction, the code size and thus, the number of SRAM source bits required decreases considerably (compare 4080 in Table 1 with the shortened [226, 86, 43]-BCH code at 2260 bits). Thus, it is clear that our construction offers considerable advantages.

Table 2. Output error probabilities for several concatenated codes with an input bit error probability of $p_b = 0.15$. Codes denoted with a star (*) have been shortened.

C_2 $[n_2, k_2, d_2]$	C_1 $[n_1, k_1, d_1]$	P_1	source bits for 171 bits
repetition $[3, 1, 3]$	$BCH[127, 29, 43]$	8.48 E-06	2286
	$RM[64, 7, 32]$	1.02 E-06	4800
	$BCH[63, 7, 31]$	8.13 E-07	4725
repetition $[5, 1, 5]$	$RM[32, 6, 16]$	1.49 E-06	4640
	$BCH[226, 86, 43]^*$	2.28 E-07	2260
repetition $[7, 1, 7]$	$G_{23}[23, 12, 7]$	1.58 E-04	2415
	$G_{23}[20, 9, 7]^*$	8.89 E-05	2660
	$BCH[255, 171, 23]$	8.00 E-05	1785
	$RM[16, 5, 8]$	3.47 E-05	3920
	$BCH[113, 57, 19]^*$	1.34 E-06	2373
repetition $[9, 1, 9]$	$BCH[121, 86, 11]$	6.84 E-05	2178
	$G_{23}[23, 12, 7]$	8.00 E-06	3105
	$RM[16, 5, 8]$	1.70 E-06	5040
repetition $[11, 1, 11]$	$G_{24}[24, 13, 7]$	5.41 E-07	3696
	$G_{23}[23, 12, 7]$	4.52 E-07	3795

4   HDA Architecture and Implementation Results

In addition to the error correcting properties of the codes that we previously considered, we also consider their performance from a hardware perspective. In particular, in this work we aim to make designs as small as possible in order to reserve space for the actual IP block to be implemented on the FPGA. We propose decoder architectures for first order Reed-Muller codes and for the binary Golay codes. For hash functions, we take the architecture proposed by Krawczyk [31] since this family accepts a more efficient implementation than all the other ones proposed or described in [32,31,33]. Due to space constraints, we refer to [28] for an exact analysis of their complexity.

Reed-Muller Codes. In this work we only consider first-order Reed-Muller codes because of their simple decoding algorithms. The procedure for decoding these codes is shown in Algorithm 3. To describe the process of generating the characteristic vectors let us denote the row of the generator matrix corresponding with the variable $\mathbf{v}_i$ by $\mathbf{v}_i^{(1)}$ and its logical negation by $\mathbf{v}_i^{(0)}$. Then the characteristic vectors of $\mathbf{v}_i$ are different vectors

$$\prod_{j=1,\cdots,m, j \neq i} \mathbf{v}_j^{(k_j)}, \tag{3}$$

where k_j is either 0 and 1. The values of k_j for each of the $m-1$ values of j assign to each characteristic vector for each variable a number between 0 and $2^{m-1} - 1$. Thus an $m - 1$ bit counter can be used to enumerate all of the characteristic

---

Algorithm 3. Decoding $\mathcal{R}(1, m)$ codes using Majority logic

---

Require: $x = (x_0, x_1, \ldots, x_{2^m-1})$ (the received vector) and $G \in \mathbb{F}_2^{(m+1) \times 2^m}$ the generator matrix of $\mathcal{R}(1, m)$

Ensure: $\hat{u} = (u_0, u_1, \cdots, u_m)$ the original message

1: **for** $i = 1$ to m do **do**
2:     Find 2^{m-1} characteristic vectors for the row i of G (the index of the rows of G begin with zero).
3:     Compute the dot product of each of these vectors with the received message.
4:     Compute the majority of the values of the dot products and assign it to u_i.
5: **end for**
6: Multiply $(u_1, \cdots u_m)$ by the sub-matrix consisting of the last m rows of G to get the vector s with 2^m entries.
7: Assign the majority of the entries in $s + x$ to u_0.

---

vectors corresponding with a variable. We are aware of two different hardware structures proposed in the literature for hardware based decoding of $\mathcal{R}(1, m)$ codes which are also described in [21, Chapter 13]. However, since we target a low resource implementation, we propose an architecture that is a factor of m (asymptotically) smaller than those proposed in [21] at the cost of additional processing time. We defer a more detailed comparison of the architectures to the full version of the paper.

The newly proposed design is based on Algorithm 3 and is shown in Fig. 1. The most important parts of this circuit are the GM-generator and the CV-generator modules. The output of the GM-module periodically consists of each column of the generator matrix. Due to the structure of the $\mathcal{R}(1, m)$ generator matrix and considering the fact that only the last m rows of the $(m+1) \times 2^m$ generator matrix are required, it is easy to verify that GM-generator can be realized using an m-bit counter. The CV-generator module generates the bits of each of the characteristic vectors using the current column of the generator matrix, based on the index of the characteristic vector, the $m - 1$ values of k_j from (3), which is the output of CV Index and the variable being currently decoded which is the output of Variable counter. CV-generator consists of several multiplexers, which output an input value or its logical inverse, and the required circuitry to compute the product in (3). The Majority Decoder is a counter which can be either m bit or $m+1$ bit wide and its content must be compared with 2^{m-1} or 2^m, respectively. Hence its output is its $(m - 1)$th or mth bit, respectively. The output of Algorithm 3 is the message corresponding to the appropriate codeword whereas for PUF applications the codeword is needed. After the message is correctly decoded it is multiplied, again using the inner product module, by the generator matrix and the result is stored in the Received Word module. Our decoder requires $m2^{m-1}2^m = m2^{2m-1}$ iterations to process each row of the generator matrix with 2^m columns for each of the 2^{m-1} characteristic vectors and each of the m decoded messages. To this time the 2^m iterations for processing each of the 2^m columns of the generator matrix should be added. The Received Word module is used for both input and output of the values. The overall complexity of the decoder is shown in Table 3.

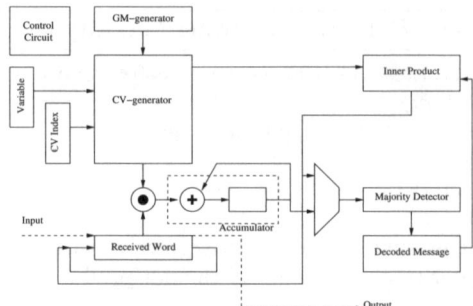

Fig. 1. Block diagram of our Reed-Muller decoder

Golay Code. An arithmetic decoder as seen in Algorithm 4 uses the weight structure of the syndrome to determine the error patterns [34]. P is the non-identity part of the generator matrix. The vector cp_i is the ith column of P and rp_i the ith row, respectively. The error vector is denoted as $e = (x, y)$ where x and y are vectors of length 12. A vector x_i is the zero vector with a 1 at the ith position. Our proposed circuit shown in Figure 2 can be derived from Algorithm 4. The main steps in the decoding process are the computation of the syndrome and helper syndrome, the determination of the Hamming weight, $GF(2)$ addition and the comparison of the Hamming weights with a constant.

We use a dot product block, which consists of 1 AND, 1 XOR and 1 FF for the serial computation of the syndrome and the helper syndrome. These syndromes are of length 12 and therefore the Hamming weight is at most 12 which can be represented with 4 bits. The result of the dot product or the $GF(2)$ addition respectively is loaded into a 12-bit shift register and a simple 4-bit counter counts the number of ones. The 4-bit counter requires 8 XOR, 8 AND and 4 OR gates. The result is then compared with a constant depending on the step of Algorithm 4. This step requires a 4-bit comparator and therefore 12 AND, 8 OR and 8 NOT gates. The constants are stored in memory and need 3 FFs. The $GF(2)$ addition is done with an XOR gate. Furthermore we need 24 FF for the error vector e, 24 FF to store the received vector and 288 FF for the generator matrix. The gate complexity without the control circuit is shown in Table 3. The above circuit can be optimized by removing the shift register and constructing the generator matrix on the fly, so we need to store only 24 bits for the first column and 23 bits for the second column. The other columns are determined by a simple shift operation. The complexity of the circuit without control can be seen in Table 3.

Universal Hashing. As previously mentioned, we use a construction due to Krawczyk [31]. This construction makes use of random binary matrices, where the hash value $h_A(x)$ is the Boolean multiplication of the matrix A by the message x. Krawczyk [31] shows how this can be implemented using a simple LFSR. We only need to store the first column of the matrix and the next columns are generated by the LFSR. The circuit is shown in Fig. 3. For a 128-bit key

---

Algorithm 4. Arithmetic Decoding of the Golay G_{24} code [34]

Require: r (the received vector), $G = [I|P]$ (the generator matrix)
Ensure: v (the encoded message)
1: Compute the syndrome $s = Gr$
2: **if** $wt(s) \leq 3$ **then**
3:      $e = (s^T, 0)$
4: **else if** $wt(s + cp_i) \leq 2$ for a column vector cp_i **then**
5:      $e = ((s + cp_i)^T, y_i)$
6: **else**
7:      Compute the helper syndrome $z = P^T s$
8:      **if** $wt(z) \leq 3$ **then**
9:          $e = (0, (z)^T)$
10:     **else if** $wt(z + rp_i^T) \leq 2$ for a row vector rp_i **then**
11:         $e = (x_i, (z)^T + rp_i)$
12:     **else**
13:         Too many errors
14:     **end if**
15: **end if**
16: $v = r + e$

Table 3. Area complexity of a serial implementation of arithmetic Golay decoding and low resources Reed-Muller decoder

Decoder Variant	FF	XOR	AND	OR	NOT
Golay store matrix	352	10	21	12	8
Golay generate matrix	99	10	21	12	8
Low resource $\mathcal{R}(1, m)$ decoder	$2^m + 6m - 1$	$\frac{m^2}{2} + \frac{13m}{2} - 2$	$9m$	$\frac{5m^2}{2} + \frac{m}{2} - 1$	m

the LFSR and the register for the accumulator need to be of size 128, thus requiring 256 FF. In addition the LFSR requires about $\frac{128}{2}$ XOR gates and the accumulator 128 XOR gates. The size of the shift register in Fig. 3 depends on the parameter n of the error correcting code used. Thus, for the Reed-Muller codes and Golay code it needs between 16 and 64 FFs depending on the code. Altogether without control the circuit requires 272-320 FFs and 192 XOR gates. *Implementation Results.* We have implemented the repetition code, Golay and Reed-Muller code decoders ($\mathcal{R}(1, 4), \mathcal{R}(1, 5), \mathcal{R}(1, 6)$) as well as the Toeplitz design for a universal hash function based on [31] in VHDL. We target the Spartan-3E 500 FPGA and use Xilinx ISE v9.2 for our tooling. We synthesized and mapped all designs. The Spartan-3E family of devices corresponds to low end FPGAs typically used in automotive and consumer electronic applications. The results are shown in Table 4. We observe that our designs our very space efficient. In particular, combining any repetition code decoder (a counter plus logic), a Reed-Muller or Golay code, any of the designs for the hash function our utilization is not greater than 10%. It seems clear that the Reed-Muller code is both superior in area but also in error correction performance (based on Table 2). Al-

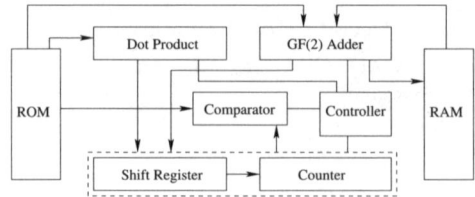

Fig. 2. Block diagram of our arithmetic Golay decoder

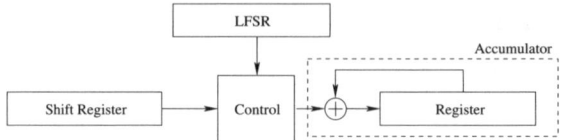

Fig. 3. LFSR-based Toeplitz hashing

Table 4. Implementation Results on Xilinx Spartan-3E-500 FPGA

Code / Hash	Output (bits)	Slices	Latency (cycles)	Critical Path (nsec)	Performance for 128-bit key@50 MHz (sec)
Repetition $[3, 1, 3]$	3	41 (1%)	6	5.3	$2.1\ 10^{-5}$
Repetition $[5, 1, 5]$	5	41 (1%)	10	5.3	$3.4\ 10^{-5}$
Repetition $[7, 1, 7]$	7	41 (1%)	14	5.3	$4.8\ 10^{-5}$
Repetition $[9, 1, 9]$	9	41 (1%)	18	5.3	$6.2\ 10^{-5}$
Repetition $[11, 1, 11]$	11	41 (1%)	22	5.3	$7.5\ 10^{-5}$
$\mathcal{R}(1, 4)$	16	69 (1%)	503	5.5	$3.5\ 10^{-4}$
$\mathcal{R}(1, 5)$	32	90 (1%)	1743	5.6	$1.0\ 10^{-3}$
$\mathcal{R}(1, 6)$	64	127 (1%)	6495	5.6	$3.2\ 10^{-3}$
Golay G_{24}	24	539 (5%)	1188	6.6	$3.6\ 10^{-4}$
Toeplitz Hash 16 [31]	128	319 (3%)	64	5.7	$1.0\ 10^{-5}$
Toeplitz Hash 24 [31]	128	327 (3%)	96	5.7	$1.2\ 10^{-5}$
Toeplitz Hash 32 [31]	128	335 (3%)	128	5.7	$1.0\ 10^{-5}$
Toeplitz Hash 64 [31]	128	367 (3%)	256	5.7	$1.0\ 10^{-5}$

though, the Golay code decoder can be optimized by generating the parity check matrix on the fly, in terms of area it is still outperformed by the Reed-Muller codes. We can estimate the complexity of the overall helper data algorithm by assuming a concatenated construction with a Repetition code, a Reed-Muller code, a Toeplitz-based hash function and 100% overhead for control. Even then, the overall fuzzy extractor requires less than 10% of the FPGA resources. Unfortunately, we have not found any BCH code implementations on FPGAs to which we can compare. However, the BCH decoding algorithms themselves are much more complex, thus, it is expected that their hardware complexity will be similarly higher. In the full version of the paper, we expect to have a full BCH decoder and thus, be able to fully compare all our constructions.

5   Conclusion

We present the first efficient implementations of helper data algorithms on FP-GAs. Helper data algorithms are used to extract cryptographic keys from the noisy response of, e.g., a Physical Unclonable Function (PUF). PUFs have become an attractive subject of research due to their nice properties for unforgeable authentication and secure key storage purposes. In particular, one can deploy them to securely bind applications to the underlying hardware, a mechanism that has various applications and most prominently IP protection. Our solution offers the last missing building block toward real world IP protection on FPGAs. Our helper data algorithms are efficient with regard to the required hardware resources, which is important for hardware design. In the design of our helper data algorithms, we make use of various linear codes constructions, each with own advantages and shortcomings. These constructions are then compared in terms of error correction capabilities and hardware resource usage, giving the designer the necessary tools to make an informed decision when implementing a helper data algorithm.

References

1. Pappu, R.S., Recht, B., Taylor, J., Gershenfeld, N.: Physical one-way functions. Science 297(6), 2026–2030 (2002)
2. Tuyls, P., Schrijen, G.-J., Škorić, B., van Geloven, J., Verhaegh, N., Wolters, R.:: Read-Proof Hardware from Protective Coatings. In: Goubin, L., Matsui, M. (eds.) CHES 2006. LNCS, vol. 4249, pp. 369–383. Springer, Heidelberg (2006)
3. Trusted Computing Group: TPM main specification. Technical Report Version 1.2 Revision 94 (March 2006)
4. Gassend, B., Clarke, D.E., van Dijk, M., Devadas, S.: Silicon physical unknown functions. In: Atluri, V. (ed.) ACM Conference on Computer and Communications Security — CCS 2002, pp. 148–160. ACM, New York (2002)
5. Guajardo, J., Kumar, S.S., Schrijen, G.-J., Tuyls, P.: FPGA Intrinsic PUFs and Their Use for IP Protection. In: Paillier, P., Verbauwhede, I. (eds.) CHES 2007. LNCS, vol. 4727, pp. 63–80. Springer, Heidelberg (2007)
6. Škorić, B., Bel, T., Blom, A., de Jong, B., Kretschman, H., Nellissen, A.: Randomized resonators as uniquely identifiable anti-counterfeiting tags. Technical report, Philips Research Laboratories (January 28, 2008)
7. Kean, T.: Cryptographic rights management of FPGA intellectual property cores. In: ACM/SIGDA International Symposium on Field-Programmable Gate Arrays — FPGA 2002, pp. 113–118 (2002)
8. Simpson, E., Schaumont, P.: Offline Hardware/Software Authentication for Reconfigurable Platforms. In: Goubin, L., Matsui, M. (eds.) CHES 2006. LNCS, vol. 4249, pp. 311–323. Springer, Heidelberg (2006)
9. Guajardo, J., Kumar, S.S., Schrijen, G.J., Tuyls, P.: Physical Unclonable Functions and Public Key Crypto for FPGA IP Protection. In: International Conference on Field Programmable Logic and Applications — FPL 2007, August 27-30, 2007, pp. 189–195. IEEE, Los Alamitos (2007)
10. Linnartz, J.P.M.G., Tuyls, P.: New Shielding Functions to Enhance Privacy and Prevent Misuse of Biometric Templates. In: Kittler, J., Nixon, M.S. (eds.) AVBPA 2003. LNCS, vol. 2688, pp. 393–402. Springer, Heidelberg (2003)

11. Dodis, Y., Reyzin, M., Smith, A.: Fuzzy extractors: How to generate strong keys from biometrics and other noisy data. In: Cachin, C., Camenisch, J.L. (eds.) EUROCRYPT 2004. LNCS, vol. 3027, pp. 523–540. Springer, Heidelberg (2004)
12. Suh, G.E., O'Donnell, C.W., Devadas, S.: AEGIS: A Single-Chip Secure Processor. IEEE Design & Test of Computers 24(6), 570–580 (2007)
13. Dijk, M.v., Lim, D., Devadas, S.: Reliable Secret Sharing With Physical Random Functions. Computation Structures Group Memo 475, CSAIL — Massachusetts Institute of Technology (2004)
14. Gassend, B.: Physical Random Functions. Master's thesis, Computer Science and Artificial Intelligence Laboratory, MIT Computation Structures Group Memo 458 (February 2003)
15. Juels, A., Wattenberg, M.: A Fuzzy Commitment Scheme. In: Motiwalla, J., Tsudik, G. (eds.) ACM Conference on Computer and Communications Security — ACM CCS 1999, November 1-4, 1999, pp. 28–36. ACM, New York (1999)
16. Hao, F., Anderson, R., Daugman, J.: Combining Crypto with Biometrics Effectively. IEEE Transactions on Computers 55(9), 1081–1088 (2006)
17. Hochquenghem, A.: Codes Correcteurs D'erreurs. Chiffres 2, 147–156 (1959)
18. Bose, R.C., Ray-Chaudhuri, D.K.: On a Class of Error-Correcting Binary Group Codes. Information and Control 3, 68–79 (1960)
19. Forney Jr., G.D.: Concatenated Codes. Research Monograph No. 37. MIT Press, Cambridge (1966)
20. Blahut, R.E.: Theory and Practice of Error Control Codes, 1st edn. Addison-Wesley Publishing Company, Reading (1985)
21. MacWilliams, F.J., Sloane, N.J.A.: The Theory of Error-Correcting Codes. North-Holland Mathematical Library, vol. 16. North-Holland/Elsevier, Amsterdam (1977)
22. Carter, L., Wegman, M.N.: Universal Classes of Hash Functions. J. Comput. Syst. Sci. 18(2), 143–154 (1979)
23. Xilinx: Device Reliability Report — Fourth Quarter 2007. Technical Report UG116 (v4.3) (February 6, 2008), http://www.xilinx.com/support/documentation/
24. Altera: Reliability Report 45 — Q2 2007. Technical report (2007), http://www.altera.com/literature/lit-index.html.
25. MacKay, D.J.C.: Good Error-Correcting Codes Based on Very Sparse Matrices. IEEE Transactions on Information Theory 45(2), 399–431 (1999)
26. Levine, B.A., Reed Taylor, R., Schmit, H.: Implementation of Near Shannon Limit Error-Correcting Codes Using Reconfigurable Hardware. In: IEEE Symposium on Field-Programmable Custom Computing Machines — FCCM 2000, April 17-19, 2000, pp. 217–226. IEEE Computer Society, Los Alamitos (2000)
27. Brack, T., Kienle, F., Wehn, N.: Disclosing the LDPC code decoder design space. In: Gielen, G.G.E. (ed.) Conference on Design, Automation and Test in Europe — DATE 2006, European Design and Automation Association, Leuven, Belgium, March 6-10, 2006, pp. 200–205 (2006)
28. Bösch, C.: Efficient fuzzy extractors for reconfigurable hardware. Master's thesis, Chair for System Security, Department of Electrical Engineering and Information Science, Ruhr-Universität Bochum (March 2008)
29. Desset, C., Macq, B., Vandendorpe, L.: Block error-correcting codes for systems with a very high BER: Theoretical analysis and application to the protection of watermarks. Signal Processing: Image Communication 17(5), 409–421 (2002)
30. Desset, C., Macq, B.M., Vandendorpe, L.: Computing the word-, symbol-, and bit-error rates for block error-correcting codes. IEEE Transactions on Communications 52(6), 910–921 (2004)

31. Krawczyk, H.: LFSR-based Hashing and Authentication. In: Desmedt, Y.G. (ed.) CRYPTO 1994. LNCS, vol. 839, pp. 129–139. Springer, Heidelberg (1994)
32. Nevelsteen, W., Preneel, B.: Software Performance of Universal Hash Functions. In: Stern, J. (ed.) EUROCRYPT 1999. LNCS, vol. 1592, pp. 24–41. Springer, Heidelberg (1999)
33. Kaps, J.P., Yüksel, K., Sunar, B.: Energy Scalable Universal Hashing.. IEEE Trans. Computers 54(12), 1484–1495 (2005)
34. Vanstone, S.A., van Oorschot, P.C.: An Introduction to Error Correcting Codes with Applications. Kluwer Academic Publishers, Dordrecht (1989)

The Carry Leakage on the Randomized Exponent Countermeasure

Pierre-Alain Fouque[1], Denis Réal[2,3], Frédéric Valette[2],
and Mhamed Drissi[3]

[1] École normale supérieure/CNRS/INRIA, 75 Paris, France
`Pierre-Alain.Fouque@ens.fr`
[2] CELAR, 35 Bruz, France
{`Denis.Real,Frederic.Valette`}`@dga.defense.gouv.fr`
[3] INSA-IETR, 20 avenue des coesmes, 35043 Rennes, France
{`Denis.Real,Mhamed.Drissi`}`@insa-rennes.fr`

Abstract. In this paper, we describe a new attack against a classical differential power analysis resistant countermeasure in public key implementations. This countermeasure has been suggested by Coron since 1999 and is known as the *exponent randomization*.

Here, we show that even though the binary exponentiation, or the scalar product on elliptic curves implementation, does not leak information on the secret key, the computation of the randomized secret exponent, or scalar, can leak useful information for an attacker. Such part of the algorithm can be not well-protected since its goal is to avoid attack during the exponentiation. Consequently, our attack can be mounted against any kind of exponentiation, even very resistant as soon as the exponent randomization countermeasure is used. We target an ℓ-bit adder which adds ℓ-bit words of the secret exponent and of a random value. We show that if the carry leaks during the addition, then we can almost learn the high order bits of each word of the secret exponent. Finally, such information can be then used to recover the entire secret key of RSA or ECC based cryptosystems.

1 Introduction

Side channel attacks are very powerful attacks and today most embedded applications that require high level of security use countermeasures against such kind of attacks. Two of the most carefully studied algorithms are the square-and-multiply algorithm and its analog on Elliptic Curve, the double-and-add algorithm, since its wide usage. There exists a classical countermeasure to avoid simple power analysis (SPA) attack, that always performs the multiply or the add operation so that all the operations of the implementation are not key dependent. This countermeasure is very efficient in practice, so that most implementations use it. However, such implementations can be attacked by using differential power analysis (DPA [13]) techniques such as in [14] and a popular countermeasure consists in randomizing the secret exponent or secret scalar by

E. Oswald and P. Rohatgi (Eds.): CHES 2008, LNCS 5154, pp. 198–213, 2008.

a multiple of the order of the elements $\varphi(N)$ in the case of RSA modulus or of the order of the base point in the case of Elliptic Curve. Such countermeasure has been proposed by Coron in [7] since 1999. With this countermeasure, the secret exponent will never be the same and DPA attacks that recover the secret bit by bit cannot be mounted.

Related Work. This well-known countermeasure has been first attacked by Fouque and Valette in [11] using the Doubling Attack. However, in such attack the adversary is assumed to be able to send many times the same message and that no randomization of the message is performed before the exponentiation. Here, our attack avoids these two drawbacks since the attack does not need the knowledge of the message.

In [10], Fouque *et al.* show that if Coron's countermeasure is used with some windowing exponentiation algorithms and a small public key e, then a simple SPA followed by a very clever attack can recover the secret key d and $\varphi(N)$ in the same time. In [10], the implementation is not protected against SPA attacks since the classical SPA attack does not work on the windowing algorithms. In this work, the authors have to solve a problem similar of that which we try to solve here, namely, recovering the secret d in RSA, knowing some *non-consecutive* bits of d. Indeed, side channel technique allows Fouque *et al.* to learn some key bits of many randomized exponents of the form $d_j = d + \lambda_j \varphi(N)$, for many λ_j in a small set, the set of 20-bit or 32-bit integers in typical implementations.

Recovering secret RSA key knowing some bits of d is an old problem starting from the pionerring work of Boneh, Durfee and Frankel in [2] since 1998. However, the techniques used in Boneh *et al.*'s paper are based on Coppersmith's lattice algorithm [5,6] that works well when the bits are *consecutive*. Later, other attacks such as [9,1] have been proposed on RSA, but no one except [10] targets the case when bits are non consecutive.

In the Elliptic Curve case, the problem of recovering secret scalar when non-consecutive bits are known has also been studied. The Baby Step Giant Step algorithm can always be used, however reducing the memory requirement is not always possible as with Pollard algorithm or the lambda method, *a.k.a.* the kangoroo algorithm in [19,15]. However, Stinson describes an algorithm due to Coppersmith in [18] that can be used to reduce the memory requirement. A similar algorithm has been devised by Coron *et al.* in [8] for RSA modulus. However, the missing bits must not be too numerous since the method is based on the birthday paradox and memory and time requirements are almost in the square root or fourth root of the number of missing bits.

Our Results. In this paper, we show that the exponent randomization countermeasure can be attacked very efficiently and the whole secret key can be recovered. The main novelty of the attack is to target the computation of the randomization itself $d_j = d + \lambda_j \cdot \varphi(N)$ in case of an RSA modulus and not the exponentiation $x \mapsto x^{d_j} \bmod N$. In the addition of a random value with a fix and secret one, the targeted operation is the sum of the secret scalar with a random number, a random multiple of the order of the base point P. Seifert in [17] and Brier *et al.* in [3] have also studied attacks on other part of the algorithm, on some public information for example. Here, our attack is less invasive since we do not change parameters and we only record some electromagnetic radiations. Finally, this attack is very efficient since it works against very secure or even "provably-secure" exponentiation that uses the exponent randomization since the side channel leakage comes from the countermeasure and not from the exponentiation algorithm.

We show that when the secret exponent, or scalar, and the randomization are cut into ℓ-bit word, then the carries of the adder can leak and such information can be used to guess the high order bits of each ℓ-bit word of the secret with a good precision. Then to recover the whole secret key, either the number of missing bits is small enough so that a classical baby step giant step method could be used or other techniques are required to find the other bits. In the case of RSA keys or large ECC keys, the idea consists in recovering the randomized value λ_j using the known bits of the order. Once the λ_j's are known, the addition or the exponentiation are unprotected against classical DPA attacks such as address-bit DPA [12] or Correlation Power Analysis (CPA) attack [4].

Organization of the Paper. The principle of the attack is presented in section 2. Then, in section 3, we theoretically explain how the knowledge of the number of carries allows us to guess the high order bits of each word of the secret key. In section 4, we show that the internal carries of the full addition involved in the masking process can be observed by SCA. Finally, in section 5 we describe the attacks against classical implementations of RSA and ECC to retrieve the whole secret key.

2   The Attack Principle

The idea of the attack is to target the countermeasure operation and not the exponentiation or scalar product operation. The former operation is usually not well protected since it is used to protect the latter one. So, in the sequel, we assume that the exponentiation is protected against SPA by using the square-and-multiply always algorithm and against DPA attack by using randomization of the message even with unknown blinding and the randomization of the exponent.

2.1   The Secret Randomization Countermeasure

It is well-known that randomizing d with $d_j = d + \lambda_j \varphi(N)$ for RSA and $d_j = d + \lambda_j \#\mathcal{E}$ for ECC leads to the same results. Furthermore, if λ_j is different at each execution of the algorithm, classical DPA attacks which retrieve the secret bit by bit become ineffective. Such a countermeasure is known as the exponent randomization. Fig. 1 describes this technique for RSA and ECC.

- **Inputs**: a message M for RSA (resp. a point P of a curve $\mathcal{E}$ for ECC), a word size in bits μ, an exponent d, a modulus N (resp. $\#\mathcal{E}$, the cardinal of $\mathcal{E}$).
- **Output**: $M^d \bmod N$ for RSA (resp. $d \cdot P$ for ECC)

1. Take a μ-bit random integer λ_j
2. Compute $d_j = d + \lambda_j \varphi(N)$ (resp. $d_j = d + \lambda_j \#\mathcal{E}$)
3. Return SCA protected exponentiation $M^{d_j} \bmod N$ (resp. $d_j \cdot P$)

Fig. 1. The Private Exponent Randomization for RSA (resp. ECC)

2.2 The Sketch of the Attack

If someone adds random integers R_i to a fixed integer S, the probability over the different values of R_i to observe a carry flag only depends on S. Indeed, on 8-bit integers, random addition with the fixed value 0xFF is more likely to raise a carry flag than with the fixed integer 0x01.

Integers are often too large to be added through a digital circuit. The operands are usually broken into ℓ-bit words and the full addition function is splitted into ℓ-bit additions. An ℓ-bit addition is the sum of two ℓ-bit integers. A carry flag is raised for a buffer overflow, *i.e.* when the ℓ-bit sum is larger or equal to 2^ℓ.

These carry flags raised during the full addition can be observed by side channel analysis. An attacker who observes a device for many secret randomizations can use the carry flag as a source of information to retrieve the secret RSA or ECC exponent. Our attack uses two stages: the side channel analysis to obtain information on the secret and the cryptographic attack which uses the information to recover the entire secret key.

2.3 The Exponent Randomization Ripple Carry Addition

This subsection describes the notations used in the rest of the paper. The attacker performs m exponent randomizations and j denotes the indice of the randomization from 0 to $m - 1$.

The addition function used for the exponent randomization is assumed to be designed as a k-word ripple carry addition. The two operands of the addition are broken in k ℓ-bit words with $\ell = 8$, 16 or 32. The full addition is then performed word by word using a ℓ-bit adder which takes as input two ℓ-bit operands and a carry-in and outputs the sum and the carry-out. The ripple strategy consists in chaining the carry-out and the carry-in together. Let i be the word indice from 0 to $k-1$. The private exponent and the mask are denoted by d and $A^{(j)} = \lambda_j \varphi(N)$ for RSA and $A^{(j)} = \lambda_j \#\mathcal{E}$ for ECC. The carry flag raised during the ith ℓ-bit addition for the jth randomization is $c_i^{(j)}$ and C_i is the sum of the carry flags raised during the m exponent randomizations, $C_i = \sum_{j=0}^{m-1} c_i^{(j)}$. The principle of the ripple adder for the jth exponent randomization is described in Fig. 2 and the notations are the following:

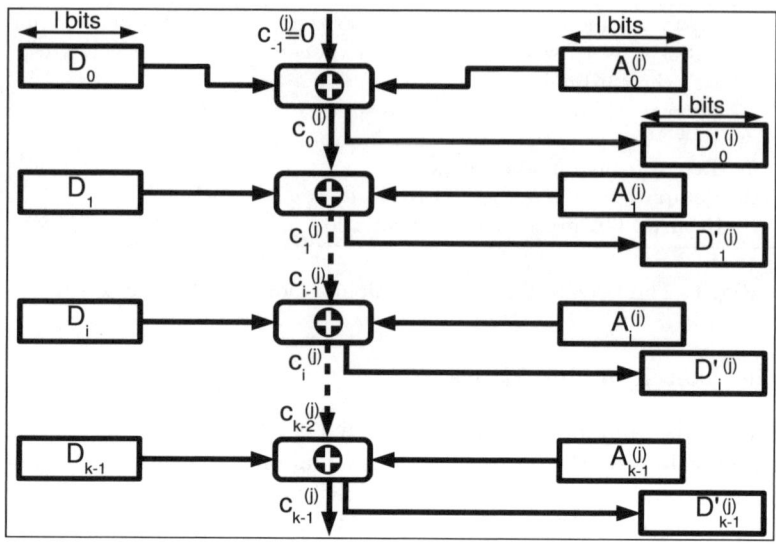

Fig. 2. j^{th} Exponent randomization

- ℓ: The atomic adder size
- k: The number of words.
- m: The number of exponent randomizations observed.
- d: The private exponent $d = \sum_{i=0}^{k-1} D_i 2^{\ell \cdot i}$.
- d': The randomized private exponent $d' = \sum_{i=0}^{k-1} D_i' 2^{\ell \cdot i}$.
- $A^{(j)}$: The jth mask $A^{(j)} = \sum_{i=0}^{k-1} a_i^{(j)} 2^{\ell \cdot i}$.
- $c_i^{(j)}$: The carry involved in the addition of the ith ℓ-bit word:
    - $c_{-1}^{(j)} = 0$ (no initial carry.)
    - $c_i^{(j)} = 1$ if $D_i + a_i^{(j)} + c_{i-1}^{(j)} \geq 2^\ell$ with $0 \leq i < k$ and $c_i^{(j)} = 0$ otherwise.
  - C_i: The number of carries in the addition of the ith ℓ-bit word: $C_i = \sum_{j=0}^{m-1} c_i^{(j)}$

3   The Exponent Randomization Attack

The exponent randomization consists in summing the private exponent with a mask. To do so, both exponent and mask are divided into k ℓ-bit words. In this section, we assumed that the attacker can observe or deduce the number C_i of carries involved on the ith ℓ-bit addition in the m exponent randomizations. In the next section, we show that such information can be observed by using side channel attack.

In the following, we assume that the randomization $\lambda_j \varphi(N)$ (or $\lambda_j \# \mathcal{E}$) are uniformly distributed values. Even though such an assumption is not correct, we can assume that it is locally correct. For each word of $\lambda_j \varphi(N)$, we can assume this property since the number of curves needed is less than the 2^{32} values of the λ_j's and the multiplication has the property to quickly spread the random values of the λ_js into all words of $\lambda_j \varphi(N)$ except maybe the first and last words.

Probability of Guessing a Word given the Number of Carries. The attacker has to guess the ith word of the secret exponent knowing the number of carries involved during the m randomizations. Theorem 1 gives us the probability of a correct guess of the probability distribution of guessing the ith word of the secret knowing the number C_i of carry flags involved in its making is given by Eq. 1.

Theorem 1. *The probability distribution of guessing the ith word of the secret knowing C_i the number of carries flags involved in the m randomizations is*

$$\Pr(D_i = n | C_i = q) = \frac{(n/2^\ell)^q (1 - n/2^\ell)^{m-q}}{\sum_{\alpha=0}^{2^\ell - 1} (\alpha/2^\ell)^q (1 - \alpha/2^\ell)^{m-q}} \tag{1}$$

Proof. First, we compute the probability distribution of the first ℓ-bit word D_0 of the secret exponent given the number of carries C_0 involved with a ℓ-bit adder implementation during m randomizations, *i.e.* we prove the above formula for $i = 0$. Then, we use an induction on i to prove the theorem for all values i.

During a *single* randomization, the probability $\Pr(C_0 = 1 | D_0 = n)$ of observing one carry for the first word is $n/2^\ell$. Indeed, let a given mask A^j, a given secret d, and their first ℓ-bit words are respectively a_0^j and D_0. These words can take 2^ℓ different values with the same probability. The value D_0 is fixed while a_0^j is purely random, thus: $\Pr(C_0 = 1 | D_0 = n) = \Pr(n + a_0^j > 2^\ell - 1) = \Pr(a_0^j > 2^\ell - n - 1)$. Then a carry is observed when a_0^j takes one of the n values larger than or equal to $2^\ell - n$ and smaller than or equal to $2^\ell - 1$. Therefore:

$$\Pr(C_0 = 1 | D_0 = n) = n/2^\ell \tag{2}$$

Now, we compute the probability distribution $\Pr(D_0 = n \cap C_0 = q)$ using the definition of the conditional probability: $\Pr(D_0 = n \cap C_0 = q) = \Pr(C_0 = q | D_0 = n) \cdot \Pr(D_0 = n)$. Since there exist $\binom{m}{q}$ possible cases where q carries are observed during m randomizations. Therefore:

$$\Pr(D_0 = n \cap C_0 = q) = \left[\binom{m}{q} \Pr(C_0 = 1 | D_0 = n)^q (1 - \Pr(C_0 = 1 | D_0 = n))^{m-q} \right] \cdot (1/2^\ell) \tag{3}$$

Then, we need to compute the probability distribution of the event $C_0 = q$. Since, the secret D_0 can take 2^ℓ different values, we can thus compute the probability by summing on all value of D_0 as follows: $\Pr(C_0 = q) = \sum_{\alpha=0}^{2^\ell - 1} \Pr(C_0 = q \cap D_0 = \alpha)$ and using (3), we get:

$$\Pr(C_0 = q) = \frac{1}{2^\ell} \cdot \binom{m}{q} \sum_{\alpha=0}^{2^\ell - 1} (\alpha/2^\ell)^q (1 - \alpha/2^\ell)^{m-q} \tag{4}$$

Finally, we compute the probability distribution $\Pr(D_0 = n|C_0 = q)$ by using (3) and (4):

$$\Pr(D_0 = n|C_0 = q) = \frac{(n/2^\ell)^q(1 - n/2^\ell)^{m-q}}{\sum_{\alpha=0}^{2^\ell-1}(\alpha/2^\ell)^q(1 - \alpha/2^\ell)^{m-q}} \tag{5}$$

Now, we prove theorem (1) for $i > 0$. For the jth randomization, the $(i+1)^{th}$ addition carry c_{i+1}^j does not only depend on the value of $D_{i+1} + a_{i+1}^j$ but also on the ith addition carry c_i^j. More precisely, the $(i+1)^{th}$ addition carry does not depend on the ith addition carry except if $D_{i+1}^j + a_{i+1}^j = 2^\ell - 1$. Then, as D_{i+1} is fixed, c_{i+1}^j depends on c_i^j one time out of 2^ℓ. If we omit this fact, then equation (5) can be generalized to:

$$\Pr(D_{i+1} = n|C_{i+1} = q) = \frac{(n/2^\ell)^q(1 - n/2^\ell)^{m-q}}{\sum_{\alpha=0}^{2^\ell-1}(\alpha/2^\ell)^q(1 - \alpha/2^\ell)^{m-q}} \tag{6}$$

$\square$

Even if this function is discrete, the probability distribution of the random variable $D_i/2^\ell$ knowing C_i can be approximated as the Beta distribution $\beta(q + 1, m - q + 1)$. This approximation is detailed in Appendix B and Fig. 3 represents the evolution of the probability distribution according to the number m of experiments.

The probability distribution shape tends to zero except on a lobe which is maximal for $\lfloor q \cdot (2^\ell + 1)/m \rfloor$ or $\lceil q \cdot (2^\ell + 1)/m \rceil$. The attacker can then take a decision. The most probable of these two words is defined as the secret estimate $\hat{D}_i$. The attacker's probability to take the right decision, i.e. the probability of $\hat{D}_i = n$, increases with m. The worst case, i.e. when the probability of $\hat{D}_i = n$ is the lowest, is for $m = 2q$ leading to $\hat{D}_i = 2^{\ell-1}$.

Furthermore, instead of choosing one single word, the attacker can select the most probable words that could match to the secret. He owns then not anymore one estimate but a set of estimates. He can then accumulate the different probabilities, meaning he tries to guess part of the secret instead of the whole secret itself. This strategy can be very efficient. Indeed, just a few words achieve a non negligible probability, the other ones having a probability close to 0. This strategy consists then in using cumulative properties instead of the density properties.

This gain can be illustrated through an example: an attacker observes $10,000$ exponent randomizations and observes $1,250$ carries on a 8-bit adder. What can he deduce? The probability that 0x20 is the secret word is 0.47. But the probability that 0x1F or 0x20 is the secret word increases to 0.7. Cumulating 4 words (0x1E,0x1F,0x20 0x21) leads to a probability of success higher than 0.99. In the worst case, $m = 2q$, the variance of $\beta(m/2+1, m/2+1)$ is $\sigma^2 = 1/4(m+3)$ [16]. Then, the number of estimates to accumulate for reaching a success probability of at least 0.99 is proportional with $2^\ell/\sqrt{m}$ by using Chebyshev bound. We verified experimentally this result: for $10,000$ exponent randomizations, 4 estimates are needed for getting a probability of 0.99 when $q = 5,000$ and $\ell = 8$.

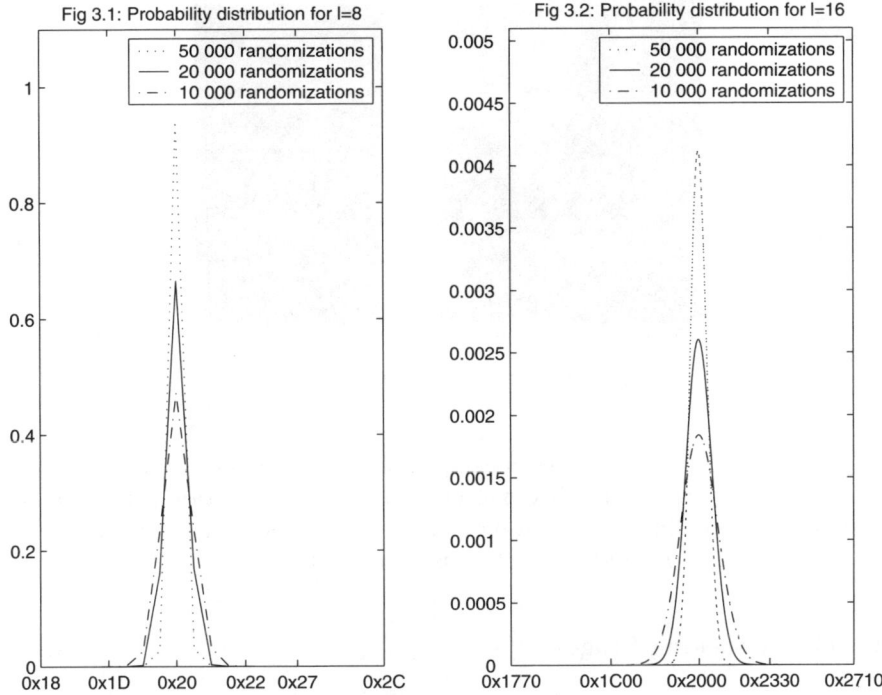

Fig. 3. Probability Distribution of $D|C$ According to the Number of Experiments with $\ell = 8$ and $\ell = 16$

4   The Exponent Randomization SCA

In this section, we show that the value C_i can be learned by the adversary. The target of our side channel attack is the carry-out of the atomic adder. We have tested its feasibility by simulating a 160-bit masking on the ProASIC 3/E starter kit from Actel which is a FPGA development kit. We have designed a full ripple addition function with a 32-bit adder. In appendix A, we give some information concerning addition design.

4.1   The Location and Profiling Stages

The SCA feasibility is demonstrated with EMA techniques, studying the electromagnetic side channel. Radiation is measured in the near field zone using a small loop probe sensitive to the horizontal magnetic field. The used test bench is represented on Fig. 4. The two operands are randomly chosen to localise in space the adder on the chip and time slot where the addition is performed during the implementation. The carry flag can then be localised more sharply by using a DPA attack.

Fig. 4. EM Test Bench

In order to build the jth 160-bit mask used for the jth exponent randomization, the random generator of the FPGA is used. The 32-bit addition is performed in two stages: the loading stage (the new operands of the adder are loaded) and the addition stage (the add instruction is executed).

4.2   The Attacking Stage

The 160-bit secret d is split in 5 32-bit words. Then, it is randomized m times and the average EMA trace Γ_m is computed. From the profiling stage, we can locate on Γ_m the carry contribution for each word D_i. This contribution is noise free. Indeed, the noise is assumed to be zero-mean. It is close to zero with m large enough. For each word D_i, the corresponding carry contribution is expected to be proportional with the carry probability. The number of carry flags raised during the m masking operations can be then deduced according to the previous section.

The previous statements are illustrated on a concrete case. We performed 1000 masking operations. The least significant bits (LSB) of each word D_i are chosen randomly, the probability to have a carry depends then only on the most significant bits (MSB) of D_i. Thus, we build d such as:

- D_0=0x00FC3478: the expected carry probability is around 0
- D_1=0x40FE56AC: the expected carry probability is around 63/256
- D_2=0x804890BD: the expected carry probability is around 127/256
- D_3=0xC0C2A4C8: the expected carry probability is around 200/256
- D_4=0xFF98ACBF: the expected carry probability is around 255/256

Fig. 5 shows Γ_{1000} where the contribution of the masking of D_0 is subtracted. To do so, an extra loading is made with D_0 parameters but the addition is not performed: this yields the characteristic of the unrelated instructions.

For a given word of d, the expected carry probability and the carry radiation are proportional as it is shown in Tab. 1. The relative amplitude difference between two consecutive maskings is $5\mu V$.

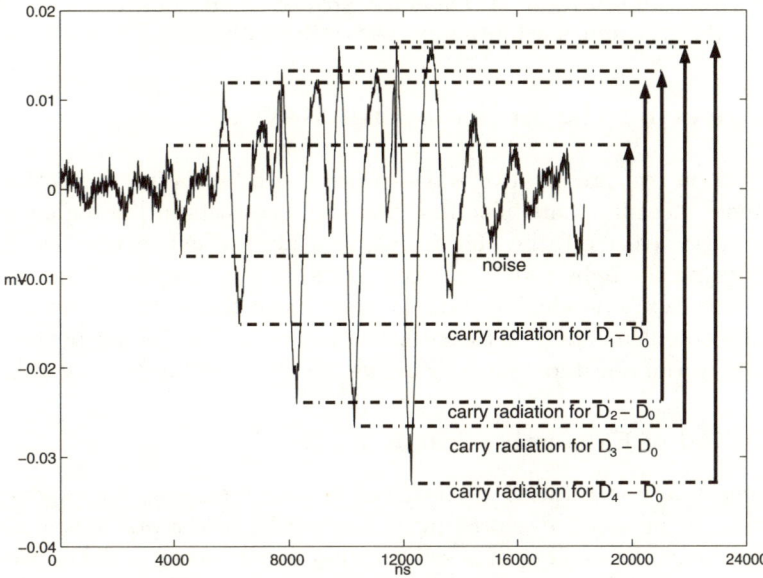

Fig. 5. Average Trace Γ_{1000} where the contribution of the masking of D_0 is subtracted

Table 1. Absolute and relative contributions of the carry on Γ_{1000}

Masking	Absolute Amplitude	Relative Amplitude
$D_0 - D_0$	0.012mV	0mV
$D_1 - D_0$	0.031mV	0.019mV
$D_2 - D_0$	0.036mV	0.024mV
$D_3 - D_0$	0.043mV	0.031mV
$D_4 - D_0$	0.049mV	0.037mV

4.3   Results and Conclusion

For a ripple carry addition, the attacker can have access to the information C_i even in the presence of noise. If the addition function has been designed another way, we claim that the attacker has access to the same amount of information. Indeed, the computational cost of the carry-out of a ℓ-bit adder depends on the way it is built. The more the carry-out is complex to obtain, the more its computation costs power and the more it leaks with the side channel. The ripple carry adder is the adder whose carry-out is the lowest side channel available. Indeed, it needs 2 OR and 3 AND while the carry-out of a 4-bit look-ahead adder costs 10 OR and 4 AND as it is stated in Appendix A.

Furthermore, independently of the addition design, it takes into account word adder whose operands are a word of the private exponent and the corresponding word of the mask: the unique difference is the carry-in treatment. However this difference is negligible: as D_i is fixed, the carry-out of the word adder depends one time out 2^ℓ on the carry-in. Then, irrespective of the addition function used, we assume that the multiple bits adder takes into account a carry-in equals to zero.

5   Recovering the Entire Secret Keys

In this section, we present two ways to use the information extracted by the side channel measurements. The first technique consists in finding enough bits with the carry leakage to be able to realize a kind of exhaustive search of the secret by using the baby step-giant step method. The second technique consists in combining two side channel attacks to retrieve the entire secret key. Both attacks are complementary as their efficiency depends on the size of the key and on the size of the registers. Some examples are discussed in the last subsection.

5.1   A Kind of Exhaustive Search

We assume that the attacker performs m measurements of the exponent randomization of the secret d, stored in k ℓ-bit words. In the previous analysis, he is able to reduce the number of possible values in each word of d. For each word, a fraction $2^\ell/\sqrt{m}$ of the corresponding key word is possible (the probability the secret is in this set is then higher than 0.99) so the number of possible values for d will be $(2^\ell/\sqrt{m})^k$. If the attacker can reduce the set of possible values for d to a subset of size lower than 2^{128}, we consider that he can find the whole secret exponent d with classical baby-step giant-step methods for a computational cost lower than 2^{64}. We can note that this attack will be more efficient on shorter keys and smaller register such as elliptic curve implementations on 8-bit or 16-bit registers. So the computational cost of the attack is $(2^\ell/\sqrt{m})^{k/2}$.

5.2   The Combined Attack

The other solution uses the carry leakage information to find partial information on d which will be used to find for each masking operation $d_j = d + \lambda_j \times \varphi(N)$ (or $d_j = d + \lambda_j \times \#\mathcal{E}$) the random value λ_j. Once sufficiently many λ_j's are known, a classical DPA attack can be mounted either on the masking operation or directly on the exponentiation to retrieve the missing bits of d. In fact, the knowledge of λ_j will unprotect the exponentiation against classical attacks such as an address bit DPA which does not need to know the value of the message. We will see in the following that the success of this attack depends more on the size of key and on the size of λ than on the number of possible measurements.

Sketch of the Attack. The attack can be divided into three steps:

- with m measurements, the attacker approximates the value D_i of each register with a precision of $\sqrt{m}$,
- with this approximation, he can try all possible values for λ and compute for the known bits of the order $Ord = \varphi(N)$ or $\#\mathcal{E}$ all the possible values for $\lambda \times Ord$. In case of RSA, only half of the bits are known as the most significant bits

of $\varphi(N)$ are equal to those of N, but in the discrete logarithm case, the order of the group is known so all the bits of Ord are known. With the approximation of d, the attacker can compute for each value λ the value of the carry of the ith register. The carry at register i will be perfectly defined excepted when it comes from the unknown bits of D_i which can happen with probability $1/\sqrt{m}$. If the number of carries information is sufficient, each curve can be associated with a single value of λ. This will happen when the number of registers where the carry is known, is larger than the size of λ.

- with the m measurements and their associated value of λ, an address-bit DPA or CPA attack can be mounted to retrieve the value of d. If the attacker targets the masking operation or the address during the exponentiation, he will have to guess recursively the unknown bits of d and eventually, the unknown bits of $\varphi(N)$ in case of RSA.

The number of measurements m is defined by the number of curves needed to complete an address bit DPA attack on the masking operation or on the exponentiation without the exponent masking protection. Usually, $10,000$ curves are sufficient to mount such an attack but this depends on the noise level. With such a number of curves, the approximation of the value D_i of each register has a precision of 2^6. If λ is a 32-bit long random value, the attacker needs the secret key to be stored on more than 32 registers in case of discrete logarithm problem or more than 64 in case of RSA as only the most significant bits of $\varphi(N)$ are known.

5.3   Results on RSA and ECC

In this section, we will present some applications of the previous attacks. The complexity in terms of measurement and computation is evaluated according to the considered attack with a λ of 32 bits.

Table 2. Attack complexity on some examples. "ES" stands for exhaustive search, "CA" for combined attacks, and "NP" for Not Practical.

Cryptographic implementation	attack	Measurements	computational cost
RSA 1024 on a 8-bit adder cell	ES	2^{16}	1
RSA 1024 on a 8-bit adder cell	CA	$10,000$	2^{32}
RSA 1024 on a 16-bit adder cell	CA	$10,000$	2^{32}
RSA 1024 on a 32-bit adder cell	NP		
RSA 2048 on a 32-bit adder cell	CA	$10,000$	2^{32}
ECC 160 on a 16-bit adder cell	ES	2^{16}	$\approx (2^{16}/\sqrt{2^{16}})^{10/2} = 2^{40}$
ECC 160 on a 32-bit adder cell	ES	2^{20}	$\approx (2^{32}/\sqrt{2^{20}})^{5/2} = 2^{55}$

6   Conclusion

In this article, we show that the addition performed during an exponent randomization is a risky operation. Indeed, the internal carries due to local buffer overflows during this operation are a side channel available and secret dependent so that the whole private exponent can be recovered for some public key implementations. The SCA feasibility has been demonstrated using near field techniques for gaining the electromagnetic radiations of a FPGA summing two 32-bit words: the presence of a carry has been detected.

This new attack is interesting since it targets the countermeasure and not the algorithm that it has to protect. Usually this operation is not well-protected and so side channel leakage can be observed. Finally, the attack can be performed on any exponentiation algorithm except the final phase which is needed only for RSA based cryptosystem. The carry leakage is in general sufficient to attack ECC based cryptosystem since the secret keys are smaller.

References

1. Blömer, J., May, A.: New Partial Key Exposure Attacks on RSA. In: Boneh, D. (ed.) CRYPTO 2003. LNCS, vol. 2729, pp. 27–43. Springer, Heidelberg (2003)
2. Boneh, D., Durfee, G., Frankel, Y.: An Attack on RSA Given a Small Fraction of the Private Key Bits. In: Ohta, K., Pei, D. (eds.) ASIACRYPT 1998. LNCS, vol. 1514, pp. 25–34. Springer, Heidelberg (1998)
3. Brier, E., Chevallier-Mames, B., Ciet, M., Clavier, C.: Why One Should Also Secure RSA Public Key Elements. In: Goubin, L., Matsui, M. (eds.) CHES 2006. LNCS, vol. 4249, pp. 324–338. Springer, Heidelberg (2006)
4. Brier, E., Clavier, C., Olivier, F.: Correlation Power Analysis with a Leakage Model. In: Joye, M., Quisquater, J.-J. (eds.) CHES 2004. LNCS, vol. 3156, pp. 16–29. Springer, Heidelberg (2004)
5. Coppersmith, D.: Finding a Small Root of a Bivariate Integer Equation; Factoring with High bits Known. In: Maurer, U.M. (ed.) EUROCRYPT 1996. LNCS, vol. 1070, pp. 155–165. Springer, Heidelberg (1996)
6. Coppersmith, D.: Small Solutions to Polynomial Equations, and Low Exponent RSA Vulnerabilities. J. Cryptology 10(4), 233–260 (1997)
7. Coron, J.-S.: Resistance against Differential Power Analysis for Elliptic Curve Cryptosystems. In: Koç, Ç.K., Paar, C. (eds.) CHES 1999. LNCS, vol. 1717, pp. 292–302. Springer, Heidelberg (1999)
8. Coron, J.-S., Lefranc, D., Poupard, G.: A New Baby-Step Giant-Step Algorithm and Some Applications to Cryptanalysis. In: Rao, J.R., Sunar, B. (eds.) CHES 2005. LNCS, vol. 3659, pp. 47–60. Springer, Heidelberg (2005)
9. Ernst, M., Jochemsz, E., May, A., de Weger, B.: Partial Key Exposure Attacks on RSA up to Full Size Exponents. In: Cramer, R.J.F. (ed.) EUROCRYPT 2005. LNCS, vol. 3494, pp. 371–386. Springer, Heidelberg (2005)
10. Fouque, P.-A., Kunz-Jacques, S., Martinet, G., Muller, F., Valette, F.: Power Attack on Small RSA Public Exponent. In: Goubin, L., Matsui, M. (eds.) CHES 2006. LNCS, vol. 4249, pp. 339–353. Springer, Heidelberg (2006)
11. Fouque, P.-A., Valette, F.: The Doubling Attack - why Upwards Is Better than Downwards. In: Walter, C.D., Koç, Ç.K., Paar, C. (eds.) CHES 2003. LNCS, vol. 2779, pp. 269–280. Springer, Heidelberg (2003)
12. Itoh, K., Izu, T., Takenaka, M.: Address-Bit Differential Power Analysis of Cryptographic Schemes OK-ECDH and OK-ECDSA. In: Kaliski Jr., B.S., Koç, Ç.K., Paar, C. (eds.) CHES 2002. LNCS, vol. 2523, pp. 129–143. Springer, Heidelberg (2003)

13. Kocher, P.C., Jaffe, J., Jun, B.: Differential Power Analysis. In: Wiener, M.J. (ed.) CRYPTO 1999. LNCS, vol. 1666, pp. 388–397. Springer, Heidelberg (1999)
14. Messerges, T.S., Dabbish, E.A., Sloan, R.H.: Power Analysis Attacks of Modular Exponentiation in Smartcards. In: Koç, Ç.K., Paar, C. (eds.) CHES 1999. LNCS, vol. 1717, pp. 144–157. Springer, Heidelberg (1999)
15. Pollard, J.M.: Kangaroos, Monopoly and Discrete Logarithms. J. Cryptology 13(4), 437–447 (2000)
16. Rade, L., Westergren, B.: Mathematics Handbook for Science and Engineering, Sudentlitteratur, Lund (1998)
17. Seifert, J.-P.: On authenticated computing and RSA-based authentication. In: Atluri, V., Meadows, C., Juels, A. (eds.) ACM Conference on Computer and Communications Security, pp. 122–127. ACM, New York (2005)
18. Stinson, D.R.: Some baby-step giant-step algorithms for the low hamming weight discrete logarithm problem. Math. Comput. 71(237), 379–391 (2002)
19. van Oorschot, P.C., Wiener, M.J.: Improving Implementable Meet-in-the-Middle Attacks by Orders of Magnitude. In: Koblitz, N. (ed.) CRYPTO 1996. LNCS, vol. 1109, pp. 229–236. Springer, Heidelberg (1996)

A   The Addition Strategy

The addition problems start when adding 2 single bits and finishes when able to add 2 words of arbitrary length.

A.1   The Single Bit Adder

The single bit adder is the most elementary logical circuit of a device. Two kinds of single bit adder exist: the half adder and the full adder. The Half Single Bit Adder (HA) has two inputs labelled a and b and two outputs: the sum s and the carry-out c_{out}. The value s is the 1-bit sum of a and b while c_{out} is the carry flag raised in case of overflow. Sum and carry-out are computed as follow : $s = a \oplus b$ and $c_{out} = a.b$ The Full Single Bit Adder (FA) is a half adder that takes into account the carry-in bit c_{in}. The different relations become $s = a \oplus b \oplus c_{in}$ and $c_{out} = (a.b) + (b.c_{in}) + (c_{in}.b)$.

A.2   The Word Adder

An ℓ-bit adder is an element used for the addition of two words of ℓ bits each, typically, $\ell = 8$, 16 or 32. Let $A = \sum_{i=0}^{\ell-1} a_i 2^i$ and $B = \sum_{i=0}^{\ell-1} b_i 2^i$ be the two ℓ-bit operands, C_{in} be the carry-in, $S = \sum_{i=0}^{\ell-1} s_i 2^i$ be the sum and C_{out} be the carry-out. The value C_{out} is the object of the side channel analysis. There is not just one way of building a word adder. Indeed, different strategies exist for dealing with internal carries. Then, the way C_{out} is computed depends on the word adder design.

The Ripple Carry Adder. This is the most straightforward implementation of a final stage ℓ-bit adder. Carry-ins and carry-outs are chained together requiring

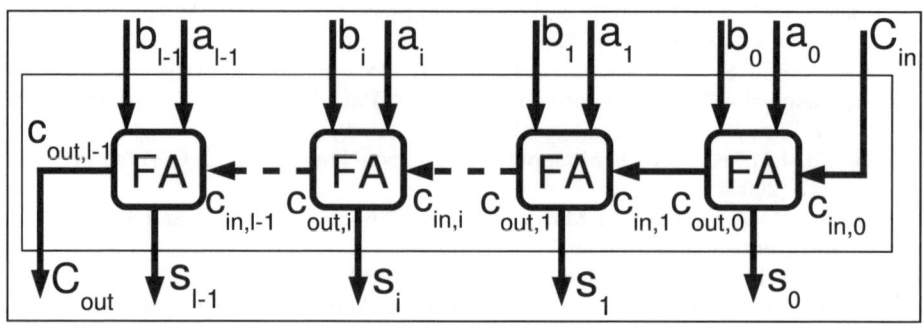

Fig. 6. The Ripple Carry Adder

ℓ FAs. Fig. 6 describes this design. Let $c_{out,i}$ and $c_{in,i}$ be respectively the carry-out and the carry-in of the ith FA.

Chaining carries together leads to the following relations: $c_{in,0} \leftarrow C_{in}$
for $0 \leq i < \ell$ $c_{in,i+1} \leftarrow c_{out,i}$
$C_{out} \leftarrow c_{out,\ell-1}$.
Then C_{out} is connected to the carry-out of the last FA.

The Carry Look-Ahead Adder. This adder aims to generate all carry-ins in parallel for not waiting until the carry propagates from the stage of the FA it has been generated. The carry propagation signal $\{P_i\}$ and the carry generation signal $\{G_i\}$ are introduced using the previous notations: $P_i = a_i \oplus b_i$, $G_i = a_i \cdot b_i$ and then $c_{in,i+1} = G_i + c_{in,i} \cdot P_i$. These expressions can be computed in parallel for all the carries. As, an example, for a 4-bit adder, we have:

$$c_{in,0} = C_{in}$$

$$c_{in,1} = G_0 + c_{in,0} \cdot P_0 = G_0 + C_{in} \cdot P_0$$

$$c_{in,2} = G_1 + c_{in,1} \cdot P_1 = G_1 + G_0 \cdot P_1 + C_{in} \cdot P_0 \cdot P_1$$

$$c_{in,3} = G_1 + c_{in,2} \cdot P_2 = G_2 + G_1 \cdot P_2 + G_0 \cdot P_1 \cdot P_2 + C_{in} \cdot P_0 \cdot P_1 \cdot P_2$$

$$c_{in,4} = G_3 + c_{in,3} \cdot P_3 = G_3 + G_2 \cdot P_3 + G_1 \cdot P_2 \cdot P_3 + G_0 \cdot P_1 \cdot P_2 \cdot P_3 + C_{in} \cdot P_0 \cdot P_1 \cdot P_2 \cdot P_3$$

$$C_{out} = c_{in,4}$$

B   The Beta Distribution

The last probability distribution of the secret estimate knowing the carry function given by formula (6) can be approximated by a discrete beta distribution. Indeed: the beta distribution is defined as

$$\beta(q+1, m-q+1) = \int_0^1 t^q (1-t)^{m-q} dt$$

and using Riemann sums, we obtain:

$$\beta(q+1, m-q+1) = \lim_{n \to \infty} \frac{1}{n} \sum_{\alpha=1}^{n} \frac{\alpha^q}{n} \left(1 - \frac{\alpha}{n}\right)^{m-q}.$$

Finally, if we assume that 2^ℓ is large enough, then

$$2^\ell \cdot \beta(q+1, m-q+1) \approx \sum_{\alpha=0}^{2^\ell-1} \frac{\alpha^q}{2^\ell} \left(1 - \frac{\alpha}{2^\ell}\right)^{m-q}.$$

Recovering Secret Keys from Weak Side Channel Traces of Differing Lengths

Colin D. Walter

Comodo CA Research Laboratory
7 Campus Road, Bradford, BD7 1HR, UK
Colin.Walter@comodo.com

Abstract. Secret key recovery from weak side channel leakage is always a challenge in the presence of standard counter-measures. The use of randomised exponent recodings in RSA or ECC means that, over multiple re-uses of a key, operations which correspond to a given key bit are not aligned in the traces. This enhances the difficulties because traces cannot be averaged to improve the signal-to-noise ratio.

The situation can be described using a hidden Markov model (HMM) but the standard solution is computationally infeasible when many traces have to be processed. Previous work has not provided a satisfactory way out. Here, instead of *ad hoc* sequential processing of complete traces, trace prefixes are combined naturally in parallel. This results in the systematic extraction of a much higher proportion of the information theoretic content of the leakage, enabling many keys of typical ECC length to be recovered with a computationally feasible search through a list of most likely values. Moreover, likely errors can now be located very easily.

Keywords: Side channel leakage, simple power analysis, SPA, Hidden Markov Models, Forward-Backward Algorithm, Viterbi Algorithm.

1 Introduction

Side channel leakage from embedded cryptographic devices may contain substantial information. When possible this is averaged to improve the signal to noise ratio and enable recovery of the secret key. However, some randomised exponentiation algorithms are designed so that averaging over contemporaneous operations reduces rather than increases the useful information [4,8,9,15]. With a perfect side channel that distinguishes squares from multiplications in each trace, it is possible to recover the secret exponent key for most of these algorithms without substantial effort [12,13,15].

In the real world the side channels are rarely so clear, especially where designers have taken steps to reduce the leakage. Then standard statistical techniques can be applied to detect correlations between possible key bits and the trace data, but they are computationally infeasible for the length of cryptographic keys and the expected level of leakage. Instead, dedicated algorithms are required to extract meaningful information and search for the most likely keys.

E. Oswald and P. Rohatgi (Eds.): CHES 2008, LNCS 5154, pp. 214–227, 2008.

Karlov and Wagner [5] modelled this using input-driven Hidden Markov Models, and suggested the sequential processing of complete traces as an effective way of limiting the computational complexity. However, they only consider traces of equal length where the ith observation always corresponds to the ith exponent digit. Green, Noad and Smart [3] show how to deal with the traces of different lengths which are more typical of randomised exponentiation algorithms, and they provide some heuristic methods for the sequential processing of complete traces. Nevertheless, even with strong leakage it is clear from their tables (e.g. *op. cit.* Table 1) that very little of the information content of the traces is successfully extracted. Moreover, it is unclear whether their methods would converge to any solution in the presence of weak leakage.

The hidden Markov model (HMM) of [5] and [3] leads to a forward algorithm that provides a *global* minimum for a metric that measures distance from a best-fit solution. A backward algorithm then generates the state sequence and hence the input key which yields that minimum value. On the other hand, the randomised exponentiation algorithms of interest perform recodings which influence the side channel traces only *locally* for a small number of operations. Therefore it seems better to attempt recovery of input key bits using a more locally-based algorithm. This, of course, is an approach which proved very successful with weak side channels in the original timing and power analysis attacks of Kocher *et al.* [6,7]. Their averaging of contemporaneous trace outputs does not work here because such values no longer correspond to the same input symbol. Thus, some new ideas are required but, to benefit from very weak leakage, averaging is still key to avoiding previous convergence problems of [5] and [3].

Here the proposed algorithm adjusts trace positions in an attempt to align outputs which correspond to the same input symbol. This allows averaging to take place and also makes it possible to take into account the influence of recoding decisions on neighbouring operations. There are a number of parameters to choose in the algorithm. Their choice enables the calculations to be kept within available computational resources. The output is a set of good guesses at the secret key. Moreover, each bit is naturally assigned a correctness probability which enables likely errors to be located easily. This seems to be a new feature: Green *et al.* [3] do not say if they can locate possible errors, but the ability enables many more errors to be corrected. Simulation results are provided to show what fraction of keys are recoverable for a given effort.

As the whole process is computationally feasible, the immediate conclusion is that designers should assume most leakage can be converted successfully into useful knowledge when a secret key is re-used with these random recoding exponentiation algorithms. Indeed, they should be able to calculate upper bounds on the number of times the key can be safely re-used.

2   The Leakage Model

The context of the attack is the repeated use of a randomised exponentiation algorithm for computing M^D in any cryptographic group where D is a fixed secret key which is not subject to blinding by a random multiple of the group order, and M is an unknown ciphertext which may vary and may be whitened. The adversary is assumed to know all the details of the exponentiation algorithm. Use of the key provides him with a side channel trace for the exponentiation itself, but no further information is assumed: he is not expected to be able to choose any input, view any output, or usefully observe any pre- and post- processing.

It is assumed that occurrences of multiplicative operations in the exponentiation can be identified accurately from the corresponding side channel trace, but that their identities as squares or multiplications can only be determined with a substantial degree of inaccuracy[1] [2]. The adversary's aim is to discover D using computationally feasible resources.

3   The Randomised Exponentiation

Examples of the randomised exponentiation algorithms which can be attacked in the way described here include those of Liardet-Smart [8], Oswald-Aigner [9] and Ha-Moon [4,15]. Their common, underlying basis is a recoding of the binary representation of the key D into a form

$$D = ((...(d_{m-1}2^{m_{m-2}} + d_{m-2})2^{m_{m-3}} + ... + d_2)2^{m_1} + d_1)2^{m_0} + d_0$$

where the digits $d_i \in \mathcal{D}$ and 2-power exponents $m_i \in \mathcal{M}$ belong to some fixed, pre-determined sets $\mathcal{D}$ and $\mathcal{M}$ respectively. Both d_i and m_i are selected according to some finite automaton which has the bits of D and the output from a random number generator (RNG) as inputs. Different bit streams from the RNG result in different recodings of D.

The exponentiation M^D begins with the pre-calculation of the table $\{M^d \mid d \in \mathcal{D}\}$. Then the main iterative step of the exponentiation consists of m_i squarings followed by a multiplication by the table value M^{d_i} when $d_i \neq 0$. This results in a sequence of multiplicative operations which is most easily presented using d_i to denote multiplication by the table entry M^{d_i} and m_i copies of 0 to denote the squarings. We call this a *recoding sequence* for D. For example, the exponent $D = 13_{10} = 1101_2$ has a recoding $D = (1.2^2+3)2^1+\bar{1}$ which gives the operation sequence $10030\bar{1}$. (Alternatives in processing the first digit are ignored.)

The exponentiation algorithms of interest here are assumed to have the property that perfect knowledge of the multiplication/squaring sequences for a small number of recodings of D yields enough information to reconstruct the secret key D with at most a small number of ambiguities. This is the case for the algorithms mentioned above: attacks on them using such information are described in [12], [13] and [15] respectively.

---

[1] For the table-driven exponentiation algorithms under attack here it may also be possible, with a degree of uncertainty, to identify which table element is used in a multiplication, and hence guess at the most likely value for the exponent digit. The methods below can be extended easily to such cases.

4   Notation for Leakage Traces

The above-mentioned exponentiation algorithms are reasonably secure when the key D is used only once, as in ECDSA [1], because a single recoding pattern does not generally yield sufficient information to determine a computationally feasible search space for the key. However, for key re-use, the pattern must be hidden. Hence implementers generally employ both hardware and software counter-measures to prevent leakage of the recoding pattern through any side channels. Consequently, an attacker only obtains partial information about any recoding through side channels. But extensive testing of the cryptographic system and some pre-computation enables the adversary to process the side channel information from each exponentiation into a sequence of probabilities that each component operation is a squaring. For convenience, this will be referred to as a *trace*. So the operation sequence $100301\bar{1}$ yields a trace such as $(0.23, 0.87, 0.69, 0.15, 0.83, 0.42)$, with the larger probabilities occurring for doublings.

For consistency, exponent bit strings, recoding sequences and traces are all written in the same left-to-right order. For convenience, this is the order in which the recoding process consumes key bits and generates operation sequences. Then, in an obvious sense, a prefix in one list always corresponds to some prefix in another. These prefixes are extended incrementally as the attack progresses.

Recodings are pairs consisting of (i) the operation sequence r which the recoding automaton has generated for D, and (ii) the state s which the automaton has entered at that point. $\mathcal{R}(D)$ denotes the set of all these recodings (r, s) of D. Let $\bullet$ denote the end-of-list symbol and also the final state of the recoding automaton. A list is called *terminated* or *un-terminated* according to whether or not it ends with this symbol. When the recoding automaton reads $\bullet$ at the end of D, it performs the post-processing stage required to reach its final state $\bullet$ and then stops. Recoding $D\bullet$ will result in a pair $(r\bullet, \bullet) \in \mathcal{R}(D\bullet)$ for which r applied to M yields M^D. r is terminated with $\bullet$ to indicate that the operation sequence is complete. If D is not terminated, the pair $(r, s) \in \mathcal{R}(D)$ has $s \neq \bullet$ and it can be extended to a recoding of any D' with prefix D.

In the above example with $D = 13_{10}$, both $r = 100301\bar{1}$ with borrow 0 and $r' = 10030$ with borrow 1 could represent the output and state of the recoding automaton after processing D when further input bits are possible. They belong to $\mathcal{R}(D)$. Reading $\bullet$ next gives $(r\bullet, \bullet) \in \mathcal{R}(D\bullet)$ from $(r, 0)$ as no further processing is required. However, from $(r', \bar{1})$ there needs to be post-processing to obtain an element in $\mathcal{R}(D\bullet)$, for example, by appending $\bar{1}$ to obtain $(r'\bar{1}\bullet, \bullet)$.

5   The Metric

A metric $\mu(D, T)$ is constructed to provide a measurement of how well a bit string D matches the side channel leakage presented in a set T of traces. Roughly speaking, the "best" guesses at the secret key D are those strings which provide the smallest distances under this metric. As indicated above, the metric for a set of traces T is just the average of the value of the metric for a single trace t:

$$\mu(D, T) = |T|^{-1} \sum_{t \in T} \mu(D, t)$$

Here $\mu(D, t)$ is the minimum of the metric applied to t and a single recoding $r \in \mathcal{R}(D)$, i.e.

$$\mu(D, t) = \mathrm{Min}\{\mu(r, t) \mid r \in \mathcal{R}(D)\}$$

If r is an un-terminated recoding which is no longer than trace t, i.e. $len(r) \leq len(t)$, then we define

$$\mu(r, t) = len(r)^{-1} \sum_{0 \leq i < len(r)} (1 - t_i(r_i))$$

where $r = (r_0, r_1, ..., r_{len(r)-1})$, $t = (t_0, t_1, t_2, ...)$, and $t_i(r_i)$ is the probability[2] observed through the side channel that the ith element of trace t corresponds to the same operation as r_i. The same definition is also used for $\mu(r, t)$ if r is a terminated recoding such that $len(r) = len(t)$. If $len(r) > len(t)$ then t is too short to correspond to the recoding r and so we define $\mu(r, t) = \infty$ whether r is terminated or not. Similarly, if r is a terminated recoding with $len(r) < len(t)$ then r is too short to correspond to trace t and again we set $\mu(r, t) = \infty$.

Scaling by $len(r)$ prevents shorter recodings of D being given an unjustified selection bias. Then, being the average of a set of probabilities in most cases, $\mu(r, t)$ lies in $[0, 1] \cup \infty$. Hence $\mu(D, t) \in [0, 1] \cup \infty$ and $\mu(D, T) \in [0, 1] \cup \infty$. Clearly $\mu(r, t)$ is small when the operations in r are those which have high probability in the corresponding initial segment of t. Thus $\mu(D, T)$ is small when an initial segment of each trace in T closely matches some recoding of D.

If trace t is too short or too long to correspond to any recoding of D, then the above definitions give $\mu(D, t) = \infty$, and therefore $\mu(D, T) = \infty$ for any T containing t. Suppose d_{max} is the largest digit in $\mathcal{D}$ and k the length of the shortest trace in T. Then the shortest trace represents the leakage from too few operations to correspond a recoding of any string satisfying $D > d_{max}2^k$. Hence $\mu(D, T)$ will only be finite for D with at most $k + \lfloor \log_2 d_{max} \rfloor$ bits.

The main problem with evaluating μ is that for cryptographically sized keys D, $\mathcal{R}(D)$ is too large a set over which to compute a minimum – it is exponential in the bit length of D. Consequently, we use an approximation

$$\mu'(D, t) = \mathrm{Min}\{\mu(r, t) \mid r \in \mathcal{S}_t(D)\}$$

to $\mu(D, t)$ which is determined iteratively by the best attempts to minimise μ for shorter strings. Specifically, for each trace and a suitable parameter R, we iteratively create a set $\mathcal{S}_t$ of up to R triples (d, i, s) which consist of the metric

---

[2] It may be desirable to augment this definition of $t_i(r_i)$ to take account of the relevant transition probability from the recoding FA, so that less likely events would yield larger contributions to the sum for $\mu(r, t)$.

value $d = \mu(r, t)$ for an underlying "good" recoding r of D, the number i of operations in r, and the state s of the recoding finite automaton after generating r from D. Set $\mathcal{S}_t$ is constructed as follows. First, for D being the empty bit string, $\mathcal{S}_t$ is initialised to contain just the triple $(0, 0, s_0)$ corresponding to the empty recoding sequence when the recoding automaton is initialised with start state s_0. For the iterative step, suppose $D = D'b$ for bit b, and $\mathcal{S}_t'$ is the set of triples constructed for D'. Then, for each $(d', i', s') \in \mathcal{S}_t'$, s' and b are fed into the FA. The output is a set of new states s and operations to extend the underlying recoding of D' to ones for D. These are used to create new triples (d, i, s) for D where i comes from increasing i' by the number of these operations, and d comes from a scaled incrementing of d' by the terms $(1 - t_{i''}(r_{i''}))$ with $i' \leq i'' < i$. As the triple also depends on a random input to the FA, there can be several new triples for each one in $\mathcal{S}_t'$. These are then rationalised by removing triples (d_2, i, s) for which there is already a triple (d_1, i, s) with $d_1 \leq d_2$. Then the R triples with the smallest values for d are chosen for inclusion in $\mathcal{S}_t$.

If the recoding automaton had s possible states and t_{max} were the maximum length of any trace, then st_{max} would be an upper bound on the size of $\mathcal{S}_t$. Hence

$$\mu'(D, T) = \mu(D, T) \quad \text{for } R = st_{max}$$

since all the smallest intermediate values for μ are retained. Whatever R is, μ' can be computed easily and accurately in time which is polynomial rather than exponential in $\log D$. It avoids enumerating all the recodings of D. R can often be picked much smaller than st_{max} without significantly affecting the accuracy of the method, and this helps reduce the complexity of the attack.

6   The Search Tree

The main phase of the attack is the construction and pruning of a (nearly) binary tree where internal edges are labelled by bits and edges to leaves by the end-of-list symbol •. Each node N is labelled with the (possibly terminated) bit string D_N given by concatenating the labels along the branch from the root to N. Nodes are also labelled with $\mu_N = \mu'(D_N, T)$ and the sets of triples $\mathcal{S}_{t,N}$ ($t \in T$) for $D = D_N$, each of which is computed incrementally as described in §5. The root ρ is labelled by the empty string $D_\rho = \epsilon$, $\mu_\rho = \mu(\epsilon, T) = 0$ and $\mathcal{S}_{t,\rho} = \{(0, 0, s_0)\}$. For each non-terminated node N, up to three child nodes are constructed with edges labelled 0, 1 and • respectively. Only the first two can grow further branches, so the tree is almost binary. Upon completion, a set of possible keys D is obtained from the labels D_N on the leaves N, and they can be arranged in order of likelihood using the values μ_N.

The tree is constructed breadth-first to aid pruning. Pruning is driven by the values of μ_N, although not quite directly. There are three pruning rules which are applied whenever possible. First, nodes N with $\mu_N = \infty$ are deleted because D_N cannot be the correct key, nor a prefix of the correct key. This limits the depth of the tree, thereby ensuring the construction terminates. It also removes leaves near the root so that leaves only appear towards the bottom of the tree.

Secondly, un-terminated nodes whose children have all been pruned are also deleted because every line of descent from them eventually leads to a problem.

The third, and final, pruning rule uses two threshold parameters. The first, B, is the maximum breadth of the tree after pruning. The second, λ, is the number of "lookahead" bits. These parameters are chosen to make the construction of the whole tree and subsequent calculations computationally feasible.

The *level* of a node N is its distance from the root, namely $len(D_N)$. Suppose the tree has been fully constructed down to level $l+\lambda$ and all pruning rules have been applied to the levels above l. For a node N at level l, let $\mathcal{N}_N$ be the set of all its un-terminated descendents at level $l+\lambda$, and its terminated descendents with level at most $l+\lambda$. Let[3] $\bar{\mu}_N = \min\{\mu_{N'} \mid N' \in \mathcal{N}_N\}$. Then the set of nodes at level l is pruned to leave the B nodes with the smallest values $\bar{\mu}_N$.

This rule removes the nodes whose recodings provide the poorest match to the observed leakage. Since recoding choices affect the pattern of subsequent operations and this effect may only become apparent in the metric after processing several more bits, larger values of λ tend to give better results in determining the best match D. Larger values of B clearly make the inclusion of the correct key D more likely. Even the best fit key with smallest value at its leaf node may not have the smallest value for μ_N or $\bar{\mu}_N$ at each intermediate node N. So B and λ must be kept large enough to include the correct key; their values can be determined only after practical experiment on the leaking device. It also pays to be increasingly light handed in pruning the final λ levels.

7   Locating Bit Errors

By their nature, all key searching algorithms suffer from unavoidable deficiencies: one is that the best fit key may not be among the good keys which they generate; another is that the correct key may not be the best fit. The first problem arises because the ultimately best fit key is not always the best at intermediate points. To ameliorate this, a number of the best keys need to be continued all the time. This action should also solve the second problem and is achieved by appropriate choice of the parameters, as illustrated in the tables of the next section.

However, there are more subtle causes of errors. A single bit error can completely de-rail the process for several reasons. Firstly, because of nature of the exponentiation algorithm, it may be possible for different key bit sequences to generate identical leakage. An example is described in Appendix 2, and it is indeed a main cause of errors when dealing with the Ha-Moon recoding algorithm. Secondly, there may be so many good choices when the wrong bit is chosen that the correct one does not survive.

Most of these bit errors are at predictable points, namely those for which the relative difference in the values of $\bar{\mu}$ for the 0-bit and 1-bit choices is very small. Specifically, the set $\mathcal{N}_N$ is partitioned into subsets $\mathcal{N}_N^{(0)}$ and $\mathcal{N}_N^{(1)}$ corresponding to the 0- and 1- branches at N and the minimum metric values are compared for

---

[3] Different definitions of $\bar{\mu}$ are possible: e.g. one might weight the metric contribution at level $l+i$ by i^{-1} instead of 1 for $i > 0$.

the two sets, where the sums only include terms $1-t_i(r_i)$ from levels $l+1$ to $l+\lambda$. The difference is a useful measure of confidence in the decision. It enables the search for the correct key to be prioritised by trying alternatives for the most doubtful bit decisions first. This reduces the search cost very considerably.

Finally we note that the smaller μ is at the end of the process, the better the fit, and so, on average, the fewer the number of errors. Hence it is possible to select the most likely candidates to break. Sometimes the traces can become incorrectly aligned during key recovery. This leads to a large number of errors and a high value for the metric, but such cases are easily detected and avoided.

8   Example Simulation

This section contains results from a simulation of the attack applied to the Ha-Moon algorithm [4], showing variations from the choice of parameters. The metric difference described in the previous section was used to order the bit decisions for 192-bit keys, and the bit error with the highest difference between the choices 0 or 1 was located. The probability of it lying at a particular point in this list was recorded. The tables show that errors are strongly associated with smaller differences. Consequently, for example, from Table 1 there is a probability of 0.3868+0.0058 that, with the stated parameters and 0.4 leakage, all the bit errors will be among the $\frac{2}{16}$th of bits with the lowest difference. In practice, this means checking the alternatives for only 24 bits in order to have a good probability of recovering a key. This is clearly computationally feasible. The last column states that on average only 9.082 of these bits will be in error, and so $\frac{1}{2}\binom{24}{9} \approx 2^{19}$ key tests is a realistic average for the effort involved. For the tabulated cases, the total number of errors is typically around 20 if the position of the worst error is anywhere in the top half of the ordered bit list, but, with extra computation, it can become under 11, as happens for the last line of Table 3, which covers 99.5% of all cases.

The investigation did not assess performance on the final λ bits, but any variation in the recovery rate of those bits would not affect the computational complexity significantly.

For the simulation, the trace probability values were approximately normally distributed with expectation $\frac{1}{2}(E+1)$ where E is the "strength of leakage" value in the first column of Table 1[4]. A leakage of 0 means probability $\frac{1}{2}$ that the operation is a squaring rather than a multiplication, i.e. no information content.

Tables 1 and 2 illustrate the effect of different amounts of leaked data on the key recovery process. Given that the work involved is proportional to the number of traces $|T|$ and to the number of recoding choices R which are stored, but exponential in the lookahead distance λ, it is clear from Tables 3 to 5 that the most efficient way of recovering the highest number of Ha-Moon recoded exponents is by increasing R.

---

[4] Green et al. [3] use a simpler model: trace probabilities are 0 or 1, with average $\frac{1}{2}(E+1)$. They need stronger leakage, and tabulate only $E = 0.6$ and $E = 0.8$.

Table 1. Distributions for the Worst Error in a 192-bit best-fit Exponent as Leakage varies for Ha-Moon Exponentiation [4] with $|T| = 10$, $\lambda = 5$, $R = 10$, $B = 2$

Leakage Level	In 1st Half	In 3rd Quarter	In 7th Eighth	In 15th Sixteenth	In last Sixteenth	#Bit errors when all in last Eighth
0.10	1.0000	0.0000	0.0000	0.0000	0.0000	—
0.20	1.0000	0.0000	0.0000	0.0000	0.0000	—
0.30	0.9697	0.0270	0.0031	0.0002	0.0000	10.00
0.35	0.5760	0.2212	0.1542	0.0478	0.0008	9.414
0.40	0.1186	0.1456	0.3433	0.3868	0.0058	9.082
0.45	0.0143	0.0358	0.1956	0.7407	0.0136	8.925
0.50	0.0019	0.0081	0.0811	0.8913	0.0176	8.853
0.60	0.0000	0.0001	0.0304	0.9500	0.0195	8.790

Table 2. Distributions for the Worst Error in a 192-bit best-fit Exponent as the Number of Traces varies for Ha-Moon Exponentiation with 0.4 leakage, $\lambda=5$, $R=10$, $B=2$

Traces $|T|$	In 1st Half	In 3rd Quarter	In 7th Eighth	In 15th Sixteenth	In last Sixteenth	#Bit errors when all in last Eighth
1	0.9994	0.0006	0.0000	0.0000	0.0000	—
2	0.9344	0.0656	0.0000	0.0000	0.0000	—
3	0.7140	0.2218	0.0642	0.0000	0.0000	—
4	0.5154	0.1986	0.2860	0.0000	0.0000	—
5	0.3873	0.2010	0.4090	0.0027	0.0000	12.07
6	0.3081	0.1984	0.4579	0.0356	0.0000	11.08
8	0.1923	0.1830	0.3849	0.2394	0.0004	10.17
10	0.1186	0.1456	0.3433	0.3868	0.0058	9.082
20	0.0095	0.0369	0.1850	0.4619	0.3067	5.847
40	0.0000	0.0025	0.0403	0.2456	0.7116	3.754

Table 3. Distributions for the Worst Error in a 192-bit best-fit Exponent as the Number of Recodings varies for Ha-Moon Exponentiation with 0.4 leakage, $|T|=10$, $\lambda=5$, $B=2$

Recodings R	In 1st Half	In 3rd Quarter	In 7th Eighth	In 15th Sixteenth	In last Sixteenth	#Bit errors when all in last Eighth
6	0.5547	0.2508	0.1599	0.0341	0.0005	9.431
7	0.3576	0.2871	0.2668	0.0864	0.0021	9.023
8	0.2541	0.2359	0.3268	0.1807	0.0025	9.264
9	0.1662	0.1929	0.3584	0.2777	0.0048	9.029
10	0.1186	0.1456	0.3433	0.3868	0.0058	9.082
12	0.0605	0.0876	0.2930	0.5516	0.0073	9.012
15	0.0228	0.0472	0.2208	0.6999	0.0093	8.945
20	0.0104	0.0175	0.1553	0.8045	0.0123	8.960
30	0.0051	0.0112	0.1087	0.8579	0.0171	8.755

Table 4. Distributions for the Worst Error in a 192-bit best-fit Exponent as the Lookahead Value λ varies for Ha-Moon Exponentiation with 0.4 leakage, $|T|=10$, $R=10$, $B=2$

Lookahead λ	In 1st Half	In 3rd Quarter	In 7th Eighth	In 15th Sixteenth	In last Sixteenth	#Bit errors when all in last Eighth
1	0.2456	0.2037	0.3370	0.2107	0.0030	9.331
2	0.2019	0.1873	0.3277	0.2782	0.0049	9.222
3	0.1632	0.1685	0.3403	0.3220	0.0060	9.269
4	0.1378	0.1572	0.3341	0.3659	0.0050	9.209
5	0.1186	0.1456	0.3433	0.3868	0.0058	9.082
6	0.0997	0.1348	0.3502	0.4095	0.0058	9.039
8	0.0829	0.1380	0.3423	0.4312	0.0056	8.977

Table 5. Distributions for the Worst Error in a 192-bit best-fit Exponent as the Tree Width B varies for Ha-Moon Exponentiation with 0.4 leakage, $\lambda=5$, $|T|=10$, $R=10$

Tree Width B	In 1st Half	In 3rd Quarter	In 7th Eighth	In 15th Sixteenth	In last Sixteenth	#Bit errors when all in last Eighth
1	0.1521	0.1534	0.3285	0.3613	0.0047	9.199
2	0.1186	0.1456	0.3433	0.3868	0.0058	9.082
4	0.0983	0.1493	0.3348	0.4103	0.0073	9.038
8	0.0882	0.1313	0.3286	0.4440	0.0079	9.012
12	0.0857	0.1325	0.3346	0.4378	0.0094	8.926
16	0.0898	0.1357	0.3233	0.4433	0.0079	8.949

In the case of Liardet-Smart recoding [8], it is much harder to extract the correct key than for the Ha-Moon recoding because it is much more difficult to align the traces correctly. For example, for a maximum base 2^4, digits 0, ± 1, ± 3, ± 5, ± 7, 0.4 leakage, $\lambda = 5$ and $B = 2$, but taking 30 traces and $R = 30$, 0.38 of 192-bit exponents have all errors located in the last eighth of the ordered bit list. For 0.38 of cases the worst error occurs in the first half of the list, but, on average key guesses have fewer than 7.5 bit errors, so it is still computationally feasible to recover almost all keys.

The Oswald-Aigner recoding [9] has comparable strength to that of Ha-Moon: with the reference values of 0.4 leakage, 10 traces, $\lambda=5$, $R=10$ and $B=2$, 0.2714 of 192-bit exponents have all errors located in the last eighth of the ordered bits.

The standard, deterministic binary method is also susceptible to the algorithm. Coding decisions are unique and do not propagate to other positions, so only $\lambda=1$, $R=1$ and $B=1$ make sense. With 0.3 leakage and 10 traces, over 98% of 192-bit exponents are recovered with no errors at all. Unlike that of Green *et al.* [3], this algorithm reduces to the obvious, and probably optimal, one for the binary algorithm: it simply averages the leakage from each operation to see if a squaring is more or less likely than a multiplication followed by a squaring.

9 Complexity

For algorithm complexity, constant time and space is assumed for individual machine-level instructions, i.e. they are independent of the volume of data and the required arithmetic accuracy. It is also assumed that generation and storage of all possible recodings of a single input digit require $O(1)$ time and space.

There are two main terms in the time complexity for processing level l of the search tree. First, tree construction consists primarily of incrementing the metric values at level $l+\lambda$ to those for level $l+\lambda+1$. This takes $O(2^\lambda BTR \log R)$ time since there are $O(2^\lambda B)$ nodes to consider, each having T traces with R recodings apiece. Each recoding is extended in all possible ways – constant time order – but it takes $O(R \log R)$ time to select the R best recodings to keep. Secondly, pruning is dominated by the $O(B \log B)$ time required to order nodes. The first of these terms is the most likely to dominate for expected choices of the parameters. Both must also be multiplied by the bit length of the key, $viz.$ $\log D$, to obtain the time for processing complete traces. The space complexity has two contributions. The first is $O(2^\lambda BRT)$ for storing details of the R recodings per trace associated with the $O(2^\lambda B)$ nodes between levels l and $l+\lambda$ during tree construction. The other is $O(B \log D)$ for storing details of nodes in the completed, pruned part.

10 Conclusion

A computationally feasible algorithm has been presented for determining the secret key used repeatedly in exponentiations where there is weak side channel leakage and randomised recoding has been employed to nullify the leakage. It has been shown that it is still frequently possible to recover the key. Moreover, it is easy to determine which results have few bit errors, and it is easy to locate the potential errors.

Acknowledgement

The author would like to thank Werner Schindler of BSI for helpful conversations.

References

1. Digital Signature Standard (DSS), FIPS PUB 186-2 (Appendix 6), U.S. National Institute of Standards and Technology (January 27, 2000)
2. Brier, E., Joye, M.: Weierstraß Elliptic Curves and Side-Channel Attacks. In: Naccache, D., Paillier, P. (eds.) PKC 2002. LNCS, vol. 2274, pp. 335–345. Springer, Heidelberg (2002)
3. Green, P.J., Noad, R., Smart, N.: Further Hidden Markov Model Cryptanalysis. In: Rao, J.R., Sunar, B. (eds.) CHES 2005. LNCS, vol. 3659, pp. 61–74. Springer, Heidelberg (2005)
4. Ha, J.C., Moon, S.J.: Randomized Signed-Scalar Multiplication of ECC to Resist Power Attacks. In: Kaliski Jr., B.S., Koç, Ç.K., Paar, C. (eds.) CHES 2002. LNCS, vol. 2523, pp. 551–563. Springer, Heidelberg (2003)

5. Karlof, C., Wagner, D.: Hidden Markov Model Cryptanalysis. In: Walter, C.D., Koç, Ç.K., Paar, C. (eds.) CHES 2003. LNCS, vol. 2779, pp. 17–34. Springer, Heidelberg (2003)
6. Kocher, P.: Timing Attack on Implementations of Diffie-Hellman, RSA, DSS, and other systems. In: Koblitz, N. (ed.) CRYPTO 1996. LNCS, vol. 1109, pp. 104–113. Springer, Heidelberg (1996)
7. Kocher, P., Jaffe, J., Jun, B.: Differential Power Analysis. In: Wiener, M.J. (ed.) CRYPTO 1999. LNCS, vol. 1666, pp. 388–397. Springer, Heidelberg (1999)
8. Liardet, P.-Y., Smart, N.P.: Preventing SPA/DPA in ECC Systems using the Jacobi Form. In: Koç, Ç.K., Naccache, D., Paar, C. (eds.) CHES 2001. LNCS, vol. 2162, pp. 391–401. Springer, Heidelberg (2001)
9. Oswald, E., Aigner, M.: Randomized Addition-Subtraction Chains as a Counter-measure against Power Attacks. In: Koç, Ç.K., Naccache, D., Paar, C. (eds.) CHES 2001. LNCS, vol. 2162, pp. 39–50. Springer, Heidelberg (2001)
10. Rabiner, L.R., Juang, B.H.: An Introduction to Hidden Markov Models. IEEE ASSP Magazine 3(1), 4–16 (1986)
11. Viterbi, A.J.: Error Bounds for Convolutional Codes and an Asymptotically Optimum Decoding Algorithm. IEEE Trans. Information Theory 13(2), 260–269 (1967)
12. Walter, C.D.: Breaking the Liardet-Smart Randomized Exponentiation Algorithm. In: Proc. Cardis 2002, San José, November 2002, pp. 59–68. Usenix Association, Berkeley (2002)
13. Walter, C.D.: Issues of Security with the Oswald-Aigner Exponentiation Algorithm. In: Okamoto, T. (ed.) CT-RSA 2004. LNCS, vol. 2964, pp. 208–221. Springer, Heidelberg (2004)
14. Walter, C.D.: Longer Randomly Blinded RSA Keys may be Weaker than Shorter Ones. In: Kim, S., Yung, M., Lee, H.-W. (eds.) WISA 2007. LNCS, vol. 4867, pp. 303–316. Springer, Heidelberg (2007)
15. Yen, S.-M., Chen, C.-N., Moon, S.J., Ha, J.C.: Improvement on Ha-Moon Randomized Exponentiation Algorithm. In: Park, C., Chee, S. (eds.) ICISC 2004. LNCS, vol. 3506, pp. 154–167. Springer, Heidelberg (2005)

Appendix 1: A Markov Model

This section describes the construction of a hidden Markov Model $\mathcal{H}$ for dealing with multiple traces [10]. We start with the case of a single trace.

The recoding automaton is a Markov process with a finite number of states and transitions which depend on the next key digit and bits from a random number generator. On entering a state after traversing the appropriate transition, the recoding algorithm generates a recoded digit which is transformed into a sequence of multiplicative operations. The attacker observes these operations with restricted clarity. Because the observations do not correspond directly to the states, the sequence of states is not known, giving a *hidden* Markov process.

Without loss of generality, we can assume that the sequence of states determines D uniquely. Then the problem is to determine the most likely sequence of states which generates the given sequence of observations. An algorithm for finding an optimal solution is due to Viterbi [11]. It computes the maximum probability $P_i(s_i)$ of any sequence of states $s_0 s_1 ... s_i$ from the start state s_0 to state s_i at the time of the ith observation, given the sequence of observations up to that point. By keeping track of which state s_{i-1} leads to $P_i(s_i)$, the optimal sequence of states can be reconstructed from the final best state.

The model $\mathcal{H}$ for many traces is constructed as follows. Assume there are $|T|$ copies of the recoding automaton indexed by the elements of the trace set T. These generate the operation sequences that are observed through the traces. Let S be the set of states of the automaton. When i digits of D have been processed by each copy of the automaton, we have an element of $S \times \mathbb{N}$ for each $t \in T$, which provides the state s_{ti} reached by the automaton of index t, and the number of operations n_{ti} so far in its recoding. This T-tuple of pairs is a state in $\mathcal{H}$. The start state has $(s_{t0}, n_{t0}) = (s_0, 0)$ for each $t \in T$. So the state set of $\mathcal{H}$ is the subset of $(S \times \mathbb{N})^T$ which is reachable from the start state. This is finite because each n_{ti} is bounded above by the length of its trace t.

Transitions in $\mathcal{H}$ are T-tuples of transitions from the basic recoding automaton, subject to the consistency requirement that they all correspond to the same input bit (or digit). So the inputs which determine a transition in $\mathcal{H}$ are a digit from D and a T-tuple of random numbers. The probability of this transition is the product of the probabilities of the $|T|$ constituent transitions of the original automaton. When the end-of-list symbol • is read from D, each finite automaton enters its final state, and the final state • of $\mathcal{H}$ is reached. The transition to this state generates any necessary final operations in the $|T|$ recoding sequences.

A path $p = s_0 s_1 ... s_i$ in $\mathcal{H}$ represents the first i recoding steps which have been performed for each of the traces. So p determines a path $p_t = s_{0,t} s_{1,t} ... s_{i,t}$ in copy $t \in T$ of the recoding automaton. If r_t is the recoding sequence along that path then it has a metric value $\mu(r_t, t)$ defined in §5. This leads to defining a path metric $\mu(p) = \sum_{t \in T} \mu(r_t, t)$. The "goodness" value of a state is the minimum $\mu(p)$ over all paths p to that state. It is easily computed incrementally by increasing path length. By keeping a pointer back to the previous state on the minimum path, the best path from start to final state can be constructed, and hence the best-fit key obtained.

If the number of operations is completely determined by the key so that all traces have the same length, then there are typically $O(|S|^{|T|})$ states which need processing for each input digit. There are more when trace lengths can vary. So, being exponential in $|T|$, the usual Viterbi algorithm becomes totally impractical when the leakage is so weak that more than a few tens of traces are needed. The algorithm in the main body of the paper is a pruned and re-organised version of this which is linear in $|T|$.

Appendix 2: Errors in Attacking Ha-Moon

In the Ha-Moon algorithm [4], the recoding automaton reads one bit at a time and the recoding state is determined by a borrow of 0 or 1. If either the guessed bit or the borrow is 1, but not both, then a given recoding can be extended in two ways: either the next re-coding digit is -1 with borrow 1, or it is $+1$ with borrow 0. Both result in a squaring and a multiplication and hence give rise to the same new metric value and the same new position along the trace, but they differ in the borrow value.

Now select a level l node N in the search tree where this property holds for the best recoding of every trace. These recodings occur in pairs with complementary borrow values. Suppose b_λ is the λ-bit label on the branch from N down to a level $l+\lambda$ node which is labelled with the minimum value $\bar{\mu}_N$ of the metric μ. This minimum arises from taking a good recoding of the prefix D_N for each trace t and appending the best recoding of $b_\lambda+b_t$ where b_t is the existing borrow for the recoding. However, using the complementary λ-bit sequence $2^\lambda-1-b_\lambda$ and complementary borrows $1-b_t$ of the other recodings in each pair, we can obtain the same value of the metric for each trace, and therefore achieve the same minimum $\bar{\mu}_N$ at the complementary level $l+\lambda$ node. This is because, for each trace t, $2^\lambda-b_\lambda-b_t$ has a recoding with the same pattern of squares and multiplications as the chosen recoding for $b_\lambda+b_t$. Specifically, interchanging digits $+1$ and -1 in a recoding of $b_\lambda+b_t$ will give a recoding of $2^\lambda-b_\lambda-b_t$ with exactly the same pattern[5] (and the complementary overflow borrow). Consequently, we obtain best metric values at level $l+\lambda$ from descending the branches corresponding to both b_λ and $2^\lambda-1-b_\lambda$. As one is odd and the other even, we don't know whether the next bit for the best choice should be 0 or 1 – both are equally likely.

If the wrong bit is chosen, the subsequent bits are all wrong until the next point at which the same problem arises. This is because, as in the branch from level l to level $l+\lambda$, the algorithm will continue to generate the best patterns of squares and multiplications, but now by choosing complementary bits, borrows and digits to those which would have been derived had the error not been made.

A consequence of this is that, if no other errors are made, roughly half the bits of the best fit guess at D are incorrect. They occur in sequences of consecutive bits, with changes occurring at predictable points, namely those for which the metric is totally inconclusive about the next bit.

---

[5] The other digits in the recoding are all 0, and they are the same for both recodings.

Attacking State-of-the-Art Software Countermeasures—A Case Study for AES

Stefan Tillich and Christoph Herbst

Graz University of Technology
Institute for Applied Information Processing and Communications
Inffeldgasse 16a, A–8010 Graz, Austria
{Stefan.Tillich,Christoph.Herbst}@iaik.tugraz.at

Abstract. In order to protect software implementations of secret-key cryptographic primitives against side channel attacks, a software developer has only a limited choice of countermeasures. A combination of masking and randomization of operations in time promises good protection and can be realized without too much overhead. Recently, new advanced DPA methods have been proposed to attack software implementations with such kind of protection. In this work, we have applied these methods successfully to break a protected AES software implementation on a programmable smart card. Thus, we were able to verify the practicality of the new attacks and to estimate their effectiveness in comparison to traditional DPA attacks on unprotected implementations. In the course of our work, we have also refined and improved the original attacks, so that they can be mounted more efficiently. Our practical results indicate that the effort required for attacking the protected implementation with the examined methods is more than two orders of magnitude higher compared to an attack on an unprotected implementation.

Keywords: Advanced Encryption Standard, smart card, side channel attacks, power analysis, software countermeasures, masking, operation randomization, advanced DPA attacks.

1 Introduction

Today, an increasing amount of data is processed and distributed in electronic form. This trend is driven by advances in digital microprocessing and network technologies, which are leading us towards visions of "ubiquitous computing" and "ambient intelligence". One of the most pressing problems on the way to realizing these visions is the challenge of security. Cryptographic algorithms are an indispensable tool to establish reasonable security assurances for digital data, e.g. privacy, integrity, and authenticity. The presumption of most cryptographic methods is that the employed key is only known to authorized entities. A fundamental principle of cryptography is that cryptographic algorithms are designed in such a way that observable cryptographic data (e.g. the ciphertext) contains as little information about the key as possible.

E. Oswald and P. Rohatgi (Eds.): CHES 2008, LNCS 5154, pp. 228–243, 2008.

However, in practice keys have to be stored on physical devices like PCs or smart cards and it has been shown that the physical properties (the so-called side channels) of these devices can be exploited to extract information about the cryptographic keys they contain. Amongst such side channel attacks, power analysis developed by Kocher et al. [8] has proven to be a very potent method. The improvement of such attacks and possible countermeasures as defence against them has since been the topic of a wide array of scientific publications.

In power analysis, an attacker has to record the power consumption of a device while it performs cryptographic operations with an unknown key. A particularly powerful attack method is Differential Power Analysis (DPA) [8], which predicts intermediate values of the cryptographic algorithm and an according power consumption and matches it against the recorded power traces. In this fashion, the used key can be recovered even if the relevant information is deeply buried within noise.

Two principal countermeasures have been proposed against power analysis: Masking and hiding [9]. Masking tries to break the link between the predicted intermediate values and the values processed by the device. Hiding seeks to minimize the effect of the processed values on the power consumption. Many specific countermeasures have been proposed on different levels for hardware and software. For software implementations on a given platform, the options tend to be limited to masking schemes and to hiding through the randomization of executed operations in time.

Masking schemes split each intermediate value in a number of shares, which are then processed independently. Only by combining all the shares, the original value can be reconstructed. In its simplest form, a value a is split into two shares $a \circ m$ and m, where m is a random mask, so that $a = (a \circ m) \circ m$. A common choice for the operation $\circ$ is the logical XOR (Boolean masking). Masking is generally susceptible to higher-order DPA attacks. Such attacks combine information of the power consumption of the different shares (higher-order DPA preprocessing) so that the resulting power consumption is again dependent on the unprotected value a and thus susceptible to a "normal" 1st-order DPA attack.

As the effort for higher-order DPA attacks is expected to grow exponentially with the order, it is assumed that a masking scheme with enough shares will make practical attacks infeasible. A higher-order masking scheme for AES [10] based on this idea has been developed by Schramm et al. [13]. However, Coron et al. have demonstrated that this scheme is susceptible to 3rd-order DPA attacks irrespective of the number of used shares [3]. Another problem is posed by the large computational overhead which is required for refreshing the masks. In [13], it has been shown that a single AES encryption with resistance against 2nd-order DPA attacks requires over 40 times more clock cycles (about 200,000 clock cycles in total).

Irrespective of the security aspects, overheads of this order are not likely to be acceptable for every implementation. Therefore, it is necessary to resort to more "light-weight" countermeasures. A possible solution which requires significantly less overhead is a combination of 1st-order masking and operation randomization as proposed in [4]. Advanced DPA attacks targeted at such a combination of masking and randomization have been proposed in [15], but so far no practical evaluation of their effectiveness has been available. The work described in this paper puts these new attacks to the practical test. Our goals were twofold: First, we sought to verify that these attacks are practicable in a state-of-the-art measurement setup. Second, we wanted to collect empirical evidence for the degree of protection offered by this combination of countermeasures. Note that we did not have the goal to develop new attacks on these countermeasures. Furthermore, we stress that—as with any practical evaluation—our results may not necessarily be optimal for the targeted device. Therefore, the increase in the number of required power traces for the protected implementation indicated in Section 5 should not be taken as a fixed "security gain factor" but only as an upper border of this factor.

The rest of this paper is organized as follows. In Section 2, we describe the protected software implementation of AES which we attacked and we give details on the countermeasures. The advanced DPA methods which have been proposed to break these countermeasures and which we have evaluated practically are presented in Section 3. Some details on the attacked smart card device (especially a characterization of its power leakage) are given in Section 4. In Section 5, we present the results of our practical work. A further discussion of some issues relating to the effectiveness of the attacks in dependence on the attacker's capabilities follows in Section 6. Finally, conclusions are drawn in Section 7.

2   Protected AES Software Implementation

The protection of our AES software implementation is based on the strategy of combining masking, shuffling and dummy operations as published in [4]. At the beginning and at the end of the AES operations there are so-called "randomization zones". Within each zone all intermediate values are protected with a single mask and the sequence of processing of the bytes of the State is randomized. In [4], the initial zone extends to the first MixColumns transformation. Jaffe showed that it is possible to attack the AES after the MixColumns operation [6]. This principally means that a protection of the first round alone would be insufficient. However, Tillich et al. showed that it is quite easy to extend this randomization zone beyond the second SubBytes operation [15], thus thwarting Jaffe's attack[1].

We are using the same masking scheme with six different random masks[2] as published in [4]. All intermediate values of the State and the key are masked. In our implementation, the randomization is achieved by shuffling of the sequence of operations on the bytes of the State. Furthermore, it would be possible

---

[1] The randomization zone at the end can be extended in a similar fashion to protect against Jaffe's attack.

[2] One mask for S-box inputs, one for S-box outputs, and one for each State row before MixColumns. All other occurring masks (e.g. after MixColumns) are derived from these six masks.

to process additional dummy States to increase the degree of randomization. The randomization is controlled by random values which are—similarly to the mask bytes—unknown to the attacker. We denote the degree of randomization with R, i.e. the number of points in time where a specific State byte can be processed during a specific AES encryption. In our case, the 16 bytes of the AES State are fully shuffled and no dummy States are added. This means that the randomization degree $R = 16$. Hence, a specific byte of the State will be processed with a probability of $p = \frac{1}{16}$ at one of the 16 possible points in time. One protected AES encryption requires less than 12,000 clock cycles on our targeted platform, which is described in Section 4. The cost per additional dummy State would be about 1,000 clock cycles.

The consequences of this randomization for a plain 1st-order DPA attack are illustrated in the following. In Figure 1, the result of an attack on the first S-box output of an unmasked and randomized implementation is shown. Note that only the section of the trace which corresponds to the SubBytes transformation was used. One can clearly identify four groups of peaks. When zooming into one of these groups, again four pairs of peaks can be identified. Each group of peaks corresponds to the transformation of a single State column, which again encompasses four State bytes. As a specific State byte can occur at any of these times, there are all in all 16 different positions where the output value of the unmasked S-box correlates. Furthermore if we compare the achieved correlation of this attack to the achieved correlation of an attack on the unprotected implementation (cf. also Figure 5 in Section 4) we end up with a correlation which is reduced by a factor of approximately 16. As expected, the correlation coefficient scales down linearly with the degree of randomization R [9].

3   Description of the Advanced DPA Attacks

From an implementor's view, a combination of masking and operation randomization countermeasures is a good bet for protecting software implementations of secret-key cryptographic algorithms against power analysis. Proper masking can prevent 1st-order DPA attacks while the randomization of operations in time can offer some protection against more elaborate attacks like higher-order DPA and template-based methods. At the same time, the implementation complexity and overhead can be kept within somewhat acceptable limits.

Higher-order DPA attacks and template attacks have been shown to be very effective to circumvent masking. In higher-order DPA attacks, power leakage of several intermediate values is combined in such a way that the resulting power consumption value is again dependent on the original unmasked value [7, 12, 14, 16]. Template-based methods can be applied to enhance higher-order DPA attacks or to make first-order DPA attacks feasible [9, 11]. On the other side, the technique known as "windowing" is a good way to limit the protection of randomization of operations [2]. In this method, all R possibilities of appearance of a protected value are considered and combined so that the effective protection of the countermeasure is lowered.

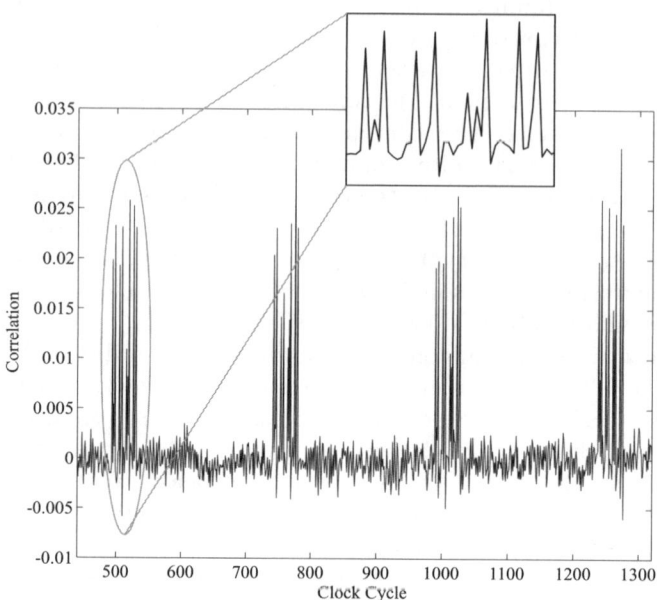

Fig. 1. Result of DPA attack on randomized AES implementation using the Hamming weight model and compressed traces

It has been shown in [15] that the attacks on masking and randomization can be combined to form effective attacks on implementations which employ a single mask and which randomize the course of operations. Three possible combinations have been presented and their effectiveness has been compared by estimations techniques and high-level simulation which neglected electronic noise.

Figure 2 shows the timeline for a part of the execution of a protected secret-key cipher implementation. Towards the beginning at time index t_0, the mask m is processed in some form (it is generated, stored, used in some precomputation, etc.). Subsequently, the intermediate value a masked with m appears. The occurrence of this masked intermediate value is protected by randomization, i.e. in each execution the specific value $a \oplus m$ can appear in any of the R points at the times $t_1..t_R$ with equal probability $p = \frac{1}{R}$. The power consumption at these

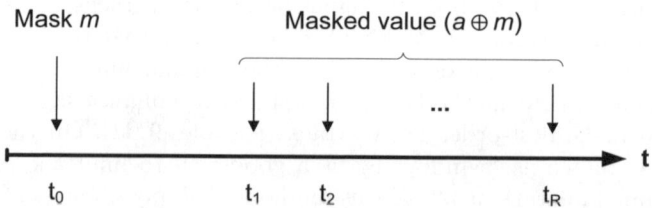

Fig. 2. Points in time relevant for an attack

points in time is used in all attacks from [15]. An adversary must therefore be able to find these points in time. As will be discussed in Section 6, the constraints for $t_1..t_R$ can be relaxed, so that knowledge of the exact time indices is not necessary. The attacks are described in the following.

3.1 Biasing Masks and Windowing Followed by 1st-Order DPA Attack

One precondition for effective masking is that the used masks must be uniformly distributed. If this condition is not met, 1st-order DPA attacks can become feasible. Therefore, the principal idea of this attack is to try to determine the Hamming weight of the used mask and to select a subset of the collected power traces, where the mask fulfills some property, e.g. has a high Hamming weight. This selection of power traces effectively equals a bias which is introduced into the distribution of the mask values. The selected power traces are then only protected by the randomization of the operations $(t_1..t_R)$, whose effect can be minimized by windowing. A subsequent 1st-order DPA attack can be successfully applied on the selected power traces. This attack has been shown to be rather effective under most circumstances in [15].

3.2 2nd-Order DPA Attack Followed by Windowing

The idea of this attack is to take the randomization of the operations into account during 2nd-order DPA preprocessing. The power consumption values for m at t_0 and $a \oplus m$ at $t_1..t_R$ are pairwise combined (2nd-order DPA preprocessing). For each pair, this preprocessing results in a joint leakage value of the two points. If the correct points in time have been chosen, one of these R joint leakage points is always dependent on the actual unmasked value. Which of these points is the correct one is determined by the randomized course of operations of the corresponding execution. When all points are windowed (i.e. summed up), the correct one is inevitably included and the resulting power consumption is to some degree dependent on the unmasked value. A 1st-order DPA attack can then be mounted to determine the correct key hypothesis. This attack has been evaluated in [15] to be less effective than the first one in most cases.

3.3 Windowing Followed by 2nd-Order DPA Attack

A third option for attacking is to reverse the order of windowing and 2nd-order DPA preprocessing. First, randomization is compensated by summing up all R points in time where the targeted masked value $a \oplus m$ can occur. Then, 2nd-order DPA preprocessing is performed with this sum and a point of the power trace which depends on the corresponding mask m. The result of this preprocessing can be attacked with a 1st-order DPA attack. In [15], this attack variant has been shown to be rather ineffective in comparison to the previous two methods.

4   Attacked Device

The device used to implement and attack the protected AES software implementation is a smart card with an ATMega163 core [1]. The ATMega163 is an 8-bit microcontroller based on AVR, which is a single-cycle instruction RISC architecture from Atmel. It is equipped with 1,024 bytes of internal RAM, 16 KB in-system self-programmable FLASH and 512 bytes of EEPROM. The core of the controller contains 32 general purpose registers which are directly connected to the arithmetic-logic unit (ALU). Three register pairs can be used to store a 16-bit address into the internal memory.

The used smart card is shipped without any software or operating system. This means the card is under full control of the designer and all parts of the software (including boot code and operating system) have to be implemented from scratch. In our scenario, there is only a minimum version of an operating system implemented which can handle the basic functions of the T=1 protocol specified in ISO 7816 [5]. The card can execute the protected AES implementation described in Section 2. For the sake of performance, the randomization parameters and mask bytes are sent to the smart card along with the plaintext. The key used for the AES encryption is stored in the EEPROM of the smart card.

In general, the device leaks the Hamming weight as well as the Hamming distance of the processed values. When attacking the non-randomized S-box output using the Hamming weight model, the maximum achievable correlation is 0.458. In a similar attack using the Hamming distance between the S-box input and the S-box output—which occur as subsequent values of a register—the maximum correlation is 0.257. The results for these attacks on uncompressed traces are displayed in Figure 3 and in Figure 4. It can be seen that for this device and the sequence of instructions used to implement the S-box lookup, the Hamming weight model leads to a higher correlation.

For minimization of the amount of data used for an attack, it is a common technique to compress the measured traces [9]. When using the compression

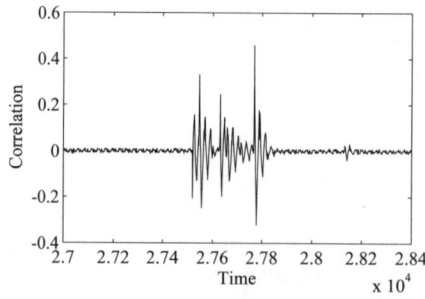 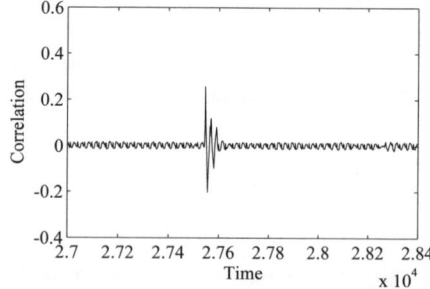

Fig. 3. Result of DPA attack on un-protected AES implementation using the Hamming weight model and uncompressed traces

Fig. 4. Result of DPA attack on un-protected AES implementation using the Hamming distance model and uncom-pressed traces

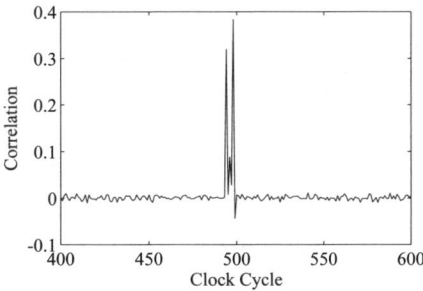

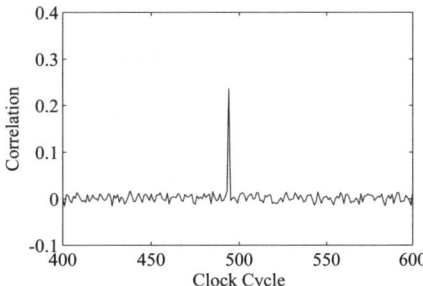

Fig. 5. Result of DPA attack on unprotected AES implementation using the Hamming weight model and compressed traces

Fig. 6. Result of DPA attack on unprotected AES implementation using the Hamming distance model and compressed traces

described in Section 5.2, the achievable correlation using the Hamming weight model reduces from 0.458 to 0.383. With the Hamming distance model the correlation reduces from 0.257 to 0.236. The results of an attack on compressed traces can be seen in Figure 5 and Figure 6. For our practical attacks, this means that most of the information is preserved in the compressed power traces.

5   Practical Results

In order to demonstrate the effectiveness and practicability of the methods described in [15], we have attacked the protected AES software implementation presented in Section 2. For the randomization of operations, we have used full shuffling of the 16 State bytes, i.e. $R = 16$. Power traces were collected with a LeCroy LC584AM digital oscilloscope and a differential probe by measurement over a $1\,\Omega$ resistor in the ground line of the smart card reader. A trigger signal has been supplied by the smart card at the beginning of encryption. We have collected a set of 500,000 power traces, which took about 134 hours in our measurement setup, i.e. a rate of approximately one trace per second. The uncompressed traces required about 50 GB of disk space. For comparison, a set of compressed traces was between 700 MB and 2 GB in size, depending on the actual compression function. An uncompressed trace contained 100,000 points, whereas a compressed trace consisted of about 1,800 points (one per clock cycle).

The power traces included about 1,800 clock cycles at the start of AES encryption spanning over various precomputations (parts of the masked key scheduling, mask preprocessing, and the masking of the plaintext), the initial AddRoundkey, and the first AES round. In order to keep the size of the traces small, the sampling rate has been limited to $200 \cdot 10^6$ samples/second.

All statistical analyses were carried out on a PC featuring a quad-core Intel Xeon processor at 2.33 GHz and 8 GB of RAM. Attack times were generally determined by the number and size of the analyzed traces, and not by the kind of statistical analysis. An attack using all 500,000 power traces took about 140 s for compressed traces and about 1,7 hours for uncompressed traces. For an attack with biased masks, the template-building took about 160 s when 100 traces were used for each of the nine templates. The time for attacks involving fewer traces would scale down almost linearly.

For our attacks we have used the S-box output of the first round as intermediate value a and the S-box output mask as corresponding m. The time indices $t_1..t_{16}$ for $a \oplus m$ were determined by 1st-order DPA attacks using the known masked S-box outputs as attacked intermediate values. Suitable indices t_0 were found accordingly by using the S-box output mask as attacked value. For both cases, the time indices resulting in high correlation values were used.

5.1   Results: Biasing Masks and Windowing Followed by 1st-Order DPA Attack

In order to introduce a bias in the mask values, we have used templates to derive the Hamming weight of the mask m. Templates were built from the uncompressed traces for each Hamming weight of the mask. We used 100 traces per template with 16 interesting points per trace. The multivariate Gaussian distribution model has been employed. The traces used for the 1st-order DPA attack have been compressed (integration of absolute values per clock cycle). Randomization has been countered by windowing, i.e. the power consumption values at times $t_1..t_{16}$ have been summed up. The Hamming weight of an unmasked S-box output byte has been used as predicted power consumption. The attack itself is therefore similar to the one described in [11] ("Templates During Preprocessing"), except for the additional compensation of the randomization countermeasure.

In practice, it is important to find a good tradeoff between a sharp bias and a minimal number of discarded traces. For example, only choosing traces with a mask Hamming weight of 8 (i.e. $m = \text{0xFF}$) will lead to the highest correlation but on the other hand, this would mean to discard $\frac{255}{256} = 99.6\%$ of the recorded power traces. Selecting masks with a Hamming weight greater or equal to six has been shown to be a good choice [9,11,15] and therefore we have also used it for our evaluations.

The effectiveness of the attack depends on the accuracy of the biasing process. In order to show the best outcome, we have also biased the masks following their actual values (ideal case). The results for biasing with the actual Hamming weights and with the Hamming weights predicted by template matching are show in Figures 7 and 8, respectively.

In the ideal case, the correlation for the correct key hypothesis was about -0.04 while the use of template matching yielded a correlation of about -0.025. With increasing accuracy of the template method in predicting the actual Hamming weight of the used mask, the result of the attack should get closer to that of the ideal case. We use the rule of thumb from [9] to estimate the required number of power traces for a successful attack. We have also taken those traces into account which were discarded during the biasing process (about 85% of

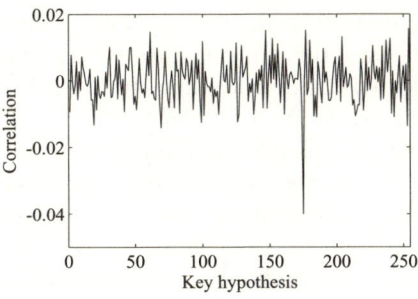

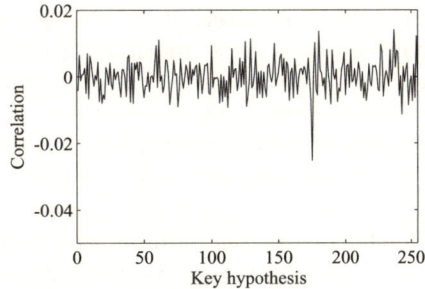

Fig. 7. Result of attack with ideal mask biasing

Fig. 8. Result of attack with mask biasing through templates

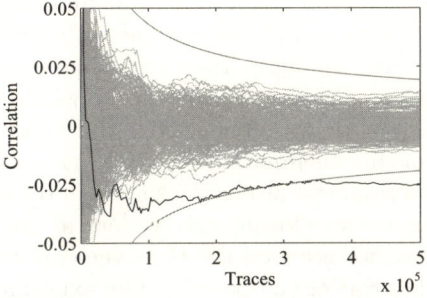

Fig. 9. Evolution of correlation in dependence on number of traces for mask biasing through templates

all traces). For ideal biasing, about 122,000 power trace are sufficient, for our biasing with templates, about 305,000 power traces are required.

Figure 9 shows the evolution of the correlation with increasing number of power traces for the attack depicted in Figure 8. Note that the trace count on the x-axis also includes the discarded traces. The correct key hypothesis is plotted in black, the incorrect hypotheses are displayed in light gray. The outer dark gray lines indicate the confidence interval for $\rho = 0$. Roughly speaking, this is the expected region for incorrect key hypotheses. The point where the correct key hypothesis leaves this region gives another estimation for the number of traces required for a successful attack. In this case, the estimate lies in the vicinity of 300,000 traces, which is in line with the result from the rule of thumb from [9].

5.2   Results: 2nd-Order DPA Attack Followed by Windowing

This attack can be seen as multiple 2nd-order DPA attacks in parallel, with their results combined by windowing. Nevertheless, a successful attack is not quite as simple to achieve as in a conventional 2nd-order DPA attack. Normally, most 2nd-order DPA attacks can be conducted in a more or less "brute-force" manner. More precisely, it is not necessary to determine the exact points in time which carry the most information about the targeted intermediate values and which are therefore suited most for 2nd-order DPA preprocessing. In fact, it is sufficient to predict the general regions of the power traces which are expected to contain the required points. By examining all possible combinations of the points of both regions in a 1st-order DPA attack, the correct key hypothesis can be identified without giving much thought to the actual points of the power trace which carry the required information.

When there is a need to compensate for the randomization countermeasure as well, it quickly becomes evident that this "brute-force" approach is no longer feasible. Even if all of the R parallel 2nd-order DPA attacks could be done in this manner, the subsequent windowing of the results requires that only those points are summed up which might contain information about the unmasked intermediate values. Our experiments have shown that the attack result is extremely sensitive even to slight variations in time of the two input points to the 2nd-order DPA preprocessing function. Therefore, choosing the best points from the power trace becomes a crucial precondition for windowing. Unfortunately, the best points only become known after a successful attack.

An effective way out of this dilemma can be made with a suitable compression function. If there is only a single point per clock cycle in the power trace, the 2nd-order DPA preprocessing and windowing can be done at the exact points in time where the maximal information is contained. However, care must be taken that not too much information is lost during compression. Our experiments have shown that none of the standard compression functions (maximum extraction, integration) [9] deliver satisfying results. After careful analysis of the 2nd-order DPA leakage profile of the attacked device, we have developed a new compression function, which retains most of the required information and hence delivers good results. Our new compression function extracts a small range of points around the maximum of each clock cycle and forms the average value of those points. At our sampling rate of $200 \cdot 10^6$ samples/second, a range of two points around the maximum (i.e. 5 points in total per clock cycle) was sufficient to achieve satisfying results.

As 2nd-order DPA preprocessing function we have employed the absolute of the difference of the two input points, as it has the best correspondence to single bits of unmasked values and still a good correspondence to the Hamming weight of larger values [9]. We have used the bit model (LSB of the S-box output) as power model for our attack. The results are shown in Figure 10.

The correlation peak for the correct key hypothesis has a height of approximately 0.024, requiring about 50,000 power traces for a successful attack [9].

The evolution of the correlation with the number of power traces used in the attack is shown in Figure 11. In this case, the correlation curve for the correct key hypothesis leaves the confidence interval for $\rho = 0$ at about 65,000 traces. Note that this number is a bit higher than the estimate from the rule of thumb from [9]. In our experience, the evolution of the correlation is quite dependent on the measurements, so the rule of thumb should normally be preferred for a more general prediction.

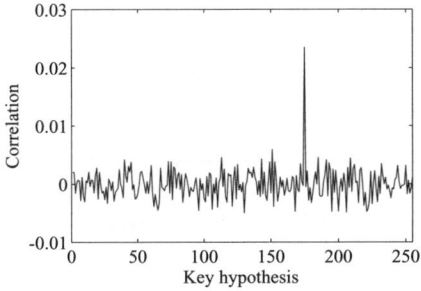
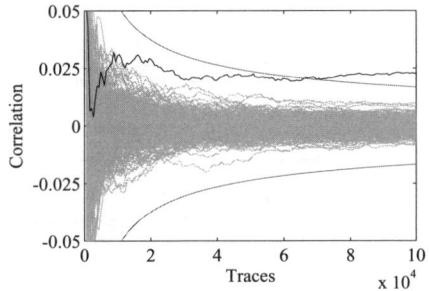

Fig. 10. Result of 2nd-order DPA attack followed by windowing

Fig. 11. Evolution of correlation in dependence on number of traces

5.3 Results: Windowing Followed by 2nd-Order DPA Attack

This attack had already a very low effectiveness in the simulated evaluation of [15]. For completeness, we have conducted attacks with this method on all 500,000 power traces. As suspected, this number of power traces was not sufficient to lead to a correct prediction of the key.

5.4 Dependence of Attack Efficiency on Randomization Degree

The AES implementation allows to change the degree of randomization R in order to trade performance against security. Table 1 shows how the effectiveness of the two attacks from Section 3.1 and 3.2 changes with increasing R. Conceptually, the correlation coefficient should scale down with a factor of $\sqrt{R}$ [15]. It can be seen from Table 1 that both attacks approximately follow this behavior, whereby the second one (2nd-order DPA attack followed by windowing), tends to perform worse at a higher R.

Table 1. Maximal absolute correlation coefficient in dependence on randomization degree R

R	1	2	4	8	16
Biasing masks	0.104	0.072	0.052	0.035	0.025
2nd-order and windowing	0.125	0.102	0.073	0.042	0.024

6 Discussion of the Practicality of the Attacks

As shown in Section 5, two of the three examined attacks succeeded with a reasonable amount of samples. Mask biasing turned out to lead to a potentially higher correlation, which is in line with the estimation results from [15]. However, this attack requires to discard a large number of power traces, which increases the total number of required power traces considerably. Furthermore, the 2nd-order DPA attack followed by windowing puts less demands on the attacker's

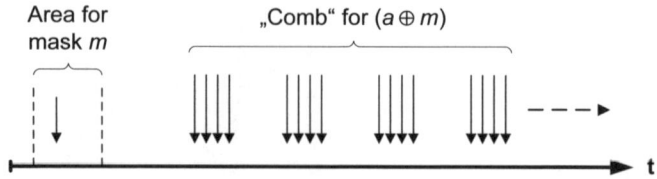

Fig. 12. Extracting viable points for 2nd-order DPA preprocessing

knowledge and control over the device. In order to introduce a bias in the mask, templates for the mask values have to be built. This requires the availability of a device for profiling which is sufficiently similar to the attacked one. Moreover, the profiling device must offer the possibility to extract some information about the actually occurring mask values in order to allow template building. Depending on the attack scenario, these preconditions might not be always given.

Both methods require a windowing for the time indices $t_1..t_R$, i.e. all points in time where the attacked masked intermediate value can occur due to the randomization countermeasure (cf. Figure 2). However, for a practical attack it is not necessary to identify the exact points in time, but it is sufficient to know the distance between those points. In our attack, we have first compressed the power traces (see Section 5.2) so that there was only a single power consumption value per clock cycle. When the distance (in clock cycles) between the R points in time is known, all possible combinations of points with this distance can be used in the attack. The selection of possible combinations of R points can be seen as pulling a comb with R teeth over the power trace. The distances between the comb's teeth correspond to the clock cycle distances between the possible occurrences of the masked value $a \oplus m$. This is illustrated in Figure 12.

For each position of the comb and each point in time where the mask value m is suspected to appear ("area for mask m" in Figure 12), a new correlation value can be calculated. Thereby, 2nd-order DPA preprocessing is applied with the current mask point and each comb tooth. The resulting 16 preprocessed points are then summed up (windowed) to produce a single predicted power consumption value for the attack.

Normally, an attacker has some general idea of the order of operations which are performed by the attacked device so that it is possible to specify some areas in the power traces where certain values are likely to appear. This limits the number of possible combinations of comb positions and mask positions and makes the attack faster. But even if all possible combinations are used in our case, the total number ranges around $3 \cdot 10^6$, which is quite feasible for an attack[3].

Depending on the scenario, an attacker can obtain information about the distance of the R randomized points (i.e. the distance between the teeth of

---

[3] There are about 1,800 points per compressed trace, which is hence the upper limit for comb positions and mask positions. The maximal number of combinations is therefore $1,800 \cdot 1,800 = 3,240,000$.

the comb) through different means. If a device is available for profiling, then the relevant points in time can be determined through a DPA attack with known intermediate values. When the relevant sections of the implementation's source code are available, the distances can be derived with a cycle-accurate simulator. Even if those options are not available, some general knowledge about the protected implementation can be enough to establish a set of "candidate combs" with different distances between the teeth. If this set is not too large, the correct comb can be determined by trying out all combs of the set in an attack.

For our protected AES implementation it would be sufficient to know that there is a randomization of the columns of the State and a randomization of the bytes within each column. The distance between the processing of the columns and between the four S-box lookups of one column are constant. Thus there are only two configuration parameters for the comb, resulting in a manageable set of candidate combs.

Hence, the method of 2nd-order DPA attack followed by windowing can be regarded as a fairly generic attack which requires only little more knowledge about the implementation than a plain 1st-order DPA attack.

7 Conclusions

In this paper we have practically demonstrated the effectiveness of advanced DPA attacks on an AES smart card implementation with state-of-the-art software countermeasures. We have evaluated the three principal attack methods described in [15], which have so far only been subject to theoretical estimation and high-level simulation. Two of these methods work well in defeating the masking and randomization of operations countermeasures of the AES software implementation. One of the methods leads to a potentially higher correlation, but requires the attacker to be able to profile the attacked device in detail. The second attack is not quite as effective but is more general. It can be mounted without profiling and requires only little knowledge about the implementation. Nevertheless, it must not be overlooked that the effort for the attacks is considerably larger than for an unprotected implementation. While 100 power traces are normally enough to break the unprotected implementation, the advanced DPA attacks on the protected implementation require a minimal number of about 50,000 traces for success. Hence, DPA becomes more than two orders of magnitude (i.e. 100 times) harder under use of the described attacks. Although there is no guarantee that there are no better attacks on a specific implementation, our work has delivered empirical evidence that a combination of masking and operation randomization can offer significant protection against advanced DPA attacks.

Acknowledgements. The research described in this paper has been supported by the Austrian Science Fund (FWF) under grant number P18321-N15

("Investigation of Side-Channel Attacks"), by the European Commission under grant number FP6-IST-033563 (Project SMEPP) and, in part, by the European Commission through the IST Programme under contract IST-2002-507932 ECRYPT. The information in this document reflects only the authors' views, is provided as is and no guarantee or warranty is given that the information is fit for any particular purpose. The user thereof uses the information at its sole risk and liability.

References

1. Atmel Corporation. 8-bit Microcontroller with 16K Bytes In-System Programmable Flash (February 2003),
   http://www.atmel.com/dyn/resources/prod_documents/doc1142.pdf
2. Clavier, C., Coron, J.-S., Dabbous, N.: Differential Power Analysis in the Presence of Hardware Countermeasures. In: Paar, C., Koç, Ç.K. (eds.) CHES 2000. LNCS, vol. 1965, pp. 252–263. Springer, Heidelberg (2000)
3. Coron, J.-S., Prouff, E., Rivain, M.: Side Channel Cryptanalysis of a Higher Order Masking Scheme. In: Paillier, P., Verbauwhede, I. (eds.) CHES 2007. LNCS, vol. 4727, pp. 28–44. Springer, Heidelberg (2007)
4. Herbst, C., Oswald, E., Mangard, S.: An AES Smart Card Implementation Resistant to Power Analysis Attacks. In: Zhou, J., Yung, M., Bao, F. (eds.) ACNS 2006. LNCS, vol. 3989, pp. 239–252. Springer, Heidelberg (2006)
5. International Organisation for Standardization (ISO). ISO/IEC 7816-3: Information technology - Identification cards - Integrated circuit(s) cards with contacts - Part 3: Electronic signals and transmission protocols (September 1997),
   http://www.iso.org
6. Jaffe, J.: Introduction to Differential Power Analysis, Presented at ECRYPT Summerschool on Cryptographic Hardware, Side Channel and Fault Analysis (June 2006)
7. Joye, M., Paillier, P., Schoenmakers, B.: On Second-Order Differential Power Analysis. In: Rao, J.R., Sunar, B. (eds.) CHES 2005. LNCS, vol. 3659, pp. 293–308. Springer, Heidelberg (2005)
8. Kocher, P.C., Jaffe, J., Jun, B.: Differential Power Analysis. In: Wiener, M.J. (ed.) CRYPTO 1999. LNCS, vol. 1666, pp. 388–397. Springer, Heidelberg (1999)
9. Mangard, S., Oswald, E., Popp, T.: Power Analysis Attacks – Revealing the Secrets of Smart Cards. Springer, Heidelberg (2007)
10. National Institute of Standards and Technology (NIST). FIPS-197: Advanced Encryption Standard (November 2001), http://www.itl.nist.gov/fipspubs/.
11. Oswald, E., Mangard, S.: Template Attacks on Masking—Resistance is Futile. In: Abe, M. (ed.) CT-RSA 2007. LNCS, vol. 4377, pp. 243–256. Springer, Heidelberg (2006)
12. Oswald, E., Mangard, S., Herbst, C., Tillich, S.: Practical Second-Order DPA Attacks for Masked Smart Card Implementations of Block Ciphers. In: Pointcheval, D. (ed.) CT-RSA 2006. LNCS, vol. 3860, pp. 192–207. Springer, Heidelberg (2006)
13. Schramm, K., Paar, C.: Higher Order Masking of the AES. In: Pointcheval, D. (ed.) CT-RSA 2006. LNCS, vol. 3860, pp. 208–225. Springer, Heidelberg (2006)

14. Standaert, F.-X., Peeters, E., Quisquater, J.-J.: On the Masking Countermeasure and Higher-Order Power Analysis Attacks. In: International Conference on Information Technology: Coding and Computing (ITCC 2005), Las Vegas, Nevada, USA, April 4-6, 2005, vol. 1, pp. 562–567. IEEE Computer Society, Los Alamitos (2005)

15. Tillich, S., Herbst, C., Mangard, S.: Protecting AES Software Implementations on 32-bit Processors against Power Analysis. In: Katz, J., Yung, M. (eds.) ACNS 2007. LNCS, vol. 4521, pp. 141–157. Springer, Heidelberg (2007)

16. Waddle, J., Wagner, D.: Towards Efficient Second-Order Power Analysis. In: Joye, M., Quisquater, J.-J. (eds.) CHES 2004. LNCS, vol. 3156, pp. 1–15. Springer, Heidelberg (2004)

Binary Edwards Curves[*]

Daniel J. Bernstein[1], Tanja Lange[2], and Reza Rezaeian Farashahi[2,3]

[1] Department of Mathematics, Statistics, and Computer Science (M/C 249)
University of Illinois at Chicago, Chicago, IL 60607–7045, USA
djb@cr.yp.to
[2] Department of Mathematics and Computer Science
Technische Universiteit Eindhoven, P.O. Box 513, 5600 MB Eindhoven, Netherlands
tanja@hyperelliptic.org, r.rezaeian@tue.nl
[3] Dept. of Mathematical Sciences, Isfahan University of Technology,
P.O. Box 85145 Isfahan, Iran

Abstract. This paper presents a new shape for ordinary elliptic curves over fields of characteristic 2. Using the new shape, this paper presents the first complete addition formulas for binary elliptic curves, i.e., addition formulas that work for all pairs of input points, with no exceptional cases. If $n \geq 3$ then the complete curves cover all isomorphism classes of ordinary elliptic curves over $\mathbf{F}_{2^n}$.

This paper also presents dedicated doubling formulas for these curves using $2\mathbf{M} + 6\mathbf{S} + 3\mathbf{D}$, where $\mathbf{M}$ is the cost of a field multiplication, $\mathbf{S}$ is the cost of a field squaring, and $\mathbf{D}$ is the cost of multiplying by a curve parameter. These doubling formulas are also the first complete doubling formulas in the literature, with no exceptions for the neutral element, points of order 2, etc.

Finally, this paper presents complete formulas for differential addition, i.e., addition of points with known difference. A differential addition and doubling, the basic step in a Montgomery ladder, uses $5\mathbf{M} + 4\mathbf{S} + 2\mathbf{D}$ when the known difference is given in affine form.

Keywords: Elliptic curves, Edwards curves, binary fields, complete addition law, Montgomery ladder, countermeasures against side-channel attacks.

1 Introduction

The points on a Weierstrass-form elliptic curve

$$y^2 + a_1 xy + a_3 y = x^3 + a_2 x^2 + a_4 x + a_6$$

[*] Permanent ID of this document: 592248bfa170d87d90a8d543cb645788. Date of this document: 2008.05.16. This work has been supported in part by the European Commission through the IST Programme under Contract IST–2002–507932 ECRYPT, in part by the National Science Foundation under grant ITR–0716498, and in part by the Ministry of Science, Research and Technology of I. R. Iran under scholarship no. 800.147.

E. Oswald and P. Rohatgi (Eds.): CHES 2008, LNCS 5154, pp. 244–265, 2008.

include not only the affine points (x_1, y_1) satisfying the curve equation but also an extra point at infinity serving as the neutral element. The standard formulas to compute a sum $P + Q$ fail if P is at infinity, or if Q is at infinity, or if $P + Q$ is at infinity, or if P is equal to Q. Each of these possibilities needs to be tested for and handled separately; a complete addition *algorithm* is produced by gluing together several incomplete addition *formulas*.

This plethora of cases has caused a seemingly neverending string of problems for implementors of elliptic-curve cryptography, especially in cryptographic hardware subject to side-channel attacks. Consider, for example, computing $nP + mQ$. A typical two-scalar-multiplication algorithm would double P, add P, add Q, etc., where the exact pattern of additions and doublings depends on the values of n and m. What happens if $3P = Q$? Does the implementation take the time to see that $3P = Q$ and to switch from the addition formulas to doubling formulas? Can the attacker detect the switch through timing analysis, power analysis, etc.? If the implementation fails to check for $3P = Q$, what does it end up computing? What about $3P = -Q$? Can an attacker trigger failure cases—and incorrect computations—by choosing inputs cleverly? Can these failures compromise cryptographic security?

Some papers have presented "unified" addition formulas that can be used for doublings. See, e.g., [27], [18], [6], [3], and [5]; for overviews see [17], [25], and [2, Section 5]. "Strongly unified" addition formulas eliminate the need to check for equal inputs. However, they do not eliminate the need to check for inputs and outputs at infinity and for other exceptional cases. The exceptional-points attack presented in [16] targets the exceptional cases in these unified formulas.

Edwards Curves. In the recent paper [2], Bernstein and Lange show for fields k with $\mathrm{char}(k) \neq 2$ that if d is not a square in k then the affine points on the "Edwards curve"

$$x^2 + y^2 = 1 + dx^2 y^2$$

form a group. The affine addition law introduced by Edwards in [10] is complete for this curve, as are the fast projective formulas introduced in [2].

"Complete" is stronger than "unified": it means that the addition formulas work for *all* pairs of input points. There are no troublesome points at infinity. In particular, the neutral element of the curve is an affine point $(0, 1)$.

If k is finite then approximately $1/4$ of all elliptic curves over k are birationally equivalent to complete Edwards curves, i.e., Edwards curves with non-square d. The formulas in [2] can therefore be used for elliptic-curve computations, and in particular for elliptic-curve cryptography.

Implementors can—although they are not forced to!—gain speed by switching from the addition formulas to dedicated doubling formulas when the inputs are known to be equal. Bernstein and Lange show, for typical scalar-multiplication problems, that their addition formulas and doubling formulas for Edwards curves use fewer multiplications than the best available formulas for previous curve shapes.

Unfortunately, $x^2 + y^2 = 1 + dx^2 y^2$ is not elliptic over fields k with $\mathrm{char}(k) = 2$.

Contributions of This Paper. We introduce a new method of carrying out computations on binary elliptic curves, i.e., elliptic curves over fields k with $\mathrm{char}(k) = 2$. In particular, we introduce "complete binary Edwards curves." We present explicit formulas for addition on these curves, an explicit birational equivalence to an elliptic curve in short Weierstrass form, explicit formulas for doubling, and explicit formulas for Montgomery-type differential addition. See Section 2 for the curve shape and birational equivalence; Sections 3 and 5 for the addition law; Section 6 for doubling; and Section 7 for differential addition.

Our curve equation has a surprisingly large number of terms but shares many geometric features with non-binary Edwards curves $x^2 + y^2 = 1 + dx^2y^2$. In particular, we prove that our formulas are complete. We also show that if $n \geq 3$ then every ordinary elliptic curve over $\mathbf{F}_{2^n}$ is birationally equivalent to a complete binary Edwards curve. See Section 4.

Our doubling formulas and differential-addition formulas are extremely fast: for example, $2\mathbf{M} + 6\mathbf{S}$ for projective doubling, and $5\mathbf{M} + 4\mathbf{S}$ for one step of a Montgomery ladder, when curves are chosen to have small parameters. Here $\mathbf{M}$ is a field multiplication and $\mathbf{S}$ is a field squaring. For comparison, state-of-the-art formulas for small-parameter Weierstrass curves—the best formulas in the literature, and some new speedups that we present—use $2\mathbf{M} + 4\mathbf{S}$ for projective doubling and $5\mathbf{M}+4\mathbf{S}$ for one step of a Montgomery ladder. There is one caveat, namely that our general addition formulas use at best $16\mathbf{M}+1\mathbf{S}$ and are therefore not as fast as previous (incomplete) formulas; we can nevertheless recommend binary Edwards curves for a wide variety of applications.

2   Binary Edwards Curves

In this section we introduce the new curve shape and show that the affine points are nonsingular. The points at infinity are singular; we give details on the blowup. To prove that the curve describes an elliptic curve we state a birational map to an ordinary elliptic curve in Weierstrass form.

Definition 2.1 (Binary Edwards curve). *Let k be a field with $\mathrm{char}(k) = 2$. Let d_1, d_2 be elements of k with $d_1 \neq 0$ and $d_2 \neq d_1^2 + d_1$. The binary Edwards curve with coefficients d_1 and d_2 is the affine curve*

$$\mathrm{E}_{\mathrm{B},d_1,d_2} : d_1(x + y) + d_2(x^2 + y^2) = xy + xy(x + y) + x^2y^2.$$

This curve is symmetric in x and y and thus has the property that if (x_1, y_1) is a point on the curve then so is (y_1, x_1). We will see in Section 3 that (y_1, x_1) is the negative of (x_1, y_1). The only curve points invariant under this negation law are $(0, 0)$ and $(1, 1)$; $(0, 0)$ will be the neutral element of the addition law while $(1, 1)$ will have order 2. We will also see that $(x_1, y_1) + (1, 1) = (x_1 + 1, y_1 + 1)$.

Theorem 2.2 (Nonsingularity). *Each binary Edwards curve is nonsingular.*

Proof. By definition the curve $\mathrm{E}_{\mathrm{B},d_1,d_2}$ has $d_1 \neq 0$ and $d_2 \neq d_1^2 + d_1$. The partial derivatives of the curve equation are $d_1 + y + y^2$ and $d_1 + x + x^2$. A singular point (x_1, y_1) must have $d_1 + y_1 + y_1^2 = 0$ and $d_1 + x_1 + x_1^2 = 0$, and therefore $(x_1 + y_1)^2 = x_1 + y_1$, implying $x_1 = y_1$ or $x_1 = y_1 + 1$.

The case $x_1 = y_1$ implies $0 = x_1^2 + x_1^4$ by the curve equation and therefore $d_1^2 = x_1^2 + x_1^4 = 0$, contradicting the hypothesis that $d_1 \neq 0$.

The case $x_1 = y_1 + 1$ implies $d_1 + d_2 = y_1^2 + y_1^4$ by the curve equation and therefore $d_1^2 = y_1^2 + y_1^4 = d_1 + d_2$, contradicting the hypothesis that $d_2 \neq d_1^2 + d_1$. $\square$

Singularities of the Projective Closure. The projective closure of the curve E_{B,d_1,d_2} is

$$d_1(X + Y)Z^3 + d_2(X^2 + Y^2)Z^2 = XYZ^2 + XY(X + Y)Z + X^2Y^2.$$

It has the points $(1 : 0 : 0)$ and $(0 : 1 : 0)$ at infinity. Both are singular. We present details on the blowup for the first point; by the symmetry of the curve equation all considerations also hold for the second point.

To study the curve around $(1 : 0 : 0)$ we consider the affine curve $d_1(1+y)z^3 + d_2(1 + y^2)z^2 = yz^2 + y(1 + y)z + y^2$. The partial derivatives $d_1z^3 + z^2 + z$ and $d_1(1+y)z^2+y(1+y)$ both vanish in $(0,0)$ which shows that the point is singular. We blow up the singularity by putting $y = tz$ and dividing by z^2, obtaining the curve

$$d_1(1 + tz)z + d_2(1 + t^2z^2) = tz + t(1 + tz) + t^2.$$

Substituting $z = 0$ produces the equation $d_2 + t + t^2 = 0$, which has two distinct roots in the algebraic closure of the base field k, corresponding to two distinct points of the blowup. These points are nonsingular since the partial derivative $d_1z^2 + z + 1$ does not vanish for $z = 0$. These blowups are defined over the smallest extension of k in which $d_2 + t + t^2 = 0$ has roots.

An Alternate Curve Shape. The curve

$$d_1(1 + x + y) + d_2(1 + x^2 + y^2) = xy + xy(x + y) + x^2y^2$$

is isomorphic to E_{B,d_1,d_2} via the map $(x, y) \mapsto (x, y + 1)$, and is another suitable generalization of Edwards curves to the binary case. Since the addition and doubling formulas look slightly simpler on E_{B,d_1,d_2} we picked that one but would like to point out here that all considerations also apply to this shifted curve.

Birational Equivalence. Traditionally elliptic curves are given in Weierstrass form; see, e.g., [9]. An ordinary elliptic curve over k can be expressed in short Weierstrass form

$$v^2 + uv = u^3 + a_2u^2 + a_6$$

with $a_6 \neq 0$. The neutral element of the addition law is the point at infinity and negation is defined as $-(u_1, v_1) = (u_1, v_1 + u_1)$.

The map $(x, y) \mapsto (u, v)$ defined by

$$u = d_1(d_1^2 + d_1 + d_2)(x + y)/(xy + d_1(x + y)),$$
$$v = d_1(d_1^2 + d_1 + d_2)(x/(xy + d_1(x + y)) + d_1 + 1)$$

is a birational equivalence from E_{B,d_1,d_2} to the elliptic curve

$$v^2 + uv = u^3 + (d_1^2 + d_2)u^2 + d_1^4(d_1^4 + d_1^2 + d_2^2)$$

with j-invariant $1/(d_1^4(d_1^4 + d_1^2 + d_2^2))$. An inverse map is given as follows:

$$x = d_1(u + d_1^2 + d_1 + d_2)/(u + v + (d_1^2 + d_1)(d_1^2 + d_1 + d_2)),$$
$$y = d_1(u + d_1^2 + d_1 + d_2)/(v + (d_1^2 + d_1)(d_1^2 + d_1 + d_2)).$$

We define a function φ on all affine points of E_{B,d_1,d_2} by extending the rational map $(x,y) \mapsto (u,v)$ given above. Specifically, the rational map is undefined at $(0,0)$; we define $\varphi(0,0) = P_\infty$. There are no other exceptional cases: if $xy + d_1(x+y) = 0$ then $d_2(x^2+y^2) = xy(x+y) + x^2y^2 = d_1(x+y)^2 + d_1^2(x+y)^2$ so $(d_2 + d_1^2 + d_1)(x^2+y^2) = 0$ so $x^2 + y^2 = 0$ so $x = y$. Use $xy + d_1(x+y) = 0$ again to see that $xy = 0$ so $x^2 = 0$ so $x = 0$ so $(x,y) = (0,0)$.

3   The Addition Law

This section presents an addition law for the binary Edwards curve E_{B,d_1,d_2} and proves that the addition law corresponds to the usual addition law on an elliptic curve in Weierstrass form. One consequence of the proof is that the addition law on E_{B,d_1,d_2} is strongly unified: it can be used with two identical inputs, i.e., to double.

Here is the addition law. The sum of two points $(x_1, y_1), (x_2, y_2)$ on E_{B,d_1,d_2} is the point (x_3, y_3) defined as follows:

$$x_3 = \frac{d_1(x_1 + x_2) + d_2(x_1 + y_1)(x_2 + y_2) + (x_1 + x_1^2)(x_2(y_1 + y_2 + 1) + y_1 y_2)}{d_1 + (x_1 + x_1^2)(x_2 + y_2)},$$

$$y_3 = \frac{d_1(y_1 + y_2) + d_2(x_1 + y_1)(x_2 + y_2) + (y_1 + y_1^2)(y_2(x_1 + x_2 + 1) + x_1 x_2)}{d_1 + (y_1 + y_1^2)(x_2 + y_2)}.$$

If the denominators $d_1 + (x_1 + x_1^2)(x_2 + y_2)$ and $d_1 + (y_1 + y_1^2)(x_2 + y_2)$ are nonzero then the sum (x_3, y_3) is a point on E_{B,d_1,d_2}: i.e., $d_1(x_3 + y_3) + d_2(x_3^2 + y_3^2) = x_3 y_3 + x_3 y_3(x_3 + y_3) + x_3^2 y_3^2$. We present a script in the Sage computer-algebra system [34] that verifies this:

```
R.<d1,d2,x1,y1,x2,y2>=GF(2)[]
S=R.quotient([
    d1*(x1+y1)+d2*(x1^2+y1^2)+x1*y1+x1*y1*(x1+y1)+x1^2*y1^2,
    d1*(x2+y2)+d2*(x2^2+y2^2)+x2*y2+x2*y2*(x2+y2)+x2^2*y2^2
])
x3 = (
    d1*(x1+x2)+d2*(x1+y1)*(x2+y2)+(x1+x1^2)*(x2*(y1+y2+1)+y1*y2)
) / (d1+(x1+x1^2)*(x2+y2))
y3 = (
    d1*(y1+y2)+d2*(x1+y1)*(x2+y2)+(y1+y1^2)*(y2*(x1+x2+1)+x1*x2)
```

```
) / (d1+(y1+y1^2)*(x2+y2))
verif = d1*(x3+y3)+d2*(x3^2+y3^2)+x3*y3+x3*y3*(x3+y3)+x3^2*y3^2
0 == S(numerator(verif))
```

Inserting $(x_1, y_1) = (0,0)$ or $(x_2, y_2) = (0,0)$ into the addition law shows that $(0,0)$ is the neutral element. Similarly $(x_1, y_1) + (1,1) = (x_1 + 1, y_1 + 1)$; in particular $(1,1) + (1,1) = (0,0)$. Furthermore $(x_1, y_1) + (y_1, x_1) = (0,0)$, so $-(x_1, y_1) = (y_1, x_1)$. We emphasize that the addition law works without change for all of these inputs.

The following lemma will be useful in Section 7 and later in this section.

Lemma 3.1. *Let k be a field with* $\text{char}(k) = 2$. *Let d_1, d_2 be elements of k with $d_1 \neq 0$ and $d_2 \neq d_1^2 + d_1$. Fix $(x_3, y_3), (x_2, y_2) \in E_{B, d_1, d_2}(k)$. Assume that $(x_3, y_3) + (x_2, y_2)$ is defined. Then $(x_3, y_3) + (y_2, x_2)$ is also defined. Furthermore define $(x_5, y_5) = (x_3, y_3) + (x_2, y_2)$ and $(x_1, y_1) = (x_3, y_3) + (y_2, x_2)$. Then $d_1^2 + w_2 w_3 (d_1 (1 + w_2 + w_3) + d_2 w_2 w_3) \neq 0$ and*

$$w_5 = \frac{d_1 (d_1(w_2 + w_3) + x_2 x_3 (x_2 + x_3 + 1) + y_2 y_3 (y_2 + y_3 + 1) + (x_2 x_3 + y_2 y_3)^2)}{d_1^2 + w_2 w_3 (d_1 (1 + w_2 + w_3) + d_2 w_2 w_3)},$$

$$w_1 w_5 = \frac{d_1^2 (w_2 + w_3)^2}{d_1^2 + w_2 w_3 (d_1 (1 + w_2 + w_3) + d_2 w_2 w_3)},$$

where $w_i = x_i + y_i$.

Proof. The denominators of the coordinates of $(x_3, y_3) + (x_2, y_2)$ are $d_1 + (x_3 + x_3^2)(x_2 + y_2)$ and $d_1 + (y_3 + y_3^2)(x_2 + y_2)$; these formulas are symmetric in x_2, y_2, so they are the same as the denominators of $(x_3, y_3) + (y_2, x_2)$. Furthermore, their product is

$$(d_1 + (x_3 + x_3^2)(x_2 + y_2))(d_1 + (y_3 + y_3^2)(x_2 + y_2))$$
$$= d_1^2 + d_1(x_3 + x_3^2 + y_3 + y_3^2)(x_2 + y_2) + (x_3 + x_3^2)(y_3 + y_3^2)(x_2 + y_2)^2$$
$$= d_1^2 + d_1(w_3 + w_3^2)w_2 + (d_1 w_3 + d_2 w_3^2)w_2^2$$
$$= d_1^2 + w_2 w_3 (d_1 (1 + w_2 + w_3) + d_2 w_2 w_3),$$

so $d_1^2 + w_2 w_3 (d_1 (1 + w_2 + w_3) + d_2 w_2 w_3)$ is nonzero. Note that we used the curve equation in the second-to-last equality.

Cross-multiplying and using the curve equation again gives the stated numerator of w_5; we omit the details. Similarly we obtain the numerator of w_1. Multiplying, using the curve equation again, and cancelling $d_1^2 + w_2 w_3 (d_1 (1 + w_2 + w_3) + d_2 w_2 w_3)$ produces the stated formula for $w_1 w_5$. □

The rest of this section is devoted to the proof that this addition law corresponds to the addition law on the elliptic curve $v^2 + uv = u^3 + (d_1^2 + d_2)u^2 + d_1^4(d_1^4 + d_1^2 + d_2^2)$ under the function φ defined in the previous section: i.e., that $\varphi(x_3, y_3) = \varphi(x_1, y_1) + \varphi(x_2, y_2)$.

Lemma 3.2. *Let k be a field with* $\text{char}(k) = 2$. *Let d_1, d_2 be elements of k with $d_1 \neq 0$ and $d_2 \neq d_1^2 + d_1$. Fix $(x_2, y_2), (x_3, y_3) \in E_{B, d_1, d_2}(k)$. If $(x_3, y_3) + (x_2, y_2) = (0,0)$ then $(x_3, y_3) = (y_2, x_2)$.*

Proof. Define w_i as in Lemma 3.1. Then $w_5 = 0$ so

$$d_1^2(w_2 + w_3)^2 = w_1w_5(d_1^2 + w_2w_3(d_1(1 + w_2 + w_3) + d_2w_2w_3)) = 0$$

so $w_2 + w_3 = 0$; i.e., $x_2 + y_2 + x_3 + y_3 = 0$. Similarly

$$d_1(d_1(w_2 + w_3) + x_2x_3(x_2 + x_3 + 1) + y_2y_3(y_2 + y_3 + 1) + (x_2x_3 + y_2y_3)^2) = 0$$

so $x_2x_3(x_2 + x_3 + 1) + y_2y_3(y_2 + y_3 + 1) + (x_2x_3 + y_2y_3)^2 = 0$. Substitute $y_3 = x_2 + y_2 + x_3$ to see that $x_2x_3(x_2 + x_3 + 1) + y_2(x_2 + y_2 + x_3)(y_2 + (x_2 + y_2 + x_3) + 1) + (x_2x_3 + y_2(x_2 + y_2 + x_3))^2 = 0$, and simplify to see that $(x_2 + y_2)(x_2 + y_2 + 1)(x_3 + y_2)(x_3 + y_2 + 1) = 0$. We now separately consider the four factors.

Case 1: $x_2 + y_2 = 0$. Then (x_2, y_2) is either $(0, 0)$ or $(1, 1)$. Furthermore $x_3 + y_3 = 0$ so (x_3, y_3) is either $(0, 0)$ or $(1, 1)$. We must have $(x_3, y_3) = (x_2, y_2)$ since $(0, 0) + (1, 1) \neq (0, 0)$. Thus also $(x_3, y_3) = (y_2, x_2)$.

Case 2: $x_2 + y_2 = 1$. Then $x_2^2 + x_2^2 = d_1 + d_2$ from the curve equation. Furthermore $x_3 + y_3 = 1$ so $x_3^4 + x_3^2 = d_1 + d_2$ so $x_3 = x_2$ or $x_3 = x_2 + 1$. If $x_3 = x_2$ then $(x_3, y_3) + (x_2, y_2) = (1, 1) \neq (0, 0)$. Thus $x_3 = x_2 + 1$ so $(x_3, y_3) = (x_2 + 1, x_2) = (y_2, x_2)$.

Case 3: $x_3 + y_2 = 0$. Then $x_2 + y_3 = 0$. Hence $(x_3, y_3) = (y_2, x_2)$.

Case 4: $x_3 + y_2 = 1$. Then $x_2 + y_3 = 1$. Hence $(x_3, y_3) + (x_2, y_2) = (y_2 + 1, x_2 + 1) + (x_2, y_2) = (1, 1)$, contradiction.   □

Lemma 3.3. *Let k be a field with* char$(k) = 2$. *Let d_1, d_2 be elements of k with $d_1 \neq 0$ and $d_2 \neq d_1^2 + d_1$. Fix $(x_1, y_1), (x_2, y_2) \in E_{B,d_1,d_2}(k)$. If $\varphi(x_1, y_1) = \varphi(x_2, y_2)$ then $(x_1, y_1) = (x_2, y_2)$.*

Proof. If $(x_1, y_1) = (0, 0)$ then $\varphi(x_1, y_1) = P_\infty$ so $\varphi(x_2, y_2) = P_\infty$ so $(x_2, y_2) = (0, 0) = (x_1, y_1)$ as claimed. Similar comments apply if $(x_2, y_2) = (0, 0)$. Assume from now on that $(x_1, y_1) \neq (0, 0)$ and $(x_2, y_2) \neq (0, 0)$.

By definition of φ we have

$$y_1(x_2y_2 + d_1(x_2 + y_2)) = y_2(x_1y_1 + d_1(x_1 + y_1)),$$
$$x_1(x_2y_2 + d_1(x_2 + y_2)) = x_2(x_1y_1 + d_1(x_1 + y_1)).$$

Note for future reference that this system of equations is symmetric between 1 and 2, and between x and y. Multiply the first equation by x_1 and the second by y_1 and add to obtain $(x_1y_2 + x_2y_1)(x_1y_1 + d_1(x_1 + y_1)) = 0$. Recall that $x_1y_1 + d_1(x_1 + y_1) \neq 0$ so $x_1y_2 + x_2y_1 = 0$. Now replace x_1y_2 with x_2y_1 in the second equation and simplify to obtain $x_2(x_1 + x_2)y_1 = 0$.

If $y_1 = 0$ then $x_1 \neq 0$. The curve equation now says $d_1x_1 + d_2x_1^2 = 0$ so $x_1 = d_1/d_2$. Furthermore $y_2 = x_2y_1/x_1 = 0$ so also $x_2 = d_1/d_2$ so $(x_1, y_1) = (x_2, y_2)$.

Assume from now on that $y_1 \neq 0$. Apply symmetry between 1 and 2, and between x and y, to obtain also $x_2 \neq 0$. Then $x_1 + x_2 = 0$. Apply symmetry between x and y to see that $y_1 + y_2 = 0$. Thus $(x_1, y_1) = (x_2, y_2)$.   □

Lemma 3.4. *Let k be a field with* char$(k) = 2$. *Let d_1, d_2 be elements of k with $d_1 \neq 0$ and $d_2 \neq d_1^2 + d_1$. Fix $(x_1, y_1) \in E_{B,d_1,d_2}(k)$. Then $\varphi(y_1, x_1) = -\varphi(x_1, y_1)$.*

Proof. If $(x_1, y_1) = (0, 0)$ then $\varphi(y_1, x_1) = P_\infty = \varphi(x_1, y_1)$. Assume from now on that $(x_1, y_1) \neq (0, 0)$. Write $(u_1, v_1) = \varphi(x_1, y_1)$ and $(u_2, v_2) = \varphi(y_1, x_1)$. Then $u_1 = u_2$ and $v_1 + v_2 = u_1$ from the definition of φ. Hence $(u_2, v_2) = (u_1, v_1 + u_1) = -(u_1, v_1)$. $\qquad\square$

Theorem 3.5. *Let k be a field with* $\mathrm{char}(k) = 2$. *Let d_1, d_2 be elements of k with $d_1 \neq 0$ and $d_2 \neq d_1^2 + d_1$. Fix $(x_1, y_1), (x_2, y_2), (x_3, y_3) \in \mathrm{E}_{B, d_1, d_2}(k)$. Assume that $(x_1, y_1) + (x_2, y_2) = (x_3, y_3)$. Then $\varphi(x_1, y_1) + \varphi(x_2, y_2) = \varphi(x_3, y_3)$.*

Proof. Write $a_2 = d_1^2 + d_2$ and $a_6 = d_1^4(d_1^4 + d_1^2 + d_2^2)$. There are two cases in the definition of φ and several cases in the definition of addition on the Weierstrass curve $v^2 + uv = u^3 + a_2 u^2 + a_6$; the proof splits into several cases correspondingly.

If $(x_1, y_1) = (0, 0)$ then $(x_2, y_2) = (x_3, y_3)$. Now $\varphi(x_2, y_2) = \varphi(x_3, y_3)$ and $\varphi(x_1, y_1) = P_\infty$, so $\varphi(x_1, y_1) + \varphi(x_2, y_2) = P_\infty + \varphi(x_2, y_2) = \varphi(x_2, y_2) = \varphi(x_3, y_3)$. Similar comments apply if $(x_2, y_2) = (0, 0)$.

If $(x_3, y_3) = (0, 0)$ then $(x_2, y_2) = (y_1, x_1)$ by Lemma 3.2. Now $\varphi(x_3, y_3) = \varphi(0, 0) = P_\infty$ and $\varphi(x_2, y_2) = \varphi(y_1, x_1) = -\varphi(x_1, y_1)$ by Lemma 3.4. Thus $\varphi(x_1, y_1) + \varphi(x_2, y_2) = \varphi(x_1, y_1) - \varphi(x_1, y_1) = P_\infty = \varphi(x_3, y_3)$.

Assume from now on that $(x_1, y_1) \neq (0, 0)$, $(x_2, y_2) \neq (0, 0)$, and $(x_3, y_3) \neq (0, 0)$. Write $(u_i, v_i) = \varphi(x_i, y_i)$.

Case 1: $(u_1, v_1) = (u_2, v_2)$. Then $(x_1, y_1) = (x_2, y_2)$ by Lemma 3.3. If $u_1 = 0$ then $x_1 = y_1$ from the definition of φ so either $(x_1, y_1) = (0, 0)$ or $(x_1, y_1) = (1, 1)$; in either case $(x_1, y_1) + (x_2, y_2) = (x_1, y_1) + (x_1, y_1) = (0, 0)$, already handled above. Assume from now on that $u_1 \neq 0$. The usual doubling formulas for Weierstrass coordinates say that $2(u_1, v_1) = (u_4, v_4)$ where $u_4 = \lambda^2 + \lambda + d_1^2 + d_2$, $v_4 = v_1 + \lambda(u_1 + u_4) + u_4$, and $\lambda = (u_1^2 + v_1)/u_1$. A lengthy but straightforward calculation then shows that $(u_3, v_3) = (u_4, v_4)$; here is the corresponding Sage script:

```
R.<d1,d2,x1,y1>=GF(2)[]
S=R.quotient([
  d1*(x1+y1)+d2*(x1^2+y1^2)+x1*y1+x1*y1*(x1+y1)+x1^2*y1^2
])
x2 = x1
y2 = y1
x3 = (
  d1*(x1+x2)+d2*(x1+y1)*(x2+y2)+(x1+x1^2)*(x2*(y1+y2+1)+y1*y2)
) / (d1+(x1+x1^2)*(x2+y2))
y3 = (
  d1*(y1+y2)+d2*(x1+y1)*(x2+y2)+(y1+y1^2)*(y2*(x1+x2+1)+x1*x2)
) / (d1+(y1+y1^2)*(x2+y2))
u1 = d1*(d1^2+d1+d2)*(x1+y1)/(x1*y1+d1*(x1+y1))
v1 = d1*(d1^2+d1+d2)*(x1/(x1*y1+d1*(x1+y1))+d1+1)
u3 = d1*(d1^2+d1+d2)*(x3+y3)/(x3*y3+d1*(x3+y3))
v3 = d1*(d1^2+d1+d2)*(x3/(x3*y3+d1*(x3+y3))+d1+1)
lam = (u1^2+v1)/u1
u4 = lam^2+lam+d1^2+d2
```

```
v4 = v1+lam*(u1+u4)+u4
0 == S(numerator(u3-u4))
0 == S(numerator(v3-v4))
```

Hence $\varphi(x_1, y_1) + \varphi(x_2, y_2) = \varphi(x_3, y_3)$.

Case 2: $(u_1, v_1) \neq (u_2, v_2)$. If $u_1 = u_2$ then $(u_1, v_1) = -(u_2, v_2)$ so $\varphi(x_1, y_1) = -\varphi(x_2, y_2) = \varphi(y_2, x_2)$ by Lemma 3.4 so $(x_1, y_1) = (y_2, x_2)$ by Lemma 3.3 so $(x_1, y_1) + (x_2, y_2) = (0, 0)$, already handled above. Assume from now on that $u_1 \neq u_2$. The usual addition formulas for Weierstrass coordinates say that $(u_1, v_1) + (u_2, v_2) = (u_4, v_4)$ where $u_4 = \lambda^2 + \lambda + u_1 + u_2 + d_1^2 + d_2$, $v_4 = v_1 + \lambda(u_1 + u_4) + u_4$, and $\lambda = (v_1 + v_2)/(u_1 + u_2)$. Another lengthy but straightforward calculation then shows that $(u_3, v_3) = (u_4, v_4)$; here is the corresponding Sage script:

```
R.<d1,d2,x1,y1,x2,y2>=GF(2)[]
S=R.quotient([
    d1*(x1+y1)+d2*(x1^2+y1^2)+x1*y1+x1*y1*(x1+y1)+x1^2*y1^2,
    d1*(x2+y2)+d2*(x2^2+y2^2)+x2*y2+x2*y2*(x2+y2)+x2^2*y2^2
])
x3 = (
    d1*(x1+x2)+d2*(x1+y1)*(x2+y2)+(x1+x1^2)*(x2*(y1+y2+1)+y1*y2)
) / (d1+(x1+x1^2)*(x2+y2))
y3 = (
    d1*(y1+y2)+d2*(x1+y1)*(x2+y2)+(y1+y1^2)*(y2*(x1+x2+1)+x1*x2)
) / (d1+(y1+y1^2)*(x2+y2))
u1 = d1*(d1^2+d1+d2)*(x1+y1)/(x1*y1+d1*(x1+y1))
v1 = d1*(d1^2+d1+d2)*(x1/(x1*y1+d1*(x1+y1))+d1+1)
u2 = d1*(d1^2+d1+d2)*(x2+y2)/(x2*y2+d1*(x2+y2))
v2 = d1*(d1^2+d1+d2)*(x2/(x2*y2+d1*(x2+y2))+d1+1)
u3 = d1*(d1^2+d1+d2)*(x3+y3)/(x3*y3+d1*(x3+y3))
v3 = d1*(d1^2+d1+d2)*(x3/(x3*y3+d1*(x3+y3))+d1+1)
lam = (v2+v1)/(u2+u1)
u4 = lam^2+lam+u1+u2+d1^2+d2
v4 = v1+lam*(u1+u4)+u4
0 == S(numerator(u3-u4))
0 == S(numerator(v3-v4))
```

Hence $\varphi(x_1, y_1) + \varphi(x_2, y_2) = \varphi(x_3, y_3)$. $\square$

4   Complete Binary Edwards Curves

If d_2 does not have the form $t^2 + t$ then the addition law on the binary Edwards curve E_{B,d_1,d_2} has the very nice feature of *completeness*. This means that there are *no* exceptions to the addition law: the denominators $d_1 + (x_1 + x_1^2)(x_2 + y_2)$ and $d_1 + (y_1 + y_1^2)(x_2 + y_2)$ never vanish. The addition law *always* produces a point on E_{B,d_1,d_2} corresponding to the usual sum of points on elliptic curves in Weierstrass form.

In this section we prove completeness for these d_2's. We also prove that over finite fields $\mathbf{F}_{2^n}$ with $n \geq 3$ all ordinary curves are birationally equivalent to complete binary Edwards curves.

Theorem 4.1 (Completeness of the addition law). *Let k be a field with* char$(k) = 2$. *Let d_1, d_2 be elements of k with $d_1 \neq 0$. Assume that no element $t \in k$ satisfies $t^2 + t + d_2 = 0$. Then the addition law on the binary Edwards curve $\mathrm{E}_{\mathrm{B},d_1,d_2}(k)$ is complete.*

Proof. We show for all $(x_1, y_1), (x_2, y_2) \in \mathrm{E}_{\mathrm{B},d_1,d_2}(k)$ that the denominators $d_1 + (x_1 + x_1^2)(x_2 + y_2)$ and $d_1 + (y_1 + y_1^2)(x_2 + y_2)$ are nonzero.

If $x_2 + y_2 = 0$ then the denominators are d_1, which is nonzero by hypothesis. Assume from now on that $x_2 + y_2 \neq 0$, and suppose that $d_1/(x_2 + y_2) = x_1 + x_1^2$. Use the curve equation to see that

$$
\frac{d_1}{x_2 + y_2} = \frac{d_1(x_2 + y_2)}{x_2^2 + y_2^2} = \frac{d_2(x_2^2 + y_2^2) + x_2 y_2 + x_2 y_2 (x_2 + y_2) + x_2^2 y_2^2}{x_2^2 + y_2^2}
$$

$$
= d_2 + \frac{x_2 y_2 + x_2 y_2 (x_2 + y_2) + y_2^2}{x_2^2 + y_2^2} + \frac{y_2^2 + x_2^2 y_2^2}{x_2^2 + y_2^2}
$$

$$
= d_2 + \frac{y_2 + x_2 y_2}{x_2 + y_2} + \frac{y_2^2 + x_2^2 y_2^2}{x_2^2 + y_2^2}
$$

and hence that $t^2 + t + d_2 = 0$ where $t = x_1 + (y_2 + x_2 y_2)/(x_2 + y_2) \in k$. Contradiction. Hence $d_1 + (x_1 + x_1^2)(x_2 + y_2) \neq 0$. Similarly $d_1 + (y_1 + y_1^2)(x_2 + y_2) \neq 0$. □

Definition 4.2 (Complete binary Edwards curve). *Let k be a field with* char$(k) = 2$. *Let d_1, d_2 be elements of k with $d_1 \neq 0$. Assume that no element $t \in k$ satisfies $t^2 + t + d_2 = 0$. The* complete binary Edwards curve *with coefficients d_1 and d_2 is the affine curve*

$$
\mathrm{E}_{\mathrm{B},d_1,d_2} : d_1(x + y) + d_2(x^2 + y^2) = xy + xy(x + y) + x^2 y^2.
$$

There is no conflict in notation or terminology here: the complete binary Edwards curve $\mathrm{E}_{\mathrm{B},d_1,d_2}$ is the same as the binary Edwards curve $\mathrm{E}_{\mathrm{B},d_1,d_2}$. The complete case has the extra requirement that $t^2 + t + d_2 \neq 0$ for *all* $t \in k$, not just for $t = d_1$. If k is a finite field $\mathbf{F}_{2^n}$ then an equivalent requirement is that $\mathrm{Tr}(d_2) = 1$, where Tr is the absolute trace of $\mathbf{F}_{2^n}$ over $\mathbf{F}_2$.

Generality of $\mathrm{E}_{\mathrm{B},d_1,d_2}$. We now study which isomorphism classes of elliptic curves over a finite field $\mathbf{F}_{2^n}$ are birationally equivalent to complete binary Edwards curves $\mathrm{E}_{\mathrm{B},d_1,d_2}$.

Theorem 4.3. *Let n be an integer with $n \geq 3$. Each ordinary elliptic curve over $\mathbf{F}_{2^n}$ is birationally equivalent over $\mathbf{F}_{2^n}$ to a complete binary Edwards curve.*

Proof. Each ordinary elliptic curve over $\mathbf{F}_{2^n}$ is isomorphic to $v^2 + uv = u^3 + a_2 u^2 + a_6$ for some $a_2 \in \mathbf{F}_{2^n}$ and $a_6 \in \mathbf{F}_{2^n}^*$. Note that if $\mathrm{Tr}(a_2) = \mathrm{Tr}(a_2')$ then the two curves $v^2 + uv = u^3 + a_2 u^2 + a_6$ and $v^2 + uv = u^3 + a_2' u^2 + a_6$ are isomorphic: there exists b such that $a_2' = a_2 + b + b^2$, and the map $v \mapsto v + bu$ is an isomorphism from $v^2 + uv = u^3 + a_2 u^2 + a_6$ to $v^2 + uv = u^3 + (a_2 + b + b^2)u^2 + a_6$.

Fix a_2, a_6 for the rest of the proof. For each $\delta, \epsilon \in \mathbf{F}_2$ define

$$D_{\delta, \epsilon} = \left\{ d_1 \in \mathbf{F}_{2^n}^* : \mathrm{Tr}(d_1) = \delta, \ \mathrm{Tr}(\sqrt{a_6}/d_1^2) = \epsilon \right\}.$$

If $d_1 \in D_{\mathrm{Tr}(a_2)+1,1}$ then the pair (d_1, d_2) with $d_2 = d_1^2 + d_1 + \sqrt{a_6}/d_1^2$ has $\mathrm{Tr}(d_2) = \mathrm{Tr}(\sqrt{a_6}/d_1^2) = 1$ and therefore defines a complete binary Edwards curve E_{B,d_1,d_2}. This curve is birationally equivalent to $v^2 + uv = u^3 + (d_1^2 + d_2)u^2 + a_6$, since $d_1^4(d_1^4 + d_1^2 + d_2^2) = a_6$, and therefore birationally equivalent to $v^2 + uv = u^3 + a_2 u^2 + a_6$, since $\mathrm{Tr}(d_1^2 + d_2) = \mathrm{Tr}(d_1) + \mathrm{Tr}(d_2) = \mathrm{Tr}(a_2)$.

Our goal is to show that $D_{\mathrm{Tr}(a_2)+1,1}$ is nonempty. We will do this by counting the number of elements in both D_{01} and D_{11}.

Observe first that $\#D_{00} + \#D_{01} = 2^{n-1} - 1$. Indeed, $\#D_{00} + \#D_{01}$ is the number of $d_1 \in \mathbf{F}_{2^n}^*$ with $\mathrm{Tr}(d_1) = 0$.

Observe next that $\#D_{01} + \#D_{11} = 2^{n-1}$. Indeed, $\#D_{01} + \#D_{11}$ is the number of $d_1 \in \mathbf{F}_{2^n}^*$ with $\mathrm{Tr}(\sqrt{a_6}/d_1^2) = 1$. As d_1 runs through $\mathbf{F}_{2^n}^*$, the quotient $\sqrt{a_6}/d_1^2$ also runs through $\mathbf{F}_{2^n}^*$, so it has trace 1 exactly 2^{n-1} times.

The heart of the proof is a bound on $\#D_{00} + \#D_{11}$, the number of $d_1 \in \mathbf{F}_{2^n}^*$ with $\mathrm{Tr}(d_1 + \sqrt{a_6}/d_1^2) = 0$. For each such d_1 there are exactly two choices of $s \in \mathbf{F}_{2^n}$ such that $s^2 + s = d_1 + \sqrt{a_6}/d_1^2$, producing two choices of point $(U_1, V_1) = (d_1, d_1 s)$ on the elliptic curve $V^2 + UV = U^3 + \sqrt{a_6}$. All points on this elliptic curve appear uniquely in this way, except that the point at infinity and the point $(0, 0)$ do not appear. By Hasse's theorem, this curve has $2^n + 1 + t$ points for some integer t in the interval $[-2\sqrt{2^n}, 2\sqrt{2^n}]$. Therefore $\#D_{00} + \#D_{11} = 2^{n-1} + (t-1)/2$.

Now $2\#D_{01} = (\#D_{00} + \#D_{01}) + (\#D_{01} + \#D_{11}) - (\#D_{00} + \#D_{11}) = 2^{n-1} - 1 + 2^{n-1} - 2^{n-1} - (t-1)/2 = 2^{n-1} - (t+1)/2$ and $2\#D_{11} = 2^n - 2\#D_{01} = 2^{n-1} + (t+1)/2$. The crude bound $(\sqrt{2^n} - 1)^2 \geq (\sqrt{8} - 1)^2 > 2$ implies $2^n > 2\sqrt{2^n} + 1 \geq |t| + 1$, so both D_{01} and D_{11} are nonempty. □

Given a_2, a_6 defining a Weierstrass curve, one can choose a random d_1 with $\mathrm{Tr}(d_1) = \mathrm{Tr}(a_2) + 1$, check whether $\mathrm{Tr}(\sqrt{a_6}/d_1^2) = 1$, and if so compute $d_2 = d_1^2 + d_1 + \sqrt{a_6}/d_1^2$, obtaining a complete binary Edwards curve E_{B,d_1,d_2} birationally equivalent to the original curve. The theorem says that this procedure succeeds for *at least one* d_1, but the proof actually shows more: the procedure succeeds for approximately 50% of all d_1 with $\mathrm{Tr}(d_1) = \mathrm{Tr}(a_2) + 1$. Computer experiments show that it suffices to search a few *small* field elements d_1, where "small" means "allowing very fast multiplications."

5 Explicit Addition Formulas

This section presents explicit formulas for affine addition, projective addition, and mixed addition on binary Edwards curves. The formulas are not as fast as known formulas for Weierstrass curves but have the advantage of being strongly unified and, for suitable d_2, the advantage of completeness. We are continuing to investigate addition speed; we have already found several speedups and incorporated those speedups into the formulas here.

See Section 6 for much faster doubling formulas, and Section 7 for much faster differential-addition formulas. We intend to incorporate all new formulas into the Explicit-Formulas Database, http://hyperelliptic.org/EFD.

Affine Addition. The following formulas, given (x_1, y_1) and (x_2, y_2) on the binary Edwards curve E_{B,d_1,d_2}, compute the sum $(x_3, y_3) = (x_1, y_1) + (x_2, y_2)$ if it is defined:

$$w_1 = x_1 + y_1, \ w_2 = x_2 + y_2, \ A = x_1^2 + x_1, \ B = y_1^2 + y_1, \ C = d_2 w_1 \cdot w_2,$$
$$D = x_2 \cdot y_2, \ x_3 = y_1 + (C + d_1(w_1 + x_2) + A \cdot (D + x_2))/(d_1 + A \cdot w_2),$$
$$y_3 = x_1 + (C + d_1(w_1 + y_2) + B \cdot (D + y_2))/(d_1 + B \cdot w_2).$$

These formulas use $2\mathbf{I} + 8\mathbf{M} + 2\mathbf{S} + 3\mathbf{D}$, where $\mathbf{I}$ is the cost of a field inversion, $\mathbf{M}$ is the cost of a field multiplication, $\mathbf{S}$ is the cost of a field squaring, and $\mathbf{D}$ is the cost of a multiplication by a curve parameter. The $3\mathbf{D}$ here are two multiplications by d_1 and one multiplication by d_2. One can replace $2\mathbf{I}$ with $1\mathbf{I} + 3\mathbf{M}$ using Montgomery's inversion trick.

For complete binary Edwards curves the denominators $d_1 + A \cdot w_2 = d_1 + (x_1^2 + x_1)(x_2 + y_2)$ and $d_1 + B \cdot w_2 = d_1 + (y_1^2 + y_1)(x_2 + y_2)$ cannot be zero. See Theorem 4.1.

Mixed Addition. The following formulas, given $(X_1 : Y_1 : Z_1)$ and (x_2, y_2) on the binary Edwards curve E_{B,d_1,d_2}, compute the sum $(X_3 : Y_3 : Z_3) = (X_1 : Y_1 : Z_1) + (x_2, y_2)$ if it is defined:

$$W_1 = X_1 + Y_1, \ w_2 = x_2 + y_2, \ A = x_2^2 + x_2, \ B = y_2^2 + y_2,$$
$$D = W_1 \cdot Z_1, \ E = d_1 Z_1^2, \ H = (E + d_2 D) \cdot w_2,$$
$$I = d_1 Z_1, \ U = E + A \cdot D, \ V = E + B \cdot D, \ Z_3 = U \cdot V,$$
$$X_3 = Z_3 \cdot y_2 + (H + X_1 \cdot (I + A \cdot (Y_1 + Z_1))) \cdot V,$$
$$Y_3 = Z_3 \cdot x_2 + (H + Y_1 \cdot (I + B \cdot (X_1 + Z_1))) \cdot U.$$

These formulas use $13\mathbf{M} + 3\mathbf{S} + 3\mathbf{D}$. As above the $3\mathbf{D}$ are two multiplications by d_1 and one multiplication by d_2. For complete binary Edwards curves the product $Z_3 = Z_1^4(d_1 + (x_2^2 + x_2)(x_1 + y_1))(d_1 + (y_2^2 + y_2)(x_1 + y_1))$ cannot be zero.

Projective Addition. The following formulas, given $(X_1 : Y_1 : Z_1)$ and $(X_2 : Y_2 : Z_2)$ on the binary Edwards curve E_{B,d_1,d_2}, compute the sum $(X_3 : Y_3 : Z_3) = (X_1 : Y_1 : Z_1) + (X_2 : Y_2 : Z_2)$ if it is defined:

$$W_1 = X_1 + Y_1, \ W_2 = X_2 + Y_2, \ A = X_1 \cdot (X_1 + Z_1), \ B = Y_1 \cdot (Y_1 + Z_1),$$
$$C = Z_1 \cdot Z_2, \ D = W_2 \cdot Z_2, \ E = d_1 C^2, \ H = (d_1 Z_2 + d_2 W_2) \cdot W_1 \cdot C,$$
$$I = d_1 C \cdot Z_1, \ U = E + A \cdot D, \ V = E + B \cdot D, \ S = U \cdot V,$$
$$X_3 = S \cdot Y_1 + (H + X_2 \cdot (I + A \cdot (Y_2 + Z_2))) \cdot V \cdot Z_1,$$
$$Y_3 = S \cdot X_1 + (H + Y_2 \cdot (I + B \cdot (X_2 + Z_2))) \cdot U \cdot Z_1, \ Z_3 = S \cdot Z_1.$$

These formulas use $21\mathbf{M} + 1\mathbf{S} + 4\mathbf{D}$. The $4\mathbf{D}$ are three multiplications by d_1 and one multiplication by d_2. For complete binary Edwards curves the product $Z_3 = Z_1^5 Z_2^4 (d_1 + (x_2^2 + x_2)(x_1 + y_1))(d_1 + (y_2^2 + y_2)(x_1 + y_1))$ cannot be zero.

The following formulas are considerably better than the previous formulas when d_1 and d_2 are small:

$$A = X_1 \cdot X_2, \ B = Y_1 \cdot Y_2, \ C = Z_1 \cdot Z_2, \ D = d_1 C, \ E = C^2, \ F = d_1^2 E,$$
$$G = (X_1 + Z_1) \cdot (X_2 + Z_2), \ H = (Y_1 + Z_1) \cdot (Y_2 + Z_2),$$
$$I = A + G, \ J = B + H, \ K = (X_1 + Y_1) \cdot (X_2 + Y_2),$$
$$U = C \cdot (F + d_1 K \cdot (K + I + J + C)),$$
$$V = U + D \cdot F + K \cdot (d_2(d_1 E + G \cdot H + A \cdot B) + (d_2 + d_1) I \cdot J),$$
$$X_3 = V + D \cdot (A + D) \cdot (G + D), \ Y_3 = V + D \cdot (B + D) \cdot (H + D),$$
$$Z_3 = U + (d_2 + d_1) C \cdot K^2.$$

These formulas use $18\mathbf{M} + 2\mathbf{S} + 7\mathbf{D}$. The $7\mathbf{D}$ are three multiplications by d_1, two multiplications by $d_2 + d_1$, one multiplication by d_1^2, and one multiplication by d_2. One can alternatively compute F as D^2, replacing $1\mathbf{D}$ with $1\mathbf{S}$. For complete binary Edwards curves the denominator Z_3 cannot be zero.

These formulas become simpler in the case $d_1 = d_2$:

$$A = X_1 \cdot X_2, \ B = Y_1 \cdot Y_2, \ C = Z_1 \cdot Z_2, \ D = d_1 C, \ E = C^2, \ F = d_1^2 E,$$
$$G = (X_1 + Z_1) \cdot (X_2 + Z_2), \ H = (Y_1 + Z_1) \cdot (Y_2 + Z_2),$$
$$I = A + G, \ J = B + H, \ K = (X_1 + Y_1) \cdot (X_2 + Y_2), \ L = d_1 K,$$
$$U = C \cdot (F + L \cdot (K + I + J + C)),$$
$$V = U + D \cdot F + L \cdot (d_1 E + G \cdot H + A \cdot B),$$
$$X_3 = V + D \cdot (A + D) \cdot (G + D), \ Y_3 = V + D \cdot (B + D) \cdot (H + D),$$
$$Z_3 = U.$$

These formulas use $16\mathbf{M} + 1\mathbf{S} + 4\mathbf{D}$. The $4\mathbf{D}$ are three multiplications by d_1 and one multiplication by d_1^2. As above one can replace $1\mathbf{D}$ with $1\mathbf{S}$. For complete binary Edwards curves the denominator Z_3 cannot be zero.

6   Doubling

This section presents extremely fast doubling formulas on the binary Edwards curve E_{B,d_1,d_2}, first in affine coordinates and then in inversion-free projective coordinates. The formulas are complete if the curve is complete.

Since the addition formulas on the curve are strongly unified, they can be used to double. This is an interesting option when doublings occur "by accident" or when side-channel uniformity is an issue. This section shows the relation of the doubling formulas to the general addition formulas.

This section also reviews the literature on doubling formulas for binary elliptic curves, presents two improvements to the best previous formulas for Weierstrass form, and compares the doubling speeds of binary Edwards curves and Weierstrass curves.

Affine Doubling. Let (x_1, y_1) be a point on E_{B,d_1,d_2}, and assume that the sum $(x_1, y_1) + (x_1, y_1)$ is defined. Computing $(x_3, y_3) = (x_1, y_1) + (x_1, y_1)$ we obtain

$$x_3 = \frac{d_2(x_1 + y_1)^2 + (x_1 + x_1^2)(x_1 + y_1^2)}{d_1 + (x_1 + y_1)(x_1 + x_1^2)}$$

$$= \frac{d_1(x_1 + y_1) + x_1 y_1 + x_1^2(1 + x_1 + y_1)}{d_1 + x_1 y_1 + x_1^2(1 + x_1 + y_1)}$$

$$= 1 + \frac{d_1(1 + x_1 + y_1)}{d_1 + x_1 y_1 + x_1^2(1 + x_1 + y_1)},$$

where the second line uses that $d_2(x_1 + y_1)^2 + x_1^2 y_1^2 + x_1 y_1^2 = d_1(x_1 + y_1) + x_1 y_1 + x_1^2 y_1$ for all points on E_{B,d_1,d_2}. Likewise we have

$$y_3 = 1 + \frac{d_1(1 + x_1 + y_1)}{d_1 + x_1 y_1 + y_1^2(1 + x_1 + y_1)}.$$

To compute the affine formulas with one inversion we note that the product of the denominators of x_3 and y_3 is

$$(d_1 + x_1 y_1 + x_1^2(1 + x_1 + y_1))(d_1 + x_1 y_1 + y_1^2(1 + x_1 + y_1))$$

$$= d_1^2 + (x_1^2 + y_1^2)(d_1(1 + x_1 + y_1) + x_1 y_1(1 + x_1 + y_1) + x_1^2 y_1^2)$$

$$= d_1^2 + (x_1^2 + y_1^2)(d_1 + d_2(x_1^2 + y_1^2)) = d_1(d_1 + x_1^2 + y_1^2 + (d_2/d_1)(x_1^4 + y_1^4)),$$

where we used the curve equation again. This leads to the doubling formulas

$$x_3 = 1 + \frac{d_1 + d_2(x_1^2 + y_1^2) + y_1^2 + y_1^4}{d_1 + x_1^2 + y_1^2 + (d_2/d_1)(x_1^4 + y_1^4)},$$

$$y_3 = 1 + \frac{d_1 + d_2(x_1^2 + y_1^2) + x_1^2 + x_1^4}{d_1 + x_1^2 + y_1^2 + (d_2/d_1)(x_1^4 + y_1^4)}$$

needing $1\mathbf{I} + 2\mathbf{M} + 4\mathbf{S} + 2\mathbf{D}$. The $2\mathbf{D}$ are one multiplication by d_2 and one multiplication by d_2/d_1. For complete binary Edwards curves all denominators here are nonzero.

If $d_1 = d_2$ some multiplications can be grouped as follows:

$A = x_1^2,\ B = A^2,\ C = y_1^2,\ D = C^2,\ E = A + C,$

$F = 1/(d_1 + E + B + D),\ x_3 = (d_1 E + A + B) \cdot F,\ y_3 = x_3 + 1 + d_1 F.$

These formulas use only $1\mathbf{I} + 1\mathbf{M} + 4\mathbf{S} + 2\mathbf{D}$. The $2\mathbf{D}$ are two multiplications by d_1.

Projective Doubling. Here are explicit formulas to compute $2(X_1 : Y_1 : Z_1) = (X_3 : Y_3 : Z_3)$ if it is defined:

$A = X_1^2,\ B = A^2,\ C = Y_1^2,\ D = C^2,\ E = Z_1^2,\ F = d_1 E^2,$

$G = (d_2/d_1)(B + D),\ H = A \cdot E,\ I = C \cdot E,\ J = H + I,\ K = G + d_2 J,$

$Z_3 = F + J + G,\ X_3 = K + H + D,\ Y_3 = K + I + B.$

These formulas use $2\mathbf{M} + 6\mathbf{S} + 3\mathbf{D}$. The $3\mathbf{D}$ are multiplications by d_1, d_2/d_1, and d_2. For complete binary Edwards curves the denominator Z_3 is nonzero.

Comparison with Previous Work. All of the doubling formulas for binary elliptic curves presented in the literature have exceptional cases, such as doubling a point of order 2. Our doubling formulas for complete Edwards curves are the first complete doubling formulas in the literature. The following comparison shows that our doubling formulas also provide quite attractive speeds.

The fastest inversion-free doubling formulas mentioned in [9, Table 13.4] are in López-Dahab coordinates and take $4\mathbf{M}+4\mathbf{S}+1\mathbf{D}$; these formulas were introduced by Lange in [26]. The $1\mathbf{D}$ is a multiplication by a_2 and is eliminated by typical curve choices. Formulas in [9, page 294], introduced by López and Dahab in [28], take $3\mathbf{M} + 5\mathbf{S} + 1\mathbf{D}$ when $a_2 \in \{0, 1\}$; here the $1\mathbf{D}$ is a multiplication by the curve parameter $\sqrt{a_6}$.

For random curves, experiments show that we can always choose d_1 to be small, so our new $2\mathbf{M} + 6\mathbf{S} + 3\mathbf{D}$ becomes at worst $4\mathbf{M} + 6\mathbf{S}$, slightly slower than $4\mathbf{M} + 4\mathbf{S}$. By choosing curves where d_1 and d_2/d_1 are both small we achieve $2\mathbf{M} + 6\mathbf{S}$, which is significantly faster than $3\mathbf{M} + 5\mathbf{S}$ and $4\mathbf{M} + 4\mathbf{S}$.

In [21] Kim and Kim present doubling formulas for curves of the form $v^2+uv = u^3+u^2+a_6$ needing $2\mathbf{M}+5\mathbf{S}+2\mathbf{D}$, where the $2\mathbf{D}$ are both by a_6. Our $2\mathbf{M}+6\mathbf{S}+3\mathbf{D}$ formulas are slightly slower but have the advantages of extra generality and completeness.

Our Improvements of Previous Work. We present here two improvements to doubling formulas in López-Dahab coordinates for binary curves in Weierstrass form. Of course, this makes the speed competition more challenging for Edwards curves! ;–)

The first improvement is an easy speedup of the Kim–Kim formulas. Kim and Kim represent an affine point (u_1, v_1) as $(U_1 : V_1 : W_1 : T_1)$, where $u_1 = U_1/W_1$, $v_1 = V_1/W_1^2$, and $T_1 = W_1^2$. Our improved formulas compute $2(U_1 : V_1 : W_1 : T_1) = (U_3 : V_3 : W_3 : T_3)$ as

$$A = U_1^2, \ B = V_1^2, \ W_3 = T_1 \cdot A, \ T_3 = W_3^2,$$
$$U_3 = (A + \sqrt{a_6}\, T_1)^2, \ V_3 = B \cdot (B + U_3 + W_3) + a_6 T_3 + T_3.$$

These improved formulas use only $2\mathbf{M} + 4\mathbf{S} + 2\mathbf{D}$, where the $2\mathbf{D}$ are one multiplication by a_6 and one multiplication by $\sqrt{a_6}$.

The second improvement achieves $2\mathbf{M} + 5\mathbf{S} + 2\mathbf{D}$ for curves of the shape $v^2 + uv = u^3 + a_6$. We represent a point by $(U_1 : V_1 : W_1 : T_1 : S_1)$, where additionally $S_1 = U_1 W_1$. The idea used by Kim and Kim does not carry over to these curves but we have developed the following formulas to compute $2(U_1 : V_1 : W_1 : T_1 : S_1) = (U_3 : V_3 : W_3 : T_3 : S_3)$:

$$A = U_1^2, \ B = V_1^2, \ W_3 = S_1^2, \ U_3 = (A + \sqrt{a_6}\, T_1)^2,$$
$$T_3 = W_3^2, \ S_3 = U_3 \cdot W_3, \ V_3 = B \cdot (B + U_3 + W_3) + a_6 T_3 + S_3.$$

We caution the reader that these formulas are not complete.

7   Differential Addition

This section presents fast explicit formulas for w-coordinate differential addition on binary Edwards curves. Here $w = x + y$. Note that $w(-P) = w(P)$, since $-(x, y) = (y, x)$.

"Differential addition" means computing $Q + P$ given $Q, P, Q - P$: e.g., computing $(2m+1)P$ given $(m+1)P, mP, P$, or computing $2mP$ given $mP, mP, 0P$. In particular, "w-coordinate differential addition" means computing $w(Q + P)$ given $w(Q), w(P), w(Q - P)$. This section also discusses "w-coordinate differential addition and doubling": computing both $w(2P)$ and $w(Q + P)$, again given $w(Q), w(P), w(Q - P)$.

More concretely, write $(x_1, y_1) = Q - P$, $(x_2, y_2) = P$, $(x_3, y_3) = Q$, $(x_4, y_4) = 2P$, and $(x_5, y_5) = Q + P$. This section presents fast explicit formulas to compute $x_5 + y_5$ given $x_1 + y_1$, $x_2 + y_2$, and $x_3 + y_3$. This section also presents fast explicit formulas to compute $x_4 + y_4$ and $x_5 + y_5$ given $x_1 + y_1$, $x_2 + y_2$, and $x_3 + y_3$. As in previous sections, the formulas are complete if the curve is complete.

We analyze the costs of our formulas in several situations. The simplest situation is that inputs $x_1 + y_1, x_2 + y_2, x_3 + y_3$ and outputs $x_4 + y_4, x_5 + y_5$ are represented in affine form, i.e., as field elements. If inversions are expensive—as they usually are—and storage is available then it is better for each input and output to be represented in projective form, i.e., as a ratio of two field elements. Some applications use mixed differential additions, where $x_1 + y_1$ is given in affine form while everything else is projective. We achieve the following speeds:

	general case	$d_2 = d_1$
affine diff addition	$1\mathbf{I} + 3\mathbf{M} + 1\mathbf{S} + 1\mathbf{D}$	$1\mathbf{I} + 1\mathbf{M} + 1\mathbf{S} + 1\mathbf{D}$
affine diff addition+doubling	$2\mathbf{I} + 4\mathbf{M} + 3\mathbf{S} + 2\mathbf{D}$	$2\mathbf{I} + 1\mathbf{M} + 3\mathbf{S} + 2\mathbf{D}$
mixed diff addition	$6\mathbf{M} + 1\mathbf{S} + 2\mathbf{D}$	$5\mathbf{M} + 1\mathbf{S} + 1\mathbf{D}$
mixed diff addition+doubling	$6\mathbf{M} + 4\mathbf{S} + 2\mathbf{D}$	$5\mathbf{M} + 4\mathbf{S} + 2\mathbf{D}$
projective diff addition	$8\mathbf{M} + 1\mathbf{S} + 2\mathbf{D}$	$7\mathbf{M} + 1\mathbf{S} + 1\mathbf{D}$
projective diff addition+doubling	$8\mathbf{M} + 4\mathbf{S} + 2\mathbf{D}$	$7\mathbf{M} + 4\mathbf{S} + 2\mathbf{D}$

Why Differential Addition Is Interesting. Montgomery in [30] presented fast formulas for u-coordinate differential addition on non-binary elliptic curves $v^2 = u^3 + a_2 u^2 + u$. As an application, Montgomery suggested what is now called the "Montgomery ladder" to compute $u(mP), u((m+1)P)$ given $u(P)$. The idea is to recursively compute $u(\lfloor m/2 \rfloor P), u((\lfloor m/2 \rfloor + 1)P)$, and then to compute $u(mP), u((m+1)P)$ with a differential addition and doubling.

The Montgomery ladder is one of the most popular scalar-multiplication methods. It has several attractive features: it is fast; it fits into extremely small hardware; and its uniform double-and-add structure adds a natural layer of protection against simple side-channel attacks. See [29], [6], [15], [11], and [19]. The input $u(P)$ is normally given in affine form, creating affine differential additions if inversions are inexpensive and mixed differential additions otherwise.

Montgomery also suggested a more complicated "PRAC" chain of differential additions to compute $u(mP)$ from $u(P)$. This chain uses more memory than the

Montgomery ladder and does not have the same simple structure, but it is faster in some situations. This chain rarely reuses the input $u(P)$; it relies mainly on projective differential additions if inversions are expensive.

Differential-Addition Formulas for Binary Elliptic Curves. Several authors have given formulas for u-coordinate differential additions on binary elliptic curves $v^2 + a_1 uv = u^3 + a_2 u^2 + a_6$. The resulting Montgomery ladders for binary elliptic-curve scalar-multiplication fit into even smaller hardware than the ladders for the non-binary case, and they have similar resistance to simple side-channel attacks.

Specifically, u-coordinate differential-addition formulas for the case $a_1 = 1$ were presented by Agnew, Mullin, and Vanstone in [1, page 808]; by Lopez and Dahab in [29, Lemma 2 and Section 4.2]; by Vanstone, Mullin, Antipa, and Gallant, according to [33]; by Stam in [33, Section 3.1], and by Gaudry in [13, page 33]. Lopez and Dahab say that their formulas use $6\mathbf{M} + 5\mathbf{S}$ for a mixed differential addition and doubling; see [29, Lemma 5]. Stam, after pointing out various speedups, says that projective differential addition takes $6\mathbf{M} + 1\mathbf{S}$; that mixed differential addition takes $4\mathbf{M} + 1\mathbf{S}$; and that a doubling takes $1\mathbf{M} + 3\mathbf{S} + 1\mathbf{D}$. Stam also presents differential-addition formulas for the case $a_6 = 1/a_1^2$, using only $5\mathbf{M}$ and an unspecified number of $\mathbf{S}$ for projective differential addition. Gaudry states a cost of $5\mathbf{M} + 5\mathbf{S} + 1\mathbf{D}$ for mixed differential addition and doubling; Gaudry and Lubicz state the same cost in [14, page 16].

All of the formulas in [1], [29], [33], and [13] fail if the neutral element on the curve appears. Our new formulas have no trouble with the neutral element, and have the advantage of completeness for suitable d_2. Our formulas are also competitive in speed with previous formulas—slightly slower in some situations but slightly faster in others.

The New Formulas. Let (x_2, y_2) be a point on the binary Edwards curve E_{B,d_1,d_2}. Assume that the sum $(x_2, y_2) + (x_2, y_2)$ is defined (as it always is on complete binary Edwards curves). Write $(x_4, y_4) = (x_2, y_2) + (x_2, y_2)$, and write $w_i = x_i + y_i$. Then $d_1^2 + d_1 w_2^2 + d_2 w_2^4 \neq 0$ and

$$w_4 = \frac{d_1 w_2^2 + d_1 w_2^4}{d_1^2 + d_1 w_2^2 + d_2 w_2^4} = \frac{w_2^2 + w_2^4}{d_1 + w_2^2 + (d_2/d_1)w_2^4}$$

by Lemma 3.1. In particular, if $d_2 = d_1$, then $d_1 + w_2^2 + w_2^4 \neq 0$ and

$$w_4 = 1 + \frac{d_1}{d_1 + w_2^2 + w_2^4}.$$

More generally, assume that $(x_1, y_1), (x_2, y_2), (x_3, y_3), (x_5, y_5)$ are points on E_{B,d_1,d_2} satisfying $(x_1, y_1) = (x_3, y_3) - (x_2, y_2)$ and $(x_5, y_5) = (x_2, y_2) + (x_3, y_3)$, and write $w_i = x_i + y_i$ as before. Then, by Lemma 3.1,

$$d_1^2 + w_2 w_3 (d_1(1 + w_2 + w_3) + d_2 w_2 w_3) \neq 0$$

and

$$w_1 + w_5 = \frac{d_1 w_2 w_3 (1 + w_2)(1 + w_3)}{d_1^2 + w_2 w_3 (d_1(1 + w_2 + w_3) + d_2 w_2 w_3)},$$

$$w_1 w_5 = \frac{d_1^2 (w_2 + w_3)^2}{d_1^2 + w_2 w_3 (d_1(1 + w_2 + w_3) + d_2 w_2 w_3)}.$$

In particular, if $d_2 = d_1$, then $d_1 + w_2 w_3 (1 + w_2)(1 + w_3) \neq 0$ and

$$w_1 + w_5 = 1 + \frac{d_1}{d_1 + w_2 w_3 (1 + w_2)(1 + w_3)},$$

$$w_1 w_5 = \frac{d_1 (w_2 + w_3)^2}{d_1 + w_2 w_3 (1 + w_2)(1 + w_3)}.$$

Cost of Affine w-coordinate Differential Addition and Doubling. The explicit formulas

$$R = w_2 \cdot w_3, \ S = R^2, \ T = R \cdot (1 + w_2 + w_3) + S,$$

$$w_5 = T \cdot \frac{1}{d_1 + T + (d_2/d_1 + 1)S} + w_1$$

use $1\mathbf{I} + 3\mathbf{M} + 1\mathbf{S} + 1\mathbf{D}$, where the $1\mathbf{D}$ is a multiplication by the curve parameter $d_2/d_1 + 1$. For complete binary Edwards curves the denominator is never zero.
  If $d_2 = d_1$ then the explicit formulas

$$A = w_2^2, \ B = A + w_2, \ C = w_3^2, \ D = C + w_3, \ w_5 = 1 + d_1 \frac{1}{d_1 + B \cdot D} + w_1$$

use just $1\mathbf{I} + 1\mathbf{M} + 2\mathbf{S} + 1\mathbf{D}$. For complete binary Edwards curves the denominator is never zero.
  Doubling: The explicit formulas

$$A = w_2^2, \ J = A^2, \ K = A + J, \ w_4 = K \cdot \frac{1}{d_1 + K + (d_2/d_1 + 1)J}$$

use $1\mathbf{I} + 1\mathbf{M} + 2\mathbf{S} + 1\mathbf{D}$, where the $1\mathbf{D}$ is a multiplication by the curve parameter $d_2/d_1 + 1$. For complete binary Edwards curves the denominator is never zero. The total cost of a differential addition and doubling is $2\mathbf{I} + 4\mathbf{M} + 3\mathbf{S} + 2\mathbf{D}$, or $1\mathbf{I} + 7\mathbf{M} + 3\mathbf{S} + 2\mathbf{D}$ with Montgomery's inversion trick.
  If $d_2 = d_1$ then the explicit formulas

$$A = w_2^2, \ B = A + w_2, \ w_4 = 1 + d_1 \frac{1}{d_1 + B^2}$$

use just $1\mathbf{I} + 2\mathbf{S} + 1\mathbf{D}$. For complete binary Edwards curves the denominator is never zero. These formulas can share the computations of A and B with differential addition, reducing the total cost of a differential addition and doubling to $2\mathbf{I} + 1\mathbf{M} + 3\mathbf{S} + 2\mathbf{D}$, or $1\mathbf{I} + 4\mathbf{M} + 3\mathbf{S} + 2\mathbf{D}$ with Montgomery's inversion trick.

Cost of Mixed w-coordinate Differential Addition and Doubling. Assume that w_1 is given as a field element, that w_2, w_3 are given as fractions $W_2/Z_2, W_3/Z_3$, and that w_4, w_5 are to be output as fractions $W_4/Z_4, W_5/Z_5$.

The explicit formulas

$$C = W_2 \cdot (Z_2 + W_2), \ D = W_3 \cdot (Z_3 + W_3), \ E = Z_2 \cdot Z_3, \ F = W_2 \cdot W_3,$$
$$V = C \cdot D, \ U = V + (\sqrt{d_1}\, E + \sqrt{d_2/d_1 + 1}\, F)^2, \ W_5 = V + w_1 \cdot U, \ Z_5 = U$$

use $6\mathbf{M} + 1\mathbf{S} + 2\mathbf{D}$, where the $2\mathbf{D}$ are multiplications by the curve parameters $\sqrt{d_1}$ and $\sqrt{d_2/d_1 + 1}$. For complete binary Edwards curves Z_5 cannot be zero.

If $d_2 = d_1$ then the explicit formulas

$$C = W_2 \cdot (Z_2 + W_2), \ D = W_3 \cdot (Z_3 + W_3), \ E = Z_2 \cdot Z_3,$$
$$V = C \cdot D, \ U = V + d_1 E^2, \ W_5 = V + w_1 \cdot U, \ Z_5 = U$$

use only $5\mathbf{M} + 1\mathbf{S} + 1\mathbf{D}$.

Doubling: The explicit formulas

$$C = W_2 \cdot (Z_2 + W_2), \ W_4 = C^2, \ Z_4 = W_4 + ((\sqrt[4]{d_1}\, Z_2 + \sqrt[4]{d_2/d_1 + 1}\, W_2)^2)^2$$

use $1\mathbf{M} + 3\mathbf{S} + 2\mathbf{D}$, where the $2\mathbf{D}$ are multiplications by the curve parameters $\sqrt[4]{d_1}$ and $\sqrt[4]{d_2/d_1 + 1}$. For complete binary Edwards curves Z_4 cannot be zero. These formulas can share the computation of C with differential addition, reducing the total cost of differential addition and doubling to $6\mathbf{M} + 4\mathbf{S} + 4\mathbf{D}$.

If $d_2 = d_1$ then the explicit formulas

$$C = W_2 \cdot (Z_2 + W_2), \ W_4 = C^2, \ Z_4 = d_1(Z_2^2)^2 + W_4$$

use $1\mathbf{M} + 3\mathbf{S} + 1\mathbf{D}$ and can share the computation of C with differential addition, reducing the total cost of differential addition and doubling to $5\mathbf{M} + 4\mathbf{S} + 2\mathbf{D}$.

Cost of Projective w-coordinate Differential Addition and Doubling. Assume that w_1, w_2, w_3 are given as fractions $W_1/Z_1, W_2/Z_2, W_3/Z_3$, and that w_4, w_5 are to be output as fractions $W_4/Z_4, W_5/Z_5$.

Replacing "$W_5 = V + w_1 \cdot U, \ Z_5 = U$" in any of the mixed formulas with "$W_5 = V \cdot Z_1 + U \cdot W_1, \ Z_5 = U \cdot Z_1$" produces projective formulas costing $2\mathbf{M}$ extra. For example, starting from the $5\mathbf{M} + 4\mathbf{S} + 2\mathbf{D}$ formulas for mixed differential addition and doubling with $d_2 = d_1$, one obtains $7\mathbf{M} + 4\mathbf{S} + 2\mathbf{D}$ formulas for projective differential addition and doubling with $d_2 = d_1$.

Our $w_1 w_5$ formulas offer an interesting alternative. For example, the explicit formulas

$$A = W_2 \cdot W_3, \ B = Z_2 \cdot Z_3, \ C = (W_2 + Z_2) \cdot (W_3 + Z_3),$$
$$W_5 = Z_1 \cdot (d_1(C + A + B)^2), \ Z_5 = W_1 \cdot (A \cdot C + (\sqrt{d_1}\, B + \sqrt{d_2/d_1 + 1}\, A)^2)$$

use only $6\mathbf{M} + 2\mathbf{S} + 3\mathbf{D}$ for differential addition. These formulas assume that w_1 is known, or checked, to be nonzero—if $w_1 = 0$ then one must resort to the previous formulas for w_5—but they still have the virtue of handling arbitrary w_2, w_3, w_4, w_5. Note that w_1 is fixed throughout the Montgomery ladder, and is 0 only if the starting point is $(0,0)$ or $(1,1)$.

Recovering $2P$ from $Q - P, w(P), w(Q)$. If $w_1^2 + w_1 \neq 0$ then

$$x_2^2 + x_2 = \frac{w_3\left(d_1 + w_1 w_2(1 + w_1 + w_2) + \dfrac{d_2}{d_1} w_1^2 w_2^2\right) + d_1(w_1 + w_2) + (y_1^2 + y_1)(w_2^2 + w_2)}{w_1^2 + w_1}.$$

One can use this formula to compute $2(x_2, y_2)$ given x_1, y_1, w_2, w_3; i.e., to recover $2P$ given $Q - P, w(P), w(Q)$. The formula produces $x_2^2 + x_2$; a "half-trace" computation reveals either x_2 or $x_2 + 1$, and therefore either (x_2, y_2) or $(x_2, y_2) + (1, 1)$. The failure case $w_1^2 + w_1 = 0$ occurs only if $4(Q - P) = (0, 0)$.

In particular, one can recover $2mP$ given $P, w(mP), w((m + 1)P)$, except in the easily recognizable case $4P = (0, 0)$. The Montgomery ladder can therefore be used not just to compute $w(mP)$ given $w(P)$, but also to compute $2mP$ given P. If P has odd order ℓ, as it does in typical cryptographic applications, then one can replace m by $(m/2) \bmod \ell$, obtaining $mP = 2((m/2) \bmod \ell)P$ from P via $w(((m/2) \bmod \ell)P)$.

References

1. Agnew, G.B., Mullin, R.C., Vanstone, S.A.: An implementation of elliptic curve cryptosystems over $F_{2^{155}}$. IEEE Journal on Selected Areas in Communications 11, 804–813 (1993); Citations in this document: §7, §7

2. Bernstein, D.J., Lange, T.: Faster addition and doubling on elliptic curves. In: Asiacrypt 2007 [24] pp. 29–50 (2007); Citations in this document: §1, §1, §1, §1

3. Billet, O., Joye, M.: The Jacobi model of an elliptic curve and side-channel analysis. In: AAECC 2003 [12] pp. 34–42 (2003), http://eprint.iacr.org/2002/125; MR 2005c:94045. Citations in this document: §1

4. Blake, I.F., Seroussi, G., Smart, N.P. (eds.): Advances in elliptic curve cryptography. London Mathematical Society Lecture Note Series, vol. 317. Cambridge University Press, Cambridge (2005); MR 2007g:94001. See [17]

5. Brier, É., Déchène, I., Joye, M.: Unified point addition formulae for elliptic curve cryptosystems. In: [32], pp. 247–256 (2004); Citations in this document: §1

6. Brier, É., Joye, M.: Weierstrass elliptic curves and side-channel attacks. In: PKC 2002 [31], pp. 335–345 (2002),
   www.geocities.com/MarcJoye/publications.html; Citations in this document: §1, §7

7. Cohen, H., Frey, G. (eds.): Handbook of elliptic and hyperelliptic curve cryptography. CRC Press, Boca Raton (2005); MR 2007f:14020. See [9], [25]

8. Desmedt, Y.G. (ed.): PKC 2003. LNCS, vol. 2567. Springer, Heidelberg (2002); See [16], [33]

9. Doche, C., Lange, T.: Arithmetic of elliptic curves. In: [7], pp. 267–302 (2005); MR 2162729. Citations in this document: §2, §6, §6

10. Edwards, H.M.: A normal form for elliptic curves. Bulletin of the American Mathematical Society 44, 393–422 (2007),
    http://www.ams.org/bull/2007-44-03/S0273-0979-07-01153-6/home.html; Citations in this document: §1

11. Fischer, W., Giraud, C., Knudsen, E.W., Seifert, J.-P.: Parallel scalar multiplication on general elliptic curves over $\mathbb{F}_p$ hedged against non-differential side-channel attacks (2002), http://eprint.iacr.org/2002/007;
Citations in this document: §7

12. Fossorier, M., Høholdt, T., Poli, A. (eds.): AAECC 2003. LNCS, vol. 2643. Springer, Heidelberg (2003); ISBN 3540401113. MR 2004j:94001. See [3]

13. Gaudry, P.: Variants of the Montgomery form based on Theta functions (2006), http://www.loria.fr/~gaudry/publis/toronto.pdf; Citations in this document: §7, §7

14. Gaudry, P., Lubicz, D.: The arithmetic of characteristic 2 Kummer surfaces (2008), http://eprint.iacr.org/2008/133; Citations in this document: §7

15. Izu, T., Takagi, T.: A fast parallel elliptic curve multiplication resistant against side channel attacks. In: PKC 2002 [31], pp. 280–296 (2002); Citations in this document: §7

16. Izu, T., Takagi, T.: Exceptional procedure attack on elliptic curve cryptosystems. In: PKC 2003 [8], pp. 224–239 (2002); Citations in this document: §1

17. Joye, M.: Defences against side-channel analysis. In: [4], pp. 87–100 (2005); Citations in this document: §1

18. Joye, M., Quisquater, J.-J.: Hessian elliptic curves and side-channel attacks. In: CHES 2001 [22], pp. 402–410 (2001); MR 2003k:94032, www.geocities.com/MarcJoye/publications.html; Citations in this document: §1

19. Joye, M., Yen, S.-M.: The Montgomery powering ladder. In: CHES 2002 [20], pp. 291–302 (2003), http://www.gemplus.com/smart/rd/publications/pdf/JY03mont.pdf; Citations in this document: §7

20. Kaliski Jr., B.S., Koç, Ç.K., Paar, C. (eds.): CHES 2002. LNCS, vol. 2523. Springer, Heidelberg (2003); See [19]

21. Kim, K.H., Kim, S.I.: A new method for speeding up arithmetic on elliptic curves over binary fields (2007), http://eprint.iacr.org/2007/181; Citations in this document: §6

22. Koç, Ç.K., Naccache, D., Paar, C. (eds.): CHES 2001. LNCS, vol. 2162. Springer, Heidelberg (2001); MR 2003g:94002. See [18], [27]

23. Koç, Ç.K., Paar, C. (eds.): CHES 1999. LNCS, vol. 1717. Springer, Heidelberg (1999); See [29]

24. Kurosawa, K. (ed.): ASIACRYPT 2007. LNCS, vol. 4833. Springer, Heidelberg (2007); See [2]

25. Lange, T.: Mathematical countermeasures against side-channel attacks. In: [7], pp. 687–714 (2005); MR 2163785, Citations in this document: §1

26. Lange, T.: A note on López-Dahab coordinates. Tatra Mountains Mathematical Publications 33, 75–81 (2006), http://eprint.iacr.org/2004/323; MR 2007f:11139. Citations in this document: §6

27. Liardet, P.-Y., Smart, N.P.: Preventing SPA/DPA in ECC systems using the Jacobi form. In: CHES 2001, [22], pp. 391–401 (2001); MR 2003k:94033, Citations in this document: §1

28. López, J., Dahab, R.: Improved algorithms for elliptic curve arithmetic in $GF(2^n)$. In: SAC 1998, [35], pp. 201–212 (1999); MR 1715809, Citations in this document: §6

29. López, J., Dahab, R.: Fast multiplication on elliptic curves over $GF(2^m)$ without precomputation. In: CHES 1999, [23], pp. 316–327 (1999); Citations in this document: §7, §7, §7, §7

30. Montgomery, P.L.: Speeding the Pollard and elliptic curve methods of factorization. Mathematics of Computation 48, 243–264 (1987),
    http://links.jstor.org/
    sici?sici=0025-5718(198701)48:177243:STPAEC2.0.CO;2-3;
    MR 88e:11130. Citations in this document: §7
31. Naccache, D., Paillier, P. (eds.): PKC 2002. LNCS, vol. 2274. Springer, Heidelberg (2002); MR 2005b:94044. See [6], [15]
32. Nedjah, N., Mourelle, L.M. (eds.): Embedded cryptographic hardware: methodologies & architectures. Nova Science Publishers (2004); ISBN 1-59454-012-8. See [5]
33. Stam, M.: On Montgomery-like representations for elliptic curves over $GF(2^k)$. In: PKC 2003, [8], pp. 240–254 (2002); Citations in this document: §7, §7, §7
34. Stein, W. (ed.): Sage Mathematics Software (Version 2.8.13). The Sage Group (2008), http://www.sagemath.org Citations in this document: §3
35. Tavares, S., Meijer, H. (eds.): SAC 1998. LNCS, vol. 1556. Springer, Heidelberg (1999); MR 1715799. See [28]

A Real-World Attack Breaking A5/1 within Hours

Timo Gendrullis, Martin Novotný, and Andy Rupp

Horst Görtz Institute for IT-Security, Ruhr-University Bochum, Germany
{gendrullis,arupp}@crypto.rub.de, novotnym@fel.cvut.cz

Abstract. In this paper we present a real-world hardware-assisted attack on the well-known A5/1 stream cipher which is (still) used to secure GSM communication in most countries all over the world. During the last ten years A5/1 has been intensively analyzed [1,2,3,4,5,6,7]. However, most of the proposed attacks are just of theoretical interest since they lack from practicability — due to strong preconditions, high computational demands and/or huge storage requirements — or have never been fully implemented.

In contrast to these attacks, our attack which is based on the work by Keller and Seitz [8] is running on an existing special-purpose hardware device, called COPACOBANA [9]. With the knowledge of only 64 bits of keystream the machine is able to reveal the corresponding internal 64-bit state of the cipher in about 6 hours on average. We provide a detailed description of our attack architecture as well as implementation results.

Keywords: A5/1, GSM, special-purpose hardware, COPACOBANA.

1 Introduction

The Global System for Mobile communications (GSM) was initially developed in Europe in the 1980s. Today it is the most widely deployed digital cellular communication system all over the world. The GSM standard specifies algorithms for data encryption and authentication. A5/1 and A5/2 are the two encryption algorithms stipulated by this standard, where the stream cipher A5/1 is used within Europe and most other countries. A5/2 is the intentionally weaker version of A5/1 which has been developed — due to the export restrictions — for deploying GSM outside of Europe. Though the internals of both ciphers were kept secret, their designs were disclosed in 1999 by means of reverse engineering [10]. In this work we focus on the stronger GSM cipher A5/1.

1.1 The A5/1 Stream Cipher

A5/1 is a synchronous stream cipher accepting a 64-bit session key $K_S = (k_0, \ldots, k_{63}) \in GF(2)^{64}$ and a 22-bit initial vector $IV = (v_0, \ldots, v_{21}) \in GF(2)^{22}$ derived from the 22-bit frame number which is publicly known. It uses three

E. Oswald and P. Rohatgi (Eds.): CHES 2008, LNCS 5154, pp. 266–282, 2008.

linear feedback shift registers (LFSRs) $R1$, $R2$, and $R3$ of lengths 19, 22, and 23 bits, respectively, as its main building blocks (see Figure 1). The taps of the LFSRs correspond to primitive polynomials and, therefore, the registers produce sequences of maximal periods. $R1$, $R2$, and $R3$ are clocked irregularly based on the values of the clocking bits (CBs) which are bits 8, 10, and 10 of registers $R1$, $R2$, and $R3$, respectively.

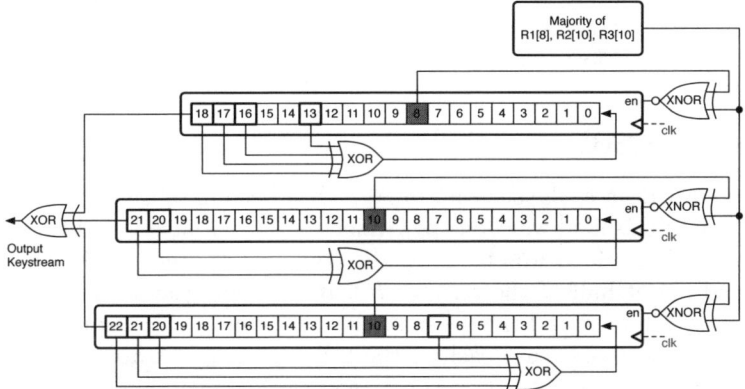

Fig. 1. Design of A5/1

The A5/1 keystream generator works as follows. First, an *initialization phase* is run. At the beginning of this phase all registers are set to 0. Then the *key setup* and the *IV setup* are performed. In the initialization phase all three registers are clocked regularly and the key bits followed by IV bits are xored with the least significant bits of all three registers. Thus, after $64 + 22 = 86$ clock-cycles the state S^i is achieved.

Based on this initial state S^i the *warm-up phase* is performed where the generator is clocked for 100 clock-cycles and the output is discarded. This results directly in the state S^w producing the first output bit 101 clock-cycles after the initialization phase. Note that already during the warm-up phase and also during the stream generation phase which starts afterwards, the registers $R1$, $R2$, and $R3$ are clocked irregularly. More precisely, the stop/go clocking is determined by the bits $R1[8]$, $R2[10]$, and $R3[10]$ in each clock-cycle as follows: the majority of the three bits is computed, where the majority of three bits a, b, c is defined by $maj(a, b, c) = ab + ac + bc$. $R1$ is clocked iff $R1[8]$ agrees with the majority. $R2$ is clocked iff $R2[10]$ agrees with the majority. $R3$ is clocked iff $R3[10]$ agrees with the majority. Regarding to Table 1 in each cycle at least two of the three registers are clocked. After these clockings, an output bit is generated from the values of $R1$, $R2$, and $R3$ by xoring their most significant bits.

After warm-up A5/1 produces 228 output bits, one per clock-cycle. 114 of them are used to encrypt uplink traffic, while the remaining bits are used to decrypt downlink traffic. In the remainder of this paper we assume that we are given at least 64 consecutive bits of such a 228 bit keystream.

Table 1. Clockcontrol of *A5/1*

CB of R1: R1[8]	0	0	0	1	0	1	1	1
CB of R2: R2[10]	0	0	1	0	1	0	1	1
CB of R3: R3[10]	0	1	0	0	1	1	0	1
Majority	0	0	0	0	1	1	1	1
Clock R1?	√	√	√	–	–	√	√	√
Clock R2?	√	√	–	√	√	–	√	√
Clock R3?	√	–	√	√	√	√	–	√

1.2 Related Work

During the last decade the security of A5/1 has been extensively analyzed. Pioneering work in this field was done by Anderson [11], Golic [5], and Babbage [12].

Anderson's basic idea was to guess the complete content of the registers $R1$ and $R2$ and about half of the register $R3$. In this way the clocking of all three registers is determined and the second half of $R3$ can be derived given 64 bits of keystream. In the worst-case each of the 2^{52} determined state candidates (i.e., candidates for S^w) needs to be verified against the keystream which imposes a high workload when done in software.

The hardware-assisted attack by Keller and Seitz [8] is based on Anderson's idea. However, they proposed a way to exclude a significant fraction of possible candidates at a very early stage of the verification process. The authors claim that their approach reduces the attack complexity to $2^{41} \cdot \left(\frac{3}{2}\right)^{11}$ with an expected computing time of 14 clock-cycles per guess. This results in a worst-case complexity of $2^{51.24}$ clock cycles. They implemented the attack on a Xilinx XC4062 FPGA. The FPGA is hosting seven instances of the guessing algorithm and operates at a frequency of 18.65 MHz leading to an attack time of about 236 days. Unfortunately, the approach given in [8] does not only immediately discard wrong candidates but a priori *restricts* the search for candidates to a certain subspace. This fact is not explicitly mentioned in the paper. Moreover, no complete analysis of the attack is given. Our analyses in Section 2 show that the success probability of their attack is only about 18% and the expected computing time for a guess is slightly higher than the stated one.

The key idea of Golic's attack [5] is to guess the lower half of each register (these bits determine the register clocking in the first few clock-cycles) and clock the cipher until the guessed bits "run-out". Each output bit immediately yields a linear equation in terms of the internal state bits belonging to the upper halves of three registers. Then we continue guessing the clocking sequence yielding again other linear equations that describe the output of the majority function. Whenever 64 linearly independent equations are obtained in this way the system is solved using Gaussian elimination. The complexity of this attack is $O(2^{40})$ steps. However, each step is fairly complex since it comprises to compute the solution of an 64×64 LSE (and the verification of the corresponding state candidate).

Pornin and Stern proposed a SW/HW tradeoff attack [7] that is based on Golic's approach but in contrast to Golic they are guessing the clocking sequence from the very first step, similarly to [13]. These guesses create a tree with 4 branches in each node (each branch represents one clocking combination, cf. Table 1). While traversing a path down the tree, three equations are obtained at each node (similarly to the second phase of Golic's method), namely two equations describing the clocking and one equation describing the output. Hence, after n steps (in depth) one collected $3n$ equations. The tradeoff parameter n is chosen such that $3n < 64$. Thus, each path in the tree leads to an underdetermined LSE that is solved in software resulting in a parametric solution on the internal state. The basis of the corresponding linear subspace containing all solutions to such an LSE consists of $(64 - 3n + 1)$ 64-bit vectors. These vectors are sent to the hardware, where a brute force attack is performed, i.e., each of the 2^{64-3n} elements of the subspace is generated and loaded to the A5/1 instance. The instance is run after each load to verify the obtained output keystream against the given keystream. The authors estimated an average running time of 2.5 days when using an XP-1000 Alpha station for the software part and two Pamettes 4010E for the hardware part of the attack (where $n = 18$).

The authors consider to place twelve A5/1 instances into one Xilinx 4010E FPGA, occupying $12 \times 36 = 432$ CLBs out of 576 (75% of the FPGA). Unfortunately, any details (especially the area) of the unit generating 2^{64-3n} internal states are missing which makes it hard to verify the stated figures. However, these figures do not seem to be based on real measurements and we consider them as too optimistic; we expect that the generator unit occupies a relatively large area. For instance, when choosing $n = 18$ the transmitted basis consists of 11 vectors, i.e., $11 \times 64 = 704$ bits. Since the deployed Xilinx 4010E FPGA contains only 1152 flip-flops, more than 60% of them would be used just for holding the coefficients of the basis. So there seems not to be enough space to place twelve A5/1 units (needing further $12 \times 64 = 768$ flip-flops) on the FPGA as stated in the paper.

Finally, there is a whole class of time-memory-data tradeoff (TMDTO) attacks on A5/1 which share the common feature that a large amount of known keystream must be available and/or huge amounts of data must be precomputed and stored in order to achieve reasonable success rates and workloads for the online phase of these attacks. Simple forms of such attacks have been independently proposed by Babbage [12] and Golic [5]. Recently, Biryukov, Shamir, and Wagner presented an interesting (non-generic) variant of an TMDTO [3] (see also [14]) utilizing a certain property of A5/1 (low sampling resistance). The precomputation phase of this attack exhibits a complexity of 2^{48} and memory requirements of only about 300 GB, where the online phase can be executed within minutes with a success probability of 60%. However, 2 seconds of known keystream (i.e., about 25000 bits) are required to mount the attack making it impractical. Another important contribution in this field is due to Barkan, Biham, and Keller [15] (see also [16]). They exploit the fact that GSM employs error correction before encryption — which reveals the values of certain linear combinations of stream bits by observing the ciphertext — to mount a ciphertext-only TMDTO. However, in the precomputation phase of such an attack huge amounts of data need to be computed and stored; even more than for known-keystream TMDTOs. For instance, if we assume that 3 minutes of ciphertext (from the GSM SACCH channel) are available in the online phase, one needs to precompute about 50 TB of data to achieve a success probability of about 60% (cf. [16]). There are 2800 contemporary PCs required to perform the precomputation within one year. These are practical obstacles making actual implementations of such attacks very difficult. In fact, to the best of our knowledge no full implementation of TMDTO attack against A5/1 has been reported yet.

1.3   Our Contribution

As seen in the previous section most of the proposed attacks against A5/1 lack from practicability and/or have never been fully implemented. In contrast to these attacks, we present a real-world attack revealing the internal state of A5/1 in about 6 hours on average (and about 12 hours in the worst-case) using an existing low-cost (about US\$ 10,000) special-purpose hardware device. To mount the attack only 64 consecutive bits of a known keystream are required and we do not need any precomputed data. Also the communication requirements with the host computer are relatively small.

On the theoretical side, we present a modification and analysis of the approach sketched in [8]. Furthermore, we propose an optimization of the attack implementation leading to an improvement of about 13% in computation time compared to a plain implementation. Both plain and optimized version of the attack have been fully implemented and tested on our target platform.

1.4   Implementation Platform

The COPACOBANA (Cost-Optimized Parallel Code Breaker) machine [9] is a high-performance, low-cost cluster consisting of 120 Xilinx Spartan3-XC3S1000 FPGAs. Currently, COPACOBANA appears to be the only such reconfigurable parallel FPGA machine optimized for code breaking tasks reported in the open literature. Depending on the actual algorithm, the parallel hardware architecture can outperform conventional computers by several orders of magnitude. COPACOBANA has been designed under the assumptions that (i) computationally costly operations are parallelizable, (ii) parallel instances have only a very limited need to communicate with each other, (iii) the demand for data transfers between host and nodes is low due to the fact that computations usually dominate communication requirements and (iv) typical crypto algorithms and their corresponding hardware nodes demand very little local memory which can be provided by the on-chip RAM modules of an FPGA. Considering these characteristics COPACOBANA appeared to be perfectly tailored for simple guess-and-determine attacks on A5/1 like the one described in the next section.

2   Analysis and Modification of Keller and Seitz's Approach

The approach is based on a simple guess-and-determine attack proposed by R. Anderson in 1994 where the shorter registers $R1$ and $R2$ are guessed and the longer register $R3$ is to be determined. But because Anderson neglected the asynchronous clocking of the registers at first, only the 12 most significant bits of $R3$ can be determined from the known keystream while the remaining bits have to be guessed as well.

Keller and Seitz's attack can be divided into two phases, into the *determination phase* in which a possible state candidate consisting of the three registers of A5/1 after its warm-up phase is generated and into a subsequent *postprocessing phase* in which the state candidate is checked for consistency.

2.1   Analysis

In the determination phase, Keller and Seitz try to reduce the complexity of the simple guess-and-determine attack further by early recognizing contradictions that can occur by guessing the clocking bit (CB) of $R3$ such that $R3$ will not be clocked. Therefore, they first completely guess the registers $R1$ and $R2$ and then derive register $R3$ in the following manner. Let $Ri^{(t)}[n]$ denote the n-th bit of register Ri at a time t, where $t = 0$ is immediately after the warm-up phase of A5/1 and increases by 1 every clock-cycle. Then, foremost compute the first most significant bit (MSB) of $R3$, which is $R3^{(0)}[22]$, immediately out of $R1^{(0)}[18]$ and $R2^{(0)}[21]$ and the first bit of the known keystream (KS). Then inspect the clocking bits of registers $R1$ and $R2$, which are $R1^{(0)}[8]$ and $R2^{(0)}[10]$, and guess the first clocking bit of $R3$, namely $R3^{(0)}[10]$. If $R1^{(0)}[8]$ and $R2^{(0)}[10]$ are not equal, $R3$ will be clocked in either way and so both possibilities for $R3^{(0)}[10]$ have to be checked. But if the CBs of $R1$ and $R2$ are identical then at least these two registers will be clocked. Assume now the CB of $R3$ is chosen to be different from the ones of $R1$ and $R2$, i.e., $R3^{(0)}[10] \neq R1^{(0)}[8]$, and as a consequence $R3$ will not be clocked. Now in one half of these cases the generated output bit of the MSBs of all three registers (which are $R1^{(1)}[18] = R1^{(0)}[17]$, $R2^{(1)}[21] = R2^{(0)}[20]$, $R3^{(1)}[22] = R3^{(0)}[22]$) does not match the given keystream bit and a contradiction occurs. As a consequence the CB of $R3$ has to be guessed in a way that $R3$ will be clocked together with $R1$ and $R2$, i.e., the CB of $R3$ is to be chosen equal to the CBs of $R1$ and $R2$, so that a new MSB can be computed.

By early recognizing this possible contradiction while guessing $R3^{(t)}[10]$, all arising states of this contradictory guess neither need to be computed further on nor checked afterwards. To further reduce the complexity of the attack they do not only discard these described wrong possibilities for the CB of $R3$ in case of a contradiction but they also limit the number of choices to the one of not-clocking $R3$ if this is possible without any contradiction. After having computed the first MSB of $R3$ the process of guessing a CB and computing another MSB of $R3$ is repeated until $R3$ is completely determined which is after having clocked $R3$ for 11 times.

This heuristic reduces the number of possibilities for $R3^{(t)}[10]$ in one half of all cases from two to one. The number of possible state candidates to be checked decreases thus from 2^{11} to $(2 - \frac{1}{2})^{11} = (\frac{3}{2})^{11} \approx 2^{6.43} \approx 86$ for every fixed guess of registers $R1$ and $R2$ in general. This results in $2^{41} \cdot 2^{6.43} = 2^{47.43}$ possible state candidates. But because they discard some valid states as well as states leading to a contradiction they have only a low success probability. The number of all valid state candidates for one fixed guess of $R1$ and $R2$ is $(2 - \frac{1}{4})^{11} = (\frac{7}{4})^{11} \approx 2^{8.88} \approx 471$. Thus, the number of state candidates inspected by Keller and Seitz in proportion to the number of valid state candidates results in a success probability of only $\frac{86}{471} \approx 0.18 = 18\%$.

Immediately after the determination phase, the A5/1 is performed with the generated state candidate in the postprocessing phase and the generated output bits are checked against the remaining bits of the 64 bit known keystream. Keller and Seitz just state that this consistency check in the postprocessing phase will proceed fast and that both, determining a state candidate and checking it against the known keystream, will take $14 \approx 2^{3.81}$ clock-cycles. This leads to a complexity of $2^{47.43} \cdot 2^{3.81} = 2^{51.24}$ clock-cycles. But with this expected amount of clock-cycles they underestimated the time complexity as will be shown in Section 2.2.

One instance of Keller and Seitz's guessing algorithm occupies 313 out of the 2304 configurable logic blocks (CLBs) of the XC4062 FPGA. It is hard to estimate how fast the original Keller-Seitz attack would be when implemented on COPACOBANA, since the architecture and the performance of the XC4062 [17] and the Spartan-3 XC3S1000 [18] FPGAs are different. For example, one XC4000 CLB only roughly corresponds to one Spartan-3 slice, because it contains two 4-input look-up tables (LUT), one 3-input LUT and two flip-flops (FF), while a Spartan-3 slice contains only two 4-input LUTs and two FFs. Because the available number of slices on a Spartan-3 XC3S1000 FPGA is 7680 and if we assume that one instance of the guessing algorithm would occupy 313 slices, a maximum number of 24 instances could be implemented on one FPGA. This leaves just 168 slices for other circuits for controlling the instances. According to the datasheets the "internal performance of XC4000 family chips can exceed 150 MHz" while the "maximum toggle frequency of Spartan-3 chips is 630 MHz". That represents a performance ratio of less than 4.2. Out of these figures we estimate that the attack would not be faster than $\frac{24}{7} \times 4.2 \times 120 = 1728$ times when run on COPACOBANA. This yields to a minimum of 3.27 hours to perform the search of Keller and Seitz. But if we recall again that (i) the attack searches only through 18% of the valid states, the search through all valid states would take at least 18.19 hours, (ii) the number of guessing instances implemented in one FPGA would be less than 24 since at least an additional control logic has to be implemented, and (iii) Keller and Seitz underestimate the time complexity as will be shown in Section 2.2, the computation time is expected to increase significantly.

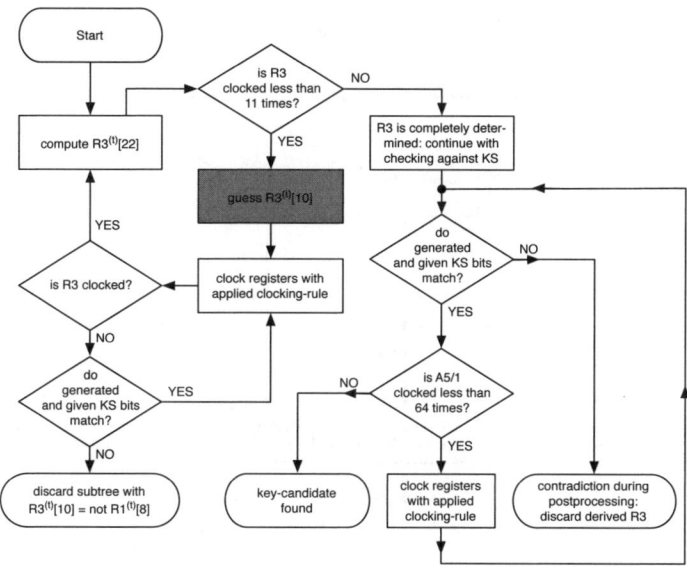

Fig. 2. Flowchart of the FSM of a guessing-engine

2.2   A Slight Modification

Our algorithm is similar to the one proposed by Keller and Seitz except that we only discard wrong possibilities for $R3^{(t)}[10]$ that would immediately lead into a contradiction. But if no contradiction appears we still check both possibilities for $R3^{(t)}[10]$, which means clocking and not-clocking $R3$. Because of this, we take every possible state candidate into account and therefore will find unlike Keller and Seitz the correct state candidate in any case. This reduces only in $\frac{1}{4}$ of all cases the number of choices from two to one and, hence, the expected number of possibilities for $R3$ that need to be checked is approximately 471 for every fixed guess of registers $R1$ and $R2$ (cf. Section 2.1).

A flowchart of the decisions during the determination phase and the post-processing phase shows Figure 2. A more detailed overview of how $R3^{(t)}[10]$ is guessed and how certain subtrees are discarded is given in Figure 3.

Example. An example for the first steps of the reduction of possibilities performed by the algorithm is given in Figure 4. It shows next to the first 4 bits of a known keystream the first 4 MSBs and the first 3 CBs of the guessed registers $R1$ and $R2$ and of the derived register $R3$. The algorithm proceeds as follows.

1. Compute $R3^{(0)}[22] = R1^{(0)}[18] \oplus R2^{(0)}[21] \oplus KS[0] = 0$.
2. $R1^{(0)}[8] \neq R2^{(0)}[10]$: Choose $R3^{(0)}[10] = 0 \neq R1^{(0)}[8]$ first and clock registers $R2$ and $R3$.
3. Compute $R3^{(1)}[22] = R3^{(0)}[21] = R1^{(0)}[18] \oplus R2^{(0)}[20] \oplus KS[1] = 0$.

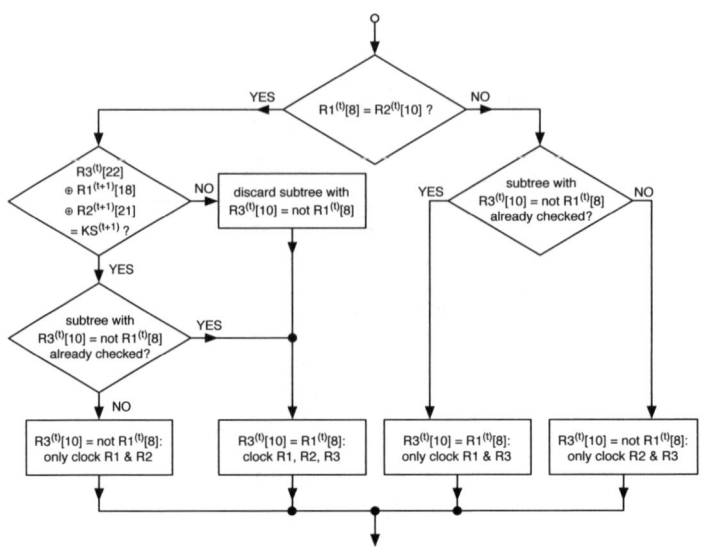

Fig. 3. Guessing the clocking bit of $R3$ in detail

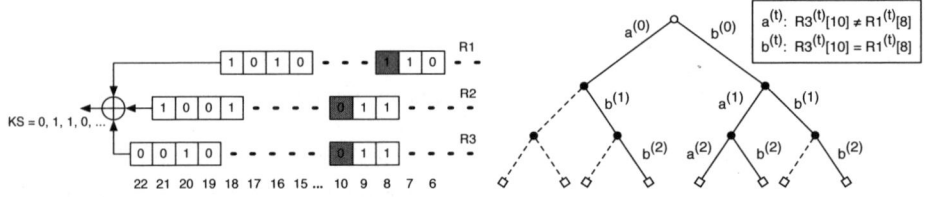

Fig. 4. An example for a generated state candidate after 3 times guessing $R3^{(t)}[10]$

Fig. 5. An example for a reduced binary decision tree of $R3^{(t)}[10]$

4. $R1^{(0)}[8] = R2^{(0)}[9]$: Not clocking register $R3$ would result in a contradiction because $R1^{(0)}[17] \oplus R2^{(0)}[19] \oplus R3^{(0)}[21] \neq KS[2]$.
   Hence, discard the possibility $R3^{(1)}[10] = 0 = R3^{(0)}[9] \neq R1^{(1)}[8]$, instead choose $R3^{(1)}[10] = 1 = R3^{(0)}[9] = R1^{(0)}[8]$, and clock all registers $R1$, $R2$, $R3$.
5. Compute $R3^{(2)}[22] = R3^{(0)}[20] = R1^{(0)}[17] \oplus R2^{(0)}[19] \oplus KS[2] = 1$.
6. ...

   The example ends here because it is apparent from Figure 5, which shows the binary decision tree for $R3^{(t)}[10]$ up to a depth of 3, that discarding possibilities for $R3^{(t)}[10]$ results in cutting whole subtrees. In the example above we chose edge $a^{(0)} = R3^{(0)}[10] = 0 \neq R1^{(1)}[8]$ at the root node first and then discarded the possibility $a^{(1)} = R3^{(1)}[10] = 0 \neq R1^{(1)}[8]$ at the corresponding node of depth 1.

Time Complexity of the Attack. Generating one possible state candidate during determination phase takes one clock-cycle for deriving $R3^{(0)}[22]$ and then eleven times clocking register $R3$ to determine the remaining MSBs of the register. With a probability of $P_{clk} = \frac{3}{4}$ for clocking a register of A5/1 it takes an expected number of $1 + \frac{4}{3} \cdot 11 = 15\frac{2}{3}$ clock-cycles to generate the state candidate for fixed registers $R1$ and $R2$ and the known keystream. Because every clock-cycle one bit of the known keystream is inspected, the expected number of needed known keystream bits to generate a state candidate corresponds to the number of clock-cycles needed for this process.

After having generated one state candidate it needs to be checked in the postprocessing phase further on against the remaining bits of the known keystream. To be able to perform this check immediately after the determination phase we additionally compute the feedback bits of register $R3$ with its linear feedback function. We start with this computation from the time when $R3^{(3)}[10] = R3^{(0)}[7]$ is guessed. So we already computed 8 of the 11 feedback bits of $R3$ when the state candidate is generated. The remaining 3 feedback bits are computed in parallel and we continue with performing A5/1. Now, the produced output is compared to the known keystream. A contradiction between the generated output and a known keystream bit is expected to occur with a probability of $\alpha = \frac{1}{2}$ in the first clock-cycle of postprocessing. Every cycle the algorithm is clocked further on, the probability of a contradiction is again $\frac{1}{2}$. Generally speaking, it is $\alpha_n = \frac{1}{2^n}$ for the n-th cycle after the determination phase and the algorithm will clock on with an expected value of $\frac{1}{\alpha} = 2$ further needed clock-cycles to inspect the output. If it is clocked without any contradiction up to the 64-th bit of the known keystream we found a valid state candidate for reconstructing the session key. Although there might be more than just one state candidate generating the same 64 bit of output, the probability for this event is negligible.

So, we get an expected number of $T = 15\frac{2}{3} + 2 = 17\frac{2}{3}$ clock-cycles to determine a state candidate and check it for consistency with the given keystream instead of just 14 clock-cycles as stated by Keller and Seitz. Thus, the time complexity of our whole attack is $C \approx 2^{41} \cdot (\frac{7}{4})^{11} \cdot 17\frac{2}{3} \approx 2^{54.02}$.

3   Breaking A5/1 on COPACOBANA

3.1   Our Hardware Architecture

This section presents an efficient implementation of a *guessing-engine* in hardware which performs the determination phase and the postprocessing phase of the attack. On every FPGA, several instances of this guessing-engine will be implemented. Therefore, we will additionally introduce a hardware-software-interface controlling these instances and providing intercommunication.

The Guessing-Engine. Figure 6 shows an overview of the guessing-engine with its different components. A large part of the architecture for implementing this guessing-engine consists of flip-flops (FFs) for storing the content of different registers. This is in detail the *state candidate register*, storing the computed register $R3$ and the fixed guess of registers $R1$ and $R2$ in 64 bits. Additionally, we need FFs to store the 64 bits of known keystream and an additional simple shift register to evaluate a different known keystream bit every clock-cycle. To perform the consistency check in the postprocessing phase, all three $A5/1$ $LFSRs$ have to be implemented, too. But the most important part of this architecture is the finite state machine (FSM) performing the determination phase and the postprocessing phase. Its functionality was already presented in Figures 2 and 3. The shown process is repeated until all possible state candidates, i.e., the whole binary decision tree of $R3^{(t)}[10]$, for one fixed guess of registers $R1$ and $R2$ have been checked. The fact, that the guess $R3^{(t)}[10] \neq R1^{(t)}[8]$ is always checked first corresponds to the binary decision tree of Figure 5. This binary decision tree storing the discarded or already checked possibilities is mapped into the *branching state register*.

The most straightforward way of mapping such a binary decision tree with a certain height h into hardware, is to use an h-bit wide binary counter. In our case all leaves are at a depth of $d = h = 11$. Turning left at a node of the tree, i.e., $R3^{(t)}[10] \neq R1^{(t)}[8]$, is represented by 0 in the corresponding counter bit and turning right at a node, i.e., $R3^{(t)}[10] = R1^{(t)}[8]$, is represented by 1. Now, to reach all leaves from the leftmost unto the rightmost one by one, we initialize the 11-bit wide counter to all 0 and read it in 11 clock-cycles bit by bit from the most significant bit (MSB) to the least significant bit (LSB). When having reached the leftmost leaf in such a manner, we increase the register by one and restart reading bit by bit at the MSB again. This will lead us to the second leaf from the left. To reach the rest of the leaves we count through this 11-bit wide register up to all bits being 1. Now it is claimed by the attack that certain subtrees of the binary decision tree are discarded (cf. Section 2.2). To be able to do that while passing through the tree, we have to set the corresponding bits of the 11-bit wide counter manually to 1 with an 1-to-11 bit demultiplexer. The FSM does this with bit number b every time a contradiction is detected at a node of depth $d = b+1$ and a possibility of $R3^{(t)}[10]$ is discarded. This results in the reduced number of leaves of the binary decision tree of $(\frac{7}{4})^{11} \approx 471$ meaning the amount of possible state candidates for a fixed guess of $R1$ and $R2$.

The Control-Interface. Because several instances of the guessing-engine are implemented on one FPGA they need to be controlled continuously. This is done by the *control-interface* and there is exactly one instance of it implemented on each FPGA of COPACOBANA. It accepts the 64 bit known keystream and a *sub-searchspace* which has to be searched by the FPGA. By sub-searchspace we mean a certain amount of fixed guesses for registers $R1$ and $R2$. Therefore, a software divides the *searchspace* consisting of the 2^{41} possibilities into these sub-searchspaces and transmits to each FPGA another one of them together with the known keystream. The control-interface of the FPGA then counts through this sub-searchspace and provides each guessing-engine with a fixed guess of registers $R1$ and $R2$ to be searched. Every time a guessing-engine finishes its search it sends a report to the control-interface whether it was successful or not on finding a state candidate and requests for another fixed guess of registers $R1$ and $R2$

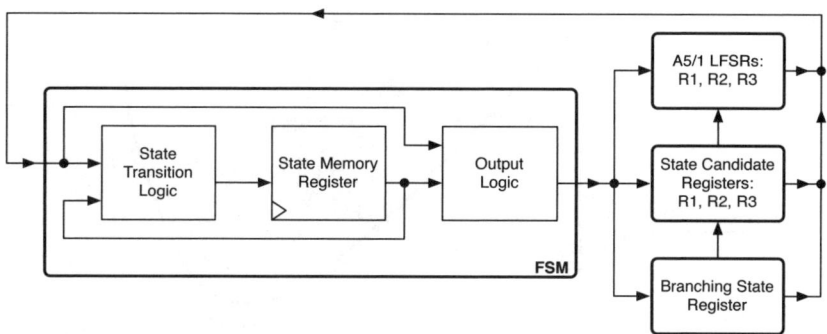

Fig. 6. An overview of the guessing-engine

out of the current sub-searchspace. In case of success the valid state candidate is propagated to the software. This is repeated until the whole sub-searchspace is searched by the FPGA. During the search, the software retrieves regularly at reasonable intervals the status information of each FPGA and assigns a new sub-searchspace to an FPGA if requested. The search is finished when all state candidates that can be generated with the 2^{41} possibilities for guessing $R1$ and $R2$, i.e., the whole searchspace, are checked for consistency.

3.2 Optimization: Storing Intermediate States

When completely passing through a binary decision tree, edges near the root node are traversed much more often than edges near the leaf nodes. The number of cycles $R3$ needs to be clocked to reach any leaf of the tree is 11 (cf. Section 3.1). For example, when inspecting the two leftmost leaves we have to go bit by bit through the states 00000000000 and 00000000001 of the 11-bit wide counter corresponding to the tree. Apparently, the first ten edges up to the node of depth 10 for both leaves are identical. Therefore, we can create *recovery points* at some depth in the search tree. More precisely, it is possible to store the intermediate state (i.e., the content of all A5/1 registers) at such a point (node of tree) and search the subtree starting at this recovery point instead of starting at the root node. This apparently demands a larger area, but saves a certain amount of clock-cycles.

Let us assume that reloading takes exactly one clock-cycle. If we store and reload the intermediate states at depth $d = 10$, then the number of clock-cycles for $R3$ reduces from 11 to $\frac{11+1+1}{2} = 6.5$ on average: 11 times clocking $R3$ to reach the first leaf, one clock-cycle reloading the intermediate state, and one time clocking $R3$ to reach the next leaf from the reloaded state. If we store the intermediate states at depth $d = 9$, the corresponding subtree has 4 leaves. To reach the leftmost one takes 11 clock-cycles, but to reach the other 3 leaves will take just $1 + 2 = 3$ clock-cycles each. Therefore, the average number of times $R3$ needs to be clocked is in this case only $\frac{11+3+3+3}{4} = \frac{8+3\cdot4}{4} = 5$.

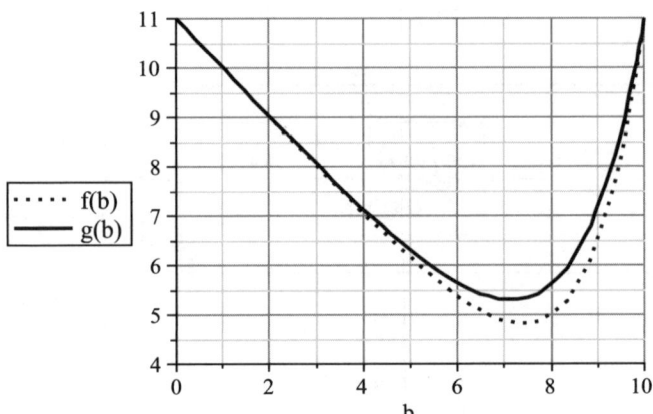

Fig. 7. Functions $f(b), g(b)$: The average number of cycles clocking $R3$ to generate a state candidate with reloading intermediate states at recovery position b

Generalizing this approach of storing and reloading intermediate states at a depth of $d = 10$ or $d = 9$ to a depth of $d = b + 1$, where b denotes the number of the bit in the 11-bit wide counter consecutively numbered from 0 to 10, we need to clock $R3$

$$f(b) = \frac{b + (11 - b) \cdot 2^{(10-b)}}{2^{(10-b)}} \tag{1}$$

times on average to reach one leaf. The function has a minimum of 4.875 times clocking $R3$ on average to reach a leaf for storing and reloading intermediate states at a depth of $b_{min} = 7$ for $b \in \mathbb{N}$.

Taking also into account that some subtrees are discarded while passing through the tree (cf. Section 2.2) and the number of possibilities is reduced from 2 to $\frac{7}{4}$ for every guess, the function needs to be adapted:

$$g(b) = \frac{b + (11 - b) \cdot \left(\frac{7}{4}\right)^{(10-b)}}{\left(\frac{7}{4}\right)^{(10-b)}}. \tag{2}$$

Both functions $f(b)$ and $g(b)$ are shown in Figure 7. The value for the minimum of the function $g(b)$ now changes to approximately 5.31 at $b_{min} = 7$ for $b \in \mathbb{N}$. Therefore, the expected number of clock-cycles for generating and checking one state candidate is now

$$T_{opt} = 1 + \frac{4}{3} \cdot 5.31 + 2 \approx 10.10 \approx 2^{3.33}$$

instead of $T = 17\frac{2}{3}$ (cf. Section 2.2). This results in an optimized time complexity of

$$C_{opt} \approx 2^{41} \cdot 2^{8.88} \cdot 2^{3.33} \approx 2^{53.21}$$

and reduces the previous complexity of $C \approx 2^{54.02}$ by 0.81 bit. But when comparing the time complexities of the standard and the optimized guessing-engine we additionally have to take the required area into account. The optimized guessing-engine is expected to occupy a larger area because of the storing elements for intermediate states of several registers. Hence, we will be able to place less instances on one FPGA. This comparison of time-area products is done after the implementation process and will be discussed in Section 3.3.

3.3   Implementation Results for COPACOBANA

We used Xilinx ISE Foundation 9.2i to synthesize and implement all components for a Xilinx Spartan3-XC3S1000-FT256 FPGA used in COPACOBANA. The simulation of the hardware model was done in MentorGraphics ModelSim SE 6.3d.

First, we implemented and tested one single instance of the standard and optimized guessing engine together with the control-interface for one instance. Therefore, Table 2 shows the post place & route results of the implementation process for a single instance of the control-interface and both guessing-engines.

Table 2. Implementation results for the control-interface and the guessing-engines

	slices	flip-flops	look-up tables	f_{max} [MHz]
control-interface	371	304	254	123.19
standard guessing-engine	202	179	256	112.84
optimized guessing-engine	311	312	412	115.01

To decide whether it is worth or not implementing the optimized guessing-engine in spite of the increased area consumption we calculated the *time-area product*. Table 3 shows a comparison of the computing time T and T_{opt} in *clock-cycles* (cf. Sections 2.2 and 3.2), the number of slices needed, and the time-area product in *clock-cycles·slices* for our standard and optimized implementation of the guessing-engine. The last row shows the quotient of the values of both designs. The quotient of the time-area products shows an overall improvement of about 12% for one single optimized guessing-engine compared to the standard one. We omitted considering the operating frequencies in the time-area product because both implementations run at nearly the same speed.

After having tested a single instance of each guessing-engine together with the control-interface on one of the *Spartan3-XC3S1000* FPGAs we attempted to maximize the utilization ratio of the available hardware resources. For this purpose, we implemented as many instances as possible of both types of guessing-engines with one instance of the control-interface. We were able to place & route 36 instances of the standard engine on one of the target FPGAs. However, the complexity of the control-interface grows with the number of guessing-engines. For 36 such engines the critical path was transfered to the control-interface creating the bottle-neck of the design. Therefore, the achieved maximum frequency

Table 3. Comparison of the implementation results of both guessing-engines

	computing-time [clock-cycles]	slices	time-area product [clock-cycles · slices]
optimized	10.10	311	3,141.10
standard	17.67	202	3,568.73
optimized / standard	0.57	1.54	0.88

Table 4. Implementation results of the maximally utilized designs

	slices	FFs	LUTs	f_{max} [MHz]	f_{test} [MHz]
1 control-engine &					
○ **36 standard**	6,953 (91 %)	10,730	10,576	81.85	72.00
○ **32 standard**	6,614 (86 %)	9,636	9,417	102.42	92.00
○ **23 optimized**	7,494 (98 %)	10,141	10,562	104.65	92.00
guessing-engines					
Spartan3-XC3S1000	7,680 (100 %)	15,360	15,360	300.00	—

of 81.13 MHz was relatively low. So we decided to implement less engines at a higher frequency instead. The best trade-off for the standard guessing-engine was to implement 32 instances at a maximum frequency of 102.42 MHz. In case of the optimized guessing-engine we were able to implement 23 instances running at 104.65 MHz. The implementation results of both complete designs are shown in Table 4. Additionally, the available resources of one FPGA are listed, too.

Table 4 also shows the frequencies the designs were tested with. Thus, we can calculate a preliminary estimation of the computation time to determine and check all possible state candidates. For the slow design with the standard guessing-engine and a time complexity of $C = 2^{54.02}$ (cf. Section 2.2) we expect a computation time of

$$t_{est} = \frac{2^{54.02}}{120 \cdot 36 \cdot 72 \cdot 10^6} \cdot \frac{1}{3600} \, h \approx 16.31 \, h.$$

This is an estimation for a fully equipped COPACOBANA with 120 FPGAs. In accordance to the previous calculation, the preliminary estimation of the computation time for the smaller but faster standard design (32 instances @ 92 MHz) is $t'_{est} \approx 14.36$ h. For the optimized guessing-engine (23 optimized instances @ 92 MHz) with a time complexity of $C_{opt} = 2^{53.21}$ we expect a computation time of $t''_{est} \approx 11.40$ h.

Time measurements of several extended test runs on COPACOBANA showed an average computation time of $t' = 13.58$ h for the small and fast standard design to perform a complete search for a given 64 bit known keystream. Comparing this result to the estimation of the computing time t'_{est} shows that the complexity differs only by 0.08 bit from our measurements. The optimized design took an average computation time of $t'' = 11.78$ h for a full search. This equals a variation of only 0.05 bit between the estimated and the measured computation time. Because these were the computation times for a full search (i.e., the worst case) the expected average time for finding the valid state candidate is 6.79 h for the standard design and 5.89 h for the optimized design, respectively.

4   Conclusion

In this paper we presented a guess-and-determine attack on the A5/1 stream cipher running on the special-purpose hardware device COPACOBANA. It reveals the internal state of the cipher in less than 6 hours on average needing only 64 bits of known keystream. We like to stress that our attack is also very attractive with regard to monetary costs which is a significant factor for the practicability of an attack: The acquisition costs for COPACOBANA are about US$ 10,000. Since COPACOBANA has a maximum power consumption of only 600 W, the attack also features very low operational costs. For instance, assuming 10 cent per kWh the operational costs of an attack are only 36 cents.

We like to note that we just provided a machine efficiently solving the problem of recovering a state of A5/1 after warm-up given 64 bits of known keystream. There is still some work to do in order to obtain a full-fledged practical GSM cracker: To finally recover the session key used for encryption, the cipher still needs to be tracked back from the revealed state to its initial state. Albeit, this backtracking and the extraction of the key can be done efficiently and in a fraction of time on almost any platform. Further technical difficulties will certainly appear when it actually comes to eavesdropping GSM calls. This is due to the frequency hopping method applied by GSM which makes it difficult to synchronize a receiver to the desired signal. Also the problem of obtaining known plaintext is still under discussion in pertinent news groups and does not seem to be fully solved. However, these are just some technical difficulties that certainly cannot be considered serious barriers for breaking GSM.

References

1. Barkan, E., Biham, E.: Conditional Estimators: An Effective Attack on A5/1. In: Preneel, B., Tavares, S. (eds.) SAC 2005. LNCS, vol. 3897, pp. 1–19. Springer, Heidelberg (2006)
2. Biham, E., Dunkelman, O.: Cryptanalysis of the A5/1 GSM Stream Cipher. In: Roy, B., Okamoto, E. (eds.) INDOCRYPT 2000. LNCS, vol. 1977. Springer, Heidelberg (2000)
3. Biryukov, A., Shamir, A., Wagner, D.: Real Time Cryptanalysis of A5/1 on a PC. In: Schneier, B. (ed.) FSE 2000. LNCS, vol. 1978, pp. 1–18. Springer, Heidelberg (2001)
4. Ekdahl, P., Johansson, T.: Another Attack on A5/1. IEEE Transactions on Information Theory 49(1), 284–289 (2003)
5. Golic, J.: Cryptanalysis of Alleged A5 Stream Cipher. In: Fumy, W. (ed.) EURO-CRYPT 1997. LNCS, vol. 1233, pp. 239–255. Springer, Heidelberg (1997)

6. Maximov, A., Johansson, T., Babbage, S.: An Improved Correlation Attack on A5/1. In: Handschuh, H., Hasan, M.A. (eds.) SAC 2004. LNCS, vol. 3357, pp. 239–255. Springer, Heidelberg (2005)
7. Pornin, T., Stern, J.: Software-hardware Trade-offs: Application to A5/1 Cryptanalysis. In: Paar, C., Koç, Ç.K. (eds.) CHES 2000. LNCS, vol. 1965, pp. 318–327. Springer, Heidelberg (2000)
8. Keller, J., Seitz, B.: A Hardware-Based Attack on the A5/1 Stream Cipher (2001), http://pv.fernuni-hagen.de/docs/apc2001-final.pdf
9. Kumar, S., Paar, C., Pelzl, J., Pfeiffer, G., Schimmler, M.: Breaking Ciphers with COPACOBANA - A Cost-Optimized Parallel Code Breaker. In: Goubin, L., Matsui, M. (eds.) CHES 2006. LNCS, vol. 4249, pp. 101–118. Springer, Heidelberg (2006)
10. Briceno, M., Goldberg, I., Wagner, D.: A Pedagogical Implementation of the GSM A5/1 and A5/2 "voice privacy" Encryption Algorithms (1999), http://cryptome.org/gsm-a512.html
11. Anderson, R.: A5 (was: Hacking digital phones). sci.crypt (17 June 1994)
12. Babbage, S.: A Space/Time Tradeoff in Exhaustive Search Attacks on Stream Ciphers. In: European Convention on Security and Detection (May 1995)
13. Golic, J.: Cryptanalysis of three mutually clock-controlled stop/go shift registers. IEEE Transactions on Information Theory 46, 1081–1090 (2000)
14. Biryukov, A., Shamir, A.: Cryptanalytic time/memory/data tradeoffs for stream ciphers. In: Okamoto, T. (ed.) ASIACRYPT 2000. LNCS, vol. 1976, pp. 1–13. Springer, Heidelberg (2000)
15. Barkan, E., Biham, E., Keller, N.: Instant Ciphertext-Only Cryptanalysis of GSM Encrypted Communications. In: Boneh, D. (ed.) CRYPTO 2003. LNCS, vol. 2729, Springer, Heidelberg (2003)
16. Barkan, E., Biham, E., Keller, N.: Instant Ciphertext-only Cryptanalysis of GSM Encrypted Communication (full-version). Technical Report CS-2006-07, Technion (2006)
17. Xilinx: XC4000E and XC4000X Series Field Programmable Gate Arrays (May 1999)
18. Xilinx: Spartan-3 FPGA Family: Complete Data Sheet, DS099 (November 2007)

Hash Functions and RFID Tags: Mind the Gap

Andrey Bogdanov, Gregor Leander, Christof Paar, Axel Poschmann,
Matt J.B. Robshaw, and Yannick Seurin

[1] Horst Görtz Institute for IT Security, Ruhr-University Bochum, Germany
[2] Orange Labs, Issy les Moulineaux, France
leander@rub.de, {abogdanov,cpaar,poschmann}@crypto.rub.de,
{matt.robshaw,yannick.seurin}@orange-ftgroup.com

Abstract. The security challenges posed by RFID-tag deployments are well-known. In response there is a rich literature on new cryptographic protocols and an on-tag hash function is often assumed by protocol designers. Yet cheap tags pose severe implementation challenges and it is far from clear that a suitable hash function even exists. In this paper we consider the options available, including constructions based around compact block ciphers. While we describe the most compact hash functions available today, our work serves to highlight the difficulties in designing lightweight hash functions and (echoing [17]) we urge caution when routinely appealing to a hash function in an RFID-tag protocol.

1 Introduction

With RFID tags on consumer items, the potential for wired-homes, and large-scale sensor networks becoming a reality, we are on the threshold of a pervasive computing environment. But along with these new applications come new, and demanding, security challenges. The cryptographic research community has been quick to identify some of the issues, and device authentication and privacy have received considerable attention. As a result a variety of new protocols have been proposed and in many of them, particularly ones intended to preserve user privacy and to anonymize tag interactions, it is assumed that a cryptographic hash function will be used on the tag.

However which hash function might be used in practice is rarely identified. Looking at dedicated hash functions from the last 20 years, we have become used to their impressive hashing speed (though this is a view that we might have to change in the future). This fast throughput might lead some designers to believe that hash functions are "efficient" in other regards and that they can be routinely used in low-cost environments. This is a mistake, a point that was convincingly made in a paper by Feldhofer and Rechberger [17]. Generally speaking, current hash functions are not at all suitable for constrained environments. They require significant amounts of state and the operations in current dedicated designs are not hardware friendly. This is not surprising since modern hash functions were designed with 32-bit processors in mind, but it means that very few RFID-oriented protocols appealing to a hash function could ever be used on a modestly-capable tag.

In this paper we consider RFID tag-enabled applications and the use of hash functions in RFID protocols. We then turn our attention to the design of hash functions in

E. Oswald and P. Rohatgi (Eds.): CHES 2008, LNCS 5154, pp. 283–299, 2008.

Table 1. An overview of the performance of some current compact algorithms where block ciphers are ordered by block and key size while hash functions are ordered by the size of the output

	Key size	Block size	Cycles per block	Throughput at 100KHz (Kbps)	Logic process	Area GE	rel.
Block ciphers							
PRESENT-80 [6]	80	64	32	200	0.18μm	1 570	1
PRESENT-80 [7]	80	64	563	11.4	0.18μm	1 075	0.68
DES [42]	56	64	144	44.4	0.18μm	2 309	1.47
mCrypton [32]	96	64	13	492.3	0.13μm	2 681	1.71
PRESENT-128 [6]	128	64	32	200	0.18μm	1 886	1.20
TEA [54]	128	64	64	100	0.18μm	2 355	1.50
HIGHT [24]	128	64	34	188.2	0.25μm	3 048	1.65
DESXL [42]	184	64	144	44.4	0.18μm	2 168	1.38
AES-128 [16]	128	128	1 032	12.4	0.35μm	3 400	2.17
Stream ciphers							
Grain [15]	80	1	1	100	0.13μm	1 294	0.82
Trivium [15]	80	1	1	100	0.13μm	2 599	1.66
Hash functions							
	Hash output size	Cycles per block	Throughput at 100KHz (Kbps)	Logic process	Area GE	rel.	
MD4 [17]	128	456	112.28	0.13μm	7 350	4.68	
MD5 [17]	128	612	83.66	0.13μm	8 400	5.35	
SHA-1 [17]	160	1 274	40.18	0.35μm	8 120	5.17	
SHA-256 [17]	256	1 128	45.39	0.35μm	10 868	6.92	
MAME [53]	256	96	266.67	0.18μm	8 100	5.16	

Section 3 and we explore whether a block cipher makes an appropriate starting point for a compact hash function instead of a dedicated design.[1]

In Section 4 we instantiate lightweight hash functions using literature-based constructions and the compact block cipher PRESENT [6]. This allows us to implement a range of representative constructions that, for their given parameter sets, are the most compact hash functions available today. In Section 5 we then look at some challenging problems in designing hash functions with greater hash output lengths. While the paper reveals positive results, our work also serves to highlight the difficult issue of compact hash functions; we therefore close the paper with problems for future research.

2 Cryptography and RFID Tags

When considering applications based around the deployment of RFID tags we are working with very specific applications with rather unique requirements. The difficulty of implementing cryptography in such environments has spurred considerable research, and this can be roughly divided into two approaches:

---

[1] This relates to proposals for future work identified in [17].

1. Devise new algorithms and protocols for tag-based applications. Such new protocols might use new cryptographic problems or might be based almost exclusively on very lightweight operations, *e.g.* bitwise exclusive-or and vector inner-products.
2. Optimise existing algorithms and protocols so that they become suitable for RFID tag-based applications. This approach might not give the compact results that some of the more exotic proposals do, but the security foundations may be more stable.

The work in this paper is more in-line with the second approach—seeing what we can do with what we have—though we hope it will be helpful to protocol designers. The current state of the art for new compact block ciphers and stream ciphers is summarised in Table 1 where most compact proposals offering 80-bit security seem to require 1 300– 1 600 *gate equivalents* (GE). For hash functions things are more complicated.

2.1   Hash Functions and Protocols for RFID Tags

Informally, a cryptographic hash function H takes an input of variable size and returns a hash value of fixed length while satisfying the properties of preimage resistance, second preimage resistance, and collision resistance [33]. For a hash function with n-bit output, compromising these should require 2^n, 2^n, and $2^{n/2}$ operations respectively. These properties make hash functions very appealing in a range of protocols. For tag-based applications, the protocols in question are often focused on authentication or on providing some form of anonymity and/or privacy [1,2,13,18,20,31,39]. However some estimates suggest that no more than 2 000 GE are available for security in low-cost RFID tags [26] and a glance at Table 1 shows that the hash functions available are unsuitable in practice. When we consider what we need from a hash function in an RFID tag-based application the following issues can be identified:

1. In tag-based applications we are unlikely to hash large amounts of data. Most tag protocols require that the hash function process a challenge, an identifier, and/or perhaps a counter. The typical input is usually much less than 256 bits.
2. In many tag-based applications we do not need the property of *collision resistance*. Most often the security of the protocol depends on the *one-way* property. In certain situations, therefore, it is safe to use hash functions with smaller hash outputs.
3. Applications will (typically) only require moderate security levels. Consequently 80-bit security, or even less, may be adequate. This is also the position taken in the eSTREAM project [14]. An algorithm should be chosen according to the relevant security level and in deployment, where success depends on every dollar and cent spent, there is no point using extra space to get a 256-bit security level if 64-bit security is all that is required.
4. While the physical space for an implementation is often the primary consideration, the peak and average power consumption are also important. The time for a computation will matter if we consider how a tag interacts with higher-level communication and anti-collision protocols.
5. Some protocols use a hash function to build a *message authentication code* (MAC), often by appealing to the HMAC construction [38]. When used as a MAC a number of interesting issues arise such as choosing an appropriate key length and understanding whether keys will be changed, something that will almost certainly be

impossible in most tag-enabled applications. There might also be the possibility of side-channel analysis on the MAC. However such attacks will rarely be worthwhile for cheap tag-enabled applications and we do not consider this issue further.

Taking account of these considerations allows us to make some pragmatic choices. There will be applications that just require one-wayness and the application may only require 80-bit or 64-bit security. Note that this is the view adopted by Shamir in the proposal SQUASH for use in RFID tags [49]. For other applications we might like to see 80-bit security against collision attacks.

Since current hash functions of dedicated design are either too big or broken, we first consider hash functions that are built around block ciphers. In particular we use the compact block cipher PRESENT [6] as a building block and we consider the implementation of a range of hash functions offering 64-bit and 128-bit outputs using established techniques. We also consider hash functions that offer larger outputs and we highlight some design directions along with their potential hardware footprint.

3   Hash Function Constructions

Hash functions in use today are built around the use of a *compression function* and appeal to the theoretical foundations laid down by Merkle and Damgård [11,34]. The compression function h has a fixed-length input, consisting of a *chaining variable* and a message extract, and gives a fixed-length output. A variety of results [12,25,27] have helped provide a greater understanding of this construction and while there are some limitations there are some countermeasures [4]. Since our goal is to obtain *representative* performance estimates, we will not go into the details of hash function designs. Instead we will assume that our hash function uses a compression function in an appropriate way and that the compression function takes as input some words of chaining variable, represented by H_i, and some words of (formatted) message extract, represented by M_i. We then restrict our focus to the cost of implementing the compression function.

In the hash function literature it is common to distinguish between two popular ways of building a compression function. The first is to use a compression function of a dedicated design and the second is to use an established, and trusted, block cipher.

3.1   Dedicated Constructions

The separation of dedicated constructions from block cipher-based constructions tends to disguise the fact that even dedicated hash functions like SHA-1 [36] and MD5 [46] are themselves built around a block cipher. Remove the feed-forward from compression functions in the MD-family and we are left with a reversible component that can be used as a block cipher (such as SHACAL [19] in the case of SHA-1). However the underlying block cipher we are left with is rather strange and has a much larger-than-normal block and key size combination. The problem with dedicated hash functions is that recent attacks [51,52] have shown that there is much to learn in designing block ciphers with such strange parameter sizes. There is therefore some value in considering approaches that use a more "classical" block cipher as the basis for a compression function.

3.2 Block Cipher Constructions

The use of a block cipher as a building block in hash function design [10] is as old as DES [35]. The topic has been recently revisited and Black *et al.* [5] have built on the work of Preneel [44] to present a range of secure $2n$- to n-bit compression functions built around an n-bit block cipher that takes an n-bit key. Among these are the well-known *Davies-Meyer*, *Matyas-Meyer-Oseas*, and *Miyaguchi-Preneel* constructions.

A hash function with an output of n bits can only offer a security level of 2^n operations for pre-image and second pre-image attacks and $2^{n/2}$ operations against finding collisions. While a security level of 128 bits is typical for mainstream applications, 80-bit security is often a reasonable target for RFID tag-based applications. Either way, there is a problem since the hash functions we need cannot always be immediately constructed out of the block ciphers we have to hand. This is not a new problem. But it is not an easy one to solve either, and there has been mixed success in constructing $2n$-bit hash functions from an n-bit block cipher [8,10,28,29,30,43,45]. While limitations have been identified in many constructions, work by Hirose [21,22] has identified a family of double-block-length hash functions that possess a proof of security. These use block ciphers with a key length that is twice the block length. Such a property is shared by AES-256 [37] and PRESENT-128 [6] and so in Section 4.2 we consider the performance of an Hirose-style construction instantiated using PRESENT-128.

When it comes to providing a replacement for SHA-1, the parameter sizes involved provide a difficult challenge. If we are to use a 64-bit block cipher like PRESENT-128, then in arriving at a hash function with an output of at least 160 bits we need a construction that delivers an output three times the block size (thereby achieving a 192-bit hash function). There are no "classical" constructions for this and so Sections 5.1 and 5.2 illustrate two possible design directions. These give representative constructions and we use them to gauge the hardware requirements of different design approaches. We hope that this will be of interest to future hash function designers.

4 Compact Hashing for 64- and 128-Bit Hash Outputs

In this section we will consider a variety of approaches to compact hashing when we use the block cipher PRESENT [6] as a building block. PRESENT is a 64-bit SPN block cipher which can be used with either an 80-bit or a 128-bit key. These will be referred to as PRESENT-80 and PRESENT-128 and full details and design rationale for these ciphers can be found in [6]. We denote encrypting a message M under the key K with PRESENT-80 or PRESENT-128 to obtain the ciphertext C as $C = E(M, K)$ and $A \| B$ denotes the concatenation of A and B.

4.1 Two Compact 64-Bit Proposals: DM-PRESENT-80 and DM-PRESENT-128

There are a variety of choices for building a 64-bit hash function from a 64-bit block cipher. We will illustrate these with the *Davies-Meyer* mode where a single 64-bit chaining variable H_i is updated using a message extract M_i according to the computation $H_i' = E(H_i, M) \oplus H_i$.

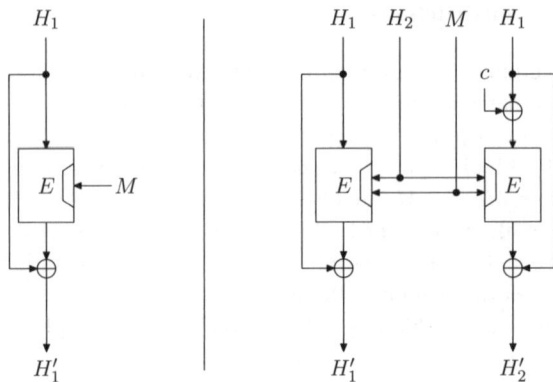

Fig. 1. Compression functions for the 64-bit and 128-bit hash functions: DM-PRESENT-80 and DM-PRESENT-128 (on the left) as well as H-PRESENT-128 (on the right)

In our case E denotes encryption with either PRESENT-80 or PRESENT-128, see Figure 1. Such hash functions will only be of use in applications that require the one-way property and 64-bit security.[2] At each iteration of the compression function 64 bits of chaining variable and 80 bits of message-related input are compressed. Therefore the two proposals DM-PRESENT-80 and DM-PRESENT-128 provide a simple trade-off between space and throughput. We also provide figures for a serial and parallel implementation of PRESENT, see Table 2.

While we have focused on using Davies-Meyer, it is important to note that these figures are a good indication of the cost for *any* single block-length hash function construction. If one prefers to implement *Matyas-Meyer-Oseas* or *Miyaguchi-Preneel* based on PRESENT (instead of *Davies-Meyer*) then the cost of DM-PRESENT-80 will be a reasonable guide. Moving away from PRESENT to a different block cipher will almost certainly cause an increase to the space required for an implementation.

4.2   A Compact 128-Bit Proposal: H-PRESENT-128

When designing a 128-bit hash function from the 64-bit output block cipher PRESENT, we have to appeal to so-called double-block-length hash function constructions. Natural candidates are MDC-2 [10] and Hirose's constructions [21,22]. These schemes possess security proofs in the ideal cipher model, where the underlying block cipher is modeled as a family of random permutations, one permutation being chosen independently for each key. However MDC-2 is not an ideal construction [50] and so we base our 128-bit hash function H-PRESENT-128 on the construction studied in [22].

The scheme H-PRESENT-128 is illustrated in Figure 1. The compression function takes as input two 64-bit chaining variables and a 64-bit message extract, denoted by the triple (H_1, H_2, M), and outputs the pair of updated chaining variables (H'_1, H'_2) according to the computation

---

[2] These properties are identical to those offered by the proposal SQUASH [49].

$$H_1' = E(H_1, H_2 \| M) \oplus H_1 \quad \text{and} \quad H_2' = E(H_1 \oplus c, H_2 \| M) \oplus H_1$$

where E denotes PRESENT-128 and c is a non-zero constant that needs to be fixed [9]. Thus the chaining variable $H_1 \| H_2$ is 128 bits long and 64 bits of message-related input are hashed per iteration.

Hirose showed that, in the ideal cipher model, an adversary has to make at least 2^n queries to the cipher in order to find a collision with non-negligible advantage, where n is the block size of the cipher. It is possible to make the same kind of analysis for preimage resistance (see proof of Theorem 4 in [23]) and to show that any adversary has to make at least 2^{2n} queries to the cipher to find a preimage. As for Section 4.1 our implementation results are presented for both a parallel and serial implementation of PRESENT-128, see Table 2. These results should be viewed as indicative of the cost of a double-block-length construction using PRESENT. Since only one key schedule needs to be computed per iteration of the compression function, the Hirose construction is probably one of the most efficient constructions of this type, e.g. in the case of PRESENT around 1 000 GE can be saved in this way.

5   Compact Hashing for $\geq$ 160-Bit Hash Outputs

It is possible that some tag-enabled applications might need collision-resistance at a security level of 2^{80} operations. For this we need a hash output of 160 bits or greater. However this is where the problems really begin and we consider two directions.

For the first, we continue the approach of the paper so far and we consider building a hash function with a hash output greater than 160 bits from PRESENT *as is*. So in Section 5.1 we try to use PRESENT in this way and, using established results in the literature, we make a proposal. However, at the same time, we use the very same results to demonstrate that this approach is unlikely to be successful, a sentiment that is supported by our implementation results. Instead, for the second direction that is described in Section 5.2, we move towards a dedicated hash function though we keep elements of PRESENT in our constructions. Our dedicated proposals are deliberately simple and obvious, and in this way we aim to provide some first results on the impact different design choices might have in moving towards a new, compact, hash function.

5.1   Longer Hash Outputs Using PRESENT

Our goal is to build a hash function out of PRESENT that offers an output of at least 160 bits. Since PRESENT has a 64-bit block size, this means that we are forced to consider a triple-block-length construction and we will end up with a 192-bit hash function.

Unfortunately very few designs for l-block length hash function with $l \geq 3$ have been studied so far. However Peyrin *et al.* [41] have identified some necessary conditions for securely combining *compression functions* to obtain a new compression function with a longer output. We can use these results and so, in the case we consider here, our constituent compression functions will be based around PRESENT-128, *i.e.* we will use DM-PRESENT-128 as the building block.

More background to the construction framework is given in [41]. However, within this framework, efficiency demands that we keep to a minimum the number of compression functions that we need to use, where each compression function is instantiated by DM-PRESENT-128. For reasons of simplicity and greater design flexibility we restrict ourselves to processing only a single 64-bit message extract, and so our inputs to C-PRESENT-192, where we use C as shorthand for "constructed", consist of a quadruplet (H_1, H_2, H_3, M) while the output is a triplet (H'_1, H'_2, H'_3). The compression function C-PRESENT-192 is illustrated in Appendix I and the output is computed as

$$H'_1 = f^{(1)}(H_3, H_1, H_2) \oplus f^{(3)}(H_3 \oplus M, H_1, H_2) \oplus f^{(5)}(H_2, H_3, M)$$
$$H'_2 = f^{(1)}(H_3, H_1, H_2) \oplus f^{(4)}(H_1, H_3, M) \oplus f^{(6)}(H_1 \oplus H_2, H_3, M)$$
$$H'_3 = f^{(2)}(M, H_1, H_2) \oplus f^{(4)}(H_1, H_3, M) \oplus f^{(5)}(H_2, H_3, M) \ ,$$

with $f^{(i)}(A, B, C) = E(A \oplus c_{i-1}, B \| C) \oplus A$ for different constants c_i and E denotes encryption with PRESENT-128.

This construction might seem too complicated, but this is exactly the point we wish to make. The particular set of parameter values that are forced upon us when trying to build a large-output hash function from a small block cipher means that there will be *no* simple construction. More precisely, work in [41] shows that for *any* construction that uses a compression function with parameters equivalent to PRESENT-128 along with linear mixing layers to combine chaining variables and intermediate values, at least six compression functions are needed to resist all currently-known generic attacks. We *must* therefore use at least six independent calls to DM-PRESENT-128. The construction C-PRESENT-192 attains this minimum and more details of the construction are given in Appendix I. Our implementation results and estimates are given in Table 2, but the performance profile for C-PRESENT-192 suggests that building directly on PRESENT is unlikely to be a good way forward. Instead we consider some dedicated elements.

5.2   Dedicated Design Elements Inspired by PRESENT

Hash function design is notoriously difficult and so an interesting first step is to identify some general approaches and to understand their security and performance trade-offs. In this section we describe the results of some prototyping which tests a range of approaches and provides good background to our ongoing work. Our basic premise is to stay close to the design elements of PRESENT and to modify the design so as to give a block cipher with a much larger block size. We then adapt the key schedule in two alternative ways with the first being a natural proposal and the second having strong similarities to Whirlpool [3]. We give implementation results for both approaches.

Our schemes will continue to be based on the Davies-Meyer (DM) scheme $H_{i+1} = E(H_i, M_i) \oplus H_i$ though the form of our encryption function E will now change. In general, the encryption function E can be described as:

$$E : \mathbb{F}_2^n \times \mathbb{F}_2^k \to \mathbb{F}_2^n \ ,$$
$$E : \text{PLAINTEXT} \times \text{KEY} \mapsto \text{CIPHERTEXT}$$

The detailed description of PRESENT can be found in [6]. At a top-level we can write the r-round encryption of the plaintext STATE as:

for $i = 1$ to r **do**
    STATE $\leftarrow$ STATE $\oplus$ eLayer(KEY, i)
    STATE $\leftarrow$ sBoxLayer(STATE)
    STATE $\leftarrow$ pLayer(STATE)
    KEY $\leftarrow$ genLayer(KEY, i)
end for
STATE $\leftarrow$ STATE $\oplus$ eLayer(KEY, $r+1$),

where eLayer describes how a subkey is combined with a cipher STATE, sBoxLayer and pLayer describe how the STATE evolves, and genLayer is used to describe the generation of the next subkey.

When used in the DM mode we recast the plaintext and ciphertext as hash function STATE and use the (formatted) message extract as the key. For ease of design we will choose the parameters k and n so that $k|n$ and $4|n$, and both our proposals will have the following (unmodified) structure:

for $i = 1$ to r **do**
    STATE $\leftarrow$ STATE $\oplus$ eLayer(MESSAGE, i)
    STATE $\leftarrow$ sBoxLayer(STATE)
    STATE $\leftarrow$ pLayer(STATE)
    MESSAGE $\leftarrow$ genLayer(MESSAGE, i)
end for
STATE $\leftarrow$ STATE $\oplus$ eLayer(MESSAGE, $r+1$)

The following building blocks are unchanged between the two proposals and are merely generalizations of the PRESENT structure to larger 160-bit block sizes.

1. sBoxLayer: This denotes use of the PRESENT 4-bit to 4-bit S-box S and it is applied $n/4$ times in parallel.
2. pLayer: This is an extension of the PRESENT bit-permutation and moves bit i of STATE to bit position $P(i)$, where

$$P(i) = \begin{cases} i \cdot n/4 \mod n-1, & \text{if } i \in \{0, \ldots, n-2\} \\ n-1, & \text{if } i = n-1. \end{cases}$$

It is in the specification of genLayer, which transforms the message of length k from round-to-round, and eLayer : $\mathbb{F}_2^k \to \mathbb{F}_2^n$, that describes how the message extract is combined with cipher state, that the two proposals differ.

PROP-1. For ease of comparison with PRESENT we keep exactly the same 80-bit key input and the same 80-bit key schedule. Thus we modify a 160-bit chaining variable using an 80-bit message input and, to make an implementation estimate, we use 64 rounds. This is equivalent to the parameters $n = 160$, $k = 80$, and $r = 64$. The sBoxLayer and pLayer are as above and eLayer and genLayer are described as follows:

1. eLayer(MESSAGE, i) = MESSAGE $\|$ genLayer(MESSAGE, i)
2. genLayer(MESSAGE, i) is defined as the 80-bit key schedule of PRESENT. Thus, MESSAGE is rotated by 61 bit positions to the left, the left-most four bits are passed through the PRESENT S-box, and the round counter i is exclusive-ored with some bits of MESSAGE.

In words, we use the key schedule of PRESENT-80 exactly as is and at each round we use what would be two successive 80-bit round keys. At each round the key schedule is updated only once, so the same subkey is used once on the right-hand side and, in the following round, on the left-hand side.

PROP-2. For the second proposal, we consider a structure that has some similarity to Whirlpool. Our parameter set is $n = 160$ and $k = 160$ which allows us to use a longer message extract at each iteration of the compression function. For prototyping and implementation estimates we set $r = 80$. The building blocks eLayer and genLayer are specified as:

1. eLayer(MESSAGE, i) = MESSAGE
2. genLayer(MESSAGE, i) = pLayer(sBoxLayer(MESSAGE $\oplus i$)), being just a copy of the data path with round constant addition.

In words, we imagine that our message extract is a 160-bit key and we process the key in a key-schedule that is identical to the encryption process.

We estimated the hardware figures for different architectures when implementing PROP-1 and PROP-2. Our implementation estimates range from a 4-bit width data path (highly serialized) up to a 160-bit width data path which offers one round of processing in one cycle. Since PROP-2 uses a very similar key schedule (*i.e.* message path) and encryption routine, we can give a further two different implementation options: one with a shared sBoxLayer between the data path and the message path and one with an individual sBoxLayer. The results are summarized below with the efficiency *eff.* being measured in bps/GE.

Understanding the best trade-offs for the different approaches is not easy. As one can see, all three implementations scale nicely, though it seems that PROP-2 is more efficient in terms of throughput per area when compared to PROP-1. On the other hand PROP-1 offers a lower minimal achievable gate count, though at the cost of a higher cycle count. Much would also depend on a thorough security analysis of any final proposal and while some initial analysis in Appendix II suggests the possibility of optimizations to an approach like PROP-2, this is something to explore in future work during the design of an explicit proposal.

data path width	PROP-1			PROP-2 (shared)			PROP-2 (ind.)		
	area (GE)	cycles	*eff.*	area (GE)	cycles	*eff.*	area (GE)	cycles	*eff.*
4	2 520	5 282	1.2	3 010	6 481	0.82	3 020	3 281	1.62
16	2 800	1 322	4.33	3 310	1 621	2.92	3 380	821	5.77
32	3 170	662	7.64	3 730	811	5.11	3 860	411	10.09
80	4 270	266	14.09	4 960	325	9.29	5 300	165	18.3
160	4 830	134	24.73	5 730	163	15.29	6 420	83	30.03

6 Implementation of the Standard Constructions

To consider the efficiency of the standard constructions, we implemented two different architectures (round-based and serial) in VHDL and simulated using *Mentor*

Table 2. The performance of different hash functions based on the direct application of PRESENT. For comparison with our hash functions with 128-bit output we include estimates for the AES-based 128-bit hash function in Davies-Meyer mode. For comparison with MAME we include estimates for the 256-bit hash function built from the AES in Hirose's construction.

	Hash output size	Data path size	Cycles per block	Throughput at 100KHz (Kbps)	Efficiency (bps/GE)	Logic process	Area GE
MD4 [17]	128	32	456	112.28	15.3	$0.13\mu m$	7 350
MD5 [17]	128	32	612	83.66	10	$0.13\mu m$	8 400
SHA-1 [17]	160	32	1 274	40.19	4.9	$0.35\mu m$	8 120
SHA-256 [17]	256	32	1 128	45.39	4.2	$0.35\mu m$	10 868
MAME [53]	256	256	96	266.67	32.9	$0.18\mu m$	8 100
In this paper							
DM-PRESENT-80	64	64	33	242.42	109.5	$0.18\mu m$	2 213
DM-PRESENT-80	64	4	547	14.63	9.1	$0.18\mu m$	1 600
DM-PRESENT-128	64	128	33	387.88	153.3	$0.18\mu m$	2 530
DM-PRESENT-128	64	4	559	22.9	12.1	$0.18\mu m$	1 886
H-PRESENT-128	128	128	32	200	47	$0.18\mu m$	4 256
H-PRESENT-128	128	8	559	11.45	4.9	$0.18\mu m$	2 330
C-PRESENT-192	192	192	108	59.26	7.4	$0.18\mu m$	8 048
C-PRESENT-192	192	12	3 338	1.9	0.41	*estimate*	4 600
AES-based *DM scheme*	128	8	> 1 032	< 12.4	< 2.8	*estimate*	> 4 400
AES-based *Hirose scheme*	256	8	> 1 032	< 12.4	< 1.3	*estimate*	> 9 800

Graphics Modelsim SE PLUS 6.3a. Synopsys DesignCompiler version *Z-2007.03-SP5* was used to synthesize the design to the *Virtual Silicon* (VST) standard cell library *UMCL18G212T3*, which is based on the *UMC L180 0.18μm 1P6M* logic process and has a typical voltage of 1.8 Volt. For synthesis we advised the compiler to use a clock frequency of 100 KHz, a typical operating frequency for RFID applications.

We used *Synopsys Power Compiler* version *Z-2007.03-SP5* to estimate the power consumption of our implementations. At a clock frequency of 100 KHz DM-PRESENT-80 consumes 6.28 μW in the round-based implementation and 1.83 μW in the serialized implementation. The figures for the other designs are as follows: DM-PRESENT-128 7.49 μW and 2.94 μW, H-PRESENT-128 8.09 μW and 6.44 μW, and C-PRESENT-192 9.31 μW (round-based). Note that it is not easily possible to compare power consumption of designs implemented in different technologies, hence we did not include these figures in Table 2. However, the figures for SHA-256 (15.87 μW) and SHA-1 (10.68 μW) provided by Feldhofer et Rechberger [17] are in the same range as ours.

The area requirements of DM-PRESENT-80 and DM-PRESENT-128 comprise of the area requirements of the appropriate PRESENT cores and a 64-bit register to store the chaining variable (around 510 GE). Additionally, in the round-based variants a 64-bit XOR gate (170 GE) is required and in the serial variants a 4-bit XOR gate (10 GE).[3]

---

[3] Note that contrary to the constructions presented in this article the round-based PRESENT cores do not require a finite state machine nor do they contain clock-gated flip-flops. Therefore all in this paper presented constructions require additional logic which increases the area.

For the area estimates of the AES-based *Davies-Meyer* and *Hirose* schemes we used the smallest known (3 400 GE) AES implementation [16]. We estimated the area requirements for storing one bit to be 8 GE as stated in [16]. For the AES-based *Davies-Meyer scheme* we assumed that at least one additional register would be required to store the 128-bit value H_1 (1 024 additional GE), summing up to at least 4 400 GE in total.

The H-PRESENT-128 implementation consists of a modified PRESENT-128 core, a PRESENT data path (1 010 GE), a 64-bit register for the chaining variable (510 GE), and two 64-bit multiplexer (340 GE). Additionally, the round-based variant requires two 64-bit XOR gates (340 GE) and the serial variant two 4-bit XOR gates (20 GE). The AES-based *Hirose scheme* requires an AES implementation with 256-bit key length. However, no such low-cost implementation has been reported so far. Therefore we estimate the area requirements starting from the Feldhofer *et al.* [16] implementation with a 128-bit key. At least 128 additional key bits (1 024 GE) have to be stored to achieve an AES implementation with 256 bits key length, summing up to at least 4 400 GE. The *Hirose scheme* requires two instantiations of the block cipher and the storage of one intermediate value H_1, which has the same size as the block size. All together we estimate the AES-based *Hirose scheme* to require at least 9 800 GE. The serial variant of C-PRESENT-192 was not implemented, because the figures for the round-based variant and the estimations indicate large area requirements with more than 4 500 GE. In fact this large area requirement for both variants of C-PRESENT-192 was the main reason to look for other constructions such as PROP-1 and PROP-2.

Table 2 summarizes our results and compares them to other hashing functions and AES-based schemes. When the hash output length is 128 bits or lower, a construction based around PRESENT seems to have potential. Certainly they are far more competitive than current hash functions, the primary reason being that there exist efficient block cipher-based constructions for this size of hash output. Even a larger block cipher such as AES makes for a more compact hash function than current dedicated designs at this security level, though the throughput suffers.

7   Conclusions

While compact hash functions are often proposed in protocols for RFID tags, there are currently no sufficiently compact candidates to hand. Here we have explored the possibility of building a hash function out of a block cipher such as PRESENT. We have described hash functions that offer 64- and 128-bit outputs based on current design strategies. For their parameter sets these are the most compact hash function candidates available today. In particular, H-PRESENT-128 requires around 4 000 GE, which is similar to the best known AES implementation and about 50% smaller than the best reported MD5 implementation. At the same time, H-PRESENT-128 requires between 20–30 *times* fewer clock cycles than compact AES and MD5 implementations, giving it a major time-area advantage.

Obviously 128-bit hash functions are relevant for applications where a security-performance trade-off is warranted. To obtain larger hash outputs there are severe complications and we suspect that dedicated designs could be more appropriate. Clearly there are many areas of open research, not least the design of very compact hash functions. In parallel, it might also be worth revisiting tag-based protocols that use hash functions to see if the same goals can be achieved in a different way.

References

1. An, Y., Oh, S.: RFID System for User's Privacy Protection. In: IEEE Asia-Pacific Conference on Communications, pp. 16–519. IEEE Computer Society, Los Alamitos (2005)
2. Avoine, G., Oechslin, P.: A Scalable and Provably Secure Hash-based RFID Protocol. In: 3rd IEEE Conference on Pervasive Computing and Communications Workshops (PerCom 2005 Workshops), pp. 110–114. IEEE Computer Society, Los Alamitos (2005)
3. Baretto, P., Rijmen, V.: The Whirlpool Hashing Function, http://paginas.terra.com.br/informatica/-paulobarreto/WhirlpoolPage.html
4. Biham, E., Dunkelman, O.: A Framework for Iterative Hash Functions - HAIFA. Presented at Second NIST Cryptographic Hash Workshop, August 24-25 (2006), csrc.nist.gov/groups/ST/hash/
5. Black, J., Rogaway, P., Shrimpton, T.: Black-Box Analysis of the Block-Cipher-Based Hash-Function Constructions from PGV. In: Yung, M. (ed.) CRYPTO 2002. LNCS, vol. 2442, pp. 320–335. Springer, Heidelberg (2002)
6. Bogdanov, A., Knudsen, L.R., Leander, G., Paar, C., Poschmann, A., Robshaw, M.J.B., Seurin, Y., Vikkelsoe, C.: Present: An Ultra-Lightweight Block Cipher. In: Paillier, P., Verbauwhede, I. (eds.) CHES 2007. LNCS, vol. 4727, pp. 450–466. Springer, Heidelberg (2007)
7. Rolfes, C., Poschmann, A., Leander, G., Paar, C.: Ultra-Lightweight Implementations for Smart Devices - Security for 1000 Gate Equivalents. In: CARDIS 2008. Springer, Heidelberg (to appear, 2008)
8. Brown, L., Pieprzyk, J., Seberry, J.: LOKI - A Cryptographic Primitive for Authentication and Secrecy Applications. In: Seberry, J., Pieprzyk, J.P. (eds.) AUSCRYPT 1990. LNCS, vol. 453, pp. 229–236. Springer, Heidelberg (1990)
9. Chang, D.: A Practical Limit of Security Proof in the Ideal Cipher Model: Possibility of Using the Constant As a Trapdoo. In: Several Double Block Length Hash Functions. IACR Cryptology ePrint Archive, Report 2006/481, http://eprint.iacr.org/2006/481
10. Coppersmith, D., Pilpel, S., Meyer, C.H., Matyas, S.M., Hyden, M.M., Oseas, J., Brachtl, B., Schilling, M.: Data authentication using modification detection codes based on a public one way encryption function. U.S. Patent No. 4,908,861 (March 13, 1990)
11. Damgård, I.: A Design Principle for Hash Functions. In: Brassard, G. (ed.) CRYPTO 1989. LNCS, vol. 435, pp. 416–427. Springer, Heidelberg (1990)
12. Dean, R.D.: Formal Aspects of Mobile Code Security. PhD thesis, Princeton University (1999)
13. Dimitriou, T.: A Lightweight RFID Protocol to Protect Against Traceability and Cloning Attacks. In: Proceedings of IEEE International Conference on Security and Privacy of Emerging Areas in Communication Networks (SecureComm 2005), pp. 59–66. IEEE Computer Society, Los Alamitos (2005)
14. ECRYPT Network of Excellence. The Stream Cipher Project: eSTREAM, http://www.ecrypt.eu.org/stream
15. Good, T., Chelton, W., Benaissa, M.: Hardware Results for Selected Stream Cipher Candidates. In: SASC 2007 (February 2007), http://www.ecrypt.eu.org/stream/
16. Feldhofer, M., Dominikus, S., Wolkerstorfer, J.: Strong Authentication for RFID Systems Using the AES Algorithm. In: Joye, M., Quisquater, J.-J. (eds.) CHES 2004. LNCS, vol. 3156, pp. 357–370. Springer, Heidelberg (2004)

17. Feldhofer, M., Rechberger, C.: A Case Against Currently Used Hash Functions in RFID Protocols. In: Meersman, R., Tari, Z., Herrero, P. (eds.) OTM 2006 Workshops. LNCS, vol. 4277, pp. 372–381. Springer, Heidelberg (2006)

18. Gao, X., Xian, Z., Wang, H., Shen, J., Huang, J., Song, S.: An Approach to Security and Privacy of RFID System for Supply Chain. In: IEEE International Conference on E-Commerce Technology for Dynamic E-Business, pp. 164–168. IEEE Computer Society, Los Alamitos (2004)

19. Handschuh, H., Knudsen, L.R., Robshaw, M.J.B.: Analysis of SHA-1 in Encryption Mode. In: Naccache, D. (ed.) CT-RSA 2001. LNCS, vol. 2020, pp. 70–83. Springer, Heidelberg (2001)

20. Henrici, D., Götze, J., Müller, P.: A Hash-based Pseudonymization Infrastructure for RFID Systems. In: Georgiadis, P., Lopez, J., Gritzalis, S., Marias, G. (eds.) SecPerU 2006, pp. 22–27. IEEE Computer Society Press, Los Alamitos (2006)

21. Hirose, S.: Provably Secure Double-Block-Length Hash Functions in a Black-Box Model. In: Park, C.-s., Chee, S. (eds.) ICISC 2004. LNCS, vol. 3506, pp. 330–342. Springer, Heidelberg (2005)

22. Hirose, S.: Some Plausible Constructions of Double-Block-Length Hash Functions. In: Robshaw, M.J.B. (ed.) FSE 2006. LNCS, vol. 4047, pp. 210–225. Springer, Heidelberg (2006)

23. Hirose, S.: How to Construct Double-Block-Length Hash Functions. In: Second Cryptographic Hash Workshop, Santa Barbara (August 2006)

24. Hong, D., Sung, J., Hong, S., Lim, J., Lee, S., Koo, B.-S., Lee, C., Chang, D., Lee, J., Jeong, K., Kim, H., Kim, J., Chee, S.: HIGHT: A New Block Cipher Suitable for Low-Resource Device. In: Goubin, L., Matsui, M. (eds.) CHES 2006. LNCS, vol. 4249, pp. 46–59. Springer, Heidelberg (2006)

25. Joux, A.: Multi-Collisions in Iterated Hash Functions. Application to Cascaded Constructions. In: Franklin, M. (ed.) CRYPTO 2004. LNCS, vol. 3152, pp. 306–316. Springer, Heidelberg (2004)

26. Juels, A., Weis, S.A.: Authenticating Pervasive Devices With Human Protocols. In: Shoup, V. (ed.) CRYPTO 2005. LNCS, vol. 3621, pp. 198–293. Springer, Heidelberg (2005)

27. Kelsey, J., Schneier, B.: Second Preimages on n-bit Hash Functions for Much Less than 2^n Work. In: Cramer, R.J.F. (ed.) EUROCRYPT 2005. LNCS, vol. 3494, pp. 474–490. Springer, Heidelberg (2005)

28. Knudsen, L.R., Lai, X.: New Attacks on all Double Block Length Hash Functions of Hash Rate 1, Including the Parallel-DM. In: De Santis, A. (ed.) EUROCRYPT 1994. LNCS, vol. 950, pp. 410–418. Springer, Heidelberg (1995)

29. Lai, X., Massey, J.L.: Hash Functions Based on Block Ciphers. In: Rueppel, R.A. (ed.) EUROCRYPT 1992. LNCS, vol. 658, pp. 55–70. Springer, Heidelberg (1993)

30. Lai, X., Waldvogel, C., Hohl, W., Meier, T.: Security of Iterated Hash Functions Based on Block Ciphers. In: Stinson, D.R. (ed.) CRYPTO 1993. LNCS, vol. 773, pp. 379–390. Springer, Heidelberg (1994)

31. Lee, S., Hwang, Y., Lee, D., Lim, J.: Efficient Authentication for Low-Cost RFID Systems. In: Gervasi, O., Gavrilova, M.L., Kumar, V., Laganá, A., Lee, H.P., Mun, Y., Taniar, D., Tan, C.J.K. (eds.) ICCSA 2005. LNCS, vol. 3480, pp. 619–627. Springer, Heidelberg (2005)

32. Lim, C., Korkishko, T.: mCrypton - A Lightweight Block Cipher for Security of Low-cost RFID Tags and Sensors. In: Song, J., Kwon, T., Yung, M. (eds.) WISA 2005. LNCS, vol. 3786, pp. 243–258. Springer, Heidelberg (2005)

33. Menezes, A.J., Vanstone, S.A., Van Oorschot, P.C.: Handbook of Applied Cryptography. CRC Press, Inc., Boca Raton (1996)

34. Merkle, R.C.: One Way Hash Functions and DES. In: Brassard, G. (ed.) CRYPTO 1989. LNCS, vol. 435, pp. 428–446. Springer, Heidelberg (1990)

35. National Institute of Standards and Technology. FIPS 46-3: Data Encryption Standard (DES) (October 1999), http://csrc.nist.gov

36. National Institute of Standards and Technology. FIPS 180-2: Secure Hash Standard (August 2002), http://csrc.nist.gov
37. National Institute of Standards and Technology. FIPS 197: Advanced Encryption Standard (AES) (November 2001), http://csrc.nist.gov
38. National Institute of Standards and Technology. FIPS 198: The Keyed-Hash Message Authentication Code (March 2002), http://csrc.nist.gov
39. Ohkubo, M., Suzuki, K., Kinoshita, S.: Cryptographic Approach to Privacy-Friendly Tags. In: RFID Privacy Workshop, MIT, Cambridge (2003)
40. Okeya, K.: Side Channel Attacks Against HMACs Based on Block-Cipher Based Hash Functions. In: Batten, L.M., Safavi-Naini, R. (eds.) ACISP 2006. LNCS, vol. 4058, pp. 432–443. Springer, Heidelberg (2006)
41. Peyrin, T., Gilbert, H., Muller, F., Robshaw, M.J.B.: Combining Compression Functions and Block Cipher-Based Hash Functions. In: Lai, X., Chen, K. (eds.) ASIACRYPT 2006. LNCS, vol. 4284, pp. 315–331. Springer, Heidelberg (2006)
42. Poschmann, A., Leander, G., Schramm, K., Paar, C.: New Lightweight DES Variants Suited for RFID Applications. In: Biryukov, A. (ed.) FSE 2007. LNCS, vol. 4593, pp. 196–210. Springer, Heidelberg (2007)
43. Preneel, B., Bosselaers, A., Govaerts, R., Vandewalle, J.: Collision-Free Hash Functions Based on Block Cipher Algorithms. In: Proceedings 1989 International Carnahan Conference on Security Technology, pp. 203–210. IEEE, Los Alamitos (1989)
44. Preneel, B.: Ph.D. thesis. Katholieke Universiteit Leuven (1993)
45. Quisquater, J.-J., Girault, M.: 2n-bit Hash-Functions Using n-bit Symmetric Block Cipher Algorithms. In: Quisquater, J.-J., Vandewalle, J. (eds.) EUROCRYPT 1989. LNCS, vol. 434, pp. 102–109. Springer, Heidelberg (1990)
46. Rivest, R.L.: RFC 1321: The MD5 Message-Digest Algorithm (April 1992), http://www.ietf.org/rfc/rfc1321.txt
47. Rogaway, P.: Efficient Instantiations of Tweakable Blockciphers and Refinements to Modes OCB and PMAC. In: Lee, P.J. (ed.) ASIACRYPT 2004. LNCS, vol. 3329, pp. 16–31. Springer, Heidelberg (2004)
48. Seurin, Y., Peyrin, T.: Security Analysis of Constructions Combining FIL Random Oracles. In: Biryukov, A. (ed.) FSE 2007. LNCS, vol. 4593, pp. 119–136. Springer, Heidelberg (2007)
49. Shamir, A.: SQUASH - a New MAC With Provable Security Properties for Highly Constrained Devices Such As RFID Tags. In: Nyberg, K. (ed.) FSE 2008, Springer, Heidelberg (to appear, 2008)
50. Steinberger, J.P.: The Collision Intractability of MDC-2 in the Ideal-Cipher Model. In: Naor, M. (ed.) EUROCRYPT 2007. LNCS, vol. 4515, pp. 34–51. Springer, Heidelberg (2007)
51. Wang, X., Yin, Y.L., Yu, H.: Finding Collisions in the Full SHA-1. In: Shoup, V. (ed.) CRYPTO 2005. LNCS, vol. 3621, pp. 17–36. Springer, Heidelberg (2005)
52. Wang, X., Yu, H.: How to Break MD5 and Other Hash Functions. In: Cramer, R.J.F. (ed.) EUROCRYPT 2005. LNCS, vol. 3494, pp. 19–35. Springer, Heidelberg (2005)
53. Yoshida, H., Watanabe, D., Okeya, K., Kitahara, J., Wu, J., Kucuk, O., Preneel, B.: MAME: A Compression Function With Reduced Hardware Requirements. In: Paillier, P., Verbauwhede, I. (eds.) CHES 2007. LNCS, vol. 4727, pp. 148–165. Springer, Heidelberg (2007)
54. Yu, Y., Yang, Y., Fan, Y., Min, H.: Security Scheme for RFID Tag. Auto-ID Labs white paper WP-HARDWARE-022, http://www.autoidlabs.org/

Appendix I

Using current best practice we outline a representative design for a 192-bit hash function, named C-PRESENT-192 in the text. Some of the background to the design and its implementation are given in Section 5.1 with some additional explanation below.

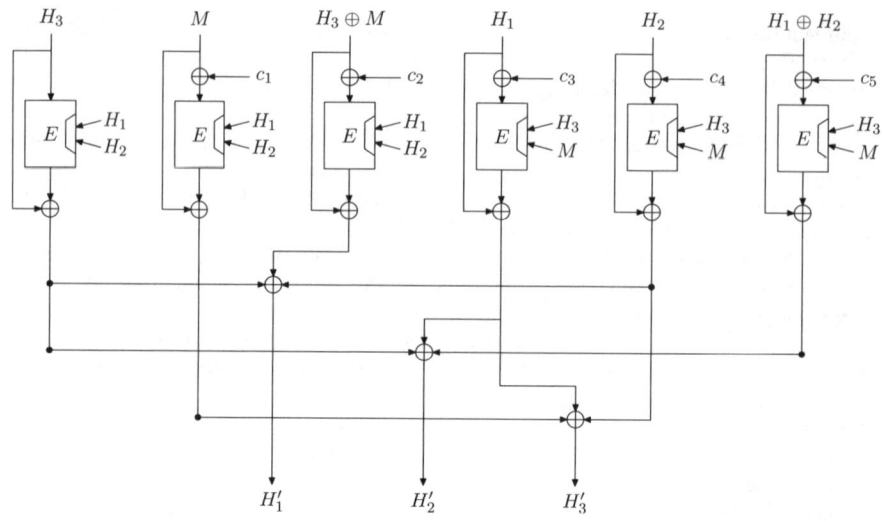

Motivation. Our goal was to design a 192-bit hash function using PRESENT as the fundamental building block and to use linear mixing layers both before and after the compression functions. Within this framework, it has been shown that the minimum number of compression functions that can be used is six. In addition, the output mapping should be a $(6,3,3)$ binary linear error-correcting code, while the input mapping must satisfy the following constraints:

1. Every external output block must depend on all external input blocks, no matter which invertible transformation of the external inputs and outputs is applied.
2. Every pair of external input blocks must appear as an identified pair for every invertible combination of external output blocks, where a pair (A,B) is said to be identified when A and B both appear within the internal inputs to some $f^{(i)}$, and this no matter which invertible transformation of the external inputs is applied.

The input mapping for our representative was selected from among those that satisfy these conditions and that also minimize the number of key schedules used to hash one block of message. By reducing the number of key schedules we increase the performance of the scheme and, potentially, reduce the space required by an implementation. It can be proved that for the parameter sets of interest to us here, the minimal number of key schedules is two.

For the results of Peyrin *et al.* to hold, the compression functions $f^{(i)}$ have to be *ideal* compression functions with respect to collision and preimage resistance (that is, finding a collision or a preimage must require on average $\Theta(2^{n/2})$ and $\Theta(2^n)$ evaluations of the function respectively) and must behave independently. Each inner compression function $f^{(i)}$ is built around PRESENT-128 in a way similar to the Davies-Meyer mode. That way, the results of Black *et al.* [5] ensure that, in the ideal cipher model, finding a collision (resp. a preimage) for the compression functions $f^{(i)}$ requires $\Theta(2^{n/2})$ (resp. $\Theta(2^n)$) queries to the cipher. Hence, in the ideal cipher model, each inner compression function $f^{(i)}$ is ideal in the sense defined above.

Making the six compression functions $f^{(i)}$ independent is not so easy. The most secure way to do this would be to "tweak" the block cipher with *e.g.* the XE or XEX construction of Rogaway [47]. However, these constructions are only efficient when one has to compute ciphertexts for the same key and many different tweaks, which is not our case. Using any known provably secure construction of a tweakable block cipher for the C-PRESENT-192 scheme would imply one supplementary cipher call for each key, thus increasing the number of block cipher calls per message block to eight. Instead we might consider using the same kind of technique that is used in the Hirose construction and we use five constants $c_1, \ldots, c_5$ to make the six instances of the compression function independent. In the absence of a structural weakness in PRESENT this is sufficient for our purposes. Further, we are trying to estimate the space required for a construction of this type and so this approach will help yield conservative estimates. The constants were chosen to be linearly independent and of low Hamming weight. They are given by $c_0 = 0$ and $c_i = (\texttt{0x0000000000000001}) \ll (i-1)$ for $i \geq 1$. While some limitations of this construction follow from [48], assuming we can consider the inner compression functions independent, Peyrin *et al.* show that there is no currently-known attack with *computational* complexity less than brute-force on the larger compression function.

Appendix II

Our proposed design elements are not intended to be specifications. Nevertheless, some preliminary analysis follows from the simple structures proposed. In particular, for a fixed message block and two different chaining values we can apply Theorem 1 of [6] directly. This states that at least 10 active S-boxes are involved in any 5-round differential characteristic. However, for the more important case of two different message blocks, the analysis has to be slightly modified. The following two results on the differential behavior of the proposals can be viewed as a first step towards a deeper analysis:

Theorem 1. *Let $P^{(3)}_{(\Delta_1,\Delta_2) \mapsto \Delta}$ be the probability of a differential characteristic over 3 rounds of PROP-1 with $\Delta_2 \neq 0$, i.e. the probability that*

$$\text{PROP-1}_3(H \oplus \Delta_1, M \oplus \Delta_2) = \text{PROP-1}_3(H, M) \oplus \Delta,$$

where PROP-1$_3$ denotes three rounds of PROP-1. Then each 3-round differential characteristic of this form has at least 4 active S-boxes and therefore $P^{(3)}_{(\Delta_1,\Delta_2) \mapsto \Delta} \leq 2^{-8}$.

Theorem 2. *Let $P_{(\Delta_1,\Delta_2) \mapsto \Delta}$ be the probability of a differential characteristic such that*

$$\text{PROP-2}(H \oplus \Delta_1, M \oplus \Delta_2) = \text{PROP-2}(H, M) \oplus \Delta$$

for $\Delta_2 \neq 0$. Then $P_{(\Delta_1,\Delta_2) \mapsto \Delta} \leq 2^{-400}$ for PROP-2.

Theorem 1 indicates that the probability of each 64-round differential characteristic can be upper-bounded by $(2^{-8})^{\frac{64}{3}} \approx 2^{-170}$. This observation as well as Theorem 2 show that the differential properties may be strong enough to thwart pre-image, second pre-image and collision attacks for the both proposals. Furthermore, Theorem 2 indicates that one could probably decrease the number of rounds in PROP-2 without unduly compromising the security. The most appropriate trade-off remains an area of research.

A New Bit-Serial Architecture for Field Multiplication Using Polynomial Bases

Arash Reyhani-Masoleh

Department of Electrical and Computer Engineering
The University of Western Ontario
London, Ontario, Canada
areyhani@uwo.ca

Abstract. Multiplication is the main finite field arithmetic operation in elliptic curve cryptography and its bit-serial hardware implementation is attractive in resource constrained environments such as smart cards, where the chip area is limited. In this paper, a new serial-output bit-serial multiplier using polynomial bases over binary extension fields is proposed. It generates a bit of the multiplication in each clock cycle with the latency of one cycle. To the best of our knowledge, this is the first time that such a serial-output bit-serial multiplier architecture using polynomial bases for general irreducible polynomials is proposed.

Keywords: Finite or Galois field, Mastrovito multiplier, polynomial basis, bit-serial multiplier.

1 Introduction

The multiplication over finite (or Galois) field $GF(2^m)$ is the main arithmetic operation in the elliptic curve cryptography [7,11] and choosing a suitable basis plays an important role in efficient implementation [6]. A field element can be represented using different bases, such as polynomial basis (PB), normal basis, and dual basis. Among them, representation of field elements using a polynomial basis is simpler and has received more attention for hardware implementation.

A hardware implementation of a finite field multiplier can be categorized either as a bit-parallel or bit-serial type. In a bit-parallel multiplier over $GF(2^m)$, once $2m$ bits of two inputs are received, m bits of the product are obtained together at the output after a propagation delay through various logic gates. Such a parallel type multiplier (see for example [16,10,15,5,18,13,12]) requires $O(m^2)$ number of gates. On the other hand, a bit-serial multiplier takes m clock cycles for one multiplication using $O(m)$ number of gates.

Bit-serial multipliers can be categorized into two types of either parallel or serial output. In the parallel-output bit-serial (POBS) multipliers, all m output bits of the product are available at the end of the m-th cycle, whereas serial-output bit-serial (SOBS) multipliers generate one bit of the product in each of these m cycles. Examples of the former type includes the well known LSB- and MSB-first bit-serial polynomial basis multipliers [14,3] and the normal basis

E. Oswald and P. Rohatgi (Eds.): CHES 2008, LNCS 5154, pp. 300–314, 2008.

multiplier due to Agnew et al. [1] while those of the latter type are Berlekamp's bit-serial dual basis multiplier [2] and Massey-Omura's original bit-serial normal basis multiplier [8]. Usually, POBS multipliers run at a much higher clock rate than their SOBS counterparts. However, the latency to generate the first bit of the product in the SOBS multipliers is one clock cycle as compared to m clock cycles for the POBS ones. Therefore, in applications that require implementation on resource constrained environment such as smart cards, SOBS multipliers result in faster overall computation than POBS multipliers since such a system is usually running at low operating clock frequency. In this paper, we propose a new SOBS PB multiplier for a general irreducible polynomial. To the best of our knowledge, this is the first time that a SOBS PB multiplier is proposed for general polynomials.

The organization of this article is as follows. In Section 2, the traditional bit-serial architectures for PB multiplication over $GF(2^m)$ are introduced. In Section 3, the matrix formulations for the PB multiplication is revisited. Then, we derive formulations for the proposed multiplier structure. A new serial-output bit-serial multiplier is proposed in Section 4. Finally, conclusions are given in Section 5.

2   Traditional Bit-Serial Multipliers over $GF(2^m)$

The finite field $GF(2^m)$ consists of 2^m field elements and is constructed by the polynomial basis $\{1, \alpha, \alpha^2, \cdots, \alpha^{m-1}\}$, where α is a root of the irreducible polynomial

$$P(x) = x^m + \sum_{i=1}^{\omega-2} x^{t_i} + 1. \tag{1}$$

In (1), $1 \le t_0 < t_1 < \cdots < t_{\omega-2}$, and ω is the number of non-zero terms. Then, each field element $B \in GF(2^m)$ can be written with respect to this basis as

$$B = (b_{m-1}, \cdots, b_1, b_0) = \sum_{i=0}^{m-1} b_i \alpha^i, \ b_i \in \{0, 1\}, \tag{2}$$

where b_is are the coordinates of B. For convenience, these coordinates will be denoted in vector notation as

$$\mathbf{b} = [b_0, b_1, \cdots, b_{m-1}]^T, \tag{3}$$

where T denotes the transposition of a vector or a matrix.

There are two types of bit-serial, namely LSB-first and MSB-first, multipliers [3]. The LSB-first bit-serial multiplier is shown in Figure 1(a). In this multiplier structure, both $X = \langle x_{m-1}, \cdots, x_1, x_0 \rangle$ and $Y = \langle y_{m-1}, \cdots, y_1, y_0 \rangle$ are m bit registers. Let $X(n)$ and $Y(n)$ denote the contents of X and Y at the n-th, $0 \le n \le m$, clock cycle, respectively. Suppose the X register in Figure 1(a) is initialized with A, i.e., $X(0) = A$, then the output of this register at the n-th clock cycle is $X(n) = X^{(n)} \in GF(2^m)$, which is calculated from the input of this register, i.e., $X^{(n-1)}$, using the α module shown in Figure 1(a) as

$$X^{(n)} = \alpha \cdot X^{(n-1)} \bmod P(\alpha), \quad 1 \le n \le m-1, \tag{4}$$

where $X^{(0)} = A$. Also, suppose that the register Y is initially cleared, i.e., $Y(0) = 0$. Then, one can obtain the content of Y at the first clock cycle as $Y(1) = b_0 A$ and in general at the n-th clock cycle as $Y(n) = b_0 A + \sum_{i=1}^{n-1} b_i X(i), 1 < n \le m$. Let C denote the PB multiplication of A and B, i.e., $C = AB \bmod P(\alpha)$. Then, using (2) and (4) recursively, one can obtain

$$C = \sum_{i=0}^{m-1} b_i \cdot ((A\alpha^i) \bmod P(\alpha)) \tag{5}$$

$$= \sum_{i=0}^{m-1} b_i \cdot X^{(i)}, \tag{6}$$

and noting the fact that $X(n) = X^{(n)}$, one can determine that after m clock cycles Y contains $C = AB \bmod P(\alpha) \in GF(2^m)$, i.e., $Y(m) = C$. The implementation of $b_i \cdot X^{(i)}$ in (6) is done using m 2-input AND gates. This is shown with the double circle module with a dot inside in Figure 1(a). Also, the sum operation in (6) is implemented with m 2-input XOR gates which is shown with a double circle module with a plus inside. Since the coordinates of B enter the multiplier from the least significant bit (LSB), i.e., b_0, this multiplier is referred to as the LSB first bit-serial multiplier.

The MSB-first bit-serial multiplier is shown in Figure 1(b). This structure implements

$$C = (((b_{m-1}A\alpha + b_{m-2}A)\alpha + b_{m-3}A) + \cdots + b_1 A)\alpha + b_0 A, \tag{7}$$

where the mod $P(\alpha)$ operations after multiplications by α are omitted for simplicity. If the registers U and V are initialized with $A = (a_{m-1}, \cdots, a_1, a_0)$ and $0 = (0, \cdots, 0, 0)$, respectively, then one can verify that after the m-th clock cycle the register V contains the coordinates of C, i.e., $V(m) = C$. It is noted that for parallel load of inputs into the registers in Figure 1, multiplexers may be used. These are not shown in the figure for simplicity.

3   Matrix Formulations for PB Multiplication Revisited

In [10,9], Mastrovito showed that the coordinates of $C = AB \bmod P(\alpha)$ are obtained from the matrix-by-vector product of $\mathbf{c} = [c_0, c_1, \cdots, c_{m-1}]^T = \mathbf{M} \cdot \mathbf{b}$, where $\mathbf{M}$ is an $m \times m$ binary matrix whose entries depend on the coordinates of A and the entries of the *reduction matrix* $\mathbf{Q} = [q_{i,j}], 0 \le i \le m-2, 0 \le j \le m-1$, defined by [9]

$$[\alpha^m, \alpha^{m+1}, \cdots, \alpha^{2m-2}]^T \equiv \mathbf{Q}[1, \alpha, \cdots, \alpha^{m-1}]^T \pmod{P(\alpha)}. \tag{8}$$

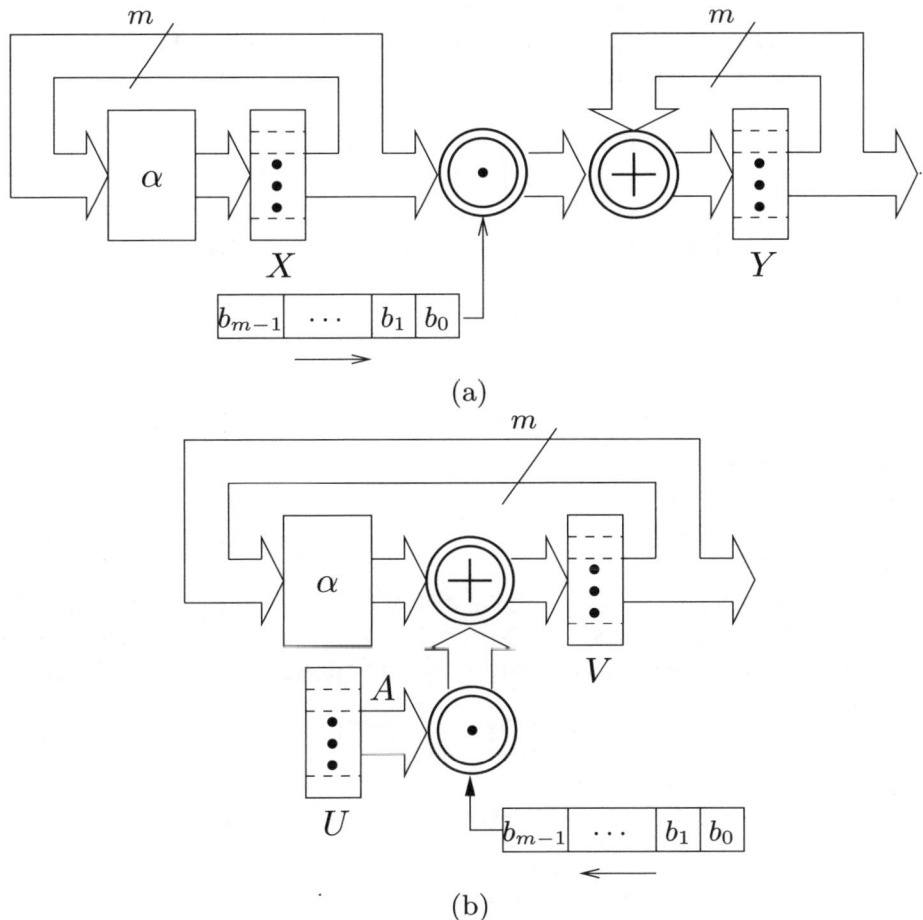

Fig. 1. (a) LSB first bit-serial multiplier. (b) MSB first bit-serial multiplier.

The Mastrovito matrix $\mathbf{M}$ has been studied in [15] and [5] for irreducible trinomials and arbitrary polynomials, respectively. Then, a systematic design to obtain the Mastrovito matrix $\mathbf{M}$ for general irreducible polynomials is presented in [18].

To find the PB multiplication, another approach is proposed in [17] and [12] for irreducible trinomials and arbitrary polynomials, respectively. The multiplication operation in this approach consists of two parts of the *product* of two field elements $A = (a_{m-1}, \cdots, a_1, a_0), B \in GF(2^m)$, i.e., AB, followed by the *modular reduction*, i.e., $C = AB \mod P(\alpha)$. Let us denote the result of the product of two polynomials

$$AB = \sum_{j=0}^{m-1} b_j \alpha^j A = D + \alpha^m E, \tag{9}$$

where $D = (d_{m-1}, \cdots, d_1, d_0)$ and $E = (0, e_{m-2}, \cdots, e_1, e_0)$ are the field elements in $GF(2^m)$. It is shown in [12] that the coordinates of E and D can be obtained from the following:

$$
\mathbf{d} = \begin{bmatrix} d_0 \\ d_1 \\ \vdots \\ d_{m-1} \end{bmatrix} = \mathbf{Lb} = \begin{bmatrix} a_0 & 0 & \cdots & 0 \\ a_1 & a_0 & \cdots & 0 \\ \vdots & \vdots & \ddots & \vdots \\ a_{m-1} & a_{m-2} & \cdots & a_0 \end{bmatrix} \begin{bmatrix} b_0 \\ b_1 \\ \vdots \\ b_{m-1} \end{bmatrix},
\tag{10}
$$

$$
\mathbf{e} = \begin{bmatrix} e_0 \\ e_1 \\ \vdots \\ e_{m-2} \end{bmatrix} = \mathbf{Ub} = \begin{bmatrix} 0 & a_{m-1} & \cdots & a_2 & a_1 \\ 0 & 0 & \cdots & a_3 & a_2 \\ \vdots & \vdots & \ddots & \vdots & \vdots \\ 0 & 0 & \cdots & 0 & a_{m-1} \end{bmatrix} \begin{bmatrix} b_0 \\ b_1 \\ \vdots \\ b_{m-1} \end{bmatrix}.
\tag{11}
$$

Then, one can calculate the coordinates of $C = (c_{m-1}, \cdots, c_1, c_0)$ from the following reduction equation [12]

$$
\mathbf{c} = [c_0, c_1, \cdots, c_{m-1}]^T = \mathbf{d} + \mathbf{Q}^T \mathbf{e}.
\tag{12}
$$

Let us define the down shift of the matrix $\mathbf{S}$ by j rows as $\mathbf{S}[\downarrow j]$ and the right shift of $\mathbf{S}$ by i columns as $\mathbf{S}[\rightarrow i]$, where the emptied positions after the shifts are filled by zeros. Then, it is shown in [4] that the $\mathbf{Q}^T$ matrix in (12) can be represented as

$$
\mathbf{Q}^T = \sum_{i \in N} \sum_{j \in \mathcal{T}} \mathbf{I}_{\mathbf{m} \times (\mathbf{m-1})} [\downarrow j][\rightarrow i],
\tag{13}
$$

where the sets $N \subset \{0, 1, \cdots, m-1\}$, $\mathcal{T} = \{0, t_1, \cdots, t_{w-2}\}$ (see $P(x)$ in (1)) and

$$
\mathbf{I}_{\mathbf{m} \times (\mathbf{m-1})} = \begin{bmatrix} \mathbf{I}_{\mathbf{m-1} \times \mathbf{m-1}} \\ ----- \\ \mathbf{0}_{\mathbf{1} \times \mathbf{m-1}} \end{bmatrix}.
\tag{14}
$$

In (14), $\mathbf{I}_{\mathbf{m-1} \times \mathbf{m-1}}$ is an $m-1 \times m-1$ unity matrix and $\mathbf{0}_{\mathbf{1} \times \mathbf{m-1}}$ is a zero row vector with $m-1$ zero entries. Then, using (13), the matrix reduction equation of (12) is simplified in [4] to

$$
\mathbf{c} = \mathbf{d} + \sum_{j \in \mathcal{T}} \mathbf{e}'[\downarrow j],
\tag{15}
$$

where

$$
\mathbf{e}'[\downarrow j] = [\underbrace{0, \cdots, 0}_{j}, e_0', \cdots, e_{m-1-j}']^T \text{ for } j > 0,
\tag{16}
$$

and

$$
\mathbf{e}' = \mathbf{e}'[\downarrow 0] = [e_0', \cdots, e_{m-2}', 0]^T = \sum_{i \in N} \mathbf{I}_{\mathbf{m} \times (\mathbf{m-1})} [\rightarrow i] \mathbf{e}.
\tag{17}
$$

It is noted that to obtain the set $N \subset \{0, 1, \cdots, m-1\}$ in (17), one can use the algorithm proposed in [18]. For the irreducible polynomial $P(x)$ with the second highest degree $t_{\omega-2} \leq (m+1)/2$, it is proved in [4] that $N = \{0, m - t_{\omega-2}, \cdots, m - t_1\}$. In the following, we show another approach to find this set for arbitrary irreducible polynomial.

For a given irreducible polynomial $P(x)$ stated in (1), the reduction matrix defined in (8) is fixed. Thus, the entries of $\mathbf{Q}$ are constant, i.e., $q_{i,j} \in \{0, 1\}$, and can be found from (8) for the underlying polynomial $P(x)$. Let us assume the entries of column 0 of $\mathbf{Q}$, i.e., $q_{i,0}$, $0 \leq i \leq m - 2$, are given. Let n and r_j $(0 \leq j \leq n - 1)$ be the number of nonzero entries and their row positions of the column 0 in this matrix, respectively, i.e.,

$$q_{i,0} = 1, \text{ for } i \in \mathcal{R}, \tag{18}$$

where

$$\mathcal{R} = \{r_0, r_1, \cdots, r_{n-1}\}.$$

This column is equal to the row 0 of $\mathbf{Q}^T$ and is obtained from (13) for $j = 0$. Then, one can easily see that $\mathcal{R} = N$, i.e., the elements of N are the locations of non-zero entries of column 0 of the reduction matrix.

Remark 1. Using (8) and $x^m = \sum_{i=1}^{\omega-2} x^{t_i} + 1$ which is obtained from (1), one can easily see that $r_0 = 0$ for any irreducible polynomial [4].

Remark 2. It is noted that for the irreducible trinomial $P(x) = x^m + x + 1$, i.e., $t_{\omega-2} = 1$, $\omega = 3$, the column 0 of $\mathbf{Q}$ has only one nonzero entry, i.e., $n = 1$, which is in the row $r_0 = 0$.

Remark 3. If $t_{\omega-2} > 1$, then the second nonzero entry in the column 0 of $\mathbf{Q}$ is $r_1 = m - t_{\omega-2}$.

In the following, we slightly simplify $\mathbf{e}'$ in (17) to present the key formulation for the proposed SOBS multiplier. Since

$$\mathbf{I}_{\mathbf{m}\times(\mathbf{m}-\mathbf{1})}[\rightarrow \mathbf{i}] = \left[\mathbf{0}_{\mathbf{m}\times\mathbf{i}} \left| \begin{array}{c} \mathbf{I}_{\mathbf{m}-\mathbf{1}-\mathbf{i}\times\mathbf{m}-\mathbf{1}-\mathbf{i}} \\ ----- \\ \mathbf{0}_{\mathbf{i}+\mathbf{1}\times\mathbf{m}-\mathbf{1}-\mathbf{i}} \end{array} \right. \right], \tag{19}$$

one can see that $\mathbf{I}_{\mathbf{m}\times(\mathbf{m}-\mathbf{1})}[\rightarrow \mathbf{i}]\mathbf{e}$ is equal to the up shift of the vector $[e_0, \cdots, e_{m-2}, 0]^T$ by i rows, i.e.,

$$\mathbf{e}[\uparrow i] = [e_i, \cdots, e_{m-2}, \underbrace{0, \cdots, 0}_{i+1}]^T. \tag{20}$$

Therefore, we conclude the above discussion to state the following.

Lemma 1. *Let the finite field $GF(2^m)$ be constructed by the general irreducible polynomial $P(x) = x^m + \sum_{i=1}^{\omega-2} x^{t_i} + 1$, then the coordinates of the PB multiplication of $C = AB \mod P(\alpha)$ can be obtained from two steps of*

$$\mathbf{e}' = [e_0', \cdots, e_{m-2}', 0]^T = \sum_{i \in \mathcal{R}} \mathbf{e}[\uparrow i] \tag{21}$$

followed by

$$c = d + \sum_{j \in \mathcal{T}} e'[\downarrow j], \tag{22}$$

where d, e, $e[\uparrow i]$ *and* $e'[\downarrow j]$ *are obtained from (10), (11), (20) and (16), respectively.*

Proposition 1. *The reduction matrix method stated by (21) and (22) in Lemma 1 requires*

$$(m-1)(n+\omega-2) - \sum_{i=1}^{n-1} r_i - \sum_{j=1}^{\omega-2} t_j \tag{23}$$

number of two-input XOR gates with the critical path delay of at most

$$(\lceil \log_2 n \rceil + \lceil \log_2 \omega \rceil) T_X, \tag{24}$$

where T_X *is the time delay of an XOR gate.*

Proof. The number of bit-wise addition (XOR gates) required for (21) is

$$\sum_{i=1}^{n-1} (m-1-r_i) = (m-1)(n-1) - \sum_{i=1}^{n-1} r_i. \tag{25}$$

Similarly, implementation of (22) requires

$$m-1 + \sum_{j=1}^{\omega-2} (m-1-t_j) = (m-1)(\omega-1) - \sum_{j=1}^{\omega-2} t_j. \tag{26}$$

Thus, by adding (25) and (26), the proof of (23) is complete. The time delay of (24) is obtained if we add the delay of (21), i.e., $\lceil \log_2 n \rceil T_X$, with the delay of (22), i.e., $\lceil \log_2 \omega \rceil T_X$.

4   New Serial-Output Bit-Serial Multiplier

Unlike the bit-serial multipliers presented in Section 2, this multiplier generates one bit of the multiplication in each clock cycle with the latency of one clock cycle.

4.1   Architecture

In order to develop a bit-serial multiplier, Lemma 1 is used to generate the coordinates of C in the order of c_0, followed by $c_1, \cdots$, and c_{m-1}. The new architecture, which is referred to as serial-output bit-serial (SOBS) multiplier, is shown in Figure 2(a). It consists of one register $B = \langle b_0, b_1, \cdots, b_{m-1} \rangle$ which contains the coordinates of the field element $B = (b_{m-1}, \cdots, b_1, b_0)$ as well as three shift registers $L = \langle l_{m-1}, \cdots, l_1 \rangle$, $U = \langle u_{m-1}, \cdots, u_1, u_0 \rangle$, and $X = \langle x_1, x_2, \cdots, x_{t_{\omega-2}} \rangle$.

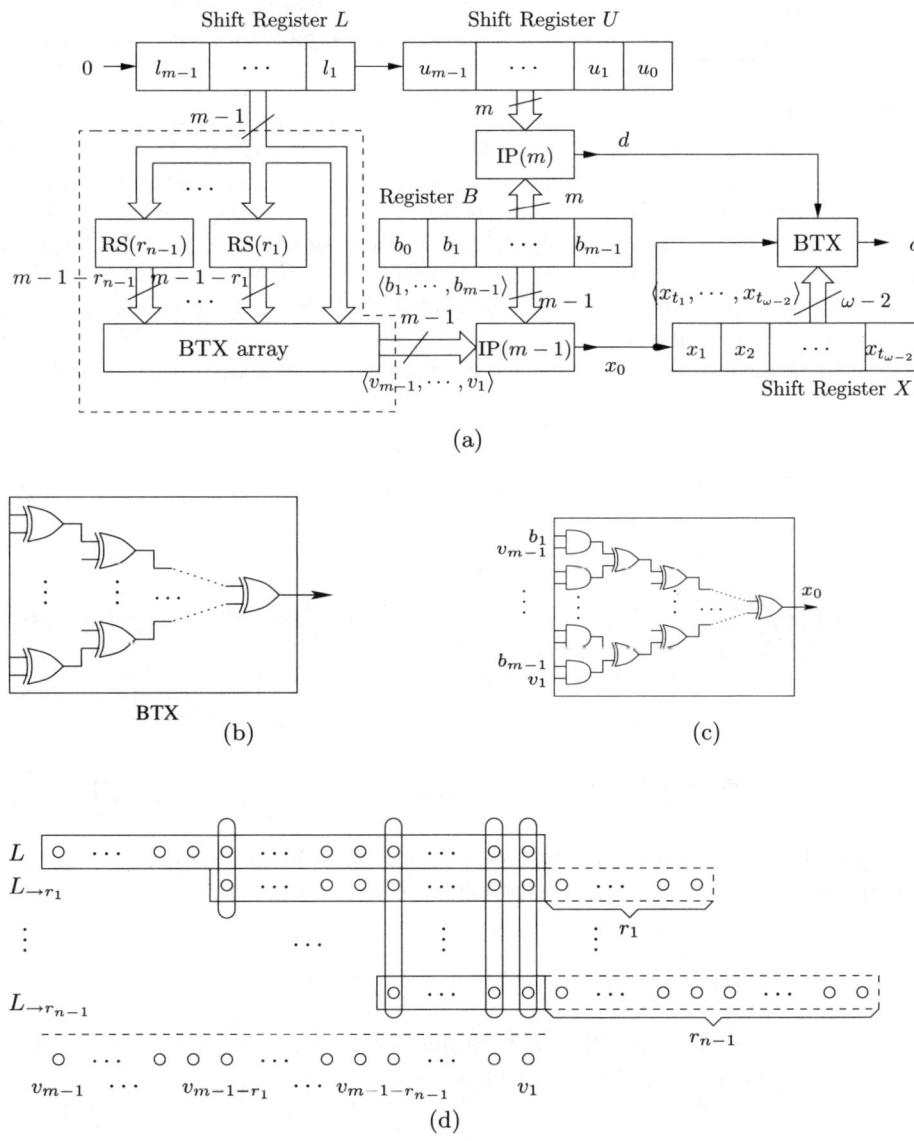

Fig. 2. (a) The architecture of serial output bit-serial (SOBS) PB multiplier over $GF(2^m)$. (b) The details of binary tree of XOR (BTX) gates. (c) The architecture of IP$(m-1)$, i.e., inner product with $m-1$ AND gates. (d) The BTX array output which requires $m-1-r_1$ BTXs.

As seen in this figure, the output of shift register L are connected to $n-1$ right shift (RS) blocks as well as the BTX array. The RS(r_i), $1 \le i \le n-1$, block shifts the $m-1-r_i$ left most input lines to the right by r_i positions. Let the input of the re-wiring $RS(r_i)$ block be $L = \langle l_{m-1}, \cdots, l_1 \rangle$, the output of the $RS(r_i)$ block is $L_{\to r_i} = \langle \underbrace{-, \cdots, -}_{r_i}, l_{m-1}, \cdots, l_{r_i+1} \rangle$, where $-$ denotes nothing is connected to those r_i left-most coordinates. The outputs of $RS(r_1)$ and $RS(r_{n-1})$ blocks, i.e., $L_{\to r_1}$ and $L_{\to r_{n-1}}$, respectively, are shown in Figure 2(b). This figure also shows how the outputs of the BTX array, i.e., $\langle v_{m-1}, \cdots, v_1 \rangle$, are obtained. As seen in Figure 2(b), the BTX array requires $m - 1 - r_1$ BTXs whose number of inputs vary from 2 to n. Specifically, it consists of $m - 1 - r_{n-1}$ BTXs with n inputs, $r_{n-1} - r_{n-2}$ BTXs with $n - 1$ inputs, $\cdots$, and $r_2 - r_1$ BTXs with 2 inputs, i.e., 2-input XOR gates. In general, the BTX array includes $r_{i+1} - r_i$ BTXs with $i + 1$ inputs for $1 \le i \le n - 1$ (assume $r_n = m - 1$). Therefore, as seen in Figure 2(b), the outputs of the BTX array, i.e., v_is, are obtain as follows:

$$
v_i = \begin{cases}
l_i, & \text{if } m - r_1 \le i \le m - 1 \\
l_i + l_{i+r_1}, & \text{if } m - r_2 \le i \le m - 1 - r_1 \\
l_i + l_{i+r_1} + l_{i+r_2}, & \text{if } m - r_3 \le i \le m - 1 - r_2 \\
\vdots & \vdots \\
l_i + \sum_{j=1}^{n-1} l_{i+r_j}, & \text{if } 1 \le i \le m - 1 - r_{n-1}.
\end{cases}
\tag{27}
$$

Using Figure 2(b) or (27), one can obtain the number of XOR gates required for realizing the BTX array in Figure 2(a) as

$$
\# \mathrm{XOR}_{BTX\ array} = \sum_{i=1}^{n-1} (m - 1 - r_i) = (n-1)(m-1) - \sum_{i=1}^{n-1} r_i.
\tag{28}
$$

Also, the time delay of the longest path between the inputs and outputs of the BTX array is $\lceil \log_2 n \rceil T_X$.

Figure 2(a) also consists of two inner product (IP) blocks as denoted by $IP(m)$ and $IP(m-1)$. Figure 2(c) shows the architecture of $IP(m-1)$ which implements

$$
x_0 = \sum_{i=1}^{m-1} b_i v_{m-i} = [v_{m-1}, \cdots, v_1][b_1, \cdots, b_{m-1}]^T
\tag{29}
$$

using $m - 1$ AND gates and $m - 2$ XOR gates with $T_A + \lceil \log_2(m - 1) \rceil T_X$ time delay. Similarly, the output of $IP(m)$ generates

$$
d = \sum_{i=0}^{m-1} b_i u_{m-i-1},
\tag{30}
$$

which requires m AND gates and $m - 1$ XOR gates with $T_A + \lceil \log_2 m \rceil T_X$ time delay.

4.2   Initialization and Multiplication Operation

In this section we show that by properly initialization of the shift registers, the bit-serial multiplier generates the coordinates of C in such a way that c_0 and c_{m-1} are the first and last bits output from c, respectively.

Let us initialize the shift register L and U with the coordinates of A as

$$L(0) = \langle a_{m-1}, \cdots, a_1 \rangle, \quad U(0) = \langle a_0, 0, \cdots, 0 \rangle. \tag{31}$$

In fact, only one bit of U, i.e., u_{m-1}, is initialized with a_0 and other bits are cleared. Also, the register B is initialized with the coordinates of B as $B(0) = \langle b_0, b_1, \cdots, b_{m-1} \rangle$ and its contents remains unchanged during each clock cycle until the end of multiplication process. Thus, we can state that $B(\tau) = \langle b_0, b_1, \cdots, b_{m-1} \rangle$ for $0 \leq \tau \leq m-1$, where τ denotes the number of clock cycles applied after initialization ($\tau = 0$). Also, we assume that the contents of the shift register X are cleared initially, i.e., $X(0) = \langle x_1, x_2, \cdots, x_{t_\omega-2} \rangle = \underbrace{\langle 0, 0, \cdots, 0 \rangle}_{t_\omega - 2}$.

It is noted that for parallel load of A and B into the registers L and B and the last bit of U, multiplexers may be used. Those are not shown in the figure for simplicity. However, for serial load such multiplexers are not needed.

Let $x_0(\tau)$ denote the output of $IP(m-1)$ in Figure 2(a) after the τ-th clock cycle. Then, by substituting (31) into (27) and using (29), one can obtain the initial value of the output of $IP(m-1)$ in Figure 2(a) as

$$x_0(0) = \left(\sum_{i \in \mathcal{R}} [\underbrace{0, \cdots, 0}_{i}, a_{m-1}, \cdots, a_{i+1}] \right) [b_1, \cdots, b_{m-1}]^T. \tag{32}$$

Using (11) and (21), one can simplify (32) to $x_0(0) = \sum_{i \in \mathcal{R}} e_i = e_0'$. Similarly, let $U(\tau)$ and $d(\tau)$ be the contents of the shift register U and signal d in Figure 2(a) after the τ-th, $0 \leq \tau \leq m-1$, clock cycle. Then, by using (10) and (30), one can see that

$$d(\tau) = \sum_{i=0}^{m-1} b_i u_{m-i-1}(\tau) = [a_\tau, \cdots, a_0, 0, \cdots, 0][b_0, b_1, \cdots, b_{m-1}]^T = d_\tau. \tag{33}$$

Thus, noting that the contents of register X are initially cleared, i.e., $x_j = 0$, $j \neq 0$, one can find that c in Figure 2(a) outputs c_0 after initialization, i.e.,

$$c(0) = \sum_{j \in \mathcal{T}} x_j(0) + d(0) = 0 + e_0' + d_0 = c_0.$$

In the following, we show that the output c in Figure 2(a) generates c_τ after the τ-th clock cycle. At this time, the coordinates of register L is changed from the initial value of $L(0) = \langle a_{m-1}, \cdots, a_1 \rangle$ to

$$L(\tau) = \left\langle \underbrace{0, \cdots, 0}_{\tau}, a_{m-1}, \cdots, a_{\tau+1} \right\rangle. \tag{34}$$

Then, using (32) with the new value of L, the output of $\mathrm{IP}(m-1)$ generates

$$x_0(\tau) = \left(\sum_{i \in \mathcal{R}} \underbrace{[0, \cdots, 0}_{i+\tau}, a_{m-1}, \cdots, a_{i+\tau+1}] \right) [b_1, \cdots, b_{m-1}]^T,$$

which simplifies to

$$x_0(\tau) = \sum_{i \in \mathcal{R}} e_{i+\tau} = e'_\tau \tag{35}$$

if (11) and (21) are used.

To obtain the output of c after the τ-th clock cycle, i.e., $c(\tau)$, we need to obtain the content of the shift register X, which are found as

$$x_i(\tau) = x_{i-1}(\tau - 1), \quad 1 \le i \le t_{\omega-2}. \tag{36}$$

By recursive using (36), one can find $x_i(\tau) = x_0(\tau - i)$ for $\tau \ge i$, which can be written to

$$x_i(\tau) = \begin{cases} e'_{\tau-i}, & \text{if } \tau \ge i, \\ 0 & \text{otherwise}, \end{cases} \tag{37}$$

if we use (35). Thus, the output of Figure 2(a) after the τ-th clock cycle is $c(\tau) = \sum_{j \in \mathcal{T}} x_j(\tau) + d(\tau)$. Therefore, by using (33), (35), (37) and Lemma 1, one can find $c(\tau) = c_\tau$.

4.3   An Example

We consider the field $GF(2^7)$ defined by the irreducible polynomial $P(x) = x^7 + x^5 + x^3 + x + 1$ for which the reduction matrix can be obtained as

$$\mathbf{Q} = \begin{bmatrix} 1 & 1 & 0 & 1 & 0 & 1 & 0 \\ 0 & 1 & 1 & 0 & 1 & 0 & 1 \\ 1 & 1 & 1 & 0 & 0 & 0 & 0 \\ 0 & 1 & 1 & 1 & 0 & 0 & 0 \\ 0 & 0 & 1 & 1 & 1 & 0 & 0 \\ 0 & 0 & 0 & 1 & 1 & 1 & 0 \end{bmatrix}. \tag{38}$$

It is seen from the column 0 of (38) that $n = 2$, $r_0 = 0$, and $r_1 = 2$. For this example, $\mathcal{R} = \{0, 2\}$ and $\mathcal{T} = \{0, 1, 3, 5\}$. Table 1 shows how Figure 2(a) generates the coordinates of C at each clock cycle τ.

4.4   Complexity Analysis

In this section, we obtain the space and time complexities of the proposed serial-output bit-serial (SOBS) multiplier.

Proposition 2. *For the finite field $GF(2^m)$ generated by the general irreducible ω-nomial $P(x) = x^m + \sum_{i=1}^{\omega-2} x^{t_i} + 1$, the SOBS PB multiplier (Figure 2(a)) requires $3m + t_{\omega-2} - 1$ 1-bit register, $2m - 1$ 2-input AND gates, and $(n+1)(m-1) + \omega - 2 - \sum_{i=1}^{n-1} r_i$ 2-input XOR gates.*

Table 1. The multiplication operation for $GF(2^7)$ generated by $x^7 + x^5 + x^3 + x + 1$

τ	$v_6, v_5, v_4, v_3, v_2, v_1$	x_0	x_1, x_2, x_3, x_4, x_5	d	$c = x_0 + x_1 + x_3 + x_5 + d$
0	$a_6, a_5, a_6 + a_4, a_5 + a_3, a_4 + a_2, a_3 + a_1$	e'_0	$0, 0, 0, 0, 0$	d_0	$e'_0 + d_0 = c_0$
1	$0, a_6, a_5, a_6 + a_4, a_5 + a_3, a_4 + a_2$	e'_1	$e'_0, 0, 0, 0, 0$	d_1	$e'_1 + e'_0 + d_1 = c_1$
2	$0, 0, a_6, a_5, a_6 + a_4, a_5 + a_3$	e'_2	$e'_1, e'_0, 0, 0, 0$	d_2	$e'_2 + e'_1 + d_2 = c_2$
3	$0, 0, 0, a_6, a_5, a_6 + a_4$	e'_3	$e'_2, e'_1, e'_0, 0, 0$	d_3	$e'_3 + e'_2 + e'_0 + d_3 = c_3$
4	$0, 0, 0, 0, a_6, a_5$	e'_4	$e'_3, e'_2, e'_1, e'_0, 0$	d_4	$e'_4 + e'_3 + e'_1 + d_4 = c_4$
5	$0, 0, 0, 0, 0, a_6$	e'_5	$e'_4, e'_3, e'_2, e'_1, e'_0$	d_5	$e'_5 + e'_4 + e'_2 + e'_0 + d_5 = c_5$
6	$0, 0, 0, 0, 0, 0$	0	$e'_5, e'_4, e'_3, e'_2, e'_1$	d_6	$e'_5 + e'_3 + e'_1 + d_6 = c_6$

Proof. The number of 1-bit registers includes the ones in the L and U shift registers, i.e., $2m - 1$, the register B, i.e., m, and the shift register X, i.e., $t_{\omega-2}$, Thus, the multiplier requires $3m + t_{\omega-2} - 1$ 1-bit registers. The $IP(m)$ and $IP(m - 1)$ blocks require m and $m - 1$ AND gates, respectively. Therefore, the multiplier requires $2m - 1$ 2-input AND gates. The number of XOR gates is obtained by adding those for the BTX array, the $IP(m)$ and $IP(m - 1)$ as well as the BTX blocks, which are (28), $m - 1$, $m - 2$, and $\omega - 1$, respectively. As a result, the number of XOR gates required in the multiplier is $(n - 1)(m - 1) - \sum_{i=1}^{n-1} r_i + m - 1 + m - 2 + \omega - 1 = (n + 1)(m - 1) + \omega - 2 - \sum_{i=1}^{n-1} r_i$ and the proof is complete.

The time complexities of the multiplier are determined by three factors: latency, the number of clock cycles required for whole multiplication, and the critical path delay. Let us define the latency as the number of clock cycles needed that the first bit of the output be available. Based on this definition, one can see that the latency of the SOBS multiplier is one and the entire multiplication requires m clock cycles. The critical path delay, which is the longest path from the registers to the output c, determines the maximum operating frequency. By properly implementation of the BTX block in Figure 2(a), one can minimize this delay to obtain it as follows.

Proposition 3. *Let T_A and T_X be the delay of an AND gate and an XOR gate, respectively. Then, the critical path delay of the SOBS PB multiplier (Figure 2(a)) is at most $T_A + \max(T_1, T_2)$, where $T_1 = (1 + \lceil \log_2(\omega - 1) \rceil + \lceil \log_2 m \rceil) T_X$ and $T_2 = (1 + \lceil \log_2(m - 1) \rceil + \lceil \log_2 n \rceil) T_X$.*

Proof. The critical path delay of the multiplier is determined by the maximum delay between the two paths from the shift registers of L and U to the output c. In order to minimize this delay, one can implement c in Figure 2(a) as $c = c' + x_0$, where

$$c' = \sum_{j \in \mathcal{T} - \{0\}} x_j + d. \tag{39}$$

Since the path delay from the shift register U to the output d is $T_A + \lceil \log_2 m \rceil T_X$ and (39) requires $\lceil \log_2(\omega - 1) \rceil T_X$ using a BTX, one can see that the delay to generate c' is at most $T' = T_A + (\lceil \log_2(\omega - 1) \rceil + \lceil \log_2 m \rceil) T_X$. Also, the delay to generate x_0 from the shift register L is $T'' = T_A + (\lceil \log_2(m-1) \rceil + \lceil \log_2 n \rceil) T_X$. Therefore, the total delay to generate c is $T_X + \max(T', T'')$ which is equal to $T_A + \max(T_1, T_2)$ and the proof is complete.

4.5 Comparison

Table 2 shows the comparison of the proposed SOBS PB multiplier with the traditional LSB-first and MSB-first ones presented in Section 2 in terms of time and space complexities for irreducible ω-nominal and trinomial. To illustrate the differences between the complexities of the proposed multiplier with the ones of other multipliers, the complexities for irreducible trinomials are also tabulated in this table. The number of XOR gates γ in this table is obtained for the irreducible trinomial $P(x) = x^m + x^k + 1$, $1 \le k < \frac{m}{2}$. For the $GF(2^{233})$ field recommended by NIST, one can use $m = 233$, $k = 74$, and $T_3 = T_A + 10T_X$ in this table. As seen from this table, the proposed SOBS multiplier has the lowest latency at the expense of longer critical path and more area requirement.

Table 2. Comparison of multipliers in terms of time and space complexities for irreducible ω-nomial and trinomial, where $\gamma = (n+1)(m-1) + \omega - 2 - \sum_{i=1}^{n-1} r_i$, $T_1 = (1 + \lceil \log_2(\omega - 1) \rceil + \lceil \log_2 m \rceil) T_X$, $T_2 = (1 + \lceil \log_2(m-1) \rceil + \lceil \log_2 n \rceil) T_X$, and $T_3 = T_A + (2 + \lceil \log_2 m \rceil) T_X$

Multiplier	Latency	Critical path	# AND	# XOR	# 1-bit Register
$P(x) = x^m + \sum_{i=1}^{\omega-2} x^{t_i} + 1$, $1 \le t_0 < t_1 < \cdots < t_{\omega-2}$					
LSB-first	m	$T_A + T_X$	m	$m + \omega - 2$	$3m$
MSB-first	m	$T_A + T_X$	m	$m + \omega - 2$	$3m$
SOBS	1	$T_A + \max(T_1, T_2)$	$2m - 1$	γ	$3m + t_{\omega-2} - 1$
$P(x) = x^m + x^k + 1$, $1 \le k < \frac{m}{2}$					
LSB-first	m	$T_A + T_X$	m	$m + 1$	$3m$
MSB-first	m	$T_A + T_X$	m	$m + 1$	$3m$
SOBS	1	T_3	$2m - 1$	$2m + k - 2$	$3m + k - 1$

5 Conclusions

A new serial-output bit-serial multiplier structure for general irreducible polynomials has been proposed. The proposed multiplier can be used for applications, such as, RFID tags, where the field size and irreducible polynomial are fixed. We have obtained the complexities of the proposed multiplier and compared them with the ones of the LSB-first and the MSB-first multipliers. Unlike the parallel-output multipliers which require m clock cycles for the latency, the proposed serial-output bit-serial multiplier has the latency of one clock cycle. This is achieved at the expense of longer critical path delay and more area requirement.

It is interesting to note that by connecting the output of the proposed multiplier to the serial-input of the LSB-first multiplier, one can obtain a hybrid structure which performs two multiplications together. The results of such a hybrid structure are available in parallel after m clock cycles and it has practical applications for fast cryptographic computations.

The proposed bit-serial multiplier can be extended to obtain a new serial-output digit-serial multiplier by replicating the BTX, IP(m), and IP($m-1$) blocks in Figure 2(a). The latency of such a digit-serial multiplier is one and it generates K bits of the multiplication in each clock cycles with the total $\lceil \frac{m}{K} \rceil$ clock cycles for the entire multiplication.

Acknowledgements

The author would like to thank the anonymous referees of CHES 2008 for their comments. This work has been supported in part by an NSERC Discovery grant awarded to the author.

References

1. Agnew, G.B., Mullin, R.C., Onyszchuk, I.M., Vanstone, S.A.: An Implementation for a Fast Public-Key Cryptosystem. Journal of Cryptology 3, 63–79 (1991)
2. Berlekamp, E.R.: Bit-Serial Reed-Solomon Encoders. IEEE Transactions on Information Theory 28(6), 869–874 (1982)
3. Beth, T., Gollman, D.: Algorithm Engineering for Public Key Algorithms. IEEE J. Selected Areas in Communications 7(4), 458–465 (1989)
4. Erdem, S.S., Yanik, T., Koç, C.K.: Polynomial basis multiplication over $GF(2^m)$. Acta Applicandae Mathematicae 93(1-3), 33–55 (2006)
5. Halbutogullari, A., Koç, C.K.: Mastrovito Multiplier for General Irreducible Polynomials. IEEE Transactions on Computers 49(5), 503–518 (2000)
6. Hankerson, D., Menezes, A., Vanstone, S.: Guide to Elliptic Curve Cryptography. Springer, Heidelberg (2004)
7. Koblitz, N.: Elliptic curve cryptosystems. Mathematics of Computation 48, 203–209 (1987)
8. Massey, J.L., Omura, J.K.: Computational Method and Apparatus for Finite Field Arithmetic. US Patent No. 4,587,627 (1986)
9. Mastrovito, E.D.: VLSI Designs for Multiplication over Finite Fields $GF(2^m)$. In: Mora, T. (ed.) AAECC-6 1988. LNCS, vol. 357, pp. 297–309. Springer, Heidelberg (1989)
10. Mastrovito, E.D.: VLSI Architectures for Computation in Galois Fields. PhD thesis, Linkoping Univ., Linkoping Sweden (1991)
11. Miller, V.S.: Use of Elliptic Curves in Cryptography. In: Williams, H.C. (ed.) CRYPTO 1985. LNCS, vol. 218, pp. 417–426. Springer, Heidelberg (1986)
12. Reyhani-Masoleh, A., Hasan, M.A.: Low Complexity Bit Parallel Architectures for Polynomial Basis Multiplication over $GF(2^m)$. IEEE Transactions on Computers 53(8), 945–959 (2004)
13. Rodriguez-Henriquez, F., Koç, C.K.: Parallel Multipliers Based on Special Irreducible Pentanomials. IEEE Transactions on Computers 52(12), 1535–1542 (2003)
14. Scott, P.A., Tavares, S.E., Peppard, L.E.: A Fast VLSI Multiplier for $GF(2^m)$. IEEE J. Selected Areas in Communications 4(1), 62–66 (1986)

15. Sunar, B., Koç, C.K.: Mastrovito Multiplier for All Trinomials. IEEE Transactions on Computers 48(5), 522–527 (1999)
16. Wang, C.C., Truong, T.K., Shao, H.M., Deutsch, L.J., Omura, J.K., Reed, I.S.: VLSI Architectures for Computing Multiplications and Inverses in $GF(2^m)$. IEEE Transactions on Computers 34(8), 709–716 (1985)
17. Wu, H.: Bit-Parallel Finite Field Multiplier and Squarer Using Polynomial Basis. IEEE Transactions on Computers 51(7), 750–758 (2002)
18. Zhang, T., Parhi, K.K.: Systematic Design of Original and Modified Mastrovito Multipliers for General Irreducible Polynomials. IEEE Transactions on Computers 50(7), 734–748 (2001)

A Very Compact Hardware Implementation of the MISTY1 Block Cipher

Dai Yamamoto, Jun Yajima, and Kouichi Itoh

FUJITSU LABORATORIES LTD.
4-1-1, Kamikodanaka, Nakahara-ku, Kawasaki, 211-8588, Japan
{ydai,jyajima,kito}@labs.fujitsu.com

Abstract. This paper proposes compact hardware (H/W) implementation for the MISTY1 block cipher, which is an ISO/IEC18033 standard encryption algorithm. In designing the compact H/W, we focused on optimizing the implementation of FO/FI functions, which are the main components of MISTY1. For this optimization, we propose two new methods; reducing temporary registers for the FO function, and shortening the critical path for the FI function. According to our logic synthesis on a 0.18-μm CMOS standard cell library based on our proposed method, the gate size is 3.95 Kgates, which is the smallest as far as we know.

Keywords: Block cipher, MISTY1, Hardware, ASIC, Compact Implementation.

1 Introduction

The MISTY1 64-bit block cipher [1] is an ISO/IEC18033 [2] standard encryption algorithm. MISTY1 can be implemented in various ways in order to meet different performance requirements, such as compact design or high-speed preference. So, MISTY1 is suitable for embedded systems, such as mobile phones.

A number of MISTY1 ASIC implementations have been studied [3] [4] [5]. In [3] [4], compact MISTY1 architectures were designed. To realize compact design, these architectures use the only one FI function module repeatedly, and use S-boxes that are implemented in combinational logic. However, these architectures do not use common methods for the compact design, in which extended keys are sequentially generated in the encryption/decryption process in order to limit the register size of extended keys to 16 bits. Furthermore, they do not optimize the implementation method of the FO/FI function in consideration of using one FI function module. This optimization is very significant for the compact MISTY1 H/W.

In this paper, we focus on four strategies for the compact design. First, we choose to implement the H/W by using one FI function. Secondly, we use S-boxes implemented in the combinational logic. Thirdly, extended keys are generated sequentially in our H/W. Fourthly, we optimize the implementation of the FO/FI function. To realize this optimization, we propose two new methods. One reduces the temporary register for the FO function by the optimization of an FO function

E. Oswald and P. Rohatgi (Eds.): CHES 2008, LNCS 5154, pp. 315–330, 2008.

structure. Another shortens the critical path around the FI function by reducing the number of XOR gates in the critical path.

With our strategies, we synthesize MISTY1 H/W by a 0.18-μm CMOS standard cell library (CS86 technology[18]), and the performance evaluations are shown. As a result, an extremely small size of 3.95 Kgatcs with 71.1 Mbps throughput is obtained for our MISTY1 H/W. This is the smallest MISTY1 H/W, as far as we know.

Our proposed methods can be applied not only to MISTY1 but also to MISTY2 [1] and KASUMI [6], which have a similarly structured MISTY1 FO function. In [7], the compact H/W of KASUMI is proposed. A further gate count reduction of the KASUMI H/W can be realized by using our proposal.

The rest of the paper is organized as follows. A survey of related work is found in Chapter 2. Chapter 3 explains the algorithm of MISTY1. Our strategy for the smallest H/W of MISTY1 is discussed in Chapter 4. Chapter 5 proposes two new methods for an effective H/W implementation of MISTY1. Chapter 6 presents evaluation results for gate counts and the performance of our H/W, compared with previous results. Finally, we conclude with a summary and comment on future directions in Chapter 7.

2   Previous Work

A large number of MISTY1 H/W implementation evaluations on FPGA and ASIC have been studied.

The implementation on FPGA platform was reported in [8] [9] [10] [11] [12] [13] [14]. In [8] [9] [10], designers of MISTY1 have implemented MISTY1 H/W based on three types of H/W architectures; the fully loop unrolled architecture, the pipeline architecture, and the loop architecture. The two former architectures allow high processing speed, while the latter architecture allows a compact circuit. The implemented H/W based on the loop architecture uses a large 128-bit register for extended keys. In [11] [12], the implemented H/W was aimed not at compact design but high H/W efficiency, and it had an encryption function without a decryption function. In [13] [14], the implemented H/W had both the encryption and decryption function. Also, RAM blocks embedded in the considered FPGA devices were used for the implementation of S-boxes, so the implemented H/W realized higher H/W efficiency.

Implementation on the ASIC platform was reported in [3] [4] [5]. In [3] [4], developers of MISTY1 implemented and evaluated MISTY1 H/W. In particular, the research purpose in [4] is to reduce the gate count, and the implementation methods of FO/FI functions are well-studied. However, the gate size of their H/W is not small enough because one large 128-bit register is used for the extended key. The H/W performances of various block ciphers including MISTY1 are compared in [5]. In [5], the MISTY1 H/W is implemented straightforwardly based on the cipher specification. S-boxes are implemented by a lookup table in consideration of the fairness among ciphers, and a 128-bit register is used for extended keys, so the gate count of the implemented H/W is not small.

3   MISTY1

Figure 1 shows the nested structure of MISTY1 excluding the key scheduler [1]. MISTY1 encrypts a 64-bit plaintext using a 128-bit secret key. MISTY1 has the Feistel network with a variable number of rounds n including FO functions and FL/FL^{-1} functions. Since $n = 8$ is recommended in [1], we set $n = 8$ in the rest of this paper. The $FO_i (1 \leq i \leq 8)$ function uses a 48-bit extended key KI_i and a 64-bit extended key KO_i. The $FL_i (1 \leq i \leq 10)$ function is used in the encryption, meanwhile the FL_i^{-1} function is used in the decryption with a 32-bit extended key KL_i. In Fig. 1, 16-bit KL_{i1} and KL_{i2} are the left and right data of 32-bit KL_i, respectively. The FO_i function has three FI functions $FI_{ij} (1 \leq j \leq 3)$. Here, $KO_{ij} (1 \leq j \leq 4)$ and $KI_{ij} (1 \leq j \leq 3)$ are left j-th 16-bit data of KO_i and KI_i, respectively. The FI function uses the 7-bit S-box S_7 and the 9-bit S-box S_9. Here, the zero-extended operation is performed to 7-bit blocks by adding two '0's. The truncate operation truncates the two most significant bits of a 9-bit string. KI_{ij1} and KI_{ij2} are the left 7 bits and the right 9 bits of KI_{ij}, respectively. Here, the key scheduler of MISTY1 is explained. $K_i (1 \leq i \leq 8)$ is the left i-th 16 bits of a 128-bit secret key. $K_i' (1 \leq i \leq 8)$ corresponds to the output of FI_{ij} where the input of FI_{ij} is assigned to K_i and the key KI_{ij} is set to $K_{(i \bmod 8)+1}$. The assignment between the 16-bit secret/extended keys K_i, K_i' and the 16-bit round key KO_{ij}, KL_{ij}, KI_{ij} is defined in Table 1, where i equals $(i - 8)$ when $(i > 8)$.

Table 1. The assignment between K_i, K_i' and KO_{ij}, KL_{ij}, KI_{ij}

Round	KO_{i1}	KO_{i2}	KO_{i3}	KO_{i4}	KI_{i1}	KI_{i2}	KI_{i3}	KL_{i1}	KL_{i2}
Secret/	K_i	K_{i+2}	K_{i+7}	K_{i+4}	K_{i+5}'	K_{i+1}'	K_{i+3}'	$K_{\frac{i+1}{2}}$ (odd i)	$K_{\frac{i+1}{2}+6}'$ (odd i)
Extended								$K_{\frac{i}{2}+2}'$ (even i)	$K_{\frac{i}{2}+4}'$ (even i)

4   Four Strategies for the Compact Design

4.1   The Number of the FO/FI Function Module

The FO/FI function is the main component of MISTY1, so the FO/FI function is one of the most influential factors for gate counts of MISTY1 H/W. Thus, it is important to decide the number of the FO/FI function module. MISTY1 has a nested structure including FO functions and FL/FL^{-1} functions, so the number of the FO/FI function module can be variously selected. When MISTY1 is implemented with a pipelined H/W architecture, eight FO function modules are performed in the same clock cycle. This is suitable for high-speed implementation, but leads to a large circuit size. Therefore, we choose to implement only one FI function module for the compact design. That is, the FO function is executed in three clock cycles by repeatedly using one FI function module. This architecture leads to low speed processing, but is suitable for compact implementation.

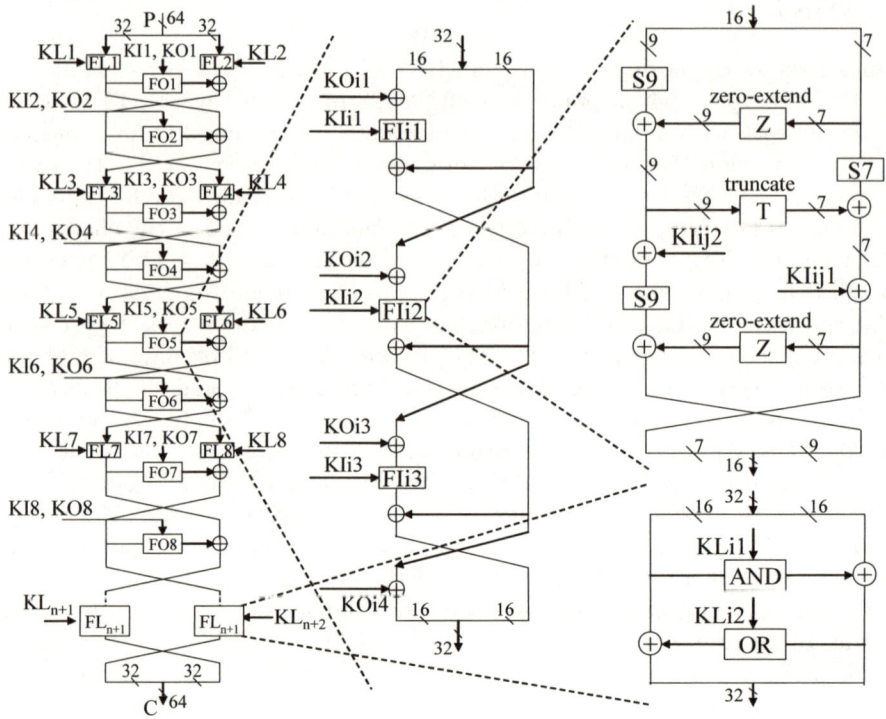

Fig. 1. MISTY1 encryption algorithm

4.2   Extended Key Generation Method

The generation method of extended keys in MISTY1 is classified into two methods; called the "register method" and the "on-the-fly method". It is important for the compact design to choose between two methods. In the register method, a 128-bit extended key is generated and stored into a 128-bit register in advance of the encryption/decryption process, and the required extended key is read directly from the register. In the on-the-fly method, a 16-bit required extended key is generated in the encryption/decryption process sequentially. The on-the-fly method is more suitable for the compact design than the register method because of the 128-bit register. Therefore, we chose the on-the-fly method, which has not been reported in the existing H/W implementation of MISTY1, but has been employed in other algorithm implementations, such as AES. That is, all of the previous architectures of MISTY1 are based on not the on-the-fly method but the register method. Also, because of the MISTY1 algorithm, the FI function is used not only in the encryption/decryption process but also in the extended key generation process. Therefore, we chose the implemented method, in which one FI function module is shared with these two processes. Thus, both the encryption/decryption process and the extended key generation process cannot be performed in the same cycle. So, a 16-bit register is required to retain a 16-bit extended key generated sequentially. Here, our on-the-fly method requiring a 16-bit register is called the "sequential method".

4.3   S-Box Implementation Method

The S-box performance of MISTY1, including gate counts, depends on the S-box implementation method, so it is important for the compact design to discuss them. The implementation method of two S-boxes (S_7 and S_9) is considered as follows. The two S-boxes of MISTY1 have been designed so that they can be easily implemented in combinational logic as well as by a lookup table [1]. On MISTY1, S-boxes in combinational logic show better performance both in terms of the area size and the delay time than that by a lookup table [3]. We confirmed that the same results are obtained when the implemented S-boxes are synthesized by using a 0.18-μm CMOS standard cell library. Therefore, we used S-boxes implemented in combinational logic.

4.4   Optimization of FO/FI Function

The proposed H/W uses one FI function module repeatedly. Furthermore, it is very significant for the smallest MISTY1 H/W to discuss the following two methods; a concrete implementation method of FO function in three cycles by using one FI function module, and the method of reducing the gate count of the FI function itself. In Chapter 5, we propose these two new methods.

5   Proposed Methods for the Compact Design

5.1   Reducing the Temporary Register for the FO Function

When an FO function is executed in three cycles by repeatedly using one FI function module, an intermediate result in each cycle must be stored into a register. The FO function transforms 32-bit data, so a 32-bit temporary register for the intermediate result (i.e., is "temporary register") is required. We reduced the size of the temporary register to 16 bits.

The concept of the proposed method is explained by reference to Fig. 2. It shows the method of dividing an FO function into three cycles. The previous method is straightforward based on MISTY1 specification. An FO function is separated horizontally for every cycle in the previous method, so a 32-bit temporary register is required for left and right 16-bit data. Meanwhile, an FO function is separated vertically for every cycle in the proposed method. In fact, the output data from the FI function in Cycle2 is directly XORed with a data register, so the 16-bit temporary register for the data is reduced by the proposed separation.

The detail and effectiveness of the proposed method is explained in the following steps. First, the straightforward architecture based on MISTY1 specification is explained as "existing method". Next, the proposed architecture based on the proposed concept shown in Fig. 2 is explained as "proposed method (a)". Then,

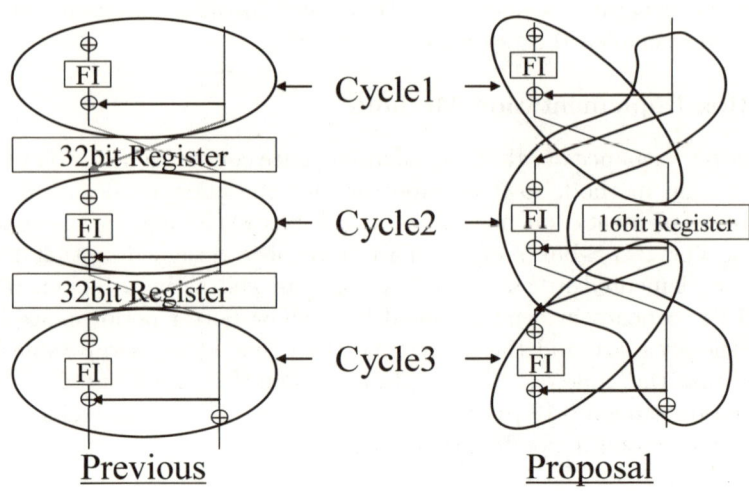

Fig. 2. Concept of temporary register reduction

we propose the second proposed architecture, which is maximally optimized for compact design as "proposed method (b)". Finally, the gate counts of FI functions are estimated. By using proposed method (b), the size of the FO function is estimated to be reduced 17% of the existing method.

Existing Method. The common partition algorithm based on MISTY1 specification is shown in Fig. 3 (I) as the existing algorithm. Equation (1) in Appendix shows each process for three cycles in this algorithm. Let $Reg\text{-}R_H$, $Reg\text{-}R_L$, $Reg\text{-}L_H$, and $Reg\text{-}L_L$ be 16-bit registers (called "Feistel data register"), respectively. The Feistel data register means the register for storing intermediate results for each round plaintext/ciphertext. Also, let $Reg\text{-}FOR$ and $Reg\text{-}FOL$ be the 16-bit temporary registers, so the total size of temporary registers is 32 bits in the existing algorithm. Next, the existing architecture based on the existing algorithm is shown in Fig. 3 (II). Note that the registers described in the following architecture figures include a 2-1MUX. This 2-1MUX can select the value stored in the register or the value of the external input. The value stored into the register can be updated to the selected value. Consequently, two 16-bit registers, $Reg\text{-}FOR$ and $Reg\text{-}FOL$, are required in the existing method.

Proposed Method (a). We discuss the proposed algorithm (a) shown in Fig. 4 (I), which is designed based on the proposed concept shown in Fig. 2. Comparing Fig. 4 (I) with Fig. 3 (I), the output data from the FI function is directly XORed with $Reg\text{-}R_H$ and $Reg\text{-}R_L$ in Cycle2 in Fig. 4 (I). This makes it possible to remove a 16-bit temporary register because the output data from the FI function in Cycle2 does not need to be stored into the temporary register. The proposed architecture (a) based on the proposed algorithm (a) is shown in Fig. 4 (II). Equation (2) in Appendix shows each process for three cycles shown in Fig. 4

(I). Although the proposed architecture (a) shown in Fig. 4 (II) can remove the 16-bit temporary register, there is another issue. The issue is that the number of MUX operators is increased compared with the existing method, because the circuit structure differs in every three cycles, which comes from the vertical separation of the proposed method. Concretely, different values are input into input1 and input4 in the FI function in three cycles, so the existing architecture has two 16-bit 2-1MUX, meanwhile the proposed architecture (a) has two 16-bit 3-1MUX. Also, the proposed architecture (a) has a 16-bit 2-1MUX instead of a 16-bit XOR operator located above $Reg\text{-}R_H$. This 2-1MUX selects the output data from the FI function in Cycle2, and the extended key KO_{i4} in Cycle3. In other words, the proposed method (a) reduces the 16-bit temporary register, but increases the 48-bit 2-1MUX compared with the existing method.

Proposed Method (b). The algorithm (b) shown in Fig. 5 (I) aims to reduce the 2-1MUX increased in the proposed method (a). One of the redundant MUX operators is a 2-1MUX located above $Reg\text{-}R_H$ in Fig. 4 (II). If KO_{i4} is XORed with $Reg\text{-}R_H$ without this 2-1MUX, then the 2-1MUX can be removed. To remove the 2-1MUX, we focused on the input4 in the FI function. KO_{i4} is input into the input4 in both Cycle2 and Cycle3 as shown in Fig. 5 (I). That is, KO_{i4} is XORed with both $Reg\text{-}R_H$ and $Reg\text{-}R_L$ in Cycle2, and KO_{i4} is XORed with only $Reg\text{-}R_L$ in Cycle3, so KO_{i4} is cancelled on $Reg\text{-}R_L$, and XORed with only $Reg\text{-}R_H$ finally. This algorithm can remove the 2-1MUX located above $Reg\text{-}R_H$. Moreover, the input4 in both Cycle2 and Cycle3 in this algorithm is the same value KO_{i4}. Therefore, not 3-1MUX but 2-1MUX is assigned above the input4 in the proposed method (b). In other words, the proposed method (b) reduces the 32-bit 2-1MUX compared with the proposed method (a). The proposed architecture (b) based on the proposed algorithm (b) is shown in Fig. 5 (II). Equation (3) in Appendix shows each process for the three cycles shown in Fig. 5 (I).

The gate counts of FI functions based on the above three architectures are estimated as shown Table 2. Let MUX, REG, and XOR be the 2-1multiplexer, the register, and the exclusive-OR, respectively. We supposed 1-bit 2-1MUX = 3.5 NAND gates, 1-bit REG = 13.5 NAND gates, 1-bit XOR = 2.5 NAND gates. In the row of MUX in Table 2, the value is based on a 1-bit 2-1MUX. For example, 16-bit 3-1MUX is regarded as two 16-bit 2-1MUX (= one 32-bit 2-1MUX). From Table 2, the gate count of the FI function based on the proposed architecture (b) is 17% smaller than the existing architecture.

5.2 Shortening the Critical Path Around an FI Function

MISTY1 has a Feistel network with eight FO functions, and an FO function comprises three FI functions. Also, MISTY1 extended key is obtained by using the FI function. Thus, the performance of any MISTY1 H/W depends on the processing speed of the FI function. The proposed method improves the processing speed, which is important as well as the area size for the compact H/W.

Table 2. Comparison of gate counts of FI function

	Existing	Proposed (a)	Proposed (b)
# 1-bit MUX	32	80	48
# 1-bit REG	64	48	48
# 1-bit XOR	80	64	64
Total [gate] (†)	1176	1088	976

(†) MUX = 3.5gate/bit (in 2-1MUX) REG = 13.5gate/bit
XOR = 2.5gate/bit

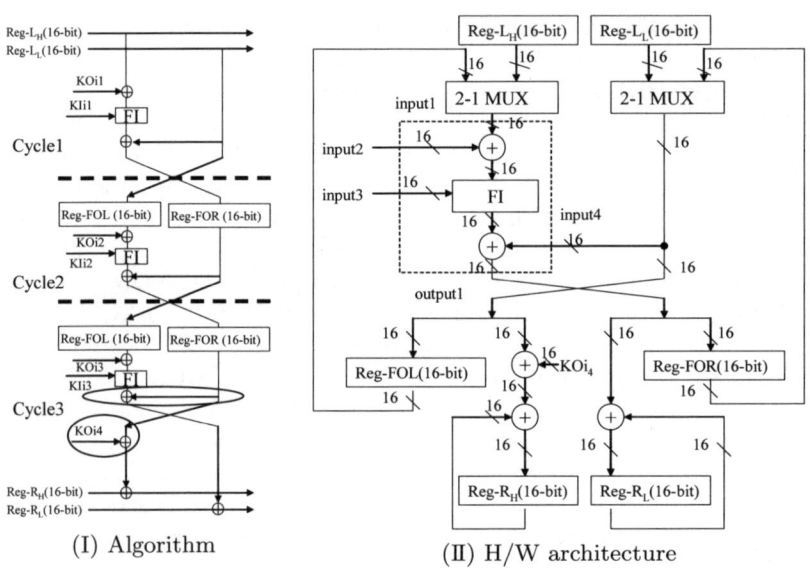

(I) Algorithm   (II) H/W architecture

Fig. 3. Existing method

Figure 6 shows the straightforward and the proposed algorithm of the FI function. XOR gates under a FI function in a FO function are described in Fig. 6. In Fig. 6, the critical path with two S-boxes S_9 in the FI function including these XOR gates is illustrated by the thick line. The XOR gate into which KI_{ij2} is input in the straightforward algorithm is transferred just below the first zero-extend operation in the proposed algorithm (Move1). This movement reduces one XOR gate on the critical path. To guarantee the logic equivalence in both algorithms of the FI function, the KI_{ij1} input in the straightforward algorithm is modified to the $(KI_{ij1}$ XOR $KI_{ij2})$ input (Move2). Here, the two most significant bits of KI_{ij2} are truncated, and XORed with KI_{ij1}. Next, the 9-bit XOR gate under the FI function is transferred just below the second zero-extend operation (Move3). In other words, the proposed algorithm reduces two XOR gates on the critical path in the FI function, and realizes higher processing speed of the FI function almost without the gate counts increase.

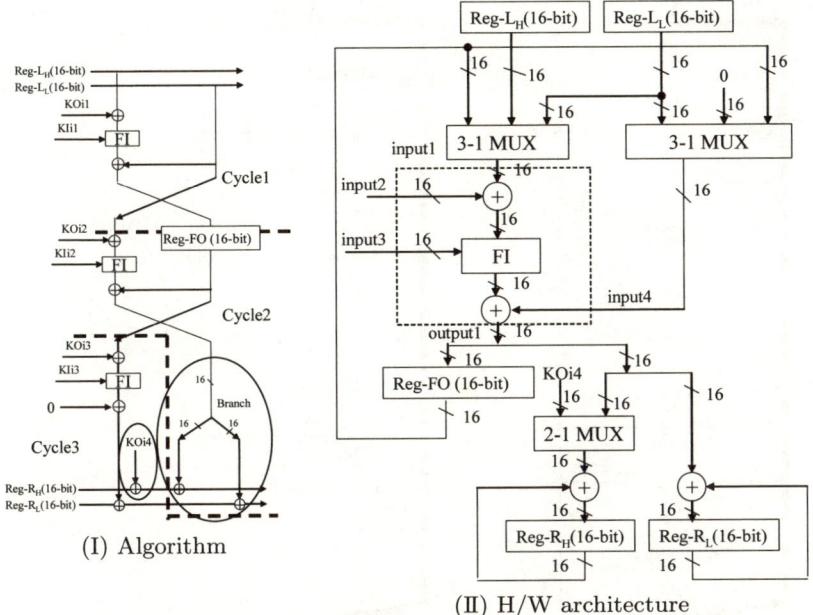

Fig. 4. Proposed method (a)

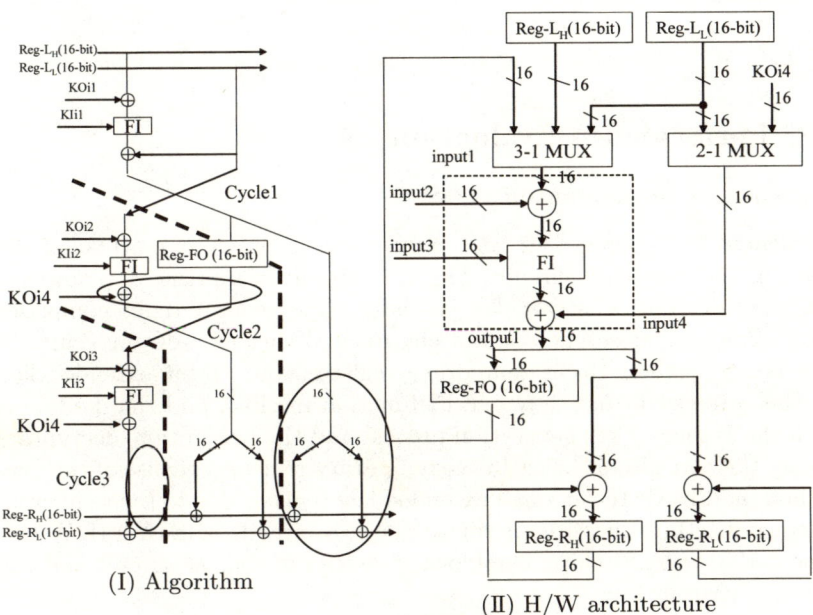

Fig. 5. Proposed method (b)

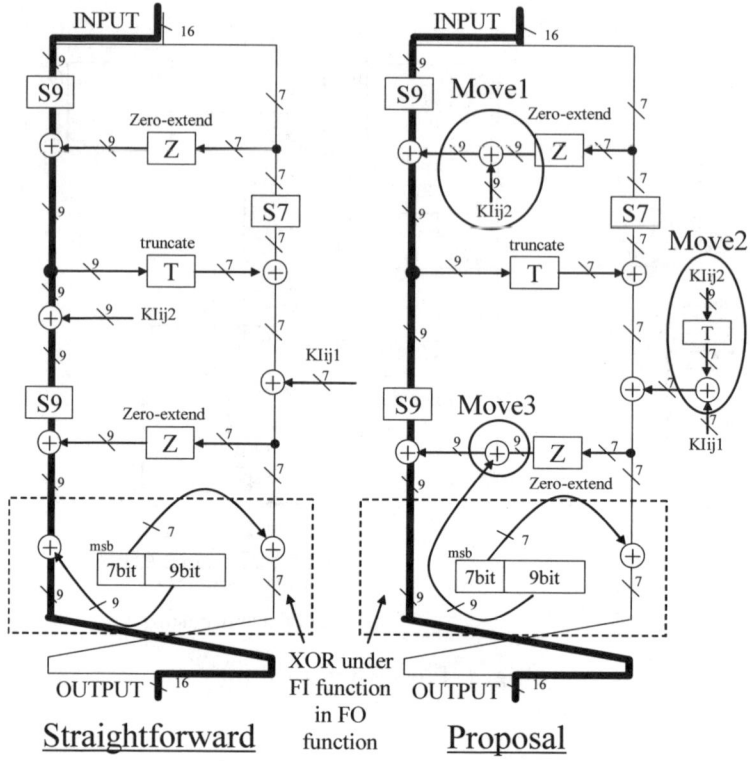

Fig. 6. Method for shortening the critical path around FI function

6 ASIC Performance Evaluation

6.1 Structure of Implemented H/W

The implemented H/W comprises two circuits; the interface circuit(called the "I/F circuit") and the core circuit. The I/F circuit comprises a plaintext/ciphertext register and a secret key register. The core circuit comprises FI/FL/FL^{-1} function, selectors, counter circuit, and various registers (four 16-bit Feistel data registers, 16-bit temporary register, and 16-bit extended key register). The core circuit has only one FI function module, and the module is shared with the extended key generation process and the encryption/decryption process. Also, the core circuit has a 16-bit temporary register because of the proposed method, and has a 16-bit small extended key register due to the sequential method. By connecting the core circuit to the I/F circuit, MISTY1 H/W can be implemented as a VLSI chip. The block structure of the I/F circuit and the core circuit is shown in Fig. 7.

The implemented H/W generates a 64-bit ciphertext (plaintext) from a 64-bit plaintext (ciphertext) in 60 clock cycles. The details are as follows. The data

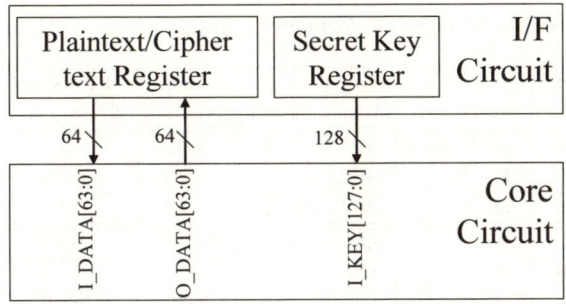

Fig. 7. The block structure of the I/F circuit and the core circuit

input and output requires 2 cycles. The encryption/decryption processes in FO and FL/FL^{-1} function require 24 cycles and 10 cycles, respectively. The extended key generation process in the FI function requires 3 (cycles) $\times$ 8 (rounds) = 24 cycles, because an extended key generated by using the FI function is input into FL/FL^{-1} function in the same cycle.

6.2 Comparison of Our MISTY1 H/W Results

This section evaluates the ASIC performance of the proposed H/W based on the structure shown in Section 6.1. The evaluation environment is as follows.

H/W description language. Verilog-HDL
Design library. Fujitsu 0.18-μm CMOS standard cell library (CS86 technology [18])
Logic synthesizer. Design Compiler 2006.06-SP5-1
Synthesis condition. Worst case condition (Supply voltage: 1.65V, Junction temperature: 125°C)

In this evaluation, the proposed H/W is not based on scan design, and is synthesized with the Design Compiler with size optimization and ungroup command. Also, one gate is equivalent to 2-1NAND gate.

Table 3 shows the ASIC performance of three types of the proposed H/W; the core circuit (Proposed 1), the core circuit with the secret key register (Proposed 2), and the core and I/F circuit (Proposed 3). In Table 3, "Block Structure" in the last column means the above-mentioned three types of the proposed H/W. Also, "H/W efficiency" means the throughput per gate, so the implementation with higher throughput and smaller gate counts show higher values. In this paper, the H/W efficiency is defined as the throughput divided by area size by reference to [5]. From Table 3, it is confirmed that a size of 3.95 Kgates with 71.1 Mbps throughput is obtained for our MISTY1 core (Proposed 1).

Table 3. H/W performance comparison in ASICs

Source	Process [μm]	Cycle	S-box	Freq. [Mhz]	Thr'put [Mbps]	Area [Kgates]	Efficiency [Kbps/gates]	Block Structure
Proposed 1	0.18	60	Logic	66.7	71.1	3.95	18.0	Core
Proposed 2	0.18	60	Logic	66.7	71.1	4.79	14.9	(‡)
Proposed 3	0.18	60	Logic	66.7	71.1	5.29	13.4	Core + I/F
[4]	0.60	35	(†)	29.9	66.3	8.099	8.19	Core
[5]	0.18	30	Table	92.6	197.5	9.3	21.3	(‡)
[15]	0.18	(†)	(†)	(†)	70.2	5.39	13.0	(†)
[16]	0.18	35	(†)	(†)	78.4	6.10	12.85	(†)

(†) Unknown, (‡) Core + Secret Key Register

6.3 Further Comparison

This section compares the performance of existing and proposed architectures. The lower rows in Table 3 show the performance of existing architectures reported in [4] [5] [15] [16]. The implemented architectures shown in [4] [5] are based on the register method and have the only one FI function module. The core circuits in [4] [5] include a 128-bit extended key register. Meanwhile, the information of implementation methods is not clear in [15] [16]. From Table 3, our H/W is implemented with the smallest size and good efficiency.

Because the synthesis condition, such as design library, S-box implementation method, and Block Structure, are different from one another, it might be difficult to fairly compare the performance of each implementation shown in Table 3. In the following evaluation, both MISTY1 H/W based on the available RTL code [17] in [5] and the proposed H/W are synthesized under the same synthesis condition in order to compare performance fairly. These two architectures are based on the same implemented method except for two differences, one is to apply the proposed methods or not, the other is the extended key generation method. The following evaluation compares the performance of three implemented architectures. First, implementation (a) is the MISTY1 H/W based on the RTL code [17], which is implemented straightforwardly based on MISTY1 specification. Second, implementation (b) is obtained from the RTL code [17], where the S-box code was changed from the lookup table to combinational logic. Finally, implementation (c) is our MISTY1 H/W (Proposed 2 in Table 3), which is the core circuit with a secret key register, because implementation (a) and (b) have the only secret key register. Here, implementation (b) and (c) are based on the same implementation methods of S-boxes and Block Structure, so the performance of both implementations can be compared fairly.

Figure 8 shows a comparison of the gate counts of the above three implementations under various delay requirements. From Fig. 8, the gate count of implementation (c) is about 2K gates smaller than that of implementation (b). The reasons are as follows. First, implementation (b) has the 128-bit extended key register due to the register method, while implementation (c) has the 16-bit

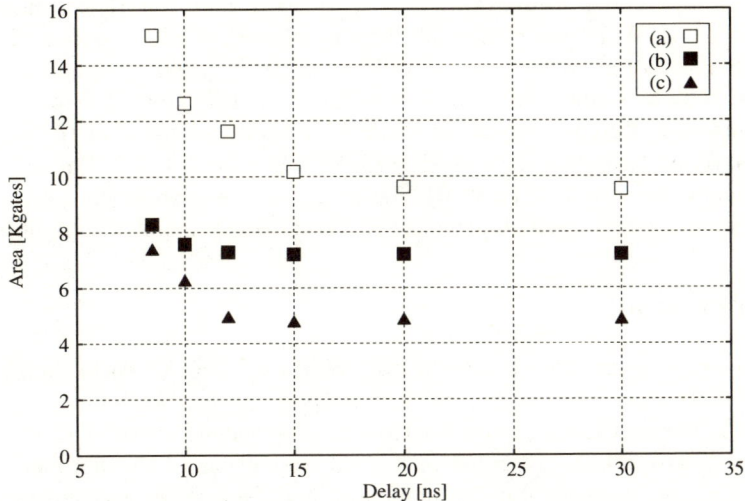

Fig. 8. Comparison of the gate counts under various delay requirements

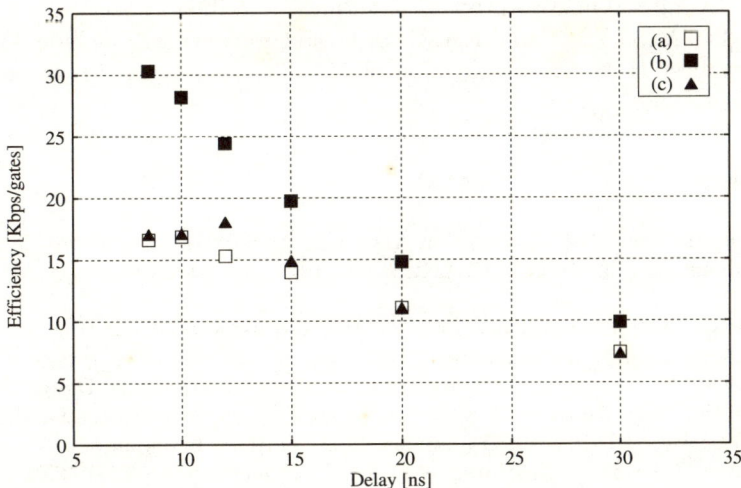

Fig. 9. Comparison of the H/W efficiency under various delay requirements

small one due to the sequential method. Second, implementation (c) has reduced the temporary register due to our proposal described in Section 5.1.

Next, Fig. 9 shows a comparison of the H/W efficiency of the above three implementations under various delay requirements. From Fig. 9, the H/W efficiency of implementation (c) is lower than that of implementation (b). This is mainly because implementation (b) is based on the register method, while implementation (c) is based on the sequential method.

Through the above evaluation, it is confirmed that the H/W efficiency of our MISTY1 H/W is lower than implementation (b), but is better than that of the other reports. The proposed H/W realized the smallest-area of less than 4K gates, which is about 2K gates smaller than the area of straightforward implementation. This is because our MISTY1 H/W is based on the sequential method and our proposed methods described in Section 5.1, 5.2. This paper aims to implement the smallest H/W of MISTY1, so it is significant to maximally reduce the gate count even though the H/W efficiency is not the highest.

7   Conclusion

In this paper, we presented the smallest H/W of the MISTY1 64-bit block cipher, and proposed two new methods. The first method reduced the temporary register for the FO function from 32 bits to 16 bits. The second method shortened the critical path around the FI function by the reduction of the number of XOR gates on the critical path. The implemented MISTY1 H/W was synthesized by a 0.18-μm CMOS standard cell library, then an extremely small size of 3.95 Kgates with 71.1 Mbps throughput was obtained for our MISTY1 core circuit. In this paper, it was first shown that MISTY1 H/W is implemented with a size of less than 4K gates. Our two proposed methods described in Section 5.1, 5.2 can be applied to MISTY2 [1] and KASUMI [6]. Future work will include discussion on the smallest H/W implementation of MISTY2 and KASUMI by using the proposed methods.

References

1. Matsui, M.: New Block Encryption Algorithm MISTY, Fast Software Encryption. In: Biham, E. (ed.) FSE 1997. LNCS, vol. 1267, pp. 54–68. Springer, Heidelberg (1997)
2. ISO/IEC18033-3, http://www.iso.org/iso/iso_catalogue/catalogue_tc/catalogue_detail.htm?csnumber=37972
3. Ichikawa, T., Sorimachi, T., Matsui, M.: A Study on Hardware Design for Block Encryption Algorithms. In: Proc. 1997 Symposium on Cryptography and Information Security, SCIS1997, 9. D (January 1997) (written in Japanese)
4. Ichikawa, T., Katoh, J., Matsui, M.: An Implementation of MISTY1 for H/W Design. In: Proc. 1998 Symposium on Cryptography and Information Security, SCIS 1998, 9.1.A (January 1998) (written in Japanese)
5. Sugawara, T., Homma, N., Aoki, T., Satoh, A.: ASIC Performance Comparison for the ISO Standard Block Ciphers. In: Proc. 2007 Joint Workshop on Information Security, JWIS 2007, pp. 485–498 (August 2007)
6. Third Generation Partnership Project: 3rd Generation Partnership Project; Technical Specification Group Services and System Aspects; 3G Security; Specification of the 3GPP Confidentiality and Integrity Algorithms; Document 2: KASUMI Specification (Release 7), 3GPP TS 35.202 v7.0.0 (June 2007)
7. Satoh, A., Morioka, S.: Small and High-Speed Hardware Architectures for the 3GPP Standard Cipher KASUMI. In: Proc. 5th International Conference on Information Security, ISC 2002, pp. 48–62 (September 2002)

8. Sorimachi, A., Ichikawa, T., Kasuya, T.: On Hardware Implementation of Block Ciphers using FPGA. In: Proc. 2003 Symposium on Cryptography and Information Security, SCIS 2003, 12D-3 (January 2003) (written in Japanese)
9. Ichikawa, T., Sorimachi, T., Kasuya, T.: On Hardware Implementation of Block Ciphers Selected at the NESSIE Project Phase I (1). In: Proc. 2002 Symposium on Cryptography and Information Security, SCIS 2002, 12C-3 (January 2002) (written in Japanese)
10. Ichikawa, T., Sorimachi, T., Kasuya, T., Matsui, M.: On the criteria of hardware evaluation of block ciphers, in Technical Report of IEICE, ISEC2001-54 (September 2001) (written in Japanese):
11. Standaert, F.-X., Rouvroy, G., Quisquater, J.-J., Legat, J.-D.: Efficient FPGA Implementations of Block Ciphers KHAZAD and MISTY1. In: The Third NESSIE Workshop (November 2002)
12. Rouvroy, G., Standaert, F.-X., Quisquater, J.-J., Legat, J.-D.: Efficient FPGA Implementation of Block Cipher MISTY1. In: Proc. Parallel and Distributed Processing Symposium 2003, IPDPS (April 2003)
13. Kitsos, P., Koufopavlou, O.: A Time And Area Efficient Hardware Implementation Of The Misty1 Block Cipher. In: Proc. 46th IEEE Midwest Symposium on Circuits and Systems 2003, ISCAS 2003 (December 2003)
14. Kitsos, P., Galanis, M.D., Koufopavlou, O.: A RAM-Based FPGA Implementation of the 64-bit MISTY1 Block Cipher. In: Proc. 46th IEEE Midwest Symposium on Circuits and Systems 2005, ISCAS 2005 (May 2005)
15. Information-technology Promotion Agency, and Telecommunications Advancement Organization of Japan: CRYPTREC Report 2002 (March 2003)
16. Mitsubishi Electric Web Site, http://global.mitsubishielectric.com/bu/security/rd/rd01_01d.html
17. HDL codes used for the performance evaluation in [5], http://www.aoki.ecei.tohoku.ac.jp/crypto/items/JWIS2007.zip
18. CS86 technology, http://edevice.fujitsu.com/fj/DATASHEET/e-ds/e620209.pdf

Appendix

Existing Method

$$\text{Cycle1}: \ Reg\text{-}FOR = \text{FI}(Reg\text{-}L_H \oplus KO_{i1}) \oplus Reg\text{-}L_L$$
$$Reg\text{-}FOL = Reg\text{-}L_L$$
$$\text{Cycle2}: \ Reg\text{-}FOR = \text{FI}(Reg\text{-}FOL \oplus KO_{i2}) \oplus Reg\text{-}FOR$$
$$Reg\text{-}FOL = Reg\text{-}FOR$$
$$\text{Cycle3}: \ Reg\text{-}R_H = Reg\text{-}R_H \oplus (Reg\text{-}FOR \oplus KO_{i4})$$
$$Reg\text{-}R_L = Reg\text{-}R_L \oplus \text{FI}(Reg\text{-}FOL \oplus KO_{i3}) \oplus Reg\text{-}FOR \qquad (1)$$

Proposed Method (a)

$$\text{Cycle1}: \ Reg\text{-}FO = \text{FI}(Reg\text{-}L_H \oplus KO_{i1}) \oplus Reg\text{-}L_L$$
$$\text{Cycle2}: \ Reg\text{-}R_H = Reg\text{-}R_H \oplus \text{FI}(Reg\text{-}L_L \oplus KO_{i2}) \oplus Reg\text{-}FO$$
$$Reg\text{-}R_L = Reg\text{-}R_L \oplus \text{FI}(Reg\text{-}L_L \oplus KO_{i2}) \oplus Reg\text{-}FO$$

$$\text{Cycle3}: \ Reg\text{-}R_H = Reg\text{-}R_H \oplus (KO_{i4} \oplus 0)$$
$$Reg\text{-}R_L = Reg\text{-}R_L \oplus \text{FI}(Reg\text{-}FO \oplus KO_{i3}) \oplus 0 \qquad (2)$$

Proposed Method (b)

$$\text{Cycle1}: \ Reg\text{-}FO = \left\{\text{FI}(Reg\text{-}L_H \oplus KO_{i1}) \oplus Reg\text{-}L_L\right\}$$
$$Reg\text{-}R_H = Reg\text{-}R_H \oplus \left\{\text{FI}(Reg\text{-}L_H \oplus KO_{i1}) \oplus Reg\text{-}L_L\right\}$$
$$Reg\text{-}R_L = Reg\text{-}R_L \oplus \left\{\text{FI}(Reg\text{-}L_H \oplus KO_{i1}) \oplus Reg\text{-}L_L\right\}$$
$$\text{Cycle2}: \ Reg\text{-}R_H = Reg\text{-}R_H \oplus \left\{\text{FI}(Reg\text{-}L_L \oplus KO_{i2}) \oplus KO_{i4}\right\}$$
$$Reg\text{-}R_L = Reg\text{-}R_L \oplus \left\{\text{FI}(Reg\text{-}L_L \oplus KO_{i2}) \oplus KO_{i4}\right\}$$
$$\text{Cycle3}: \ Reg\text{-}R_H = Reg\text{-}R_H$$
$$Reg\text{-}R_L = Reg\text{-}R_L \oplus \left\{\text{FI}(Reg\text{-}FO \oplus KO_{i3}) \oplus KO_{i4}\right\} \qquad (3)$$

Light-Weight Instruction Set Extensions for Bit-Sliced Cryptography

Philipp Grabher, Johann Großschädl, and Dan Page

University of Bristol, Department of Computer Science
Merchant Venturers Building, Woodland Road, Bristol, BS8 1UB, U.K.
{grabher,johann,page}@cs.bris.ac.uk

Abstract. Bit-slicing is a non-conventional implementation technique for cryptographic software where an n-bit processor is considered as a collection of n 1-bit execution units operating in SIMD mode. Particularly when implementing symmetric ciphers, the bit-slicing approach has several advantages over more conventional alternatives: it often allows one to reduce memory footprint by eliminating large look-up tables, and it permits more predictable performance characteristics that can foil time based side-channel attacks. Both features are attractive for mobile and embedded processors, but the performance overhead that results from bit-sliced implementation often represents a significant disadvantage. In this paper we describe a set of light-weight Instruction Set Extensions (ISEs) that can improve said performance while retaining all advantages of bit-sliced implementation. Contrary to other crypto-ISE, our design is generic and allows for a high degree of algorithm agility: we demonstrate applicability to several well-known cryptographic primitives including four block ciphers (DES, Serpent, AES, and PRESENT), a hash function (SHA-1), as well as multiplication of ternary polynomials.

1   Introduction

In some sense, the provision of cryptographic schemes to secure information being communicated or stored is a compromise: higher levels of security necessitate higher levels of computational overhead. Given this fact, the study of low-cost implementation techniques that improve the efficiency and/or memory footprint of cryptographic schemes remains an ongoing research topic. In this context one can consider a spectrum of approaches. At one extreme are software-based techniques to manipulate algorithms so they are more efficient or more easily map to the capabilities of the host platform; at the other are hardware-based techniques which re-design or extend the platform to better suit algorithms. Somewhere in this design space is the technique of identifying and implementing Instruction Set Extensions (ISEs) [16,27,35]. The premise is that, after a careful workload characterisation, it is possible to identify a small set of operations that dominate the execution time of a software implementation. By supporting these specific operations using additional or modified hardware and exposing their behaviour to the programmer via the Instruction Set Architecture (ISA), performance can

E. Oswald and P. Rohatgi (Eds.): CHES 2008, LNCS 5154, pp. 331–345, 2008.

be significantly improved. This is often possible with only minor penalties in terms of datapath disruption and logic overhead; ideally a generic ISE is more attractive than one which is suited for use in only a single algorithm.

The design of custom instructions to support the execution of cryptographic workloads has been actively researched in the recent past. Previous work on cryptography extensions for general-purpose processors covered both public-key [2,16,30] and secret-key algorithms [9,15,8]. An example for the former are the Cryptography Instruction Set (CIS) extensions to the SPARC V8 architecture [17]. The CIS extensions consist of only six custom instructions, but allow one to accelerate the full range of public-key algorithms standardised in IEEE 1363 [20]; these include RSA, DSA, Diffie-Hellman, as well as elliptic curve schemes over prime and binary fields. Therefore, the CIS extensions are referred to as *domain-specific extensions*, in contrast to application-specific extensions like the ones described in [2,30], which support just a single public-key algorithm. The idea of domain-specific extensions is based on the observation that virtually all public-key algorithms of practical importance use either a multiplicative group ($\mathbb{Z}_p^*$ or $\mathbb{Z}_n^*$), a prime field, or a field of characteristic 2 as underlying algebraic structure. Thus, by designing custom instructions that accelerate the arithmetic of large integers and binary polynomials, it is possible to support a wide range of public-key cryptosystems.

Previous work on optimised architectures for secret-key cryptography considered the design Application-Specific Instruction set Processors (ASIPs) and the integration of custom instructions into general-purpose processors. Most of the published instructions are optimised for a single secret-key algorithm such as DES [12] or AES [4,13,35]. Among the few exceptions are the instruction sets of CryptoManiac [36], MOSES [32,33], and PAX [14], which were designed with the objective of more general applicability. CryptoManiac's architecture consists of a conglomeration of different sets of custom instructions, each set crafted for a specific algorithm based on its performance-critical core functions. Unfortunately, the design of custom instructions for a whole domain of algorithms is much harder for secret-key cryptography than for public-key cryptography, mainly due to the large number of different design strategies and underlying basic operations: instructions for accelerating the execution of one secret-key algorithm are in most cases useless for other algorithms.

Look-up tables are a generic and low-cost processor extension to increase the performance of various classes of applications, including secret-key algorithms [38]. These look-up tables can be configured to implement different dataflow subgraphs depending on the application being executed. Using this mechanism reduces the latency of the subgraph's execution and the number of temporary values that need to be stored to the register file. In [29], Patterson demonstrated the merits of this approach taking Serpent as example, whereby he achieved a throughput of 10 Gbit/sec on an FPGA implementation.

In this paper we introduce an ISE which can be used to accelerate a range of cryptographic algorithms that operate on data in a bit-oriented (rather than word-oriented) manner. In particular, we consider bit-sliced algorithms [5]. The exemplar use of bit-slicing is given by Biham, who extracted a 5-fold performance gain from DES [5]. However, beyond pure performance, one can identify another more subtle advantage from the general approach. By, for example, eliminating a (potentially very large) table used to represent S-box content, a typical bit-sliced implementation will have a smaller data memory footprint; despite the fact that the code memory footprint may slightly increase, the overall effect is usually a net gain. Furthermore, elimination of such tables also eliminates the need to execute instructions that access them. Depending on the exact memory hierarchy, this can result in (more) predictable, data-independent execution and thus prevent cache-based side-channel attacks [7,28]. Our proposed ISE capitalises on these significant advantages of bit-sliced implementation while further improving their performance, a factor which is often perceived as a disadvantage.

We organise the rest of this paper as follows. In Section 2 we recap on the concept of bit-slicing and introduce the design of our ISE and the host platform it is embedded into. We then use Section 3 to evaluate the ISE, demonstrating its generic nature by presenting application in six different case studies; in each case we are able to improve performance and reduce memory footprint versus an implementation on the same platform without the use of our ISE. Finally, in Section 5 we conclude and present some areas for further work.

2   ISE Definition

2.1   Bit-Sliced Implementation

Imagine a scalar processor with a w-bit word size, let x_i denote the i-th bit of a machine word x where i is termed the index of the bit. Such a processor operates natively on word-sized operands. For example, with a single operation one might perform addition of w-bit operands x and y to produce $r = x + y$, or component-wise XOR to produce $r_i = x_i \oplus y_i$ for all $0 \leq i < w$. This ability is restricted however when an algorithm is required to perform some operation involving different bits from the same word. For example, one might be required to combine x_i and x_j, where $i \neq j$, using an XOR operation in order to compute the parity of x. In this situation one is required to shift (and potentially mask) the bits so they are aligned at the same index ready for combination through a native, component-wise XOR. The technique of bit-slicing, proposed by Biham for efficient implementation of DES [5], offers a way to reduce the associated overhead. Instead of representing the w-bit value x as one machine word, we represent x using w machine words where word i contains x_i aligned at the same fixed index j. As such, there is no need to align bits ready for use in a component-wise XOR operation. Additionally, since native word-oriented logical operations in the processor operate on all w bits in parallel, one can pack w different values (say $x[k]$ for $0 \leq k < w$) into the w words and proceed using an analogy of a SIMD-style parallelism. Conversion to and from a bit-sliced representation can represent an overhead but this can be amortised if the cost of computation using the bit-sliced values is significant enough.

2.2   CRISP

A quarter century after many design decisions and assumptions were made by the pioneers of RISC, we are still using largely similar processor designs. One expects that such decisions were initially made using a mix of research and common sense based on prevailing technologies of the time. Despite the huge success of these assumptions, the technology landscape has now changed radically: the types of program we execute today are different and many of the constraints which guided initial thinking have disappeared. This is certainly true of cryptographic workloads as evidenced by previous work on application specific processors such as CryptoManiac [36] and Cryptonite [8].

CRISP (short for Cryptographic RISc Processor) represents an attempt to reassess some of these design decisions in the context of cryptography. The aim is to produce a processor design which is general purpose, but unencumbered by the constraints of history. For this paper, it suffices to consider CRISP as a conventional five-stage pipeline which, in contrast with the more conventional 3-address form, allows 6-address instructions. There are 16 general-purpose registers; this enables instructions to be encoded using a fixed 32-bit format. The philosophy is that, although this approach might, for example, dictate a lower clock frequency, central operations are more naturally described. Let the i-th entry in the general-purpose register file be denoted by $GPR[i]$, the datapath width be w and x_j denote the j-th bit of some w-bit word x. A representative example of said philosophy is the instruction for addition which uses three source operands (a, b and c) and two target operands (p and q). A conventional processor would maintain, and specify instruction for manipulating, a carry-flag; since an instruction can produce two results, CRISP treats the carry-flag as a general purpose register. The addition is therefore specified as

$$ADD\ p, q, a, b, c \ \mapsto \ \begin{aligned} t \quad &= \ (GPR[a] + GPR[b]) + GPR[c] \\ GPR[p] &= \ t_{w-1...0} \\ GPR[q] &= \ t_{2w-1...w} \end{aligned}$$

such that the three source operands are added together and low and high w-bit halves of the result are stored using the two target operands p and q. The clear disadvantage of such an instruction is higher latency; the advantages include removal for special-case management of the carry-flag and higher instruction throughput. We are aiming to improve the instruction throughput with a level of overhead somewhere between single issue and much more expensive multiple issue. Although the 6-address instruction format of CRISP is unconventional, one can imagine mechanisms to specify similar instructions in conventional 3-address architectures. One example is the use of SIMD instructions that pack multiple operands into registers addressed as one unit. Another approach is to serialise the operand transfers from/to the register file, which effectively relaxes the port constraints of instruction set extensions [31].

Within the general CRISP design we include three instructions which target bit-sliced implementation of cryptography. The processor includes two special purpose registers $LUT0$ and $LUT1$, which are used as 4-input, 1-output Look-Up Tables (LUTs). Configuration of the LUTs is performed by two instructions

$$CLUT0 \; a \quad \mapsto \quad LUT0_i = a_i$$
$$CLUT1 \; a \quad \mapsto \quad LUT1_i = a_i$$

each of which load the given LUT with a 16-bit immediate operand a, essentially configuring the LUTs. Use of the LUTs is performed with a third instruction

$$ULUT \; p, q, a, b, c, d \quad \mapsto \quad \begin{aligned} GPR[p]_i &= LUT0[8 \cdot a_i + 4 \cdot b_i + 2 \cdot c_i + 1 \cdot d_i] \\ GPR[q]_i &= LUT1[8 \cdot a_i + 4 \cdot b_i + 2 \cdot c_i + 1 \cdot d_i] \end{aligned}$$

which takes the i-th bit of each source operand and concatenates them to form an index into each LUT; the LUT output forms the i-th bit of the result, two of which are computed in parallel.

To illustrate the benefit of our approach, we use the dataflow subgraph in Figure 1(a) as example, which takes four inputs and produces two outputs via a series of simple logical instructions. On a general-purpose RISC processor, the cost of evaluating this subgraph is exactly six instructions as depicted in Figure 1(b). However, this form of subgraph can be implemented naturally using the LUTs described above; Figure 1(c) shows that the corresponding implementation consists of only two CLUT instructions and one ULUT instruction.

Since many important block ciphers rely on the efficient computation of bit-level permutations, we include architectural support for this type of operation within our design. Extensive research in this area has been conducted by Lee et al. [23,37,34]. In [23], Lee et al. described how a combination of GRP and SHIFT PAIR instructions can be used to perform arbitrary bit permutations. The GRP instruction is defined as follows

GRP Rs, Rc, Rd

It moves the bits in the source register Rs to the most significant bit positions and to the least significant bit positions according to the control bits in Rc. On

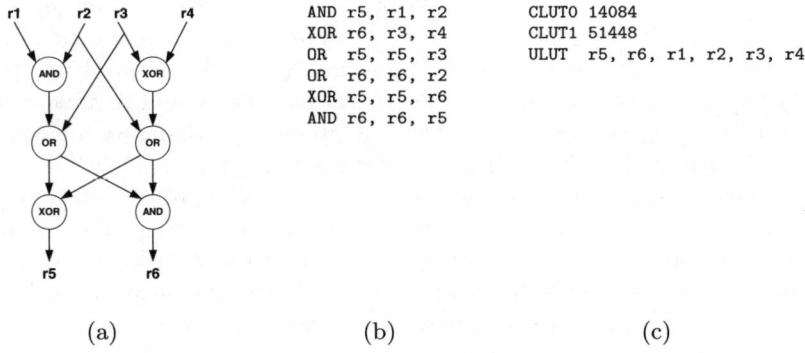

(a)   (b)   (c)

Fig. 1. An example dataflow subgraph (a) with the corresponding pseudo assembly code for a basic RISC machine (b) and for a LUT-based implementation (c)

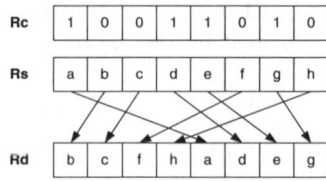

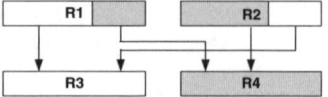

Fig. 2. GRP instruction [23]   **Fig. 3.** Shift Pair instruction [23]

an n-bit processor, no more than $\log(n)$ GPR instructions are required to perform an arbitrary n-bit permutation. Figure 2 illustrates the functionality of the GRP instruction in case of 8-bit registers. The SHIFT PAIR instruction is instrumental in supporting permutations that cross word boundaries. It concatenates two source registers and separates the contiguous bit regions into two destination registers as depicted in Figure 3.

3   Performance Evaluation

We implemented an early prototype of the CRISP processor using the Processor Designer tool-chain from CoWare. The tool-chain is based on the Language for Instruction Set Architectures (LISA), which allows one to describe a processor architecture at a high level of abstraction; the description allows automatic generation of an instruction set simulator, a complete suite of software development tools, and synthesisable VHDL code. As such, although the results are often less optimal than a hand-written alternative, the tool-chain allows one to quickly explore the ISE design space in order to identify and assess the relative merits of different custom instructions.

Starting with a LISA description of the CRISP 5-stage pipeline, we equipped the processor with Harvard-style data and instruction RAMs, each of 4KB, and synthesised the generated VHDL code using Xilinx ISE 7.3. Our experimental platform was an ADM-XRC-II PCI card which hosts a Xilinx Virtex-II FPGA (XC2V6000-4FF1152) device with $33,000$ slices. The synthesis report indicated that the processor core can operate at a maximum clock frequency of 30 MHz and occupies a total of roughly $9,500$ slices. The integration of our proposed LUTs has no negative impact on the critical path delay and requires about 280 slices. In order to demonstrate correct in-circuit behaviour, we augmented the processor core to include an interface with Xilinx Chipscope. In terms of both performance and area we posit that there is room for improvement: the automatically generated VHDL code is not ideal in a number of cases. For instance, the register file and RAM components are implemented as distributed RAM instead of dedicated block RAM; this leads to a significant overhead in terms of slices occupied by RAM resources and to long routing delays. Moreover, the tool-chain is not able to identify exclusive read operations to the register file from different instructions; it generates a total of 20 read ports although at most four would be sufficient. As a consequence, the critical path of the design lies in this specific part of the implementation and not in the ALU which would allow an operating frequency of nearly 50 MHz. We plan to address these issues at a later stage of the project when the definition of the instruction set architecture has been finalised.

Regardless of the implementation quality, our functional processor model is sufficient to accurately assess the merits of our LUT-based ISE. We developed six case studies which represent different cryptographic primitives with different demands; the results presented below identify each algorithm, the potential for LUT-based acceleration within the algorithm, and compare implementation results (in terms of performance and memory footprint) versus a non-LUT-based alternative. It should be mentioned that bit-sliced ciphers use a non-traditional format to represent data; hence, the format conversion from standard into the bit-sliced domain introduces additional overhead before and after the encryption operation. However, in a closed environment the data can be kept in bit-sliced representation and so the need for a data conversion is omitted. In the following performance evaluation we do not consider the overhead caused by conversion to and from bit-slice representation.

3.1   SHA-1

SHA-1 is a cryptographic hash function which was designed and published by the NIST in 1995. Although SHA-1 is today considered to be cryptographically insecure, it is still employed in a vast range of standard applications and protocols such as SSL, SSH, and IPSec. The algorithm accepts an arbitrary length input message, split into 512-bit blocks, and produces a 160-bit message digest. The state of computation is held in five 32-bit chaining variables a, b, c, d and e which the algorithm processes in four rounds each composed of twenty operations. A different nonlinear function is used in each of the four rounds; for instance the nonlinear function for the third round is given by

$$f_3(a, b, c) : (a \wedge c) \vee ((a \vee b) \wedge c).$$

Using a conventional RISC processor the evaluation of this function takes four instructions; with our LUT-based approach the same function can be realised with one ULUT instruction plus one initial CLUT instruction to configure the LUT before the round starts. In Table 1, we compare results using our LUT-based approach with the performance of SHA-1 on the same CRISP pipeline without using LUTs; the ISE permits a performance improvement by a factor of 1.11 while code memory footprint is reduced by 21%.

Table 1. Implementation results for SHA-1 compression function

Implementation	Performance (cycles)	Code footprint (bytes)
Standard SHA-1	1602	2620
SHA-1 with LUTs	1441	2060

3.2 Multiplication of Ternary Polynomials

Fast arithmetic in finite fields of characteristic three is important for efficient pairing evaluation using particular parameterisations. In algorithms for pairing evaluation, multiplication in some extension field represents the time-critical operation; the performance of this operation in turn depends on the efficiency of the underlying base field arithmetic.

Using a polynomial basis representation, one can hold an element $a \in \mathbb{F}_{3^n}$ as two n-element bit-vectors a^H and a^L [19]. Using a_i^H and a_i^L to denote the i-th bit of a^H and a^L, respectively, the vectors a^H and a^L are constructed from a such that for all i

$$a_i^H = a_i \text{ div } 2$$
$$a_i^L = a_i \text{ mod } 2.$$

That is, a^H and a^L are a bit-sliced representation of the coefficients of a where a^H and a^L hold the high and low bits of a given coefficient, respectively. Given such a representation, one can construct component-wise addition using logical operations. For example, a component-wise addition $r_i = a_i + b_i$ of two field elements a and b is specified by

$$r_i^H = (a_i^L \vee b_i^L) \oplus t$$
$$r_i^L = (a_i^H \vee b_i^H) \oplus t$$

where $t = (a_i^L \vee b_i^H) \oplus (a_i^H \vee b_i^L)$.

Using a conventional RISC processor, the cost of each component-wise addition is seven logical operations; with our LUT-based approach the same addition can be collapsed to obtain the high and low bits with two CLUT instructions and one ULUT instruction. To demonstrate the impact of this, we implemented the comb method for field multiplication in $\mathbb{F}_{3^{97}}$ (the characteristic-two analogue is detailed in [18, Algorithm 2.35]). A summary of the results is shown in Table 2; in comparison to the CRISP processor without LUTs, the LUT-based approach improves performance by a factor of 1.51 while code memory footprint is reduced by 33%.

Table 2. Implementation results for multiplication in $\mathbb{F}_{3^{97}}$

Implementation	Performance (cycles)	Code footprint (bytes)
Standard Multiply	8652	2656
Multiply with LUTs	5750	1784

3.3 Serpent

Serpent was one of five finalists in the AES competition; it is a 32-round substitution-permutation block cipher that operates on 128-bit data blocks. Anderson et al. [1] describe an efficient bit-sliced implementation in which each round is constructed from three layers: a key mixing operation, an S-box operation, and a linear transformation operation. In particular, the S-box layer is realised using a sequence of logical instructions that are applied to four 32-bit input words to produce four output words; each S-box is represented, on average, by about 17 logical instructions.

Implementing each S-box operation on a conventional RISC processor is hampered by the resulting register pressure which, in turn, can enforce costly spills to memory. The advantage of using our LUTs for the S-box layer in Serpent is two-fold: firstly, a series of logical operations can be implemented with only four CLUT and two ULUT instructions; secondly, we reduce the number of temporary variables such that there is less need to spill values into memory. To further improve the performance of the Serpent encryption operation, specific portions of the linear transformation layer can also be implemented with LUTs.

In Table 3 we compare the LUT-based approach to the original, reference approach of Anderson et al. [1]. The LUT-based approach improves performance by a factor of 2.2 and reduces code memory footprint by 53%.

Table 3. Implementation results for Serpent encryption

Implementation	Performance (cycles)	Code footprint (bytes)
Bit-sliced Serpent	2031	2112
Bit-sliced Serpent with LUTs	922	984

3.4   AES

AES can, by design, be implemented efficiently on 8-bit or 32-bit platforms. In order to perform encryption (resp. decryption), the AES algorithm iteratively applies a round function (resp. inverse round function) to a 4×4 state matrix of elements in $\mathbb{F}_{2^8}$. The round function is composed of four steps: SubBytes, a non-linear substitution via an S-box that roughly equates to inversion in $\mathbb{F}_{2^8}$; AddRoundKey, the addition of key material via XOR; ShiftRows, which simply rotates rows of the state; and MixColumns, which multiplies columns of the state by a constant matrix.

An 8-bit implementation typically represents the state matrix as an array of sixteen bytes and implements each step of the round function in a direct fashion [11, Section 4.1]. A 32-bit implementation typically packs the columns of the state matrix into four words and combines the round function steps into a set of table look-ups [11, Section 4.2]. Previous work has developed effective alternatives for bit-sliced implementations of AES [24,25,21]. Könighofer [21] gives a detailed description of a fast bit-sliced AES implementation on a 64-bit AMD Opteron processor. In this work, the state matrix is stored in eight different registers throughout the encryption routine and four blocks are processed in parallel. We implemented Könighofer's method on our CRISP processor; the half-sized datapath width means we process two blocks at a time.

In a bit-sliced AES implementation, SubBytes represents the time-critical operation. In contrast to conventional implementations that usually store the S-box as a table in memory, the S-box is expressed by a series of logical operations according to the description of Canright [10]. The basic idea is to decompose the calculation of the multiplicative inverse in $\mathbb{F}_{2^8}$ into the calculation of the inverse in $\mathbb{F}_{2^4}$ and $\mathbb{F}_{2^2}$, respectively. Certain parts of these subfield computations can be mapped efficiently to our LUTs, for instance the inverse of $x = (x_0, x_1, x_2, x_3) \in \mathbb{F}_{2^4}$ is given by

$$e = ((x_3 \oplus x_2) \wedge (x_1 \oplus x_0)) \oplus x_3 \oplus x_1$$
$$d_1 = (x_3 \wedge x_1) \oplus e$$
$$d_0 = (x_2 \wedge x_0) \oplus e \oplus x_2 \oplus x_0$$

On a conventional RISC processor, the cost of computing the inverse in $\mathbb{F}_{2^4}$ is eleven instructions; using a LUT-based approach the computation can be performed with as little as two CLUT instructions and one ULUT instruction. Similar to the Serpent case, the LUTs are useful in terms of both reducing the number of logical instructions as well as reducing the spills into memory. However, the ShiftRows operation requires a closer examination. Each single byte within a register that holds the state needs to be rotated by a different distance; on a conventional RISC processor this can require a number of shift-and-mask type operations. To overcome this problem, one can integrate a custom instruction for efficient bit-level permutation, as proposed by Lee et al. [37], which reduces the cost of ShiftRows dramatically. The execution times of these implementations are given in Table 4; comparing our LUT-based implementation to the standard bit-sliced AES implementation of Könighofer [21], we improve performance by a factor of 1.23 and reduce code memory footprint by 36%. Having a dedicated instruction for efficient bit-level permutation further improves performance by a factor of 2.21 and reduces code memory footprint by some 59%. In [3], Bertoni et al. describe a fast non-bit-sliced software implementation of the AES for a 32-bit RISC processor. Comparing this implementation to the fastest bit-sliced version, our ISE permits a performance improvement by a factor of 1.36 on a per-block basis and reduces code memory footprint by 26%.

Table 4. Implementation results on a per-block basis for AES encryption

Implementation	Performance (cycles)	Code footprint (bytes)
Standard AES [3] (i.e. 32-bit)	1662	1160
Bit-sliced AES [21]	2699	2080
Bit-sliced AES with LUTs	2203	1328
Bit-sliced AES with LUTs & perm.	1222	858

3.5 PRESENT

Bogdanov et al. [6] describe PRESENT, a light-weight block cipher that can be efficiently implemented in hardware. PRESENT is a 31-round substitution-permutation network block cipher operating on 64-bit blocks. The S-box layer is realised as a table which maps 4-bit inputs to 4-bit outputs. In a bit-sliced implementation, the 64-bit blocks are stored in sixty four different words such that the i-th bit of each block is held in the i-th word; on a 32-bit datapath this allows us to process thirty two blocks in parallel. The S-box layer is expressed by a sequence of thirty logical operations; in a LUT-based implementation this is realised using four `CLUT` instructions and two `ULUT` instructions. The results are summarised in Table 5; compared to the reference implementation executed on CRISP, our ISE improve performance by a factor of 1.42 and reduce code memory footprint by 18%.

Table 5. Implementation results for PRESENT encryption

Implementation	Performance (cycles)	Code footprint (bytes)
Bit-sliced PRESENT	39986	500
Bit-sliced PRESENT with LUTs	28082	408

3.6 DES

The performance-critical operations in a standard DES software implementation are bit-oriented (e.g. permutation); in some sense this is a result of the hardware based origins of the algorithm. These sorts of operation are costly in software when implemented on a conventional RISC processor. As mentioned previously, Biham [5] described a fast implementation of DES using bit-slicing where the overhead caused by bit-oriented permutations is vastly reduced. Each S-box operation maps a 6-bit input to a 4-bit output and use of bit-slicing means their application is a bottleneck; the S-boxes require at most 132 logical operations and 100 instructions on average.

To reduce this cost, Kwan [22] presented an algorithm to generate S-boxes with an average of 56 logical operations. We examined each S-box using the Mimosys Clarity tool-chain [26] to identify where our ISE could be applied. The tool-chain takes C source code as input and analyses the data-flow graph to find subgraphs which can be implemented using a given ISA; in our case we had it search for 4-input, 2-output subgraphs consisting only of logical operations. The obtained speed-up factors of the bit-sliced DES S-boxes are detailed in Table 6; compared to Kwan's implementation we improve the performance of the S-box layer by a factor of 1.12 using the LUT-mechanism.

Table 6. Analysis of bit-sliced DES S-Boxes

S-Box	S1	S2	S3	S4	S5	S6	S7	S8
Speed-up factor	1.10	1.11	1.09	1.12	1.12	1.13	1.13	1.13

4 Comparison and Discussion

In recent years, custom instructions for secret-key cryptography have been integrated into a wide variety of platforms, ranging from high-performance ASIPs to

Table 7. Comparison of general-purpose processors with crypto extensions

Design	Base arch.	Algorithms and throughput (in cycles per byte)
MOSES [32]	Xtensa (32-bit)	3DES: 42.1 cpb, AES: 87.5 cpb
PAX [15]	RISC (64-bit)	3DES: 79.5, AES: 7.86, Twofish: 39.0, Mars: 85.21
O'Melia [27]	SPARC (32-bit)	3DES: 56.1 cpb, AES: 47.5 cpb, IDEA: 60.6 cpb
CRISP	RISC (32-bit)	SHA-1: 45.0 cpb, AES: 76.4 cpb, Serpent: 57.6 cpb

embedded processors optimised for small area and low power consumption. The plethora of target applications makes a fair comparison of the different designs very difficult, if not impossible. For example, Cryptonite [8] is an ASIP dedicated to cryptographic algorithms[1] and not a general-purpose processor with crypto extensions like CRISP. On the other hand, the custom instructions described in [4,13,35] were designed for integration into general-purpose processors, but their applicability is restricted to a single cryptosystem (AES), while the instructions introduced in this paper allow one to accelerate any cryptographic algorithm that can be implemented via bit-slicing.

Table 7 shows a comparison of CRISP with other general-purpose processors with crypto extensions which followed a similar design strategy, namely support of more than just a single cryptographic algorithm and orientation towards the embedded domain, which requires to consider both performance and hardware cost rather than focussing solely on the former. We omitted CryptoManiac as it is a 4-way VLIW processor optimised for high-bandwidth applications. Even though we restrict our comparison to closely related designs, the figures in Table 7 should be taken with a pinch of salt due to differences in the respective base architectures (e.g. 32-bit vs. 64-bit). MOSES supports only two secret-key algorithms (3DES and AES) while the instruction set of PAX is applicable to a wider range of algorithms of which seven were evaluated in [15] on basis of a 64-bit version of the architecture. The throughput figures of all four designs lie between 40 and 90 cycles per byte for the different algorithms, except of AES on PAX, which is extremely fast. In summary, the results of CRISP compare very well with that of previous work, especially when considering the flexibility and cost-efficiency of its crypto instructions.

5   Conclusions

We have presented a light-weight, generic instruction set extension for a 32-bit RISC processor with a 6-address instruction format (four source registers and two destination registers). Focusing on bit-sliced implementation, the ISE helps to address the disadvantages of this technique; for example, it improves performance and reduces code memory footprint, while maintaining all the advantages including low data memory footprint and predictable execution. Thanks to the

---

[1] The programmability of an ASIP is limited to applications within the application domain it has been designed for (e.g. cryptography), while a general-purpose processor can execute any kind of application.

generic nature of the proposed extensions, our processor architecture allows for a high degree of algorithm agility. This is a desirable feature when executing algorithm-independent security protocols, such as SSL/TLS or IPSec, where the support of several secret-key algorithms is essential. Moreover, the flexibility of our design can even be exploited by next-generation algorithms rather than being restricted to current-generation algorithms. In terms of hardware cost, the implementation of our ISE represents a modest overhead (just 280 slices of a Virtex-II device). Even though the proposed ISE might not be applicable in a high-performance processor design, it represents an excellent trade-off between implementation quality and cost for embedded and mobile processors.

Acknowledgements

The work described in this paper has been supported by the EPSRC under grant EP/E001556/1 and, in part, by the European Commission through the IST Programme under contract IST-2002-507932 ECRYPT. The information in this document reflects only the authors' views, is provided as is and no guarantee or warranty is given that the information is fit for any particular purpose. The user thereof uses the information at its sole risk and liability.

References

1. Anderson, R., Biham, E., Knudsen, L.: Serpent: A proposal for the Advanced Encryption Standard. Technical report,
   http://www.cl.cam.ac.uk/~rja14/serpent.html
2. Bartolini, S., Branovic, I., Giorgi, R., Martinelli, E.: A performance evaluation of ARM ISA extension for elliptic curve cryptography over binary finite fields. In: Proceedings of the 16th Symposium on Computer Architecture and High Performance Computing (SBAC-PAD 2004), pp. 238–245. IEEE Computer Society Press, Los Alamitos (2004)
3. Bertoni, G., Breveglieri, L., Fragneto, P., Macchetti, M., Marchesin, S.: Efficient software implementation of AES on 32-bit platforms. In: Kaliski Jr., B.S., Koç, Ç.K., Paar, C. (eds.) CHES 2002. LNCS, vol. 2523, pp. 129–142. Springer, Heidelberg (2003)
4. Bertoni, G.M., Breveglieri, L., Farina, R., Regazzoni, F.: Speeding up AES by extending a 32-bit processor instruction set. In: Proceedings of the 17th IEEE International Conference on Application-Specific Systems, Architectures and Processors (ASAP 2006), pp. 275–279. IEEE Computer Society Press, Los Alamitos (2006)
5. Biham, E.: A fast new DES implementation in software. In: Biham, E. (ed.) FSE 1997. LNCS, vol. 1267, pp. 260–272. Springer, Heidelberg (1997)
6. Bogdanov, A., Knudsen, L.R., Leander, G., Paar, C., Poschmann, A., Robshaw, M.J., Seurin, Y., Vikkelsoe, C.: PRESENT: An ultra-lightweight block cipher. In: Paillier, P., Verbauwhede, I. (eds.) CHES 2007. LNCS, vol. 4727, pp. 450–466. Springer, Heidelberg (2007)
7. Bonneau, J., Mironov, I.: Cache-collision timing attacks against AES. In: Goubin, L., Matsui, M. (eds.) CHES 2006. LNCS, vol. 4249, pp. 201–215. Springer, Heidelberg (2006)

8. Buchty, R., Heintze, N., Oliva, D.: Cryptonite – A programmable crypto processor architecture for high-bandwidth applications. In: Müller-Schloer, C., Ungerer, T., Bauer, B. (eds.) ARCS 2004. LNCS, vol. 2981, pp. 184–198. Springer, Heidelberg (2004)
9. Burke, J., McDonald, J., Austin, T.: Architectural support for fast symmetric-key cryptography. In: Proceedings of the 9th International Conference on Architectural Support for Programming Languages and Operating Systems (ASPLOS 2000), pp. 178–189. ACM Press, New York (2000)
10. Canright, D.: A very compact S-box for AES. In: Rao, J.R., Sunar, B. (eds.) CHES 2005. LNCS, vol. 3659, pp. 441–455. Springer, Heidelberg (2005)
11. Daemen, J., Rijmen, V.: The Design of Rijndael: AES – The Advanced Encryption Standard. Springer, Heidelberg (2002)
12. Davies, P.L., Robsky, S.R.: Customized processor extension speeds network cryptology. Electronic Design 50(19), 83–88 (2002)
13. Elbirt, A.J.: Fast and efficient implementation of AES via instruction set extensions. In: Proceedings of the 21st International Conference on Advanced Information Networking and Applications (AINA 2007), vol. 1, pp. 481–490. IEEE Computer Society Press, Los Alamitos (2007)
14. Fiskiran, A.M., Lee, R.B.: PAX: A datapath-scalable minimalist cryptographic processor for mobile devices. In: Embedded Cryptographic Hardware: Design and Security, pp. 19–34. Nova Science Publishers (2004)
15. Fiskiran, A.M., Lee, R.B.: On-chip lookup tables for fast symmetric-key encryption. In: Proceedings of the 16th IEEE International Conference on Application-specific Systems, Architectures and Processors (ASAP 2005), pp. 356–363. IEEE Computer Society Press, Los Alamitos (2005)
16. Großschädl, J., Savaş, E.: Instruction set extensions for fast arithmetic in finite fields GF(p) and GF(2^m). In: Joye, M., Quisquater, J.-J. (eds.) CHES 2004. LNCS, vol. 3156, pp. 133–147. Springer, Heidelberg (2004)
17. Großschädl, J., Tillich, S., Szekely, A., Wurm, M.: Cryptography instruction set extensions to the SPARC V8 architecture (preprint submitted for publication, 2007)
18. Hankerson, D., Menezes, A., Vanstone, S.: Guide to Elliptic Curve Cryptography. Springer, Heidelberg (2004)
19. Harrison, K., Page, D., Smart, N.P.: Software implementation of finite fields of characteristic three, for use in pairing pased cryptosystems. LMS Journal of Computation and Mathematics 5(1), 181–193 (2002)
20. Institute of Electrical and Electronics Engineers (IEEE). IEEE Std 1363-2000: IEEE Standard Specifications for Public-Key Cryptography
21. Könighofer, R.: A fast and cache-timing resistant implementation of the AES. In: Topics in Cryptology — CT-RSA 2008. LNCS, vol. 4964, pp. 187–202. Springer, Heidelberg (2008)
22. Kwan, M.: Reducing the gate count of bitslice DES. Cryptology ePrint Archive, Report 2000/051 (2000), http://eprint.iacr.org
23. Lee, R.B., Shi, Z., Yang, X.: Efficient permutation instructions for fast software cryptography. IEEE Mirco. 21(6), 56–69 (2001)
24. Matsui, M.: How far can we go on the x64 processors? In: Robshaw, M.J.B. (ed.) FSE 2006. LNCS, vol. 4047, pp. 341–358. Springer, Heidelberg (2006)
25. Matsui, M., Nakajima, J.: On the power of bitslice implementation on Intel Core2 processor. In: Paillier, P., Verbauwhede, I. (eds.) CHES 2007. LNCS, vol. 4727, pp. 121–134. Springer, Heidelberg (2007)
26. Mimosys. Clarity Product Datasheet (July 2006),
    http://www.mimosys.com/pdf/Mimosys_Clarity_Product_Datasheet.pdf

27. O'Melia, S.R.: Instruction Set Extensions for Enhancing the Performance of Symmetric-Key Cryptography. M.Sc. Thesis. University of Massachusetts, Lowell (2007)
28. Osvik, D.A., Shamir, A., Tromer, E.: Cache attacks and countermeasures: The case of AES. In: Pointcheval, D. (ed.) CT-RSA 2006. LNCS, vol. 3860, pp. 1–20. Springer, Heidelberg (2006)
29. Patterson, C.: A dynamic FPGA implementation of the Serpent block cipher. In: Paar, C., Koç, Ç.K. (eds.) CHES 2000. LNCS, vol. 1965, pp. 141–155. Springer, Heidelberg (2000)
30. Phillips, B.J., Burgess, N.: Implementing 1,024-bit RSA exponentiation on a 32-bit processor core. In: Proceedings of the 12th IEEE International Conference on Application-specific Systems, Architectures and Processors (ASAP 2000), pp. 127–137. IEEE Computer Society Press, Los Alamitos (2000)
31. Pozzi, L., Ienne, P.: Exploiting pipelining to relax register-file port constraints of instruction-set extensions. In: Proceedings of the 8th International Conference on Compilers, Architecture and Synthesis for Embedded Systems (CASES 2005), pp. 2–10. ACM Press, New York (2005)
32. Ravi, S., Raghunathan, A., Potlapally, N.R., Sankaradass, M.: System design methodologies for a wireless security processing platform. In: Proceedings of the 39th Design Automation Conference (DAC 2002), pp. 777–782. ACM Press, New York (2002)
33. Ravi, S., Raghunathan, A., Potlapally, N.R.: Securing wireless data: System architecture challenges. In: Proceedings of the 15th International Symposium on System Synthesis (ISSS 2002), pp. 195–200. ACM Press, New York (2002)
34. Shi, Z., Lee, R.B.: Bit permutation instructions for accelerating software cryptography. In: Proceedings of the 12th IEEE International Conference on Application-Specific Systems, Architectures, and Processors (ASAP 2000), pp. 138–148. IEEE Computer Society Press, Los Alamitos (2000)
35. Tillich, S., Großschädl, J.: Instruction set extensions for efficient AES implementation on 32-bit processors. In: Goubin, L., Matsui, M. (eds.) CHES 2006. LNCS, vol. 4249, pp. 270–284. Springer, Heidelberg (2006)
36. Wu, L., Weaver, C., Austin, T.M.: CryptoManiac: A fast flexible architecture for secure communication. In: Proceedings of the 28th Annual International Symposium on Computer Architecture (ISCA 2001), pp. 110–119. ACM Press, New York (2001)
37. Yang, X., Vachharajani, M., Lee, R.B.: Fast subword permutation instructions based on butterfly networks. In: Media Processors 2000. Proceedings of the SPIE, vol. 3970, pp. 80–86. SPIE (1999)
38. Yehia, S., Clark, N.T., Mahlke, S.A., Flautner, K.: Exploring the design space of LUT-based transparent accelerators. In: Proceedings of the 8th International Conference on Compilers, Architecture and Synthesis for Embedded Systems (CASES 2005), pp. 238–249. ACM Press, New York (2005)

Power and Fault Analysis Resistance
in Hardware through Dynamic Reconfiguration

Nele Mentens[1,2], Benedikt Gierlichs[1], and Ingrid Verbauwhede[1]

[1] Katholieke Universiteit Leuven, ESAT/SCD-COSIC and IBBT
Kasteelpark Arenberg 10, B-3001 Leuven-Heverlee, Belgium
{firstname.lastname}@esat.kuleuven.be
[2] Katholieke Hogeschool Limburg, IWT
Agoralaan Gebouw B bus 3, B-3590 Diepenbeek, Belgium
nele.mentens@iwt.khlim.be

Abstract. Dynamically reconfigurable systems are known to have many
advantages such as area and power reduction. The drawbacks of these
systems are the reconfiguration delay and the overhead needed to provide
reconfigurability. We show that dynamic reconfiguration can also improve
the resistance of cryptographic systems against physical attacks. First,
we demonstrate how dynamic reconfiguration can realize a range of countermeasures which are standard for software implementations and that
were practically not portable to hardware so far. Second, we introduce a
new class of countermeasure that, to the best of our knowledge, has not
been considered so far. This type of countermeasure provides increased
resistance, in particular against fault attacks, by randomly changing the
physical location of functional blocks on the chip area at run-time. Third,
we show how fault detection can be provided on certain devices with negligible area-overhead. The partial bitstreams can be read back from the
reconfigurable areas and compared to a reference version at run-time
and inside the device. For each countermeasure, we propose a prototype
architecture and evaluate the cost and security level it provides. All proposed countermeasures do not change the device's input-output behavior,
thus they are transparent to upper-level protocols. Moreover, they can
be implemented jointly and complemented by other countermeasures on
algorithm-, circuit-, and gate-level.

1 Introduction

After the production of the first Complex Programmable Logic Devices (CPLD)
and Field Programmable Gate Arrays (FPGA) in the 1980s, research in programmable devices has evolved in many directions. To put our idea in context,
the following advances are worth mentioning. Partial reconfiguration increases
the performance of a reconfigurable system by reducing the reconfiguration time.
This can be done dynamically at run-time and without user interaction, while
the static part of the chip is not interrupted. The idea we put into practice is
a coarse-grained partially dynamically reconfigurable implementation of a cryptosystem. Our prototype implementation consists of a FPGA which is partially

E. Oswald and P. Rohatgi (Eds.): CHES 2008, LNCS 5154, pp. 346–362, 2008.

reconfigured at run-time to provide countermeasures against physical attacks. The static part is only configured upon system reset.

Some advantages of dynamic reconfiguration for cryptosystems have been explored before. In such systems, the main goal of dynamic reconfigurability is to use the available hardware resources in an optimal way. This is the first work that considers to use a coarse-grained partially dynamically reconfigurable architecture in cryptosystems to prevent physical attacks by introducing temporal and/or spatial jitter. Note that the proposed countermeasures do not represent an all embracing security solution and should be complemented by other countermeasures.

The first experimental results of power analysis attacks on FPGAs were given by Örs et al. [20]. Standaert et al. examined the effect of pipelining and unrolling techniques on the power consumption of FPGAs [23]. Power analysis countermeasures based on the random pre-loading of pipelining registers are evaluated in [22]. Successful fault injection on FPGAs is reported by Maingot et al. in [16]. The concept of spatial jitter for hardware implementations has been addressed in [2] and [8], where architectures are proposed that consist of several identical elementary cells. An algorithm's suboperations are randomly mapped on these cells. In our solution, the suboperations are always performed in the same functional blocks, but these blocks are randomly relocated.

This paper is organized as follows: Section 2 gives an overview of the physical attacks and countermeasures relevant for this work. Section 3 describes the initial assumptions and the setup. Sections 4, 5, and 6 introduce the countermeasures temporal jitter, combination of spatial and temporal jitter, and fault detection for partially dynamically reconfigurable systems. Finally, Sect. 7 concludes the paper.

2   Physical Attacks and Countermeasures

Differential Side Channel Attacks (DSCA), as introduced by Kocher et al. [14], are passive attacks. They exploit the fact that there exists a relation between the bit-flips in an electronic cryptographic device and its instantaneous power dissipation. Since the bit-flips in the device depend on the values it is processing, and since these data depend on a secret, e.g. a cryptographic key, there exists a link between the secret and the power dissipation. First, an adversary observes the target device's power dissipation during the encryption of several messages X. She targets an intermediate result $f_{k_c}(X)$ of the cryptographic computation that depends on the known and varying data X and a (small) part of the secret key k_c. At the time instant t_c when this particular value is computed, there exists a significant correlation between the intermediate values $f_{k_c}(X)$ and the observed power dissipation $O(t_c)$. Since, in general, both t_c and k_c are unknown, the adversary performs an exhaustive search over all time instants t and key hypotheses k. For this search, she computes the values of $f_{k'}(X)$ based on a key guess k' and applies a power consumption model to derive hypothetical power consumption values $h(\cdot)$. Then, she applies a statistical test to measure the correlation between the predicted and the observed power dissipation at all instants t. For one combination of the parameters t and k', the correlation will be significantly higher than for all others. This reveals not only the correct key k_c but also the time instant t_c when the targeted intermediate result is computed. We apply Correlation Power Analysis [7], predict the hypothetical power dissipation $h(f_{k'}(X), R)$ as the Hamming distance between $f_{k'}(X)$ and a reference state R, and use the Pearson correlation coefficient $\rho(h(\cdot), O(t))$ as statistical test.

In practice, countermeasures aim at making an attack more difficult and ideally infeasible. In this context infeasible means to raise the cost of an attack beyond the gain due to a success. A metric for measuring the difficulty of an attack is the number of samples required. Although this is not an ideal metric (the number depends on too many factors which are difficult to rate) it is often applied in practice. Hence, DSCA countermeasures aim at increasing the number of required samples. There exist many approaches to achieve this goal. They can be categorized along the implementation axis (algorithm-, circuit-, and gate-level) or according to their functionality (masking and hiding), see Table 1.

Table 1. Overview of Differential Side Channel Analysis Countermeasures

	Algorithm	Circuit	Gate
Masking	Algorithmic masking	–	Gate level masking
Hiding	Random precharge	Noise Generators	Dual-Rail Precharge
	Dummy cycles	Decoupled power	Logic
	Random Order Execution	supply	Current Mode Logic

Reference [18] presents a coarse-grained architecture that uses reconfigurability to provide an algorithmic masking scheme. In this work we focus on power analysis countermeasures that aim at introducing temporal jitter into the sequence of operations, $i.e.$ distributing the instant t_c over time for several observations. Such countermeasures are effective because the intermediate result $f_{k_c}(X)$ is no longer computed at a fixed instance. It rather occurs at a set of different time instants $\mathcal{T}$ with probability distribution $\mathcal{P}$. Examples of this type of countermeasure for software implementations are Random Process Interrupts (Dummy Cycles) [10], and Random Order Execution [24]. Reference [1] presents a "Smart Processor" that inserts random delays autonomously and code independent. For hardware implementations the only countermeasure of this category we are aware of are asynchronous circuits [6]. Note that they can introduce vulnerabilities to timing attacks, since the execution time of the implementation might depend on the processed data itself. Moreover, asynchronous circuits generally require a longer design time than synchronous circuits. While the software countermeasures are easy to implement and virtually platform independent, an asynchronous circuit needs to be designed from scratch and implemented carefully.

Fault attacks are active attacks. In the broadest sense, they expose the target device to physical stress in order to provoke abnormal behavior. An additional information flow can be caused, if the cryptographic device returns erroneous cryptograms or a modified execution path is entered. The exploitation of faulty cryptograms may involve mathematical cryptanalysis. We distinguish between transient and permanent faults. A fault is transient if the device remains fully functional and the effect is of short duration (*e.g.* one clock cycle). A fault is permanent if its effect persists during the lifetime of the device. We also distinguish two classes of attacks. One class is composed of attacks that require a single successful fault injection to achieve the goal as for example the Bellcore attack [5] against a RSA-CRT implementation. Attacks in the other class usually require many successfully injected faults to achieve their goal. As examples we mention Collision Fault Analysis (CFA) [12], Differential Fault Analysis (DFA) [3], and Ineffective Fault Analysis (IFA) [9, 4].

Fault analysis countermeasures can be divided in at least three categories. Countermeasures of the first kind do not aim at preventing fault injection and the fault's effect, but intend to make the exploitation of the fault difficult and ideally infeasible. These countermeasures aim, as in the context of DSCA, at distributing the instant t_c at which a given operation is executed over a time interval. The second kind of countermeasure aims at detecting a fault injection by, for instance, introducing redundancy and checking for errors. This can be done at the data level using a suitable code and at the software level by executing the algorithm twice and comparing the results. In hardware, one can also implement the circuit twice and run both executions in parallel, or implement the circuit in dual-rail logic with a dedicated error state. The third kind of countermeasure aims at detecting the fault injection attempt. Usually, dedicated sensors are integrated into the circuit and/or the chip package.

In this paper we introduce countermeasures of all aforementioned types for partially dynamically reconfigurable devices.

3   Setup and Assumptions

3.1   Adversarial Model

The adversary is a malicious user of the device under attack, though she can be the legitimate owner. She wants to extract confidential data, *e.g.* cryptographic keys. The adversary can perform all kinds of passive attacks, in particular power analysis.

With respect to fault analysis, we apply the notions of the adversarial model introduced by Lemke-Rust and Paar in [15]. The adversary can also perform a range of active attacks, namely those categorized as semi-invasive. Summarizing this means, that the adversary can penetrate the device as much as to open the chip's package. Penetration of what is called the cryptographic boundary is not included. However, the adversary may use fault injection mechanisms that cross this line, *e.g.* photons.

An attack is successful, if enough key information is obtained to recover the entire key with or without further cryptanalysis. The adversary is able to inject at most q faults per second, where q is a small number. The adversary can use r fault injection setups in parallel where again r is a small number. Fault injection is a probabilistic process with success rate p. Complementary events with probability $1-p$ have no or not the intented effect and cannot be exploited. In specific attack scenarios, unsuccessful fault injection can even turn an attack infeasible because the adversary can not distinguish a cryptogram where the fault effect is as desired from a cryptogram where the fault effect is different.

Faults can be injected by precisely timed modifications of the clock signal or the power supply (glitches), intense illumination with focused white light or a laser beam, intense electromagnetic fields, rapid changes of the temperature, *etc.* Note that we exclude precise and deterministic permanent modification of the chip, *e.g.* cutting and re-wiring using a focused ion beam, from the adversary's capabilities. That is, we do not consider invasive adversaries. For all fault injection techniques, we assume that a successfully injected fault has a random and non-predictable effect on the targeted volume in the device. Although this makes the adversary appear weaker than she might be, it allows a compact analysis of the security level of the proposed countermeasures. Further, it is without doubt the most general and realistic model. Considering more specific fault models, such as deterministic bit-set and bit-reset, is beyond the scope of this work. To evaluate the adversary's success probability, we use the following definitions from [15].

Spatial resolution: let dA denote the target area at depth z with depth dz so that $dA \cdot dz$ is the target volume. ΔA is the area and Δz is the depth affected by the fault. The probability to stimulate the correct area on the chip surface is given as $p_{area} = 1$ if $\Delta A \leq dA$, and as $p_{area} = dA/\Delta A$ else. Since the penetration depth depends on various technological factors and cannot be estimated for a general case, we conservatively assume that the fault injection process always penetrates to the right depth, *i.e.* $p_{depth} = 1$. Combining the probabilities for area and depth therefore leads to $p_{volume} = p_{area}$.

Temporal resolution: let dt denote the targeted time interval during which a fault must be injected in order to be successful. Let ΔT denote the time resolution of the fault injection process. The probability to inject a fault at an instant where it leads to success is given as $p_{time} = 1$, if $\Delta T \leq dt$, and as $p_{time} = dt/\Delta T$ else.

The overall success probability is a function of (at least) these two probabilities. Thus in our case and given that they are independent $p = p_{volume} \cdot p_{time}$.

3.2   Reference Architecture and System Overview

To explain our countermeasures, we assume that the cryptographic algorithm to be implemented is a repetitive instruction that consists of a number of subfunctions. This is a realistic assumption for both symmetric and public key cryptosystems. Figure 1 shows the general architecture (bottom right) and floorplan (top right), respectively, consisting of n blocks each representing a subfunction.

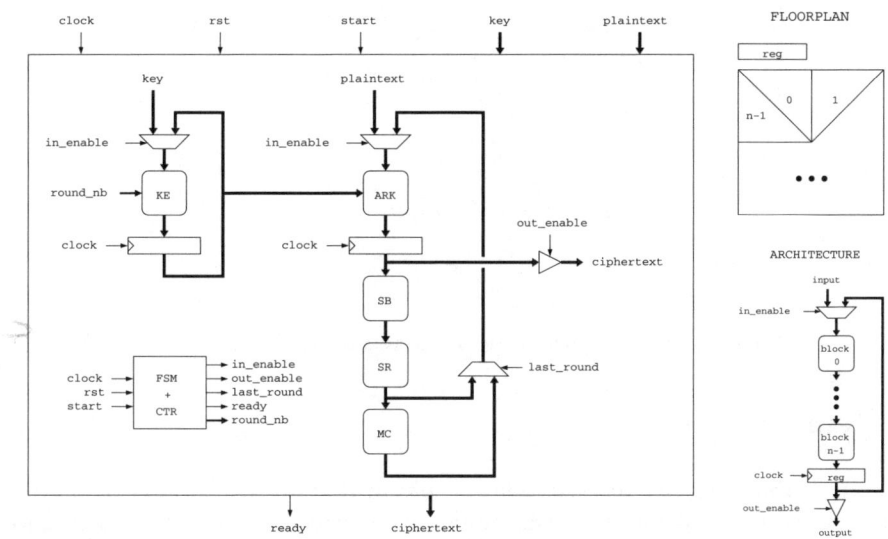

Fig. 1. General architecture and floorplan for the implementation of a repetitive algorithm consisting of n subfunctions (right) and reference architecture for our AES-128 prototype implementation (left)

These n blocks are executed a number of times and the intermediate result is saved in a register.

Moreover, we propose prototype implementations of AES with a 128-bit key [19]. The architecture of the fully parallel reference design of AES is depicted in Fig. 1 (left), where ARK, SB, SR and MC denote the subfunctions AddRoundKey, SubstituteBytes, ShiftRows and MixColumns, respectively. AES-128 consists of 10 rounds, where the round results are stored in an intermediate register. The roundkeys are computed on-the-fly using the KeyExpansion (KE) function and stored in the roundkey register. The intermediate register, the roundkey register, the multiplexors and the output buffer are controlled by the Finite State Machine (FSM) in combination with the round counter (CTR).

Our reference and prototype architectures are implemented on a Virtex-II Pro FPGA of Xilinx. In order to provide self-reconfiguration, an Internal Configuration Access Port (ICAP) [25] is added to the design. Figure 2 shows how a softcore MicroBlaze (μB) processor is connected to the partially reconfigurable AES coprocessor, the True Random Number Generator (TRNG) and the ICAP through the On-chip Peripheral Bus (OPB). The connection of the processor to the data and instruction memory (block RAM or BRAM) is realized over the Local Memory Bus (LMB). Since this paper only focuses on the security of the AES coprocessor, the bitstreams for our prototype implementations are stored in an external flash memory. More secure solutions include storing the bitstreams in the internal block RAM, although this has a limited capacity, or using secure external flash memory, as for example described by Handschuh and Trichina in [11].

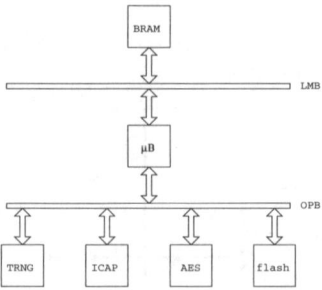

Fig. 2. Architectural view of the reconfigurable system

4   Temporal Jitter

As stated above, many attacks against physical implementations of crypto-graphic algorithms require that the timing of the executed operations is aligned for multiple executions. Since software countermeasures are flexible to apply and provide a high level of protection at the same time, we dedicate this section to the application of these well studied techniques to hardware implementations.

4.1   Description of a Generic Architecture

To port the idea of temporal jitter to hardware implementations, many registers could be foreseen in combination with multiplexors deciding whether to bypass a register or not. Because this would create a large overhead in resources, this option is highly impractical. We propose an architecture with a dynamically re-configurable switch matrix to avoid such a problem. The matrix determines the position of one or more registers in between functional blocks. Since a register causes a delay of one clock cycle, randomly positioning registers in between sub-functions de-synchronizes the observations. Our architecture is shown in Fig. 3. It is an improvement of the reference architecture shown in Fig. 1 in Sect. 3.2.

The number of possible configurations depends on the number m of registers and the number n of blocks. The value n depends on the number of reasonable subfunctions in the algorithm, which may depend on the width of the data-path. The number of options increases if we allow cascaded registers in between func-tional blocks. This is shown in the third option for the switch matrix in Fig. 3. Note, however, that if we allow cascaded registers, there exist several configu-ration options that lead to identical sequences of combinatorial and sequential logic. Concerning this matter and allowing up to m cascaded registers, the num-ber c of *distinct* configurations is $\binom{n+m-1}{m}$, *i.e.* the number of combinations of m elements out of n, where the order does not matter and repetition is allowed. The probability to observe the same configuration twice is $1/c$. However, the number of possible configurations determines the size of the memory needed to store the configuration data and is therefore bounded. Further, an increasing number of intermediate registers increases the number of cycles needed for one

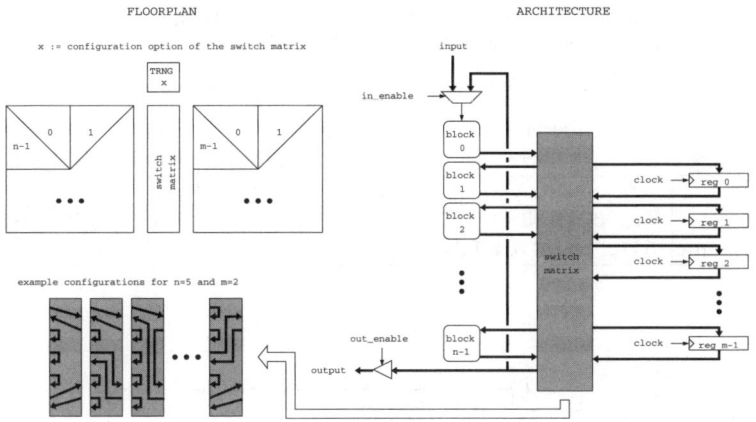

Fig. 3. Modified architecture for improved side channel analysis attack resistance

encryption. The number of registers, however, does not affect the maximal clock frequency, because we allow more than one register to be cascaded. In general, the number of options for the temporal shift is determined by the number m of registers and the number n of blocks, and is bounded above by c.

As illustrated in Fig. 3, a True Random Number Generator (TRNG) is used to select the next configuration of the switch matrix. It is important to note that the security of the architecture depends on strength of the TRNG and its resistance against fault and power analysis attacks. In this paper, we assume that the TRNG provides strong random numbers and withstands all adversaries covered by our model.

4.2   Example for AES-128 Encryption

In the fully parallel implementation of AES-128 in Fig. 1, four obvious subfunctions can be distinguished: AddRoundKey (ARK), SubstituteBytes (SB), ShiftRows (SR), and MixColumns (MC). We implemented a prototype based on the generic architecture proposed in the previous section where $n = 4$ and $m = 2$. The prototype and some options for the reconfiguration matrix are shown in Fig. 4. In this particular case and if we allow up to m cascaded registers in between functional blocks, the number of distinct configurations is $c = \binom{4+2-1}{2} = 10$.

The performance results of our implementation are compared to a static design in Table 2. The static design contains one register after each AES round, while the partially reconfigurable design contains $m = 2$ registers. The reconfiguration time of the switch matrix is approximately 3 ms. However, technological improvements reduce this number by a factor of at least 10. We also observed a decrease of the maximal clock frequency by a factor of more than 3. This is due to the communication between the static and the dynamic part of the design. The static part of the prototype design is larger than the fully static design. This

Table 2. Implementation results for the static design (one register) and the prototype dynamic design (two registers) on a Virtex-II Pro FPGA

	occupied area (# slices)	max. clock frequency (MHz)	through- put (Mbit/s)	reconf. time (ms)	reconf. data size (kB)	# conf. options
Static design	685(5%)	111	10			1
Prototype: static/dynamic	3251(23%) 1547(11%)/1704(12%)	33	1.5	3	91	10

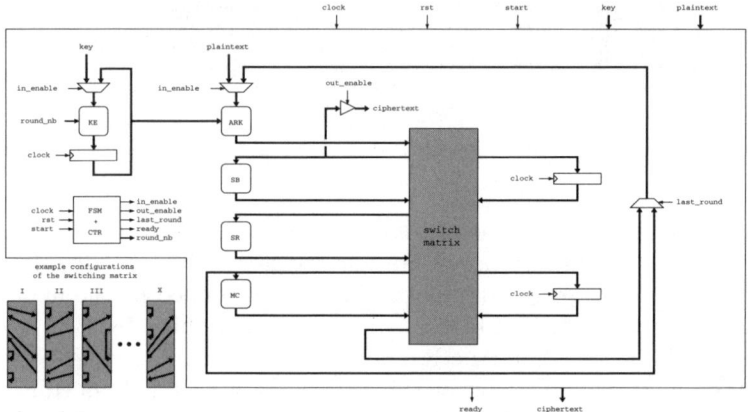

Fig. 4. Modified AES architecture for improved side channel analysis attack resistance

is because of the extra 128-bit register and because of the logic that is needed for the communication over the boundaries between the static and the dynamic part of the design.

4.3   Can the Countermeasure Be Circumvented?

An obvious approach to circumvent the countermeasure is to distinguish the different active configurations. If that is possible, an adversary can entirely undo the effect of the countermeasure by using only an appropriate subset of the observations that represent a single configuration. Therefore we examine, whether such a distinction is feasible using Timing Analysis (TA) [13] and Simple Power Analysis (SPA) [14].

The overall encryption time is constant and does therefore not reveal information about the circuit's internal configuration. The execution time is equal to $11 \cdot m$ cycles, where $m \geq 1$ is the number of intermediate registers.

Figure 5 shows power traces obtained from the prototype implementation while performing AES encryption in 2 out of 10 possible configurations. The two intermediate registers are pre-loaded with random data before the encryption starts. In this way, an attacker cannot deduce the position of the registers from the height of the first two peaks. This technique is similar to randomly pre-loading registers in a pipeline, as described in [22]. The plots support our claim that all implementations execute the algorithm in the same constant time. Additionally one can see that both plots look very similar, though not exactly the same. The slight differences are due to the pre-loading with random data and they are not configuration dependent features. These observations hold for all 10 possible configurations. Hence the power traces do not allow the distinction of the circuit's internal configuration. However, both TA and SPA allow an adversary to find out the number m of registers, which was fixed at design time.

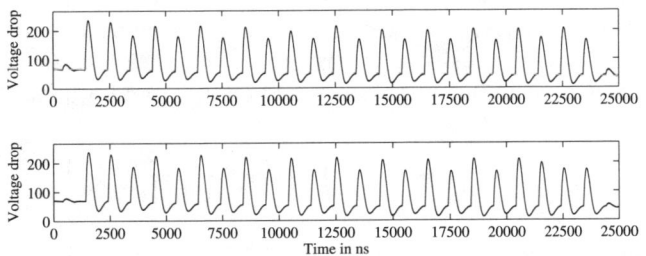

Fig. 5. Power traces of AES encryption in 2 configurations, with $n = 4$, $m = 2$ and a clock frequency of 1 MHz

Another approach to circumvent the countermeasure could consist of analyzing the circuit during dynamic reconfiguration. If an adversary can distinguish the different configurations, an attack as outlined above is feasible. We examine whether TA or SPA of the reconfiguration process might leak information about the circuit's current or next configuration. The spatial size of the reconfigurable area is constant and so is the size of the different bitstreams. Therefore, the timing of the entire reconfiguration process is constant and TA cannot reveal the circuit's current or next configuration. Similarly, the power consumption during reconfiguration does not show obvious configuration dependent features.

Without having exhausted all possibilities of TA and SPA, we assume that more elaborate analysis of both, the reconfiguration process and the actual encryption, does not allow to distinguish the configurations with a significant rate of success.

4.4   Resistance against DSCA

In this section we evaluate the level of protection that our countermeasure provides against DSCA. Recall that (standard) DSCA requires intermediate results to be synchronized in the time domain and that our countermeasure introduces time jitter.

In [17], Mangard studies the effectiveness of temporal de-synchronization as a DSCA countermeasure. He derives that, in the case of insertion of random delays, t_c is binomially distributed over time. Our proposal has the same effect.

Note that he implicitly assumes that t_c occurs at each $t \in \mathcal{T}$ equally likely, which is the most obvious choice. He derives a formula which allows to easily estimate the maximum correlation coefficient ρ_{max} as seen by an adversary. Taking his further simplifying steps into account and adapting to our notation, the equation becomes

$$\rho_{max} = \frac{\rho(h(f_{k_c}(X), R), O(t_c))}{\sqrt{1 + \frac{1}{SNR}}} \cdot \hat{p} = \rho' \cdot \hat{p} \tag{1}$$

where $\rho(h(f_{k_c}(X), R), O(t_c))$ is the correlation coefficient achieved for the correct key hypothesis k_c at the correct time instant t_c at an unprotected implementation and SNR is the signal to noise ratio. $\hat{p}$ is the the maximum probability in $\mathcal{P}$ and indicates the time instant $\hat{t}_c \in \mathcal{T}$ at which the targeted intermediate result occurs most likely. It is further possible to estimate the number S of samples required to break the protected implementation based on ρ_{max} and a quantile Z_α:

$$S = 3 + 8 \left(\frac{Z_\alpha}{\ln(\frac{1+\rho_{max}}{1-\rho_{max}})} \right) = 3 + 8 \left(\frac{Z_\alpha}{\ln(\frac{1+\rho' \cdot \hat{p}}{1-\rho' \cdot \hat{p}})} \right). \tag{2}$$

The probability α expresses the likelihood of an attack to be successful.

We evaluate our AES-128 prototype implementation w.r.t. these figures. When an attacker focuses on the storage of an intermediate result in a register, the first round is hard to attack, since all intermediate registers are pre-loaded with random values. Attacking the second round is difficult because of the diffusion property of AES. Therefore, we evaluate the effectiveness of our countermeasure under the assumption that an attacker analyzes the power consumption of the combinatorial logic. In our prototype design, the number of options for the temporal shift depends on which functional block is analyzed. Since SB is a common choice, we evaluate the number of options for the temporal shift of the computation of SB. We take into account that SB and SR can be swapped, which doubles the number of distinct configuration options and leads to $c = 20$. However, since t_c only depends on the number of registers preceding SB and the position of the last register, some configurations lead to the same temporal shift. In fact, there are 8 options with probabilities between $1/20$ and $6/20$, thus $\hat{p} = 6/20$. Under the conservative assumption of $\rho' = 1$, ρ_{max} decreases to $6/20$ and S, the amount of measurements required to break the implementation, increases by a factor of more than 3 for $Z_{alpha} = 0.5$ (the median). This number is not impressive at first sight, but note that this countermeasure can be complemented with for example a masking scheme and that we assumed $\rho' = 1$.

In [10], Clavier et al. propose the Sliding Window DPA. Although this attack is smarter since it takes into account what is actually happening in the target device, it is also much more difficult to mount in practice. The basic idea is to jointly analyze several time instants where the target value might occur, therefore effectively reversing the process of de-synchronization. The attack consists of a usual DSCA attack and a postprocessing of the differential traces. Clavier et al.

suggest to choose a suitable number of instants with a suitable distance between them to form a "comb". They suggest to slide the comb over each differential trace with a given offset and, at each position, to integrate the trace at all instants selected by the comb. As a result, one obtains the same number of integrated traces as differential traces. The integrated trace corresponding to the correct key guess does not show not a spike, but a clearly visible Gaussian 'peak'. They conclude that if the targeted intermediate result is spread over g consecutive cycles (a cycle is the smallest time unit for a software implementation) their attack requires g times more measurements. It remains, however, unclear how to choose the number of instants or their distance in practice, when one has little knowledge about the device and the implementation. For our prototype with two registers the spreading factor g is 8.

We also note that this countermeasure does not protect the functional blocks but rather the overall architecture.

4.5   Resistance against Fault Analysis

Here we evaluate the level of protection against fault attacks provided by the time jitter countermeasure. Using the definitions introduced in Sect. 3.1, the probability of a successful fault injection is $p = p_{volume} \cdot p_{time} = 6/20$, since we assume $p_{volume} = 1$. However, it is not necessarily possible for the adversary to distinguish between a successful and a non-successful fault injection. This can have a major impact if the fault attack requires multiple successful fault injections and further mathematical cryptanalysis, which is sensitive to incorrect input data. DFA, for example, usually requires several successful fault injections and might sieve out the correct key if a non-successfully faulted cryptogram is amongst the input data. Therefore, the countermeasure is effective although $p = 6/20$ is not that small in this example.

An adversary could also try to inject a fault that alters the circuit's behavior. The effect of a successfully injected fault on the switch matrix would only remain until the next dynamic reconfiguration of the matrix. Since the fault is transient, reconfiguration will bring the circuit back to its normal behavior. A successfully injected fault on any other functional block, on the other hand, remains until system reset. However, since we assume the random fault model and do not consider invasive adversaries it is highly unlikely that an adversary can modify the circuit's behavior in an exploitable way. Nevertheless, the functional blocks can be protected with complementary countermeasures.

We want to mention here one specific attack, though out of the model, that can pose a great risk. Should it be possible to inject a fault that flips a random number of bits in the key register to either zero or one with high probability, an attack as described in [3] can be carried out. Therefore a system designer might want to add further protection. For instance this can be done by duplicating the key register and comparing the contents to the original key register or applying the techniques described in the next section. These countermeasures can in general be applied to the static control part of the design.

5   Spatial and Temporal Jitter

In this section, we protect the cryptographic implementation using both temporal and spatial jitter. To achieve this, not only the moment in time when a value is stored or computed needs to be determined by dynamic reconfiguration, but also the position of the functional blocks. Therefore the time and place when/where a subfunction is executed in the resulting architecture is based on the reconfiguration option.

5.1   Description of a Generic Architecture

In order to further improve the resistance of the implementation against fault analysis attacks, we propose a dynamically reconfigurable architecture in which the location of the subfunctions and intermediate registers is altered randomly based on the output of a TRNG. The general architecture of a system including this countermeasure is depicted in Fig. 6. For each functional block, both a registered and a non-registered variant can be inserted dynamically, depending on the output of the TRNG, causing temporal jitter as described in Sect. 4.1. Moreover, the position of the blocks can be altered depending on a second output of the TRNG, causing spatial jitter. In order to connect the output of the last subfunction in the algorithm to the output of the design, all blocks have an extra output, which is connected to an OR-gate that combines all these extra outputs. Only the last block sends a value to the output, while the other blocks provide the OR-gate with zeros.

Suppose that the order of execution of the subfunctions in the algorithm is fixed and equal to f_0, f_1, ..., f_{n-1}, where f_i is the function that is implemented in block i. Then the number of possible positions of the functional blocks is

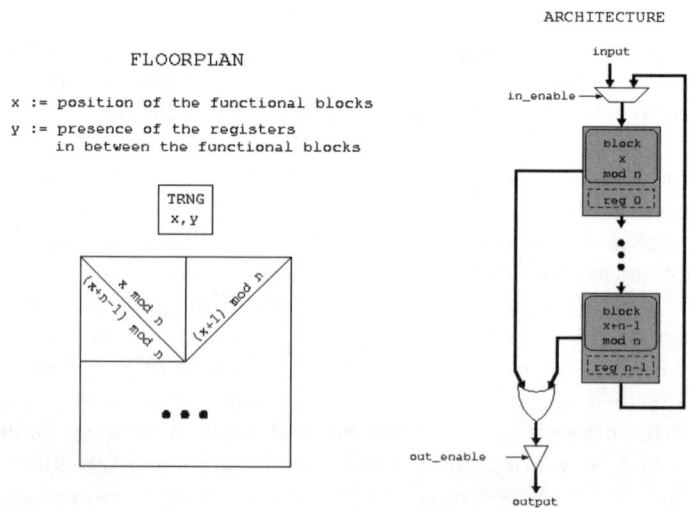

Fig. 6. Modified architecture for improved fault attack resistance

n. The probability of injecting a fault at a certain intended area on the chip surface, as denoted by p_{area} in Sect. 3.1, depends on the technology and the fault injection process. This countermeasure aims in particular at preventing local fault injection processes such as optical fault injection. We assume that the typical spatial focus in such an attack, *e.g.* the focus of a laser, is so small that the probability that a laser fault injection at the same (x,y) coordinates would still affect the same functional block after it has been relocated is negligible. Hence we have $p_{area} = 1/n$.

Suppose that each block can be followed by at most one register. Then the number of possible positions for the intermediate registers is n. The probability of injecting a fault at a certain intended moment in time, as denoted by p_{time} in Sect. 3.1, depends on the targeted subfunction and has a lower bound of $1/(m + 1)$.

5.2   Example for AES-128 Encryption

The high-level architecture of our AES-128 prototype is the same as the one in Fig. 2 in Sect. 3.2. The AES coprocessor is implemented according to the general architecture in Fig. 6 with $n = 4$. This means there are four regions which can be configured in eight possible ways, *i.e.* each region can be loaded with ARK, SB, SR, or MC, and each of these functions can be followed by a register. In this case, $p_{area} = 1/4$ and $p_{time} = 1/3$ with $m = 2$. Note that SR and SB can also be interchanged in the round sequence of AES, which increases the number of possible configurations even more. The reconfiguration time for this design is significantly higher than for the one shown in Fig. 4, since more regions need to be reconfigured. The maximal clock frequency on the other hand is similar.

5.3   Can the Countermeasure Be Circumvented?

Again we examine whether the countermeasure can be undone using TA or SPA. The results are similar to those presented in Sect. 4.3. In summary we observed a constant execution time both of the encryption and the partial reconfiguration process and no remarkable patterns in the power traces in either case. Therefore we conclude that neither TA nor SPA enables an adversary to distinguish the configurations with a significant rate of success.

5.4   Resistance against Fault Analysis

Here we evaluate the level of protection against fault attacks provided by the combined spatial and temporal jitter countermeasure. Most of the analysis presented in Sect. 4.5 also applies in this case. However, thanks to the jitter in both domains, the probability of a successful fault injection is $p = p_{volume} \cdot p_{time} = 1/12$.

Another interesting property of the spatial jitter is, that all functional blocks of the cryptosystem are now implemented in reconfigurable areas. Since the effect of a long-lasting transient fault can be undone by dynamic partial reconfiguration, the circuit can effectively recover from an injected fault. For the proposed fault attack countermeasure, the trade-off between security and reconfiguration delay should be seen in the context of the fault injection frequency. For example: the optical fault injection setup presented in [21] has a maximum laser pulse frequency of 50 Hz. Assuming a fault injection process with this kind of laser, the reconfiguration frequency can be lowered to 50 Hz (plus an additional security margin).

6   Fault Detection

In particular for FPGAs, fault detection can be realized by reading back one, some, or all bitstreams from the reconfigurable areas and comparing them with the reference copy stored in the block RAM. Certain FPGAs already allow to read back bistreams. Comparison to the reference bitstream can be done using (protected) logic gates inside the FPGA. Some vendors provide the stored bitstream with redundant CRC bits. In this case, it is more efficient to examine the bitstream that is read back based on its CRC value. The procedure of reading back the bitstream and comparing it (through logic or CRC check) to the reference copy of the bitstream only detects faults if the reference bitstream cannot be altered in the same way as the bitstream in the reconfigurable area. In our fault model, it is practically infeasible to insert a fault in the reconfigurable area and on the bitstream stored in block RAM with the same effect. Therefore, the probability that this kind of fault detection fails is negligible. Moreover, the scheme can be complemented with traditional fault detection mechanisms such as dual-rail precharge logic with an error state. Another option is to execute the implemented algorithm twice, either in parallel (which doubles the area) or sequentially (which doubles the execution time). In the architectures that we propose, both executions can run in different configurations, which increases the probability of fault detection.

All methods mentioned in this section focus on fault detection. It remains the system designer's choice how to react to an alarm signal. We note that for some attacks outputting the result first and then checking the bitstream for faults might raise an alarm when it is already too late. Checking before outputting seems to be more appropriate in such cases.

7   Conclusion

This paper introduces the use of partial dynamic reconfigurability as a countermeasure against physical attacks. On the one hand, side channel attack resistance can be improved by introducing temporal jitter. On the other hand, fault attack resistance can be improved by introducing spatial and/or temporal jitter. We also suggest a method to add a fault detection mechanism to a reconfigurable hardware design with negligible area overhead.

Acknowledgements

The authors would like to thank Kazuo Sakiyama and Frederik Gommé for their input and support.

This work was supported in part by the IAP Programme P6/26 BCRYPT of the Belgian State (Belgian Science Policy), by FWO projects G.0475.05, and G.0300.07, by the European Comission through the IST Programme under Contract IST-2002-507932 ECRYPT NoE, and by the K.U. Leuven-BOF.

The information in this document reflects only the authors' views, is provided as is and no guarantee or warranty is given that the information is fit for any particular purpose. The user thereof uses the information at its sole risk and liability.

References

1. Ambrose, J.A., Ragel, R.G., Parameswaran, S.: A Smart Random Code Injection to Mask Power Analysis Based Side Channel Attacks. In: Proceedings of CODES+ISSS, pp. 51–56. ACM, New York (2007)
2. Bajard, J.-C., Imbert, L., Liardet, P.-Y., Teglia, Y.: Leak Resistant Arithmetic. In: Joye, M., Quisquater, J.-J. (eds.) CHES 2004. LNCS, vol. 3156, pp. 62–75. Springer, Heidelberg (2004)
3. Biham, E., Shamir, A.: Differential Fault Analysis of Secret Key Cryptosystems. In: Kaliski Jr., B.S. (ed.) CRYPTO 1997. LNCS, vol. 1294, pp. 513–525. Springer, Heidelberg (1997)
4. Blömer, J., Seifert, J.P.: Fault Based Cryptanalysis of the Advanced Encryption Standard (AES). In: Wright, R.N. (ed.) FC 2003. LNCS, vol. 2742, pp. 162–181. Springer, Heidelberg (2003)
5. Boneh, D., DeMillo, R.A., Lipton, R.J.: On the Importance of Eliminating Errors in Cryptographic Computations. Journal of Cryptology 14(2), 101–119 (2001)
6. Bouesse, G.F., Renaudin, M., Sicard, G.: Improving DPA Resistance of Quasi Delay Insensitive Circuits Using Randomly Time-shifted Acknowledgment Signals. In: da Luz Reis, R.A., Osseiran, A., Pfleiderer, H.J. (eds.) Proceedings of VLSI-SoC. IFIP, vol. 240, pp. 11–24. Springer, Boston (2005)
7. Brier, E., Clavier, C., Olivier, F.: Correlation Power Analysis with a Leakage Model. In: Joye, M., Quisquater, J.-J. (eds.) CHES 2004. LNCS, vol. 3156, pp. 16–29. Springer, Heidelberg (2004)
8. Ciet, M., Neve, M., Peeters, E., Quisquater, J.-J.: Parallel FPGA Implementation of RSA with Residue Number Systems – Can side-channel threats be avoided? Cryptology ePrint Archive, Report 2004/187 (2004), http://eprint.iacr.org/
9. Clavier, C.: Secret External Encodings Do Not Prevent Transient Fault Analysis. In: Paillier, P., Verbauwhede, I. (eds.) CHES 2007. LNCS, vol. 4727, pp. 181–194. Springer, Heidelberg (2007)
10. Clavier, C., Coron, J.S., Dabbous, N.: Differential Power Analysis in the Presence of Hardware Countermeasures. In: Paar, C., Koç, Ç.K. (eds.) CHES 2000. LNCS, vol. 1965, pp. 253–263. Springer, Heidelberg (2000)
11. Handschuh, H., Trichina, E.: Securing Flash Technology. In: Breveglieri, L., Gueron, S., Koren, I., Naccache, D., Seifert, J.P. (eds.) Proceedings of FDTC, pp. 3–17. IEEE Computer Society, Los Alamitos (2007)
12. Hemme, L.: A Differential Fault Attack Against Early Rounds of (Triple-)DES. In: Joye, M., Quisquater, J.-J. (eds.) CHES 2004. LNCS, vol. 3156, pp. 254–267. Springer, Heidelberg (2004)

13. Kocher, P.: Timing Attacks on Implementations of Diffie-Hellman, RSA, DSS and other systems. In: Koblitz, N. (ed.) CRYPTO 1996. LNCS, vol. 1109, pp. 104–113. Springer, Heidelberg (1996)

14. Kocher, P., Jaffe, J., Jun, B.: Differential Power Analysis. In: Wiener, M.J. (ed.) CRYPTO 1999. LNCS, vol. 1666, pp. 388–397. Springer, Heidelberg (1999)

15. Lemke-Rust, K., Paar, C.: An Adversarial Model for Fault Analysis Against Low-Cost Cryptographic Devices. In: Breveglieri, L., Koren, I., Naccache, D., Seifert, J.-P. (eds.) FDTC 2006. LNCS, vol. 4236, pp. 131–143. Springer, Heidelberg (2006)

16. Maingot, V., Ferron, J.B., Leveugle, R., Pouget, V., Douin, A.: Configuration Errors Analysis in SRAM-based FPGAs: Software Tool and Practical Results. Microelectronics Reliability 47(9-11), 1836–1840 (2007)

17. Mangard, S.: Hardware Countermeasures against DPA – A Statistical Analysis of Their Effectiveness. In: Okamoto, T. (ed.) CT-RSA 2004. LNCS, vol. 2964, pp. 222–235. Springer, Heidelberg (2004)

18. Mesquita, D., Badrignans, B., Torres, L., Sassatelli, G., Robert, M., Moraes, F.: A Cryptographic Coarse Grain Reconfigurable Architecture Robust Against DPA. In: Proceedings of IPDPS, pp. 1–8. IEEE, Los Alamitos (2007)

19. NIST. Advanced Encryption Standard (AES). FIPS Publication 197 (2001)

20. Örs, S.B., Oswald, E., Preneel, B.: Power-Analysis Attacks on an FPGA – First Experimental Results. In: Walter, C.D., Koç, Ç.K., Paar, C. (eds.) CHES 2003. LNCS, vol. 2779, pp. 35–50. Springer, Heidelberg (2003)

21. New Wave Research. Quiklaze ST,
    http://www.new-wave.com/1nwrProducts/QuikLaze.htm

22. Standaert, F.-X., Mace, F., Peeters, E., Quisquater, J.-J.: Updates on the Security of FPGAs Against Power Analysis Attacks. In: Bertels, K., Cardoso, J.M.P., Vassiliadis, S. (eds.) ARC 2006. LNCS, vol. 3985, pp. 335–346. Springer, Heidelberg (2006)

23. Standaert, F.-X., Örs, S.B., Preneel, B.: Power Analysis Attack on an FPGA Implementation of Rijndael: Is Pipelining a DPA Countermeasure?. In: Joye, M., Quisquater, J.-J. (eds.) CHES 2004. LNCS, vol. 3156, pp. 30–44. Springer, Heidelberg (2004)

24. Tillich, S., Herbst, C., Mangard, S.: Protecting AES Software Implementations on 32-bit Processors against Power Analysis. In: Katz, J., Yung, M. (eds.) ACNS 2007. LNCS, vol. 4521, pp. 141–157. Springer, Heidelberg (2007)

25. Xilinx. OPB HWICAP,
    http://www.xilinx.com/bvdocs/ipcenter/data_sheet/opb_hwicap.pdf

RFID and Its Vulnerability to Faults

Michael Hutter[1], Jörn-Marc Schmidt[1,2], and Thomas Plos[1]

[1] Institute for Applied Information Processing and Communications (IAIK),
Graz University of Technology, Inffeldgasse 16a, 8010 Graz, Austria
{Michael.Hutter,Joern-Marc.Schmidt,Thomas.Plos}@iaik.tugraz.at
[2] Secure Business Austria (SBA),
Favoritenstraße 16, 1040 Vienna, Austria

Abstract. Radio Frequency Identification (RFID) is a rapidly upcoming technology that has become more and more important also in security-related applications. In this article, we discuss the impact of faults on this kind of devices. We have analyzed conventional passive RFID tags from different vendors operating in the High Frequency (HF) and Ultra-High Frequency (UHF) band. First, we consider faults that have been enforced globally affecting the entire RFID chip. We have induced faults caused by temporarily antenna tearing, electromagnetic interferences, and optical inductions. Second, we consider faults that have been caused locally using a focused laser beam. Our experiments have led us to the result that RFID tags are exceedingly vulnerable to faults during the writing of data that is stored into the internal memory. We show that it is possible to prevent the writing of this data as well as to allow the writing of faulty values. In both cases, tags confirm the operation to be successful. We conclude that fault analysis poses a serious threat in this context and has to be considered if cryptographic primitives are embedded into low-cost RFID tags.

Keywords: RFID, Fault Analysis, Antenna Tearing, Optical Injections, Electromagnetic Analysis, Implementation Attacks.

1 Introduction

Fault analysis is a powerful technique to reveal secret information out of cryptographic devices. Instead of passive techniques where power or electromagnetic side channels are exploited, fault attacks make use of active methods to cause errors during the processing of cryptographic primitives. This article focuses on such active methods that have been applied to RFID, a technology that has become more security related over the last time.

RFID devices consist of a small microchip attached to an antenna. These so-called tags can be powered actively or passively. Actively powered tags use an own power supply, typically a battery. Passive ones are powered by the electromagnetic field generated by a reader. This field is also used for data communication and the transmission of the clock signal. There are numerous types of tags available that can be differentiated depending on the application. They differ in

E. Oswald and P. Rohatgi (Eds.): CHES 2008, LNCS 5154, pp. 363–379, 2008.

their size, shape, functionality, prize, and operating frequency. However, the use of RFID tags is already widespread not only in industry but also in everyday life. They are used in applications such as inventory control, pet identification, e-passports, or in pharmaceutical products. In particular, as RFID is more widely integrated into sensitive areas such as health care or access-control systems, the question of security becomes increasingly important. Currently, there has been much effort to make cryptography applicable to RFID devices. While the integration of cryptographic functions in many typical applications is somewhat straightforward, it is not in the field of RFID. Implementations must have a small footprint not to exceed the costs, and they have to be designed for low power in order to allow a certain reading range. A lot of proposals have been published so far that deal with lightweight cryptography for RFID by using coupon-based signature functions like GPS [23,18], stream ciphers [7,12,9], asymmetric algorithms like ECC [30,4], or symmetric algorithms like AES [10], PRESENT [6], SEA [28], HIGHT [13], or DES variants [22]. At the time, the security features of conventional RFID tags range from simple secure memory-lock functionalities to integrated cryptographic engines like Mifare [19], SecureRF [26], or CryptoRF [2].

Nevertheless, in the last decade, a lot of articles have been published that point out specific physical weaknesses of cryptographic implementations. Initiated by the pioneering work of Kocher et al. [15,16], a lot of attacks have been proposed on different kinds of devices that emphasize the need for hardware and software countermeasures. Especially fault attacks provide a variety of attacking possibilities that can evade effective side-channel countermeasures. Therefore, they are a field of increasing interest. S. Skorobogatov et al. [27] induced optical faults on microcontrollers. J.-J. Quisquater et al. [24] made use of active sensors to inject eddy currents. They have been able to insert permanent faults as well as transient faults into a circuit. Glitch attacks have been performed, for example, by O. Kömmerling et al. [17] or H. Bar-El et al. [3]. In the light of RFID, only a few articles have been published so far that focus on side-channel attacks. In [14], M. Hutter et al. discussed power and EM attacks on passive HF tags. Y. Oren et al. [20] and T. Plos [21] focused on power analysis of UHF tags. However, there is no dedicated article covering the topic of fault injections on RFID so far.

In this article, we introduce fault-analysis attacks performed on different kinds of commonly-used passive RFID tags in the form of adhesive labels. Several tags from various vendors have been examined including HF and UHF tags. The tags include neither cryptographic primitives nor countermeasures against fault-analysis attacks. The main intention of this article is to investigate the susceptibility of faults on RFID devices. This enables the verification whether the threat of faults on such kind of devices is realistic or not. We have focused on the writing of data since this operation is considered critical in respect of power consumption and execution time. Therefore, the target of the analysis has been the time between a reader request and the tag response.

Fault-injection methods can be divided into two categories dependent on how they are injected: globally and locally. For global fault injections, we have analyzed the impact of temporarily antenna tearing as well as electromagnetic interferences and optical laser-beam inductions. Temporarily antenna tearing has been obtained by simply interconnecting the antenna pins of the RFID chip. Electromagnetic interferences have been caused by a high-voltage generator. Optical faults have been induced by irradiating the chip using a simple laser diode. For local fault injections, a microscope has been used in order to get a focused laser beam. This beam has been concentrated on the control logic of the internal memory. The experiments have led us to several interesting results. At first, all investigated tags are vulnerable to faults during the writing of data. We show that fault-injection methods allow the prevention of writing data into the tag memory and, even worse, to allow the writing of faulty values. In both scenarios, the tags confirm the write operation to be successful. This is the first article that discusses fault analysis on RFID and emphasizes the need of countermeasures against fault-analysis attacks based on practical experiments.

This article is structured as follows. Section 2 gives an overview to the state-of-the-art security mechanisms of common RFID tags. Section 3 focuses on different fault-injection methods that can be applied on RFID tags. In Section 4, the performed analyses are described in detail. Section 5 deals with the measurement setups that are needed for fault analyses. The obtained results are given in Section 6. Section 7 summarizes the results and conclusions are drawn in Section 8.

2   State-of-the-Art Security Mechanisms for Passive RFID Tags

It is somehow evident that wireless devices like passive RFID tags require special efforts to reach a comparable security level as contact-based powered devices like smart cards and conventional microcontrollers. While these devices require physical contact to the power supply, passive tags gain their power from the radio frequency (RF) field generated by a reader. This field is rather unstable due to noise and interferences of the proximity. The certainty of the proper tag operation becomes therefore largely infeasible. Thus, conventional tags commonly include protection mechanisms against unintended failures. One of the most sensitive tag operations are the reading and writing of data. This data can be verified by using, for example, cyclic redundancy checks (CRC). The CRC is commonly used to detect failures during RFID-protocol communication but can also be applied to internal memory structures to prevent the storing of faulty values. There also exist so-called anti-tearing mechanisms that provide the verification of data integrity and data consistency when the tag is pulled out of the reader field or if the tag has not enough power to complete a certain operation. These tags may include data backup and shadow-memory techniques that allow the recovery of the data when the tag is powered up the next time after the occurrence of an interruption. In view of intended intervention, tags often

support password protection mechanisms to restrict the reading or writing into
the memory. If a transmitted password is valid, the corresponding memory zone
becomes accessible as long as the tag is powered up and in active state. The
major concern of this weak authentication is the insufficient protection against
passive eavesdropping and the potential use of replay attacks. In order to prevent any attempt of impersonalization, one-time passwords or challenge-response
protocols are commonly used to proof the origin of the transmitted data from
either the tag, the reader, or both. In many cases these protocols implement
zero-knowledge concepts or make use of symmetric or asymmetric cryptography
to offer strong authentication. There are actually tags available that support
the encryption of the transmitted data stream which prevents from skimming
attacks or eavesdropping. There are only a few tags available on the market that
provide countermeasures against active attacks by using, for example, tamper
sensors [2].

3   Fault Analysis on RFID Tags

As soon as security becomes a major concern in an application, the perspective of
adversaries has to be taken into account. When having physical interaction with
the device under attack, a lot of possibilities arise with respect to compromise
secret information. Faults pose one of these threats that are caused by either intended or unintended misuse of the system. In the following, we focus on intended
fault injections as a method for active attacks. Essentially, faults can be induced
globally or locally. Global fault-injection methods influence the entire device and
are therefore quite imprecisely. Local fault-injection methods, in contrast, affect
only specific parts of the device. There, it is possible to focus on specific regions
that are assumed to contain sensitive information. The control of an adversary
depends on the fault-injection method which can be non-invasive, semi-invasive,
or invasive. While non-invasive methods leave the package of a device untouched,
semi-invasive as well as invasive techniques apply a decapsulation procedure to
expose the chip surface. Invasive methods also establish direct electrical contact
to the chip. In addition to the control of fault injections, the precision of timing
constitutes an important factor for an attack. In the following, the structure of an
RFID tag is analyzed. After that, the most promising fault-injection methods are
described and they are further related to RFID tags.

In general, there are two proven approaches for the manufacturing of an RFID
tag. The first one directly mounts the chip onto its antenna. However, this
method needs a high precision in the handling and the operating condition and
is therefore often outsourced by companies using the second approach. There, a
special flip-chip package called *strap* is used which is typically a small Printed
Circuit Board (PCB). First, the RFID chip is bonded onto that strap PCB.
Second, the strap is mounted onto the antenna. In Figure 1, the cross section of
a tag is shown where the chip is interconnected to the antenna circuit. Often,
a special ink layer is inserted between the chip and the antenna circuit and a
Polyethylene Terephthalate (PET) film is used as a carrier for RFID inlays [11].

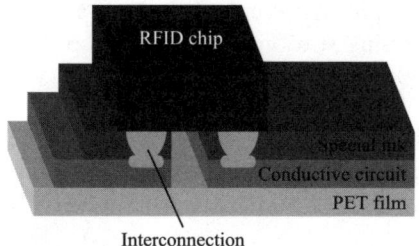

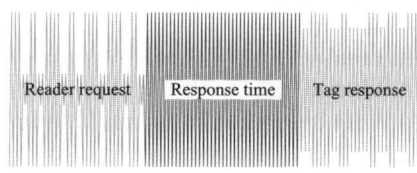

Fig. 1. Cross section of a tag where the RFID chip is interconnected to a conductive circuit (antenna)

Fig. 2. The tag performs computational work in the response time that is located between reader request and tag response

Temperature Variations. The heating of cryptographic devices Variations in the operating temperature of cryptographic devices cause faulty computations or random modifications of memory cells. Although CMOS technology is quite resistant to low temperatures, high temperatures lead to variances in the device characteristics like circuit conductance, leakage current, or diode voltage drops [24,3]. Nevertheless, the heating of semiconductors can only be achieved by global means. The adversary has no precise control concerning the timing and the resulting behavior.

In the light of the fact that RFID tags include analog circuits and that these circuits are quite susceptible to temperature variations, tags in high temperature conditions will not be able to communicate with the reader anymore. At a certain temperature, tags are unable to write data into the memory. For common passive RFID tags this is typically around 180 °C. Exceeding higher temperature limits will lead to a complete blackout of tags. In order to avoid the deformation of the tag antenna and the destruction of the inlay label, the chip has to be preferably separated from its antenna before it is stressed with heating.

Power and Clock Variations. Sudden changes in power levels or signal clock cycles are called spikes and glitches, respectively. These variations may cause the chip to either misinterpret instructions or to modify the values of internal data-bus lines of semiconductors [1,3]. This form of intervention can only be performed in a global manner but have to be injected very precisely in time.

In the context of RFID, both the power supply and the clock signal are extracted out of the reader field. The RFID tag only possesses two input pads that are normally connected to the tag antenna. By temporarily conducting these input pads, the antenna is bypassed for a certain amount of time. Tearing attacks like on smart cards focus on such supply interruptions and have to be considered especially in contact-less powered devices.

Electromagnetic Interferences. A fast-changing electromagnetic field induces current into conductors. Such a field is generated by a fast-changing current that is flowing through a coil. The characteristic of the coil, its windings, and the distance from the coil to the chip surface define the pulse strength and efficiency of the electromagnetic injection [24,25]. Although there is no need for a chip-decapsulation procedure, a proper probing station is necessary in order to be able to precisely place the probe. Thus, global as well as local fault injections are feasible both with precise timing.

As stated in [5], RFID devices that operate in higher frequencies like UHF tags, are considered to be more sensitive to electromagnetic interferences. Their antenna is largely receptive to high-frequency signals, which are around 900 MHz.

Optical Inductions. Light that hits the surface of a chip induces current. This current is often referred to as Optical Beam Induced Current (OBIC) [29]. This optical injection leads transistors to switch and causes faults during the processing of the chip [27]. In order to induce faults, the light beam has to be focused on the chip surface. Thus, it is essential to have intervisibility to regions that are intended to be attacked. As already described in Section 3, many RFID tags are only covered by a transparent PET inlay. Parts of the chip are also hidden by the antenna circuit. Remaining PET layers, adhesive, and dirt can be either removed by carefully scratching off or by using chemicals. Optical faults can be induced very precisely in time and can be applied globally and locally. Moreover, they are semi-invasive and need the decapsulation of the chip. For tags that use transparent inlays, optical inductions are performed innately without further de-packaging. In this context, they are therefore considered to be non-invasive.

4   Performed Analyses

There exist many possibilities to induce faults on RFID devices. In this article, we focus on power and clock variations as well as on electromagnetic interferences and optical laser-beam inductions. Power and clock variations have been achieved by temporarily interconnecting the antenna pins of the RFID tag. Electromagnetic injections have been carried out with the help of a self-designed high-voltage generator that is capable of producing sharp-edged EM pulses. Optical laser-beam inductions have been conducted globally by using a simple low-cost laser diode as well as locally by using an additional microscope. In Figure 2, the basic communication process in an RFID system is shown. At first, the reader interrogates the tag by sending a request to the tag. The tag receives and processes the request accordingly and sends the response back to the reader. The time when the tag processes the request of the reader is called the response time. During this time, the tag performs some computational work like writing data into the internal memory or calculating the CRC that is needed and used in the tag response. In our experiments, we have induced faults during this response time in order to disturb the writing of data into the internal memory of the tag. In this time, no RF communication is done neither from reader to tag nor from tag to the reader. The faults have been induced only in the response time after which the tag sends a response back to the reader, if the faults have not caused a reset of the tag actually. Furthermore, the faults have been induced in a very short period of time that is defined by the trigger width. In addition to the trigger width, we have also varied the point in time at which a fault injection is performed. We have implemented an automatic fault-injection sweep that covers the whole response time from its beginning to its end. The whole response time depends on the memory programming time, the underlying protocol, and the used data rate. In our experiments the response time takes a few milliseconds. The memory programming time, in particular, has taken a few hundred microseconds. We have analyzed tags using the ISO 15693 protocol for HF tags and the ISO 18000-6C (EPC Gen2) protocol for UHF tags. The data rate for HF tags has been 26.48 kbps (fast mode) for both reader to tag and tag to reader communication. For the UHF tags, a data rate of 26.67 kbps for reader to tag communication and 40 kbps for tag to reader communication has been used.

5   Measurement Setups

In order to perform fault injections, various measurement setups have been used in our experiments. All measurement setups use a PC, a standard RFID reader, a tag emulator, and the device under attack. The PC controls the devices using appropriate measurement scripts. Therefore, Matlab has been used which provides serial-connection options as well as useful functionalities like plotting and post-processing facilities. For both HF and UHF frequencies, a tag emulator has been used that is capable of eavesdropping the reader-to-tag communication. The emulators include an antenna, an analog front-end, and a programmable microcontroller. They are used to provide a trigger event that gets activated at the beginning of the response time. The trigger offset is then increased by steps of about 300 ns until the end of the response time is reached and the modulation of the tag response starts. Thus, a precise event is provided in order to trigger the antenna tearing, electromagnetic injection, and the optical induction performed by using the setups described in the following. First, the measurement setups for global fault injections are described. Second, the measurement setup for the local fault injections is described.

5.1   Setups for Global Fault Injections

The setups for global fault injections and the setup for local fault injections differ in several ways. One of the major advantages of global injections is the fact that no sophisticated equipment like probing stations or microscopes are required. The location of the fault induction is therefore fairly imprecise. Faults affect the entire chip and make an accurate knowledge of the chip circuit unessential. In fact, global faults can be performed using low-cost equipment and are rather versatile compared to immotile equipment.

Temporarily Antenna Tearing. For this setup, we have separated the chip from the tag antenna in a similar way as done by [8]. Between the chip and the

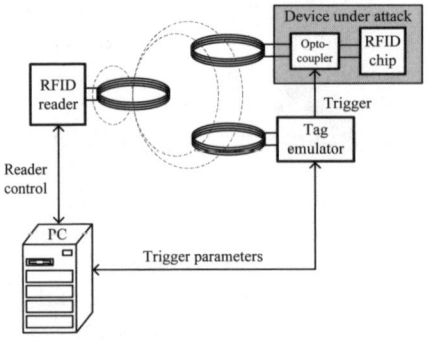 

Fig. 3. Schematic view of the measurement setup for performing antenna-tearing attacks using an optocoupler that is placed between tag antenna and chip

Fig. 4. Picture of the antenna-tearing setup where the chip has been separated from its antenna

antenna an optocoupler has been placed that is used to temporarily interconnect the antenna pins of the RFID chip. Optocouplers, in general, use a short optical transmission path that allows the transmission of signals without having electric contact. On the one hand, this is useful to protect the tag emulator against high-voltage interferences. On the other hand, it prevents against additional capacitive coupling through the galvanic isolation. This is especially necessary for antenna circuits that are matched for higher frequencies as it is used in UHF tags. In Figure 3, the used measurement setup is shown. A PC is used to control the overall measurement process. The PC is connected to an RFID reader and to the tag emulator. For UHF measurements, a reader has been used that has a field strength of about 60 mW. The distance between the reader and the device under attack and the tag emulator has been about 10 cm. For HF measurements, a field strength of about 400 mW was chosen and the device under attack and the tag emulator have been placed directly upon the reader antenna. However, the PC has been used to send write commands to the reader and to set trigger parameters to the tag emulator which has been programmed to perform the triggering. The tag emulator has therefore been placed inside the reader field to identify the beginning of the response time. Furthermore, it is connected to the optocoupler which allows us to interconnect the antenna of the chip for a user-defined interval. In Figure 4, a picture is given that shows the detachment of the tag antenna and the integration of an optocoupler.

Electromagnetic Interferences. A high-voltage generator has been built to achieve electromagnetic fault injections (see Figure 5). This device is capable of generating up to 18 kV. The circuit consists of a digital part that is used to produce a pulsating square wave of about 100 V. This pulse is then amplified using a DC voltage converter and a charge-pump circuit. However, the Electrostatic Discharge (ESD) of the high voltage generates electromagnetic interferences that can influence or damage electronic devices in the proximity. So as to protect all

Fig. 5. High-voltage generator that produces fast-changing discharges through a probe needle (upper left)

Fig. 6. Measurement setup for local fault injections on RFID tags using a microscope to focus the light of a laser diode

involved measurement devices and to produce electromagnetic injections only at a dedicated location, which is the top layer of the RFID tag, we have shielded the circuit using an aluminium case. The case has been connected to the earth ground. The output of the high-voltage generator is connected to a probe coil using a high-voltage shielded cable. As soon as the current flows through the coil, an eddy current is induced into the chip that influences the processing of operations. Electromagnetic fault injections using high-voltage pulses are more dangerous but offer a non-invasive technique as opposed to antenna tearing.

Optical Inductions. Like electromagnetic interferences, optical inductions on RFID tags with transparent inlays provide a non-invasive injection technique. We have placed a simple laser diode directly upon the chip surface. The diode emits an optical output power of 100 mW with a wavelength of 785 nm. In fact, the light of the laser diode illuminates the whole chip surface at once. Since RFID chips are typically mounted between a metallic thin-film antenna circuit and the transparent PET layer, no decapsulation procedure has to be performed. In our experiments, not all but a few regions of the chip die have been susceptive to the light beam.

5.2   Setup for Local Fault Injections

For local fault injections, we have used an optical microscope. The microscope has an integrated incident illumination device as well as a camera port. Instead of a camera, a laser diode has been used and mounted on top of the port. A collimator lens is used to parallelize the laser beam. Furthermore, the beam is focused using an optical objective which has a magnification of 50 diameters. Using the microscope it is possible to explore the device under attack very accurately. It allows the injection of focused laser beams into specific chip-circuit locations. In addition to that, it is possible to interfere data and control lines as well as memory blocks and driver circuits. Figure 6 shows the measurement setup for our local fault-injection experiments. The focused laser beam illuminates an RFID tag that lies upon an HF RFID-reader antenna. The tag emulator has also been placed inside the reader field in order to determine the beginning of the response time. The reader and the tag emulator are connected to the PC using a serial interface.

6   Results

In our experiments, different kinds of passive tags have been analyzed. Various faults have occurred that are described in the following.

Generally, five fault types have emerged during the injection of faults and are listed in Table 1. Each tag has its own behavior pattern such as the writing time, the duration of writing, and the writing strategy, for example, erasing the memory before writing. There are tags that are more sensitive to certain classes of faults while there exist other tags that are less sensitive. Once the offset and the length of the fault-injection trigger is adjusted accordingly, all examined tags show the same faulty behavior and the same results have been obtained during all our tests. Note that the microchips of the tags are different and are definitely not the same. Two types of faults occurred that are also defined in common RFID-protocol standards. We have denoted these faults by *Unconfirmed Lazy Write* and by *Unconfirmed Successful Write*. *Unconfirmed Lazy Write* indicates an unsuccessful write operation where the tag does not confirm the write-operation request. The value of the tag memory remains untouched. *Unconfirmed Successful Write*, in contrast, represents a successful write operation but the tag does not confirm the operation. Though, the new value is stored into the memory. In case of errors, protocol standards provide a certain waiting time in which tags can send an error response like *insufficient power*.

However, our experiments have shown also other tag behaviors when they are stressed within a write operation. *Unconfirmed Faulty Write* indicates the behavior where the tag does not confirm the reader request but different values are stored into the memory. These values are not random and depend on the trigger delay, the trigger width, the original memory value, the value that has to be written, and the type of fault injection. Another interesting fault that has occurred has been denoted by *Confirmed Lazy Write*. Thereby, the tag did not perform the memory writing but confirms the operation to be successful. At last,

Table 1. Overview of the specified fault types and the resulting EEPROM values

Fault type	EEPROM value
Unconfirmed Lazy Write	old
Unconfirmed Successful Write	new
Unconfirmed Faulty Write	influenced by adversary
Confirmed Lazy Write	old
Confirmed Faulty Write	influenced by adversary

we have observed the case where the tag writes different values to the memory but confirms the operation to be successful. This case is denoted by *Confirmed Faulty Write* and is one of the most critical type of faults.

6.1 Global Fault Injections

For all global injection methods, the same results have been obtained. We have induced faults by temporarily antenna tearing, electromagnetic interferences, and optical inductions. By using an automatic sweep, faults have been induced during the response time of a tag as already described in Section 5. Thus, the width as well as the offset of the trigger signal have been varied. First, we discuss the impact of the trigger-width variation. Second, results are given that have been obtained by varying the trigger offset.

The duration of an injected fault is an important factor for an attack. If it is chosen too short, it does not have an impact on the device under attack. If the fault duration is chosen too long, the tag performs a reset due to the absence of power supply and will not answer to reader requests anymore. The time when the tag actually causes a reset due to these induced faults depends on several factors. These factors are, for example, the field strength of the reader device and the distance between the tag and the reader, respectively, or the fault-injection technique (antenna tearing, optical inductions, or electromagnetic interferences). If the distance between the tag and the reader is chosen short, the duration of the fault has to be longer as compared to the scenario where the distance between the tag and the reader is chosen long. In general, the more power is available for the tag, the longer must be the fault-injection duration to cause the chip to fail. However, while the duration of the fault is important for antenna tearing and optical inductions, it is not for electromagnetic injections. The high-voltage generator produces EM pulses which have a fixed pulse width of only a few nanoseconds. Our experiments have shown that even one pulse is sufficient to force a reset of the tag. For antenna tearing, the trigger width constitutes the time in which the tag is not supplied by the field anymore. For optical inductions, the trigger width defines the period of time when the laser diode is illuminating the chip. During our experiments on antenna tearing and optical inductions, we finally have chosen a fault-injection period (trigger width) of about 100 μs which essentially causes the tags to force a reset.

Next, we have varied the trigger offset by starting at the beginning of the response time. Figure 7 shows different types of occurred faults. Depending on the offset value, we observed the occurrence of three different fault types: *Unconfirmed Lazy Write*, *Unconfirmed Faulty Write*, and *Confirmed Successful Write*. In fact, if the offset is chosen small, the reset is performed before the writing of data. Thus, the tag does not send an answer anymore and the content of the memory keeps the same. If the offset is chosen very high, the tag performs a reset after the writing of data. The tag is able to write the new memory content but is disturbed before sending the answer. However, if the offset of the fault trigger is chosen to occur during the writing of data, the content of the memory becomes modified. In addition, varying the offset very slightly leads to different

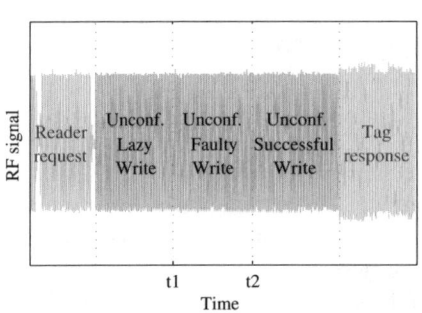 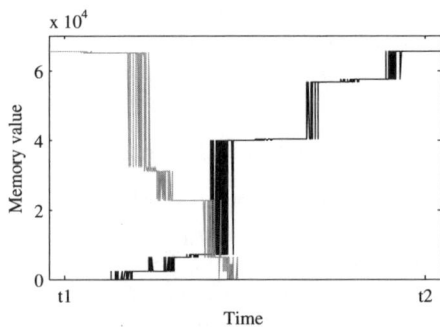

Fig. 7. Types of faults occurred at different points in time within the response time

Fig. 8. Memory value during *Unconfirmed Faulty Write* after writing two different values (black curve: 0xFFFF; gray curve: 0x0000) by varying the delay of the fault injection

memory contents. In Figure 8, the memory values are depicted as a function of the trigger offset. The black curve has been achieved by initializing two bytes of the memory with zero and setting all bits of them to one during an *Unconfirmed Faulty Write* operation. The gray curve describes the same for writing zeros to the memory that was first initialized with ones. It can be observed that the data bits are serially written into the memory and that different bits are flipped at different positions in time. The more time is proceeded the more bits are actually written. In fact, 16 bits are written while the Most-Significant Bit (MSB) makes the highest value step. The Least-Significant Bits (LSB) have only a small impact on the written value and thus cause only small value steps which are not clearly discernable in the given figure. Nevertheless, note that we have influenced the bits not sequentially (i.e. from the LSB to the MSB) but we have rather influenced specific bits at specific points in time.

With the help of an automatic sweep, we are able to detect the writing of data into the memory within a few minutes. It is possible to determine the time when the writing of data starts and how long it takes. It is further possible to detect if the memory content is cleared before the real writing of data. This allows fingerprinting of tags by identifying device-specific patterns for operations like writing to the memory.

While the same results have been obtained for all three injection methods, optical inductions have led us to further interesting findings. Besides *Unconfirmed Faulty Write* faults, we have been able to produce *Confirmed Lazy Write* and even *Confirmed Faulty Write* faults. This has been achieved by accurately adjusting the trigger width of the fault to a limit where the tag has barely enough power to confirm the write operation but it is not able to write the exact value. The tag either keeps the old value or it stores a different one. However, by choosing the right trigger width and by varying the trigger delay we have been able to roughly influence the modification of individual bits that have to be written. Following these facts, it appears that this allows the modification of memory content at several points in time during one tag operation. Hence, it is possible to bypass common security features which make use of backup facilities or memory-shading techniques. It is further possible to skip the increasing or decreasing of counter values. Counters are commonly used in cashing applications or they are used to limit the number of authentication steps to avoid differential side-channel attacks.

As a simple countermeasure against these attacks, a comparison of the value that has to be written and the actually written value becomes reasonable. However, if the register that stores the new value is modified by faults before the writing into non-volatile memory, a comparison does not help to detect the failure, obviously. This article focuses only on the modification of writing into the non-volatile memory and does not analyze the susceptibility of faults on register-values. This point keeps unclear at this stage but is marked for future work.

6.2 Local Fault Injections

Next, we focus on local fault injections using an optical laser beam. In fact, the injection of local faults offers more control for an adversary. Depending on the position of the light beam, different components of the integrated circuit are affected. The occurred faults range from simple resets to definite modifications of tag memory contents. We have been able to generate all kinds of faults that have been described in the section above.

By increasing the power of the light or by broadening the beam of the laser, simple resets have been enforced. As soon as the laser beam has been focused on the memory control logic, various faults are initiated such as they have been obtained by global fault injections. All in all, for local fault injections the timing of faults is not that relevant as the issue of fault-injection location. Once the laser beam has been focused to a specific position, injecting faults is rather easy. The fault type *Confirmed Faulty Write* has been achieved without accurately adjusting the illumination time to a certain period. However, this convenience is compensated by higher costs for the equipment.

7 Summary of the Results

In Table 2, a summary of the occurred fault types and their fault-reproducibility rate is given for different fault-injection techniques. For the antenna tearing, which has a global fault-injection scope, *Unconfirmed Lazy Write*, *Unconfirmed Successful Write*, and also *Unconfirmed Faulty Write* types have been obtained. All faults occurred with a reproducibility rate of more than 95 %. Note that especially in UHF measurements the distance between the tag and the reader antenna constitutes an important factor for a successful attack. If the tag is placed very close to the reader antenna, the tag-antenna de-tuning becomes ineffective due to parasitic inductions that inhibit further power losses on the tag side. The reproducibility of electromagnetic interferences, in contrast, is rather

Table 2. Summary of the occurred fault types and their fault-reproducibility rate

Fault type	Antenna tearing *global*	Electromagnetic interferences *global*	Optical inductions *global*	*local*[1]
Unconfirmed Lazy Write	> 95 %	< 10 %	> 95 %	> 95 %
Unconfirmed Successful Write	> 95 %	< 10 %	> 95 %	> 95 %
Unconfirmed Faulty Write	> 95 %	< 10 %	> 95 %	> 95 %
Confirmed Lazy Write	—	—	> 90 %	> 95 %
Confirmed Faulty Write	—	—	> 90 %	> 95 %

low (< 10 %) for our experiments. This has its reason in the imprecise timing of our EM fault-injection setup. Nevertheless, we have obtained the same fault types as obtained by antenna tearing.

For optical inductions, we have to distinguish between global as well as local fault injections. Both fault-injection techniques led to all types of faults. However, the laser beam has to be adjusted accordingly before the attacks. After the adjustment, each kind of fault type is reproducible with high probability (> 90 %) depending on the time and duration of the fault injection.

8 Conclusions

This article presents fundamental observations about the vulnerability of commonly-used passive RFID tags. It is the first work that provides concrete results of practical experiments in the context of fault analysis on RFID devices. We have demonstrated global as well as local fault-injection methods on HF and UHF tags. Global fault-induction methods affect the whole chip at once, local-fault induction methods apply only to dedicated parts of the chip. Beside temporarily antenna tearing, we have analyzed the impact of electromagnetic interferences as well as optical inductions. In particular, optical inductions pointed out to be a very convenient fault-injection method because of its non-invasive and effective manner. The main intention of this article is to investigate the susceptibility of faults on RFID devices and to identify potential weaknesses. Thus, we have only examined tags that do not include any countermeasures against fault-analysis attacks at this stage. Instead, we have focused on write operations which are considered critical in respect of power consumption and execution time. We have shown that fault-injection methods allow the prevention of writing data into the tag memory and, even worse, to allow the writing of faulty values. In both scenarios, the tag confirms the write operation to be successful. Hence, countermeasures have to be integrated that have to contend with limited resources as well as limited power supply and their price has to be

---

[1] For local optical inductions, the focus and position of the laser beam has to be adjusted accordingly to achieve high reproducibility.

competitive for a large deployment. This article demonstrates potential weaknesses of RFID tags to faults and provides a basis for future work like analysis of the susceptibility of cryptographic-enabled RFID tags to faults. We conclude that countermeasures against fault analysis have to be considered especially in applications where security is of increasing interest.

Acknowledgements

We would like to thank Kerstin Lemke-Rust for improving the editorial quality of this article. This work has been funded by the European Commission under the Sixth Framework Programme (Project BRIDGE, Contract Number IST-FP6-033546), by the Secure Business Austria (SBA) research center, and by the Austrian Science Found (FWF) under the grant number P18321.

References

1. Anderson, R.J., Kuhn, M.G.: Tamper Resistance - a Cautionary Note. In: Second Usenix Workshop on Electronic Commerce, pp. 1–11 (November 1996)
2. Atmel Corporation. Website atmel.com - Secure RFID: CryptoRF, http://www.atmel.com/products/SecureRF
3. Bar-El, H., Choukri, H., Naccache, D., Tunstall, M., Whelan, C.: The Sorcerer's Apprentice Guide to Fault Attacks. Cryptology ePrint Archive Report 2004/100 (2004), http://eprint.iacr.org/
4. Batina, L., Guajardo, J., Kerins, T., Mentens, N., Tuyls, P., Verbauwhede, I.: Public-Key Cryptography for RFID-Tags. In: Workshop on RFID Security 2006 (RFIDSec 2006), Graz, Austria, July 12-14 (2006)
5. Blitshteyn, M.: Mastering RFID Label Converting: Where Understanding Static Control Can Help Prevent RFID Transponder Failures. Technical report, Ion Industrial (2005)
6. Bogdanov, A., Knudsen, L.R., Leander, G., Paar, C., Poschmann, A., Robshaw, M.J.B., Seurinand, Y., Vikkelsoe, C.: PRESENT: An Ultra-Lightweight Block Cipher. In: Paillier, P., Verbauwhede, I. (eds.) CHES 2007. LNCS, vol. 4727, Springer, Heidelberg (2007)
7. Cannière, C.D., Preneel, B.: TRIVIUM Specifications. eSTREAM, ECRYPT Stream Cipher Project Report 2005/030 (April 2005), http://www.ecrypt.eu.org/stream
8. Carluccio, D., Lemke, K., Paar, C.: Electromagnetic Side Channel Analysis of a Contactless Smart Card: First Results. In: Oswald, E. (ed.) Workshop on RFID and Lightweight Crypto (RFIDSec 2005), Graz, Austria, July 13-15 (2005)
9. Feldhofer, M.: Comparing the Stream Ciphers Trivium and Grain for their Feasibility on RFID Tags. In: Posch, K.C., Wolkerstorfer, J. (eds.) Proceedings of Austrochip 2007, Graz, Austria, October 11, 2007, pp. 69–75. Verlag der Technischen Universität Graz (2007) ISBN 978-3-902465-87-0
10. Feldhofer, M., Dominikus, S., Wolkerstorfer, J.: Strong Authentication for RFID Systems using the AES Algorithm. In: Joye, M., Quisquater, J.-J. (eds.) CHES 2004. LNCS, vol. 3156, pp. 357–370. Springer, Heidelberg (2004)

11. God, R.: Lean Manufacturing of RFID Products - Put the Chip on the Box. In: Electronics Systeminteg ration Technology Conference, Proceedings of IEEE Conference, September 2006, pp. 1118–1121. IEEE Computer Society, Los Alamitos (2006)
12. Hell, M., Johansson, T., Meier, W.: Grain - A Stream Cipher for Constrained Environments. eSTREAM, ECRYPT Stream Cipher Project, Report 2006/010 (revised version 2005) (2006), http://www.ecrypt.eu.org/stream
13. Hong, D., Sung, J., Hong, S., Lim, J., Lee, S., Koo, B., Lee, C., Chang, D., Lee, J., Jeong, K., Kim, H., Kim, J., Chee, S.: HIGHT: A New Block Cipher Suitable for Low-Resource Device. In: Goubin, L., Matsui, M. (eds.) CHES 2006. LNCS, vol. 4249, pp. 46–59. Springer, Heidelberg (2006)
14. Hutter, M., Mangard, S., Feldhofer, M.: Power and EM Attacks on Passive 13.56 MHz RFID Devices. In: Paillier, P., Verbauwhede, I. (eds.) CHES 2007. LNCS, vol. 4727, pp. 320–333. Springer, Heidelberg (2007)
15. Kocher, P.C.: Timing Attacks on Implementations of Diffie-Hellman, RSA, DSS, and Other Systems. In: Koblitz, N. (ed.) CRYPTO 1996. LNCS, vol. 1109, pp. 104–113. Springer, Heidelberg (1996)
16. Kocher, P.C., Jaffe, J., Jun, B.: Differential Power Analysis. In: Wiener, M.J. (ed.) CRYPTO 1999. LNCS, vol. 1666, pp. 388–397. Springer, Heidelberg (1999)
17. Kömmerling, O., Kuhn, M.G.: Design Principles for Tamper-Resistant Smartcard Processors. In: USENIX Workshop on Smartcard Technology (Smartcard 1999), pp. 9–20 (May 1999)
18. McLoone, M., Robshaw, M.J.B.: Public Key Cryptography and RFID Tags. In: Abe, M. (ed.) CT-RSA 2007. LNCS, vol. 4377, pp. 372–384. Springer, Heidelberg (2007)
19. NXP Austria GmbH. Website mifare.net - contactless smart cards, http://www.mifare.net
20. Oren, Y., Shamir, A.: Remote Password Extraction from RFID Tags. IEEE Transactions on Computers 56(9), 1292–1296 (2007)
21. Plos, T.: Susceptibility of UHF RFID Tags to Electromagnetic Analysis. In: Malkin, T. (ed.) Topics in Cryptology - CT-RSA 2008, The Cryptographers' Track at the RSA Conference 2008, San Francisco, CA, USA, April 8-11, 2008. LNCS, vol. 4964, pp. 288–300. Springer, Heidelberg (2008)
22. Poschmann, A., Leander, G., Schramm, K., Paar, C.: A Family of Light-Weight Block Ciphers Based on DES Suited for RFID Applications. In: Workshop on RFID Security 2006 (RFIDSec 2006), Graz, Austria, July 12-14 (2006)
23. Poupard, G., Stern, J.: Security Analysis of a Practical "on the fly" Authentication and Signature Generation. In: Nyberg, K. (ed.) EUROCRYPT 1998. LNCS, vol. 1403, pp. 422–436. Springer, Heidelberg (1998)
24. Quisquater, J.-J., Samyde, D.: Eddy Current for Magnetic Analysis with Active Sensor. In: Proceedings of Esmart, pp. 185–194 (2002)
25. Schmidt, J.-M., Hutter, M.: Optical and EM Fault-Attacks on CRT-based RSA: Concrete Results. In: Posch, K.C., Wolkerstorfer, J. (eds.) Proceedings of the Austrochip 2007, October 2007, pp. 61–67. Verlag der Technischen Universität Graz (2007) ISBN 978-3-902465-87-0
26. SecureRF. SecureRF - Secure RFID Solutions, http://www.securerf.com
27. Skorobogatov, S.P., Anderson, R.J.: Optical Fault Induction Attacks. In: Kaliski Jr., B.S., Koç, Ç.K., Paar, C. (eds.) CHES 2002. LNCS, vol. 2523, pp. 2–12. Springer, Heidelberg (2003)

28. Standaert, F.-X., Piret, G., Gershenfeld, N., Quisquater, J.-J.: SEA: a Scalable Encryption Algorithm for Small Embedded Applications. In: Domingo-Ferrer, J., Posegga, J., Schreckling, D. (eds.) CARDIS 2006. LNCS, vol. 3928, pp. 222–236. Springer, Heidelberg (2006)
29. Tan, K., Tan, S., Ong, S.: Functional failure analysis on analog device by optical beam induced current technique. In: Proceedings of the 1997 6th International Symposium on Physical & Failure Analysis of Integrated Circuits, 1997, pp. 296–301. IEEExplore (July 1997)
30. Tuyls, P., Batina, L.: RFID-Tags for Anti-counterfeiting. In: Pointcheval, D. (ed.) CT-RSA 2006. LNCS, vol. 3860, pp. 115–131. Springer, Heidelberg (2006)

Perturbating RSA Public Keys: An Improved Attack

Alexandre Berzati[1,2], Cécile Canovas[1], and Louis Goubin[2]

[1] CEA-LETI/MINATEC, 17 rue des Martyrs, 38054 Grenoble Cedex 9, France
{alexandre.berzati,cecile.canovas}@cea.fr
[2] Versailles Saint-Quentin-en-Yvelines University,
45 Avenue des Etats-Unis, 78035 Versailles Cedex, France
Louis.Goubin@prism.uvsq.fr

Abstract. Since its first introduction by Bellcore researchers [BDL97], fault injections have been considered as a powerful and practical way to attack cryptosystems, especially when they are implemented on embedded devices. Among published attacks, Brier *et al.* followed the work initiated by Seifert to raise the problem of protecting RSA public elements.

We describe here a new fault attack on RSA public elements. Under a very natural fault model, we show that our attack is more efficient than previously published ones. Moreover, the general strategy described here can be applied using multiple transient fault models, increasing the practicability of the attack.

Both the theoretical analysis of the success probability, and the experimental results – obtained with the GMP Library on a PC –, provide evidence that this is a real threat for all RSA implementations, and confirm the need for protection of the public key.

Keywords: RSA, fault attacks, DFA, public key.

1 Introduction

Since the advent of fault attacks, most cryptographic algorithms have been endangered [BECN+04, BS97, CJRR99]. The difficulty of modeling the fault, depending on the attacker abilities, makes it uneasy to define countermeasures [Gir05b]. It is particularly the case for the RSA algorithm, which has been shown vulnerable to many attacks injecting faults on temporary values during the computation, or on value of the private key itself.

Moreover, the vulnerability of the public key elements has been recently proved to be a new security potential threat against various RSA implementations [Sei05, Mui06, BCMCC06]. As the effect of a computation perturbation can take multiple forms, mounting an attack based on the use of an altered public modulus is quite realistic.

In this context we describe here a new efficient attack that exploits a few faults on the modulus and leads to a full recovery of the private exponent in a very reasonable time.

E. Oswald and P. Rohatgi (Eds.): CHES 2008, LNCS 5154, pp. 380–395, 2008.

After a brief presentation of RSA, Sect. 3 provides an overview of the previous attacks on standard RSA. We particularly focus on modulus attacks so as to compare them with our new attack. Then we will explain the principle of our method, and give a detailed theoretical analysis of its complexity, based on a detailed computation of the involved probabilities.

2   Background

Let N, the public modulus, be the product of two large prime numbers p and q. The length of N is denoted by n. Let e be the public exponent, coprime to $\varphi(N) = (p-1) \cdot (q-1)$, where $\varphi(\cdot)$ denotes Euler's totient function. The public key exponent e is linked to the private exponent d by the equation $e \cdot d \equiv 1 \bmod \varphi(N)$. The private exponent d is used to perform the following operations:

RSA Decryption: Decrypting a ciphertext C boils down to compute $\tilde{m} \equiv C^d \bmod N \equiv C^{\sum_{i=0}^{i=n-1} 2^i \cdot d_i} \bmod N$ where d_i stands for the i-th bit of d. If no error occurs during computation, transmission or decryption of C, then $\tilde{m}$ equals m.

RSA Signature: The signature of a message m is given by $S = \dot{m}^d \bmod N$ where $\dot{m} = \mu(m)$ for some hash and/or deterministic padding function μ. The signature S is validated by checking that $S^e \equiv \dot{m} \bmod N$.

2.1   Modular Exponentiation: *"Right-To-Left"* Algorithm

In all the paper, we will consider the *"Right-To-Left"* algorithm (see for instance [YKLM02]), which is one of the most used algorithm to perform the modular exponentiation. This algorithm scans the bits of the private exponent d from the least to the most significant ones.

Algorithm 1. *"Right-To-Left"* modular exponentiation

INPUT: m, N, d

OUTPUT: $A \equiv m^d \bmod N$

---

1 : $A:=1$;
2 : $B:=m$;
3 : **for** i **from** 0 **upto** $(n-1)$
4 :   **if** $(d_i == 1)$
5 : $A := (A \cdot B) \bmod N$;
6 :   **endif**
7 : $B := B^2 \bmod N$;
8 : **endfor**
9 : **return** A;

---

3   Previous Work

3.1   Bellcore's DFA against Standard RSA

Bellcore's researchers not only introduced the concept of Differential Fault Analysis [BDL97] by attacking RSA in CRT mode but they also showed how this new side channel attack can be applied to many public key cryptosystems and their various implementations, such as standard RSA. They explain in [BDL97] and [BDL01] how to advantageously analyse the injection of a fault during the standard RSA signature process to recover the secret exponent. Their attack is described against a particular exponentiation algorithm: the *"Right-To-Left"* one (see Sect. 2.1).

 The considered fault model is a transient or permanent bit modification of the memory area containing the current value of the exponentiation algorithm. According to [BDL97, BDL01], recovering d by using windows of length l with a probability greater than $1/2$ requires $(n/l) \cdot \log(2n)$ (message, faulty signature) pairs. In terms of complexity, this attack needs to perform $\mathcal{O}(n^3 \cdot 2^l \cdot \log^2(n)/l^2)$ modular exponentiations. It is worth noticing that the choice of the window length l has an impact on the global complexity of the attack.

 This attack principle was later studied and generalized by J. Blömer and M. Otto [Ott04].

Bellcore's Attack Principle. The attack can be divided into two parts. The first one is *"on-line"* and consists in getting sufficiently many erroneous signatures $\hat{S}_i$ from known plaintexts m_i that are randomly distributed over $\mathbb{Z}/N\mathbb{Z}$. The second part is completely *"off-line"* and consists in analysing the previously obtained faulty signatures. The attack principle is described below in the case of a transient fault model:

1. Getting sufficiently many $(m_i, \hat{S}_i)$ pairs, by injecting a transient fault on the current value during each signature execution.
2. Error analysis. Let S_v be the correct signature and $\varepsilon = \pm 2^b$ the induced error with $0 \leq b < n$. The effects of such a transient error, that has occurred during some unknown iteration j, can be modeled as:

$$\hat{S}_v \equiv \left[\left(\prod_{i=0}^{j-1} \dot{m}_v^{2^i d_i} \right) \pm 2^b \right] \cdot \prod_{i=j}^{n-1} \dot{m}_v^{2^i d_i} \tag{1}$$

$$\equiv S_v \pm \left(2^b \cdot \prod_{i=j}^{n-1} \dot{m}_v^{2^i d_i} \right) \bmod N \tag{2}$$

$$\Rightarrow S_v \equiv \hat{S}_v \pm 2^b \cdot \dot{m}_v^{\,w} \bmod N, \text{ where } w = \sum_{i=j}^{n-1} 2^i d_i \tag{3}$$

Using the public exponent e, we finally obtain:

$$\dot{m}_v \equiv (\hat{S}_v \pm 2^b \cdot \dot{m}_v^{\,w})^e \bmod N \tag{4}$$

One can notice from the previous equation that it only depends on the message $\hat{m}_v$ and its faulty signature $\hat{S}_v$.

The analysis consists in recovering the whole private exponent d by scanning l-bit long windows from the most to the least significant bits. To reach this goal, the values of b and w satisfying (4) are simultaneously searched. The value of w contains a known part of d and at most l unknown bits. These bits are recovered by testing values in $[\![0; 2^l - 1]\!]$ until one of them satisfies (4). A priori, from a given pair $(m_i, \hat{S}_i)$, an attacker can not guess when the fault occurs during the signature's computation. So, for each searched value of w, he has to test all the obtained couples $(m_i, \hat{S}_i)$.

In [BDL01], Boneh et al. proved that this method allows an attacker to recover the whole private exponent d with a probability greater than $1/2$.

3.2   Fault Attack on RSA Private Exponent

This attack was published by F. Bao et al. in [BDJ$^+$96, BDJ$^+$98] and then in [BECN$^+$04]. The principle is to induce a transient error during the decryption, that produces the same effect as a bit modification of the private exponent. In practice this fault will be a *shunt* of the conditional test on the private bit value during the binary exponentiation algorithm.[1] Note that this attack is suitable for multiple errors [BDJ$^+$98]. Moreover the principle can be adapted to attack cryptosystems based on discrete logarithm (DSA, El-Gamal, ...). The following paragraph only describes the attack for a bit error on the exponent d.

Attack Principle. In case of a faulty computation, the deciphered text $\hat{m}$ is:

$$\hat{m} \equiv C^{\hat{d}} \bmod N$$

The fault is exploited by dividing the erroneous result by a correct one: $\frac{\hat{m}}{m}$. The induced error can be modeled as a *bit-flip* of the j-th bit of d. We thus have:

$$\hat{m} \equiv C^{\sum_{i=0, i \neq j}^{i=n-1} 2^i \cdot d_i + 2^j \bar{d}_j} \bmod N$$

That implies, either $\frac{\hat{m}}{m} \equiv \frac{1}{C^{2^j}} \bmod N \Rightarrow d_j = 1$,

or $\frac{\hat{m}}{m} \equiv C^{2^j} \bmod N \Rightarrow d_j = 0$.

This method can be repeated until we obtain enough information on the private exponent. This attack strategy was later extended and generalized by M. Joye et al. [JQBD97], who describes an improved attack relying on the mere knowledge of the faulty deciphered text.

3.3   J-P. Seifert and J. Muir's Attacks

Seifert's attack on RSA signature [Sei05] was the first one using a modification of some public parameter (*i.e.* the modulus N). Unlike the previously described attacks, the objective does not consist in retrieving the secret key, but in compromising the signature verification mechanism.

---

[1] Algorithms *"Right-To-Left"* or *"Left-to-Right"*.

Attack Principle. Seifert's attack is composed of two different phases.

The first – *"off-line"* – phase consists in finding an altered modulus $\hat{N}$, that satisfy some interesting properties, and generating the corresponding signature. In practice the attacker modifies the modulus $\hat{N}$ so that e is coprime to $\varphi(\hat{N})$ [2] and $\hat{N}$ is a possible altered value of N. Then the attacker has to choose an adequate model for the fault that will disrupt the signature verification mechanism. Seifert proposes to require $\hat{N}$ to be prime, so that the previous condition is satisfied and $\hat{d} \equiv e^{-1} \mod \varphi(\hat{N})$ is easily computable. Muir generalizes the condition and imposes that $\hat{N}$ should be easily factorized [Mui06]. The attacker signs a message m with the computed $\hat{d}$ value and saves the signature with its corresponding message $(m,\hat{S})$.

In the second – *"on-line"* – phase, the attacker inputs $(m,\hat{S})$ into the signature's verification mechanism and tries to inject a fault during the loading of the N value, so that all computations are performed with this altered modulus. The generated fault has to correspond to the chosen fault model (*i.e.* the altered N value equals to previously computed $\hat{N}$ value). In that case, the signature $\hat{S}$ will be accepted by the algorithm. Otherwise, the attacker performs the *"on-line"* phase until its faulty signature is accepted.

The success rate of this attack and the average number of faults depends on the suitability of the chosen fault model. Moreover the attacker must be able to induce a fault corresponding to $\hat{N}$ with a reasonable probability. The resulting implementation of this attack and a further optimization are proposed in [Mui06].

3.4   E. Brier *et al.*'s Attack

Whether it is necessary or not to protect RSA public elements was an open question until Brier *et al.* attack proposal for recovering the whole private key. This attack, inspired from Seifert's one [Sei05], was published in [BCMCC06] and reviewed in [Cla07]. It makes it possible to extract the private key using a modulus perturbation. Moreover, in its simplest version, it does not require any hypothesis on the type of induced fault during the signature process. This represents a significant advantage, compared to Seifert's attack.

Attack Principle without Dictionary. The attacker proceeds in two distinct phases. The feature of this method (without dictionary) is that it does not require any fault model.

In the first *"on-line"* phase, the attacker conducts a perturbation campaign in order to obtain a large enough number of (message, faulty signature) pairs of the form $(m_i, \hat{S}_i)_{1 \leq i \leq K}$, corresponding to computations with unknown (modified) moduli $\hat{N}_i \neq N$. As in Seifert's attack, the N value is modified during its loading, so that each pair satisfies the following relation:

$$\forall i \in [\![1; K]\!], \ \hat{S}_i \equiv \dot{m}_i{}^d \mod \hat{N}_i$$

---

[2] This is equivalent to e being invertible in $\mathbb{Z}/\varphi(\hat{N})\mathbb{Z}$.

The *"off-line"* phase consists in analysing the gathered data in order to retrieve the secret key, by an application of the Chinese Remainder Theorem. The value $d \bmod r_k$ is gradually determined for small power of some small prime numbers r_k. When $R = \prod_k r_k$ is greater than N (and so than $\varphi(N)$), the Chinese Remainder Theorem is applied for finding d. The way the values $d_k \equiv d \bmod r_k$ are found, is based on a probabilistic approach that is described in [BCMCC06, Cla07]. We note that the method does not require to model the induced fault.

Implementing the attack shows that approximately 25000 faults are necessary to recover 512 bits of exponent d. In comparison, approximately 60000 faults (more than twice) are necessary to extract 1024 bits.

Attack Principle with a Dictionary. The attack with dictionary requires the choice of a fault model. From this model and the correct modulus N, the attacker builds a list of possible modified moduli, called modulus dictionary. As in the previous case, this attack is divided into two phases.

The first phase is *"on-line"*. As before, the attacker conducts a fault campaign in order to obtain sufficiently many (message, faulty signature) pairs, denoted by $(m_i, \hat{S}_i)_{1 \leq i \leq K}$.

The attacker begins the *"off-line"* phase by building the dictionary. To do so, the attacker experiments and validates an adequate fault model. Then he lists all the possible values for a modified public modulus. Next, for each dictionary entry v_j, he identifies the pairs $(m_i, \hat{S}_i)$ satisfying $v_j = \hat{N}_i$. Each pair that matches a value in the dictionary, a so-called *"touch"*, brings some information about d as shown in [BCMCC06, Cla07].

In terms of performance the use of a dictionary is advantageous, because 1100 faults and 28 *"touches"* are necessary to retrieve 1024 key bits. On the other hand, it requires a relevant fault model.

A third attack proposed in [BCMCC06] and revisited in [Cla07] explains how to optimally exploit fault injections. Authors claims that, in good conditions, this allows to reduce the number of fault injections from 1100 to a dozen.

3.5   Summary

The RSA standard algorithm is not immune to fault attacks. The previously presented attacks show that the protection of the public modulus during the decryption or signature processing has to be considered. Now we will present a brand new attack on the public modulus that have some advantages over the previous methods because of the use of a realistic fault model and greater performance.

4   Principle of Our Attack

4.1   Fault Model

Our attack is based on modifying the public modulus during the computation of the exponentiation corresponding to the signature scheme. The injected fault affects a byte of the modulus by modifying it in a random way, namely:

$$\hat{N} = N \oplus \varepsilon \tag{5}$$

where $\varepsilon = R_8 \cdot 2^{8i}, i \in [\![0; \frac{n}{8} - 1]\!]$ and R_8 is a non-zero random byte value. These two values are supposed unknown by the attacker because they depend on the fault injection itself. The fault is supposed to be transient, and the modified value $\hat{N}$ is used until the end of the exponentiation. The consistency of this model was already checked in the smart card context, leading to successful applications [BECN+04, Gir05a, BO06].

To make our description easier, we assume that the "Right-To-Left" algorithm is used for the exponentiation and the attack will be presented in that specific context. Moreover, whereas the transient fault can first occur during the computation of a square or a multiplication, we will focus on the effect of the perturbation on the square. Perturbating the multiplication will be treated in Appendix A.

4.2   Faulty Computation

Let $d = \sum_{i=0}^{n-1} 2^i \cdot d_i$ be the binary representation of d. Then an RSA signature can be written as:

$$S \equiv \dot{m}^{\sum_{i=0}^{n-1} 2^i \cdot d_i} \bmod N \tag{6}$$

If a fault occurs j steps before the end of the exponentiation, then this step will begin with a faulty square, whatever the value of d_{n-j} may be:

$$\hat{B} \equiv \left(\dot{m}^{2^{(n-j-1)}} \bmod N \right)^2 \bmod \hat{N} \tag{7}$$

Then the algorithm continues its execution by computing faulty operations. Denoting by $A \equiv \dot{m}^{\sum_{i=0}^{(n-j-1)} 2^i \cdot d_i} \bmod N$ as the correct beginning of the computation, we finally obtain:

$$\hat{S} \equiv ((A \cdot \hat{B})...)\hat{B}^{2^{j-1}} \bmod \hat{N} \tag{8}$$

$$\equiv A \cdot \hat{B}^{\sum_{i=(n-j)}^{n-1} 2^{[i-(n-j)]} \cdot d_i} \bmod \hat{N} \tag{9}$$

$$\equiv [(\dot{m}^{\sum_{i=0}^{(n-j-1)} 2^i \cdot d_i} \bmod N) \tag{10}$$

$$\cdot (\dot{m}^{2^{(n-j-1)}} \bmod N)^{\sum_{i=(n-j)}^{n-1} 2^{[i-(n-j)+1]} \cdot d_i}] \bmod \hat{N}$$

As a consequence, the fault injection splits the computation into a correct part and a faulty one. For a given faulty signature $\hat{S}$, the value of j is supposed to be known by the attacker. This assumption comes from the fact that an attacker can trigger its fault injection using a Simple Power Analysis. Hence, he can know which step of the computation was first infected by the fault and – as a consequence – the number of bits of d that are handled with the wrong modulus.

4.3   Cryptanalysis

The attack consists in recovering a part of the private exponent using the effects of the fault. It is a pure differential analysis because it requires the knowledge of both the correct signature S and the faulty one $\hat{S}$. Indeed, the difference between these two computations resides in the end of the exponentiation (which is faulty in the case of $\hat{S}$). Therefore if the attacker chooses a candidate value for the faulty modulus $\hat{N}'$, and another candidate for the first part of d: $d'_{(1)} = \sum_{i=n-j}^{n-1} 2^i \cdot d_i'$, he can then compute:

$$S'_{(d'_{(1)}, \hat{N}')} \equiv [(S \cdot \dot{m}^{-d'_{(1)}}) \bmod N \cdot (\dot{m}^{2^{(n-j-1)}} \bmod N)^{2^{[1-(n-j)] \cdot d'_{(1)}}}] \bmod \hat{N} \quad (11)$$

The idea of the attack consists in simulating a faulty computation from a correct one. The first multiplication in $\mathbb{Z}/N\mathbb{Z}$ is done to go backwards to the perturbated step of the computation, whereas the second multiplication simulates the effects of the induced fault. Then he checks whether the following equation is satisfied or not:

$$S'_{(d'_{(1)}, \hat{N}')} \equiv \hat{S} \bmod \hat{N} \quad (12)$$

If it is the case, this means that the chosen candidates are the searched values with high probability. If no solution is found among the candidate pairs, this means that the attack occurs during a multiplication and the attacker has to perform the cryptanalysis described in Appendix A.

The attacker can optimize the search of candidates for $\hat{N}'$ by noticing that the faulty modulus, has to be greater than $\hat{S}$. Indeed, $\hat{S}$ is a result of a modular reduction by the faulty modulus. This simple property can dramatically reduce the search space for a suitable $\hat{N}$ candidate.

The subsequent secret bits will be found by repeating this attack using the knowledge of the (already found) most significant bits of d and a signature faulted earlier in the process. As a consequence, the attacker has to gather a set of faulty signatures $\hat{S}_k$ obtained by injecting faults at different steps j_k before the end of the exponentiation. Then, the collected information $(\hat{S}_k, j_k)_{1 \leq k \leq n/l}$ are sorted in descending fault location.

The number of bits recovered each time corresponds to the window length denoted by l. Hence, the k-th l-bit part of d recovered is $d_{(k)} = \sum_{i=n-j_k}^{n-j_{(k-1)}-1} 2^i \cdot d_i$. For the sake of clarity, we assume that $j_0 = 0$ and $\forall k \in [\![0; \frac{n}{l}]\!]$, $j_{k+1} - j_k = l$. But, this assumption can be easily extended to a more general case where faults are not injected regularly: $\forall k \in [\![0; \frac{n}{l}]\!]$, $j_{k+1} - j_k < l_{max}$.

4.4   Attack Algorithm

In this section, we detail the implementation of our new Differential Fault Analysis, described above. It generalizes the analysis to recover the whole private exponent by taking advantages of faults injected during squaring operations of the "Right-To-Left" algorithm. The following attack algorithm has been successfully implemented on PC using the GMP Library. We assume that, in input, the set of pairs (faulty signature, fault location) is sorted in descending fault location.

From our presented algorithm, one can notice that correct and faulty signatures are obtained from the same plaintext m. But, the attacker can recover

---

Algorithm 2. DFA against RSA in Standard mode

INPUT: N, $\dot{m}$, the correct signature S, the set of pairs $(\hat{S}_k, j_k)_{1 \le k \le n/l}$
OUTPUT: the private exponent d

1: //Initialisation
2: $d := 0$;
3: **for** k from 1 **upto** $\lfloor n/l \rfloor$
4:     //We want to recover the next l-bit window $d_{(k)}$ of d
5:     **for** $d'_{(k)}$ from 0 **upto** $(2^l - 1)$
6:         $d' := [d'_{(k)} << (n - j_k)] + d$;
7:         //We search a suitable value for $\hat{N}$
8:         **for** R_8 from 1 **upto** $(2^8 - 1)$
9:             **for** pos from 0 **upto** $(\frac{n}{8} - 1)$
10:                 $\hat{N}' := N \oplus (R_8 << 8.pos)$;
11:                 $S'_{(d',\hat{N}')} := [(S \cdot \dot{m}^{-d'}) \bmod N$
12:                     $\cdot (\dot{m}^{2^{(n-j_k-1)}} \bmod N)^{2^{[1-(n-j_k)].d'}}] \bmod \hat{N}$;
13:                 //We test if the rebuilt value equals the faulty one
14:                 **if** $(S'_{(d',\hat{N}')} == \hat{S} \bmod \hat{N})$
15:                     //If the condition is satisfied, the current value of d' suits
16:                     $d := d'$;
17:                     //So, we can search the next l-bit of d
18:                     **goto** line_3;
19:                 **end if**
20:             **end for**
21:         **end for**
22:     **end for**
23: **end for**
24: //Don't forget the purpose of our attack ...
25: **return** d;

---

parts of d from different plaintexts and their associated correct and faulty signatures. To perform this he has to replace the algorithm's input by the quadruplets $(\dot{m}_k, S_k, \hat{S}_k, j_k)_{1 \le k \le n/l}$.

4.5   Complexity

Computational Complexity. To perform our attack, we need to recover both the induced fault and the part of d affected by the perturbation. For each possible candidate pair, a modular exponentiation is performed. Therefore, according to the previously presented algorithm, the complexity C_{attack} of our attack is :

$$C_{attack} \sim \mathcal{O}(\frac{n^2 \cdot 2^l \cdot (2^8 - 1)}{8.l}) \text{ exponentiations} \qquad (13)$$

Observing the algorithm, one can notice that the computation of candidates for the faulty modulus can be replaced by a precomputed dictionary of candidates $\hat{N}'$. But, such a time optimisation has to be done according to the chosen fault model.

As a comparison, the attack presented by Bellcore researchers against a standard RSA [BDL97, BDL01] requires $\mathcal{O}(n^3 \cdot 2^l \cdot \log^2(n)/l^2)$ full modular exponentiations (*i.e.* mod N), which is more complex. Concerning the attack of Brier *et al.* [BCMCC06], it needs to resolve $\mathcal{O}(n)$ discrete logarithm problems of reasonable sizes (*i.e.* less than 2^{30} bits). If the Shank's Baby-Step Giant-Step algorithm $(\sim \mathcal{O}(\sqrt{N} \cdot \log(N))$ is used, the associated complexity is in $\mathcal{O}(n \cdot 2^{30} \cdot 30 \cdot \log(2))$. If the chosen window length l is small enough (*i.e.* $l \leq 20$ bits for a 1024-bit RSA) this computational complexity is bigger than our attack's one.

Number of Required Faults. The principle of our algorithm is based on recovering the secret exponent by using windows of bits. Each faulty signature is used to recover a different window of d. Therefore, if l is the length of the window, recovering the whole secret exponent requires:

$$\text{Number of faults} \sim \mathcal{O}(n/l) \tag{14}$$

For Bellcore's attack against a plain RSA [BDL97, BDL01], the number of required faults is $\mathcal{O}((n/l) \cdot \log(2n))$ and for Brier *et al.* [BCMCC06] it is $\mathcal{O}(n)$.

4.6   Performance

The performance of our proposed attack are evaluated according to our detailed cryptanalysis (see Sect. 4.3). So, to determine the real $(d_{(1)}, \hat{N})$ pair among all possible candidates, the attacker tests if (12) is satisfied by its rebuilt value $S'_{(d'_{(1)}, \hat{N}')}$ (see (11)). However this equation is checked in $\mathbb{Z}/\hat{N}\mathbb{Z}$, so that some wrong candidates for the searched values $d_{(1)}$ and $\hat{N}$ could be accepted by mistake. This is the problem of false-acceptance. We thus have to evaluate the probability for a given (accepted) pair to be a false one. This phenomenon can be modeled as the probability to pass the test knowing that the values are incorrect:

$$\Pr[\text{Equation (12) is satisfied} \mid (d'_{(1)}, \hat{N}') \neq (d_{(1)}, \hat{N})] \tag{15}$$

$$\Longleftrightarrow \Pr[\text{Equation (12) is satisfied} \mid (d'_{(1)} \neq d_{(1)} \text{ or } \hat{N}' \neq \hat{N})] \tag{16}$$

Since, this probability is quite difficult to evaluate, we propose in next section a method to maximize it. First, we use the well-known property of conditional probability. If A and B are two dependent events, then, the probability of the event A to occur knowing that B has occurred is:

$$\Pr[A|B] = \frac{\Pr[A \cup B]}{\Pr[B]} \tag{17}$$

This property can be applied to evaluate our probability of false-acceptance by substituting:

- A by the event: "Equation (12) is satisfied";
- B by the event: "$d'_{(1)}$ or $\hat{N}'$ is a false candidate value respectively for $d_{(1)}$ and $\hat{N}$".

Our probability will be given by computing $\Pr[A \cup B]$ and $\Pr[B]$. For the sake of clarity, both computations are detailed in Appendix B. The obtained results are summarized below:

- $\Pr[A \cup B]$: This represents the probability that (12) is satisfied if at least one candidate is not equal to its expected value. Hence:

$$0 < \Pr[A \cup B] < min\left(\frac{\hat{N}-1}{\hat{N}}, \frac{2^l \cdot n \cdot (2^8-1)-1}{8 \cdot \hat{N}}\right) \qquad (18)$$

- $\Pr[B]$: Applying the B's above definition, this is the probability that at least one candidate is not equal to its expected value.

$$\Pr[(d'_{(1)}, \hat{N}') \neq (d_{(1)}, \hat{N})] = \frac{n \cdot (2^8-1) \cdot 2^l - 8}{n \cdot (2^8-1) \cdot 2^l} \qquad (19)$$

The False-Acceptance Probability. Using the two partial results, established in Appendix B, and the property of conditional probabilities, the false acceptance probability can be approximated by:

$$0 < \Pr[A|B] < min\left(\frac{n \cdot (\hat{N}-1) \cdot (2^8-1) \cdot 2^l}{n \cdot \hat{N} \cdot (2^8-1) \cdot 2^l - 8}, \frac{(n \cdot (2^8-1) \cdot 2^l - 1) \cdot n \cdot (2^8-1) \cdot 2^l}{\hat{N} \cdot (n \cdot (2^8-1) \cdot 2^l - 8))}\right) \qquad (20)$$

Even though the false-acceptance probability is bounded by a value close to 1 when $n < 16$ bits, it is interesting to notice that this probability decreases with $\hat{N}$ (and so exponentially with n). As a consequence, the false-acceptance probability rapidly becomes negligible. These theoretical results have been confirmed by our GMP implementation of the attack.

5   Extension of the Attack Model

5.1   Extension of Our Fault Model

The fault model we have chosen to present our attack principle can be extended to another transient fault model. Such a fault can be induced by the perturbation of a read-access to the public modulus N before computing a square or a multiplication. The perturbation has to influence only the current operation. Indeed, subsequent accesses to N must remain *error-free* [Wag04]. As previously described, the fault still modifies a byte of N by adding a random byte value. With this new assumption, the attacker has to face different cases, depending on the value of d and on the targeted operation. These cases are described below for a fault injected j steps before the end of the exponentiation:

1. $d_{n-j} = 0$ or 1 and the square is perturbated. Whatever the value of d_{n-j} may be, A keeps the same expression: $A \equiv \dot{m}^{\sum_{i=0}^{(n-j-1)} 2^i \cdot d_i} \bmod N$. Moreover, the fault injection modifies the value of B such that the square is computed with

a faulty modular reduction $\hat{B} \equiv (\dot{m}^{2^{(n-j-1)}} \bmod N)^2 \bmod \hat{N}$. This faulty computation then spreads in the exponentiation:

$$\hat{S} \equiv ((A \cdot \hat{B})...) \cdot \hat{B}^{2^{j-1}} \bmod N \tag{21}$$

$$\equiv A \cdot \hat{B}^{\sum_{i=(n-j)}^{n-1} 2^{[i-(n-j)] \cdot d_i}} \bmod N \tag{22}$$

$$\equiv (\dot{m}^{\sum_{i=0}^{(n-j-1)} 2^i \cdot d_i} \bmod N) \tag{23}$$

$$\cdot [(\dot{m}^{2^{(n-j-1)}} \bmod N)^2 \bmod \hat{N}]^{\sum_{i=(n-j)}^{n-1} 2^{[i-(n-j)] \cdot d_i}} \bmod N$$

This case differs from the previously described one by the modular reduction by $\hat{N}$ applied to the second part of the expression. Moreover, the main product is done here in the finite field $\mathbb{Z}/N\mathbb{Z}$ instead of $\mathbb{Z}/\hat{N}\mathbb{Z}$. Hence, under this transient fault model, the attacker has to apply small changes on the cryptanalysis described in Sect. 4.3 to recover l bits of d.

2. $d_{n-j} = 1$ and the multiplication is perturbated. This second case deals with a perturbation of the multiplication performed j steps before the end of the exponentiation. If $\hat{A}$ stands for the faulty result, then:

$$\hat{A} \equiv [(\dot{m}^{\sum_{i=0}^{[(n-j-2)]} 2^i \cdot d_i} \bmod N) \cdot (\dot{m}^{2^{(n-j-1)}} \bmod N)] \bmod \hat{N} \tag{24}$$

$$\equiv (\dot{m}^{\sum_{i=0}^{(n-j-1)} 2^i \cdot d_i} \bmod N) \bmod \hat{N} \tag{25}$$

No more error occurs during the end of the computation. As a consequence, $B \equiv \dot{m}^{2^{n-j}} \bmod N$ and the faulty signature $\hat{S}$ can be explained as:

$$\hat{S} \equiv ((\hat{A} \cdot B)...)B^{2^{j-1}} \bmod N \tag{26}$$

$$\equiv \hat{A} \cdot B^{\sum_{i=(n-j)}^{n-1} 2^{[i-(n-j)] \cdot d_i}} \bmod N \tag{27}$$

$$\equiv [(\dot{m}^{\sum_{i=0}^{(n-j-1)} 2^i \cdot d_i} \bmod N) \bmod \hat{N} \tag{28}$$

$$\cdot (\dot{m}^{\sum_{i=(n-j)}^{n-1} 2^i \cdot d_i} \bmod N)] \bmod N$$

This expression can also be cryptanalyzed as described in Sect. 4.3 to obtain l bits of d by noticing that a modular reduction by $\hat{N}$ is applied to A whereas B is not infected by the fault. Moreover the main multiplication is, in this case, computed in $\mathbb{Z}/N\mathbb{Z}$.

Finally, one can notice that the case "$d_j = 0$ and the multiplication is perturbated" is missing. In fact, this case can not occur if we consider the previously presented "Right-To-Left" algorithm.

The previous analysis shows that our new attack is not limited to a unique transient fault model. Accordingly, this increases the practicability of the attack on cryptographic devices that implement the "Right-To-Left" algorithm.

6   Conclusion

This paper introduces a new fault attack against the "Right-To-Left" implementation of RSA. We detail a new way of exploiting faulty RSA public elements (*i.e.* the public modulus N). We show in our theoretical analysis that our attack is more efficient than previously published ones [Sei05, Mui06, BCMCC06]. Moreover its GMP implementation as well as the use of practicable fault models demonstrate that this new attack represents a real threat for RSA public elements. As a consequence, the protection of RSA public key elements against Differential Fault Analysis is more than ever a hot topic.

References

[BCMCC06] Brier, E., Chevallier-Mames, B., Ciet, M., Clavier, C.: Why One Should Also Secure RSA Public Key Elements. In: Goubin, L., Matsui, M. (eds.) CHES 2006. LNCS, vol. 4249, pp. 324–338. Springer, Heidelberg (2006)

[BDJ+96] Bao, F., Deng, R.H., Jeng, A., Narasimhalu, A.D., Ngair, T.: Another New Attack to RSA on Tamperproof Devices (1996)

[BDJ+98] Bao, F., Deng, R.H., Jeng, A., Narasimhalu, A.D., Ngair, T.: Breaking Public Key Cryptosystems on Tamper Resistant Devices in the Presence of Transient Faults. In: Lomas, M., Christianson, B. (eds.) Security Protocols 1997. LNCS, vol. 1361, pp. 115–124. Springer, Heidelberg (1998)

[BDL97] Boneh, D., DeMillo, R.A., Lipton, R.J.: On the Importance of Checking Cryptographic Protocols for Faults. In: Fumy, W. (ed.) EUROCRYPT 1997. LNCS, vol. 1233, pp. 37–51. Springer, Heidelberg (1997)

[BDL01] Boneh, D., DeMillo, R.A., Lipton, R.J.: On the Importance of Eliminating Errors in Cryptographic Computations. Journal of Cryptology 14(2), 101–119 (2001)

[BECN+04] Bar-El, H., Choukri, H., Naccache, D., Tunstall, M., Whelan, C.: The Sorcerer's Apprentice Guide to Fault Attacks. Cryptology ePrint Archive, Report 2004/100 (2004)

[BO06] Blömer, J., Otto, M.: Wagner's Attack on a secure CRT-RSA Algorithm Reconsidered. In: Breveglieri, L., Koren, I., Naccache, D., Seifert, J.-P. (eds.) FDTC 2006. LNCS, vol. 4236, pp. 13–23. Springer, Heidelberg (2006)

[BS97] Biham, E., Shamir, A.: Differential Fault Analysis of Secret Key Cryptosystems. In: Kaliski Jr., B.S. (ed.) CRYPTO 1997. LNCS, vol. 1294. Springer, Heidelberg (1997)

[CJRR99] Chari, S., Jutla, C., Rao, J.R., Rohatgi, P.: A Cautionary Note Regarding Evaluation of AES Candidates on Smart-Cards. In: Second Advanced Encryption Standard (AES) Candidate Conference (1999)

[Cla07] Clavier, C.: De la sécurité physique des crypto-systèmes embarqués. PhD thesis, Université de Versailles Saint-Quentin (2007)

[Gir05a] Giraud, C.: DFA on AES. In: Dobbertin, H., Rijmen, V., Sowa, A. (eds.) AES 2005. LNCS, vol. 3373, pp. 27–41. Springer, Heidelberg (2005)

[Gir05b] Giraud, C.: Fault-Resistant RSA Implementation. In: Breveglieri, L., Koren, I. (eds.) Fault Diagnosis and Tolerance in Cryptography, pp. 142–151 (2005)

[JQBD97] Joye, M., Quisquater, J.J., Bao, F., Deng, R.H.: RSA-types Signatures in the Presence of Transient Faults. In: Darnell, M.J. (ed.) Cryptography and Coding 1997. LNCS, vol. 1355, pp. 155–160. Springer, Heidelberg (1997)

[Mui06]   Muir, J.A.: Seifert's RSA Fault Attack: Simplified Analysis and Gener-
           alizations. Cryptology ePrint Archive, Report 2005/458 (2006)
[Ott04]   Otto, M.: Fault Attacks and Countermeasures. PhD thesis, University
           of Paderborn (December 2004)
[Sei05]   Seifert, J.-P.: On Authenticated Computing and RSA-Based Authenti-
           cation. In: ACM Conference on Computer and Communications Security
           (CCS 2005), pp. 122–127. ACM Press, New York (2005)
[Wag04]   Wagner, D.: Cryptanalysis of a provably secure CRT-RSA algorithm. In:
           Proceedings of the 11th ACM Conference on Computer Security (CCS
           2004), pp. 92–97. ACM Press, New York (2004)
[YKLM02]   Yen, S.-M., Kim, D., Lim, S., Moon, S.: A Countermeasure Against One
           Physical Cryptanalysis May Benefit Another Attack. In: Kim, K.-c. (ed.)
           ICISC 2001. LNCS, vol. 2288, pp. 414–427. Springer, Heidelberg (2002)

A   Fault Injection before a Multiplication

The principle of our attack was described for a permanent fault injected before a
square. But, if $d_{n-j} = 1$, then a multiplication is done and can be the first operation modified. So, in this appendix, we present the effects of such a perturbation
and how to take advantage of it to recover the bits of the private exponent d.

A.1   Faulty Computation

Our attack is performed against the *"Right-To-Left"* exponentiation algorithm
with the fault model previously described (see Sect. 4.1). In this case, the fault
first occurs during a multiplication, j steps until the end of the exponentiation,
so:

$$\hat{A} \equiv (\dot{m}^{\sum_{i=0}^{n-j-2} 2^i \cdot d_i} \bmod N) \cdot B \bmod \hat{N} \tag{29}$$

$$\equiv [(\dot{m}^{\sum_{i=0}^{n-j-2} 2^i \cdot d_i} \bmod N) \cdot \dot{m}^{2^{(n-j-1)}} \bmod N] \bmod \hat{N} \tag{30}$$

Then, this operation is followed by a square:

$$\hat{B} \equiv (\dot{m}^{2^{(n-j-1)}} \bmod N)^2 \bmod \hat{N} \tag{31}$$

After, the cryptographic device finishes the exponentiation:

$$\hat{S} \equiv ((\hat{A} \cdot \hat{B})...) \cdot \hat{B}^{2^j} \bmod \hat{N} \tag{32}$$

$$\equiv \hat{A} \cdot \hat{B}^{\sum_{i=n-j}^{n-1} 2^{i-(n-j)} \cdot d_i} \bmod \hat{N} \tag{33}$$

$$\equiv [(\dot{m}^{\sum_{i=0}^{n-j-2} 2^i \cdot d_i} \bmod N) \tag{34}$$

$$\cdot (\dot{m}^{2^{(n-j-1)}} \bmod N)^{\sum_{i=n-j-1}^{n-1} 2^{i-(n-j)+1} \cdot d_i}] \bmod \hat{N}$$

where $d_{n-j} = 1$

A.2   Cryptanalysis

As shown in Sect. 4.3, the cryptanalysis consists in guessing possible values for the private exponent's value $d'_{(1)} = \sum_{i=n-j-1}^{n-1} 2^i \cdot d'_i$ and the public modulus one $\hat{N}'$. Then the attacker uses the correct signature to forge a possible faulty one. If this forged signature equals to the real faulty one, this means that the chosen candidates are probably the searched values. As described before, the attacker has to compute:

$$S'_{(d'_{(1)}, \hat{N}')} \equiv [(S \cdot \dot{m}^{-d'_{(1)}}) \bmod N \cdot (\dot{m}^{2^{(n-j-1)}} \bmod N)^{2^{-(n-j)} \cdot d'_{(1)}}] \bmod \hat{N}' \quad (35)$$

And then, he checks if the following equation is satisfied :

$$S'_{(d'_{(1)}, \hat{N}')} \equiv \hat{S} \bmod \hat{N}' \quad (36)$$

In that case, the value $d'_{(1)}$ gives $l - 1$ bits of d (and d_{n-j} is already known).

B   Details of Performance Evaluation

B.1   Evaluation of $\Pr[A \cup B]$

According to A and B's respective definitions (see Sect. 4.6), $\Pr[A \cup B]$ represents the probability that the equation is satisfied if at least one candidate, $d'_{(1)}$ or $\hat{N}'$, is not equal to its expected value. This probability is quite difficult to evaluate since it depends on all the unknown values of (12). However, we can find a maximum and a minimum for this probability. Indeed, this equation is satisfied in the finite field $\mathbb{Z}/\hat{N}\mathbb{Z}$, so that, if the correct value is removed, the probability of this event to occur is at least $(1 - 1)/\hat{N} = 0$. But $d'_{(1)}$ is a l-bit value and so, can take 2^l possible values. $\hat{N}'$ can take $(2^8 - 1) \cdot \frac{n}{8}$ values (possible values and position for the error ε). Hence, at most, the equation can be satisfied for $\frac{2^l \cdot n \cdot (2^8 - 1) - 1}{8 \cdot \hat{N}}$ different values. As a result, the probability can be upper-bounded:

$$0 < \Pr[A \cup B] < min \left(\frac{\hat{N} - 1}{\hat{N}}, \frac{2^l \cdot n \cdot (2^8 - 1) - 1}{8 \cdot \hat{N}} \right) \quad (37)$$

B.2   Evaluation of $\Pr[B]$

This probability seems easier to evaluate than the last one. Indeed, it is the probability that at least one of the two candidates $d'_{(1)}$ or $\hat{N}'$, is not equal to its expected value. But one can notice that this event can be divided into two independent events. Hence, we have:

$$\Pr[(d'_{(1)}, \hat{N}') \neq (d_{(1)}, \hat{N})] \quad (38)$$

$$= 1 - \Pr[(d'_{(1)} = d_{(1)}) \text{ and } (\hat{N}' = \hat{N})] \quad (39)$$

$$= 1 - \Pr[d'_{(1)} = d_{(1)}] \cdot \Pr[\hat{N}' = \hat{N}] \quad (40)$$

As seen in the previous paragraph, $d'_{(1)}$ and $\hat{N}'$ can take respectively 2^l and $(2^8 - 1) \cdot \frac{n}{8}$ possible values. In both cases, there is only one correct value to find. As a consequence, we finally obtain:

$$\Pr[(d'_{(1)}, \hat{N}') \neq (d_{(1)}, \hat{N})] = 1 - \frac{8}{n \cdot (2^8 - 1) \cdot 2^l} \tag{41}$$

$$= \frac{n \cdot (2^8 - 1) \cdot 2^l - 8}{n \cdot (2^8 - 1) \cdot 2^l} \tag{42}$$

Divided Backend Duplication Methodology for Balanced Dual Rail Routing

Karthik Baddam and Mark Zwolinski

Electronics Systems and Devices Group,
School of Electronics and Computer Science,
University of Southampton,
SO17 1BJ, UK
{kb04r,mz}@ecs.soton.ac.uk
http://www.esd.ecs.soton.ac.uk/

Abstract. Dual Rail Precharge circuits offer an effective way to address Differential Power Analysis Attacks, provided routing of differential signals is fully balanced. Fat Wire [1] and Backend Duplication [2] methods address this problem. However they do not consider the effect of coupling capacitance on adjacent differential signals. In this paper we propose a new method, Divided Backend Duplication, which is based on Divided Wave Dynamic Differential Logic [3] and Backend Duplication [2], that effectively addresses balanced routing problem of Dual Rail Precharge circuits. Experimental results on an AES test circuit in 130nm technology show improvements in achieving a balanced dual rail design. Further our method can also be successfully applied to FPGAs. Results from an sbox test circuit implementation on a Xilinx FPGA are presented.

Keywords: Differential Power Analysis, Dual Rail Routing, Dual Rail FPGA Implementation.

1 Introduction

Security is an important and often primary design goal in embedded systems such as smart-cards [4] sidelining other design parameters such as cost, performance and power consumption. Differential Power Analysis Attack (DPA) [5] pose a serious threat to secure embedded systems such as smart-cards. As a result, researchers have developed several DPA countermeasures [3,6,7,8,9,10,11]. Of these, the logic level countermeasures that fall under Dynamic and Differential logic (also referred to as Dual Rail Precharge - DRP) style, theoretically offer more resistance to DPA. The basic principle behind DRP logic is to eliminate any information leaks, by consuming the same amount of power in every clock cycle. DRP circuits have been proved to prevent DPA, provided the routing of differential nets is balanced [12].

Balancing differential nets (balanced Dual Rail routing) is not, however, a trivial task. To address the routing problem, to date the following proposals have been put forward: DWDDL [3], FatWire [1], Backend Duplication [2], Three

E. Oswald and P. Rohatgi (Eds.): CHES 2008, LNCS 5154, pp. 396–410, 2008.

Phase Dual Rail [13], Path Switching [9], Double WDDL [14] and an iterative correction flow [15]. Of these, three proposals [1,2,3] impose some constraints on backend implementation flows. Three Phase Dual Rail [13] tries to avoid the routing problem by introducing a third phase, which is an additional overhead. Path Switching [9] offers an improvement to dual rail circuits and only protects registers and buses with high capacitance. Double WDDL, as the name implies, has two separate WDDL implementation thereby increasing the area overheads by four times. Double WDDL was developed mainly for use in FPGAs [14]. The first WDDL part is implemented using normal place & route flow. The second WDDL part is obtained by copying the first WDDL part, including the routing details, and reversing the orginal and complementary logic [14]. Backend correction flow, described in [15], is iterative and can consume a significant amount of time to implement a design.

In this paper we concentrate on the implementation of balanced Dual Rail Precharge logic styles rather than the alternatives. We try to present a simple yet effective solution to improve Dual Rail circuit routing capacitance. In Section 2 we discuss Dual Rail Precharge Logic Styles, give a brief introduction to backend design flow, and discuss existing methods and their shortcomings. In Section 3 we present the inversion problem and discuss its solutions. In Section 4 we present our proposed methodology. In Section 4.1 & Section 4.2 we present ASIC & FPGA implementations respectively and then conclude the paper.

2 Background

2.1 Dual Rail Precharge Logic Styles

Dynamic and Differential Logic (also referred to as Dual Rail Precharge - DRP) [3,7,8] has been proposed to prevent DPA. The idea is to consume the same amount of power for any combination of inputs. This is achieved by using differential logic (two signals instead of one) and by precharging both the differential nets in every clock cycle. In DRP circuits for every logic gate, a complementary gate exists, usually referred to as *false* logic (or *false* part).

Dual Rail Precharge logic styles can be classified into two types based on the way precharge is applied. Sense Amplifier Based Logic (SABL) is a DRP logic based on the principles of domino logic, where a special precharge signal is applied to every gate to force the gate to precharge. Wave Dynamic Dual Rail (WDDL) and Dual Spacer Dual Rail (DSDR) on the other hand propagate the precharge signal from a design's primary inputs and state-elements (flip-flops). WDDL and DSDR have the following differences over SABL: 1) WDDL and DSDR can be constructed using existing CMOS standard cells and 2) that the *true* logic and *false* logic are two different cells. The second point is not true in all cases. WDDL and DSDR both need special inverters, where the *true* and *false* wires are cross connected. As differential logic has both *true* and *false* outputs, an inverter is implemented by exchanging the outputs. Moreover an inverter is an inverting gate, it will stop the precharge wave propagation. Fig. 1 shows the basic building blocks of WDDL with master slave WDDL flip-flops. Although

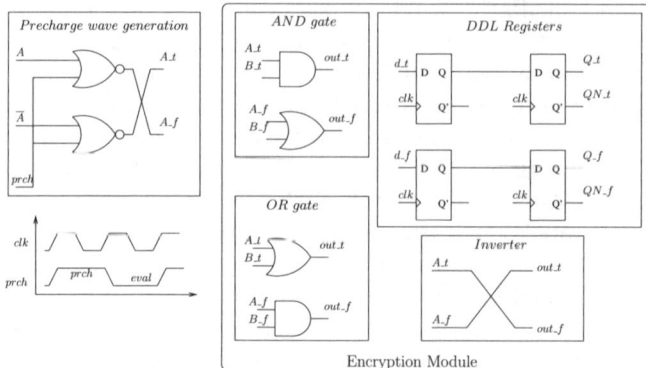

Fig. 1. Building blocks of WDDL,with Master Slave WDDL flip-flops

double the clock frequency is required to get same data rate using master slave flops, these are recommended [3]. All primary inputs are driven by a 'precharge wave generation' block, so that individual gates will propagate the precharge. Note that the inverter is implemented by exchanging the dual rail pairs.

2.2   Backend Design Flow

Most of the digital designs implemented today are based on a standard cell flow. A set of commonly used standard cells are designed and characterized such that CAD tools can be used to automate most of the design flow. Design entry is typically in behavioral HDL and is synthesized and mapped to the target technology's standard cells. After the synthesis, the resulting netlist is placed and routed to get the final design. Backend design is usually referred to the implementation of the design after the synthesis phase and mainly involves floorplanning, placement and routing. A placer partitions the available core area into rows, where the standard cells are placed. In a similar fashion, a router partitions the core area into horizontal and vertical routing grids. Each grid has a minimum size defined by the target technology's wire pitch size.

The place and route flow usually involves the following steps, shown in Fig. 2. First a floorplan is made (Fig. 2(a)). This is where the aspect ratio (or the dimensions) of the chip are determined. Next the standard cells are placed (Fig. 2(b)) and finally the wires are routed (Fig. 2(c)).

2.3   Existing Methods

Divided Wave Dynamic Differential Logic (DWDDL) was proposed by *Tiri and Verbauwhede* [3] to address routing imbalances in DRP logic styles. DWDDL's idea is to place and route a single ended design (the *true* part), copy it and replace the complementary cells (for example 'and' with 'or' and vice versa) to get the *false* part. However, this method assumes that there is no inversion in the single rail design, as an inverting cell would stop the precharge wave propagation. However, in practice it is difficult to have logic without inversion. This is

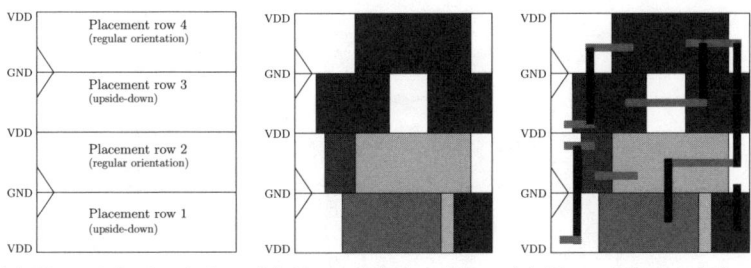

(a) Normal Backend flow: (b) Normal Backend flow: (c) Normal Backend flow:
Create a Floor plan   Place the standard cells   Route the wires

Fig. 2. Normal Backend flow overview

the only known limitation for DWDDL and no further work has been reported on it.

Fat Wire was proposed by *Tiri and Verbauwhede* [1] to address routing imbalances in DRP logic styles. In this methodology a Fat Wire is constructed by two adjacent normal wires. For the Fat Wire method to work, first the dual rail netlist, instantiating dual rail cells, has to be placed. Then instead of routing two differential wires (for the *true* and *false* signals) a single Fat Wire is routed and later decomposed into two normal single wires which will have same wire length.

Backend Duplication was proposed by *Guilley et al.* [2] to address routing imbalances in DRP logic styles. The basic idea of backend duplication is based on placement and routing obstructions (constraints to the CAD tool). The first step of Backend Duplication is to constrain the CAD tool (1) to only use alternate rows for placing cells and routing horizontal routes (2) and to use the alternate routing pitches for routing vertical routes. Thus, when the placer has finished placing the single rail design, a dual rail design can be obtained from copying (and transforming) the single rail into the previously obstructed rows. Note that this operation is a simple shift in coordinates of the placed cells. Duplicating the routes is done in two steps. Once the design is routed, horizontal routes are duplicated in the same way as cells. Vertical routes are duplicated by simple shift in the x-axis of the routing pitch.

2.4 Shortcomings of the Existing Methods

Coupling capacitance (crosstalk) has become one of the most critical issues in deep sub micron physicaql designs because of 1) interconnect dominated circuit delay and 2) strong coupling effects between intqerconnect wires [16]. As technology scales the wire widths, their height is increased and coupling capacitance between wires increases [16] (Fig. 3(a)).

In the Fat Wire and Backend Duplication methods (vertical routes) dual rail wires end up next to each other, as shown in Fig. 3(b). With coupling capacitances increasing, the effective capacitance seen by a *true* and *false* signal will vary. For

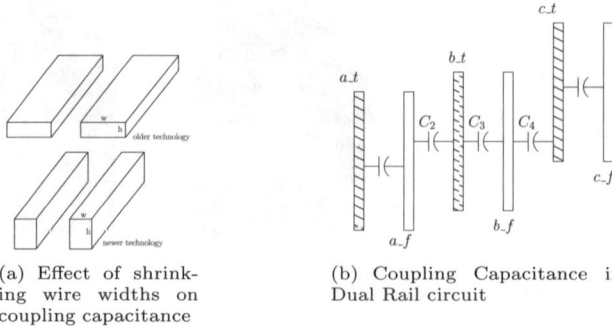

(a) Effect of shrinking wire widths on coupling capacitance

(b) Coupling Capacitance in Dual Rail circuit

Fig. 3. Coupling Capacitance effects

example consider dual rail pairs b_t & b_f. The coupling capacitance seen by b_t is C_2 & C_3 whereas the coupling capacitance seen by b_f is C_3 & C_4. Now if the capacitances C_2 & C_4 vary by a huge difference, the resulting design can have unbalanced wire capacitance and can lead to information leaks. Note that this effect becomes more and more dominant as technology scales down. The effect of coupling between differential wires is more significant in the Fat Wire method than in Backend Duplication as the horizontal wires are also next to each other.

Of course spacing between dual rail wires can always be increased to reduce the coupling capacitance, however such an increase comes at the expense of increased area and reduced routing resources. Of the three methods to address routing problems, DWDDL is the simplest and most effective. However practical designs will always have inversion and hence will not be able to use the DWDDL method.

3   Inversion Problem in DRP Logic

Inversion in Dual Rail Precharge Logic styqles is considered as a free operation, as dual rail signal pairs are coqmplementary; inversion is simply obtained by exchanging the dual rail pairs. On the other hand an inverter cannot exist in a WDDL or DSDR style design as it would stop the precharge wave propagation. In other words, inversion is only possible by exchanging the dual rail pair. This property of WDDL and DSDR logic styles prevents designs from using a DWDDL style of implementation. Of course dual rail pairs can be exchanged after DWDDL implementation, but there is no systematic way of doing this. Moreover the extra wire capacitance from this exchange can add to the critical path delay of a design and can introduce unbalanced wires. This issue of exchanging wires can be worst when the number of unused inverters in a design increases. As an example a 8ns clock period, 128 bit AES had 5,762 inverters from a total gate count of 22,704, excluding buffers used for the clock tree. For this example, we increased the area and delay cost of the original inverter by 10 times so that synthesis tool will use it only when inversion is needed and not for buffering.

3.1   Mitigating the Inversion Problem in DRP Logic

Inverters cannot exists in WDDL and DSDR style designs as they would stop the precharge wave propagation. On the other hand, designing logic without inversion is difficult. It is possible to have a cell that behaves as an inverter and still not prevent the precharge wave propagation. This is possible by using a two input Exclusive-OR (XOR) gate instead of an inverter and connecting the second input of XOR to the negated precharge signal that is used in generating the precharge wave (Fig. 1).

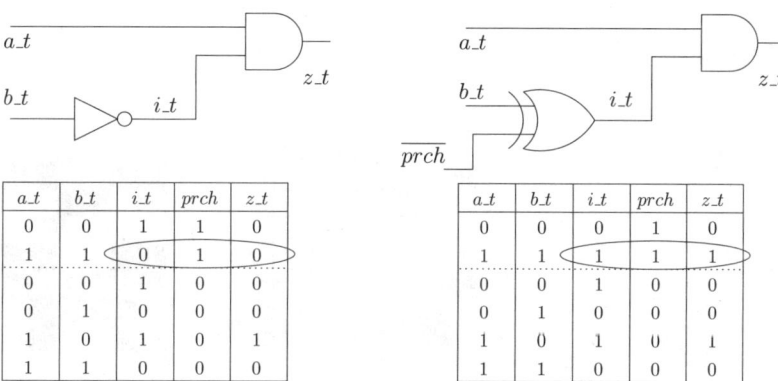

a_t	b_t	i_t	prch	z_t
0	0	1	1	0
1	1	0	1	0
0	0	1	0	0
0	1	0	0	0
1	0	1	0	1
1	1	0	0	0

a_t	b_t	i_t	prch	z_t
0	0	0	1	0
1	1	1	1	1
0	0	1	0	0
0	1	0	0	0
1	0	1	0	1
1	1	0	0	0

Fig. 4. Using XOR instead of Inverter (Inputs a_t & a_f are driven by Precharge Wave Generation Block shown in Fig. 1)

Consider the example circuit on the left side of Fig. 4, with the truth table shown. When the $prch$ signal is high all primary inputs are set to logic 1 (Inputs a_t & a_f are driven by Precharge Wave Generation Block shown in Fig. 1). However intermediate signal i_t (output of the inverter) will not propagate the precharge wave and the output signal z_t will not be precharged. Now consider the circuit on the right of Fig. 4. A two input Exclusive-Or (XOR) gate is used instead of an inverter. The original input and output of the inverter are connected as before to the XOR. The second input of the XOR is connected to the $\overline{prch}$ signal, which is used in precharge wave propagation. When $prch$ is high the XOR will act as a buffer allowing the precharge wave to propagate and when $prch$ is low XOR will act as an inverter as intended in the original circuit.

It is also possible to use a Domino-style inverter (similar to the one presented in [13]) instead of an XOR gate. As in the case of the XOR, $\overline{prch}$ is used to precharge the domino-inverter. In the case of a domino style inverter, the timing of $\overline{prch}$ is important for the circuit to work. Because of this, we prefer to use an XOR gate and in the rest of this paper we use XOR gates to replace inverters. Note that inverters that are used in clock tree synthesis need not be replaced, as the clock signal is not precharged like normal inputs. Based on this, we now present a method to implement a fully balanced dual rail design.

4   Proposed Method: Divided Backend Duplication

With XOR gates replacing inverters, a dual rail circuit can be implemented as physically separate (without any connections) *true* part (original single-ended part) and *false* part (complementary part). The primary inputs and outputs will still remain common for both the *true* and *false* parts. With this advantage the Divided WDDL implementation, [3], can now be implemented provided that 1) the pins of complementary standard cells should be same, i.e at same location and same metal layer and 2) the size of the complementary standard cells are the same.

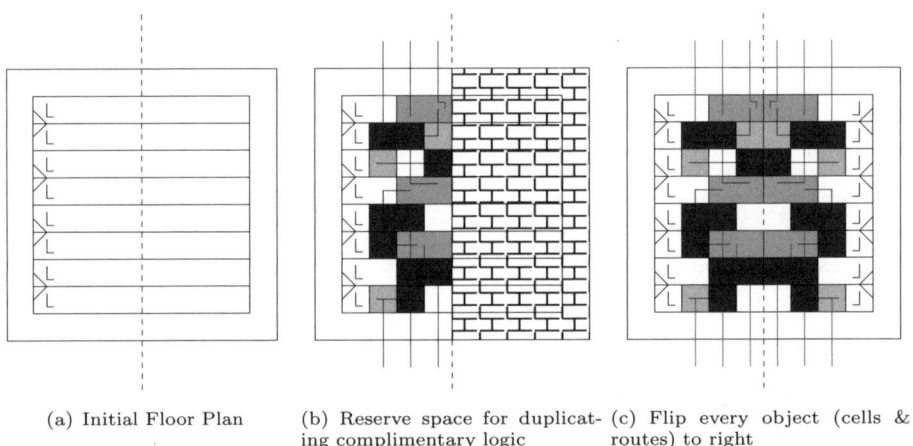

(a) Initial Floor Plan   (b) Reserve space for duplicat- (c) Flip every object (cells &
                             ing complimentary logic   routes) to right

Fig. 5. Proposed method overview

Fig. 5 shows the overview of our proposed method for balanced dual rail routing. This method is similar to the Backend Duplication method, [2]. A single ended design is used for the initial place and route process and then duplicated to get the final dual rail design. The process can be divided into the following steps (shown in Fig. 6).

1. A WDDL-compliant single rail design is processed to replace the inverter cells with XOR cells (Fig. 4). A program has been written for this conversion, based on OPENACCESS [17]. At this stage the design is still single rail.
2. A floorplan is made for the processed single rail design, with utilization of half the required final utilization. This ensures that there is enough space for duplicating the complementary part (Fig. 5(a)).
3. Half of the floorplan area is reserved (obstructed) for the complementary part (Fig. 5(b)).
4. The Single Rail design is implemented in the usual way, i.e place and route, timing analysis, SI analysis, ECO fixes, etc.

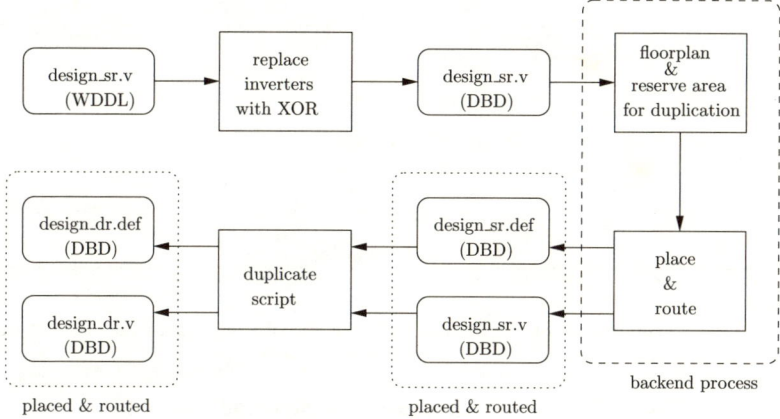

Fig. 6. Divided Backend Duplication implementation overview

5. After the Single Rail design is finalized, the complementary part can be obtained by flipping every object in the single rail design to the right and by replacing the complementary cells, *AND* with *OR* and vice versa, as shown in Fig. 5(c). This step can be done by processing the DEF file and is similar to the process used in Fat Wire [1] and Backend Duplication [2].

As our proposed method is derived from DWDDL and Backend Duplication, we call it Divided Backend Duplication (DBD). A small variation to the duplication process can be made: 1) Instead of flipping the design objects to right, they can be shifted by half of the core width. 2) Instead of flipping the design objects along the x-axis, this can be done on the y-axis too (flipping to top or bottom).

4.1 ASIC Implementation

To show the effectiveness of Divided Backend Duplication, we implemented an AES test circuit with 20k+ gates in a 130nm process. Three different designs are implemented. All designs have the same constraints and netlist. The difference is in implementation. The first implementation, which we call "regular place & route design", is implemented without any special techniques. The second implementation, which we call "backend duplicated design", is implemented as suggested in [2] and is based on the WDDL logic style [3]. The third design, which we call "divided backend duplicated design", is implemented as suggested in Section 4 and is also based on WDDL logic style [3]. All the designs aspect ratios are set to 1. The row utilization of "regular place & route design" is set to 0.70 while for "backend duplicated design" and "divided backend duplicated design" it is set to 0.35 (half the required utilization, so that enough room is available for duplication). We used Cadence Encounter tools [18] to perform the backend implementation. For parasitic extractions we used Encounter's

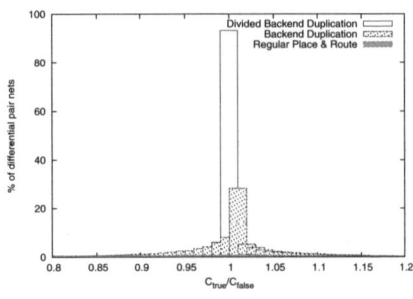 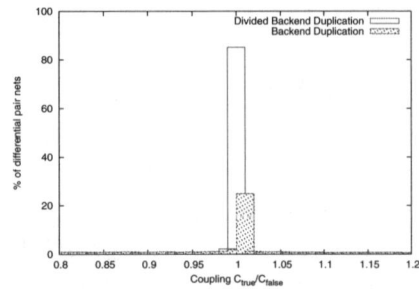

(a) Ratio of Total Capacitance of Differential Pair nets

(b) Ratio of Coupling Capacitance of Differential Pair nets

Fig. 7. Ratio of Capacitance of Differential Pair nets

native extractor and set the "detailed" and "coupling" switches to true. After the parasitic extraction, all the parasitic information was exported into a Standard Parasitic Exchange Format (SPEF) file containing the ground capacitance, coupling capacitance and resistance of every wire.

Fig. 7 shows histograms in which the internal interconnect capacitance of the regular place and route design, the Backend Duplicated design and Divided Backend Duplicated (DBD) design are compared. We have not implemented Fat Wire [1] as the effect of coupling on dual rail signal pairs from Fat Wire should be similar to that of the Backend Duplication method [2]. The capacitance per net was extracted from the SPEF file, which in turn was reported from Encounter. Fig. 7(a) shows the distribution of the ratio between the capacitance at the *true* signal net and the capacitance at the corresponding *false* signal net (C_{true}/C_{false}). The ratio C_{true}/C_{false} for regular place & route method is between 0.01 & 10 and for the backend duplication method it is between 0.70 & 1.5. On the other hand, for the divided backend duplication method this ratio is only between 0.90 & 1.1. The percentage of nets that have a ratio of 1 for Divided Backend Duplication is 93.25% when compared to 28.34% for backend duplication.

Fig. 7(b) is similar as Fig. 7(a) except that coupling capacitance is only considered instead of total capacitance. The cumulative coupling capacitance per net was extracted from SPEF file, which in turn was reported from Encounter. Coupling capacitance ratio, $Coupling\ C_{true}/C_{false}$ for regular place & route method are not shown as the ratio for some nets was as high as 70. For the backend duplication method, the ratio $Coupling\ C_{true}/C_{false}$ is between 0.22 & 3.52 while for divided backend duplication is 0.60 & 1.9. The percentage of nets that have a ratio of 1 for Divided Backend Duplication is 85.15% when compared to 24.86% for Backend Duplication. As discussed in Section 2.4, this increase in capacitance ratio for Backend Duplication method is due to unevenly distributed coupling capacitance, whereas the Divided Backend Duplication method shows much less variation.

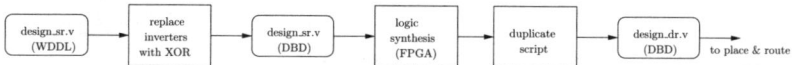

Fig. 8. Divided Backend Duplication Synthesis for FPGAs

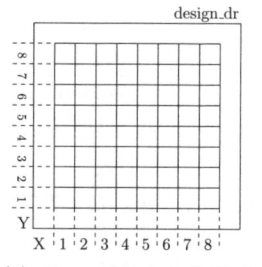

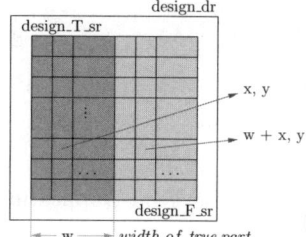

(a) Unconstrained Initial Floorplan for dual rail module

(b) Constrained Floorplan for dual rail module, with boundaries for *true* and *false* part

Fig. 9. Floorplanning to implement Divided Backend Duplication Dual Rail design on FPGAs

4.2   FPGA Implementation

Differential routing on FPGAs is more difficult than on ASICs as the routing resources are limited. *Tiri and Verbauwhede* [19] have discussed a WDDL implementation on FPGAs and proposed a synthesis flow. However, the differential routing problem in FPGAs has not been addressed to the best of our knowledge. In this section we discuss how the Divided Backend Duplication method can be applied to get balanced differential routing in FPGAs.

Before implementing a design in FPGA, it has to be synthesized to the target FPGA. Synthesizing for a secure dual rail implementation has been discussed in detail in [19]. We adopt the flow presented in [19] to synthesize for Divided Backend Duplication implementation with the modifications shown in Fig. 8. After replacing the inverters with XORs, FPGA synthesis can be done with a commercial CAD tool or "Clustering" technique described in [19]. Care needs to be taken if Commercial CAD tools are used, to preserve the wave dynamic nature of the design. Note that the structural *true* and *false* part are identical for FPGAs, the only difference being the LUT programming value.

FPGAs have highly regular structure as shown in Fig. 9(a). Each box in Fig. 9(a) corresponds to a Configurable Logic Block (CLB) and its associated routing resources. Unlike ASICs, the place & route process of FPGAs is not standardized. This makes it difficult to duplicate the placement and routing information for complementary parts of a dual rail design. Although each FPGA vendor has a specific implementation tool, most of the tools offer procedures to 1) floorplan and 2) constrain a design's instance to a specific location. However, constraining a net to a specific routing resource is not supported. Based on this,

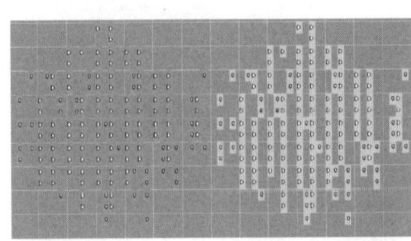
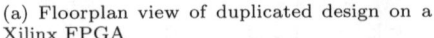
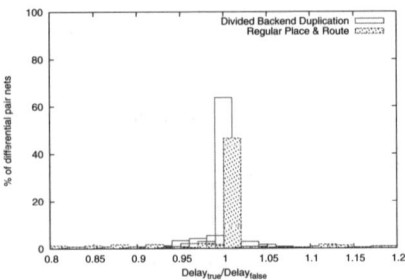

(a) Floorplan view of duplicated design on a Xilinx FPGA

(b) Ratio of Delay of Differential Pair nets

Fig. 10. Divided Backend Duplication implementation results on a Xilinx FPGA

the process to implement a balanced dual rail design in FPGAs can be divided into the following steps.

1. The WDDL-compliant single rail design is processed to replace the inverter cells with XOR cells and to transform the netlist into a FPGA-specific netlist (Fig. 8).
2. The floorplan area is divided into two equal parts (for the *true* and *false* parts), comprising equal number of CLBs, local routing resources and global routing resources (Fig. 9(b)).
3. The top-level dual-rail design is implemented in the usual way, without violating the boundary constraints set above. The implementation steps usually are place & route, timing analysis, ECO fixes, etc.
4. After the top-level dual-rail design is successfully implemented, locations of all the instances of *true* part are saved to a file. Based on the location of a *true* part's instance, the corresponding *false* part's instance is calculated and written to a constraint file.
5. Based on the new constraints, the *false* part is re-implemented.

To see the effectiveness of backend duplication, we implemented a DES sbox on a Xilinx FPGA [20]. Xilinx's XST tool was used for synthesis and ISE was used for implementation. The Xilinx Floorplan editor was used to constrain the floorplan. After the initial place & route Xilinx's Floorplan editor was used to save all the instance locations. The final place & route process was constrained by using Xilinx's UCF file. Fig. 10(a) shows a floorplan view of such a duplicated design. Although FPGA implementation tools do not report detailed parasitic information, they report delays associated with an instance and interconnect in a Standard Delay File (SDF). This SDF file was analyzed and the resulting distribution of the ratio between the delay at the *true* signal net and the delay at the corresponding *false* signal net ($Delay_{true}/Delay_{false}$) is shown in Fig. 10(b). The delay ratio $Delay_{true}/Delay_{false}$ for the regular place & route method is between 0.40 & 2.7 and for the divided backend duplication method it is between 0.8 & 1.2. The percentage of nets that have a ratio of 1 for Divided Backend Duplication is 64.25%

compared to 46.34% for regular place & route. Although we have constrained an instance to be at a specific location, the implementation tool is free to connect the wires and may be the reason for only 64.25% of nets to have a ratio of 1. Note that we are not constraining the FPGA tool to duplicate the routes, as we could not find a way to achieve this. *Yu and Schaumont* have implemented a duplication method for Double WDDL style on Xilinx FPGAs [14] that can be used to completely balance the routing of differential nets on FPGAs.

4.3   Advantages of Divided Backend Duplication

The main advantage of Divided Backend Duplication is that both the *true* and *false* parts see the same environment. The coupling capacitance problem discussed in Section 2.4 is now eliminated. As Divided Backend Duplication is based on standard cells implementation styles such as WDDL and DSDR, it can be adapted to both ASICs and FPGAs.

Divided Backend Duplication will not have a problem with diagonal routing, an upcoming interconnect technology (already available in Xilinx FPGAs and supported by the Cadence X architecture router), whereas Backend Duplication currently cannot handle it. Implementing Divided Backend Duplication process is a straightforward process. Neither specific design rules need to be changed nor specific routing blocks have to be imposed on the design. In our example implementation for ASIC, the run time was 3 times less when compared to Backend Duplication. As the *true* and *false* parts are not interleaved, implementing any Engineering Change Orders (ECOs) is also simple and straightforward.

The only requirements to implement Divided Backend Duplication are that 1) the pins of complementary standard cells should be same, i.e. at same location and same metal layer and 2) the size of complementary standard cells are the same. This is an advantage when compared to the requirements imposed by Fat Wire [1] and Backend Duplication [2].

As Divided Backend Duplication separates the *true* and *false* part, a by-product is that two separate data sets can be processed at the same time, instead of one. Divided Backend Duplication designs can have a *random mode* where one part can process the required data and the other can process random data. Further the entire design can be configured such that the design can randomly switch from *dual rail mode* to *random mode* and back. Divided Backend Duplication designs can even be configured to operate either the *true* or *false* part at a given time to reduce power consumption, when DPA countermeasure is not required. The only requirement to achieve this is to change the input/output interface to the dual rail design.

4.4   Disadvantages of Divided Backend Duplication

The main disadvantage of the Divided Duplication method is the additional area and delay overhead introduced by replacing inverters with XOR gates. The number of XOR cells used depends on the design and cannot be generalized. For our AES test circuit about 25% of cells were XORs. This increased the critical

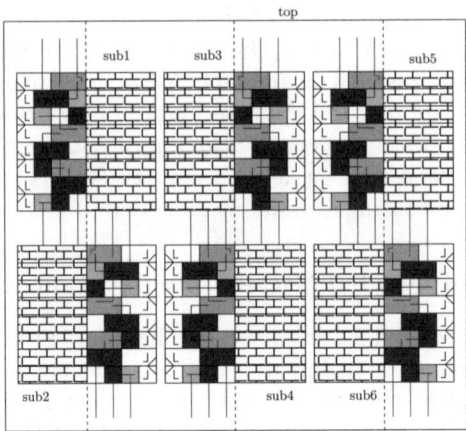

Fig. 11. Hierarchical Divided Backend Duplication

path delay by 1.2 times. The delay and area overhead introduced by XOR can be minimized by using a domino style inverter instead of XOR. Also the *prch* signal needs to be buffered as it drives all the extra XOR cells.

As the *true* and *false* part of the design are physically separated, there may be a concern that EM analysis attacks [21] may be successful, by only observing the *true* or *false* part. Although this may seem unlikely, one may minimize the extent of this concern by taking a hierarchical approach to implementing Divided Backend Duplication compared with that shown in Fig. 6. An example floorplan for a hierarchical Divided Backend Duplication is shown in Fig. 11. Another approach would be to use the Backend Duplication method [2], but with the following difference for duplication: instead of shifting to the right, every object can be flipped to the right.

5   Conclusion

We have shown that coupling capacitance between dual rail nets can cause routing imbalances. To address this, we have proposed a new method, called Divided Backend Duplication. We have shown that the Divided Backend Duplication method can be applied to get a balanced dual rail design in both ASICs and FPGAs and that it offers a significant improvement in balancing routing capacitance compared to previous methods. Divided Backend Duplication is the first method to address routing imbalances in FPGAs. Divided Backend Duplication has an area overhead of around 25% and a delay overhead of around 1.2 times.

Acknowledgments

We are very thankful to Sylvain Guilley for his valuable discussions & suggestions regarding implementation of Backend Duplication and for sharing his Perl script to implement Backend Duplication. We would also like to acknowledge the anonymous referees for their valuable comments & suggestions.

References

1. Tiri, K., Verbauwhede, I.: Place and Route for Secure Standard Cell Design. In: 6th International Conference on Smart Card Research and Advanced Applications (CARDIS 2004), August 2004, pp. 143–158 (2004)
2. Guilley, S., Hoogvorst, P., Mathieu, Y., Pacalet, R.: The Backend Duplication Method. In: Rao, J.R., Sunar, B. (eds.) CHES 2005. LNCS, vol. 3659, pp. 383–397. Springer, Heidelberg (2005)
3. Tiri, K., Verbauwhede, I.: A Logic Level Design Methodology for a Secure DPA Resistant ASIC or FPGA Implementation. In: DATE 2004: Proceedings of the conference on Design, automation and test in Europe, pp. 246–251. IEEE Computer Society, Washington (2004)
4. Ravi, S., Raghunathan, A., Kocher, P., Hattangady, S.: Security in embedded systems: Design challenges. Trans. on Embedded Computing Sys. 3(3), 461–491 (2004)
5. Kocher, P.C., Jaffe, J., Jun, B.: Differential Power Analysis. In: Wiener, M.J. (ed.) CRYPTO 1999. LNCS, vol. 1666, pp. 388–397. Springer, Heidelberg (1999)
6. Bucci, M., Guglielmo, M., Luzzi, R., Trifiletti, A.: A power consumption randomization countermeasure for DPA-resistant cryptographic processors. In: Macii, E., Paliouras, V., Koufopavlou, O. (eds.) PATMOS 2004. LNCS, vol. 3254, pp. 481–490. Springer, Heidelberg (2004)
7. Sokolov, D., Murphy, J., Bystrov, A., Yakovlev, A.: Design and Analysis of Dual-Rail Circuits for Security Applications. IEEE Transactions on Computers 54(4), 449–460 (2005)
8. Tiri, K., Verbauwhede, I.: Securing Encryption Algorithms against DPA at the Logic Level: Next Generation Smart Card Technology. In: Walter, C.D., Koç, Ç.K., Paar, C. (eds.) CHES 2003. LNCS, vol. 2779, pp. 125–136. Springer, Heidelberg (2003)
9. Baddam, K., Zwolinski, M.: Path switching: a technique to tolerate dual rail routing imbalances. Design Automation for Embedded Systems (accepted for publication) (2008), http://www.springerlink.com/content/32181g28411w2121, doi:10.1007/s10617-008-9017-z
10. Pramstaller, N., Oswald, E., Mangard, S., Gürkaynak, F.K., Haene, S.: A Masked AES ASIC Implementation. In: Ofner, E., Ley, M. (eds.) Proceedings of Austrochip 2004, Villach, Austria, October 2004, pp. 77–82 (2004)
11. Popp, T., Mangard, S.: Masked Dual-Rail Pre-Charge Logic: DPA-Resistance without Routing Constraints. In: Rao, J.R., Sunar, B. (eds.) CHES 2005. LNCS, vol. 3659, pp. 172–186. Springer, Heidelberg (2005)
12. Tiri, K., Verbauwhede, I.: Prototype IC with WDDL and Differential Routing DPA Resistance Assessment. In: Rao, J.R., Sunar, B. (eds.) CHES 2005. LNCS, vol. 3659, pp. 354–365. Springer, Heidelberg (2005)
13. Bucci, M., Giancane, L., Luzzi, R., Trifiletti, A.: Three-Phase Dual-Rail Pre-charge Logic. In: Goubin, L., Matsui, M. (eds.) CHES 2006. LNCS, vol. 4249, pp. 232–241. Springer, Heidelberg (2006)
14. Yu, P., Schaumont, P.: Secure FPGA circuits using controlled placement and routing. In: CODES+ISSS 2007: Proceedings of the 5th IEEE/ACM international conference on Hardware/software codesign and system synthesis, pp. 45–50. ACM, New York (2007)

15. Bouesse, G.F., Renaudin, M., Dumont, S., Germain, F.: DPA on Quasi Delay Insensitive Asynchronous Circuits: Formalization and Improvement. In: DATE 2005: Proceedings of the conference on Design, Automation and Test in Europe, pp. 424–429. IEEE Computer Society, Washington (2005)
16. Weste, N., Harris, D.: CMOS VLSI Design A Circuits and Systems Perspective, 3rd edn. Addison-Wesley, Reading (2004)
17. Si2.org: OpenAccess Coalition (April 2007), http://openeda.si2.org/
18. Cadence Design Systems: ENCOUNTER DIGITAL IC DESIGN PLATFORM (April 2007),
http://www.cadence.com/products/digital_ic/index.aspx?lid=dic
19. Tiri, K., Verbauwhede, I.: Synthesis of Secure FPGA Implementations. In: International Workshop on Logic and Synthesis (IWLS 2004), June 2004, pp. 224–231 (2004)
20. Xilinx Inc: Xilinx Inc. (April 2007), http://www.xilinx.com/
21. Gandolfi, K., Mourtel, C., Olivier, F.: Electromagnetic Analysis: Concrete Results. In: Koç, Ç.K., Naccache, D., Paar, C. (eds.) CHES 2001. LNCS, vol. 2162, pp. 251–261. Springer, Heidelberg (2001)

Using Subspace-Based Template Attacks to Compare and Combine Power and Electromagnetic Information Leakages

François-Xavier Standaert[1,*] and Cedric Archambeau[2]

[1] UCL Crypto Group, Université catholique de Louvain
[2] Centre for Computational Statistics and Machine Learning,
University College London
fstandae@uclouvain.be, c.archambeau@cs.ucl.ac.uk

Abstract. The power consumption and electromagnetic radiation are among the most extensively used side-channels for analyzing physically observable cryptographic devices. This paper tackles three important questions in this respect. First, we compare the effectiveness of these two side-channels. We investigate the common belief that electromagnetic leakages lead to more powerful attacks than their power consumption counterpart. Second we study the best combination of the power and electromagnetic leakages. A quantified analysis based on sound information theoretic and security metrics is provided for these purposes. Third, we evaluate the effectiveness of two data dimensionality reduction techniques for constructing subspace-based template attacks. Selecting automatically the meaningful time samples in side-channel leakage traces is an important problem in the application of template attacks and it usually relies on heuristics. We show how classical statistical tools such as Principal Component Analysis and Fisher Linear Discriminant Analysis can be used for efficiently preprocessing the leakage traces.

1 Introduction

Power Analysis Attacks have been introduced in the late nineties as a powerful cryptanalytic technique to extract secret data from cryptographic hardware devices [12,13]. Shortly after, the ElectroMagnetic (EM) radiation of a chip appeared as an alternative source of physical leakages [8,16]. Since the publication of these seminal papers, different lines of research have been followed, mainly ranging between attempts to prevent and counteract side-channel attacks and attempts to develop their understanding and discuss their optimality.

For example, Template Attacks (TAs) were introduced in [7] as the most powerful type of side-channel attack from an information theoretic point of view. TAs assume a probabilistic noise model for the leakages and use maximum likelihood as a similarity measure between actual leakage traces and their key-dependent predictions. Because of computational restrictions, TAs usually rely on heuristics

---

* Postdoctoral researcher of the Belgian Fund for Scientific Research (FNRS).

E. Oswald and P. Rohatgi (Eds.): CHES 2008, LNCS 5154, pp. 411–425, 2008.

in order to determine the leakage samples for which a model will be estimated. A more systematic approach is to use dimensionality reduction techniques for this purpose. Assuming that the information content of a leakage trace resides mainly at the time instants of maximum variability, Principal Subspace Template Attacks (PSTAs) have been introduced in [4]. Principal Component Analysis (PCA) [11] is then used to find the linear transformation that maximizes the inter-class distance when projecting the data into a low-dimensional subspace. Finally, Multi-Channel Attacks (MCAs) [2] exploit similar statistical techniques as TAs, but utilize simultaneously several side-channels like power and EM.

In parallel to these algorithmic advances, a number of practical experiments have been conducted and underlined the advantages of EM attacks compared to power analysis. For example, the ability to carefully position a small probe in the near field of a chip and to defeat certain countermeasures against power analysis attacks has been exhibited [1]. More recently, the exploitation of better leakage models than the usual Hamming weight/distance ones by monitoring the EM field sign has been detailed in [14]. Such improved models involve the improvement of non-profiled side-channel attacks, *e.g.* using the correlation coefficient [6]. They suggest that the EM leakage of a chip generally provides the adversary with more information than the power consumption of the same chip.

In this paper, we first intend to take both the comparison of the power and EM leakages and their combination one step further. For this purpose, we use different types of template attacks to evaluate the information theoretic and security metrics introduced in [18]. We apply these tools and metrics to an exemplary leaking implementation and bring a quantified confirmation of the previous intuitions: when accessible, near-field EM measurements provide more information than power leakages. Our results also demonstrate that the real power and EM channels are significantly more informative than their idealized models based on Hamming weights/distances (or even signed distances [14]). Similarly, we confirm the advantages of a multi-channel approach in which one channel is used to correct/improve the weaknesses of the other one.

In addition, we take advantage of the available power and EM measurements to compare different data dimensionality reduction techniques. PSTAs are very powerful in practice since a "small sample size" PCA can be applied in cases where there are much more time samples in the traces than key classes in the attack. But PSTAs only maximize the variance between average traces (each trace corresponding to a key class candidate) without considering the intra-class scatter. Hence, the resulting subspace might be suboptimal. Fisher's Linear Discriminant Analysis (LDA) [10] is more appropriate with this respect. LDA seeks the subspace that maximizes the ratio between inter-class and intra-class scatter. It finds the subpace in which the average traces are maximally separated, while minimizing the spread of the individual traces within their respective classes.

The rest of this paper is structured as follows. Section 2 describes our target implementation. Section 3 defines the evaluation metrics for the analysis of our experiments. Section 4 describes the PCA- and LDA-based template attacks. Experimental results are presented in Section 5 and conclusions are in Section 6.

2   Target Implementation

Our target device for the following experiments is a PIC 16F877 8-bit RISC-based microprocessor. Our measurements exploit the setup described in [14]. The microchip was clocked at a frequency around 4 MHz. We monitored the power consumption by inserting a small resistor at the ground pin of the device. The value of the resistor was chosen so that it disrupts the voltage supply by at most 5% of its reference. In order to get accurate near field EM measurements, the chip was depackaged following the guidelines given in [3]. We monitored the EM leakages with a small hand-made loop probe that was soldered on a coax mounted on a SMA connector. The signal was then amplified with a large band, low noise pre-amplifier and sampled with a 1 GHz bandwidth oscilloscope.

Since the primary goal of this paper is to evaluate the effectiveness of the power consumption and EM side-channels and to discuss their relation with different leakage models, we did not directly target a cryptographic algorithm. Rather, we programmed the microchip so that it processed all the possible 4-bit transitions in order to determine the extent to which these transitions could be recovered through physical observations. That is, we targeted the 256 possible transitions between two 4-bit values x_1 and x_2 on the bus. Considering 4-bit (rather than 8-bit) transitions was justified by the need to keep a reasonable number of transitions (hence, templates) under investigation. In practice, recovering a transition through side-channel measurements can be straightforwardly exploited *e.g.* to recover the secret key of a block cipher. This is similar to recovering, *e.g.* the Hamming weight of a key dependent intermediate value after the application of a substitution box. Consequently and for simplicity, we will denote each 4-bit transition as a a key class s in the rest of the paper.

3   Evaluation Metrics

Following the framework introduced in [18], we will evaluate our different experiments with a combination of information theoretic and security metrics.

Information Theoretic Metric. Let S be a discrete random variable indicating the target key class associated to a side-channel attack and s be a realization of this variable corresponding to one particular transition $x_1 \rightarrow x_2$ on the bus. Let $\mathbf{L}_q$ be a random vector denoting the side-channel observations generated with q queries to the target physical computer and $\mathbf{l}_q = [l_1, l_2, \ldots, l_q]$ be a realization of this random vector. Let finally $\Pr[s|\mathbf{l}_q]$ be the conditional probability of a key class s given a leakage $\mathbf{l}_q$. We first define a conditional entropy matrix as:

$$\mathbf{H}_{s,s^*}^q = -\sum_{\mathbf{l}_q} \Pr[\mathbf{l}_q|s] \cdot \log_2 \Pr[s^*|\mathbf{l}_q], \tag{1}$$

where s^* denotes a possible key class candidate in the attack. Second, we derive Shannon's conditional entropy as follows:

$$\mathrm{H}[S|\mathbf{L}_q] = -\sum_s \Pr[s] \sum_{\mathbf{l}_q} \Pr[\mathbf{l}_q|s] \cdot \log_2 \Pr[s|\mathbf{l}_q] = \underset{s}{\mathbf{E}} \ \mathbf{H}_{s,s}^q,$$

where $\mathbf{E}$ denotes the mathematical expectation and $\Pr[s|\mathbf{l}_q]$ is derived from the Bayes law. We note that this definition is equivalent to the classical one since:

$$H[S|\mathbf{L}_q] = -\sum_{\mathbf{l}_q} \Pr[\mathbf{l}_q] \sum_s \Pr[s|\mathbf{l}_q] \cdot \log_2 \Pr[s|\mathbf{l}_q]$$

$$= -\sum_s \Pr[s] \sum_{\mathbf{l}_q} \Pr[\mathbf{l}_q|s] \cdot \log_2 \Pr[s|\mathbf{l}_q]$$

Then, we define an entropy reduction matrix: $\widetilde{\mathbf{H}}^q_{s,s*} = H[S] - \mathbf{H}^q_{s,s*}$, where $H[S]$ is the entropy of the key class variable S before any side-channel attack has been performed: $H[S] = \mathbf{E}_s - \log_2 \Pr[s]$. It directly yields the mutual information:

$$I(S; \mathbf{L}_q) = H[S] - H[S|\mathbf{L}_q] = \mathbf{E}_s \ \widetilde{\mathbf{H}}^q_{s,s} \tag{2}$$

Security Metric. We consider a side-channel key recovery adversary of which the aim is to guess a key class s with non negligible probability. For this purpose and for each candidate $s*$, he compares the actual observation of a leaking device $\mathbf{l}_q$ with some key dependent model for these leakages $\mathsf{M}(s*, .)$. The construction of these models (otherwise said templates) will be detailed in the next section. Let $\mathsf{T}(\mathbf{l}_q, \mathsf{M}(s*, .))$ be the statistical test used in the comparison. We assume that the highest value of the statistic corresponds to the most likely key candidate. For each observation $\mathbf{l}_q$, we store the result of the statistical test T in a vector $\mathbf{g}_q = \mathsf{T}(\mathbf{l}_q, \mathsf{M}(s*, .))$ containing the key candidates sorted according to their likelihood: $\mathbf{g}_q := [g_1, g_2, \ldots, g_{|\mathcal{S}|}]$ (*e.g.* in our present context $|\mathcal{S}|=256$). Then, for any side-channel attack exploiting a leakage vector $\mathbf{l}_q$ and giving rise to a result $\mathbf{g}_q$, we define the success function of order o against a key class s as: $\mathsf{S}^o_s(\mathbf{g}_q) = 1$ if $s \in [g_1, \ldots, g_o]$, else $\mathsf{S}^o_s(\mathbf{g}_q) = 0$. It directly leads to the oth-order success rate:

$$\mathbf{Succ}^o_S = \mathbf{E}_s \ \mathbf{E}_{\mathbf{l}_q} \ \mathsf{S}^o_s(\mathbf{g}_q) \tag{3}$$

Intuitively, a success rate of order 1 (*resp.* 2, ...) relates to the probability that the correct key is sorted first (*resp.* among the two first ones, ...) by the adversary. From a theoretical point of view, the information theoretic metric is purposed for the comparison of different implementations. It is therefore convenient to compare different side-channels and is central in the present analysis. A security metric is additionally provided for discussion (but we do not consider all the success rate orders and the guessing entropy defined in [18]).

4   Statistical Tools

In this section, we present the different tools that will be used to extract the side-channel information from the actual observations of our target device. We first describe a classical template attack as it is the strongest form of side-channel attack from an information theoretic point of view. Hence, it provides the best way to evaluate the information theoretic metric of the previous section. Then we discuss how to solve the main practical problem that arises in the application of template attacks, namely the automatic selection of meaningful samples in a leakage trace. For this purpose, we propose to use PCA or LDA.

4.1 Template Attacks

Templates construction. Suppose that an adversary is provided with N_t leakage vectors for a given operation, *e.g.* the transition between two values $x_1 \to x_2$ on the bus of a microchip represented by a key class s. In template attacks, a multivariate Gaussian noise model is generally considered, which means that these vectors $\{1_q^{s,i}\}_{i=1}^{N_t}$ are assumed to be drawn from the multivariate distribution:

$$
\mathcal{N}(1_q^{s,i}|\boldsymbol{\mu}_s, \boldsymbol{\Sigma}_s) = \frac{1}{(2\pi)^{\frac{N}{2}}|\boldsymbol{\Sigma}_s|^{\frac{1}{2}}} \exp\left\{-\frac{1}{2}(1_q^{s,i} - \boldsymbol{\mu}_s)^\top \boldsymbol{\Sigma}_s^{-1}(1_q^{s,i} - \boldsymbol{\mu}_s)\right\},
$$

where the mean $\boldsymbol{\mu}_s$ and the covariance matrix $\boldsymbol{\Sigma}_s$ specify completely the noise distribution associated to each key class s. Constructing the templates consists then in estimating the sets of parameters $\{\boldsymbol{\mu}_s\}_{s=1}^{|\mathcal{S}|}$ and $\{\boldsymbol{\Sigma}_s\}_{s=1}^{|\mathcal{S}|}$. A standard approach is to use the empirical mean and covariance matrix associated to the observations $\{1_q^{s,i}\}_{i=1}^{N_t}$: $\hat{\boldsymbol{\mu}}_s = \frac{1}{N_t}\sum_{i=1}^{N_t} 1_q^{s,i}$, $\hat{\boldsymbol{\Sigma}}_s = \frac{1}{N_t}\sum_{i=1}^{N_t}(1_q^{s,i} - \hat{\boldsymbol{\mu}}_s)(1_q^{s,i} - \hat{\boldsymbol{\mu}}_s)^\top$.

Attack. Assume now that there are $|\mathcal{S}|$ possible secret key classes. In order to determine by which secret signal a new vector 1_{new} was generated, we apply Bayes' rule. This leads to the following classification rule:

$$
\tilde{s} = \underset{s^*}{\operatorname{argmax}} \hat{\Pr}[s^*|1_{\text{new}}] = \underset{s^*}{\operatorname{argmax}} \hat{\Pr}[1_{\text{new}}|s^*]\Pr[s^*], \tag{4}
$$

where $\hat{\Pr}[1_{\text{new}}|s^*] = \mathcal{N}(1_{\text{new}}|\hat{\boldsymbol{\mu}}_{s^*}, \hat{\boldsymbol{\Sigma}}_{s^*})$ and $\Pr[s^*]$ is the prior probability of the class candidate s^*. The classification rule assigns 1_{new} to the candidate s^* with the highest posterior probability. In general, we have $\Pr[s^*] = \frac{1}{|\mathcal{S}|}$.

Limitations. Although template attacks are theoretically the strongest ones, computational issues arise in their application. Mainly, the number of samples N per leakage trace can be very large which prevents the direct computation of a leakage covariance matrix. As a consequence, a number of heuristics are usually deployed in order to reduce the dimensions of the traces before the construction of the templates. In summary, the first template attacks (*e.g.* in [7]) selected the time samples showing the largest difference between the mean traces $\{\hat{\boldsymbol{\mu}}_s\}_{s=1}^{|\mathcal{S}|}$ associated to the classes $[1, 2, \ldots, s]$. The PCA-based attacks [4] that are described below were suggested as a way to improve and automatize this process.

4.2 PCA-Based Template Attacks

Consider the 256 mean (power and EM) traces associated to the 256 possible transitions $x_1 \to x_2$ on the microchip bus that are represented in Figure 1. PCA

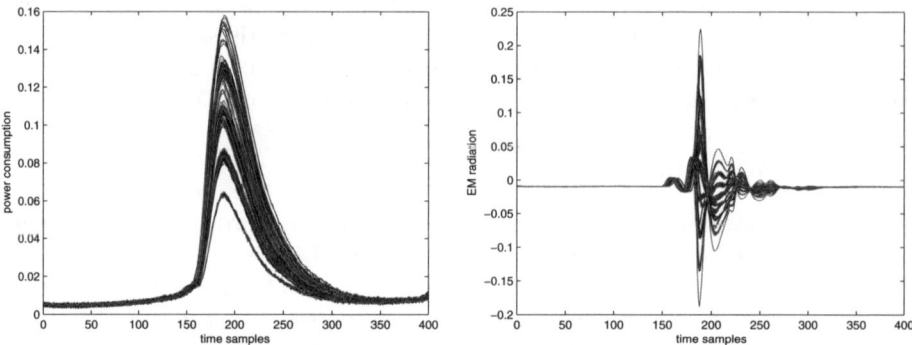

Fig. 1. Average power and EM traces

can be applied in order to find a single linear transform that maximizes the inter-class variance between these different empirical mean traces $\{\hat{\boldsymbol{\mu}}_s\}_{s=1}^{|\mathcal{S}|}$ associated to the classes $[1, 2, \ldots, s]$. PCA looks for the first principal directions $\{\mathbf{w}_m\}_{m=1}^{N_c}$ such that $N \geq N_c$ and which form an orthonormal basis of the N_c-dimensional subspace capturing maximal variance of $\{\hat{\boldsymbol{\mu}}_s\}_{s=1}^{|\mathcal{S}|}$. It can be shown [11] that the principal directions are the eigenvectors $\mathbf{U}$ of the empirical covariance matrix:

$$\bar{\mathbf{S}} = \frac{1}{|\mathcal{S}|} \sum_{s=1}^{|\mathcal{S}|} (\hat{\boldsymbol{\mu}}_s - \bar{\boldsymbol{\mu}})(\hat{\boldsymbol{\mu}}_s - \bar{\boldsymbol{\mu}})^\top, \qquad \bar{\mathbf{S}} = \mathbf{U}\boldsymbol{\Delta}\mathbf{U}^\top.$$

The quantity $\bar{\boldsymbol{\mu}} = \frac{1}{|\mathcal{S}|} \sum_{s=1}^{|\mathcal{S}|} \hat{\boldsymbol{\mu}}_s$ is the average of the mean traces. The principal directions $\{\mathbf{w}_m\}_{m=1}^{N_c}$ are the columns of $\mathbf{U}$ corresponding to the N_c largest eigenvalues of $\boldsymbol{\Delta}$. We denote these eigenvalues by the diagonal matrix $\boldsymbol{\Lambda} \in \mathbb{R}^{N_c \times N_c}$ and the corresponding matrix of principal directions by $\mathbf{W} \in \mathbb{R}^{N \times N_c}$.

In order to built principal subspace templates, we simply estimate the projected means $\{\boldsymbol{\nu}_s\}_{s=1}^{|\mathcal{S}|}$ and the covariance matrices of the projected traces along the (retained) principal directions $\{\boldsymbol{\Lambda}_s\}_{s=1}^{|\mathcal{S}|}$. These parameters are given by:

$$\boldsymbol{\nu}_s = \mathbf{W}^\top \hat{\boldsymbol{\mu}}_s, \qquad \boldsymbol{\Lambda}_s = \mathbf{W}^\top \widehat{\boldsymbol{\Sigma}}_s \mathbf{W}.$$

As in standard template attacks, the noise model is a multivariate Gaussian distribution. However, the number of principal directions N_c is much smaller than N. In practice, a direction can be considered as not being principal if the associated eigenvalue is small compared to the largest one.

Then, in order to classify a new trace $\mathbf{l}_{\text{new}}$, we apply Bayes theorem in the principal subspace of the empirical means which leads to the following rule:

$$\tilde{s} = \underset{s^*}{\operatorname{argmax}} \; \hat{\Pr}[\mathbf{W}^\top \mathbf{l}_{\text{new}} | s^*] \Pr[s^*], \tag{5}$$

with (as in classical template attacks) $\hat{\Pr}(\mathbf{W}^\top \mathbf{l}_{\text{new}} | s^*) = \mathcal{N}(\mathbf{W}^\top \mathbf{l}_{\text{new}} | \boldsymbol{\nu}_{s^*}, \boldsymbol{\Lambda}_{s^*})$.

Properties and Limitations. PSTAs improve simple heuristics selecting time samples according to the variance between the mean traces $\{\hat{\boldsymbol{\mu}}_s\}_{s=1}^{|\mathcal{S}|}$ because they first project the traces in a subspace where these variances are maximized. Additionally, they have the significant advantage of having a "small sample size" variant (see [4] for details), which is particularly useful in contexts where there are much more time samples in the traces than key classes in the attack. However, PSTAs do not consider the intra-classes variance which may theoretically result in poor classification performances. A natural extension (described in the next section) is to exploit LDA [5,10], which allows projecting the traces in a subspace that maximizes the ratio between the inter- and intra-class variance.

4.3 LDA-Based Template Attacks

Instead of seeking the directions maximizing the variance of the mean traces, it is intuitively more appropriate to seek for the directions $\{\tilde{\mathbf{w}}_m\}_{m=1}^{N_c}$ that maximize the ratio between the inter-class scatter $\mathbf{S}_B$ and the total intra-class scatter $\mathbf{S}_W$ after projection. That is, to maximize the objective: $\frac{\tilde{\mathbf{w}}^\top \mathbf{S}_B \tilde{\mathbf{w}}}{\tilde{\mathbf{w}}^\top \mathbf{S}_W \tilde{\mathbf{w}}}$, where:

$$\mathbf{S}_B = \sum_{s=1}^{|\mathcal{S}|} N_t (\hat{\boldsymbol{\mu}}_s - \bar{\boldsymbol{\mu}})(\hat{\boldsymbol{\mu}}_s - \bar{\boldsymbol{\mu}})^\top,$$

$$\mathbf{S}_W = \sum_{s=1}^{|\mathcal{S}|} \sum_{i=1}^{N_t} (\mathbf{l}_q^{s,i} - \hat{\boldsymbol{\mu}}_s)(\mathbf{l}_q^{s,i} - \hat{\boldsymbol{\mu}}_s)^\top.$$

Note that these quantities are equal to covariances up to multiplicative constants that do not play a role in the subsequent derivation. Since $\mathbf{S}_B$ is positive definite and symmetric and since $\tilde{\mathbf{w}}$ is scale invariant, the maximization problem can be replaced by the following eigendecomposition:

$$\mathbf{S}_B^{1/2} \mathbf{S}_W^{-1} \mathbf{S}_B^{1/2} = \tilde{\mathbf{U}} \tilde{\boldsymbol{\Delta}} \tilde{\mathbf{U}}^\top,$$

where $\mathbf{S}_B = \mathbf{U}_B \boldsymbol{\Delta}_B \mathbf{U}_B^\top \rightarrow \mathbf{S}_B^{1/2} = \mathbf{U}_B \boldsymbol{\Delta}_B^{1/2} \mathbf{U}_B^\top$. The projection directions are subsequently given by $\tilde{\mathbf{V}} = \mathbf{S}_B^{-1/2} \tilde{\mathbf{U}}$. We denote the directions corresponding to the N_c largest eigenvalues of $\tilde{\boldsymbol{\Delta}}$ as $\{\tilde{\mathbf{w}}_m\}_{m=1}^{N_c}$ and stack them in a projection matrix $\widetilde{\mathbf{W}} \in \mathbb{R}^{N \times N_c}$. The templates are then constructed as in PSTAs, but in the subspace obtained by LDA. Therefore and as previously, the parameters of the multivariate Gaussian noise model are given by:

$$\tilde{\boldsymbol{\nu}}_s = \widetilde{\mathbf{W}}^\top \hat{\boldsymbol{\mu}}_s, \qquad \widetilde{\boldsymbol{\Lambda}}_s = \widetilde{\mathbf{W}}^\top \hat{\boldsymbol{\Sigma}}_s \widetilde{\mathbf{W}}.$$

Finally, the attack is also performed in the same way as in PSTAs, *i.e.* by applying (5), but using the projection matrix $\widetilde{\mathbf{W}}$ found by LDA, as well as the projected means $\{\tilde{\boldsymbol{\nu}}_s\}_{s=1}^{|\mathcal{S}|}$ and the projected covariances $\{\widetilde{\boldsymbol{\Lambda}}_s\}_{s=1}^{|\mathcal{S}|}$.

Properties and Limitations. While PSTAs can perform well in practice, LDA-based TAs (LDTAs for short) optimize an objective function which is more meaningful. Its limitation arises from the fact that we have to compute the (total) intra-class scatter matrix, which becomes singular when the number of traces N_t is smaller than the number of time samples in the traces N. Hence, for very long traces, one needs to take a lot of measures which may be a practical issue. Also, the resulting matrices have to be computed and stored which may be another issue. In other words, LDA is not suitable in the "small sample size" case in contrast to PCA. But this is not always a problem since side-channel traces can be reasonably short (as in the next section). And when they are not, they can always be divided into several pieces or preliminarily reduced by heuristics or PCA. In summary, LDTAs bring another tradeoff to the side-channel toolbox: they optimize a more meaningful criteria at the cost of more constraints on the size and amount of measurements performed by the adversary.

5   Experimental Results

In this section, we present our experimental results for which we used the following parameters. For each of the 256 possible transitions on the bus, we generated simultaneously 1000 traces (such as those illustrated in Figure 1). Among those traces, N_t=500 were used for the construction of the PCA-based and LDA-based templates. The remaining 500 traces were used for testing the templates and evaluate the information and security metrics of Section 3. From these experiments, we detail both the comparison of the PCA and LDA dimensionality reductions and the comparison/combination of the power and EM side-channels. Note that for the combination of the power and EM leakages, we simply use straightforwardly concatenated traces containing an EM leakage followed by a power one, as initially suggested in [2]. This leads to 800-sample traces that are illustrated in Figure 2. In order to keep $N < N_t$, we simply rejected one every two samples.

5.1   PCA Versus LDA

Selection of the Time Samples. Before detailing the information theoretic and security metrics, an intuitive way to analyze the behavior of the PCA and LDA is to observe how they select the meaningful time samples in the traces. For this purpose, it is convenient to plot the eigenvectors of the transforms, as in Figures 3 and 4 for the power + EM combination.

It yields the following observations:

1. In Figure 3, the eigenvectors corresponding to the first three components of the PCA and LDA are pictured. They clearly show that the EM leakage is dominating in the first component while the power one comes as a backup in the second component. The same figure shows that PCA and LDA select time samples in a similar (and intuitive) way. Namely, they select the points where most of the variability occurs in the curves.
2. In Figure 4, the same eigenvectors are pictured for the last three components of the PCA and LDA. They confirm the expectation that these last

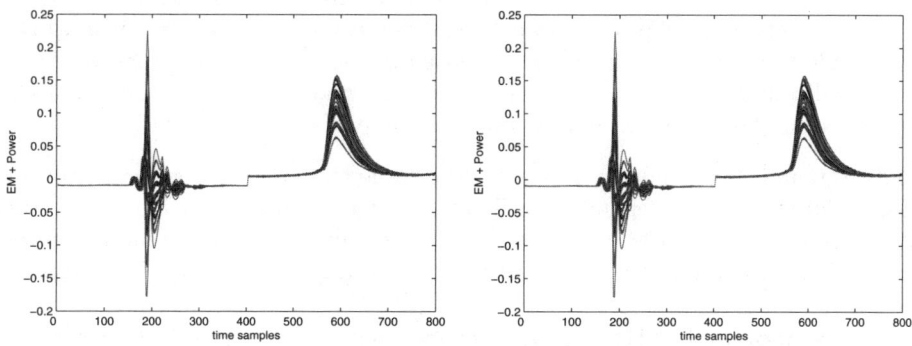

Fig. 2. Average combined power and EM traces

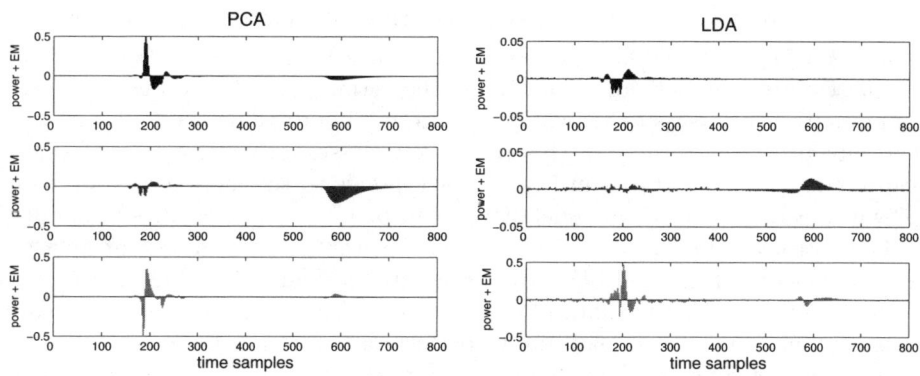

Fig. 3. Eigenvectors for the combined power and EM leakage, first three components

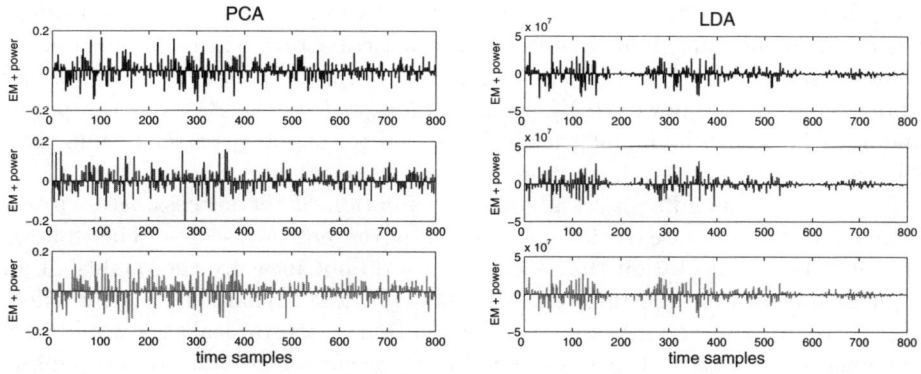

Fig. 4. Eigenvectors for the combined power and EM leakage, last three components

components mainly (only) contain noise and therefore can be discarded. Interestingly, these figures show a clear difference between the PCA and LDA. While the noise is uniformly distributed in the PCA eigenvectors, there is a significant absence of noise in the (intuitive) regions of interest for the LDA. This suggest a possibly better information extraction for LDTAs.

Figures 6 and 7 in appendix represent the same eigenvectors for the power and EM channels taken independently. They highlight similar intuitions. Note that the dominance of the EM channel in the first component of the combined power and EM eigenvectors already suggest that EM leakages are the most informative.

Entropy Scores. Let $\mathbf{H}^1_{s,s^*}$ be the entropy matrix defined in Section 3, Equation (1), where the superscript 1 comes from the fact that we classify the different transitions on the bus based on single traces (or queries). From the estimated probability distributions $\hat{\Pr}[l_1|s]$ that are provided by the PCA- or LDA-based templates and the set of 500 traces to test these templates, one can derive an estimation $\hat{\mathbf{H}}^1_{s,s^*}$ of this matrix. We say that a leakage model is (*i.e.* that our templates are) sound if for each line of the estimated entropy matrix (corresponding to a key class or transition s), the minimum value occurs for $s^* = s$. The entropy score is simply the fraction of key classes for which this condition is respected. As demonstrated in [18], it corresponds to the faction of key classes for which a Bayesian side-channel attack will be be asymptotically successful.

The entropy scores of the power, EM and power + EM template attacks exploiting both the PCA and LDA are represented in Figure 5. A first observation from these pictures is that none of these channels leads to a 100% entropy score. This is natural since we do not aim to perform a real attack but to evaluate the effectiveness of different side-channels. Similarly, *e.g.* in the Hamming weight leakage model, some key classes will remain undistinguishable (*i.e.* those corresponding to the same Hamming weight values). But since in a real attack, each actual key class (that are not transitions as in this paper but real parts of *e.g.* a block cipher key) can be identified thanks to all the transitions possibly generated by different input plaintexts, a practical attack will be successful.

More importantly, these pictures exhibit (as expected) that the best entropy score occurs for the power + EM channel, followed by the EM and the power channels. They also highlight that LDTAs lead to (slightly) better results than PSTAs, in particular for the combination of the power and EM channels.

Figure 8 in appendix shows a similar evaluation of the success rates. Interestingly, they do not reach as high values as the entropy scores. This follows the theoretical expectation that success rates do not measure the quality of an implementation (nor the information leakage of a side-channel) but the effectiveness of an adversary. Again, the combination of several leakages would lead to higher success rates. Under the conditions discussed in [18], the more information leaked (measured with the conditional entropy defined in Section 3), the faster a Bayesian adversary exploiting a sound leakage model will converge towards a 100% success rate. Note that even if the success rates are lower than the entropy scores, they underline that the EM side-channel leads to extremely

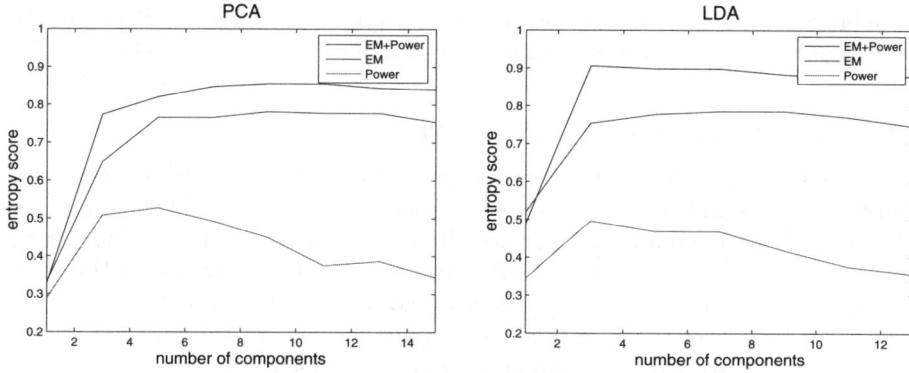

Fig. 5. Entropy scores for the PCA and LDA

powerful attacks. Indeed, even the leakage of a single clock cycle leads to a non negligible success rate in the recovery of the transitions on the bus.

Entropy Values. Since as previously mentioned, less entropy in the traces involves (under certain conditions) a more efficient Bayesian side-channel attack, this section finally provides the conditional entropy values extracted from the leakage traces for both the PCA- and LDA-based templates and different number of components. They are summarized in Table 1.

It yields the following observations:

1. This table confirms all the previous conclusions. Namely, LDA leads to a better information extraction than PCA; the EM channel is significantly more informative than the power one; and the combination of both channels (*i.e.* power + EM) leads to the most powerful type of attack.

2. The lowest conditional entropy values and the maximum entropy scores do not occur for the same number of components (although they are strongly correlated). This highlights that there exist situations where more key classes can be asymptotically recovered, but reaching a 100% success rate will be slower than in a context where less classes can be asymptotically recovered.

3. Compared to previous works on multi-channel or template attacks, this quantified comparison is justified by theoretical statements on the evaluation

Table 1. Conditional entropy of the power, EM and power + EM traces

Number of components	3	5	7
power (PCA)	4.62	4.49	4.57
power (LDA)	**4.41**	4.48	4.62
EM (PCA)	3.92	3.65	3.55
EM (LDA)	3.21	**3.15**	3.24
power + EM (PCA)	3.57	3.36	3.20
power + EM (LDA)	2.92	**2.80**	2.87

metrics. Therefore, it is expected that Table 1 provides the best possible comparison of the information leakages for the different channels.

5.2   Power Versus EM, Power + EM

While comparing LDA and PCA in the previous section, most important quantitative analyzes and conclusions on the respective effectiveness of the power and EM channels have already been drawn. However, one question that has not yet been tackled is: "how far as these real leakages from the idealized (*e.g.* Hamming weight) models that are frequently considered in the side-channel literature?".

In order to answer this question, we can fortunately use the same framework again. Let us start with the power channel for which a usual assumption is to correlate it with the Hamming distances of the transitions on the bus. In our present example, 5 possible Hamming distances can be observed (*i.e.* $h_d \in [0 \ldots 4]$) which leads to the following conditional entropy:

$$\mathrm{H}[S|\mathbf{L}_1] = - \sum_{h_d=0}^{4} \frac{2^4 \cdot \binom{4}{h_d}}{2^8} \cdot \log_2 \left(\frac{1}{2^4 \cdot \binom{4}{h_d}} \right) = 5.9694$$

This indicates that such a model is significantly less informative than a real power consumption channel which would reduce the conditional entropy down to 4.41 in exactly the same context. Looking back at Figure 1, this simply means that traces corresponding to the same Hamming distance $H_W(x_1 \oplus x_2)$ can actually be distinguished by a carefully profiled template adversary. Such traces can be seen as included in one of the packets of curves in the figure.

A very similar analysis can be performed for the EM channel. Let us for example take the signed distance model proposed in [14]. Such a model is purposed to better incorporate the specificities of the EM channel since it allows to distinguish between $x_1 \to x_2$ and $x_2 \to x_1$ transitions. In practice, it means that 9 possible signed distances can be observed by the adversary (*i.e.* $s_d \in [-4, \ldots, 4]$) which leads to the following conditional entropy:

$$\mathrm{H}[S|\mathbf{L}_1] = - \sum_{s_d=-4}^{4} \frac{\binom{8}{s_d+4}}{2^8} \cdot \log_2 \frac{1}{\binom{8}{s_d+4}} = 5.4558$$

While such a model is slightly more informative than the standard Hamming distance model, it is again by far less informative than the real EM channel that would reduce the entropy down to 3.15 in exactly the same context.

6   Conclusions

Following recent developments in physically observable cryptography, this paper provides theoretical and practical insights in the analysis of the power and EM side-channels and their efficient exploitation with powerful statistical tools.

First, we use fair information theoretic and security metrics to evaluate and compare these two side-channels. The resulting analysis demonstrates the significantly higher information leakages of the EM channel when near field measurements of a cryptographic chip are available.

Second, we propose the Linear Discriminant Analysis as an alternative to the Principal Component Analysis for the best selection of the meaningful leakage samples in template attacks. We apply these tools to both the power and EM channels as well as to their comparison in a multi-channel attack context. The results show that Linear Discriminant Analysis is an interesting alternative, bringing a better information extraction at the cost of more constraints in the size and amount of measurements performed by a side-channel adversary. It is therefore a very interesting tool to combine with Principal Component Analysis in any practical application of the template attacks.

Finally, we compare the information leakages of the power and EM channels with some idealized (e.g. Hamming weight) models used to predict these leakages. Our results confirm that not only the distinguishers that usually exploit these models (e.g. the correlation coefficient) are suboptimal, but also that the models themselves are far less informative than the actual power and EM observations. This highlights the importance of template attacks when the provable (or arguable) security of cryptographic implementations is discussed and the relevance of strong models such as the noisy identity leakages introduced in [15] in this context. In summary, if you are an adversary trying to recover the key of a cryptographic device, Hamming weight (or similar) models can be useful. But if you are a designer trying to convince that your cryptographic implementation is secure against side-channel attacks, they are definitely not sufficient.

We note that these results only considered the application of PCA and LDA to the original template attacks of [7]. However, these techniques could be similarly applied to the stochastic models of [9,17]. The direct use of templates in our experiments was reasonable since we were not limited in the number of samples to build the templates (due to our evaluation goal). But stochastic models could be very efficient in more constrained contexts. Combining data dimensionality reduction techniques with stochastic models is a scope for further research.

References

1. Agrawal, D., Archambeault, B., Rao, J., Rohatgi, P.: The EM Side-Channel(s). In: Kaliski Jr., B.S., Koç, Ç.K., Paar, C. (eds.) CHES 2002. LNCS, vol. 2523, pp. 29–45. Springer, Heidelberg (2003)
2. Agrawal, D., Rao, J.R., Rohatgi, P.: Multi-Channel Attacks. In: Walter, C.D., Koç, Ç.K., Paar, C. (eds.) CHES 2003. LNCS, vol. 2779, pp. 2–16. Springer, Heidelberg (2003)
3. Anderson, R., Kuhn, M.: Tamper Resistance - a Cautionary Note. In: The Proceedings of USENIX Electronic Commerce, Oakland, CA, USA, pp. 1–11 (November 1996)
4. Archambeau, C., Peeters, E., Standaert, F.-X., Quisquater, J.-J.: Template Attacks in Principal Subspaces. In: Goubin, L., Matsui, M. (eds.) CHES 2006. LNCS, vol. 4249, pp. 1–14. Springer, Heidelberg (2006)

5. Bishop, C.M.: Pattern Recognition and Machine Learning. Springer, Heidelberg (2006)
6. Brier, E., Clavier, C., Olivier, F.: Correlation Power Analysis with a Leakage Model. In: Joye, M., Quisquater, J.-J. (eds.) CHES 2004. LNCS, vol. 3156, pp. 16–29. Springer, Heidelberg (2004)
7. Chari, S., Rao, J.R., Rohatgi, P.: Template Attacks. In: Kaliski Jr., B.S., Koç, Ç.K., Paar, C. (eds.) CHES 2002. LNCS, vol. 2523, pp. 13–28. Springer, Heidelberg (2003)
8. Gandolfi, K., Mourtel, C., Olivier, F.: Electromagnetic Analysis: Concrete Results. In: Koç, Ç.K., Naccache, D., Paar, C. (eds.) CHES 2001. LNCS, vol. 2162, pp. 251–261. Springer, Heidelberg (2001)
9. Gierlichs, B., Lemke, K., Paar, C.: Templates vs. Stochastic Methods. In: Goubin, L., Matsui, M. (eds.) CHES 2006. LNCS, vol. 4249, pp. 15–29. Springer, Heidelberg (2006)
10. Hastie, T., Tibshirani, R., Friedman, J.: The Elements of Statistical Learning: Data Mining, Inference and Prediction. Springer, Heidelberg (2001)
11. Jolliffe, I.T.: Principal Component Analysis. Springer, New York (1986)
12. Kocher, P., Jaffe, J., Jun, B.: Differential Power Analysis. In: Wiener, M.J. (ed.) CRYPTO 1999. LNCS, vol. 1666, pp. 398–412. Springer, Heidelberg (1999)
13. Messerges, T.S., Dabbish, E.A., Sloan, R.H.: Examining Smart-Card Security under the Threat of Power Analysis Attacks. IEEE Transactions on Computers 51(5), 541–552 (2002)
14. Peeters, E., Standaert, F.-X., Quisquater, J.-J.: Power and Electromagnetic Analysis: Improved Models, Consequences and Comparisons. VLSI Journal 40, 52–60 (2007)
15. Petit, C., Standaert, F.-X., Pereira, O., Malkin, T.G., Yung, M.: A Block Cipher based PRNG Secure Against Side-Channel Key Recovery. In: The Proceedings of ASIACCS 2008 (to appear, 2008), http://eprint.iacr.org/2007/356
16. Quisquater, J.-J., Samyde, D.: ElectroMagnetic Analysis (EMA): Measures and Counter-Measures for Smart Cards. In: Attali, S., Jensen, T. (eds.) E-smart 2001. LNCS, vol. 2140, pp. 200–210. Springer, Heidelberg (2001)
17. Schindler, W., Lemke, K., Paar, C.: A Stochastic Model for Differential Side-Channel Cryptanalysis. In: Rao, J.R., Sunar, B. (eds.) CHES 2005. LNCS, vol. 3659, pp. 30–46. Springer, Heidelberg (2005)
18. Standaert, F.-X., Malkin, T.G., Yung, M.: A Unified Framework for the Analysis of Side-Channel Key Recovery Attacks, Cryptology ePrint Archive, Report 2006/139 (2006)

Appendix

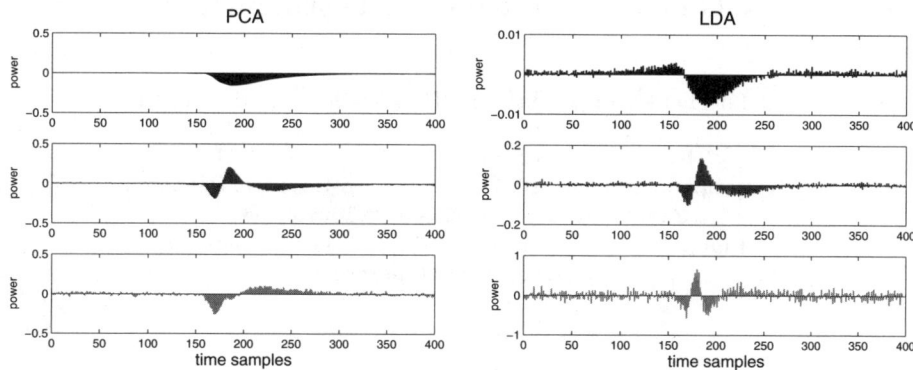

Fig. 6. Eigenvectors for the power leakage, first three components

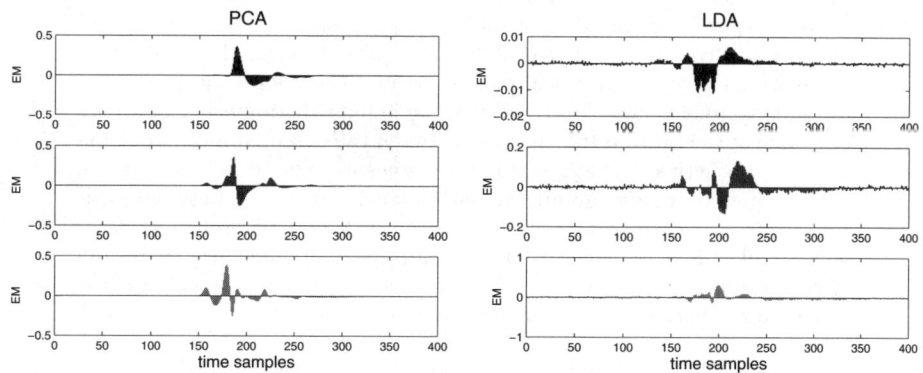

Fig. 7. Eigenvectors for the EM leakage, first three components

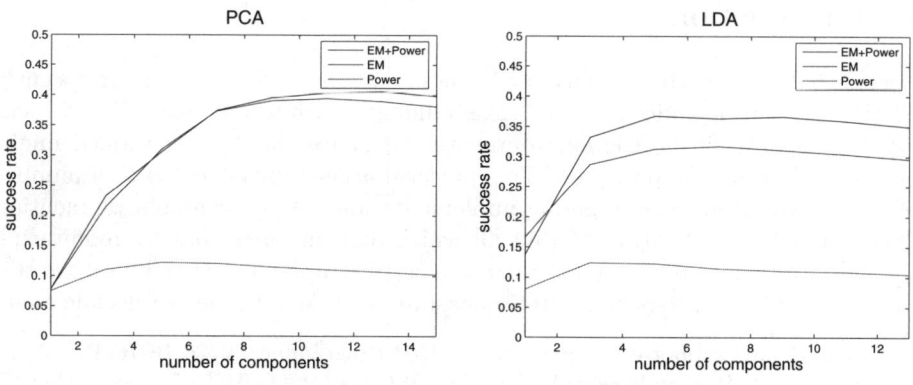

Fig. 8. Success rates for the PCA and LDA

Mutual Information Analysis*
A Generic Side-Channel Distinguisher

Benedikt Gierlichs[1], Lejla Batina[1], Pim Tuyls[1,2], and Bart Preneel[1]

[1] K.U. Leuven, ESAT/SCD-COSIC and IBBT
Kasteelpark Arenberg 10, B-3001 Leuven-Heverlee, Belgium
firstname.lastname@esat.kuleuven.be
[2] Philips Research Europe, Eindhoven, The Netherlands
pim.tuyls@philips.com

Abstract. We propose a generic information-theoretic distinguisher for differential side-channel analysis. Our model of side-channel leakage is a refinement of the one given by Standaert *et al.* An embedded device containing a secret key is modeled as a black box with a leakage function whose output is captured by an adversary through the noisy measurement of a physical observable. Although quite general, the model and the distinguisher are practical and allow us to develop a new differential side-channel attack. More precisely, we build a distinguisher that uses the value of the Mutual Information between the observed measurements and a hypothetical leakage to rank key guesses. The attack is effective without any knowledge about the particular dependencies between measurements and leakage as well as between leakage and processed data, which makes it a universal tool. Our approach is confirmed by results of power analysis experiments. We demonstrate that the model and the attack work effectively in an attack scenario against DPA-resistant logic.

Keywords: Differential Side-Channel Analysis (DSCA), Information Theory, Mutual Information, DPA-resistant logic.

1 Introduction

Pervasive devices such as smart cards, mobile phones, PDAs and more recently RFIDs and sensor nodes are now closely integrated into our lives. The devices typically operate in hostile environments and hence the data contained might be relatively easy compromised. This physical accessibility has led to a number of very powerful attacks targeting implementations. As an example we mention Differential Power Analysis (DPA) [9] which demonstrates that by monitoring the power dissipation of a smart card, the cryptographic keys can be rather efficiently extracted if no special countermeasures are taken. In the last decade many

* This work was supported in part by the IAP Programme P6/26 BCRYPT of the Belgian State (Belgian Science Policy), by FWO projects G.0475.05, and G.0300.07, by the European Comission through the IST Programme under Contract IST-2002-507932 ECRYPT NoE, and by the K.U. Leuven-BOF.

E. Oswald and P. Rohatgi (Eds.): CHES 2008, LNCS 5154, pp. 426–442, 2008.

other side-channels have been described such as electromagnetic emanation [15], timing [8], acoustics [16] *etc.* Both theory and practice have been developed and as a consequence several more advanced power analysis attacks such as correlation [2], template [3], and higher-order attacks [11] have been proposed as well as a broad range of countermeasures [4,6,7,10]. For all side-channels we use the terminology Differential Side-Channel Analysis (DSCA) when we refer to differential attacks.

DSCA attacks as introduced by Kocher *et al.* [9] use a boolean partitioning function to sort a set of power curves into two subsets. The function is usually defined on an intermediate value which can be predicted on the basis of a key hypothesis and known data. The difference between the averages of the power consumption curves of the two subsets shows a clear peak for the correct key guess. In this context, we refer to a statistical test, *e.g.* difference of means [9], Pearson correlation coefficient [2], Bayesian classification [3], as a side-channel distinguisher.

Micali and Reyzin propose theoretical models for side-channel security in [14]. In the model, the assumptions are very strong and in particular the adversary is the strongest possible, which makes their model hard to work with in practice. This was the motivation for the work of Standaert *et al.* [17]. They also use theoretical concepts such as Mutual Information to investigate side-channel leakage and attacks. In their work, the Mutual Information only measures the average amount of information present in measurements.

We introduce a Mutual Information-based distinguisher that constitutes the core of a new and generic differential side-channel attack: Mutual Information Analysis (MIA). In contrast to [17], we apply information theory to develop a powerful attack without any device characterization. The distinguisher uses only generic assumptions and is therefore more effective. Yet, the lack of assumptions may sometimes result in less efficient attacks. Further on, our model and the attack are successfully tested in practice. In general, while previous side-channel attacks tried to keep reducing the number of measurements needed by ever more sophisticated power consumption models, we take the opposite direction: we attempt to produce attacks that are still effective in more realistic attack scenarios, at the cost of a limited increase in the number of measurements.

This paper is organized as follows. Section 2 recalls the basic notions of information theory and introduces our information-theoretic model for side-channel leakage and analysis. In Sect. 3 we outline the construction of a distinguisher and we give a theoretical reasoning for our approach. Sect. 4 discusses practical aspects of MIA. In Sect. 5 we compare MIA with other known distinguishers. Sect. 6 gives empirical evidence for the correctness of our model and for the effectiveness of the proposed attack. We conclude our work in Sect. 7.

2 Preliminaries

2.1 Information Theory

We introduce some notions of information theory. For more details we refer to [5] and to the Appendix.

Let $\mathbf{X}$ and $\mathbf{Y}$ be random variables on the (discrete) spaces $\mathcal{X}$ and $\mathcal{Y}$ with probability distributions $\mathbb{P}_{\mathbf{X}}$ and $\mathbb{P}_{\mathbf{Y}}$ respectively. The reduction in uncertainty on $\mathbf{X}$ that is obtained by having observed $\mathbf{Y}$, is exactly equal to the information that one has obtained on $\mathbf{X}$ by having observed $\mathbf{Y}$. Hence the formula for the Mutual Information $\mathbf{I}(\mathbf{X}; \mathbf{Y})$ is given by

$$\mathbf{I}(\mathbf{X}; \mathbf{Y}) = \mathsf{H}(\mathbf{X}) - \mathsf{H}(\mathbf{X}|\mathbf{Y}) = \mathsf{H}(\mathbf{X}) + \mathsf{H}(\mathbf{Y}) - \mathsf{H}(\mathbf{X}, \mathbf{Y}) = \mathbf{I}(\mathbf{Y}; \mathbf{X}). \qquad (1)$$

The Mutual Information satisfies $0 \leq \mathbf{I}(\mathbf{X}; \mathbf{Y}) \leq \mathsf{H}(\mathbf{X})$. The lower bound is reached if and only if $\mathbf{X}$ and $\mathbf{Y}$ are independent. The upper bound is achieved when $\mathbf{Y}$ fully determines $\mathbf{X}$. Hence, the larger the Mutual Information, the more close the relation between $\mathbf{X}$ and $\mathbf{Y}$ is to a one-to-one relation.

2.2   Side-Channel Model

In this section we introduce our information-theoretic model for side-channel leakage of cryptographic devices, which is a refinement of the model proposed by Standaert et al. in [17].

We consider a device (e.g. an IC) that carries out a cryptographic operation E_k, depending on a secret key k from a key space $\mathcal{K} = \{0,1\}^m$. The unknown key is modeled as a random variable $\mathbf{K}$ on $\mathcal{K}$. In order to analyze the impact of an adversary who can (up to a certain extent) observe the device's internal state, the device's side-channel leakage is modeled by a side-channel leakage function L. We assume that the values $\mathbf{L}$ of the leakage function depend on state transitions $\mathbf{W}$ (e.g. bit flips) in the device. The physical observable $\mathbf{O}$ represents (possibly noisy) measurements of $\mathbf{L}$.

Summarizing, we have the following model which consists of a cascade of two channels (see also Fig. 1): $\mathbf{W} \to \mathbf{L} \to \mathbf{O}$.

1. $\mathbf{W} \to \mathbf{L}$: The leakage channel through which information on the words $\mathbf{W}$ is leaked in $\mathbf{L}$.
2. $\mathbf{L} \to \mathbf{O}$: The (possibly noisy) observation channel through which $\mathbf{O}$ provides information on $\mathbf{L}$. An adversary has access to the output of this channel.

In the following we make these ideas more precise. We assume that the values of L are determined by state transitions (e.g. bit flips) in the device. These state transitions are provoked by a pair of words $(v_1, v_2) \in \{0,1\}^n \times \{0,1\}^n = \mathcal{W}$, where n is the device's word length, (e.g. previous and next state) being processed by the device. When a cryptographic operation E_k is executed, the pair (v_1, v_2) of words usually depends on the secret key k and is randomly distributed from an adversary's point of view. Therefore we model the occurring pairs as the random variable $\mathbf{W}$ on $\mathcal{W}$. The values of the leakage function L contain information on $\mathbf{W}$ and hence, while E_k is executed, information on the secret key k used in the device. Therefore we model the images of $\mathbf{W}$ under L as a random variable $\mathbf{L}$ on a discrete space $\mathcal{L}$

$$\mathsf{L} : \mathcal{W} \to \mathcal{L}; \quad \mathbf{W} \mapsto \mathbf{L} = \mathsf{L}(\mathbf{W}). \qquad (2)$$

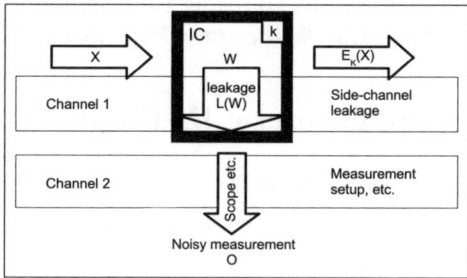

Fig. 1. Schematic illustration of the cascaded channels

Later, we will make the dependency of $\mathbf{L}$ on the key k explicit and denote it by $\mathbf{L}_k$. It is furthermore assumed that $\mathcal{L}$ is at most of size 2^{2n}, *i.e.* the leakage function L is surjective. For example, the Hamming weight model implies $\mathcal{L} = \{0, 1, \ldots, 7, 8\}$. The random variable $\mathbf{L}$ is observed by measuring a physical observable (voltage, radiation, *etc.*). The physical observable is modeled as the random variable $\mathbf{O}$ on a space $\mathcal{O}$.

Before an attack, the adversary obtains $q > 0$ measurement traces $o_{x_i}(t)$, $i = 1 \ldots, q$, by measuring $\mathbf{O}(t)$ while the device processes known data x_i with the cryptographic operation E_k over time t. During the attack, the adversary uses the information on $\mathbf{L}$ contained in $\mathbf{O}$ and aims at reconstructing the word sequence $\mathbf{W}$, which would allow to discriminate the secret key k.

The real side-channel leakage function of the device might not be known to the adversary. We thus denote her guess, *i.e.* the hypothetical leakage function, by $\hat{\mathsf{L}}$. For the sake of explanation, we assume $\hat{\mathsf{L}} = \mathsf{L}$ for the moment and address this issue later in Sect. 4.1. The adversary makes a guess $\hat{k} \in \mathcal{K}$ on the key k stored in the device. This implies a guess $\mathbf{W}_{\hat{k}}$ on the occurred pairs of words $\mathbf{W}$. The guess $\mathbf{W}_{\hat{k}}$ in turn implies a guess $\hat{\mathbf{L}}_{\hat{k}} = \hat{\mathsf{L}}(\mathbf{W}_{\hat{k}})$ on the output values $\mathbf{L}_k$ of the real leakage function. In the last step the adversary checks whether her guess $\hat{\mathbf{L}}_{\hat{k}}$ is compatible with the observed measurement values $\mathbf{O}$.

In order to explain the attack, we first restrict ourselves to the interesting point(s) in time $t = \tau_j$ when the pair of words $\mathbf{W}$ being processed depends on the result of a function $f_k : \{0,1\}^m \to \{0,1\}^n, \mathbf{X} \mapsto f_k(\mathbf{X})$ applied to a known input $\mathbf{X}$. We assume that the cryptographic primitive E_k and its implementation are known to the adversary, that $f_k(\cdot)$ is a suitable intermediate result of $E_k(\cdot)$, and that the inputs $\mathbf{X}$ are chosen uniformly at random from $\{0,1\}^m$. Further, we assume that the key space is $\{0,1\}^m$.

2.3   Side-Channel Attack

We denote by $\mathcal{M} = \{o_{x_1}, \ldots, o_{x_q}\}$ the multiset of q measurements of the physical observable $\mathbf{O}$ obtained when the known inputs $x_1, \ldots, x_q$ were processed by the device. Our side-channel adversary uses a distinguisher $\mathcal{D}$, which takes as input the measurements $o_{x_1}, \ldots, o_{x_q}$ and the inputs $x_1, \ldots, x_q$, and outputs the key guess k^*. The adversary's advantage of using this distinguisher is defined as the probability that the distinguisher's key guess k^* is indeed the correct key k.

3   The Information-Theoretic Distinguisher

In this section we derive our distinguisher and analyze it formally in our attack scenario.

3.1   Construction

Let $L_0, \ldots, L_l$ be subsets of the space $\mathcal{L}$. The set $\{L_0, \ldots, L_l\}$ is a partition of $\mathcal{L}$ and the elements $L_i, i = 0, \ldots, l$ are called atoms.

To each possible key guess $\hat{k} \in \mathcal{K}$, which implies a guess $\mathbf{W}_{\hat{k}}$ on the pairs of words, we associate a partition $\{L_0^{\hat{k}}, \ldots, L_l^{\hat{k}}\}$ of $\mathcal{L}$ which is defined by $L_i^{\hat{k}} = \{x \in \{0,1\}^m \mid \hat{L}(\mathbf{W}_{\hat{k}}) = i \wedge \mathbf{W}_{\hat{k}} = (v_1, f_{\hat{k}}(x))\}$ for $i = 0, \ldots, l$. That is, we associate all inputs values $\mathbf{X} = x$ that leak $\hat{\mathbf{L}}_{\hat{k}} = i$ under the key guess $\hat{k}$ to $L_i^{\hat{k}}$. Each partition $\{L_0^{\hat{k}}, \ldots, L_l^{\hat{k}}\}$ of $\mathcal{L}$ induces a subdivision[1] of the measurement space $\mathcal{O}$, since each measurement is associated with an input x.

Let $\mathbb{P}_{\hat{\mathbf{L}}_{\hat{k}}}$ and $\mathbb{P}_{\mathbf{O}}$ denote the probability distributions of the random variables $\hat{\mathbf{L}}_{\hat{k}}$ and $\mathbf{O}$ respectively.

Given the multiset of measurements $\mathcal{M} = \{o_{x_1}, \ldots, o_{x_q}\}$ and a partition of $\mathcal{L}$, we define the following set of conditional distributions $\{\mathbb{P}_{\mathbf{O}|L_i^{\hat{k}}}\}_{i=0}^l$. The distributions $\mathbb{P}_{\mathbf{O}|L_i^{\hat{k}}}$ describe the random variable $\mathbf{O}$ given the atoms $L_i^{\hat{k}}$ for a hypothetical key $\hat{k}$. They represent a (possibly noisy) observation channel $\hat{\mathbf{L}}_{\hat{k}} \to \mathbf{O}$ which depends on the hypothetical key $\hat{k}$ and the actual key k. The attacker will look for the distribution that is most likely compatible with the measurement results.

We compute an estimation of the Mutual Information $\mathbf{I}(\hat{\mathbf{L}}_{\hat{k}}; \mathbf{O})$ under the key guess $\hat{k}$ while the actual key is k as

$$\tilde{\mathbf{I}}(\hat{\mathbf{L}}_{\hat{k}}; \mathbf{O}) = \tilde{\mathsf{H}}(\mathbf{O}) - \tilde{\mathsf{H}}(\mathbf{O}|\hat{\mathbf{L}}_{\hat{k}}), \tag{3}$$

where $\tilde{\mathsf{H}}(\cdot)$ denotes an estimated entropy.

The distributions $\mathbb{P}_{\mathbf{O}|L_i^{\hat{k}}}$ are determined empirically by generating the histograms of the measurements $o_{x_1}, \ldots, o_{x_q}$ associated to the atoms of the partition $\{L_0^{\hat{k}}, \ldots, L_l^{\hat{k}}\}$. They are estimated by

$$\tilde{\mathbb{P}}_{\mathbf{O}|L_i^{\hat{k}}} = \frac{|\{o_{x_j} = o \mid x_j \in L_i^{\hat{k}}\}|}{|L_i^{\hat{k}}|}$$

---

[1] In contrast to a partition, the atoms of a subdivision do not necessarily have an empty intersection.

where $|\{\cdot\}|$ denotes the cardinality of a set. The distribution $\mathbb{P_O}$ is determined empirically as $\tilde{\mathbb{P}}_{\mathbf{O}} = |\{o_{x_j} = o\}|/q$.

We define our distinguisher $\mathcal{D} : \mathcal{O}^q \times \{0,1\}^m \to \mathcal{K}$ as follows: given a multiset $\mathcal{M} = \{o_{x_1}, \ldots, o_{x_q}\}$ of observations and the corresponding plaintexts $x_1, \ldots, x_q$, it outputs the key guess k^* that maximizes the mutual information between the observations and the hypothetical leakage values,

$$\mathcal{D}(o_{x_1}, \ldots, o_{x_q}; x_1, \ldots, x_q) \to k^* \quad \text{iff} \quad \tilde{\mathbf{I}}(\hat{\mathbf{L}}_{k^*}; \mathbf{O}) = \max_{\hat{k}} \tilde{\mathbf{I}}(\hat{\mathbf{L}}_{\hat{k}}; \mathbf{O}). \quad (4)$$

We extend the distinguisher $\mathcal{D}$ defined above to retrieve also the interesting point(s) in time $t = \tau_j$ when the intermediate result $f_k(\cdot)$ is computed. It takes as input the multiset of observed traces $\mathcal{M} = \{o_{x_1}(t), \ldots, o_{x_q}(t)\}$ and the inputs $x_1, \ldots, x_q$. The extended distinguisher is defined by,

$$\mathcal{D}(o_{x_1}(t), \ldots, o_{x_q}(t); x_1, \ldots, x_q) \to (k^*, \tau_j) \quad \text{iff}$$
$$\tilde{\mathbf{I}}(\hat{\mathbf{L}}_{k^*}; \mathbf{O}(\tau_j)) = \max_{(\hat{k}, t)} \tilde{\mathbf{I}}(\hat{\mathbf{L}}_{\hat{k}}; \mathbf{O}(t)). \quad (5)$$

Note that there may exist additional points in time where $\mathbf{O}(t)$ (partially) depends on $\mathbf{L}_k$ but where $\tilde{\mathbf{I}}(\hat{\mathbf{L}}_k; \mathbf{O}(t))$ is not maximal. To cover this case we denote τ_j as all instants when $\mathbf{O}(t)$ (partially) depends on $\mathbf{L}_k$.

3.2 Theoretical Reasoning

We consider the Mutual Information between the output of a guessed leakage function $\hat{\mathbf{L}}_{\hat{k}}$ and an observable $\mathbf{O}(t)$, *i.e.* the reduction in the uncertainty on $\hat{\mathbf{L}}_{\hat{k}}$ due to the knowledge of $\mathbf{O}(t)$ for a key hypothesis $\hat{k}$. There exist four interesting combinations of time instants and key candidates to study.

1) incorrect key hypotheses $\hat{k} \neq k$ and wrong time instants $t \neq \tau_j$
In this case $\mathbf{I}(\hat{\mathbf{L}}_{\hat{k}}; \mathbf{O}(t)) = 0$ because the two variables are independent (see Appendix). However, the equality holds only theoretically. In practice we compute $\tilde{\mathbf{I}}(\hat{\mathbf{L}}_{\hat{k}}; \mathbf{O}(t))$ close to 0 as we are working with estimates of entropy.
2) correct key guess $\hat{k} = k$ and wrong time instants $t \neq \tau_j$
In this case $\mathbf{I}(\hat{\mathbf{L}}_{\hat{k}}; \mathbf{O}(t)) = 0$ because the two variables are independent. Recall that $t \neq \tau_j$ implies independence by definition. Again, in practice we obtain values only close to 0.
3) correct key guess $\hat{k} = k$ and correct instant(s) $t = \tau_j$
In this case $\mathbf{I}(\hat{\mathbf{L}}_{\hat{k}}; \mathbf{O}(\tau_j)) = \mathsf{H}(\mathbf{O}(\tau_j)) - \mathsf{H}(\mathbf{O}(\tau_j)|\hat{\mathbf{L}}_{\hat{k}}) > 0$ because the variables are dependent by definition. The value of $\mathsf{H}(\mathbf{O}(\tau_j)|\hat{\mathbf{L}}_{\hat{k}})$ is minimized. So, at the right point(s) in time $t = \tau_j$, the correct key guess $\hat{k} = k$ leads to the highest Mutual Information. In practice, high values of Mutual Information can appear for several points in time if the targeted intermediate result is computed, stored, and reused later. Both facts are empirically confirmed in Sect. 6.
4) incorrect key guess $\hat{k} \neq k$ and correct time instants $t = \tau_j$
In this case $\mathbf{I}(\hat{\mathbf{L}}_{\hat{k}}; \mathbf{O}(t)) = 0$ if and only if an incorrect key guess leads to random

hypothetical leakage values. In practice we might observe Mutual Information values greater than zero. These "ghost peaks" occur if a wrong key guess does not lead to hypothetical leakage values that are independent of the real leakage values. This phenomenon is also observed for other distinguishers and studied in detail in [2].

4   Practical Aspects of Mutual Information Analysis

In this section we address aspects of Mutual Information Analysis that are of importance for its practical application.

The Mutual Information distinguisher, as most statistical tests, is bounded in its efficiency to recover keys by the hypothetical leakage function $\hat{L}$. The closer the partition induced by $\hat{L}_{\hat{k}}$ is to the *a priori unknown* physical data-dependency inherent in $O(t)$, the more efficient and effective the statistical test will be.

Hence, a side-channel analyst faces several problems which we will summarize using our model's notation. The flow of information from k to $O(t)$ has to be examined via the transition caused by W. It involves the hypothetical leakage function $\hat{L}$ and the electrical properties of the observation channel. The choice of $f_{\hat{k}}(\cdot)$ is usually an easy task and can be performed device independently. Any intermediate result that combines a small part of the (constant) unknown key and a known varying value may be chosen (here "small" means that exhausting all $\hat{k}$ should be feasible). On the other hand, the choice of $\hat{L}$ as well as the abstraction of the observation channel pose a non-trivial task. Typically, the latter is modeled as a (linear) one-to-one relation (one-to-many if noise is considered) such that the model's complexity is concentrated in $\hat{L}$. Based on the choice of $\hat{L}$ and a key guess $\hat{k}$ an adversary predicts the device's power dissipation and uses a statistical test to quantify the fitness of her simulation. However, obviously this approach requires an engineer's insight into the device's leakage behavior if the goal is to obtain significant results. As long as the target device has been built in standard CMOS technology, this behavior can be *approximated* by the Hamming weight [13] or Hamming distance [2] model. Then, the complexity is shifted to the architecture level as one has to define the exact transition (v_1, v_2) that leaks, which usually involves previously computed values, counters, conditional branches, or memory addresses (*cf.* [2]).

The approach for our attack follows the opposite idea. Instead of crafting an attack for a specific device and implementation, we propose to shift the complexity from the modeling step into the distinguisher. Rather than trying to model the leakage function and the system's electrical properties as good as possible and measuring the (linear) correlation between the simulated and the observed power dissipation, we propose the following. Assume a one-to-many relation between the leaked and observed values, *i.e.* do not average measurements unless the Gaussian assumption is justified. Assume a suitable leakage function $\hat{L}$. Compute an estimation of the Mutual Information $\tilde{I}(L_{\hat{k}}, O(t))$ between the hypothetical leakage and the observations and use it as a distinguisher to discriminate keys.

4.1   Hypothetical Side-Channel Leakage

Up to now we assumed that $\hat{L} = L$ which reflects a powerful adversary that knows the exact side-channel leakage function of the device under attack. Although this assumption might be justified in some cases, *e.g.* it might be known that the target device leaks the Hamming distance of v_1 and v_2, we relax the assumption and hence also cover cases where the real leakage function is unknown.

There exist two important restrictions for the adversary'y choice of $\hat{L}$. By assumption, L is a surjective mapping $\mathcal{L} : \mathcal{W} \to \mathcal{L}$; $\mathbf{W} \mapsto \mathbf{L} = L(\mathbf{W})$. The best the adversary can do in order not to deliberately loose information and to ensure that the distinguisher $\mathcal{D}$ works as expected is to ensure that $\hat{L}$ does not produce collisions where L does not. Since L is unknown, the only way to guarantee this property is to choose $\hat{L}$ as a bijective mapping of $\mathbf{W}$. Such a setting suggests that $\hat{L}$ might produce less collisions than L, which makes our distinguisher less efficient but does not tackle its effectiveness.

The second restriction arises due to the generic character of the distinguisher. $\hat{L}$ must be chosen such that different key hypotheses $\hat{k}$ do not yield a permutation of $\hat{\mathbf{L}}_{\hat{k}}$. If this would happen, $\tilde{\mathbf{I}}(\hat{\mathbf{L}}_{\hat{k}}; \mathbf{O})$ would be constant and more important, independent of the guess $\hat{k}$. The distinguisher would not be able to discriminate key candidates.

In the following example, the choice of $\hat{L}$ does *not* allow to discriminate key candidates using our distinguisher: suppose that E_k is AES encryption and that the targeted transition $\mathbf{W}$ is $(v_1, f_{\hat{k}}(\cdot))$ for a constant reference state $v_1 \in \{0, 1\}^n$ and for $f_{\hat{k}}(\cdot)$ being a Sbox lookup during the first round. The AES Sbox is a bijective map. Therefore, different key candidates $\hat{k}$ lead to permutations of the guess $\mathbf{W}_{\hat{k}}$. Choosing $\hat{L}$ as a bijective map of $\mathbf{W}_{\hat{k}}$ implies that the partition $\{L_i^{\hat{k}}\}_{i=0}^l$ is merely permuted, which has no effect on the entropy $\tilde{\mathsf{H}}(\mathbf{O}|\hat{\mathbf{L}}_{\hat{k}})$ and thus no effect on $\tilde{\mathbf{I}}(\hat{\mathbf{L}}_{\hat{k}}; \mathbf{O})$. A simple workaround for this problem is to choose $\hat{L}$ as a bijective map of a subspace of $\mathcal{W}$, *e.g.* one could choose $\hat{\mathbf{L}}_{\hat{k}} :=$ the seven least significant bits of $\mathbf{W}_{\hat{k}}$. In the same context, the DES Sboxes do not lead to a problem since they are not bijective.

Another interesting property of bijective hypothetical leakage functions is, that the sometimes unknown reference state v_1 is transparent to them and can simply be ignored, as long as it is constant.

4.2   Estimation of Probability Densities

In practice, an adversary does not know the probability distributions $\mathbb{P}_{\mathbf{O}|\hat{\mathbf{L}}_{\hat{k}}}$ and $\mathbb{P}_{\mathbf{O}}$ and has to estimate them. Since all successive computations are based on these estimations, the estimation of probability densities is a key issue.

The estimation technique we use relies on histograms. In our experience, it is a simple and efficient technique to address the issue. A histogram estimates the probability distribution of data in a given sample set by counting how many samples fall into a certain bin.

The arising questions are: "How many bins should be used?" and "Should all bins be equally wide?". As far as we know, there exists no strategy that leads to the best estimation in all scenarios. By applying this technique in numerous side-channel attack scenarios we extracted the following basic guidelines.

1) The first design principle of Mutual Information Analysis is the exploitation of information. We thus aim at estimating the probability distributions as good as possible. This means to use as many bins as there are distinct values in the domain covered by the sample set. This approach may require a limited increase of measurements, but it ensures that no information is lost.

2) Generating histograms is different depending on whether the observations of the random variable are deterministic or probabilistic (noisy). In the deterministic case, we can at least be sure about the value of an observed datum while this does not hold in the probabilistic case.

3) We usually work with bins of equal width. In general, less bins imply less information and vice versa. If we work with noisy observations, choosing less bins may have the effect of noise reduction. In practice this means that several distinct samples can fall into the same bin, which reflects the assumption that they stem from the same datum.

5   Contrasting MIA and Other Distinguishers

In the seminal paper on Differential Power Analysis [9], Kocher *et al.* suggest to use a single-bit partitioning function. In our notation this is the hypothetical leakage function. An advantage of a single-bit approach is that it does not require an assumption on the real leakage function. One merely assumes that different bit values leak differently. A disadvantage is the loss of information due to ignoring all other bits.

The extension to consider several bits at once was first proposed by Messerges *et al.* in [12]. More precisely, the authors proposed to use a partitioning function based on more than one bit and to analyze those atoms that are maximal different (*e.g.* all zeros vs. all ones). However, this approach requires an assumption on the real leakage function to identify those two atoms. Further, it does not allow to exploit the available information in an optimal way, since only to atoms of the partition are considered.

Other methods, *e.g.* the Hamming models, require even more sophisticated assumptions on the real leakage function and try to estimate it as good as possible. A disadvantage of these methods is, that they can only be applied if the assumptions are justified.

Independent of single- or multi-bit partitioning functions, an adversary can choose amongst several distinguishers. Kocher et *al.* suggested the difference of means test. Later publications suggested further distinguishers including the t-test [1] and the Pearson correlation coefficient [2]. These distinguishers analyze a probability distribution at most by its mean and variance (Gaussian assumption). Hence they do not exploit all information available and are inappropriate if the Gaussian assumption does not hold. Pearson's correlation coefficient requires the additional assumption of a linear relation between leakage and observation.

Template Attacks [3] are a different kind of attack. They assume a powerful adversary that fully controls a training device which is used to estimate the probability densities of the physical observable for each L_i^k. Effectively this is equivalent to knowing L. For a side-channel measurement from a target device, the maximum-likelihood test derives which previously estimated probability density is the most likely origin of the sample. Template attacks constitute the strongest form of side-channel attacks, if the Gaussian assumption holds. A disadvantage of the approach is the need for a training device.

In contrast, MIA requires neither a training device, nor a restrictive assumption about the real leakage function, nor the Gaussian assumption. MIA estimates the full probability density for each L_i^k from observations of the target device's leakage. Due to the lack of reference data, e.g. templates, MIA cannot apply the maximum-likelihood test. Instead, MIA uses our information-based distinguisher. An important advantage of MIA is, that it can exploit arbitrary relationships between $\mathbf{L}_k$ and $\mathbf{O}$.

The work of Standaert et al. [17] is different from ours in the following sense: they propose a Mutual Information-based metric for measuring an amount of side-channel leakage. That is, they do not propose an attack but a leakage analysis/evaluation tool.

6   Experimental Results for Mutual Information

In this section, we apply the theoretical framework from Sect. 2 and   3 and provide experimental results based on power measurements from an AT90S8515 micro controller ($n = 8$ bit) performing $E_k := $ AES-128 encryption in software[2]. The measurements $\mathbf{O}(t)$ represent the voltage drop over a 50Ω resistor inserted in the smart card's ground line. We sample the power consumption at instants $t = 1, \ldots, 1800$ during the first round of the AES-128 encryption of randomly chosen plaintexts with a constant key. Our experiments focus on the first key byte denoted by $\mathbf{K} \in \{0, 1\}^8$ and the first plaintext byte denoted by $\mathbf{X} \in \{0, 1\}^8$.

6.1   Mutual Information Applied to Side Channel Leakage

We empirically confirm that Mutual Information Analysis is indeed effective using relaxed assumptions with the following experiment:

- population size $q = 1000$ power curves $o_{x_i}(t)$, $i = 1, \ldots, q$
- $f_{\hat{k}}(\mathbf{X}) = \text{Sbox}(\mathbf{X} \oplus \hat{k})$, $\mathbf{W}_{\hat{k}} = (v_1, f_{\hat{k}}(\mathbf{X}))$, v_1 constant and unknown
- $\hat{\mathsf{L}}(\mathbf{W}_{\hat{k}}) :=$ the rth bit of $f_{\hat{k}}(\mathbf{X})$, where $r = 0$ denotes the LSB.

Hence, each $o_{x_i}(t)$ is associated to an atom of $\{L_i^{\hat{k}}\}_{i=0}^1$ by $\hat{\mathsf{L}}(\mathbf{W}_{\hat{k}})$ which is the rth bit of $\text{Sbox}(\mathbf{X} \oplus \hat{k})$. For the dependence between leaked value and observed power dissipation we assume a one-to-many relation due to noise, i.e. each distinct value of $\mathbf{L}_k$ leads to exactly one power consumption value under noise-free conditions,

---

[2] We would like to point out that the AES encryption terminates in constant time.

but in reality it might lead to differing observations. The probability densities $\tilde{\mathbb{P}}_{\mathbf{O}}$ and $\tilde{\mathbb{P}}_{\mathbf{O}|\hat{\mathbf{L}}_{\hat{k}}}$ are empirically determined by sampling the distributions of $\hat{\mathbf{L}}_{\hat{k}}$ and $\mathbf{O}$ with histograms. The number of bins for the histograms is chosen according to size of $\mathcal{L}$, *i.e.* the number of distinguishable values in $\hat{\mathbf{L}}_{\hat{k}}$, which is two.

We compute the Mutual Information $\tilde{\mathbf{I}}(\hat{\mathbf{L}}_{\hat{k}}; \mathbf{O}(t))$ for $\hat{k} = k$ according to Eq. (1) and (3) for each t. Figure 2 shows the resulting Mutual Information traces for $r = 0, 1, 2$. The obvious peaks in the upper plot ($r = 0$) appear during the jointly implemented SubBytes and ShiftRows operations as well as during the MixColumn operation, which involve the targeted value $\mathbf{W}_{\hat{k}}$ several times. These peaks are less significant in the plots for $r = 1$ and $r = 2$ which clearly indicates that the single bits leak different amounts of information.

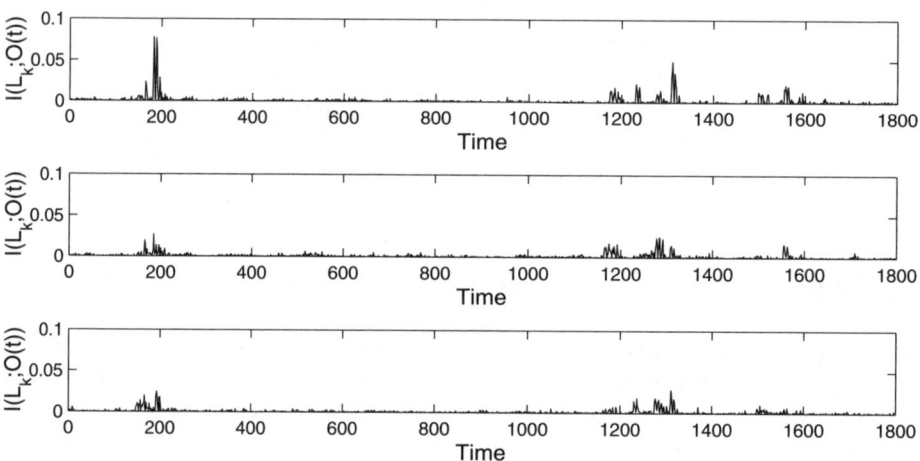

Fig. 2. Mutual Information of 1-bit leakages for bit $r = 0, 1, 2$, from top to bottom

However, the information leaked adds up as shown in Fig. 3 which depicts the Mutual Information trace of the 2-bit leakage function $\hat{\mathsf{L}}(\mathbf{W}_{\hat{k}}) :=$ the two LSBs of $f_{\hat{k}}(\mathbf{X})$. We used four bins to estimate the probability distributions.

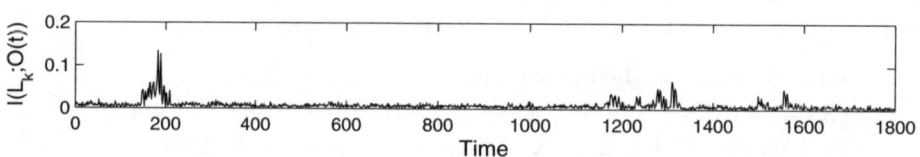

Fig. 3. Mutual Information for 2-bit leakages

6.2 Empirical Evidence

This section provides empirical evidence showing that the attack and the distinguisher are effective and hence confirms the theoretical considerations of

Sect. 3.2. We empirically verify that our distinguisher is effective in our general setting with the following experiment:

- population size $q = 1000$ power curves $o_{x_i}(t)$, $i = 1, \ldots, q$
- $f_{\hat{k}}(\mathbf{X}) = \mathrm{Sbox}(\mathbf{X} \oplus \hat{k})$, $\mathbf{W}_{\hat{k}} = (v_1, f_{\hat{k}}(\mathbf{X}))$, v_1 constant and unknown
- $\hat{\mathsf{L}}(\mathbf{W}_{\hat{k}}(\cdot)) :=$ the three MSBs of $f_{\hat{k}}(\mathbf{X})$.

As before, we assume a one-to-many relation between leaked and observed values due to noise. Based on a key guess $\hat{k} \in \mathcal{K}$, each $o_{x_i}(t)$ is associated to an atom of $\{L_i^{\hat{k}}\}_{i=0}^7$ by $\hat{\mathsf{L}}(\mathbf{W}_{\hat{k}})$ which is equal to the three MSBs of $\mathrm{Sbox}(\mathbf{X} \oplus \hat{k})$. We estimate the probability distributions $\mathbb{P}_{\mathbf{O}}$ and $\mathbb{P}_{\mathbf{O}|\hat{\mathbf{L}}_{\hat{k}}}$ with histograms for which we use eight bins and compute the Mutual Information of $\hat{\mathbf{L}}_{\hat{k}}$ and $\mathbf{O}(t)$ according to Eq. (1) and (3). Figure 4 depicts the resulting Mutual Information trace for the correct key guess $\hat{k} = k$.

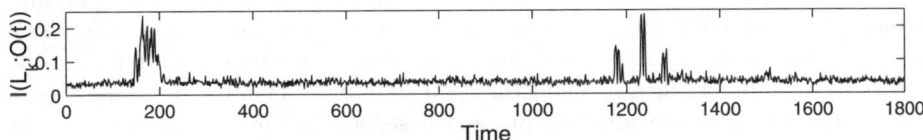

Fig. 4. Mutual Information over time for the correct key hypothesis

As can be seen when comparing to Fig. 2 and 3 the trace shows clear peaks at the points of interest $t = \tau_j$ where the targeted intermediate result $f_{\hat{k}}(\cdot)$ is processed. Next, we compute the same Mutual Information trace for all other key hypotheses $\hat{k}$ and test, if the highest derived Mutual Information value for any wrong $\hat{k}$ is lower than the one for $\hat{k} = k$. More formally that is: $\mathrm{argmax}_{t, \hat{k}=k}$ $\tilde{\mathbf{I}}(\hat{\mathbf{L}}_{\hat{k}}, \mathbf{O}(t)) > \mathrm{argmax}_{t, \hat{k} \neq k}$ $\tilde{\mathbf{I}}(\hat{\mathbf{L}}_{\hat{k}}, \mathbf{O}(t))$. Figure 5 shows the highest Mutual Information value (selected from the whole time frame t) for every key hypothesis. The peak for the correct key hypothesis $\hat{k} = k$ is clearly distinguishable.

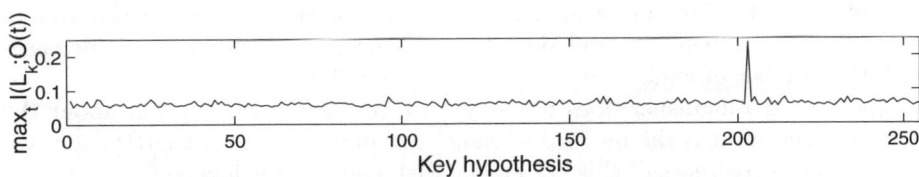

Fig. 5. Maximum Mutual Information per key hypothesis

6.3   MIA and Dual Rail Precharge Logic

In this section we apply our distinguisher in a scenario for which it seems particularly promising: special logic, $e.g.$ Wave Dynamic Differential Logic (WDDL)

[18], designed to resist differential side-channel analysis. While the assumption of the Hamming weight or distance leakage function is justified and leads to efficient attacks against devices implemented in standard CMOS, the situation is very different when facing dual rail precharge (DRP) logic. Let us look back to the initial foundations of those models. In standard CMOS, the instantaneous dynamic power dissipation of a logic or sequential gate is directly linked to whether the bit-pattern on the inputs lead to a transition (bit-flip) in the gate and/or on the output wire(s) or not. Although the energy required to perform the flip is not equal amongst cell types and not even amongst equal cells spread over the silicon area with process variations, the differences are usually negligible in a power analysis attack context. In particular, this is the case for sets of gates that drive large capacitive loads, *e.g.* bus lines in a microcontroller. This is why attacking a microcontroller when performing a memory lookup instruction with a correlation attack and the Hamming weight or distance leakage model can lead to correlation coefficients of almost one.

However, these models and assumptions do not hold for DRP logic. The fundamental idea of DRP logic is to encode one bit of information in a differential pair, *e.g.* 0 = (0,1) and 1 = (1,0), that is signaled over a wire pair. Further, the entire circuit is precharged to a constant pair (0,0) or (1,1) in the first half of each clock cycle. During the evaluation phase, the second half of each clock cycle, the logic evaluates and each wire pair takes either (0,1) or (1,0) depending on the bit value that is encoded. Doing so ensures that, whether the logical input to a gate changes or not, the gate performs exactly one bit flip in each evaluation phase. Obviously, hypothetical leakage functions that relate to the *number* of "logical" bit flips only are meaningless in this context. The circuit performs a constant number of bit flips per cycle, independent of the logical data values. Still, DRP logic leaks information. The relatively small differences that we neglected in the standard CMOS context now have a major impact.

For simplicity, consider two gates in DRP logic that each drive two differential outputs with capacities (α, β) and (γ, δ). If $\alpha > \beta$ and $\gamma > \delta$ holds, the Hamming models do not describe the power dissipation well, but they will work because the direction of the differential is the same for both logical output bits. The same holds if we replace $>$ with $<$. In the case that the directions of the differentials are not equal, the Hamming models no longer represent effective estimators of power dissipation behavior and side-channel leakage. This discrepancy increases with the number of logical bits, starting from two bits.

Since our distinguisher does not rely on a restrictive assumption about the leakage function, it is the method of choice for an attack against DRP logic. We confirm the correctness of this statement with empirical evidence.

The experimental platform is an 8051 microcontroller implemented in a DRP variant with differentially routed wire pairs. We implemented a simple yet representative test program which consists of a single table lookup of the Sbox S1 of the Data Encryption Standard. We obtained power measurements while the microcontroller performed lookups for randomly chosen plaintexts and a constant key. Before each measurement, the memory bus and the target register were reset to zero. Thus the previous state is zero. The measurements represent the voltage drop over a 50Ω resistor inserted in the microcontrollers V_{DD} line. We sampled the voltage drop at a rate of $2\mathrm{GS/s}$.

Let $\mathbf{X}$ be the six plaintext bits and k be the 6-bit subkey. Further experimental settings are:

- population size $q = 100\,000$ power curves $o_{x_i}(t)$, $i = 1, \ldots, q$
- $f_{\hat{k}}(\mathbf{X}) = \mathrm{S1}(\mathbf{X} \oplus \mathrm{k})$, $\mathbf{W}_{\hat{k}} = (v_1, f_{\hat{k}}(\mathbf{X}))$, $v_1 = 0$
- $\hat{\mathsf{L}}(\mathbf{W}_{\hat{k}}(\cdot)) := $ all four bits of $f_{\hat{k}}(\mathbf{X})$.

Figure 6 shows the result of a standard correlation attack, where we used the Hamming weight of $\mathrm{S1}(\mathbf{X} \oplus \hat{k})$ as the predicted power dissipation. The correlation trace for the correct key is plotted in black, for all other key candidates in gray. As can be seen, the correct key hypothesis does not lead to a maximal or minimal correlation coefficient with respect to the whole period.

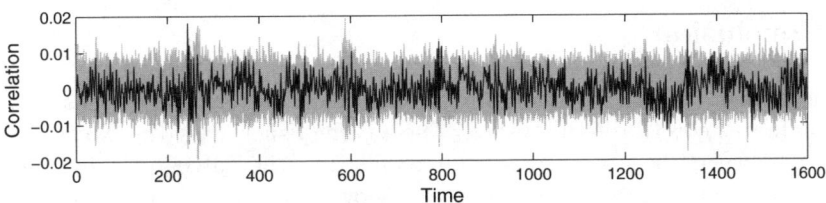

Fig. 6. Correlation traces: correct key in black, all other in gray

Figure 7 on the other hand shows the result of an attack with the Mutual Information-based distinguisher. The Mutual Information trace for the correct key is plotted in black, for all other key candidates in gray. At time index 600

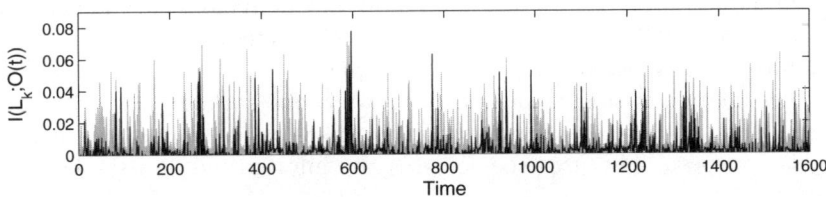

Fig. 7. Mutual Information traces, correct key in black, all other in gray

the correct key hypothesis leads to a Mutual Information value that is maximal for all key hypotheses and the whole time.

To emphasize the difference, we present in Fig. 8 plots of the maximal and minimal correlation values as well as of the maximal Mutual Information values per key hypothesis, chosen from the overall time frame.

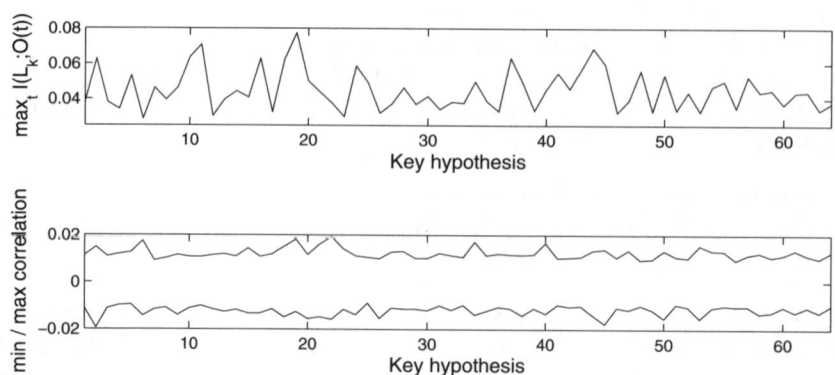

Fig. 8. Maximum Mutual Information per key hypothesis (upper plot); Maximal and minimal correlation coefficient per key hypothesis (lower plot)

7   Conclusion

We described a generic differential side-channel attack that is based on an information-theoretic distinguisher. The distinguisher uses the Mutual Information between the observed measurements and the values of a hypothetical leakage function to rank key guesses. We showed why the attack is particularly promising when the target device is implemented in dual rail precharge logic. The effectiveness of our approach is confirmed by results of power analysis experiments.

Acknowledgements

The authors would like to thank J.R. Rao for shepherding this paper, François-Xavier Standaert for fruitful discussions, and the anonymous reviewers of CHES 2007, AsiaCrypt 2007, Eurocrypt 2008, and CHES 2008 for their insightful comments. Most of them helped to improve the paper.

The information in this document reflects only the authors' views, is provided as is and no guarantee or warranty is given that the information is fit for any particular purpose. The user thereof uses the information at its sole risk and liability.

References

1. Aigner, M., Oswald, E.: Power Analysis Tutorial, http://www.iaik.tugraz.at/aboutus/people/oswald/papers/dpa_tutorial.pdf
2. Brier, E., Clavier, C., Olivier, F.: Correlation power analysis with a leakage model. In: Joye, M., Quisquater, J.-J. (eds.) CHES 2004. LNCS, vol. 3156, pp. 16–29. Springer, Heidelberg (2004)

3. Chari, S., Rao, J.R., Rohatgi, P.: Template attacks. In: Kaliski Jr., B.S., Koç, Ç.K., Paar, C. (eds.) CHES 2002. LNCS, vol. 2523, pp. 172–186. Springer, Heidelberg (2003)
4. Coron, J.-S., Goubin, L.: On Boolean and Arithmetic Masking against Differential Power Analysis. In: Paar, C., Koç, Ç.K. (eds.) CHES 2000. LNCS, vol. 1965, pp. 231–237. Springer, Heidelberg (2000)
5. Cover, T.M., Thomas, J.A.: Elements of Information Theory. John Wiley & Sons, Chichester (2006)
6. Golić, J.D., Tymen, C.: Multiplicative masking and power anaylsis of AES. In: Kaliski Jr., B.S., Koç, Ç.K., Paar, C. (eds.) CHES 2002. LNCS, vol. 2523, pp. 31–47. Springer, Heidelberg (2002)
7. Goubin, L.: A sound method for switching between boolean and arithmetic masking. In: Koç, Ç.K., Naccache, D., Paar, C. (eds.) CHES 2001. LNCS, vol. 2162, pp. 3–15. Springer, Heidelberg (2001)
8. Kocher, P.: Timing attacks on implementations of Diffie-Hellman, RSA, DSS and other systems. In: Koblitz, N. (ed.) CRYPTO 1996. LNCS, vol. 1109, pp. 104–113. Springer, Heidelberg (1996)
9. Kocher, P., Jaffe, J., Jun, B.: Differential power analysis. In: Wiener, M.J. (ed.) CRYPTO 1999. LNCS, vol. 1666, pp. 388–397. Springer, Heidelberg (1999)
10. Messerges, T.S.: Securing the AES finalists against power analysis attacks. In: Schneier, B. (ed.) FSE 2000. LNCS, vol. 1978. Springer, Heidelberg (2001)
11. Messerges, T.S.: Using second-order power analysis to attack DPA resistant software. In: Koç, Ç.K., Paar, C. (eds.) CHES 2000. LNCS, vol. 1965, pp. 238–251. Springer, Heidelberg (2000)
12. Messerges, T.S., Dabbish, E.A., Sloan, R.H.: Investigations of power analysis attacks on smartcards. In: WOST 1999: Proceedings of the USENIX Workshop on Smartcard Technology on USENIX Workshop on Smartcard Technology, Berkeley, CA, USA, p. 17. USENIX Association (1999)
13. Messerges, T.S., Dabbish, E.A., Sloan, R.H.: Examining smart-card security under the threat of power analysis attacks. IEEE Trans. Comput. 51(5), 541–552 (2002)
14. Micali, S., Reyzin, L.: Physically observable cryptography. In: Naor, M. (ed.) TCC 2004. LNCS, vol. 2951, pp. 278–296. Springer, Heidelberg (2004)
15. Quisquater, J.-J., Samyde, D.: ElectroMagnetic Analysis (EMA): Measures and Couter-Measures for Smard Cards. In: Attali, I., Jensen, T.P. (eds.) E-smart 2001. LNCS, vol. 2140, pp. 200–210. Springer, Heidelberg (2001)
16. Shamir, A., Tromer, E.: Acoustic cryptanalysis, http://theory.csail.mit.edu/~tromer/acoustic/
17. Standaert, F.-X., Malkin, T.G., Yung, M.: A formal practice-oriented model for the analysis of side-channel attacks. Cryptology ePrint Archive, Report 2006/139 (2006), http://eprint.iacr.org/
18. Tiri, K., Hwang, D., Hodjat, A., Lai, B.-C., Yang, S., Schaumont, P., Verbauwhede, I.: Prototype IC with WDDL and differential routing - DPA resistance assessment. In: Rao, J.R., Sunar, B. (eds.) CHES 2005. LNCS, vol. 3659, pp. 354–365. Springer, Heidelberg (2005)

Appendix

Let $\mathbf{X}$ be a random variable on a (discrete) space $\mathcal{X}$ with probability distribution $\mathbb{P}_{\mathbf{X}}$. The uncertainty that one has about the value of such a random variable when an experiment is performed, is expressed by the Shannon entropy of $\mathbf{X}$ which is usually denoted by $H(\mathbf{X})$ or $H(\mathbb{P}_{\mathbf{X}})$. It is defined by the following equation

$$H(\mathbf{X}) = - \sum_{x \in \mathcal{X}} \mathbb{P}_{\mathbf{X}}[\mathbf{X} = x] \log_2 \mathbb{P}_{\mathbf{X}}[\mathbf{X} = x] \, . \tag{6}$$

$H(\mathbf{X})$ expresses the uncertainty in bits. The entropy of the pair of random variables $(\mathbf{X}, \mathbf{Y})$ (where $\mathbf{Y}$ is a random variable on a space $\mathcal{Y}$) is denoted by $H(\mathbf{X}, \mathbf{Y})$ and it expresses the uncertainty one has about both. We note that the entropy of two random variables is sub-additive $i.e.$

$$H(\mathbf{X}, \mathbf{Y}) \leq H(\mathbf{X}) + H(\mathbf{Y}) \tag{7}$$

with equality if and only if $\mathbf{X}$ and $\mathbf{Y}$ are independent. Often one is interested in the uncertainty about $\mathbf{X}$ given that one has obtained the outcome of an experiment on a related random variable $\mathbf{Y}$. This is expressed by the conditional entropy $H(\mathbf{X}|\mathbf{Y})$ which is defined as follows,

$$H(\mathbf{X}|\mathbf{Y}) = - \sum_{x \in \mathcal{X}, y \in \mathcal{Y}} \mathbb{P}_{\mathbf{X}, \mathbf{Y}}[\mathbf{X} = x, \mathbf{Y} = y] \log_2 \mathbb{P}_{\mathbf{X}|\mathbf{Y}}[\mathbf{X} = x|\mathbf{Y} = y], \tag{8}$$

where $\mathbb{P}_{\mathbf{X}, \mathbf{Y}}$ denotes the joint probability distribution of $\mathbf{X}$ and $\mathbf{Y}$ and $\mathbb{P}_{\mathbf{X}|\mathbf{Y}}$ stands for the conditional probability distribution of $\mathbf{X}$ given $\mathbf{Y}$. When $\mathbf{Y}$ can be considered as an observation of $\mathbf{X}$ over a noisy channel, then one often characterizes the channel by its set of conditional distributions $\{\mathbb{P}_{\mathbf{Y}|\mathbf{X}=x}\}_{x \in \mathcal{X}}$.

RSA—Past, Present, Future

Adi Shamir

Weizmann Institute of Science, Israel
`Adi.Shamir@weizmann.ac.il`

In 2008 we are celebrating the 10-th anniversary of CHES and the 30-th anniversary of the publication of the RSA paper at CACM. In this talk I will survey some of the major RSA-related papers published at CHES during the last 10 years, describe my own research on security and implementation issues, introduce some new attacks, and make predictions about the future of RSA.

E. Oswald and P. Rohatgi (Eds.): CHES 2008, LNCS 5154, p. 443, 2008.
© International Association for Cryptologic Research 2008

A Vision for Platform Security

Ernie Brickell

Intel, United States
ernie.brickell@intel.com

Intel has recently produced several new capabilities to enhance security on the platform that have been released or will be released in the near future. In this presentation I will give a review of these capabilities and discuss their benefit to the security of the platform.

E. Oswald and P. Rohatgi (Eds.): CHES 2008, LNCS 5154, p. 444, 2008.

Author Index

Printing: Mercedes-Druck, Berlin
Binding: Stein+Lehmann, Berlin

Lecture Notes in Computer Science

Sublibrary 4: Security and Cryptology

For information about Vols. 1– 3956
please contact your bookseller or Springer

Vol. 4593: A. Biryukov (Ed.), Fast Software Encryption. XI, 467 pages. 2007.

Vol. 4586: J. Pieprzyk, H. Ghodosi, E. Dawson (Eds.), Information Security and Privacy. XIV, 476 pages. 2007.

Vol. 4582: J. López, P. Samarati, J.L. Ferrer (Eds.), Public Key Infrastructure. XI, 375 pages. 2007.

Vol. 4579: B.M. Hämmerli, R. Sommer (Eds.), Detection of Intrusions and Malware, and Vulnerability Assessment. X, 251 pages. 2007.

Vol. 4575: T. Takagi, T. Okamoto, E. Okamoto, T. Okamoto (Eds.), Pairing-Based Cryptography – Pairing 2007. XI, 408 pages. 2007.

Vol. 4567: T. Furon, F. Cayre, G. Doërr, P. Bas (Eds.), Information Hiding. XI, 393 pages. 2008.

Vol. 4521: J. Katz, M. Yung (Eds.), Applied Cryptography and Network Security. XIII, 498 pages. 2007.

Vol. 4515: M. Naor (Ed.), Advances in Cryptology - EUROCRYPT 2007. XIII, 591 pages. 2007.

Vol. 4499: Y.Q. Shi (Ed.), Transactions on Data Hiding and Multimedia Security II. IX, 117 pages. 2007.

Vol. 4464: E. Dawson, D.S. Wong (Eds.), Information Security Practice and Experience. XIII, 361 pages. 2007.

Vol. 4462: D. Sauveron, K. Markantonakis, A. Bilas, J.-J. Quisquater (Eds.), Information Security Theory and Practices. XII, 255 pages. 2007.

Vol. 4450: T. Okamoto, X. Wang (Eds.), Public Key Cryptography – PKC 2007. XIII, 491 pages. 2007.

Vol. 4437: J.L. Camenisch, C.S. Collberg, N.F. Johnson, P. Sallee (Eds.), Information Hiding. VIII, 389 pages. 2007.

Vol. 4392: S.P. Vadhan (Ed.), Theory of Cryptography. XI, 595 pages. 2007.

Vol. 4377: M. Abe (Ed.), Topics in Cryptology – CT-RSA 2007. XI, 403 pages. 2006.

Vol. 4356: E. Biham, A.M. Youssef (Eds.), Selected Areas in Cryptography. XI, 395 pages. 2007.

Vol. 4341: P.Q. Nguyên (Ed.), Progress in Cryptology - VIETCRYPT 2006. XI, 385 pages. 2006.

Vol. 4332: A. Bagchi, V. Atluri (Eds.), Information Systems Security. XV, 382 pages. 2006.

Vol. 4329: R. Barua, T. Lange (Eds.), Progress in Cryptology - INDOCRYPT 2006. X, 454 pages. 2006.

Vol. 4318: H. Lipmaa, M. Yung, D. Lin (Eds.), Information Security and Cryptology. XI, 305 pages. 2006.

Vol. 4307: P. Ning, S. Qing, N. Li (Eds.), Information and Communications Security. XIV, 558 pages. 2006.

Vol. 4301: D. Pointcheval, Y. Mu, K. Chen (Eds.), Cryptology and Network Security. XIII, 381 pages. 2006.

Vol. 4300: Y.Q. Shi (Ed.), Transactions on Data Hiding and Multimedia Security I. IX, 139 pages. 2006.

Vol. 4298: J.K. Lee, O. Yi, M. Yung (Eds.), Information Security Applications. XIV, 406 pages. 2007.

Vol. 4296: M.S. Rhee, B. Lee (Eds.), Information Security and Cryptology – ICISC 2006. XIII, 358 pages. 2006.

Vol. 4284: X. Lai, K. Chen (Eds.), Advances in Cryptology – ASIACRYPT 2006. XIV, 468 pages. 2006.

Vol. 4283: Y.Q. Shi, B. Jeon (Eds.), Digital Watermarking. XII, 474 pages. 2006.

Vol. 4266: H. Yoshiura, K. Sakurai, K. Rannenberg, Y. Murayama, S.-i. Kawamura (Eds.), Advances in Information and Computer Security. XIII, 438 pages. 2006.

Vol. 4258: G. Danezis, P. Golle (Eds.), Privacy Enhancing Technologies. VIII, 431 pages. 2006.

Vol. 4249: L. Goubin, M. Matsui (Eds.), Cryptographic Hardware and Embedded Systems - CHES 2006. XII, 462 pages. 2006.

Vol. 4237: H. Leitold, E.P. Markatos (Eds.), Communications and Multimedia Security. XII, 253 pages. 2006.

Vol. 4236: L. Breveglieri, I. Koren, D. Naccache, J.-P. Seifert (Eds.), Fault Diagnosis and Tolerance in Cryptography. XIII, 253 pages. 2006.

Vol. 4219: D. Zamboni, C. Krügel (Eds.), Recent Advances in Intrusion Detection. XII, 331 pages. 2006.

Vol. 4189: D. Gollmann, J. Meier, A. Sabelfeld (Eds.), Computer Security – ESORICS 2006. XI, 548 pages. 2006.

Vol. 4176: S.K. Katsikas, J. López, M. Backes, S. Gritzalis, B. Preneel (Eds.), Information Security. XIV, 548 pages. 2006.

Vol. 4117: C. Dwork (Ed.), Advances in Cryptology - CRYPTO 2006. XIII, 621 pages. 2006.

Vol. 4116: R. De Prisco, M. Yung (Eds.), Security and Cryptography for Networks. XI, 366 pages. 2006.

Vol. 4107: G. Di Crescenzo, A. Rubin (Eds.), Financial Cryptography and Data Security. XI, 327 pages. 2006.

Vol. 4083: S. Fischer-Hübner, S. Furnell, C. Lambrinoudakis (Eds.), Trust and Privacy in Digital Business. XIII, 243 pages. 2006.

Vol. 4064: R. Büschkes, P. Laskov (Eds.), Detection of Intrusions and Malware & Vulnerability Assessment. X, 195 pages. 2006.

Vol. 4058: L.M. Batten, R. Safavi-Naini (Eds.), Information Security and Privacy. XII, 446 pages. 2006.

Vol. 4047: M. Robshaw (Ed.), Fast Software Encryption. XI, 434 pages. 2006.

Vol. 4043: A.S. Atzeni, A. Lioy (Eds.), Public Key Infrastructure. XI, 261 pages. 2006.

Vol. 4004: S. Vaudenay (Ed.), Advances in Cryptology - EUROCRYPT 2006. XIV, 613 pages. 2006.

Vol. 3995: G. Müller (Ed.), Emerging Trends in Information and Communication Security. XX, 524 pages. 2006.

Vol. 3989: J. Zhou, M. Yung, F. Bao (Eds.), Applied Cryptography and Network Security. XIV, 488 pages. 2006.

Vol. 3969: Ø. Ytrehus (Ed.), Coding and Cryptography. XI, 443 pages. 2006.

Vol. 3958: M. Yung, Y. Dodis, A. Kiayias, T. Malkin (Eds.), Public Key Cryptography - PKC 2006. XIV, 543 pages. 2006.

Vol. 3957: B. Christianson, B. Crispo, J.A. Malcolm, M. Roe (Eds.), Security Protocols. IX, 325 pages. 2006.